MW00439435

Ballot Battles

Ballot Battles

The History of Disputed Elections in the United States

EDWARD B. FOLEY

OXFORD
UNIVERSITY PRESS

Oxford University Press is a department of the University of Oxford. It furthers the University's objective of excellence in research, scholarship, and education by publishing worldwide. Oxford is a registered trade mark of Oxford University Press in the UK and in certain other countries.

Published in the United States of America by Oxford University Press
198 Madison Avenue, New York, NY 10016, United States of America

The cartoon on the front cover, by Thomas Nast, was captioned "A National Game That Is Played Out" and appeared in Harper's Weekly, December 23, 1876, p. 1044.

Library of Congress Cataloging-in-Publication Data
Foley, Edward B.
Ballot battles : the history of disputed elections in the United States / Edward B. Foley.
pages cm
Summary: "The 2000 presidential election, with its problems in Florida, was not the first major vote-counting controversy in the nation's history—nor the last. Ballot Battles traces the evolution of America's experience with these disputes, from 1776 to now, explaining why they have proved persistently troublesome and offering an institutional solution"—Provided by publisher.
ISBN 978-0-19-023527-7 (hardback)—ISBN 978-0-19-023528-4 (ebook)
1. Elections—Corrupt practices—United States—History. 2. Election monitoring—United States—History. 3. Political corruption—United States—History. I. Title.
JK1994.F65 2016
324.973
2015025434

3 5 7 9 8 6 4 2
Printed in the United States of America
on acid-free paper

For Miranda,
with love and gratitude

CONTENTS

ACKNOWLEDGMENTS

This book, almost a decade in the making, has a multitude of benefactors. Foremost are the students who, through their seminar papers and research assistance, should recognize their contributions reflected in these pages. The many upon whose work I have relied include Bryan Becker (Pennsylvania), Jason Blake (1806), Derek Clinger (Virginia), Bradley Cromes (Georgia), Kathryn DeWeese (Colorado), David Dirisamer (Illinois), Brittany Doggett (West Virginia), Ethan Evans (Michigan), William Froehlich (Brightly), Zachary Gwin (O'Farrell-Landis), T. J. Hess (1781), Kevin Hidas (Canada), Lauren Huddleston (New Jersey), Marleen Kindel (Senate), Jared Klaus (the Bloody Eighth), Stephanie Klupinski (New Hampshire), Dania Korkor (New Mexico), Kristen Maiorino (a myriad of races), Amanda Mallot (1876), Kerry McNally (the Buckshot War), Sean Morrison (Massachusetts), Caitlyn Nestleroth (George Norris), Matt Provance (1792), Jordan Riviello (Florida), James Saywell (federal jurisdiction), Maxwell Stearns (congressional elections, among others), Natasha Szalacinski (Kentucky), Dave Twombly (Missouri), Laura Willis (Mexico), Nadia Zaiem (Maine), and Chenwei Zhang (South Carolina, Rhode Island).

Several students deserve extra recognition. Nathan Colvin did the bulk of the research and writing for two articles we coauthored that form a pillar upon which large portions of this book rest. Owen Wolfe's superb work on the Progressive Era pervades Chapter 7. Kyle Kopko researched with painstaking care and much exuberance innumerable episodes discussed in this book.

The tables in the Appendix are the accumulated efforts of many, including Trevor Covey, Alexander Darr, Jared Hasson, Andrew Ironside, Susan Allyn Johnson, Henry Phillips-Gary, Brendan Schlauch, and Stephen Wolfson. Above all, these tables and the notes that accompany them reflect the extraordinary effort of James Hafner, who put them in their final form and undertook the research necessary to pin down every last detail. The Appendix truly reflects Jimmy's principal authorship.

Down the stretch, Jimmy together with Brian Kelso and Elizabeth Young formed a phenomenal team that worked with me to prepare the final draft of the manuscript. What a team they were! I could not have been more fortunate, or grateful, to have such a dedicated and meticulous crew to pore over the notes for each chapter, to review the manuscript for accuracy and consistency, and to conduct extensive research on various matters that arose during the editing process. I have enjoyed and will cherish the camaraderie that the four of us have forged over these months.

The Ohio State University Moritz College of Law has been blessed this past decade to have a stellar library, under the leadership of first Bruce Johnson and now Sara Sampson. During this time, I have had the great privilege to work with outstanding librarians, without whom this book could not have been written: Matt Steinke, Kathy Hall, and most recently Matt Cooper, who never ceases to amaze me with his ability to find what I had thought to be the untraceable. I especially appreciate Matt's patience and persistence, as well as our friendship that has developed while working together. Kaylie Vermillion, who manages circulation for the library, has been an absolute saint, given the volume of history books we have had to borrow and keep organized throughout the duration of this project; in addition to the superb efficiency with which she has handled the project, I am especially grateful for her cheerfulness and tolerance of my often unorthodox methods of keeping track of books in use.

The Moritz College of Law has supported this project in multiple ways, including several semesters of dedicated research assignments. Especially important has been the intellectual climate of *Election Law @ Moritz*, and the ideas and values underlying this book have been shaped by a multitude of conversations and exchanges over the years with Terri Enns, Nancy Rogers, Peter Shane, Dan Tokaji, Chris Walker, and other Moritz colleagues. Daphne Meimaridis, program administrator for *Election Law @ Moritz*, is too modest to take credit for the work done under her auspices, but she maintains the logistical platform from which the rest of us can undertake our scholarly pursuits. Latonga Croomes and Cathy Thompson, who provide secretarial and other office support for our wing of the building, know how much we value the communal culture they have created for us and the positive tone they set for all that we do.

The collection of photographs, cartoons, and other images has been a particular project for which the Moritz College of Law has provided extraordinary support. At the wise and considerate direction of Associate Dean Chris Fairman (whose untimely death while this book has been in production is a devasting blow to all of us at Moritz), Katy Gullo has orchestrated an entire group to assist in obtaining the necessary digital files and, where applicable, permissions: Allyson Hennelly, Laju Mansukhani, Ingrid Mattson, Jeremiah Moebs, and especially Dawn Parker. It has been a huge endeavor, and I am deeply appreciative of all the extra steps this group, under Katy's leadership, has taken to complete it. Once again, Matt Cooper has stepped up in a major way, hunting down images that seemed impossible to find. Jenny Robb of Ohio State's Billy Ireland Cartoon Library and Museum also provided great assistance in identifying and scanning some of the key cartoons included in the book. I am, of course, very grateful to all the individuals and organizations that gave permission to reproduce images, as indicated where each such image appears. The inclusion of these images adds an important dimension to the story the book tells.

I am extremely fortunate to be able to work with Dave McBride and Katie Weaver at Oxford. Their guidance, kindness, and patience throughout the entire process have made it instructive and enjoyable. Every author should be so lucky.

This book has received generous research support from the American Philosophical Society (a Franklin Research Grant), the Smith Richardson Foundation, the Tobin Project, and especially in the last few years the American Law Institute. The ability to present different parts of the book, at different stages of development, at the University of Maryland and the University of Iowa came at especially auspicious moments, as did a workshop at Ohio State's History Department. Similarly beneficial was the opportunity to present the keynote address at a University of California, Irvine conference, which formed the basis for a key component of Chapter 5.

Readers of earlier drafts include my friends and colleagues Les Benedict, Michael Flamm, Rick Hasen, and Dave Stebenne—as well as my wife, Miranda Cox, whose contributions to this book go far beyond her careful reading of it to include her loving support for the project over its many years. I am enormously indebted to all of these readers for their extensive and insightful comments, as I am to those who reviewed a previous draft for Oxford. This valuable feedback helped me keep sight of the forest, not just the trees, and has produced a book that conveys more useful information and ideas in a significantly smaller package. Other scholars have graciously shared their time and expertise in connection with specific sections of the book, including Josiah Daniels, Nicole Etcheson, Heather Gerken, Ed Kallina, Kent Newmyer, and Rick Pildes. All remaining shortcomings are, of course, my responsibility.

To Susan Johnson at the University of Iowa, I owe my ability to develop and maintain schedules that have enabled me to complete various manuscripts by targeted deadlines. As a result of working with her over the past few years, I have gained a friend as well as an improved capacity for organizing and managing large projects. I hope she knows just how essential her role has been to getting this book finished.

Steve Huefner has been a crucial part of this project from the very beginning all the way to its completion. A great friend and collaborator in so many ways, he and I shared the vision for this book from its earliest inception, even before it took on its historical orientation, when it was just going to be an analysis of existing recount laws in an effort to discern and distill best practices. He has been an enthusiastic interlocutor as I have dived deeper into historical details in an effort to understand (for example) why our Founders did not provide a better vote-counting process to begin with, why those who lived through the Hayes-Tilden dispute did not develop a better reform, why the Progressive Era did not provide an improved institution, and so forth. I have been blessed to travel this intellectual journey with him, to whom I owe so much, and am elated that we will continue to collaborate in ongoing and future endeavors, including the American Law Institute's Election Law Project. May our mutual passion for nonpartisan fairness in the counting of votes, as well as in the operation of democracy more generally, keep our joint efforts productive for many years to come.

Ballot Battles

Prologue

The Missing Institution of Impartiality

On November 6, 2012, Apryl Babarcik went to her local polling place to vote in the election held that day. Apryl lived in New Philadelphia, Ohio, a town of 17,000 residents in the eastern part of the state, a little south of Canton and a little north of Interstate 70 (which bisects the state, east to west). Apryl went to the correct polling location for her address, 231 3rd Drive SE (Southeast), but the poll workers there mistakenly sent her to a different polling place—the one for a resident of 231 3rd Drive, NE (Northeast). As a result, Apryl cast a "provisional" ballot, which as its name indicates is not immediately counted but instead set aside for evaluation by local election officials.[1]

On the ballot was not only that year's presidential election, but also, among many "down ticket" races, one for a seat in Ohio's House of Representatives. Ohio has 99 members in its House of Representatives. Apryl's dwelling was in the 98th district, which encompassed all of Tuscarawas County (where Apryl's town, New Philadelphia, is the county seat) as well as part of neighboring Holmes County. In 2012, the race for the 98th House District was between the Republican incumbent, Al Landis, and his Democratic challenger, Josh O'Farrell. The race was a rematch: two years earlier, Landis had been the challenger and had ousted the then-incumbent O'Farrell.

The Tuscarawas County Board of Elections did not count Apryl's ballot. Ohio law requires voters to cast their ballots in the correct polling location for their address, and the Tuscarawas elections board relied upon this law as the sole reason for rejecting Apryl's ballot. They applied the law to her situation even though on Election Day she first had gone to the correct polling place for her address, only to be told incorrectly by the poll workers there to go to a different location that caused her ballot to be cast in the wrong place.[2]

Apryl's ballot did not make a difference in the presidential election of 2012. (Barack Obama beat Mitt Romney in Ohio by 166,214 votes,[3] and won the Electoral College 322–206.) But Apryl's ballot, and others like it, did matter in the Landis-O'Farrell race for Ohio's 98th House District. That race, to invoke a reliable cliché, came down to a photo finish: after a recount, Landis had only eight more votes than O'Farrell (23,393 to 23,385).[4]

An eight-vote margin of victory, while superclose, is not *that* unusual for a state legislative election. Every election year, somewhere in the country there is a state legislative race (or some other form of local election) that gets decided by just a handful of votes. Occasionally, there is even an actual tie, which in most jurisdictions is resolved by a flip of the coin.

But the Landis-O'Farrell election was exceptional because, in addition to being so close, it also would be decisive for determining a pivotal measure of control within Ohio's legislative process. Without Landis in the legislature, Ohio Republicans would have 59 House seats, one short of the number needed to override a gubernatorial veto or, even more importantly, to put a constitutional amendment on the ballot for voters to ratify.[5] Thus Ohio's Democrats saw the seat as very much worth fighting for. If they could get O'Farrell rather than Landis in that seat, then they at least could block constitutional amendments proposed by Republicans—and, when the more moderate Republican governor vetoed Tea Party-type measures coming out of the more conservative legislature, the Democrats would be able to block overrides of those vetoes as well.

Therefore, O'Farrell and the Democrats sought to contest Landis's officially certified eight-vote victory. They identified 52 specific uncounted ballots that they said had been improperly rejected. Among these were Apryl's, as well as 17 others that were similarly rejected for having been cast at the wrong polling place. The Democrats said these ballots should be counted because it was poll worker error that had caused the mistake.[6] The Democrats acknowledged that there was a state statute that required ballots to be cast at the proper polling location, but they pointed to another state statute that obligated poll workers to direct to the correct location voters who show up at the wrong polling place. A proper interpretation of all relevant state laws considered in combination, the Democrats claimed, was to count the ballot when it was a poll worker's fault that it had been cast in the wrong place. At the very least, the Democrats argued, a voter like Apryl should not be disenfranchised when she went to the right polling place initially, only to be told to go elsewhere by a mistaken poll worker.

The Essence of the Problem

The Democrats filed their contest with the chief justice of the state supreme court, but the chief justice declared that under Ohio law the House of

Figure P.1 Telecast of the Ohio House of Representatives' speaker announcing the 58–32 partisan roll call over the disputed election for the 98th district. The Ohio Channel.

Representatives itself had exclusive jurisdiction to rule on the merits of the contest.[7] Being one member shy of a 60-seat supermajority, Republicans already controlled the Ohio House. Consequently, they used this power to award themselves the coveted sixtieth seat. On a straight party-line vote of 58–32, the House rejected O'Farrell's contest.[8]

How would an impartial tribunal have handled O'Farrell's contest? Would it have agreed with the Democrats that Apryl's ballot, along with others like it, should have been counted—so that she did not suffer disenfranchisement caused by an administrative error made by the government's own election workers? Or instead, would an impartial tribunal have accepted the Republican position that no matter how harsh it might seem with respect to the individual voter in a situation like Apryl's, it is nonetheless preferable—and indeed necessitated by the rule of law—to abide by the requirements laid down in advance of the election itself, which in this case included the requirement that all ballots must be cast in the correct polling location? Plausible legal arguments could be—and were—made on both sides, and thus some institution of government was needed to adjudicate the vote-counting dispute.

One will never know how an impartial tribunal would have handled this issue, for the Ohio House of Representatives was far from an impartial tribunal. On the contrary, like other legislative bodies in the United States the Ohio House was organized along inherently partisan lines, with its Majority and Minority caucuses led by the Majority and Minority Leaders. Given this intrinsic partisan structure, as well as the supermajority status at stake, the House itself was the least trustworthy and most self-interested body to adjudicate the O'Farrell-Landis matter. Yet it was the one with the authority to do so, and that is the key point.

To be sure, although an injustice may have been done in this particular Ohio election, there was no threat of civil disorder. In that respect, it was a tamer affair than other episodes in the past. Earlier in the nation's history, when a comparable ballot-counting dispute would determine which party controlled the state's legislature or governorship (or in some instances both branches), there had been outbreaks of violence or serious risk of such tumult. That is what happened, for example, in Pennsylvania's Buckshot War of 1838, and it happened in multiple states in the 1890s, including Connecticut, Colorado, Kansas, Kentucky, Montana, New Jersey, Rhode Island, and West Virginia.[9]

Thus what occurred in the fight for Ohio's 98th House seat in 2012 was mild compared to these other occasions. Perhaps that is partly because at stake was "only" the supermajority status of the sixtieth vote; while important, this is not nearly as critical as which party has majority control of the chamber (or full rein over both legislative chambers as well as the governorship, a trifecta so tempting that when in reach it can cause direct disobedience to judicial decrees, as in New York's "Stolen Senate" debacle of 1891).[10] But it is also true that Ohio, like the rest of the United States, is much less prone to political violence in the early twenty-first century than it was in the nineteenth.[11] Americans may continue to employ political institutions that are patently unfair to one side or the other in their handling of ballot-counting disputes, but they are much less likely to react violently as a result of this unfairness.

This increased civic self-restraint is something to be applauded. But is it enough? Can Americans not hope for more? Can Americans not expect, for the resolution of ballot-counting disputes in elections where the outcome really matters, the use of political institutions that would be fair to both sides in the dispute?

No Grenville Act in America

George Grenville, Prime Minister of Britain in 1765, was a much-loathed figure in the American colonies for his sponsorship of the Stamp Act, which helped to precipitate the Revolutionary War.[12] But in 1770 he authored an act on disputed parliamentary elections for which he has since been revered by his British compatriots. The Grenville Act, as it has since been called in his honor, responded to the problem that the adjudication of disputed elections had become entirely partisan propositions. Rather than being decided "with the strictest impartiality" and according to the "principles of justice," Grenville lamented, these disputes caused "both parties" in Parliament to heed the "impulse of [their] own inclinations"—to act out of "private interest" or what he termed the "self-elective" sense that those in power were entitled to perpetuate their rule.[13] To redress this condition, Grenville proposed that a randomly selected committee, rather than the whole Parliament, decide these disputes.

Although Grenville's particular method proved inadequate (and received subsequent repairs), it enshrined impartiality as the overarching ideal for the resolution of these disputes. In particular, the Grenville Act recognized the need for a new institution. An impartial result required an impartial tribunal. Thus as jealously as the House of Commons guarded its historic prerogative of having the "sole right over the determination of its membership," Commons as an inherently partisan body needed to be supplemented by an additional body constructed in a nonpartisan fashion.[14] For recognizing this need and making this institutional move, subsequent generations in Britain have celebrated the Grenville Act as "one of the noblest works, for the honor of the house of commons, and the security of the constitution, that was ever devised by any minister or statesman."[15]

The Grenville Act, however, was essentially ignored in America.[16] Whether this was because Grenville himself was despised or otherwise, the consequence has been that the adjudications of disputed legislative elections in the United States have been the partisan affairs that Grenville decried. Legislative chambers in America, including the two houses of Congress, have insisted upon maintaining complete authority to judge "the elections, returns, and qualifications" of their own members and have not attempted to create nonpartisan tribunals to assist with these adjudications. "The child" thus "still clings" to "an idea which has been discarded by the parent who originated it."[17] As a result, toward the end of the nineteenth century, a leading American historian observed:

> Now the American House of Representatives and the legislatures of the States, are, in this matter, in almost as bad a state as the House of Commons was before the passage of the Grenville Act, when all such cases came before the whole House, and were decided by the House on party motives . . . . Something like this is true to-day of American legislative bodies.[18]

Over a century later, it is still true.

It is not that Americans do not care about impartiality in the administration of elections. In 1784, even as the United States was ratifying the Treaty of

Figure P.2 George Grenville led Britain's effort to remove partisanship from the resolution of disputed parliamentary elections, but America did not follow his lead. Portrait by William Hoare; permission of Governing Body of Christ Church, Oxford.

Paris to end the Revolutionary War with Britain, the newly liberated state of Virginia was enacting a statute that prohibited its sheriffs "to shew partiality to any candidates" in elections for either house of the state's legislature.[19] The leading early Virginian jurist St. George Tucker, in his annotation of Blackstone's Commentaries for American readers, cited this statute as an example of how America was attempting to implement what Blackstone proclaimed as the "essential" requirement "that elections should be absolutely free."[20]

But in setting up its newly independent government, Virginia did not adopt Grenville's institutional innovation or, indeed, anything like it. Thus if one attempts to reconstruct what the Founding Fathers from Virginia—Madison, Jefferson, Monroe, and the like—would have thought on the topic of disputed elections, one is left with the impression that their ideas would have been rather inchoate. They believed that the resolution of disputed elections should be fair to the candidates and voters involved, without bias toward one side or another. During a disputed 1791 congressional election, for example, Madison declared that the US House of Representatives should follow "the general rule, that whosoever had the majority of sound votes was the legal Representative."[21]

Yet the Founding Generation lacked any sophisticated sense of the institutional arrangements necessary to instantiate this ideal of impartiality. Indeed, in the context of the 1791 election, which involved a clear case of ballot-box stuffing in Georgia, the US House of Representatives split 29–29, with the Speaker needing to break the tie, on whether to award the disputed seat to the candidate who was the victim of this flagrant fraud. This split vote in Congress seems tainted by partisanship, as those members who voted against letting the genuinely victorious candidate take his seat—including the Speaker with his tiebreaking vote—appeared motivated largely by the desire to prevent the opposing political party from increasing its ranks in the legislature. Had the Grenville Act governed this disputed congressional election from Georgia, it would have been handled very differently.

The Particular Challenge of Presidential Elections

The United States is often heralded as a model of democracy for the rest of the world. After the end of the Cold War, America's constitutional scholars developed something of a cottage industry in exporting American principles of constitutional law to Eastern European countries previously under the domination of the Soviet Union. This dissemination of American constitutional values, however, focused primarily on judicial review pursuant to *Marbury v. Madison*, particularly judicial enforcement of basic individual rights enshrined in a constitutional charter like America's Bill of Rights. Propagating US constitutional law in this way conveniently overlooked the hole in America's own Constitution concerning the institution for resolving a disputed presidential election.[22]

Perhaps it is time for the balance of trade in constitutional principles to flow in the opposite direction. After all, in the early part of the twenty-first century, American democracy no longer looks like much of a model for the rest of the world. With perennial paralysis in Congress over fiscal and other policy matters (like climate change and immigration reform), American-style constitutionalism—emphasizing as it does the separation of powers and its attendant checks and balances—seems a recipe for gridlock rather than good government.[23] Maybe the lack of an institution for resolving disputed presidential elections is merely one of many weaknesses in America's constitutional design, which is showing the adverse effects of being the oldest still in existence. It potentially could be a welcome change of pace if the United States were able to learn a thing or two from other constitutional democracies, including what kind of institution is optimal for the resolution of disputed elections.[24]

Other nations that have inherited their legal systems from Britain do better in this regard than the United States. Canada, Australia, and India, among others, including Britain itself, employ ostensibly nonpartisan institutions to handle election issues.[25] In essence, these other Anglo-inheritance countries have adopted updated versions of the principle at the core of the Grenville Act.

But the United States differs from all these other Anglo-inheritance nations in another crucial respect. The United States has a powerful elected president who serves as head of government, not merely a ceremonial head of state. These other Anglo-inheritance nations have essentially parliamentary systems in which a prime minister, appointed within the legislature itself, is head of government. Even the president of India, an office with considerable executive powers (although the prime minister is India's head of government), is selected by the India's Parliament and the legislatures of India's constituent states.[26] Thus no other Anglo-inheritance nation has an elected chief executive anything like the president of the United States. This point is true quite apart from the fact that since 1945 the US president has been the so-called leader of the free world in command of an unprecedented military arsenal. Even in 1876, when the Hayes-Tilden election erupted into a four-alarm conflagration, the US president was a uniquely powerful elected chief executive within the English-speaking world.[27]

The power of the US presidency is all the more reason why disputed presidential elections should be resolved by an impartial institution derived from the principle at the core of the Glenville Act. Yet perhaps perversely the more such an impartial institution is needed, the harder it is to adopt. The incentive for resisting the imposition of a biased outcome in a disputed presidential election is far greater than in a congressional election, because the cost of losing the White House is so much larger than with an ordinary single legislative seat; but so too is the incentive for controlling whatever institution will have the final say on who is president, since the gain from winning is also so much greater. Quite possibly, America has been unable to adopt an impartial institution for resolving disputed presidential elections precisely because the temptation to control the process has been too great, even with the inevitable risk that one's political opponents might end up controlling the process instead. Greed, in other words, seems to have trumped fear as the predominant emotion among American politicians when it comes to the question of what kind of institution should possess the power to determine the winner.[28]

There are other nations besides the United States with elected presidents who wield strong powers within their systems of government. Many Latin American as well as African nations have such "presidentialist" systems. The constitutions of these nations often purport to empower impartial tribunals in the event of a disputed presidential election. It is not dismissive of these developing democracies to recognize that their track record in handling disputed presidential elections is mixed. African elections, regrettably, often end in violence. Latin America recently has done much better. In 2006 both Mexico and Costa Rica had disputed presidential elections, and both with considerable success used impartial tribunals to resolve the disputes.[29] Still, this success was not entirely unblemished: shortly thereafter, the head of the Mexican tribunal "had to resign after being exposed by the press for corruption."[30] Although the United States should continue to monitor the experience of other democracies in the Western Hemisphere, it is too soon to be confident that they provide a method of resolving disputed presidential elections that is exportable to the United States.[31]

Arguably the nation with a well-developed democratic system most similar to the United States is France. America inherited its idea of separation of powers from Montesquieu, and France was hugely instrumental to the success of America's revolutionary independence from Britain. France today has an elected president, although not one as powerful within its system of government as the US president. France places the authority to resolve a disputed presidential election in its Conseil Constitutionnel, an appointed body of prominent dignitaries as well as all former presidents who refrain from further office-seeking. The goal is to have this body act in the interest of the nation, without regard to party. But the body, created in 1958 as part of the Fifth Republic, has yet to be tested in a situation like *Bush v. Gore* or the earlier Hayes-Tilden election of 1876. France has never had a presidential election close enough to require invocation of this dispute-resolution mechanism.[32]

Thus at this stage in world history, the United States is largely without guidance from other well-established democracies on how best to handle a disputed presidential election. Impartiality, nonpartisanship, and fairness are the obvious objectives, but the best means to achieve them are not readily borrowable from abroad. For the foreseeable future, the United States will need to look within its own democratic tradition to see if it has the capacity to develop an optimal tribunal for this kind of dispute.

Introduction

Understanding the Past for the Sake of the Future

This book concerns one facet of democracy. It does not cover all aspects of democracy. Gerrymandering is a particular pathology that has afflicted American democracy since its inception. The very term, after all, derives from the name of Elbridge Gerry, who signed the Declaration of Independence and attended the Constitutional Convention of 1787 and who thus numbers among the nation's Founders—and yet who was willing to manipulate the drawing of legislative districts to achieve a partisan advantage. This book, however, does not address the particular pathology of gerrymandering, although the historical absence of impartial institutions for the drawing of legislative districts (an absence that enables partisan gerrymanders to fester) shares some affinity with the lack of impartial institutions for the resolution of vote-counting disputes.[1]

Campaign finance is another important dimension of democracy that this book does not address. Many contemporary commentators are concerned, especially after the US Supreme Court's decision in *Citizen United,* that unregulated spending of behalf of candidates can distort the marketplace of political ideas, with pernicious consequences for popular sovereignty. This concern, too, has historical roots, as nineteenth-century observers fretted over the potentially corrupting influence of campaign spending by the robber barons of the Gilded Age. This book, however, addresses not what influences the electoral choices that voters make on the ballots they cast, but the procedures for counting those ballots.[2]

Even with respect to the ballots that voters cast, this book is not directly concerned with the rules and procedures for casting them. To be sure, many ballot-*counting* controversies turn on ballot-*casting* problems. The example with which the prologue began illustrates this point. The dispute over whether to count Apryl Babarcik's ballot arose because Apryl cast her ballot at the wrong polling place after having been misdirected there by poll workers. Improving the nation's administration of ballot-*casting* processes undoubtedly would reduce the risk of ballot-*counting* disputes. Accordingly, this book applauds all efforts at ballot-casting improvement. Nonetheless, the focus of this book is not the optimal design of ballot-casting rules and procedures. Rather, the book focuses on the vote-counting controversies that arise because, at least in part, the rules and procedures for the casting of ballots have fallen short of optimality.[3]

The significance of this book's topic is not diminished by its specificity. The history detailed in this book reveals this truth: no matter how earnest and energetic may be the efforts to devise better ballot-casting rules and procedures, there inevitably will be the necessity of sound mechanisms for resolving ballot-counting disputes as well. It is impossible to reduce the risk of a vote-counting dispute to zero, just as it is impossible to build an unsinkable ocean liner. While we can admire the desire to build a ship with minimal risk of sinking, it is still necessary to put enough lifeboats on board the Titanic in case the unthinkable actually occurs. The mechanisms for resolving vote-counting disputes are the lifeboats of the electoral system. One hopes never to have to use them. But they need to be there just in case, and sure enough once every so often they are actually put to use.

To further clarify the focus of this book, it is necessary to recognize that not every election that is still unsettled after Election Day ends up being *disputed*. Sometimes the candidates placidly observe a recount and accept its result without ever challenging anything about the recount. Conversely, however, all elections that hinge on a ballot-counting dispute are among the extra-competitive races that end up in overtime. In this sense, then, elections with disputed outcomes are a subcategory of elections that carry over into extra innings. Thus, insofar as they become disputed, they invariably raise the question why: what causes their extra innings to become contentious?

They raise other questions as well. How long will the dispute last? Does it risk extending beyond the date on which the winner of the election is supposed to take office? And whenever the dispute is finally resolved, what kind of victory will it produce? Will the losing candidate accept the outcome as valid? Or, instead, will the losing candidate treat the result as imposed by force (requiring submission but not acceptance)?

As these questions indicate, the resolution of vote-counting disputes is a function that goes to the core of why the electoral system exists in the first place. Above all else, the purpose of an election is to choose a winning candidate to hold a public office in the government of the society. If the election cannot do that, it fails in its essential purpose.

Furthermore, the very existence of elections invites competition. As long as there is more than one candidate for an office, the voters have a choice, and the system needs to work when two or more candidates are closely matched in their ability to appeal to the median voter. An electoral system that cannot identify the electorate's preference when the electorate is narrowly divided over which of two options is superior can hardly claim to be a well-functioning electoral system. Thus, examining the mechanisms by which a democracy handles its most competitive elections—the ones where the outcome remains contested even after the ballots are counted (and even recounted)—provides a valuable perspective on how robust is the health of self-government in the society.

The Venerable Ideal of an Honest and Accurate Count

There is an additional reason, and an especially compelling one, to focus specifically on vote-counting disputes without delving into all other aspects about the operation of a democracy. As the history described in this book will show, there is a distinctive morality to the counting of ballots that is independent of views concerning other elements of a democracy, including who is entitled to exercise the franchise. At the time of the Founding, the franchise was severely limited in comparison to today. Women could not vote. Nor could most African Americans. Property qualifications excluded the impoverished from the right to vote.[4] Still, the Founders believed that the competing candidates and the qualified electorate were entitled to a fair count, meaning that the ballots cast by eligible voters (and only those ballots) should be counted honestly according to how they were cast. Thus quite apart from the extent of voter eligibility—whether the almost universal adult suffrage of today, or all the earlier periods that fell far short—electoral integrity has been a professed national value.

Elections should not be stolen, in other words. This basic idea has existed throughout American history, from the time of the Founding up through today. It has not always been honored. Rather, for much of the nation's existence—even as the franchise steadily expanded—adherence to this elementary tenet has proved more difficult than most Americans would care to admit.[5] Indeed, as we shall see, the most significant vote-counting disputes in each era of American history are usually *either* those in which one side believes it has been robbed of a major election *or* those in which some individual or institution thwarts an attempt to steal an election through a distortion of the vote-counting. The former are perceived failures to abide by the ideal of an honest count; the latter are successes in which the ideal, when threatened, prevailed. Even so, the simple moral principle that it is wrong to steal an election has been ever-present and unassailable as a standard to which the electoral system should conform.

Electoral theft can surface in different forms. There is outright stuffing of the ballot box with fake votes or, its equivalent, the padding of tally sheets with phantom votes never actually cast. But there is also the manipulation of the count through dishonestly selective application of vote-counting rules. To count some, but only some, of the ballots that should be treated the same under the rules (*either* all in *or* all out) is tantamount to either discarding ballots entitled to be counted or padding the count with ineligible ballots; either way, the result does not conform to the standard of counting all eligible ballots, but only eligible ballots, according to how they were cast. If the manipulation is part of an intentional effort to sway the result to one side, the other side will perceive it as a form of electoral theft. The means might be different than pure ballot-box stuffing, but the mendacity will seem the same.

Although dishonesty in vote-counting has precipitated greater crises than inaccuracy, the foundational idea of a fair count has encompassed accuracy as well as honesty. Ballots counted incorrectly can deprive candidates of victories that were deservedly theirs, simultaneously depriving the valid voters who cast those ballots of the actual choice they made (and were entitled to make). Moreover, counting mistakes can invite recounting dishonesty. For example, when absentee ballots are supposed to be verified for eligibility before being counted, but some local jurisdictions fail to conduct this verification and irretrievably commingle unverified ballots with all the rest of counted ballots, the question arises about what to do with similar absentee ballots that elsewhere were properly checked before counting: should they also be put into the mix because equivalent ballots already were, or should they be kept from being counted if the check shows them ineligible? In the abstract, this question might be considered on the merits, without regard to which candidate in the race the answer would favor. But, in reality, partisans will know which answer will benefit their side. If partisans are in a position of power that enables them to answer the question authoritatively, they will be tempted to answer that question solely with the view of helping their party's candidate and irrespective of the merits. History shows that partisans in power have great difficulty resisting this temptation, even when to hold a public office that gives them this vote-counting power they have sworn to act honestly on behalf of the public as a whole.

To minimize occasions where this kind of temptation arises requires minimizing the antecedent administrative errors that create the enticing circumstances. For this reason, among others, the transcendent ideal of a fair count encompasses the twin goals of eliminating both dishonesty and inaccuracy from the count. Both goals, moreover, point to the desirability of pinning down to the greatest degree possible the rules for counting ballots before they are cast. But one of the overarching themes of this book is that reality inevitably falls short of this ideal. This is true for the goal of maximizing the precision of vote-counting rules, just as it is for the goal of optimizing the administration of the vote-casting process. Accordingly, there will always remain the need for fallback institutions to cope with issues not adequately accounted for in advance.

The Challenges of Implementing the Ideal

The ideal of a fair count might seem clear enough in principle, but in practice it can break down into subsidiary issues for which there is no transcendently obvious answer. For example, chain-of-custody rules exist to protect against ballot tampering. Ballots, especially after they have been cast, should be stored securely and safeguarded to prevent nefarious partisans from manipulating them to alter the outcome. Suppose, however, that election officials in a particular locality violate these chain-of-custody rules in a way that leaves potentially decisive ballots vulnerable to tampering, even though there is no proof of actual tampering. Should these ballots be deemed uncountable because the chain-of-custody rules were improperly breached and there is a risk that the ballots no longer reflect the true choices of the voters who cast them? Or should the ballots be counted on the grounds that absent evidence that the ballots have been altered in a way that negates the will of the valid voters who cast them, these voters should not suffer the consequence of disenfranchisement because of the chain-of-custody breach committed by the local election officials?

As James Monroe observed about an early gubernatorial election that we shall examine closely (New York's in 1792), "general principles" do not supply a ready answer in this situation. The idea of a fair count encompasses *both* the value of preserving the integrity of the ballots as cast through enforcement of sound chain-of-custody rules *and* the value of protecting valid voters from disenfranchisement at the hands of errant election officials. In this particular situation the two subsidiary values are in tension with each other, and the basic idea of a fair count does not contain a rule by which to resolve this intramural tension. Moreover, although examples of this subsidiary conflict within the general concept of a fair count have abounded throughout American history, the nation and the states have had difficulty settling upon a set of specific rules to provide clear outcomes when these situations arise. The general trend has been to favor protecting voters from disenfranchisement, but the decisions have not been uniform in that direction even recently, as our analysis of Minnesota's 2008 US Senate election will demonstrate.

Furthermore, the goal of protecting valid voters from wrongful disenfranchisement can conflict not only with the goal of thwarting ballot-box tampering but also with the even more fundamental principle of counting ballots in accordance with rules established before the casting of those ballots. Counting rules, in other words, should not change after ballots are cast. To permit them to change is to invite dishonest manipulation of the count in order to secure a partisan advantage. And yet there can arise situations in which there is pressure to alter, or at least refine, the counting rules in order to protect innocent eligible voters from disenfranchisement at the hands of errant election officials. Arguably, the specific Ohio example in the prologue is an instance of this kind. The preexisting rules appeared categorically to require the disqualification of ballots cast in the wrong precinct, but strict enforcement of those preexisting rules would seem to perpetrate an injustice against innocent voters who went to the right precinct but who were misdirected to the wrong location by errant local election officials. There is no easy solution in this situation. The basic idea of a fair count does not say whether to prioritize faithful enforcement of preexisting rules however harsh doing so might appear in the particular instance, or instead to prioritize protecting the innocent voters from wrongful disenfranchisement even if doing so requires bending (if not outright breaking) the preexisting rules for counting ballots.

The idea of a fair count also does not straightforwardly dictate when to declare that an election must be deemed void and a new election held. Assume, for example, that the post office has lost a batch of ballots that might, or might not, make a difference to the outcome of an election. A fair count of the ballots actually on hand will not include these lost ballots. But it is impossible to count ballots that never arrive and cannot be found. Should a winner of the election be declared based on a fair count of the eligible ballots that do exist to be counted? Or should the election be declared null and void because of the uncountable missing ballots that might, or might not, have made a difference? The answer to these questions does not lie within the concept of a fair count alone, but in ideas about whether voters may have assumed the risk when entrusting the post office with their ballots, and whether the costs of holding a new election are worth paying (especially when it is possible that administrative errors might also afflict the do-over election). As we shall see, history reveals that America has had a particularly hard time making judgments about when to declare elections void and thus when to require new elections.[6]

Fairness, Impartiality, and Legitimacy

When it is unclear what fairness requires regarding the substance of a vote-counting dispute, it is possible to turn to the procedural value of impartiality as the best means of resolving the conflict. If a neutral arbiter is forced to choose between two contending and plausible claims of fairness, one of which will cause one candidate to win while the other will yield a victory for the opposing candidate, at least the neutral arbiter's choice will be unbiased and thus procedurally impartial toward both sides. At the very least, in this situation the result will not be rigged in advance by an adjudicatory tribunal predisposed to rule in one side's favor.[7]

The progress that America has made in its history of handling vote-counting disputes, as fitful and uneven as it has been over now more than two centuries, can be seen as having two dimensions. One is the dimension of clarifying and specifying the substantive standards for the adjudication of ballot-counting litigation, so that what result the adjudicatory tribunal must reach will be straightforward and uncontestable regardless of the tribunal's procedural impartiality. The other is the dimension of procedural innovation to increase the likelihood that the tribunal responsible for adjudicating a major vote-counting dispute will be unbiased and impartial—and perceived as such—in the event that the substance of what the tribunal should do is not straightforward and uncontestable. At this stage in American history, the progress achieved along both dimensions remains incomplete, and further progress along both is worth pursuing. Neither dimension deserves emphasis to the point that its advancement comes to the detriment of the other.

In addition to fairness and impartiality, the idea of legitimacy is often invoked. Associated with lawfulness, legitimacy is sometimes taken to mean that a ballot-counting dispute is resolved pursuant to the rule of law, even if it cannot comport with ideal standards of fairness or impartiality.[8] America is praised for settling its ballot-counting disputes through the instruments of lawful power, rather than by means of lawless militarism. While this record of lawfulness is indeed to be commended, especially when compared to coups d'état that often occur when ballot-counting disputes arise elsewhere in the world, one should not too quickly equate mere lawfulness with electoral legitimacy.[9]

A stolen election lacks legitimacy even when a government body wielding lawful power is the instrument of the theft. American history is replete with examples of such theft, or at least instances where the losing side reasonably believed that such theft was perpetrated by a government body under the control of its electoral opponents. Consider, for example, the circumstance in which a canvassing board dominated by members of one political party selectively manipulates the counting rules to assure that its candidate prevails. That result is undoubtedly pursuant to law, given the authority vested in the canvassing board. But is it legitimate? Doubtful, given that the board deliberately distorted the ballot-counting rules to achieve its predetermined result. In any event, this kind of conduct by a canvassing board—which certainly occurred in the presidential election of 1876, among other episodes that form our story—is in flagrant disregard of the basic idea of a fair count. Thus, when a losing candidate is asked to accept a count that is *legitimate* even if *unfair*, should the idea of legitimacy encompass a deliberately stolen election accomplished by means of a lawfully authoritative canvassing board? If so, then the gap between legitimacy and fairness would seem to stretch too far; at least, legitimacy has lost its potential appeal as a normative concept capable of conveying electoral acceptability distinct from a more stringent standard of electoral fairness. A deliberately stolen election should be condemned as not merely falling below a benchmark of fairness, but sinking below even an acceptable level of legitimacy. And this is true even if the electoral theft is not part of a coup d'état.

Whether we speak in terms of fairness, impartiality, or legitimacy, America has struggled to abide by its professed commitment to electoral integrity (defined, again, as an honest and accurate count of valid ballots). This struggle has persisted, moreover, even as the nation has made great progress in expanding voter eligibility. Why fulfillment of one core component of democracy has lagged behind achievement of the other is a complicated inquiry. A partial explanation lies in the fact that exceptionally close elections—those that yield ballot-counting disputes—are relatively infrequent. Every election, whether close or not, exposes who among the citizenry is not entitled to participate. (This remains true today with respect to felon disenfranchisement: the ineligibility of former felons is abundantly apparent in each election, whether or not their participation might have made a difference in the outcome.) When an entire category of citizens is unjustly excluded from the electorate, as African Americans and women were, every election no matter how competitive is a reminder of the unjust exclusion. Hence, momentum for reform is more easily generated, and sustained, on an eligibility issue concerning unjust exclusion. By contrast, electoral injustice in the form of unfairly manipulating the counting of ballots in an exceptionally close race is a sin not soon to be repeated, at least for the same kind of race, because such exceptionally close races are so few and far between. (If one state has a disputed gubernatorial election in a given year, for example, that same state is unlikely to have another disputed gubernatorial election for decades.) The impetus for reform of the vote-counting process is enervated by the sheer infrequency of the problem.

The difficulty of achieving vote-counting reforms, however, does not justify abandoning the effort. It is difficult to adopt precautionary measures to protect against an earthquake measuring 9.0 on the Richter scale, and mercifully earthquakes of that enormous magnitude are exceedingly infrequent. But the potential consequences of that large an earthquake are so severe that, despite the remoteness of the risk, it remains worth striving for protective measures. The analogy holds for major vote-counting disputes. Especially in the context of a presidential election, as became apparent in both 1876 and 2000, such disputes can function as a kind of massive electoral earthquake. It is preferable, if possible, to have in place an impartial vote-counting institution that can dissipate the disruptive, even potentially cataclysmic, effects of such an electoral tremor.

Moreover, as already mentioned, the ability to handle a major vote-counting dispute is the ultimate test of a democracy's capacity to accurately measure the electorate's will when the candidates are most evenly matched and their competition is most intense. For the sake of perfecting the system of democracy to which the society has professed its commitment, pursuit of improved vote-counting procedures—including impartial institutions for the resolution of these disputes—is a worthy endeavor. Perhaps, too, the kind of commitment to electoral fairness and impartiality that would be necessary to achieve such vote-counting reforms could carry over into other areas of electoral reform, including even gerrymandering and campaign finance. If the design of electoral institutions and procedures is guided by a spirit of fair competition regulated by impartial referees—so that the candidates and parties themselves can be appropriately aggressive in their efforts to win, while the system as a whole is governed by evenhandedness toward the contestants—then society would be in a position to improve its operation of democracy along multiple dimensions.

The Reform-Minded Goal and the Historical Method

This book, as should be clear by now, is motivated by the goal of improving the procedures by which America resolves vote-counting disputes in high-stakes elections. If that goal could be achieved without need for extended historical inquiry, this book would not undertake that inquiry. In other words, if simply surveying existing procedures that currently exist among the fifty states would suffice as a basis of recommending a best practice for all states to emulate, this book would exhibit a very different methodological approach in pursuit of its objective.

History is aesthetically and intellectually enriching in its own right, but the fields of law and public policy tend to treat history in a strictly utilitarian manner. History is relevant to these practical-minded disciplines if history is helpful; otherwise, it is left for leisure. Lawyers, indeed, generally pursue their craft in reverse chronological order: all else being equal, the most recent precedent is the most germane, and one need not search further back in time once one has found a newer case on point.

That this book starts with the Founding of the Republic signifies a key claim that the book makes: to achieve progress in improving the nation's processes for resolving ballot-counting controversies, it is necessary to go all the way back to the nation's beginning. The institutional inadequacies that exist today for handling disputes over election outcomes have their origins in choices made, as well as options overlooked, at the nation's Founding. Thus, this book returns to those origins to consider the extent to which our current conditions are still shaped by them. At the same time, the book also considers the extent to which we have the capacity to overcome deficiencies associated with the creation of the constitutional structures that launched the United States of America, a federal republic, as a great experiment in popular sovereignty.

The story that this book tells, however, does not ends with the Founding. Instead, it is a story about how the nation, and the states within it, have reworked the constitutional apparatus bequeathed by the Founders. Each generation of Americans has needed to adapt that constitutional legacy to the unexpected circumstances that emerged in the context of intense two-party competition over the counting of ballots in major elections. The Founders had hoped to avoid ongoing head-to-head competition over electoral outcomes between two established political parties. Yet almost from the beginning that dynamic is what took root—and began to evolve into the form of two-party competition that presently exists.[10]

For those who pursue history for its own appeal, the story of the nation's experience with vote-counting disputes should have intrinsic interest. While lacking the drama of military battles, they are a form of competition and as such have the narrative structure of any athletic contest. Indeed, this book functions as a highlights reel from the sport of electoral prizefighting. The episodes in this book concern the biggest bouts, when the competition is the stiffest. For the winners and losers of these particular elections the fight-to-the-finish could not be more dramatic or, often, more ferocious.

But this book seeks more than drama. Its story has the capacity to increase national self-understanding. Because ballot-counting disputes in high-stakes elections are the ultimate test of a democracy's capacity to identify accurately the electorate's choice, the story of how our nation has handled these tests teaches us about the strength of our mechanisms for self-government. Insofar as the story is one of increasing capacity to meet these tests successfully, the lesson helps us comprehend the nation's evolving maturation as a democracy. We deepen our understanding of America's democracy as an ongoing work-in-progress.

This understanding, in turn, is what facilitates the possibility of further growth. Armed with the insights this book offers, political leaders of the nation and its states can carry forward the project started at the Founding. To the extent that existing institutions for resolving vote-counting disputes remain less than ideal, current and future generations of Americans can continue to improve these institutions. In this way, they can enhance the commitment to democracy that forms the core of our national identity.

This book's story thus takes us through the transformations that have occurred in the nation's conception and implementation of democracy over the two-and-a-quarter centuries of its existence. It is a story that encompasses the unique pathology of slavery that severed the nation, to be restitched in Reconstruction but not altogether successfully. Running through this story is the question whether the nation as a whole shares a conception of representative democracy, or whether the South as a distinct region has had its own separate vision of what elections are for and how to conduct them. Despite the South's return to the Union after the Civil War, the enterprise of counting ballots in the former Confederacy may not be the same sort of enterprise as counting ballots in the North, at least not until the end of the twentieth century.[11]

The Gilded Age of the late nineteenth century emerges as a period of particularly divisive and destabilizing vote-counting disputes. The Progressive Era that followed attempted improvements in recount procedures but most significantly adopted other electoral reforms, especially the enfranchisement of women, which transformed cultural conditions so as to increase the insistence upon fairness in the vote-counting process. But it was the Civil Rights Era of the 1960s that elevated democratic expectations to the point that successful recounts in major races became routine.[12] During this time of renewed flourishing of political rights, several states—with Minnesota in the lead—adopted exemplary institutional innovations that would serve as a model to other states on how best to adjudicate a high-stakes vote-counting dispute.

Bush v. Gore at the close of the century,[13] rather than being an aberration, is an outgrowth of the transformation wrought by the Civil Rights Era and a key component of the overall institutional improvements that America has made since the Founding to address the challenge of counting disputed ballots fairly. In the nineteenth century, state supreme courts played an increasingly important role to compensate for the obvious inadequacies of state legislatures as the locus of authority to decide which ballots should count. State supreme courts, however, had their own limitations, often being susceptible to some of the same partisan pressures as state legislatures, in part because they—unlike the federal judiciary—were often elected rather than appointed bodies.[14]

For most of this history, however, the federal courts had no role to play, because the US Supreme Court ruled them impotent to address any dispute that arose in the context of a state's ballot-counting procedures. This ruling came in *Taylor v. Beckham*,[15] a case involving Kentucky's gubernatorial election of 1899 (a literally fatal contest, as described in Chapter 6). This ruling held sway for a full century, until *Bush v. Gore*, and was decisive in some of the lowest moments of American democracy in the twentieth century, including the blatant ballot-box stuffing that tainted the 1948 election that propelled Lyndon Johnson to the US Senate (see Chapter 8).

Justice John Marshall Harlan was the lone dissenter in *Taylor v. Beckham*, just as he was the lone dissenter in the infamous segregation case of *Plessy v. Ferguson*.[16] Harlan's dissent in *Plessy* received its vindication in *Brown v. Board of Education*.[17] His dissent in *Taylor v. Beckham* was similarly vindicated in *Bush v. Gore*, where seven Justices recognized that the federal courts have the power to enforce the federal Constitution to constrain improprieties in a state's vote-counting processes.

This vindication of Justice Harlan in *Bush v. Gore* would not have been possible, however, without the development of the one-person-one-vote doctrine in the US Supreme Court during the Civil Rights Era. One-person-one-vote was the Court's tool for insisting that states comply with the essential prerequisites of democratic government, whether in the drawing of legislative districts or rules governing access to the ballot. *Bush v. Gore* invoked the same tool to insist that states comply with the basic prerequisites of a democracy in the particular context of counting ballots. It was exactly what Harlan had called for a century earlier. When seen in the light of this history, *Bush v. Gore* is the culmination of a jurisprudential transformation that took a full century to complete.

To be sure, as *Bush v. Gore* itself shows, the federal judiciary is not a perfect institution for the adjudication of intense ballot-counting disputes. Federal judges are not immune from partisanship, even though they are appointed rather than elected. But compared to state courts, and especially compared to state legislatures, the federal judiciary is a far superior institution for increasing the likelihood that a vote-counting fight will be resolved fairly and impartially. Unless and until an even better institution is developed to handle these high-stakes cases, the federal judiciary is the best of the available institutions.[18]

The relatively short period since *Bush v. Gore* tends to confirm this point, as explained in Chapter 12. In 2008, Minnesota again was especially successful in resolving a major disputed election precisely because it used a special-purpose panel to do so—one that was intentionally and transparently structured to be balanced and neutral toward both sides. By contrast, Washington's experience with its gubernatorial recount in 2004 showed that when states use institutions that are structurally tilted toward one side, the result is inevitably a lingering perception of unfairness on the other side. A federal court, however imperfect, is more likely to be perceived as fair than a structurally biased state tribunal.

The historical journey undertaken in this book offers hope that America can continue to improve its record of compliance with the abiding ideal of honest and accurate ballot-counting. Like the expansion of the franchise, thus far much more successful, this trajectory has not been entirely uniform in its forward movement over the entire course of American history.[19] There have been steps backward, even well into the middle of the twentieth century, as well as steps forward. Nonetheless, when one considers the totality of the trajectory, from the Founding to the present, the overall motion has been toward greater achievement of vote-counting fairness, not less. Recognition of this trend gives one reason for optimism that even further progress toward fulfillment of the ideal is possible.

Hamilton or Madison?

Despite providing grounds for optimism, the history detailed in this book also offers a basis for challenging the quest for a fair count in high-stakes disputed elections. The challenge starts with the proposition that it is quixotic to expect a truly fair count in the rare case when an election is so exceptionally close that fighting over the outcome might actually change the outcome. In this situation, the argument goes, the counting process inevitably will descend into a partisan brawl, where one side will prevail based solely on political strength rather than based on any assessment of the merits that is even remotely impartial. In this situation, theft of the result—if by "theft" one means a partisan power-grab regardless of what the valid voters actually wanted as expressed through their ballots—is to be expected and tolerated, *so long as it is confined to the unique circumstances of the exceptionally close election and does not extend to normal circumstances, when margins of victory are much more decisive.*

On this view, the health of a vote-counting system should not be measured by how it handles the exceptionally close election that is rare, but instead only by how it handles all the other routine elections. A system is inappropriately rigged if in a routine election a candidate decisively chosen by valid voters, based on what a fair count would show to be a clear-cut margin, can be "counted out" through manipulation of the counting process.[20] That routine frustration of the electorate's choice may occur in other countries, but it does not occur in America, and the fact that it does not is the hallmark of America's success at operating an electoral democracy. Just because there are exceptions to this routine success, when a candidate who might have won a fair count is instead deliberately counted out in an exceptionally close race, should not be taken to negate the importance of this routine success.

This view leads to some practical advice to a candidate who is the victim of such rare counting out in America. Do not harp over the unfairness of being counted out in this one unusual election. Instead, come back next time and win decisively. Given the system's routine capacity to achieve an accurate and honest count when the win is decisive, the counted out candidate and fellow partisans should devote all their energies to convincing enough voters to make sure their win is decisive enough next time.

This pragmatic view is hardly an idiosyncratic outlier in American history. On the contrary, it has a pedigree going all the way back to Alexander Hamilton, the nation's archetypal Founding pragmatist. As we shall see, when John Jay believed that he had been robbed of a victory the voters had given him in 1792 election for governor of New York, Hamilton urged Jay to acquiesce in the defeat and then run again next time and win decisively, which Jay did. Hamilton's advice to Jay is wisdom that many successful American politicians have profited from since then (including Richard Nixon, who chose to run again and win in 1968 after declining to press the case that he had been cheated of a victory in 1960).

But Hamilton's view is not the only standard by which to measure America's vote-counting capacity. James Madison offers a useful contrast to Hamilton on this point. Just as we can juxtapose the divergent views of Hamilton and Madison on other aspects of America's political system (Hamilton favoring a national bank, Madison initially not, and so forth), we can do so in the vote-counting context as well. Madison believed that in each election, the vote-counting process should strive as best it can to produce a fair count—meaning awarding the victory to the candidate who genuinely received the most valid votes—and if it did not, that was an inappropriate result regardless of what might happen in the next election.

Both the Hamilton and Madison views on how to judge the merits of the vote-counting process have existed throughout US history, and both are likely to continue long into the future. The relative dominance of one view over the other has changed over time, and from place to place within different regions of the country. The relative strength of each view may also depend on the particular office that is at stake at any given time. To invoke again the Ohio example in the prologue, Hamilton's advice may be sound when what is at stake is a single seat in a state's legislature (even if winning the seat would give one's party a significant degree of power within the legislature). The unfair loss of a single legislative seat is one that a political party can redress in the next election. But when the office at stake is the presidency—especially in the twenty-first century, with all the enormous power of the presidency in both domestic and foreign affairs—is it really good enough to be told one has another chance to win decisively next time and thus one should accept being counted out (if that is what happened) this time?

Bush v. Gore is a multifaceted story (as we shall see in Chapter 11). One point it illustrates is the fact that in contemporary times it appears to be too

Figure I.1 Hamilton and Madison offer different visions of how to judge America's success in the resolution of disputed elections. (a) Hamilton's portrait by John Trumbull; National Gallery of Art. (b) Madison's portrait by Gilbert Stuart; Colonial Williamsburg Foundation, gift of Mrs. George S. Robbins.

much to expect a presidential candidate to give up quickly. George W. Bush would not accept the prospect that the Florida Supreme Court might engineer a recount that would give Al Gore the lead, and thus Bush went to federal court to block the Florida Supreme Court from doing so. Similarly, Gore refused to accept Bush's certified victory, but instead sought a state court remedy to overturn that result. Next time America has a disputed presidential election, whenever that occurs, would we expect a candidate to take the Hamiltonian view of acquiescing until the quadrennial cycle repeats itself, or instead demand a Madisonian fair count in the immediate election?

Regardless of what the candidates themselves would do, how should we as citizens judge the merits of our nation's vote-counting system? Should we accept the Hamiltonian perspective that the system is successful as long as it avoids rigged results in routine elections? Or should we instead embrace the Madisonian perspective that the system should strive as best it can to achieve a fair count in each election, no matter how close the particular election may be? Indeed, should we insist that a fair count is especially essential when the election is exceptionally close, because that is when the system most needs to show its capacity for an honest and accurate count?

We should keep these basic questions in mind as we embark on our historical journey to consider how our nation has fared when its vote-counting procedures have been put to the ultimate test.

1

Uncertain Vote-Counting in the Founding Era

The most significant ballot-counting disputes of the young Republic arose in two gubernatorial elections: New York's in 1792 and Massachusetts's in 1806. These two episodes will be discussed in the next chapter. First, it is important to set the stage for that discussion. The gubernatorial disputes did not arise in a vacuum. Instead, as this chapter shows, the Founders struggled with vote-counting disputes generally.

Some, but certainly not all, of that struggle can be attributed to the fact that the Founders were inventing a new kind of federal system, one characterized by the split sovereignty between the states and the national government. When the Founders first encountered vote-counting disputes in congressional elections, they were forced to consider federalism issues that simply had not existed before. For example, if the US House of Representatives determined a state's count of ballots inaccurate, could the House award the seat to a different candidate than the one the state certified as winning; or, instead, could the House only void the result and send the matter back for the state to fill the seat another way, including by choosing to hold a new election?

Other ballot-counting issues that confounded Congress in its early years had nothing to do with federalism but instead were inherent in the nature of counting ballots for any form of elective office. For example, when the military improperly attempted to influence voters at the polls, should the election be voided when it is uncertain whether the military's improper conduct actually determined the election's outcome? As we shall see, that same issue proved difficult both in Congress and within the states. Thus, implementing the basic principle of electoral integrity challenged the Founders in ways that had nothing to do with the particular type of election at stake (whether congressional, gubernatorial, or otherwise; whether statewide or local). Rather, the Founders' difficulties with the task reveal a fundamental incompleteness in their own conception of elections as a means to achieve "republican" government, as they called it.[1] Their own theory of government was incomplete in the specific sense that although collectively committed to popular sovereignty, they had no shared understanding of what method of resolving ballot-counting controversies was more faithful to this fundamental commitment to republicanism.

Consequently, we will commence our exploration not with a congressional or gubernatorial election, but instead an even more elementary one. We will begin with a local, district-based election for a seat on a multimember body—not unlike an election to a seat in a legislative chamber, although the particular government body wielded the state's executive power and, with its seats few in number, winning each one carried considerable political weight. The election we will start with, moreover, occurred in the earliest years of our nation's independent existence. Indeed, arising in 1781, it came before the creation of the federal Constitution in 1787, at a time when the thirteen states were operating under the antecedent Articles of Confederation and before their independence from Britain was even fully secured. The essential features of this early dispute establish its significance: the participants were leading members of the Founding Generation, and they vigorously debated the principles that should apply in the adjudication of the ballot-counting dispute. Moreover, the procedural method they employed to resolve the dispute was far from satisfactory; one side walked out in protest. The fact that even this basic, early election proved unexpectedly difficult for the Founders to handle vividly demonstrates the incompleteness of the republican government they were establishing. They wanted elections as a way to achieve republican government; of that there is no doubt. But they did not know how best to achieve republican government when there emerged a controversy over the outcome of an important election.

Pennsylvania, 1781

Philadelphia is the birthplace of both the Declaration of Independence and the US Constitution. It also can claim the dubious honor of being the location of the new nation's first major ballot-counting dispute. The colonial legislatures had seen their share of ballot-counting disputes pursuant to the parliamentary principle that a legislative chamber shall judge the qualification and elections of its members.[2] But the colonial legislatures had not been uniform in their handling of these disputes; some "displayed a tendency toward harshness and some toward leniency."[3] Left unanswered was the question what principles would govern after independence.

The year was 1781, and the election was for a seat on the Supreme Executive Council of Pennsylvania. The state's constitution of 1776 had adopted this multimember body to exercise executive power in lieu of a single governor. Each of the state's twelve counties, as well as the city of Philadelphia, had a seat on the council, for a total of thirteen. The seat for the *county* of Philadelphia was thus distinct from the city's seat, and the county's seat was the disputed one.[4]

At the time, there were two loosely organized political parties in Pennsylvania. One party supported the 1776 state constitution, which was especially egalitarian in its extension of the franchise. The other party, more conservative in its conception of republicanism, wanted to amend the state constitution to limit the right to vote based on economic qualifications: "Fundamentally, it was a fight between classes, between the 'haves and have nots.'"[5] Historians have labeled the two parties Radicals and Conservatives, and with the fluidity of the politics then at play, moderates straddled these two main groups.[6]

The Radical candidate for the seat was John Bayard, a colonel in the American Revolution and a previous speaker of Pennsylvania's then-unicameral legislature, the Assembly.[7] The Conservatives were split between two candidates, John Dickinson and Thomas Mifflin. Dickinson, a major figure of the Founding era, famously refused to sign the Declaration of Independence while serving in the Continental Congress, but nonetheless joined the military to fight the British in the Revolutionary War. Later, he would hold high office in both Pennsylvania and Delaware, as well as represent the latter state in the 1787 convention that drafted the federal Constitution (which, unlike the Declaration of Independence, he would sign).[8] Mifflin, likewise, fought in the Revolutionary War, serving as one of Washington's aides. He, too, signed the US Constitution as a delegate to the convention (representing Pennsylvania). After Pennsylvania replaced its Supreme Executive Council with a single governor in 1790, Mifflin would be the first to hold the office.[9] Thus the three candidates vying for this particular council seat in 1781 were a highly distinguished trio, with Bayard at the time being as prominent as his two opponents.

Voting in this election took place on October 9, 1781. The split in Conservative support between Dickinson and Mifflin caused Bayard to receive the most votes:[10]

Bayard	604
Mifflin	425
Dickinson	278

Conservatives, however, immediately condemned the result as invalid because of improprieties at the polls. Their claims included allegations that the polls had opened two hours late, that some "lads under twenty-one years of age" had been permitted to cast ballots, that some polling inspectors "were asleep" or had abandoned their duties before counting the ballots, that other inspectors had not taken their proper oaths, and that some individuals acted as inspectors even though they were not entitled to do so.[11]

The most serious charge, by far, was that leading officers of Pennsylvania's militia—including General John Lacey, who served on the Supreme Executive Council in the seat from Bucks County—had organized and implemented a plan to march their soldiers to the polls and force them to cast ballots in favor of Bayard. America was still at war against the British, and Pennsylvania's militia had taken up positions to defend the state (and particularly Philadelphia) from the possibility of another British attack. Conditions were favorable enough, however, that the Supreme Executive Council had ordered Lacey to furlough his men for enough time that they might vote in the election. Lacey then colluded with other top officers to make sure that his soldiers voted the way he wanted.[12]

Conservatives filed a petition in the Supreme Executive Council detailing their allegations.[13] Some soldiers refused to cast a ballot "by reason of there being no freedom of election."[14] When other soldiers attempted to alter their tickets, so that the names listed would be their own preferred candidates, one officer "reprimanded and abused them" and "tore the tickets they were getting, to pieces, and ordered his clerks to write new ones."[15] Other military officers, furthermore, were among those who unlawfully "acted as Inspectors" even though they had no authority to serve as "officers of the election."[16] Based on the totality of their allegations, including the "irregularities of the time and manner of holding the election" as well as the "abuses" of "military authority . . . by General Lacey and the officers under his command," the Conservative petitioners asked the council to "set aside" the election and to order a new one.[17]

The council considered the petition at many meetings from November 1781 to March of the following year. Two prominent Conservative attorneys, Jacob Rush and William Lewis, presented the evidence and arguments in support of the petition.[18] Rush's brother, Benjamin, was an especially influential Founding Father in the fields of education and medicine.[19] Jacob himself later became a distinguished judge on the state's supreme court.[20] Lewis also would become a distinguished jurist, serving on the federal court in Philadelphia.[21]

Bayard's victory in the election was defended by counsel of equal if not greater prominence. One of the three lawyers on that side of the case was William Bradford, attorney general for the state and later for the United States. Another was Jonathan Sergeant, Bradford's predecessor as Pennsylvania's attorney general.[22] The third was Jared Ingersoll, who also signed the US Constitution as one of Pennsylvania's delegates to the constitutional convention (and who afterward would litigate some of the most important early cases in federal constitutional law, including *Chisholm v. Georgia* and

Hylton v. United States).[23] The quality of the attorneys on both sides indicates the significance of the case.

During this period, the council was controlled by Radicals, although some were more moderate than others.[24] They divided into two groups in response to the petition. Five of them—including Lacey, who astonishingly did not recuse himself from the proceedings—wanted the council to request an opinion from the Pennsylvania Supreme Court on the matter. Another five, including the more moderate Radicals, saw no need for an opinion. These moderates had already determined that the evidence clearly showed that the election had been corrupted by the conduct of the military and thus should be annulled. Because two council members were absent, and because Bayard also did not recuse himself (having been seated almost immediately after the election in October), the five-to-five split in the council defeated the motion to seek the supreme court's opinion.[25]

The five who had supported this motion published a dissent in response to its defeat. Much of what they said warrants consideration over two centuries later. They understood the implications of the case: "We apprehend the present determination will become a precedent in all future elections." They knew that the controversy had already attracted widespread attention and unrest, characterizing it as "a cause . . . of such magnitude and importance [that it] has drawn the attention of other States, and raised so great a ferment in this." Professing that the dispute should be resolved with "impartiality," they asserted that the supreme court was the best body for that purpose. They argued that the issue was not merely whether wrongdoing had occurred but whether it was enough "to invalidate an election." "The law," they stressed, "should be plain, clear, and explicit" on this point. For extra emphasis, they repeated their fear of pernicious consequences if the law did not sufficiently distinguish between "irregularities of time and place in holding of elections, and manner of conducting them," on the one hand, and "the operation of law upon these [irregularities] so as to vacate an election," on the other.[26]

The moderates issued their own separate opinion, and theirs also commands the attention of posterity. They put the essence of their position plainly: "We are fully satisfied in our judgment, that the facts proved before us render the election unconstitutional and void."[27] They had no doubt that Lacey's soldiers had been coerced and deprived of their constitutional right to a "free election."[28] They expressly quoted Pennsylvania's constitution of 1776: "The necessary & essential properties of an election in this Commonwealth are, 'That it be by ballot—that it be free—that it be voluntary.' "[29] If an election lacked these qualities, the moderates argued, then it "ought to be set aside."[30]

After the 5–5 defeat of the motion to seek the supreme court's opinion, the more staunchly Radical group went ahead and obtained one anyway. They

Figure 1.1 Thomas McKean, chief justice of the Pennsylvania Supreme Court, was called upon to provide the first judicial opinion on a disputed election in the new Republic. Portrait by Charles Wilson Peale; Fogg Museum, Harvard University, bequest of Grenville L. Winthrop.

may have been sincere in their professed desire for the impartiality of a judicial opinion, but the two judges who complied with their request—Chief Justice Thomas McKean and Associate Justice George Bryan—happened to have solid Radical credentials.[31] In any event, the opinion delivered took the position that this group sought: the election should not be nullified just because some wrongdoing had occurred.

Considering the petition only, and not the evidence presented to the council in support of it, the opinion took apart the petition's allegations one by one. "It does not seem to be a sufficient ground to set the election aside because it was not opened till after two o'clock," even though the relevant statute "directs that the election shall begin before that hour." Drawing a distinction that would become pervasive in American election law, the judges said that this statute "is only directory" and thus "not . . . of so much consequence as that the election should be void in case it was begun after [the specified] hour." Invoking an ancient canon of statutory construction, the judges reasoned: "If this had been the intention of the Legislature, they certainly would have made it so by express words." The judges also relied upon a policy argument often made in support of viewing requirements of election law as merely "directory" in this fashion: "The people are not to be deprived of Representatives on account of this omission."[32]

The opinion disposed of the petition's other allegations similarly: "The election ought not to be declared void because some of the Inspectors left their stations before the election was ended." To support this point, the opinion added another policy argument that would reappear throughout American history in cases of disputed elections:

> If elections were to be set aside for irregularities which do not affect, obviously and materially, the truth of the poll, the craft of the Judges or Inspectors might lead them to contrive such departure from duty, or to commit some irregularity, in order to overturn an election, in case they dislike the event of it. *The rights of the people do not depend upon so precarious a foundation.*[33]

The law must be concerned, according to this policy argument, about the incentives it gives to poll workers. If the incentives run in the wrong direction, the right to vote itself may be undermined. Therefore, it is sometimes necessary to overlook breaches committed by poll workers in the performance of their duties, in order to uphold the fundamental right to vote. Moreover, this point applies especially when the poll workers' breach does not affect an accurate determination of which candidate won the election.

For the same reason, it was not enough that some voters were "under age." Rather, the result of an election should stand whenever the winning candidate's margin of victory exceeds the number of invalid ballots: "It would be very wrong to set aside an election for a whole county, upon proof of a single instance of this kind, especially if the sitting member has more than a bare majority." The remedy, instead, simply "would be to subtract the vote from the sitting member."[34]

Even the fact that military officers acted as inspectors, "depositing the tickets in the box," was "no[t] the least foundation for vacating the election." The statute charged "the Sheriff, Judges and Inspectors" to preside over the conduct of the elections, but "not that they shall personally perform every immaterial little act relating to it." One might wonder why the two supreme court judges thought that depositing the ballots of voters into the ballot box was an "immaterial little act," but they were willing to consider it so.[35]

Nor were these two judges moved by the petition's description of particularly egregious behavior: "Though Colonel Bitting reprimanded a man for altering his ticket, and tore it to pieces at the place of election, yet this is not a good reason for vacating the election." Their opinion speculated that perhaps "the man may have procured another ticket and delivered it to the proper Inspector." Alternatively, more speculation: "It might not have been a ticket for a Councilor," but instead only for another office up for election at the same time.[36]

As a general matter, the judges acknowledged that "fraud, force, or undue influence, may in some instances be sufficient reasons for declaring an election void." In order for this condition to obtain, however, the irregularities must "render it uncertain whether the candidate returned had a majority of the free votes of qualified electors (that being the substantial point)."[37] Error alone is not enough; it must be consequential. The judges added that voters and candidates should not suffer a deprivation of their electoral rights on account of misdeeds committed by others: "No irregularity . . . ought in our opinion, to affect the rights of the representative or represented, especially where they had no share in it."[38]

While the opinion's general principles were sound, their application to the particular case was more doubtful. The dissenting moderates on the council were particularly upset about the opinion's divide-and-conquer approach. They thought, instead, that the case should be decided based on the totality of the evidence ("the whole truth," as they put it).[39]

On March 12, a previously absent council member broke the five-to-five tie in favor of accepting the supreme court opinion. The moderates walked out in protest. The remainder of the council then dismissed the petition, and Bayard thus kept his council seat.[40]

This fight over Bayard's election was significant to the people of Pennsylvania at the time. One self-described "bystander" to the dispute, who had expressed his "hope" that "a new election" for the seat would occur, saw "party spirit" rather than "deliberate Judgment" as the reason why the council did not adopt this position.[41] But this election did not provide enough of a warning to cause the Founders to question the adequacy of their existing institutions for handling this type of dispute. Even if members of the council had acted as "the mere children of party zeal" in dealing with this dispute,[42] their partisanship did not cripple the council or affect its essential character. In 1781, the fight for this one council seat was not nearly as momentous as the fight for the governor's office in New York a decade later. Thus, as significant and precedent-setting as this Pennsylvania dispute was, it did not prepare the Founders for what was to come.

Ultimately, the greatest significance of this early dispute lies in the sheer indeterminacy of the law as it then existed on how to resolve such disputes. There was no obvious answer that both sides were compelled to accept regardless of whether it helped or hindered their particular partisan perspective. The two judges of the Pennsylvania Supreme Court had articulated broad jurisprudential principles that sounded unobjectionable in the abstract—do not overturn elections where the problems did not affect the outcome, or do not punish voters for mistakes made by election officials—but their invocation in this case did not yield an unobjectionable conclusion.

Whether the disagreement between the two sides was a consequence of self-interested partisanship or sincere beliefs about the merits of the case, it ultimately did not matter. The disagreement existed, and it meant that the Founding itself—the creation of the republican government upon independence from Britain—did not entail a self-enforcing conception of electoral representation, one that would automatically yield results when disputes arose over counting ballots. This indeterminacy in the applicable election law meant that candidates and their supporters would be able to take divergent self-serving positions, including in circumstances where the stakes were immeasurably higher. Although the participants in this early dispute knew they were setting a precedent, a precedent of unsettling indeterminacy is not what they had in mind. Yet that is the most significant legacy that they bequeathed.

Original Sin: Early Disputed Congressional Elections

The constitutional convention in Philadelphia unanimously adopted the provision that makes each house of Congress "the Judge of the Elections, Returns, and Qualifications of its own Members."[43] Because it received little attention and debate, this provision did not address what rules or principles each house should apply when exercising this power. The Constitution also gives each house the authority to adopt its own rules, and thus implicitly left to each chamber's unfettered discretion the choice of these rules and principles. Unlike with other elements of the constitutional design, there would be no checks and balances on each chamber's exercise of this discretion. Could the body be trusted to exercise this power wisely and consistently with the basic norms of electoral representation? Almost immediately, the task proved more of a challenge than had been anticipated.[44]

The First Congress and New Jersey's Election of 1789

The Constitution was ratified by the requisite ninth state, New Hampshire, on June 21, 1788. The old Congress set up by the Articles of Convention then passed an Election Ordinance that, in addition to setting the dates for the presidential election, set March 4, 1789, as the date for the new Congress to meet after congressional elections to be held in each state. The ordinance did not specify a date for the congressional elections, nor a method, and states varied widely on how they conducted these first congressional elections. Some states chose to elect all their representatives statewide, while others decided to divide themselves into districts. The choice, in some instances, reflected nascent partisanship rather than neutral principles of good government: in Pennsylvania, the Federalists chose statewide elections to prevent Antifederalists from winning any seats; in South Carolina, the Federalists chose districts for fear of losing all the seats there to Antifederalists.[45] The first gerrymander of the new Republic, even before the term was coined in response to Elbridge Gerry's manipulation of legislative districts in 1812, occurred in Virginia's initial congressional election, when Patrick Henry endeavored (unsuccessfully) to prevent James Madison from winning by putting him in a district where he would have to run against James Monroe.[46]

New Jersey was allocated four seats in the new Congress and, like Pennsylvania, chose to elect all of them statewide. The political division in the state at the time was regional as much as it was ideological. The split was between what was then called East and West Jersey, but today would be considered the northern and southern parts of the state. East Jersey, within New York's sphere of influence, favored economic policies that promoted easier credit. West Jersey, more agrarian and conservative, preferred tighter money. These economic interests caused West Jersey to align with the political faction that would emerge as the Federalist Party, while an East Jersey faction harbored Antifederalist sympathies. Recently ascendant in the state's legislature, the western-led Federalists thought they could win all four seats if the elections were statewide.[47]

This Federalist faction nominated a slate of candidates, two from the east, Elias Boudinat and James Schureman, and two from the west, Lambert Cadwallader and Thomas Sinnickson. This slate was sometimes called the "Junto ticket." The Antifederalists did not organize a four-man slate, but rallied around two East Jersey candidates: Abraham Clark and Jonathan Dayton.[48]

Under New Jersey law, the election began as scheduled on February 11, 1789. The law, however, did not specify a date or time for the election to end, and this omission would prove to be the predicate for the dispute that developed. Governor William Livingston and his council met on March 3 to canvass the returns, as was their responsibility under the law. Livingston chose that date because the new Congress was to convene in New York the next day. By then only seven of New Jersey's counties had closed their polls and submitted their returns. These seven were all the eastern counties except for Essex (home to Newark). Supporters of Clark and Dayton on the governor's council wanted Livingston to declare the election over without waiting for the five western counties and Essex to report. They knew that Clark and Dayton, given their popularity in the east, would win two of the four seats if results were calculated based on only those seven counties. Livingston, however, rejected this idea and deferred consideration of the election for another two weeks.[49]

When Livingston met with his council again on March 18, returns from all five of the western counties had arrived, but none yet from Essex. The western returns, indeed, strongly favored the Junto ticket, enough to elect all four of them, outweighing the strength of Clark and Dayton in the east. Knowing this, Essex was still keeping its polls open, in the hope of rustling up enough additional votes for Clark and Dayton to secure two of the four seats for them. The councilors supporting Clark and Dayton wanted the governor to wait for Essex to report before declaring the results. Again, Livingston rejected their position and the next day proclaimed that all four of the Junto ticket had received the most votes in the election. His proclamation asserted that "this state may suffer detriment by remaining unrepresented in the Congress of the United States."[50]

There was, however, no need to worry about New Jersey being late in sending its representatives to New York. On March 4, the date the new Congress was supposed to start, only thirteen members showed up. It was not until April 1 that a quorum appeared and the body began to organize itself by electing Frederick Augustus Muhlenberg as its first Speaker. On April 13, the House created a committee on elections, its first standing committee. Five days later, the committee reported: "It appears that the credentials" of all the members who had arrived thus far, including the four from New Jersey, "are sufficient to entitle them to take their seats in this House."[51] In that way, the Junto foursome began serving as the representatives of New Jersey in Congress.

Another ten days passed, and on April 28, the House received a petition "complaining of illegality in the late election of Representatives for [New Jersey] to this House."[52] The petition, which the House referred to its elections committee the next day, had not come as a surprise. Governor Livingston's own proclamation, in addition to claiming to be "for the public good," acknowledged that its questionable "legality" would be taken up in the House itself.[53] On the very same day that Livingston issued the proclamation, Madison wrote to George Washington to comment on the New Jersey election. Madison, having defeated Monroe for his own seat in the first Congress, was at that time waiting in New York for a quorum to arrive. Washington, still in Mount Vernon, was preparing to come to New York for his inauguration as the first president under the new Constitution.[54]

"In New Jersey," Madison told Washington, "the election has been conducted in a very singular manner." Well informed of the situation, Madison explained: "The law having fixed no time expressly for closing the polls, they have been kept open three or four weeks in some of the Counties by a rival jealousy between the Eastern & Western divisions of the State." Hinting some support for Governor Livingston's position, Madison continued: "And it seems uncertain when they would have been closed, if the Governour had not interposed by fixing on a day for receiving the returns, and proclaiming the successful candidates." Madison told Washington that he believed, but was not certain, that the "Western ticket" of the Junto foursome "is supposed to have prevailed." He quickly added, however, the key point: "But an impeachment of the election by the unsuccessful competitors has been talked of."[55] In other election news, Madison told Washington that "the federal party" in New York believed that they have won three of the six of that state's seats in the new House.[56] This reference to the federal party reflected Madison's recognition that competitive partisanship had already developed to some extent in this very first set of congressional elections—or at least had carried over from debates on whether to ratify the new Constitution.[57]

The citizens of Essex were outraged that their votes in the election would not be counted. "New Jersey is all in an uproar," one army officer reported.[58] Remonstrations published in newspapers invoked the idea that "the liberties of every free People depend on the freedom of Elections." Considering themselves robbed of a "FAIR election," the protestors asserted that "the present Election involves in it, matters of the greatest importance."[59] The distinguished New Jersey historian Richard McCormick, reviewing the record a century-and-a-half later, concluded: "If the canvass had been conducted with normal honesty," in a way that permitted Essex to participate on equal terms with the other twelve counties of the state, "Clark and Dayton would doubtless have been victorious."[60] But saying that a fair ballot-casting process would have yielded a different result, while obviously important, is not the same as saying that Essex should have been permitted to keep its polls open and hold its returns back after the other twelve had submitted theirs. Given the inadequacy of New Jersey law on when the polls were supposed to close, the question had become what was fairness under the existing circumstances, not what would have been fair from the outset.

Clark and Dayton pursued the possibility that Alexander Hamilton, soon to become the first secretary of the treasury, might represent them in the House's proceedings on the election. But Hamilton demurred. He wrote Dayton that although he agreed that the election had been mishandled in New Jersey, it did not warrant a fight in Congress at the very moment of that institution's inception. "I continue strongly inclined to the opinion that [Governor Livingston and his] Council ought to have canvassed prior to the day appointed for the Meeting of Congress upon the returns then before them"—in other words, Livingston should have ended the election at the Council's first meeting on

March 3. "But as to the second point," Hamilton continued, "the prudence of an appeal to Congress, in this commencement of the Government, my doubts have been rather strengthened than diminished by reflection."[61] Hamilton, recognizing the uncertainty of how Congress would—or should—handle the tricky situation, did not want to rock the proverbial boat just as it was starting to set sail on its maiden voyage.

Clark was disgusted with Hamilton's response, calling him a "shim sham politician" in his own letter to Dayton, his fellow candidate. Directly addressing Hamilton's caution, Clark sarcastically observed that Hamilton "thinks prudence requires our acquiescence in the last advice of Council for fear of making a Noise that will disturb this young infant child of his." Clark's rejoinder: "If it is to be so nursed and raised by our giving up all our liberties most dear and valuable—a fair representation—we had better let the Creature die."[62] Strong words indeed, given that "the Creature" was the new federal government under the new Constitution. In any event, Clark and Dayton were not going to let Hamilton dissuade them from pursuing their case in Congress.

On May 21, almost a full month after receiving the petition challenging the New Jersey election, the fledgling elections committee reported back to the House, asking for permission to appoint a subcommittee to hear evidence and arguments from both sides in the dispute. The elections committee was proceeding slowly, both because the House was preoccupied with all the various matters of setting up the new government and because the House shared some of Hamilton's sense of caution about the inevitably precedent-setting importance of this case. The House also had before it a challenge to the citizenship—and thus eligibility to serve—of a representative from South Carolina, but that petition did not carry nearly the significance of the New Jersey dispute. All the inaugural members of Congress recognized that at stake in the New Jersey case were two fundamental points: first, the proper conduct of a free and fair election so that citizens collectively could choose their representatives; and, second, the role that Congress itself would have in the Constitution's new federal system when a state was flawed in performing this essential electoral function.[63]

On May 25, the House approved the elections committee's request. After this preliminary inquiry was conducted, on July 14 the elections committee asked the House for authority to investigate further, including by collecting testimony of witnesses in New Jersey. The next day the House debated what to do. Elias Boudinot, defending the validity of his election in New Jersey, argued against setting a "precedent"—an "extremely dangerous" one—of expecting the House to "send a commission" to "New Hampshire or Georgia" "if a contested election should take place" in those far-flung states. He thought that Governor Livingston's certification of his election should suffice as "the best evidence the nature of this case requires." Unnecessary delay and expense would be the pernicious consequences of pursuing the kind of investigation the committee was contemplating.[64]

Fisher Ames, the highly respected representative from Massachusetts and a member of the elections committee, spoke in favor of "empowering the judges of New-Jersey" to take the relevant testimony and submit it to Congress. John Vining of Delaware opposed Ames's proposal for fear that "Judges in Jersey might be interested and biassed." Because this disputed election had "agitated the whole state," Vining continued, it was possible that judges were "themselves parties concerned." Vining's view prevailed; the elections committee would have witnesses come to New York to present their evidence.[65]

The public, as much as Congress, continued to agitate about what the House should do. In late July and early August, newspapers contained a missive urging "members of that house" to "dare do right, even if in doing it, should be involved the unpleasant task and the disagreeable necessity of depriving of their seats certain persons who have been associated with them as members." The House must not "depart" from "the path of rectitude," for otherwise its "precedent" among other consequences "will encourage illegal and irregular elections" and "contaminate the purity of representation." Thus, "a spirit of justice and of independency" must prevail in the House to protect "the dearest interests of the union."[66]

On August 13, the elections committee held a hearing in New York, at which witnesses described the two meetings of Governor Livingston's council on March 3 and 18. Supporters of Clark and Dayton continued to press the point that Livingston must have acted incorrectly: if it was not proper for the governor to call the election over on March 3 (because the returns were incomplete), then it was equally improper for him to call it over on March 18 (when they were still incomplete).[67] On August 18, the elections committee reported the basic facts to the House, but made no recommendation.[68]

The House took up the matter on September 1. Several members, including Vining, expressed the view that they were inclined to deem that "all the votes taken in at the election subsequent to the third of March are void and of no effect." But Vining thought it might be necessary to gather additional evidence to know "how the votes stood on the 4th of March." Others, including Ames, opposed any further fact-finding "as it would probably give an improper bias." Better for Congress to declare a rule, without knowing which candidate would prevail under that rule: "To know the state of votes might affect the determination of the principles from personal considerations."[69] This insight has proven true throughout American history; the more vote-counting rules can be set in ignorance of how those rules will affect the fortunes of particular candidates and political interests, the fairer those rules will be.[70]

John Laurence of New York gave an extended speech taking the position that New Jersey's election must be declared void.[71] He thought the best reading of the state's law was that legislative elections are to end "previous to the meeting of the legislature," and the expectation of the governor and others was that this principle would apply to the new Congress as well as the state legislature. To permit the governor to extend the election beyond March 3 "would lead to abuses" because "he might extend it a day, or he might protract it a month" for political reasons, with the consequence being "the power of the governor to determine who should be the sitting members." But even if the governor "had a right to delay," Laurence continued, he should have waited for the votes from all the counties. He concluded: "The time fixed by the Governor for the second meeting of the council was arbitrary," and consequently the certificate of election dependent on that date was "not valid" and could not stand.[72]

The House continued its deliberations the next day, and by this time it had become evident that Laurence was outnumbered in his views, however cogent they might be. Vining had come to believe that if further evidence could not be ascertained, there was not enough to set aside the election and thus he moved that the election should be sustained. William Loughton Smith of South Carolina spoke at length in support of Vining's motion. He explained that after hearing Laurence's speech the day before he had doubts, but overnight had become convinced that under New Jersey law Governor Livingston and his council were entitled on March 3 to "exercise their discretion, in postponing the determination for such a reasonable time as would allow the returns to be sent in." Having done so, on March 18, "the Governor was then justified in announcing the election" because "he waited a reasonable time, so that the returns might all have been made [and] twelve out of the thirteen were actually made, [and] Congress were assembling." Rebutting Laurence's point "that this discretionary power might be abused, because the governor might watch for the opportunity when his friends were highest on the list, and then close the election," Smith answered: "True, such abuse was possible, and were it proved, would be a good ground of setting [the election] aside." But absent such specific proof, in theory "all power is liable to abuse," including the fact that "the returning officers have it in their power to commit abuses at all elections, and yet they must be trusted." In sum, Smith saw no evidence that Livingston had "acted unfairly"; rather, "he seems to have consulted the interests of his state, by sending its representatives in proper time to Congress, and at the same time receiving the suffrages of his fellow citizens, as long as was consistent with the public good."[73]

At the end of the debate, Vining's motion carried, with only Laurence opposed. What is striking is how hesitant and uncertain the House members were, notwithstanding this lopsided vote.[74] Even a day later, Fisher Ames disclosed that he was still unsettled about what the right answer was: "I have seldom kept my mind in suspense till the vote was called. In this case I remain still in suspense, inclining sometimes *pro*, sometimes *con*."[75]

Moreover, as Ames recognized, it was not just the federalism dimension of the issue—the House for the first time reviewing a state's certificate on which candidate won the most votes—that made the matter difficult. "The case, though confined to the construction of their State law, was very complex," Ames relayed to a colleague in Massachusetts.[76] In other words, if the members of Congress had been sitting in a state's legislature instead, and the same issue concerning the validity of a state election (perhaps for governor) had arisen on similar facts, these Founding Era statesmen would have been confused about how to handle the situation. The issue of whether the election should have been declared final on March 3 and, if not, whether it should have been extended beyond March 18, easily could have applied to an election for state rather than federal office. The same risk of abuse would be present. They all knew that, and yet they remained perplexed on the legal rule or principle to apply in the situation.

The election law that America had inherited from Britain was not sufficiently well developed for these statesmen to know what to do. Of course, the problem easily could have been avoided if New Jersey had specified clearly the date on which the election must end. But the issue before Congress concerned what to do in the absence of that clarity, and on that crucial remedial question the nascent legal system had no ready answer.

Georgia, 1791

The House displayed a mostly superficial consensus in its ultimate disposition of the New Jersey election. But it took only until the next Congress, the second, for the House to split in half, straight down the middle, over a disputed seat from Georgia. Unlike the New Jersey case, this one involved clear evidence of outright ballot-box stuffing. Even so, the new Speaker, John Trumbull of Connecticut, had to break a tie vote over how the House would handle the matter. He broke the tie in favor of leaving the seat vacant, instead of awarding the seat to the petitioning candidate.[77]

This Georgia election was between two war heroes. James Jackson, the incumbent, had helped to recapture from the British both Augusta and Savannah, the state's two principal cities at the time. Anthony Wayne, the challenger, initially had served in Pennsylvania but later fought in Georgia, where he was attempting to launch a political career. Although the two officers had been friends, Wayne's ambition and politics caused him to seek the seat that Jackson held. It would be inaccurate to say that the men considered themselves the candidates of two organized political parties, as would develop subsequently. Still, Wayne's views and allegiances were an incipient version of what would soon characterize the Federalist party, while Jackson's were proto-Jeffersonian.[78]

The Georgia legislature declared Wayne the winner by 21 votes.[79] The testimony in Congress, however, established that some of Wayne's supporters had undertaken to steal the election on his behalf. In one Georgia county, after the polls had closed at sunset, a local judge "had not returned the first or legal return, having made out another more to his mind." Among other things, this local judge discovered "the names of those who were not present at the first election, and that their names were likewise set down as voters."[80] In all, the falsified return showed 89 votes cast in this remote rural county, even though it had only 81 male inhabitants. Moreover, another magistrate testified that there were only 25 votes cast before sunset,[81] making the submitted return "sixty-four more than the legal poll." That low turnout of valid votes corroborated with the numbers from other counties, causing Jackson to ask rhetorically, "Is it not extraordinary that, whilst other counties have polled one-half, and in some not one-fourth of its citizens, this county should have every elector attending?"—indeed, even "eight more votes than the whole" number of eligible citizens.[82]

Jackson served as his own attorney in presenting his case in Congress. He passionately urged the House to prevent this "wicked judge," who was motivated "by prejudice and party," from getting away with "barefacedly breaking" the law and subverting the "liberty" of the election.[83] Calling his case "the first of its kind"—because it was the House's first experience of outright election fraud—Jackson implored that "there would be no safety for the liberties of the people, if such corruptions could be permitted."[84]

In urging Congress to set the precedent that it would not permit itself to be tainted by a stolen election, Jackson appealed directly to the legacy of the Revolution:

> The right of representation was what America fought [for] for seven long years, for which so many States were desolated, and for which so many heroes fell. Yet, strange as it might appear, scarce half a score years had passed away ere this right had been violated and trampled on.[85]

He referred explicitly to the "democratic" character of the government established by the Constitution, starting with its "We the People" preamble.[86]

He made the direct connection between a functioning democracy and the free elections necessary to sustain it:

> The only safety to the People, is in their free elections of members to represent them. If elections are pure and free, the People are free; but if the elections are corrupt—I beg pardon of the House—but this honourable House must be corrupt likewise.[87]

It was not difficult for Jackson to convince the House to unseat Wayne. Given the clear evidence of enough wrongdoing to affect the election's outcome, the House voted unanimously to void the election.[88] What divided the House was the further question of whether to seat Jackson instead.

The House split 29–29. Insofar as two political parties were beginning to emerge in this second Congress, this vote broke out along largely partisan lines. Of the 29 in favor of seating Jackson, all but six are identified as being with the "anti-administration" (or proto-Jeffersonian) party; Jackson was seen as a foe of President Washington's administration.[89] Of the 29 against seating him, all but two were pro-administration (or proto-Federalist). Another way to look at these numbers: pro-administration members voted 27–6 against seating him, while anti-administration members voted 23–2 for seating him.[90] Moreover, the Speaker's tiebreaking vote was consistent with his partisan allegiances: he was himself pro-administration, and he sided with those against seating Jackson.[91]

It is possible, however, that the positions of at least some House members may have been motivated by principle rather than partisanship. There was a plausible argument, advocated by some, that Congress had the power only to declare the seat vacant, with only Georgia having the power to fill the seat with a different candidate. William Loughton Smith of South Carolina, who had spoken in favor of upholding the validity of the New Jersey election, was one of several who took this view:

> The business before the House was not to take cognizance of Mr. Jackson's right to a seat, it had been no more than to investigate the legality of Mr. Wayne's seat, which was now decided in the negative; it was not a contest between Mr. Wayne and Mr. Jackson, but an inquiry into a return.[92]

Samuel Livermore of New Hampshire likewise thought that "unless a majority of votes in favor of Mr. Jackson had been returned to the Governor, and from him transmitted officially to the Speaker, &c., he could not suppose him entitled to a seat."[93]

Others, including James Madison, expressed the opposite view. Indicating that he wished to be principled about the matter, Madison announced on Friday, March 16, that he was not ready to vote on this issue.[94] His papers disclose that before his speech the following Tuesday, Madison took extensive notes, citing several authoritative sources on *lex parliamentaria,* including William Blackstone's *Commentaries on the Law of England* and a treatise on British election law.[95] When he addressed the House after doing this homework, Madison invoked the "general rule, that whosoever had the majority of sound votes was the legal Representative." He cited a British case "wherein corruption appeared in both candidates, and a seat was adjudged to him who had the greatest number of sound votes." Apart from this British precedent, Madison thought that "the Constitution and right reason" called upon the House to "admit the petitioning member to a seat," on the grounds that the evidence showed that Jackson had received more lawful votes.[96]

William Findley of Pennsylvania echoed Madison's position, reporting that the precedents of his state "ever since the colony was settled" supported it. Emphasizing that this principle was up-to-date, he continued: "In most counties ever since the revolution, and agreeably to every decision that I recollected in Pennsylvania, General Jackson would have been admitted to his seat without opposition." It was routine for the legislature to "change the state of the return" based on "setting aside the bad votes, or restoring such as the [local election] judges had improperly rejected."[97]

The Madison-Findley position fell one vote short of prevailing in this congressional case. Yet this outcome did not set a precedent that prevented Congress from seating a candidate without a new certificate from the state. On the contrary, in the very next Congress (the third), the House decided to seat a candidate other than the one certified under state law as the winner.

This new case came from Delaware, and in it the House determined that local officials had counted ballots that violated state law.[98] Removing the invalid ballots reversed the result, and thus the House did not merely void the election, but instead awarded the seat to the winner based on its new count limited to valid ballots. Again, the House was far from unanimous (57–31), and again the split was largely partisan.[99] Ironically, though, this time it was the pro-administration members who favored (40–4) seating the candidate, one of their own, while the anti-administration members (27–17) tended to oppose this position.[100]

Madison, at least, displayed the virtue of consistency, voting to seat the pro-administration candidate as he had voted to seat Jackson. In doing so in the Delaware case, Madison was acting contrary to his own partisan leanings, as by 1793 Madison already had come to recognize himself as a leader of the newly emerging anti-administration party.[101] Madison, moreover, was not alone in this consistency, and at least one other anti-administration member chided the pro-administration party for acting in the Delaware case contrary to their position in the Georgia case.[102] But this charge of inconsistency did not dissuade the proto-Federalists from achieving their desired outcome in the case at hand.

Virginia, 1793

The House faced another disputed election in the third Congress, this one from Virginia. In its disposition, the House reverted to letting the election stand as certified in the state, the same result as in its first case from New Jersey. Yet the misconduct at the Virginia polls, although not outright ballot-box stuffing as in Georgia, was more egregious than what had occurred in New Jersey. Indeed, the case involved the same sort of military coercion of specific voters that had happened in Pennsylvania a dozen years earlier. Here the House was unwilling to adopt the remedy of voiding the election that it had used in the Georgia case. Instead, as in the Pennsylvania case, the decision was to consider the election's outcome as unaffected by the military impropriety.[103]

The candidates in this Virginia election were Francis Preston and Abram Trigg. The count of the ballots showed Preston beating Trigg by only ten votes. Trigg challenged the result, primarily on the ground that Preston's brother, a captain in the federal military, had marched troops to one of the polling places for the purpose of preventing pro-Trigg voters from casting ballots. Trigg complained that this and other improprieties deprived him of "a sufficient number of votes to have given me the majority."[104]

The House's Committee on Elections, focusing on the allegations of military coercion, found that the facts were essentially as Trigg had alleged. The committee's report found it "well-established" that soldiers under Captain Preston's command "threatened to beat any person who should vote in favor of the petitioner." When these soldiers were "afterwards interrogated why they would beat any man who voted for Trigg," they replied that they were under orders to do so. As it was very likely that more voters were "prevented from voting" than Preston's "majority of ten votes," the consequence was that "the election was unduly and unfairly biased by the turbulent and menacing conduct of the military."[105]

Eager to avoid the creation of an adverse "precedent," the report was emphatic in condemning this "dangerous" breach in the "freedom and fairness which ought to prevail at elections." The report was clear-sighted about the principle at stake: "The inestimable principle of free suffrage ought never to be violated by any military interposition." Noteworthy also is the report's invocation of equality as an essential precondition of electoral fairness: "Petitioner ought to have a chance of obtaining a seat on equal terms." Moreover, the House had a duty to annul the election, given "that the sitting member may have obtained a majority by undue influence."[106]

This report thus saw the situation essentially in the same way as had the moderates in Pennsylvania a decade earlier, but as before this position did not prevail. On the floor of the House, William Loughton Smith, the proto-Federalist from South Carolina who now chaired the Committee on Elections, tried valiantly to convince his colleagues to accept the report. But other members were unconcerned by the military presence at the polls.[107]

Samuel Smith of Maryland (a proto-Jeffersonian) observed that coercion at the polls was commonplace, at least in the South. He explained that "it was the custom, and perfectly known to be so," that a "man of influence came to the place of election at the head of two or three hundred of his friends." The objective was the intimidation and disenfranchisement of opponents: "To be sure they would not, if they could help it, suffer anybody on the other side to give a vote, as long as they were there." This Marylander acknowledged that this practice "was certainly a very bad custom, and must very much surprise an Eastern [meaning Northern] member." Then, asserting that the South did not abide by the same standards of republican government that prevailed in the North, he frankly declared "that an election in the Southern States is nothing but a nursery of superlative mischief." Thus, he could not see the facts found by the committee "as a pretense for dissolving the election" because if such conduct "be sufficient for putting an end to an election, the Committee may begin by dissolving mine."[108]

William Smith's fellow delegate from South Carolina, Alexander Gillon, went even further in this vein. He said that he had witnessed "a riot at [William Smith's] own election, and in his own favor." Moreover, "the riot was raised by a Magistrate, who, with his own hand, dragged one of the opposite party out of the Church." Gillon "saw, therefore, no reason why there should be such a noise about this election in particular, when others were just as bad, or a great deal worse."[109]

The debate in Congress continued. Despite the accusation against him personally, as well as the ugly portrait of electoral practices in the South generally, William Smith never disavowed his stance against Preston's election "since it was not conducted with that fairness, that regularity, and that equality of chances, requisite upon Republican principles." On the floor of the House, the committee chair defended the report by quoting Blackstone "on the peculiar impropriety of military imposition" at the polls. The numbers mattered to him: because "Mr. Preston had only a majority of ten votes; and when the circumstances of sixty or seventy soldiers driving off the voters of Mr. Trigg was opposed to such a narrow majority," he asked rhetorically, "could anybody

Figure 1.2 Samuel Smith, representative from Maryland, confessed to his colleagues in Congress that elections in Southern states were not conducted with the same standard of fairness as expected in Northern ones. Portrait by Rembrandt Peale; Maryland Historical Society.

call this transaction legal?"[110] But when "the question was at last called for," his position was defeated: "The petition of Mr. Trigg, and the report of the Committee upon it, were rejected, without a division."[111]

Fisher Ames of Massachusetts had "proposed that the yeas and nays should be taken, but this was not done."[112] We cannot tell, therefore, whether the vote in the House may have been affected by some partisan sentiment. The historian Edmund Morgan reports little difference in the ideological position of the two candidates. If one had to guess, there might have been something of a pro-administration tilt toward Trigg's petition, with an anti-administration tilt against.

Madison may have favored Preston's candidacy for partisan reasons.[113] It is disappointing, therefore, that Madison did not express his views, at least not to posterity, on this electoral dispute. Trigg wrote to him in October of 1793 seeking his support for overturning the outcome in the House. In his effort to persuade Madison, Trigg appealed directly to the outrage committed against republican principles: it is "essential to the existence of a republican Government that Election's [*sic*] of representatives of the people should be absolutely free, and that therefore this attempt by a military force to prescribe to free men who they shall choose will meet with your disapprobation."[114] But if Madison ever replied, his letter is lost. There is no record of his speaking in Congress during the debates on this election, nor of his vote.

Collectively, the experience of the US House of Representatives with disputed elections in the first three Congresses shows the Founding Generation struggling to get its bearings. Individual members were divided within each of their own minds, the House as a whole repudiated its election committee's report, and the House itself was deeply fractured more than once. In short, the Founding Generation lacked collective wisdom on how to handle a ballot-counting dispute consistent with the republican ideas upon which they were creating their new nation. In each of these disputes, participants on one side or the other—and often on both—would appeal to the shared republican heritage of their Revolution and the shared republican underpinnings of their new Constitution. But the lesson of these cases is that it was not at all self-evident how those shared republican ideals and values, including a commitment to free and fair elections, translated into specific answers to ballot-counting questions.

It did not take long for a pattern of partisanship to prevail in the federal House of Representatives' adjudication of disputed elections. As Henry Dawes, a later chair of the House Committee on Elections, would lament, "partisan zeal was entering more and more into every contest before the House, and the law and the evidence were made to bend more and more to the necessities or advantages of majorities."[115] In 1813, the House defeated a proposal to have its Committee on Elections selected by lot, the closest that the early Republic came to adopting anything like the Grenville Act. The same year the House also rejected a requirement that it be guided by precedent in its adjudication of disputed elections. With these two miscues, the Founding Generation cemented its legacy that neither by institution nor rule would it foster impartiality as the guiding value for the disposition of these cases.

Thus, as each subsequent generation of Americans would need to learn for themselves, they could not turn to the Founders to discover the proper principles upon which to resolve disputed elections. The story this book tells is not one of America trying to return to a condition of purity in a Garden of Eden, from which it later fell. There was no paradise at the time of the Founding in terms of handling ballot-counting disputes in important elections. The Pennsylvania dispute of 1781, along with the early congressional elections, shows that. Whether at the state or federal level, the Founders themselves were struggling in a condition of confusion on this topic. If there was to be enlightenment, it would need to come later, after the Founding, as Americans transformed their own Republic as a work-in-progress.

2

The Novelty of Chief Executive Elections

The Founders faced an even bigger problem when they started electing their chief executives. Not all the newly independent states embraced this experiment. The South preferred legislative appointment of governors. But New England and New York opted for direct election of their governors by all eligible voters in the state.[1]

New York and Massachusetts, moreover, made their elected governors especially powerful, enabling them to veto legislation.[2] This gubernatorial power in these two states made the office very much worth fighting for. As head-to-head political competition began to develop between two enduring political parties, capturing the governor's office in these two states became a primary focus of battle. Thus it was no coincidence that New York and Massachusetts experienced the nation's first major disputes over counting ballots in a gubernatorial election.[3]

The Founders who decided that these powerful governors should be elected did not anticipate the need for impartial institutions to resolve a disputed gubernatorial election. Neither New York nor Massachusetts had constitutions or laws that prepared them for the intensity of this new kind of statewide vote-counting dispute. John Jay had drafted New York's first constitution in 1776, but it contained nothing concerning a disputed gubernatorial election.[4] Ironically, Jay would be the gubernatorial candidate victimized by the lack of an impartial tribunal when a dispute arose in 1792 over that year's election. John Adams was the primary author of the 1780 constitution in Massachusetts, which did nothing more than leave a disputed gubernatorial election for the legislature to resolve. It would be John Quincy Adams who would most succinctly articulate the embarrassment caused when, in 1806, the legislature attempted to abuse this power for partisan ends.[5]

The shortsightedness of the Founders with respect to the distinctive dangers of disputed gubernatorial elections stems largely from their naïve belief that the constitutional arrangements they were assembling would keep the formation of organized political parties in check. As explained in *The Federalist Papers*, the Founders expected the constitutional separation of powers to keep political factions fluid and disorganized, preventing them from coalescing into two regularly oppositional parties.[6] If two-party competition did not materialize, then these two parties could not array themselves against each other like warring armies in scorched-earth fighting for every ballot in the state that might decide a disputed gubernatorial election. If organized political parties did not exist, then they could not control whatever institution had the authority to resolve a ballot-counting dispute in a gubernatorial election, and then that institution would be free to decide the matter on the merits rather than based on partisan impulse.

As much as this naïveté is to blame, a more elemental factor may have been the sheer novelty of the experiment the Founders were undertaking. They simply had no previous experience electing the kind of powerful chief executive that they had created for New York and Massachusetts. In any event, whatever the best explanation for their oversight, the Founders left the states—and thus themselves, as John Jay personally would experience—unprepared and ill-equipped. Both New York and Massachusetts lacked a tribunal suited to the adjudication of a gubernatorial vote-counting dispute. This unpreparedness would pose great difficulties for both states when suddenly confronted with this momentous political battle. Even worse, this unpreparedness signaled that the Founders similarly had left the nation as a whole without an adequate mechanism for resolving a ballot-counting dispute in a presidential election.

New York, 1792

Compared to the well-organized machines that later came to dominate electoral politics in the nineteenth century, the competition between Federalists and Republicans in New York's 1792 election was more amorphous.[7] Still, there is no doubt that a form of direct two-party competition had already developed. In January of that year Madison had written an essay on *Parties*, recognizing that "parties are unavoidable" and the best to be hoped is that "they would counteract each other."[8] Gone was the expectation of the *Federalist Papers* that the constitutional separation of powers would keep a plurality of interest groups, "factions," from forming into two directly competitive parties. In September, Madison was even more explicit on this point in *A Candid State of Parties*. "From 1783 to 1787," before the adoption of the Constitution, "there were parties [or, to use his earlier term "factions"] in abundance, but being rather local than general," and that was the condition that had formed his thinking in the *Federalist Papers*. By 1792, however, circumstances had changed. Now there was direct competition between "the republican party," representing the "interest of the many," and "the rival party," reflecting the "influence of money" and thus attendant to the aristocratic "interest . . . of a few." Moreover, Madison now saw this direct two-party rivalry as "natural" and "likely to be of some duration" in the system of government that the Founders had established.[9]

New York was at the forefront of this emerging two-party competition in 1792. The Yale historian Frank Monaghan, writing early in the twentieth century, described the 1792 election as the "ominous beginning of modern party politics in New York."[10] Jabez Hammond, who in 1842 wrote an important study, *The History of Political Parties in the State of New York*, described how "both political parties" engaged in "most intense" activities in preparation for the gubernatorial election of 1792.[11] Alexander Hamilton was the leader of the Federalists and believed that John Jay was the best chance his party had to defeat George Clinton, the fifteen-year incumbent whom Federalists increasingly saw as allied with their Republican opponents. Jay as the nation's first chief justice was initially reluctant to seek the governorship, but he eventually let the Federalists nominate him as their candidate to challenge Clinton (thereby reflecting the relative stature of the two offices in the Founding Era).[12]

In 1787, New York's legislature had enacted a new statute to regulate the conduct of elections. The statute required the sheriff of each county, after collecting the returns from all the municipalities in the county, to assemble these returns "without opening or inspecting the same" into "one box, which shall be well closed and sealed up by him under his hand and seal, with the name of his county wrote [*sic*] on the box." The statute required the sheriff to deliver this box to the secretary of state, who would "safely" keep the boxes from all the counties "unbroken and unopened" until the meeting of the state's canvassing committee.[13] The sheriff's duties pursuant to this statute would become the focus of the ballot-counting dispute.

For gubernatorial elections, the statute vested the authority to count the ballots in a joint legislative canvassing committee, made up of six state senators and six members of the assembly, the state's other legislative chamber. The canvassing committee was to meet in the secretary of state's office, open the boxes from the sheriffs, and count "the votes therein contained." Immediately upon counting the votes, and taking no more than two weeks to do so, the canvassers were to issue a certificate publicly declaring who was elected governor. The statute provided the canvassers were to resolve any questions concerning the counting of the votes according to majority rule. Furthermore, "their judgment and determination shall in all cases be binding and conclusive," meaning that no appeals from their certificates of election could be taken to any court or the legislature itself.[14]

The dispute over the outcome of the 1792 election centered on a problem that occurred in Otsego County, home to Cooperstown (and, much later, its Baseball Hall of Fame). The problem was that the outgoing sheriff of the county, a Federalist named Richard Smith, purported to retain the powers of his office even though his commission had expired. Consequently, when Smith performed the duties of the sheriff under the 1787 statute, he was violating the statute because he was no longer the sheriff.

By a 7–4 vote (with one member not participating), the joint canvassing committee decided to invalidate all of Otsego County's ballots on the grounds that Smith was not sheriff, and thus he had handled and delivered the ballots unlawfully. The consequence of this decision was to swing the election to Clinton, by 108 votes out of 16,772 counted.[15] If the canvassers had counted the Otsego ballots, Jay would have won by at least 200 votes.[16]

The canvassing committee's decision had the effect of disenfranchising the entire electorate of Otsego County. Moreover, these voters were obviously not responsible for the defect in Smith's status as their sheriff. Consequently, Federalists excoriated this wholesale disenfranchisement of innocent voters on what they deemed "a mere law quibble."[17]

Rufus King, US senator from New York and a leading Federalist who had actively participated in drafting and ratifying the federal Constitution, had urged the canvassers to consider Smith a "de facto sheriff" so that "the votes of that county may lawfully be canvassed." Thus "when he received and delivered the votes," Smith's acts "ought to be deemed valid" to protect "the rights of suffrage of the citizens of that county." King emphasized: "The election law is intended to render effectual the constitutional right of suffrage. It should therefore be construed liberally."[18]

John Trumbull was one of many lawyers, both in and out of New York, whom the Federalists enlisted to provide public refutations of the canvassing committee's decision. Trumbull, who had briefly practiced law with John Adams, was then serving in the Connecticut legislature and later would become a Connecticut judge. Trumbull's critique of the canvassers was particularly eloquent in its explication of why protecting the fundamental right to vote required excusing the defect in Sheriff Smith's status.

"The existence of all representative republics is founded on the rights of suffrage," Trumbull began, in language bearing remarkable resemblance to twentieth-century voting rights jurisprudence. Like that later jurisprudence, Trumbull was making more than a philosophical claim. "This right is fully established in the Constitution of the State of New-York."[19]

Turning to the 1792 election itself, Trumbull observed: "Had the Legislature directly enacted that the votes of Otsego Count[y] should not be canvassed, every person would consider this act unconstitutional and void." It followed "therefore" that if it "becomes impossible, in any case, that the statute relative to the return of the ballots should be literally complied with, I should consider the law in that instance void." The statute, in other words, is unconstitutional insofar as its construction causes the disenfranchisement of innocent voters, who have a constitutional right to elect their governor. This constitutional right, accordingly, necessitates a different principle for construing election statutes: "All votes fairly given and honestly returned ought to be canvassed, for the rights of free electors ought always to be preferred to the mere forms of law."[20]

Trumbull then offered an analogy to seal his case: "Had the Sheriff of any County died before the day of the Election, and no new Sheriff be appointed before the day of return, in which case the County would clearly be without a Sheriff, I should consider a return by the Inspectors as valid."[21] Otsego was the same situation, Trumbull reasoned. Its "late Sheriff" was not personally deceased, but his commission had expired. In neither circumstance should the eligible electors be disenfranchised, and thus the county's ballots "ought to have been canvassed" just the same.

Expressions similar to Trumbull's and King's filled newspapers throughout the summer and fall of 1792. Whole pamphlets were published on the subject, including one explicitly entitled *The Right of Suffrage*.[22] Towns around the state issued proclamations denouncing the canvassers for "arbitrarily disenfranchising" the citizens of Otsego.[23]

The Federalists were especially outraged that the canvassing committee's 7–4 decision fell along party lines. Although the six senators on the committee were split 3–3 between Federalists and Republicans, the assembly in a partisan move had put six Clinton loyalists on the committee. Thus, the seven in the majority on the committee were all "devoted Clintonians."[24] Of the four dissenters, three were the Federalist senators (joined by one Clintonian, with another Clintonian absent).[25]

Robert Troup, who orchestrated the Federalist attack on the canvassers, repeatedly denounced "the deep corruption of Clinton & his party."[26] A self-organized group of Albany voters, one of many such groups, wondered "whether a Chief Magistrate is to be elected by their voice, or by a Committee, the majority of whom were selected and named by a party."[27] Ebenezer Foote, another Federalist, explained how his side had been hoodwinked: "The Clintonian party in the assembly have by a damned Maneuvre got the better of us in appointing Canvassers."[28]

Jay's wife, too, vehemently castigated "the partizans of Clinton" for their determination "to give the people a Governor of *their* election, not the one the people preferred."[29] She bewailed: "Those shameless men, blinded by malice, ambition, and interest, have conducted themselves with such indecency," and "Clinton steals" back into office. Even the Clintonian canvassers knew beforehand that they would be vilified for a biased decision: "If we decide in favor of Clinton, it is ascribed to partiality."[30]

One correspondent told Clinton that he should step aside unless "you are so compleatly fettered by a party, some of whom have made the most deadly sacrifices for your support, that you cannot forsake them."[31] Thomas Jefferson shared that sentiment: "It does not seem possible to defend Clinton as a just or disinterested man if he does not decline the office."[32] James Madison, too, saw the New York election as suffused with "the spirit of party," and agreed that "Clinton ought certainly not to force himself on the people" assuming "that a majority of *legal* honest votes was given agst. him."[33] (Clinton's obligations would be different, Madison acknowledged, if the facts were otherwise.)

James Kent provided the most thorough condemnation of the canvassing committee's partisan composition and conduct. Kent would later become a preeminent jurist of his generation, "the American Blackstone."[34] In 1792, he was a youthful legislator allied with Jay and the Federalists. Three days after the canvassers announced their decision, Kent deemed "corrupt" the choice of the assembly to fill all of its six seats on the committee with Clinton supporters. "The Senate did as they ought to," by contrast, in giving each party three seats each. Kent's reasoning was rooted in the nature of the function the canvassers were to perform. "These canvassers form *a court* of the highest importance, a court to decide on the validity of elections *without appeal*." Their "strong bias of party" was entirely antithetical to their mission: "I believe a more partial tribunal cannot be found in the annals of freedom."[35]

Even more significant is Kent's view that the tribunal should have been evenly balanced between the two parties. "They ought at least to have been equally biassed," is how he put the point.[36] "Equally biassed" may be an odd way to phrase it, especially to modern ears, but it captures the essential requirement of impartiality that Kent considered necessary for the tribunal to perform its function. The problem was that the committee could not be trusted given the partisan imbalance of its members, and they proved their untrustworthiness by their "repugnant" decision. (Kent did not explain what should happen if an equally balanced tribunal deadlocks in a tie vote—a concern to be considered as we examine subsequent disputes, including the presidential election of 1876.)

Kent, like the other Federalists, presumed that an impartial tribunal would have counted the Otsego votes. Jabez Hammond, the fair-minded early historian, certainly thought so, essentially for the "right of suffrage" reasons offered by the Federalists.[37] But the arguments at the time were not as one-sided

Figure 2.1 James Kent, who later would become "America's Blackstone," wanted an evenly balanced tribunal to adjudicate the dispute over New York's 1792 election. Portrait by James Sharples (1798); Avery Architectural & Fine Arts Library, Columbia University, gift of Edmund Astley Prentis.

as the Federalists (and some historians) have portrayed them.[38] Upon a review of all available evidence, the administration of the election in Otsego County—including specifically the reason why Smith's commission as sheriff had lapsed without the installation of his successor—was highly suspicious and improper, perhaps even to the point of negating the reliability and validity of the election in the county.

Otsego County in 1792 was the personal fiefdom of William Cooper (the Cooper of Cooperstown).[39] He lorded over his domain in ways that were obnoxious in general and oppressive in the specific context of an election. He bullied his tenants to vote according to his dictates,[40] and he rustled to the polls voters whom he knew to be ineligible.[41] Were his extensive and egregious improprieties enough to explain the 200-vote victory that Jay would have had if Otsego's ballots had been counted? It seems doubtful. Otsego was genuinely a Federalist stronghold, notwithstanding Cooper's elements of tyranny. But the case can be made that Otsego County under Cooper's domination did not run a free and fair election, even by the rather imperfect standards of the day, and thus its ballots were irredeemably tainted and uncountable—although that entailed the disenfranchisement of the entire county in the gubernatorial election.[42]

Even worse is the role that the delayed replacement of Smith as sheriff played in the administration of the election. Smith had resigned his position as sheriff in order to be supervisor of a town within the county. Smith was Cooper's crony. As town supervisor, he would run the polls in the way that Cooper wished. The constitution and laws of New York explicitly prohibited an individual from serving as town supervisor and county sheriff simultaneously. A separation-of-powers principle at the local level, this prohibition protected the integrity of the election by assuring that the person responsible for delivering all of the county's ballots to the secretary of state, the sheriff, was not the same person who packaged a town's returns. Otherwise, a nefarious sheriff could manipulate a particular town's returns to achieve a desired result before sending the whole county's returns to the secretary of state. But at Cooper's bidding, Smith took it upon himself to play both roles in this gubernatorial election. It could be described as comical: "Smith, acting as supervisor, sealed the Otsego Township ballot box for transfer to the county sheriff; becoming sheriff, he received the ballot box from himself." But Smith's dual roles also created a serious conflict-of-interest: "As Otsego Township supervisor," he made a "ruling on challenges to voters" and determined which set of locally disputed votes to count; when someone complained that Smith could not do this "because he was still the county sheriff, he countered that he had resigned as sheriff and been replaced"; yet, "two days later Smith acted as sheriff to forward the ballots to the secretary of state's office in Albany." In short, Smith was willing to oscillate "between the legally incompatible offices of town supervisor and county sheriff, depending on the needs of the Federalist cause."[43]

The Federalists, moreover, were determined that Smith's replacement as sheriff be unable to take office until after the election. Clintonians in charge of the appointment had picked Benjamin Gilbert as Smith's successor. Cooper and Smith then conspired with Stephen Van Rensselaer, Jay's running mate for lieutenant governor, to prevent Gilbert from receiving his commission. Van Rensselaer, the only Federalist on the appointments board, said he would deliver the commission to Gilbert. But giving it to Cooper instead, he told Cooper to keep it out of Gilbert's hands until Smith, the loyal Federalist, had delivered Otsego's ballots to the secretary of state.[44] Van Rensselaer was entirely candid with Cooper that he "delayed sending Sheriff Gilbert's commission till after the Election" because he knew that Otsego's votes "in all probability will turn the Election." Ironically, Van Rensselaer professed that he did not want Gilbert committing "some irregularity" that would cause "your Poll" to "be rejected"—when that is exactly what happened as a result of letting Smith continue to act as sheriff after his commission expired. Whether Van Rensselaer wanted Smith to manipulate the Otsego returns in favor of the Federalists, or he only wanted to prevent a Clintonian sheriff from manipulating the returns in favor of the other side, is ultimately unknowable. But either way, what these three Federalists (Van Rensselaer, Cooper, and Smith) did to prevent Gilbert from serving as sheriff for the election was a partisan subversion of the applicable election laws, which had been adopted to protect elections from such mischief.

There was even more suspicious behavior on the part of Cooper and Smith. As part of his purporting to act as sheriff during the election, Smith kept the county's ballots at a store that he and Cooper owned together.[45] He also picked a Van Rensselaer associate as the one to physically transport the ballots to the secretary of state. Although there is no evidence that any of these Federalists actually broke the seals on the packages from the towns and tampered with contents of those returns, their possession of the ballots violated basic chain-of-custody precepts designed to protect the integrity of the election. Simply put, agents of one party's candidates should not be sole custodians of ballots for lengthy periods in which ballot tampering easily could occur.[46]

The Clintonian canvassers had heard reports of the various misdeeds that the Federalists had committed in the administration of the Otsego balloting. Indeed, these reports had reached Jefferson, then in Philadelphia, who relayed to Madison: "The Clintonians again tell strange tales about these votes of Otsego."[47] In their written explanation of their decision, the seven-member majority of the canvassing committee adverted to the "questionable" Otsego "circumstances" as justification for strictly enforcing the statutory requirement that a duly authorized sheriff be the intermediary to transfer the ballots from the town supervisors to the secretary of state. "The assumption of power by Mr. Smith," the seven canvassers observed, "appears to have been warranted by no pretense or colour of right."[48]

The facts were enough for the canvassers to declare that the "defect" of the Otsego ballots was not "*in form only* of the return" but "substantial" and thus requiring their rejection, "especially as the law regards the custody of the ballots as a trust of high importance." The canvassers reasoned that the purpose of the ballot-custody rules were to protect the integrity of the election.[49] It would be wrong, therefore, to convert "a provision intended a security against impositions" into an "engine to promote them" by exonerating noncompliance with those rules "in a case where the question was raised" whether the returns were "fraudulently obtained" and the facts "at least" indicated that noncompliance "must have arisen from gross misrepresentation or wilful error."[50]

Figure 2.2 William Cooper supervised his town's voting in such a suspicious way as to make plausible the claim that the ballots there should be disqualified. Portrait by Gilbert Stuart; Fenimore Art Museum, Cooperstown, New York (gift of Dr. Henry S.F. Cooper; photograph by Richard Walker).

Would an evenly balanced tribunal, one with equal numbers from both parties (and a neutral member, to break any possible tie), have disqualified the Otsego ballots? Maybe, maybe not. Yet this much is clear: if the tribunal had been evenly balanced, as Kent demanded, and if that evenhanded tribunal had invalidated the ballots, the impartial structure of the body would have undercut the Federalists' complaint that the actual ruling was biased against them. They still would have denounced the decision as wrongful disenfranchisement, but they could not have claimed—as they did—that the ruling was a partisan *theft* of the election.

Viewing the election as stolen, the Federalists did not merely rail against the ruling. They considered how they might overturn it, notwithstanding the statutory provision that the canvassing committee's "determination shall, in all cases, be binding and conclusive."[51] With the legislature in Clinton's control (and thus unwilling to amend this statute to permit any judicial review of the canvassing committee's determination), the Federalists developed the idea of pursuing a special-purpose constitutional convention to undo the canvassing committee's decision. Even Jay embraced the idea, although reluctantly, being the principal author of the state's constitution. But urged on by mass demonstrations in towns along the Hudson River from Albany to Manhattan, Jay had come to see his constitution as subverted by the partisanship of the Clintonians and thus in need of repair by the only means available, a new constitutional convention.

A constitutional convention is, by its very nature, an extralegal measure, a resort to "first principles," as the Federalists proclaimed.[52] The Federalists knew that calling for a constitutional convention to unseat Clinton risked civil instability, perhaps even civil war, in New York. Cooper himself called for armed resistance: "A Face of Flint ought to be set against the insult."[53] Ebenezer Foote was even more forceful: "Clinton must quit the Chair, or blood must and will be shed."[54] Fights between groups of Jay and Clinton supporters broke out, including one in which pistol shots were fired. King was fearful of the consequence if "the sword be drawn," but saw no way out as Clinton "will not willingly relinquish the office."[55] Observers near and far saw New York on the brink of "anarchy" and in the midst of a "constitutional quagmire."[56]

Alexander Hamilton, observing from his post as federal secretary of the treasury, was particularly resistant to all the "talking of Conventions and the Bayonet." He was open to "impeachment of some of the Canvassers who have given proofs of *premeditated* partiality." Taking the long view, he wanted to "keep alive within proper bounds the public indignation" against "Clinton and his party." He knew that Jay could run again and win in three years if this "spirit of dissatisfaction" was kept simmering. But it need not boil over. That, indeed, could risk Jay's political future: "Mr. Jay's character is likely in a degree to suffer by the idea that he fans the flame a little more than is quite prudent." Too much turmoil, moreover, would be dangerous to the "friends to order & good Government," which "the opposers of Clinton" were. A single-purpose convention easily could "produce more than it is intended," Hamilton also warned, ultimately convincing Jay to abandon the idea.[57]

Instead, pursuing Hamilton's more limited public relations strategy, the Federalists went to the legislature to seek an official rebuke of the canvassing committee. They knew that the legislature would decline, but it would be a convenient forum for airing their grievances. Their plan partially backfired in that the legislature also decided to air its own grievances about the improprieties of Cooper and his allies in Otsego. But Hamilton's plan worked insofar as Jay indeed was elected governor in 1795 (and again in 1798).

New York also changed its canvassing procedure. A 1799 statute required that the local inspectors of the elections publicly canvass their own returns, rather than sending them to the secretary of state. What the inspectors would

Figure 2.3 John Jay, who was willing to give up being the first chief justice of the United States to become governor of New York, thought he had been cheated of victory by partisan canvassers, but ultimately acquiesced. Portrait by Gilbert Stuart; National Gallery of Art.

send to the secretary of state would be certificates of these local tallies, and the role of the state canvassers would be merely the ministerial duty of aggregating the local tallies. The sheriff no longer played any role in the process, as a county clerk (not sheriff) merely assembled all the local certificates of election from the towns, transmitting them (and not the ballots) to the secretary of state.[58]

The identity of the state canvassers changed as well. Instead of twelve members of the legislature, the new ministerial body was just three statewide officers: secretary of state, treasurer, and comptroller. The statute also eliminated the provision that its decisions would be "binding and conclusive," thereby paving the way for a potential judicial remedy to challenge the legality of its decisions.[59]

In adopting these amendments, the legislature thought it was eliminating the problems that triggered the crisis of 1792. The legislature, indeed, achieved a measure of success. A century would pass before New York would suffer another major electoral crisis, in its Stolen Senate episode of 1891 (discussed in Chapter 7). That episode would point to the reform that New York's legislature did not adopt after 1792: James Kent's plea for an impartial tribunal. The legislature in 1795 thought that changing the rules to make the state canvassers a merely ministerial body, with no discretion to manipulate the local returns, would suffice as a remedy. But what 1891 would show is that as long as one of two competing parties dominates the state's canvassing board, it can connive to manipulate the election returns regardless of what the rules might say.

The furious fight over New York's 1792 gubernatorial election vividly illustrated the Founding Generation's uncertainty about what principles should apply (even more so than the first congressional vote-counting disputes, discussed in Chapter 1). James Monroe, writing to James Madison, candidly confessed: "Tis difficult to estimate the merits of this controversy." His doubt depended in part of a lack of "sufficient data": what was the true extent of the malfeasance in Otsego itself? But Monroe suggested that his doubt extended also to the "general principles" at stake.[60]

Leading members of the Founding Generation lined up on opposite sides of 1792 controversy. Rufus King and Aaron Burr, the state's two US senators, offered opposing opinions on whether the law required counting or rejecting Otsego's ballots. For all the lawyers that the Federalists mustered to support their position (especially Trumbull), the Republicans summoned their own legal luminaries. Edmund Randolph, the nation's first attorney general and a major figure in the Constitutional Convention of 1787, led the Republican effort. Randolph, like Burr, answered the Federalist invocation of the fundamental right to vote with a call to safeguard the integrity of elections. It is a debate that would continue, unsettled, throughout US history. Because the Founders themselves had this debate, a resolution does not lie within the Founding itself, but instead must come from subsequent generations of Americans revising the basic precepts of their democracy to suit their own purposes.

Yet if one adopts Hamilton's perspective on what he called the "political squabble" of 1792, the uncertainty of principle that Monroe—and many of the Founders—felt over the proper resolution of the dispute is not so disquieting.[61] Hamilton believed that as long as his Federalists could win the next election, they could tolerate the injustice of this one being stolen from them. This Hamiltonian attitude, too, has appeared throughout US history in response to other episodes of partisan electoral theft. From this perspective, the health of American democracy, particularly when evaluated in relationship to the regimes of other nations, is to be judged not by the resolution of vote-counting disputes when high-stake elections are exceptionally close. Rather, the health of American democracy is to be measured by its ability to accept the results of decisive electoral victories that are not close enough to be contestable and to permit the peaceful transfer of power from one party to another in those uncontestable situations.

That measure of success is surely not to be taken for granted, as reminders from around the globe continue to occur with regrettable frequency. But is the best that American democracy can do merely not to permit two stolen elections in a row? Is that the standard by which Americans should judge the health of their republican form of government?

James Kent certainly did not think so. He, like Madison, believed that voters and candidates are entitled to a fair result in the immediate election, and should not be required to wait until the next one.[62] Do Kent and Madison have the better view, compared to Hamilton's? In making that judgment for themselves, Americans present and future would benefit from comparing New York's election in 1792 with the Massachusetts election in 1806. Simply put, the people of Massachusetts refused to settle for the prospect of a fairer election next time. Instead, collectively adopting the attitude of Kent and Madison, they insisted on a fair count in the election immediately at stake.

Massachusetts, 1806

The two-party electoral competition between Federalists and Republicans that was just beginning in 1792 had hardened by 1806. "Never has political partisanship been so virulent, or language so vituperative," wrote Samuel Eliot Morison of Massachusetts about the decade between 1800 and 1810, "when Federalists fought desperately to retain power, and the Democrats as desperately to capture state government" (using the term "Democrats" interchangeably with "Republicans," as many did then and still do, to describe the Jeffersonian party in opposition to the Federalists). One anecdote proved the point: "To accommodate commuters, Hingham maintained rival Federalist and Republican sailing packets to Boston; and if a member of one party missed his packet home he would spend the night on Long Wharf rather than patronize the other."[63]

By 1806 the Republicans had captured control of both houses of the Massachusetts legislature and were aiming for the governor's office, which had been held by Caleb Strong, a Federalist, since 1800. Even before that, Federalists had dominated the office, and Republicans now were more than eager to have their turn. They were tempted to take it by foul means if they could not have it by fair.[64]

The story starts as if to repeat the script of New York's tale from 1792. A joint committee with members from both houses of the state's legislature canvassed the returns submitted from the localities. Because Republicans controlled both legislative chambers, they dominated this canvassing committee, with five of them on it and only two Federalists. One of the Republicans on the committee was a young Joseph Story, future Justice on the US Supreme Court, and he is an interesting figure in this drama.

Unlike in New York, the canvassing committee did not have final and unreviewable authority. Rather, its rulings on whether to count or reject a town's ballots needed approval of the legislature itself. But that seemed no obstacle to Republicans, given their control of both chambers. Also unlike New York, a gubernatorial candidate needed to win an outright majority of votes counted to secure the office; a plurality would not suffice. Otherwise, the legislature itself was entitled to choose which candidate would become governor. This rule made it even easier for the Republicans to grab the governorship. They did not need to canvass the returns in such a way that their candidate, James Sullivan, ended up with more votes than Strong. They only needed to disqualify enough ballots to deprive Strong of a majority. They could then exercise the constitutional authority of the legislature to pick Sullivan instead of Strong, despite Strong's undeniably winning more valid votes than Sullivan. (A "scattering" of votes for others besides Strong and Sullivan made it possible for Strong to defeat Sullivan decisively but still come up short of an outright majority.)

The canvassing committee made four dubious decisions that collectively caused Strong to fall just fourteen votes shy of the majority he needed for an outright victory. Although one of the four received by far the most attention at the time, and will do so here, a second decision was especially egregious and is necessary to describe for an understanding of Joseph Story's role in the proceedings. Had the committee taken the opposite position on any of the four issues, it would have yielded a majority for Strong. The committee divided 5–2 along party lines on three of the issues, including the one that dominated the discussion. But the committee split 4–3 on the second issue (in its most flagrant decision, as described below).[65] The best evidence is that Story was the Republican who in committee diverged from his fellow partisans on this issue.[66] If so, then Story was prepared to accept Strong's victory as called for by the legal merits of the issues, regardless of the consequence to his party's quest for the governorship. Such dedication to the merits without regard to party is certainly admirable and befits the future jurist. Nevertheless, it does not account for Story's agreement with his Republican colleagues on the other three issues, including the dominant one.

The main issue concerned misspellings of the candidates' names by town clerks on the returns they submitted. Some had written "Stron," "Srong," or even "Stoon," instead of Strong; others had put "Sulivan" or "Sulvan" instead of Sullivan. These misspellings were not committed by the voters on the ballots themselves. Even so, the Republican canvassers, including Story, sought to invalidate votes based on these clerical errors, and their basis for invalidation conveniently corresponded to their partisan interest in enhancing Sullivan's

Figure 2.4 James Sullivan and Caleb Strong, both painted by Gilbert Stuart, were the two candidates for governor of Massachusetts in 1806, when the election hinged on clerical misspellings of their names. (a) Massachusetts Historical Society. (b) Courtesy of Frederick S. Moseley III.

prospects over Strong's. They adopted a rule that would count misspelled returns only if phonetically the same as the correct spelling. Thus, "Sulivan" would count, but not "Stron."[67]

A phonetic rule might be reasonable in the context of write-in ballots submitted by voters, as Alaska would adopt for the recount of its 2010 US Senate election, when the incumbent Lisa Murkowski won as a write-in candidate after losing the Republican primary.[68] But in the context of the 1806 election in Massachusetts, the phonetic rule had the effect of disenfranchising eligible voters who had cast valid ballots—and doing so solely because of a town clerk's trivial spelling mistake. Making this point, an editorial in the June 9 edition of the *Boston Gazette* vividly told the affected voters:

> You, who are the inhabitants of the towns of Isleboro', Davistown, Lynn, and Otisfield, must be informed that notwithstanding you regularly gave in your votes for Caleb Strong and James Sullivan, the influence of your votes on the election of your First Magistrate, has been perverted, by this headstrong committee, and the current of your opinion has been turned into an opposite course; because your ignorant Town Clerk, has mis-spelt the names of your candidates.[69]

Moreover, context matters. When everyone knew that the race for governor was between Strong and Sullivan, and each of these candidates received almost half the votes cast statewide, then when a single town also submits that about half its ballots were cast for "Stron"—but simultaneously records no votes for a separate "Strong"—one can be sure beyond a reasonable doubt that these "Stron" votes actually belong to Strong. When it came time to debate the issue in the house of representatives, one member explained:

> Gentlemen should consider who were the great rival candidates in this State; that every town contained more or less friends to each of them; that in every town regularly returned, each of them had more or less votes; that it was not probable, that in the town in question one of the prominent candidates should have votes, and the other should not, although the majority of the votes in that town should be given for some person whom nobody knew, but whose name should happen to be similar, with the exception of a single letter, to that of the candidate last alluded to.[70]

Sophistry could concoct circumstances in which a misspelling might be so different from the actual spelling as to require the rejection of a town's return, but not in this case.

The second issue—the especially egregious one, on which Story apparently broke ranks—involved a twist on the misspelling matter. The town of New Bedford recognized that it had misspelled "Sullivan" as "Sullings" in its initial return and therefore submitted a second return, with the same vote count and the correct spelling. The vote count favored Strong by a margin of 266 ballots.[71] The canvassing committee decided to disqualify all the votes from this town on the pretext that it could not decide which of the two official returns was the valid one. This the *Boston Gazette* condemned as "the most glaring instance of political turpitude."[72]

The third and fourth issues were more technical in nature.[73] Suffice it to say that on each the reasoning of the five Republicans on the committee, including Story, was rather flimsy. Taken together with the first two rulings, they reeked of flagrantly partisan manipulation of the returns in order to reach the conclusion that Strong fell barely short of a majority.[74] One of the two Federalists on the committee, Senator Enoch Titcomb, expressly accused the Republican majority of precisely that. He had tried to persuade the other committee members "before they proceeded to examine the returns, to establish some general and fixed principles, by which they should be governed in all cases wherever they might apply," but "the majority of the Committee would not agree to this proposal."[75]

In the senate debate on the committee's report, the Federalists beseeched their Republican counterparts to "bear in mind the importance of adhering conscientiously to principle, which would conduct them safely and honourably through the perplexities of party collisions, and justify them to their constituents and the world." In this vein Harrison Gray Otis, the prominent leader of the Federalists, exhorted "that the gentlemen who compose this honourable body, however zealous they may feel for the success of their respective candidates, will still suffer no party considerations to sway them, one moment, from the paths of reason, justice, and solemn obligation; and that when the question is taken, they will so act as to feel fully justified in their own consciences." Otis, however, was enough of a realist to acknowledge that "there is unfortunately a political division in this Commonwealth, which has engaged the attention and feelings of almost every individual" and that "the election of a chief Magistrate has called forth the strongest exertions of parties." But he endeavored to turn this regrettable reality of intense two-party competition into a reason why the misspellings must not disqualify the returns. Tell "all the facts to any man not interested" in the outcome:

> Let him be informed that the state is divided into two great contending parties—that the candidate supported by the one is Caleb Strong; the candidate supported by the other is James Sullivan; lay before him this return, stating that in a certain town a number of votes were given for Caleb Stron, the r of which appears merely to have been blurred or blotted, and a number of votes for James Sullivan; then let this man be asked for whom he believed the votes were given. I am certain he would say, for the rival candidates.[76]

An impartial observer, Otis was saying, would conclude from the very condition of head-to-head partisan rivalry that the votes, despite the clerical defect in the town's return, must be counted as the voters undoubtedly cast them.

But these admonitions were unavailing. Every Republican in the senate voted to accept the committee's report in its entirety, including its preposterous rejection of the New Bedford ballots.[77] It was embarrassing that they pretended not to know which New Bedford return should be accepted—the original misspelled one, or the corrected one with the same vote count—and therefore were obligated to disqualify them both. But the Republican senators were willing to be embarrassed.

They miscalculated on the ferocity of public outrage their brazen disingenuousness provoked. Editorials characterized the senate's conduct as "disgraceful" and "disgusting."[78] One imagined these Republican senators "ashamed" that "they have sold their reputations for the mere purposes of forcing a partisan into the Chief Magistracy, against the will of the majority of the freemen of the State."[79] Other writers were still fuming over committee's "partisan report" that predicated this Republican plot to steal the election from the people:

> It appears evident to me, that the object of the majority of the committee was to keep carving, culling, and disqualifying the returns, until some plausible pretext could be hit upon, to fritter away Governor Strong's majority; and to report that no choice had been made by the people.—Confident, from their known majority in both branches of the Legislature, that they could then elect any one of the Candidates they pleased.

This writer, like others, warned that the "People" would not "bear such conduct."[80]

Two days after the senate vote, on June 9, the house took up the matter. Here, too, the Federalists echoed their earlier hopes that virtue would overcome partisanship. "Party feelings," one of them observed, "may, and do often impel men, in the fervor of their zeal, to the adoption of things, which, in their cooler moments, they will reject as unsound."[81]

At first, it appeared as if these entreaties would be just as unavailing in the house as they had been in the senate. On June 10, with Story joining his Republicans colleagues in the majority, the house voted 234–195 to disqualify the misspelled returns for Strong.[82] Story, in an "animated speech," defended his position on this issue: "He thought [as he did] because the sound of *Stoon* and *Stron* was so very different from that of STRONG." He asserted "that in the Committee," as on the house floor, "he acted from pure motives and not then, nor now, from petty feelings."[83]

But the tide was beginning to turn. Even as he defended "his honor," Story was distancing himself from the committee's report. He "declared that he was not pledged to support this report in all its parts."[84]

At the same time, some other Republicans were already willing to go further. David Goodwin of Charlestown announced that "until Saturday [just three days earlier], he was in favor of the report of the Committee, but he had now altered his opinion." He must vote against the report because "he preferred the support of his conscience and honor, to the opinion of his party."[85] Embracing the same argument that Otis and others had made, Goodwin "had no doubt the People intended Governor Strong by the votes." Not only were "the two great parties in the State" and "the names of their candidates" common knowledge among men, "even the boys in the streets knew who were the candidates for Governor." "It was common for the children to ask each other, whether they were for Strong or Sullivan." In this situation, "could any person at such a time, believe that votes were given for Caleb Stoon or Stron and Srong, and not in reality by the voters be intended for Caleb Strong"? He answered his own rhetorical question: "For his part he could not."[86]

Goodwin was not the only Republican to break ranks that day. "Six of the party, to their eternal honour, voted from principle," as one paper described it.[87] But that was just a signal of what was about to follow.

Overnight, as Republicans felt the heat of rising public anger, they latched on to a new discovery that two other returns, one from Cambridge and the other from Lincolnville, were defective. The Cambridge return was unsealed, the Lincolnville return undated. The effect of disqualifying these returns, by changing the denominator as well as the numerator, would be to give Caleb Strong the majority.[88] On Wednesday, June 11, the house unanimously embraced this solution to the crisis.[89] Sullivan, the Republican candidate, also may have played a major role in curbing the avarice of his fellow partisans in the house.[90]

If Sullivan exercised forbearance, he was rewarded for it. Like Jay, Sullivan ran again in the next election and won. To be sure, unlike Jay, Sullivan had no claim of being robbed of a victory that the electorate, by their votes, had given him. If anything Sullivan was the candidate of the robbers, not the robbed. Still, Hamilton's insight was that the public values patience in a candidate who refrains from forcing himself into office. Sullivan's example supports that view.

But the experience of Massachusetts in 1806 also supports the demand for a fair resolution to the immediate election without having to wait for the next one. The voters in Massachusetts refused to abide by the attempted theft of Strong's victory even knowing that they had the opportunity to vote again just one year later. They were under no obligation to accept, even in the short term, the "oppression and tyranny" that the Republicans, through "party violence," were attempting to impose.[91]

Massachusetts was able to achieve, albeit belatedly, a fair outcome without need of Kent's evenly balanced tribunal. That is because Republicans in Massachusetts ultimately were able to do what was *right* rather than simply assert *power* (to invoke the dichotomy of one editorialist during the dispute), even if they were far too slow in reaching the right result. In this respect, Massachusetts can claim superiority over New York in how the two states resolved these first disputed gubernatorial elections. Neither side in Massachusetts was left with a sense that the outcome was illegitimate, whereas in New York that was very much the case. Jay and his Federalist followers acquiesced, but they did so still feeling very strongly that they had been robbed of a governorship that was rightfully theirs. Thus, if the resolution of a major vote-counting dispute is to be judged successful based on the extent to which both sides perceive the resolution legitimate, then 1806 was a success while 1792 was a failure.

In fairness to New York, however, the specific circumstances made it much easier for Massachusetts to achieve this measure of success. Unlike in New York, there were not two plausible positions to the controversy in Massachusetts (as much as the Republicans there attempted to pretend otherwise until they could sustain the pretense no longer). By contrast, in New York, although the Federalists there were reluctant to admit it, there *was* another side to the story. The serious improprieties in Otsego at least gave plausibility to the Republican claim that the Otsego ballots properly were rejected and that Clinton was the rightful winner of the election based on a fair count of authentic votes. New York showed that when there are two plausible sides to the dispute, a neutral arbiter was necessary for a fair outcome. No appeal to rectitude or honor would cause Republicans in New York to abandon a *plausible* claim to the governorship, whether or not the Federalists' claim arguably might have more merit.[92]

John Quincy Adams was the one who best summarized what Massachusetts experienced in 1806. He was observing the events from his perch as Harvard's new Boylston Professor, and he was able to employ a tone of detached bemusement. On June 15, just four days after the house acquiesced in Strong's reelection, he wrote to his wife:

> An attempt was made and pushed with an unusual violence of party spirit to reject a number of votes sufficient to prevent [Strong] from having a majority of the whole number. A committee of the two houses of the legislature, five demos against two federalists, did accomplish the object as far as depended on them. They contrived to reject just enough votes to leave the governor short of the complete majority by fourteen; and it is amusing to observe the expedients to which they resorted for that purpose. The Senate after long and warm debates accepted the report of the committee in all its parts. . . . When the report however pass'd down to the House of Representatives, many of the party began to stagger. The general sentiment abroad was much against them, and their own partisans were ashamed to support what they were doing.[93]

Adams learned from watching this episode the consequence of partisan overreaching in a major ballot-counting controversy. It would be a lesson that he would need to heed much later in his career, when serving in the US House of Representatives after his presidency (as we shall see in Chapter 3). His observation of the 1806 episode deepened his sense that the constitutional architecture that his father, and his father's generation, had devised did not suffice to guarantee a proper functioning of the political process; instead, it was necessary to rely upon a sufficient degree of honor and virtue on the part of those, like him, who were called upon to operate the political machinery that the Founders had built.[94]

But one is still left wondering about Joseph Story.[95] Did he not feel some shame, or at least remorse, for the position he took on the issue of the misspelled returns? No evidence has come to light that he did. Still, he acquitted himself with a measure of fair-mindedness by refusing to go along with preposterous disenfranchisement of New Bedford.

Undoubtedly, moreover, Story's experience in 1806 helped him to recognize, when he was writing his *Commentaries on the Constitution of the United States* in 1833, that a similar dispute might arise in a presidential election.[96] James Kent likewise had realized, in his own *Commentaries on American Law* in 1826, that a ballot-counting dispute in a presidential election will "eventually . . . test the goodness and try the strength of the Constitution."[97] Kent achieved this insight no doubt in part because of living through New York's

Figure 2.5 Joseph Story, later a Supreme Court justice and constitutional scholar, struggled to be fair in the 1806 Massachusetts dispute, an experience reflected in his subsequent concerns about the dangers of a disputed presidential election. Portrait by Gilbert Stuart (1819); Historical & Special Collections, Harvard Law School Library.

trauma of 1792. Thus, both Kent and Story—the two great constitutional scholars of their generation—understood, based on first-hand experience, that the Constitution did not equip the nation for the situation and thus might not be adequate to the task.[98]

The Possibility of a Disputed Presidential Election

By 1806, the nation had actually suffered, and survived, a constitutional crisis in the context of a presidential election. But that crisis did not involve the counting of ballots that ordinary citizens had cast to choose their state's presidential electors (the single-purpose and temporary office that the federal Constitution had created in an effort to insulate the selection of the president from untempered public opinion). That crisis did not even involve some other kind of challenge to the eligibility of those presidential electors or their own Electoral College votes for who should be president. Instead, the crisis involved the Electoral College tie in 1800 between Thomas Jefferson and Aaron Burr, Jefferson's designated running mate for vice president—a crisis caused by the original Constitution's flaw in having each presidential elector cast two votes (each for a different candidate), with the runner-up in total votes becoming vice president.[99]

Reflecting the failure of the Constitution's authors to anticipate the development of two-party competition, the original plan did not expect an organized majority of electors—all belonging to the same party—to cast their Electoral College votes in lockstep for the same two candidates, thereby invariably producing a tie between a party's presidential and vice presidential nominees. Instead, the Founders expected that with a multiplicity of factions never coalescing into two perpetually contesting parties, the presidential electors each would vote for candidates they thought best based on their considered judgment, and the overall top two choices resulting from this collective wisdom would ascend to the presidency and vice presidency respectively. It did not work out that way. Instead, by 1800, two ferociously antagonistic parties were in direct competition with each other, and the Electoral College system established by the Constitution was entirely ill-suited for the situation.[100]

Even worse was the Constitution's mechanism for breaking the Electoral College tie. The Constitution specified that the US House of Representatives would pick the president from the two tied candidates, but would do so using a special procedure in which each state's delegation to the House would share a single vote (not the normal procedure of each representative having one vote). The Constitution also required that "a Majority of all the States be necessary" to break the tie. In an environment without two adversarial parties, this tiebreaker system might not be so bad. But when two parties were determined to defeat each other, the Constitution's tiebreaker created a dangerous incentive. If the losing party in the Electoral College preferred the winning party's vice presidential candidate, then the losing party could look to the House to see if it controlled enough state delegations to prevent a majority of state delegations from voting for the winning party's presidential candidate.

That is what happened when the Federalists gleefully found themselves handed an Electoral College tie between Jefferson and Burr. Jefferson needed nine of the sixteen states in February of 1801, when the House entered its special session to break the Electoral College tie. But the Republicans controlled only eight state delegations. The Federalists controlled six, and two were evenly split. With Republicans one state short of the necessary majority, the Federalists could block Jefferson from becoming president for as long as they held together in the House.

Thirty-five times, eight Republican states voted for Jefferson, six Federalist states for Burr, with two abstentions. Finally, James Bayard, the sole representative from Delaware and a Federalist, believing he had struck a deal with Jefferson through an intermediary, announced an end to the stalemate. Jefferson denied that he bargained for the presidency. Whether Jefferson did or not, Bayard caved, paving the way for Jefferson to become president on the House's thirty-sixth vote.[101]

With the constitutional crisis averted, Congress adopted and the states ratified the Twelfth Amendment in time for the next presidential election in 1804.[102] Acquiescing to the reality of two-party competition, the Twelfth Amendment requires presidential electors to cast two "distinct ballots," one for president and the other for vice president. This change permits a party's two candidates to run together as a ticket without competing against each other in the Electoral College, as Jefferson and Burr were forced to do. Thus, the Twelfth Amendment fixed the specific defect in the Constitution's original design that precipitated the electoral stalemate of 1800.

The Twelfth Amendment, however, did not address any of the problems that might arise in a dispute over the counting of ballots cast by citizens to choose a state's presidential electors. Indeed, the Twelfth Amendment left intact the original Constitution's indeterminate use of the passive voice in its scanty description of the congressional procedure for counting the Electoral College votes from the states. The Twelfth Amendment says only that after the presidential electors "sign and certify, and transmit sealed to the seat of the government of the United States, directed to the President of the Senate," their "distinct lists" of votes for president and vice president, then "the President of the Senate shall, in the presence of the Senate and House of Representatives, open all the certificates *and the votes shall then be counted*."[103] As Joseph Story explained in 1833, this utterly vague formulation presumed that counting the Electoral College votes from the states would be entirely straightforward and uncontroversial: "It seems to have been taken for granted that that no question could ever arise on the subject." But as New York and Massachusetts already had proven with their disputed gubernatorial elections, it "easily is to be conceived" that an equivalent dispute could occur over ballots cast to choose a state's presidential electors.[104]

The best that can be said of both the original Constitution and the Twelfth Amendment in this regard is that their authors assumed that any such dispute would be entirely and definitively resolved within the particular state in which it occurred. Evidence of this original assumption comes in the form of a bill that Congress contemplated, but did not adopt, in advance of the 1800 election. Known as the Ross Bill after its sponsor, James Ross of Pennsylvania, it would have created a Grand Committee to adjudicate various forms of disputes that might arise concerning the eligibility of presidential electors or the validity of the Electoral College votes that they cast. Notably, however, the Ross Bill explicitly exempted from the Grand Committee's jurisdiction any "dispute" over "the number of votes given for an elector in any of the States, or the fact whether an elector was chosen by a majority of votes in his State or district."[105] Thus, like the original Constitution and the subsequent Twelfth Amendment, the Ross Bill intended to leave these disputes to the states themselves to resolve without any congressional involvement whatsoever.[106]

But Story's insight was that it was not so simple to contain within a state a ballot-counting dispute over the choice of that state's presidential electors. First, the state itself would need a procedure for dealing with that dispute. How adequate would that procedure be, and how well would the state handle the dispute using that procedure, given the track record of the disputed gubernatorial elections in New York and Massachusetts? What if a controversy arose over the state's procedure or how the state applied it? Worse yet, what if there were a controversy over which of two state procedures Congress should recognize? As Story explained, "very delicate and interesting questions may occur, fit to be debated and decided by some deliberative body" on "the regularity and authenticity of the returns of the electoral votes, or of the right of the persons who gave those votes."[107] The Twelfth Amendment created no such deliberative body to such matters and provided no guidance at all on what to do if the two houses of Congress disagreed on how to proceed.[108]

The Twelfth Amendment also did not address the possibility that March 4 would arrive without a president elected, not because of the House's failure to elect (as almost happened in 1800), but because of a dispute over counting ballots cast for presidential electors. Moreover, given the extraordinary vagueness of the Twelfth Amendment itself, there might even be a dispute about whether or not Congress already had resolved an underlying ballot-counting controversy. Imagine one chamber of Congress claiming on March 4 that no president has yet been elected (and thus provisions for an "acting president" apply), while the other chamber of Congress claims the opposite and is ready to move forward with the inauguration of the president it claims has been duly elected. What happens then?[109]

While this concern would remain theoretical until 1876, it shows the inability of the Founding Generation—even when revising the Electoral College procedures with the Twelfth Amendment—to prepare for the risk of a ballot-counting dispute in a presidential election. Late in life, Madison himself admitted that the Founders had not adequately considered the topic of presidential elections. In 1823 he reflected that the adoption of the Electoral College at the Convention of 1787 "took place in the latter stage of the Session," and thus "it was not exempt from a degree of the hurrying influence produced by fatigue and impatience in all such Bodies."[110]

Madison's observations were prompted by the political conditions in the 1820s that led to the second, and only other time, that the House of Representatives has elected a president: 1824, when the House chose John Quincy Adams instead of Andrew Jackson after neither achieved an Electoral College majority as required by the Twelfth Amendment.[111] Madison let it be known that he favored a constitutional amendment that would have required voting for presidential electors by district rather than statewide.[112]

Madison's ruminations in the 1820s on improving the processes for presidential elections also make clear that by then he was particularly concerned about the possibility of a presidential vote-counting dispute. In an 1824 letter, he expressed doubts about a proposed constitutional amendment, different from his own, because it "might give rise to disputes as to the validity of an Election." Reflecting his earlier experience with disputed congressional elections, as well as his observations of New York's experience in 1792, Madison amplified his concern: "The distinction between a regulation which is directory only, and one a departure from which would have a viciating [*sic*] effect, is not always obvious; and in the delicate affair of electing a Chief Magistrate it will be best to hazard as little as possible a discussion of it."[113] Here Madison was explicitly acknowledging that the jurisprudence on whether to count or reject disputed ballots remained uncertain in principle, and difficult in application. This jurisprudential indeterminacy would be particularly problematic in a presidential election. In 1826, Madison reiterated his concern: "In arranging the delicate task of appointing a President, as little room as possible ought to be left for abortive or controvertible results."[114]

Madison was as familiar as any member of the Founding Generation with disputed elections. He had been directly involved in resolving some of them as a member of Congress. He had commented on New York's then-unprecedented statewide dispute in the 1792 election, and these comments had occurred precisely when he was beginning to revise his thinking on the role of political parties under the Constitution that he had a primary hand in creating. By the 1820s, after serving as president himself, he had more than enough experience with both the practice and theory of politics to know—and to articulate—that the problem of a ballot-counting dispute in a presidential election would be a particularly trying test for the nation.

Yet despite his explicit recognition of the problem and its severity, he never offered a solution. In this respect, like others, Madison exemplifies the Founding Generation. He and they bequeathed to the nation a political system, not to revere, but to improve. Madison, a principal author of the Constitution, knew it to be flawed in fundamental respects, particularly its machinery for the election of presidents. He explicitly said so himself.

Thus, neither Madison individually nor the Foundation Generation collectively adopted a remedy for the problem of two-party conflict over statewide ballot-counting disputes. This problem had caught them by surprise in 1792. Massachusetts's flirtation with partisan theft of a gubernatorial election was only the second of many such challenges to unsettle the young nation as it moved forward into the nineteenth century. The question, then, was what would subsequent generations make of the legacy they inherited from the Founders? Would they remain mired within a political system now recognized as seriously flawed? Or would they find the capacity to identify and implement the improvements that Madison himself had hoped for but had been unable to provide?

3

The Entrenchment of Two-Party Competition

The 1806 disputed gubernatorial election in Massachusetts was the last major disputed election of the Founding Era. Between then and 1876, when the crisis over the Hayes-Tilden presidential election occurred, the most prominent vote-counting disputes were characterized by two opposing tendencies. One tendency was for these disputes to degenerate into political violence, of a kind the nation was fortunate to avoid in the twentieth century. The opposite tendency was to call upon the judiciary to provide a peaceful and fair-minded resolution of the dispute. Both of these tendencies shall be on display in this chapter.

In the 1830s violence erupted (or seriously threatened to erupt) over the counting of ballots in the North, including Pennsylvania and New York. These episodes show that vote-counting violence in the United States has not been limited to the South or to circumstances involving slavery or race. This point is often overlooked, because subsequent outbreaks of vote-counting violence did concern slavery and race, and they have tended to overshadow what came before. To be sure, immigration into the growing cities in these Northern states was a factor in making electoral politics more prone to outbreaks of violence. But even more significant was the basic solidification of continuous competition between two major political parties, which took hold in this period.[1]

America's first party system, involving competition between the Federalists and the Jeffersonian Democratic-Republicans, had collapsed with the demise of the Federalists after the War of 1812. The so-called Era of Good Feelings followed, in which the Jeffersonian party reigned without organized opposition. Then in the 1830s came the second party system, marked by competition between the Democrats led by Andrew Jackson and Martin Van Buren, on the one hand, and the Whigs led by John Quincy Adams and Henry Clay, on the other.[2]

This second party system was more developed, organized, and ingrained than the first. The parties themselves were more sophisticated and elaborate organizations, with mass mobilization of rank-and-file recruits as well as office-holders and statesmen. Expectations concerning the role of the two parties also had changed. No longer did the belief prevail that competition between two parties was a temporary condition, to be eliminated as soon as another Era of Good Feelings could occur. Instead, the recognition set in that two-party competition would be a regular, ongoing feature of American politics.[3]

These conditions intensified the competitiveness of elections in the 1830s. This intensification in turn increased the risk that a vote-counting dispute in a close and important race would escalate into violent confrontation, with the party regulars arming themselves and becoming militia-like bodies. Thus, when a state now was confronted with a situation like New York had faced in 1792—one party believing that it had been robbed of a gubernatorial election because the opposing party abused its control of the state's vote-counting process—the organized anger provoked by this perception of electoral theft became much more dangerous. Fueled by this organized anger, the cauldron of electoral competition was much more likely to boil over into civil unrest or bloodshed.[4]

In the early years of this second party system, it became increasingly evident that state governments generally lacked an institutional arrangement suited to handle a ballot-counting dispute in a gubernatorial election. As the so-called Broad Seal War of 1838–1839 would show, the nation also lacked the institutional capacity to handle similarly high-stakes disputes affecting control of Congress. Until such institutional innovation could occur, both states and the nation would be dependent upon the political virtue of individual statesmen—their capacity to rise above partisanship in pursuit of the public interest more generally—to diffuse vote-counting crises before they might erupt into violence. Although such altruistic virtue would be in short supply among politicians, as the philosophy of the *Federalist Papers* had predicted, it was not entirely nonexistent. Edward Everett, governor of Massachusetts in 1839, would provide the leading example of this infrequent, but commendable, virtue.

As the second party system matured, however, the institutional vacuum for major vote-counting disputes began to be filled by the judiciary. The expectation of the Founding Generation had been that conventional courts would have no authority to adjudicate these political disputes. Although James Kent had characterized New York's canvassing committee in 1792 as a court-like tribunal, he recognized that it was not actually a judicial court of the state, and he did not believe that the state's regular courts had any jurisdiction over the ballot-counting dispute in the gubernatorial election that year. Indeed, from the perspective of the twenty-first century, perhaps the most remarkable fact about both the 1792 and 1806 gubernatorial disputes taken together is the absence of any inkling that a conventional court might become involved. The single offhand suggestion in 1792 that Jay's supporters might consider a *quo warranto* petition is hardly an indication that anyone really thought that the idea was even remotely realistic. Moreover, although one side sought the opinion of the Pennsylvania Supreme Court in the disputed election of 1781 over a seat on the state's Supreme Executive Council, that opinion did not conciliate the particular conflict, and the example of seeking an advisory judicial opinion was not replicated in either 1792 or 1806.

By the 1850s, however, it was not far-fetched that a conventional court might step into the breach to settle a major ballot-counting controversy in a gubernatorial election. It would not be the federal judiciary that would do so. The "political question doctrine," articulated by the US Supreme Court during Rhode Island's Dorr War in the 1840s, would keep ballot-counting cases off-limits to federal courts for over a century. But courageous state supreme courts did not necessarily see themselves as similarly constrained. The prime example is the Wisconsin Supreme Court, which in the celebrated case of *Bashford v. Barstow* intervened to prevent the state's incumbent governor from stealing another term based on falsified returns in the election of 1855.

Litigation is a kind of combat. But it is combat without weapons. The move to take vote-counting disputes out of the arena of armed conflict and place them in courtrooms was a major step forward in bringing these intensely political disputes under the rule of law. Although the subsequent track record of the judiciary after *Bashford v. Barstow* with similar cases has hardly been perfect, as will be evident throughout the rest of this book, it is nonetheless better to have courts settle these cases than to have belligerent confrontation determine their outcome.

Electoral Violence in the 1830s

1834 was the year that the serious troubles began, as the Whigs had just organized themselves in opposition to the Democrats and were eager to test themselves in a series of significant local elections before taking on a major national campaign. New York City's mayoral election in April of that year was a foreboding example of what could occur when the stakes were especially high.[5] Under a new provision in the city's charter, this year was the first in which the mayor would be directly elected rather than appointed by the city's council, thereby making the mayor independently powerful. The race was seen at the time as "one of the rich against the poor" and the "bank aristocracy against the people."[6] To increase their popular support, the Whigs played the anti-immigration card. As the leading history of New York City explains:

> Whigs also appealed to American-born workers' growing resentment of the Catholic Irish. Tammany, they said, was using the new immigrants to consolidate municipal power, and in fact Irishmen had flocked to the party that had courted them.[7]

Voting took place from April 8 through April 10, and all three days were marred with violence. Rioting erupted on the first day at a polling place in a strongly Democratic neighborhood, with a pro-Whig mob attempting to prevent the residents from casting ballots. (Merchant sailors, whose livelihood was tied to trade, tended to support the Whigs, and they were instrumental in instigating the electoral riots.) Democrats then attacked Whig headquarters, and shots were fired there. Scores were injured, some severely or even fatally.[8] The incumbent mayor attempted to intervene, but he too was badly beaten.[9] Thousands were involved in the mayhem, armed and aroused by political leaders on both sides.

The invocation of a military guard was necessary to complete the casting and counting of votes.[10] Whigs complained of "illegal voting."[11] They threatened to attack the ballot boxes as they were being transported from polling places to City Hall for counting.[12] Conditions could have deteriorated even further, as multitudes took to the streets to await the outcome.[13] But when the results of the election were announced over the next two days, the Whigs were satisfied because they had won control of the city council. Although the Whigs lost the mayor's race by a mere 181 votes out of 35,000 cast, they did not press the matter further, and effectively declared a truce in order to avoid further bloodshed.

In assessing the significance of New York City's 1834 election riot, one historian has observed: "The extent and violence of the disturbance went well beyond any riot of the eighteenth century and far exceeded any previous political tumult in New York."[14] To be sure, there had been isolated incidents of polling place violence in the 1810s and 1820s. "But never before had an election pushed the city so near the brink."[15] It was "anarchy" more than democracy, and certainly not any kind of well-functioning democracy that conformed to ideals about how a polity should handle a close electoral contest.[16]

When Philadelphia conducted its own elections in October of that same year, it suffered even more severe unrest. At least four citizens were killed and five buildings were burned, as the two parties waged an armed battle while the voting process was underway. In addition to attacking Whig headquarters (as they had in New York City), the Democrats also destroyed ballots cast by

Whigs. But there were not significant disputes over the election's results after they were announced, and the violence over Philadelphia's 1834 election was essentially confined to the casting rather than counting of ballots.[17] Thus, as bad as it was, the civil disorder attendant to this election was nothing compared to what confronted Pennsylvania just four years later.

The Buckshot War: Pennsylvania, 1838

Pennsylvania's gubernatorial election of 1838 became ensnared in a vote-counting dispute that made New York's in 1792, as precarious as it had been, seem placid by comparison. In his 1871 treatise on election law (the first of its kind in the country), Frederick Brightly called it "the most remarkable attempt to overthrow the legitimate state government that has occurred in the political history of Pennsylvania."[18] Known as the Buckshot War, this struggle to control the governor's office had both Whigs and Democrats gathering weapons and taking to the streets in preparation for organized military conflict.[19] The incumbent governor and secretary of state, both Whigs, deliberately attempted to use the power of their offices to distort the outcome in their favor. Brightly again captured the essence of the problem: "The party in power sought, by every means, without regard to fairness or honesty, to perpetuate their hold on state government."[20]

Control of the state legislature also depended on the outcome of the vote-counting dispute. For a while two separate bodies—both purporting to be the official Pennsylvania House of Representatives—attempted to declare their own preferred gubernatorial candidate the official winner. (This phenomenon, known as "rival legislatures," would become particularly virulent in the hyperpolarized electoral competition of the Gilded Age in the late nineteenth century.[21] Here, in the 1830s, the phenomenon was just emerging in the context of the new partisan conflict between the Whigs and the Democrats.) There was an assassination attempt on some of the leading figures involved, and a call for the intervention of federal troops. Eventually, however, several moderate Whigs broke ranks with their party in order to diffuse the crisis, and they were successful in doing so before major bloodshed occurred.

The dispute started with accusations of rampant fraud at the polls in Philadelphia. One account, written in 1905 by a Republican politician, saw both political parties in 1838 equally at fault: "In Philadelphia both sides gave a pretty free range to election frauds."[22] The participants involved lived by the old adage that the ends justify the means: "So intense was the political bitterness of the time that party advantage was sought by leaders and excused by followers generally, regardless of the methods adopted to attain it."[23]

The fight quickly focused on one particular district, known as Northern Liberties. Democrats claimed that Whigs had bribed election officials there to discard Democratic votes. One election inspector allegedly boasted of stuffing a ballot box with 120 extra votes. Democrats also complained that Whig thugs stationed outside the local polling place prevented anyone from voting unless they would vote for Joseph Ritner, the incumbent Whig governor.[24] Because of all the wrongdoing that allegedly occurred in Northern Liberties, Democrats argued that the entire return from this district should be discarded. Doing so would cause the Democrats to win a coveted congressional seat that otherwise would go to the Whigs. But eight seats in the state's house of representatives also became entangled in the fight. Even more significantly, whichever party prevailed in the fight over these eight seats would obtain majority control of the house.[25]

Democrats controlled Philadelphia County's Board of Return Judges, which was responsible for canvassing the county's returns and reporting the result to the secretary of state.[26] The board split on a party-line vote. Ten Democrats voted to disqualify the Northern Liberties ballots, and seven Whigs voted to count them. Moreover, six of these Whigs protested that the board was not entitled to disqualify these ballots and therefore purported to send their own separate return to the secretary of state, Thomas Burrowes.[27]

Burrowes received two documents each claiming to be the official return from Philadelphia County. One, from the ten Democrats forming the majority of the board, showed the eight Democratic candidates winning the swing seats in the state's house of representatives. The other, from the six dissenting Whig board members, reported numbers that would cause the Whig candidates to win these same seats. In an apparently retaliatory tit-for-tat, because the Democrats had disqualified the Northern Liberties vote, the Whig members decided not to count ballots from any district except those that the Whig candidates had carried.[28] The Democrats immediately and persistently characterized the conduct of these six Whig board members as an effort to steal the election of their eight house candidates.[29]

Because of this controversy, the Pennsylvania House of Representatives was unable to organize itself and elect a speaker. A majority of the 100-seat house was necessary for a quorum. Two separate bodies met, each claiming to constitute the required majority of the new house. The eight Democratic candidates from Philadelphia claiming to have been elected met with 48 other Democrats from elsewhere in the state, while the eight Whig claimants from Philadelphia met with 44 other Whigs. Before they began their separate deliberations, both groups attempted to occupy the physical building in which the official Pennsylvania House of Representatives was to meet, with some pushing and shoving as their two different speakers simultaneously took to the podium.[30]

If this situation were not bad enough, the gubernatorial election got caught up in the dispute. The disputed votes from Northern Liberties were not enough to control which side won the governorship. On the contrary, statewide returns showed David Porter, the Democratic challenger, defeating the incumbent Joseph Ritner by 5,540 votes.[31] Nonetheless, Whigs attempted to use the Northern Liberties dispute as a pretext for keeping Ritner in office.

Under Pennsylvania's constitution, both houses of the state's legislature would need to vote to declare which gubernatorial candidate was the lawful winner. Whigs held an indisputable majority in the state's senate. Therefore, if they could also control the state's house of representatives, then they could have both chambers reinstall Ritner as governor. Consequently, Burrowes, the incumbent Whig secretary of state, announced that he was accepting the Whig return from Philadelphia as valid. At the same time, he openly told Whigs to ignore Ritner's apparent defeat by more than 5,000 votes, urging them to act "as if we had not been defeated."[32] His blatant partisanship as a secretary

Figure 3.1 Joseph Ritner, incumbent governor of Pennsylvania, instigated the state's Buckshot War by refusing to accept his apparent defeat at the polls. State Museum of PA.

of state remains unsurpassed in US history, even by Florida's controversial Katherine Harris in the 2000 presidential election.

Perhaps Burrowes sincerely believed that he was only resisting what he perceived to be greater fraud committed by Democrats throughout the state. In his exhortation to his fellow Whigs, he claimed that an honest count would put Ritner ahead of Porter by 10,000 votes. He itemized a litany of polling place abuses that he said had been committed by Democrats throughout the state. Whatever the merits of his allegations, however, he was not even purporting to be an impartial public servant. Instead, Burrowes used his office to advance the Whig's cause and to rally party loyalists. Democrats perceived his conduct as equivalent to a coup d'etat.[33]

Thaddeus Stevens, who later would become famous as a leader of the Radical Republicans during Reconstruction, was a central figure in the dispute. A Whig at the time, he was hoping that the Whigs would control the house for the additional reason that they could then secure his appointment to the US Senate.[34] As he and Burrowes were plotting their moves, they learned that an armed gang was coming to assassinate them. They made a narrow escape only by climbing through a window and outrunning their assailants.[35]

The situation became especially tense as both Democrats and Whigs, at the direction of their political leaders, began to arm themselves and descend on the state capitol in force. At one point, open warfare almost broke out as the two sides sought control over the state's arsenal. Delicate negotiations secured a temporary arrangement whereby the arsenal was unavailable to both sides.

Governor Ritner called out the state militia, ostensibly to keep the peace, but actually in an attempt to give the upper hand to the Whig group claiming to be the Pennsylvania House of Representatives. To his credit, General Robert Patterson, who commanded the state militia, told the governor that he would act only to protect lives and property but he would support neither side in the political controversy. (Patterson's order that his men should arm themselves with buckshot gave the episode its name.) In a remarkable meeting of Ritner's cabinet, Patterson was persistently pressed to declare that he would support the governor's position. Patterson repeatedly resisted: "If ordered to clear the Capitol and install in the chair either or both of the Speakers, he would not do it." Likewise, "if ordered to fire upon those [the Whigs] chose to call rebels, he would not do it." Ritner, dissatisfied with Patterson's position, "abruptly" ended the meeting and ordered the state militia to stand down.[36]

Ritner also sought the intervention of federal troops, but this request was denied on the grounds that it would be improper for the federal military to involve itself in the state's political dispute. The federal officer in charge of the local garrison put the point bluntly in his reply to Ritner: "As the disturbance at the Capitol of this state appears to proceed from political differences

Figure 3.2 General Robert Patterson, commander of the state militia, heroically refused Governor Ritner's orders to use force against Ritner's political opponents. Historical Society of PA.

alone, I do not feel that it would be proper for me to interpose my command between the parties."[37] The federal secretary of war, on behalf of himself and President Martin Van Buren (a Democrat), backed up this officer's decision with a similar response: "To interfere in [this] commotion," which "grows out of a political contest," would have "dangerous consequences to our republican institutions."[38]

The dispute ended when three Whigs defected from their own self-proclaimed house of representatives, thereby bringing its number down to 49 and thus depriving it of a majority of the whole 100-member house even counting the eight Whigs from Philadelphia whose claims to seats were disputed. Moreover, when these three Whigs went over to join the Democratic body, their addition gave that body 51 members—a bare majority of the whole house—not even counting the eight Democrats who claimed the disputed Philadelphia seats. At the same time, six moderate Whigs in the senate joined with Democrats there to recognize this Democratic-dominated body as the official Pennsylvania House of Representatives. The two houses then proceeded to certify Porter's election as governor, and Ritner vacated the office without further incident.[39]

Although Pennsylvania managed to avoid all-out civil war, thanks primarily to the individual heroism of General Robert Patterson, the state came much closer to the brink of that calamity than New York had in 1792. One key difference is that New York's canvassing committee, while also splitting along party lines in its key vote over the Otsego ballots, took a plausible position given the contested facts, and thus had the veneer of legitimacy as the officially authoritative body to adjudicate the dispute. In Pennsylvania, conversely, the secretary of state seemed to transgress the legitimate scope of his public office, and thus appeared to usurp power on behalf of his party.

A comparison between Pennsylvania in 1838 and Massachusetts in 1806 is also instructive. While partisans in Massachusetts also attempted to steal the governorship based on a pretext derived from a problem with local election returns, the Massachusetts attempt never spun out of control or escalated into armed conflict in the way Pennsylvania's did. The reason is that the Jeffersonian Republicans in Massachusetts abandoned their attempted electoral theft much more quickly than the Whigs in Pennsylvania did three decades later. When public opinion immediately turned against the Republicans in 1806, they essentially reversed course overnight. By contrast, the Whigs in Pennsylvania pushed their plan to retain power well past the bounds of civic tranquility, and control was restored only after military maneuvers had occurred.

That is why the episode is called the Buckshot War, reflecting the inability of Pennsylvania's institutions of government to handle the electoral dispute peaceably.

The Epitome of Magnanimity: Massachusetts, 1839

Just one year after Pennsylvania's Buckshot War, Massachusetts again showed itself capable of handling a disputed gubernatorial election much more successfully than the Quaker State. In fact, learning from its experience in 1806, Massachusetts disposed of its 1839 gubernatorial election without much of a ruffle, even though the race had the closest statewide margin in US history—just one vote—and even though local returns once again furnished a pretext for challenging the outcome. But Massachusetts, unlike Pennsylvania, had an incumbent governor who was a magnanimous statesman and refused to cling to power on a pretext.

In 1839, as in 1806, the constitution of Massachusetts required a candidate to receive a majority of votes cast in order to win the office outright; otherwise, the legislature would have the authority to choose among the leading candidates. The incumbent Whig, Edward Everett, was running for the fifth time against Democratic challenger Marcus Morton. Everett, the quintessential Boston Brahmin, had been a Harvard professor and would go on to be the university's president. Morton championed the causes of the less affluent, having risen from a more modest background to become a justice of the state's supreme court.[40]

Everett had easily defeated Morton in each of their four previous races, but this time it was too close to call. In January 1840, when the state's legislature convened to review the returns, the Whigs controlled both houses. Although Morton undoubtedly had received more votes than Everett, it was unclear whether he had received the majority necessary to win outright and thus deprive the legislature of a chance to reelect Everett.

The legislature appointed a joint committee to examine the returns, just as it had three decades earlier. Once the committee commenced its work, it became clear that the legislature could successfully deprive Morton of a majority if it disqualified the return from the town of Westfield. There was, moreover, an argument for doing so: the Westfield return was irregular and improper under the laws of the state because the attestation of its authenticity was not under seal. Instead, the return had been sealed first, and only afterward affixed with an attestation from the relevant local official. Whigs in the legislature were tempted to use this procedural defect as a means of throwing out the Westfield votes and keeping Everett in office.[41]

To their credit, however, most Whigs—both on the committee and in the legislature as a whole—suppressed partisan impulses and refused to invalidate the Westfield return. All available evidence indicated that the procedural defect was merely a clerical mistake, and the Whigs did not want to disenfranchise the town's innocent voters because of this inadvertent official error. As was described about one member of the Massachusetts House of Representatives:

> He would like to have all the forms to be observed in the returns, but when he was satisfied that the form in reference to the return of a town

> was all the objection to it, and that the votes as stated were actually given as so stated, he would not vote merely for form's sake to deprive a town of its vote, *let it make what difference it might to his own or any other party.* He was satisfied in his own mind that the vote of Westfield was given as stated, and he should vote for acceptance of the Report.[42]

Likewise, another house member explicitly "urged acceptance of the report, notwithstanding, by doing so, the political character of the Governor elect was different from that of the majority of the members of the House."[43]

Not every Whig was willing to be so magnanimous. Three of the joint committee's thirteen members (including its chair) published a dissent, claiming that the state's constitution required rejection of returns that did not comply with the requirement that the attestation be under seal. More ominously, the Whig speaker of the house apparently was itching for a partisan fight. But on January 15 the senate voted 29–10 to defeat a motion that would have excluded the Westfield return contrary to the joint committee's report, and the next day the house voted overwhelmingly to accept the report.[44]

Based on the joint committee's complete calculations of all the returns, including Westfield's, Morton had the exact number of votes needed to make an outright majority: 51,034. In that sense, Morton won the election by a single vote, even though Everett had only 50,725 and there were a "scattering" of 307 other counted ballots. Had just one Morton voter cast a ballot for Everett instead, Morton would have lost his majority. It was excruciatingly ironic to Everett that his own brother had voted for Morton. This statewide election was truly one in which every single vote mattered, and his own brother's betrayal caused his defeat. Perhaps even worse, although such would seem hardly possible, Everett's own secretary of state failed to cast a ballot. At least, his brother's defection was based on contrary political convictions. The secretary of state, a fellow Whig, had no excuse; he had intended to vote in the afternoon but had run out of time.[45]

Everett himself supported the counting of the contested Westfield votes, and his leadership on this issue was instrumental in causing the Whigs as a party to accept his defeat. In his diary on January 13, he wrote:

> As the votes were unquestionably given in Westfield, and as Judge Morton has a majority of all the votes, I think it is decidedly best that this return should not be rejected, although its admission costs my election.[46]

Everett's biographer observes: "The fact stood out that above all else that Judge Morton had received the larger number of votes."[47] This fact made it

Figure 3.3 Edward Everett, governor of Massachusetts in 1839, needed only one more vote to win another term, but he refused to prevail by invaliding votes for clerical defects. Portrait by Richard Morrell Staigg, in *American Eloquence* (vol. III, 1897).

unpalatable to Everett to try to deprive Morton of his victory based on a technicality. Also relevant was the fact that Everett had served four terms, and thus it was time to give the other side a turn. Still, in the annals of American history there is not an equivalent example of a candidate in a major statewide election willing to forego a victory so tantalizingly within reach based on, first, such a narrow a margin and, second, such a readily available legal argument for invalidating disputed ballots.

The Broad Seal War: New Jersey, 1838 and Congress, 1839

Although handled very differently, the Pennsylvania election of 1838 and Massachusetts election of 1839 were symptoms of just how evenly matched and tenacious the electoral competition between Whigs and Democrats could be in this era. Other states were affected, and so too was Congress. In 1838 the election of New Jersey's entire congressional delegation became tangled in a vote-counting dispute, and the following year that dispute ensnared Congress.

Establishing which party controlled the US House of Representatives required determining which of the disputed representatives from New Jersey were entitled to take their seats. It was a vicious circle: the House could not act until the representatives from New Jersey were seated, but they could not be seated until the House acted. Chaos reigned, exposing a flaw in the constitutional design.

Once again, the conduct of a particular individual contributed significantly to the outcome of the conflict. Whereas Pennsylvania had avoided even worse calamity in its Buckshot War because of General Patterson, and while Edward Everett's magnanimity helped avert any crisis in Massachusetts, in Congress John Quincy Adams stepped forward to break the deadlock over New Jersey's delegation. Although Adams acted outside the bounds of strict procedural regularity and although his role could not be described as entirely nonpartisan, some sort of intervention was necessary, and his was undertaken in a statesmanlike spirit of assisting the nation to resolve the impasse.

Just as New Jersey in 1789 had given the House of Representatives its first ballot-counting dispute, now New Jersey triggered the House's most crippling vote-counting crisis. In 1838 New Jersey elected all six of its federal representatives at-large rather than by district, meaning that the entire state voted for each of them. The Whig candidate won one of these seats indisputably, but the outcome of the other five depended on the status of ballots from two towns in the state. In both instances, the town's election officials had failed to authenticate the town's election returns in the specific form required by state law. In one case, the town clerk failed to affix the necessary local seal; in the other, the town's election officials failed to certify and sign the returns properly. In essence, it was a repeat of the problem that afflicted New York's gubernatorial election of 1792: there were formal deficiencies in the officials' delivery of election returns, which risked the disenfranchisement of all voters from those localities, but which also might signal (at least in theory) a problem with the returns' reliability. Indeed, with respect to the returns from each of these New Jersey towns, the county clerk to whom the returns were sent refused to accept them on account of their deficiencies.[48]

Both county clerks were Whigs, and rejecting the returns from these two towns caused the Whig candidates to have a majority of counted ballots in these five disputed congressional seats, whereas accepting the returns would have caused the Democratic candidates to have a majority of votes. Democrats immediately and vehemently protested the partisanship of these two county clerks' decisions.

The partisanship continued at the state level. The state's governor, a Whig, certified the victory of the five Whig congressional candidates based on the submissions from the two Whig county clerks. In doing so the governor affixed the "broad seal" of the state, thereby giving the controversy its name. (In contrast to the Buckshot War, the term Broad Seal War was entirely metaphorical.) Meanwhile, the secretary of state was a Democrat, and he submitted to Congress his own dueling certificate of the election, which included the returns from the two towns and thus declared the five Democratic candidates to be victorious.[49]

December 2, 1839, was the date for the new House of Representatives in the 26th Congress to convene—over a year after the New Jersey voters had cast their ballots. The five Whig claimants to the disputed New Jersey seats presented their Broad Seal certificates to the Clerk of the House, Hugh Garland. The five Democratic claimants likewise presented their competing certificates from the secretary of state. Everyone was aware that whichever set of claimants was seated, even if only provisionally, would likely determine which party would be able to elect a Speaker and appoint committee chairs and members. The only significant uncertainty was whether some Southern Democrats would break from their party if it took too much of a pro-Northern stance on issues relating to slavery and states' rights. The situation had the potential for the kind of "rival legislature" scenario that Pennsylvania had witnessed a few months earlier: two different bodies each purporting to be the majority of the US House of Representatives and thus a sufficient quorum to do business.[50]

The Whigs argued that their claimants should be seated solely by virtue of possessing the Broad Seal certificates, since they were appropriate and conventional in form and obviously superior (as a purely formal matter) to the unconventional and dubious certificates from the secretary of state. Garland, however, was a Democrat, having been appointed Clerk at the end of the previous Congress by the slimmest of margins, 106–104, in an intensely partisan vote.[51] As Garland called the roll to seat the representatives from each state, when he got to New Jersey he announced that he would skip it on account of the dispute, rather than seating either set of claimants even provisionally.[52]

"The [House] chamber erupted," as one account of the episode puts it.[53] Both sides attempted to control the situation, but with the status of the New Jersey seats unsettled neither side was able to surmount the parliamentary impasse. The Clerk took the position that no business could be done until there was a quorum, which could not occur until after he resumed calling the roll. But he would not resume calling the roll while there were objections to his doing so, and there were plenty of objections based on his handling of the disputed seats from New Jersey.

Garland disclaimed any partisan motives for his conduct. On the contrary, he asserted that leaving the seats vacant until completion of the roll call was the best method to avoid any "party advantage."[54] Others, however, have accused Garland of being disingenuous in this respect. They argue that the nonpartisan position would have been for him to seat the Whig claimants according to the formal propriety of their certificates, and that his deviation from that course demonstrated his own partisanship.[55] While precedent concerning single seats arguably supported seating of the Whigs, the situation was itself unprecedented as never before had partisan control of the entire House turned on a Clerk's initial decision on whether or not to seat a member during the roll call.

On December 5, after three days of intransigence, John Quincy Adams, the former president and now a Whig member of Congress from Massachusetts, took the chair in an effort to obtain some order whereby the House could vote on various motions concerning the status of the New Jersey seats. Although there was no official parliamentary mechanism for this move, the Democrats acquiesced in order to avoid sheer anarchy. Still, there were some protests. The *Congresssional Globe* reports:

> Much confusion and noise being heard [when Adams took the chair,] and some hissing, Mr. THOMPSON of South Carolina said that he announced to galleries that if there was the slightest interruption to the business of the meeting he would call on the President for a military force to preserve order.[56]

(The president in 1839 was Martin Van Buren, a Democrat. Thompson, however, like Adams, was a Whig.) The next day, Adams continued to act as "Chairman *pro tempore*" of the meeting. Ignoring the Clerk's position that there was no quorum until he resumed calling the roll, Adams put to the entire body assembled the question of whether the five Whig claimants should be seated immediately. He was of the view that they should be and would rule from the chair to that effect unless and until overruled by the entire body. There was considerable uncertainty on whether any of the New Jersey claimants, Whig or Democrat, would be permitted to vote on these irregular procedural motions, which concerned the very question of their entitlement to be seated during the calling of the roll.

On December 10, there was a vote on whether to sustain Adams's decision as chair that the five Whig claimants would be permitted to participate in the vote on their right to take their seats. This vote was 108 to 114, meaning that "the decision of the CHAIR was reversed."[57] As it turned out, for this particular vote four of the Whig claimants participated and also four of the Democratic claimants. Obviously, it could not be the case that both groups of four were entitled to participate, and yet such was the disarray that the House was then in. Over the next two days, there were several other extraordinarily close votes on procedural skirmishes that proved inconclusive because of the participation of competing claimants. "Great disorder was now prevailing in the House."[58]

The situation came to a head late on December 11 after much "noise and confusion" and the belligerent disturbance of one member who threatened Adams and others with physical violence.[59] The House conclusively voted to deny all of the claimants the right to participate on whether they would be seated. The key vote was 118 to 122 on the question of the claimants' right to participate, with four Whig claimants voting in favor and three Democratic claimants against. Adams, as chair, declared that the decision must stand that the claimants could not participate. The House then voted to leave the New Jersey seats vacant until completion of the roll call.[60]

Two days later, after completion of the roll call, the Whigs attempted again to seat their claimants, at least provisionally until such time as the House ruled on the issue of the disputed election itself. This motion failed by a tie vote, 117–117. With the New Jersey seats still empty, the Democrats thought they had a chance to elect one of themselves Speaker, but their members from South Carolina refused to go along with the party's choice, John Jones. After much jockeying, the South Carolinians defected from their party and voted with the Whigs to elect a Virginian Whig, Robert Hunter, as Speaker.[61] Eventually, however, the House accepted the Democratic claimants to the disputed New Jersey seats, on the grounds that the returns from the two towns should not have been excluded.[62]

Figure 3.4 John Quincy Adams, serving in the House of Representatives after his presidency, asserted himself chair of the chamber to diffuse a crisis when the House was unable to elect a Speaker because of disputed elections. Portrait by Asher Brown Durand, N.Y. Historical Society.

The significance of the Broad Seal War is that it shows the US House of Representatives institutionally ill-equipped to handle a conflict of this kind. The Whig-Democrat conflict within New Jersey had precipitated the problem, and the same Whig-Democrat competition left the House in paralysis. The House needed some sort of procedure to settle a dispute over specific seats that would determine which party was the majority in the chamber. Having a nonpartisan Clerk apply a clear and predetermined rule for the situation—for example, that claimants with certificates of election bearing the official seal of the state must be seated at least provisionally regardless of the merits of a challenge to the underlying circumstances upon which those certificates rest—would go a long way to enable the House to manage the situation. But in 1839 the Clerk could not be trusted to be nonpartisan, and a clear rule had not been laid down with sufficient precision in advance.

It was salutary that a figure of such stature as John Quincy Adams, the only ex-president to serve in the House, was available and willing to step into the breach. Adams, moreover, despite being a Whig, conducted himself as provisional chair of the House without undue bias in favor of his own party, sustaining the key preliminary motions he put to a vote of the House, even though they went against the Whigs.[63] As impressive as his own personal conduct may have been, however, it would have been better for the House to have adopted institutional procedures and rules that were fair to both sides of the dispute and did not depend on the personal virtues of any particular individual—and especially did not depend on the personality of whoever stepped forward to take control of an anarchic situation.

The Triumph of Judicial Intervention: *Bashford v. Barstow*, 1856

The convulsive electoral competition between Democrats and Whigs in the late 1830s cried out for some new institution to arbitrate the vote-counting conflicts this competition precipitated. The first sign that a state supreme court could constructively play that role occurred in 1837, when Maine faced a potentially divisive gubernatorial election like the one that would occur in Pennsylvania the following year. As elsewhere in that era, the fight was over whether to disqualify local returns from particular towns because of formal deficiencies in the official certificates accompanying them. With Whigs controlling one chamber of the state's legislature and Democrats the other, the state risked deadlock over the partisan conflict, as the assent of both houses was necessary for a new governor to take office. Rather than letting the dispute fester—or worse, become violent (as it was threatening to do)—the legislature turned to the state's supreme court for an advisory opinion on the validity of the disputed ballots. When the court unanimously ruled them valid (on the ground that there was no evidence to indicate that the technically deficient returns did not authentically reflect the will of the electorate in those localities), the entire controversy immediately evaporated. It was a signal of the great power of submitting this kind of ballot-counting dispute to the rule of law rather than the force of arms or the mercy of particular politicians.[64]

Using the judiciary to resolve a vote-counting dispute did not immediately become the norm. Pennsylvania, for example, did not similarly turn to its supreme court to diffuse the Buckshot War of 1838. (Perhaps Pennsylvania's less-than-ideal experience in 1781 with seeking an advisory opinion from its supreme court, as described in Chapter 1, soured the state on this approach.) No court did—or could have—become involved to resolve the congressional impasse in the Broad Seal War. Two constitutional obstacles precluded that solution: first, the constitutional prerogative of each house of Congress to judge elections of its own members; and, second, the constitutional prohibition against advisory opinions on the part of the federal judiciary.[65]

Moreover, in the 1849 case of *Luther v. Borden*,[66] the US Supreme Court ruled the federal judiciary off-limits in a case concerning which claimant to a state's governorship had the better title. Articulating what would come to be known as the "political question doctrine," the Court determined that Congress and the president—and not the judiciary—were the branches of the federal government with the power to recognize which of competing claimants was the valid governor of a state. The case did not involve a conventional ballot-counting dispute. Instead, arising from Rhode Island's Dorr War of 1842, the controversy concerned which of two state constitutions was the authoritative one at the time.[67] Nonetheless, a half century later, in *Taylor v. Beckham* (discussed in Chapter 6), the Court would apply the political question doctrine of *Luther v. Borden* to a more typical dispute over which candidate won more votes in a gubernatorial election.

The unavailability of the federal judiciary to adjudicate these vote-counting disputes did not necessarily apply to a state's own supreme court, as Maine's example showed. Furthermore, state courts were empowered with the ancient writ of *quo warranto*, which entitled the court to determine an officeholder's title to the office. Although this writ historically had applied to local rather than statewide offices, it was susceptible to further refinement and development as a component of the common law. If held applicable to a disputed gubernatorial election, this writ would mean a state court's jurisdiction was not merely advisory. Rather, invoking the writ, the court would have the power to order which candidate was entitled to serve as the duly elected governor. Even more powerfully, the court potentially could order an incumbent governor to vacate the office upon a determination that the incumbent's bid for reelection failed, contrary to the incumbent's own contention regarding the proper count of the votes.[68]

This potential came to fruition in the watershed case of *Bashford v. Barstow*, an 1856 decision of the Wisconsin Supreme Court involving the state's gubernatorial election of the previous year.[69] The incumbent William Barstow, a Democrat, was being challenged by Coles Bashford, a candidate representing the recently formed Republican Party. The election was extremely close, and amidst allegations of fraud the state's canvassing board announced that Barstow has been reelected by only 157 votes (36,355 to 36,198).[70] The Republicans decided to contest the result by pursuing a writ of *quo warranto* in the Wisconsin Supreme Court. The fact that two of the court's three members were Republicans, while the other was a Democrat who disagreed with his party on the key question of states' rights, made the judicial option attractive to Bashford's partisans. Bashford's attorneys were able to procure clear evidence of fraud, including the wholesale fabrication of returns from entirely fake precincts.[71]

Barstow did all that he could to maintain his grip on power. Much like Rittner in Pennsylvania during the Buckshot War, Barstow threatened to use the state militia to keep himself in office by force: "Militia units from areas supporting Barstow came to Madison for his inauguration and stayed to fight for him if necessary."[72] He also refused to acknowledge the authority of the state's supreme court to adjudicate whether he had won the election. Invoking the doctrine of separation of powers, Barstow asserted that only the executive branch could determine which candidate had received more lawful votes for the office of chief executive.

The Wisconsin Supreme Court, however, unanimously rejected Barstow's argument. It would be wrong, the chief justice wrote on behalf of the court, to let an incumbent governor unilaterally decide whether illegal votes had been cast on his behalf. An unscrupulous incumbent could abuse that power to stay in office "by usurpation and intrusion, and without any legal right whatsoever."[73] The ultimate sovereignty of the people, the chief justice continued, required that the judiciary—not the executive—determine which gubernatorial candidate received the most legal votes; otherwise, the executive would exercise unilateral power inconsistent with popular sovereignty. The court, moreover, explicitly rejected the governor's invocation of the "political question doctrine" that had prevailed in *Luther v. Borden*, saying instead that the state's constitution authorized the court to adjudicate the legal question of whether or not the incumbent had been duly reelected by winning more lawful ballots.[74] In this way, the court turned the governor's separation of powers argument on its head, explaining that the constitutional division of official power on behalf of the people required the court to assure the lawful status of the individual purporting to maintain a hold on the governor's office.[75]

After the Wisconsin Supreme Court issued its decision on this proposition of constitutional principle, it ordered a trial on Bashford's factual allegations concerning which candidate received more lawful votes. Barstow's attorneys, however, did not bother to show up for the trial.[76] But Bashford's evidence was compelling, and the court—again unanimously—ordered Barstow removed from office. Before doing so, the court on its own initiative considered whether it should view the determinations of the state's canvassing board as conclusive and binding on it. The court held that it should not, viewing the canvassing board's tasks as merely ministerial. The true issue, according to the court, was which candidate actually won the election, not which candidate prevailed in the canvass. In short, the same rules of *quo warranto* should apply even though the office at stake was the highest one in the state:

> This court has, in repeated instances, decided that the failure of the officers appointed by law to canvass the votes given at an election, to perform their duty, does not deprive a person who has been duly elected of his right to the office. We have in all cases given effect to the election, and have uniformly decided that a person who proved the fact of his election to an office, by competent testimony, was entitled to the office, although another person might have the certificate of the canvassers.[77]

The same principle should apply in this case, the Wisconsin Supreme Court unanimously ruled.

Barstow more than hinted that he might disobey the court's order removing him from office. He even told the court that he would resist its ruling against him "with all the force vested in this department."[78] But the court did not back down, and ultimately Barstow acquiesced. Public opinion had turned against him, "and moreover it was evident that the legislature would not support him in the use of force."[79] (The Democrats controlled the lower house, but the Republicans had a one-vote majority in the state senate.[80])

Bashford v. Barstow has been called the *Marbury v. Madison* of Wisconsin's jurisprudence.[81] Yet truly it deserves even higher praise than that. *Marbury v. Madison*, after all, was an inconsequential decision practically: the US Supreme Court there ruled that it lacked any power to order Madison to give Marbury the commission to which he was entitled.[82] An order removing an incumbent from office, especially from the office of chief executive, is quite the opposite: it is the most potent of judicial decisions in a polity and thus requires "considerable political courage."[83]

Figure 3.5 The three members of the Wisconsin Supreme Court, who in *Bashford v. Barstow* (1856) overturned the reelection of the incumbent governor because it rested on fraudulent returns. J.B. Winslow, *The Story of a Great Court.*

The Wisconsin Supreme Court's order had the effect of diffusing the political crisis without violence. There was a real risk that the outcome in Wisconsin might not have been so auspicious: "There can be no doubt that there was grave danger of an armed conflict between the partisans of Barstow and Bashford at this time."[84] But Wisconsin was able to avoid the extreme precariousness that characterized the Buckshot War, when Pennsylvania's armory literally was a powder keg about to explode upon the slightest move of either party's encamped militia. However virtuous General Patterson's personal conduct was during the Pennsylvania crisis, it lacked the legal imprimatur of the Wisconsin Supreme Court's unanimous opinion. *Bashford v. Barstow* was publicly embraced as representing the peaceful transition of power according to the rule of law.[85]

The decision, moreover, received great acclaim among leading legal commentators. Thomas Cooley, dean of the University of Michigan Law School and chief justice of the Michigan Supreme Court (and preeminent jurist of his generation), enthusiastically praised *Bashford v. Barstow* in his 1868 treatise,

Constitutional Limitations, propounding that Barstow's assertion of executive authority to preclude judicial review of the ballot-counting was a "strange doctrine in this country of laws! but which, of course, received no countenance from the able court to which it was addressed."[86] George McCrary, a member of Congress who would play a crucial role in the resolution of the disputed presidential election of 1876 (and who would go on to serve as secretary of war and a federal appeals court judge), was even more effusive in praising *Bashford v. Barstow* in his own 1875 treatise on *The American Law of Elections*: "It matters not how high and important an office may be, an election to it must be by the majority or plurality of the legal votes cast" and "if anyone without having received such majority or plurality intrudes himself into an office, whether with or without a certificate of election, the Courts have jurisdiction to oust him."[87]

Thus, *Bashford v. Barstow* was a shining vindication of principle in a constitutional democracy. As the historian Tracy Campbell has observed, "the Wisconsin Supreme Court displayed how an independent judiciary can play a vital constitutional role in overseeing contested elections and can resolve them without regard to partisan motivations."[88] The question remained, however, to what extent the principle would take root and receive similar, and regular, judicial vindication in future gubernatorial (and other high-stakes) elections.

4

Counting Votes at Times of Crisis

Most of the vote-counting disputes discussed in this book occur in circumstances involving normal political conditions, with normality understood in terms of the nature of partisan competition as it existed at the time. While vote-counting disputes can trigger crises even in such normal circumstances, as did Pennsylvania's Buckshot War, they are not themselves the product of crisis conditions. A close election in normal times is enough to spark the conflagration.

The disputes in this chapter are different. They occurred in the Civil War era, defined broadly to encompass the antecedent to the war in Bleeding Kansas as well as Reconstruction in its aftermath. Throughout this period the body politic was in a pathological state, and the vote-counting disputes that arose in this context reflected that pathology. The very survival of the Union was at stake.

At issue also was the status of white supremacy, whether in the form of slavery or Jim Crow, its successor. When elections will determine whether or not slavery will take root in the new territory of Kansas, with all the implications that determination will have for the potential further expansion of slavery westward, one cannot expect a dispute over ballots in that election to be a model of democratic deliberation. When the Ku Klux Klan and other white supremacists, as part of their crusade to "redeem" the South and nullify Reconstruction, are perpetrating widespread terrorism in order to prevent freedmen from exercising their right to vote—newly guaranteed in the Fifteenth Amendment—it is inevitable that the disputes over the outcome of elections held in those conditions will be tainted by the terror campaigns.

Even assuming that the pathological conditions of the Civil War era will never recur, the history remains relevant. Not only does it teach something of our national character—holding elections in the midst of a Civil War is the ultimate test of a country's commitment to democracy—but there are relationships between extreme and normal conditions to pursue. Take, for example, the Hayes-Tilden presidential election of 1876, the subject of the next chapter. Being part of the demise of Reconstruction, it shares features with the terror-afflicted electoral disputes of 1872, which are discussed in this chapter. At the same time, the Hayes-Tilden debacle has elements that undoubtedly remain relevant today and into the future. Florida, after all, was the key pivotal state in both 1876 and 2000, and the constitutional apparatus that formed the foundation for the congressional crisis over Hayes-Tilden remains unchanged and provided justification for the US Supreme Court's intervention in *Bush v. Gore*. If we are to fully and accurately assess the ongoing relevance of the Hayes-Tilden dispute, we must consider it in relationship to the intense vote-counting battles of Reconstruction that preceded it.

More broadly, even if more uncomfortably, we must consider the extent to which issues of race relations continue to play a role in vote-counting disputes. Race is a major factor in other elements of voting law, as is evident from the Voting Rights Act of 1965 and its application to voter eligibility rules as well as to redistricting.[1] There is no reason, a priori, why race might not be a factor in vote-counting controversies, at least in some circumstances.

Likewise, one recurrent theme of this book is to consider whether the South has its own particular challenges with respect to the counting of ballots. We have seen evidence of that already, in the very early days of the Republic. And we will see further evidence of that subsequently. It remains open to consideration whether today and in the future, the South still has special challenges in this regard, or whether it has come to resemble the rest of America with respect to this particular aspect of electoral democracy.[2]

Historically, the special situation of the South has largely been a story about race. Thus, in grappling with the question whether the South continues to face vote-counting challenges distinct from the rest of the nation, we need to consider the special vote-counting challenges that slavery and Jim Crow generated. This inquiry, for the sake of the present and the future, provides another reason to understand the events described in this chapter.

No *Bashford v. Barstow* for Bleeding Kansas

The contrast between Wisconsin and Kansas in 1855 could hardly be sharper. Wisconsin's election that year produced *Bashford v. Barstow*, a glorious precedent for how to protect the electorate's democratic choice through the rule of law. Kansas, conversely, suffered that same year one of the nation's worst electoral failures, a failure that in turn would further propel the nation toward its Civil War.[3]

The Kansas failure stemmed from elections held on March 30, 1855, for the new legislature of the territory. Congress had passed the Kansas-Nebraska Act to permit settlers to exercise "popular sovereignty" on whether Kansas would be a free or slave state. Before passage of this Act, Kansas would have been a free state pursuant to the Missouri Compromise of 1820, and so the move to popular sovereignty was already a victory for proslavery forces. What Congress did not adequately anticipate is that Kansas was incapable of employing elections to exercise popular sovereignty in 1855. The will of Kansans could not be determined at the ballot box because the polls were overrun by non-Kansans, especially proslavery marauders crossing the border from Missouri, who wanted to control the choice of whether Kansas would be a slave or free state. The breakdown of basic electoral democracy was so severe that the existing mechanisms available for addressing the dispute were unable to undertake any meaningful remedial measures. As a consequence, majority rule under constitutional law was incapable of taking root in Kansas soil. The territory quickly descended into the armed conflict between the two sides—proslavery and free state—that came to be called Bloody Kansas.

Before the election, the territory's governor, Andrew Reeder, had decreed that would-be voters were required to swear that they actually resided in Kansas and intended to stay there in order to be eligible to cast a ballot. This decree, however, was flagrantly defied. Although a prevoting census had established that there were only 2,905 residents in the territory eligible to vote, 6,307 ballots were cast.[4]

These fraud-infested returns showed proslavery candidates winning the vast majority of seats in the new legislature. Reeder announced that he would consider challenges to the returns. But he received challenges affecting only a small portion of the seats. In some districts, Free Soil forces were intimidated against filing challenges by proslavery thuggery. In other districts, Free Soilers missed the deadline, or thought that a challenge would be futile.[5] Reeder invalidated the returns and ordered new elections in all the districts for which he had challenges. But he felt powerless to order new elections in unchallenged districts. For those, he certified the returns he had received, despite the transparency of the fraud on which they rested. These certified returns gave the proslavery party control of the new territorial legislature.

That moment marked the start to the territory's "reign of anarchy."[6] The proslavery forces took the position that the governor was powerless to invalidate even the few returns that were challenged. Thus, they refused to participate in the new elections he ordered. Furthermore, controlling the legislature, they refused to seat the Free Soil candidates who won unopposed in those new elections. The proslavery party still would have had a sizable majority of the legislature based on the governor's certifications even if they had seated these few Free Soilers, but they were in no mood for any kind of gesture of good will. As a result, the Free Soilers retaliated by claiming the proslavery legislature illegitimate—the Bogus Legislature, they called it—and organized a constitutional convention to set up their own entirely separate government. With that, the violence erupted.

The US House of Representatives created a three-member committee to investigate the Kansas chaos. Although the committee produced thousands of pages of testimony, much of it uncontradicted, the committee itself was divided 2–1 in both its membership and its conclusion. The majority of the committee were two Northerners committed to Free Soil, one of whom was a young John Sherman of Ohio (whom we will encounter again in Chapter 6).[7] The committee's dissenter was a proslavery Missourian.[8]

The majority found that 4,908 ballots cast in the March 30 election were invalid, over three-quarters of the total; only 1,410 were valid. Moreover, based on its district-by-district analysis of evidence, the majority concluded that this monumental fraud had a decisive effect on which party ended up in control of the legislature. The majority report stated:

> If the election had been confined to the actual settlers, undeterred by the presence of non-residents, or the knowledge that they would be present in numbers sufficient to outvote them, the testimony indicates that the council [which was the legislature's upper chamber] would have been composed of seven in favor of making Kansas a free state [while] three members would have been doubtful [and three other districts] would have elected three pro-slavery members.

Similarly, for the legislature's lower house, the majority concluded that a free and fair election would have produced "fourteen members in favor of making Kansas a free state," while "five members would have been doubtful" and the rest "would have elected seven pro-slavery members." [9] In short, a fraud-free election would have produced a Free Soil victory.

The committee's dissenter objected on multiple grounds. First and foremost, the dissent said that once the governor certified the bulk of the returns, all objections to the composition of the legislature were waived.[10] Second, the dissent emphatically maintained that if it were permissible to undertake an inquiry into the certified seats, a proper analysis would show that "the majority of the legal voters . . . were in favor of the [proslavery] party electing a majority of the legislature, as returned and certified to by the governor."[11] The dissent seemingly based its own analysis on the number of eligible residents as identified in the census, not the number of voters who actually cast ballots. In any event, the dissent was not subscribing to the majority's conclusion that the massive fraud made a difference in which party controlled the legislature.

Even with the hindsight of history, it is difficult to see how a different resolution of the disputed election could have avoided the "reign of anarchy" that ensued. Arguably, Governor Reeder should have ordered a new election for all the seats in the legislature based on the mere fact that ballots cast exceeded eligible residents by more than two to one (again, 6,307 compared to 2,905). Some have defended Reeder on the ground that he could not have been expected to invalidate unchallenged returns.[12] But this defense seems weak in light of the atrocious conditions that occurred at the polls, of which he had at least some knowledge, as well as the sheer impropriety of the returns across-the-board given the recent census that he had ordered.[13] Nonetheless, would a new election have prevented Bloody Kansas? It seems highly doubtful. Although it might have forestalled the Free Soilers from setting up their own alternative government, it would have only made the proslavery forces all the more furious. Either they would have inundated the new election with ineligible voters, just as they had done before, or they would have been the ones to set up their own rival legislature, creating a mirror image of the conditions that in fact occurred. Only a strong military presence of federal troops might have prevented the situation from becoming as violent as it did.[14] But that kind of heavy-handed military occupation is hardly consistent with the optimal conditions for operating democracy, and it is not clear that even a large-scale military presence would have guaranteed untainted elections. Simply put, it is hard to believe that in 1855 Kansas was capable of conducting democratic elections, with or without federal military oversight.[15]

The Wakarusa War. The Sack of Lawrence. The Pottawatomie Massacre. The Battle of Osawatomie. These are events of terror and combat, most intense in 1856, by which Bloody Kansas came to be known. John Brown slaughtered innocents in the name of Free Kansas. His motto "fight fire with fire" was matched by his proslavery adversaries, who committed their own "Le Marais du Cygne" Massacre in retaliation for the atrocities committed by Brown and his allies.[16]

In all, it took a succession of nine territorial governors and fourteen trips to the ballot box, most marred by some variation on the fraud with which the ordeal began, until Kansas quieted down under a Free State regime in 1859.[17] Most significant was the election held on October 5, 1857, for the next term of the territorial legislature. The key question was whether the Free Staters were going to bother to participate this time. They had already boycotted several elections held under the Bogus Legislature's authority, including one to choose delegates to another constitutional convention.[18] This convention, held at Lecompton, was inevitably dominated by proponents of slavery and thus drafted a thoroughly proslavery document. Persuaded partly by the new territorial governor, Robert Walker, and partly by some of their own leaders,

Free Staters decided to go to the polls on October 5, 1857, as a way to subvert ratification of the despised Lecompton Constitution.

Once again, there was flagrant fraud, in two precincts in particular. In one of them, names from a Cincinnati directory were simply copied into the poll books with little effort to conceal this ballot-box stuffing. In the other, over a thousand ballots were cast for a locale of only 50 residents.[19] These two precincts were well targeted insofar as the fraud, unless corrected, would enable the proslavery party to retain control of the legislature. Governor Walker, however, refused to certify the returns from these precincts, thereby giving the Free State Party controlling majorities in the legislature. A proslavery local judge ordered Walker to certify the fraudulent returns, but he disobeyed that judicial decree—conduct normally deserving of severe condemnation, but in this case exonerated by the pathological conditions in Kansas at the time.

The legislature, now under Free State control, convened for a special session to put to the voters the question whether the Lecompton Constitution should be repudiated. Although Lecompton supporters boycotted this vote

Figure 4.1 Robert Walker, governor of Kansas, thwarted voting fraud in the territory by refusing to obey a judicial decree to count fabricated votes. Kansas Historical Society.

and instead held their own separate vote to ratify the document, the strength of numbers turning out against Lecompton sent a strong message that Free State forces were consolidating power in Kansas: their rejection of Lecompton numbered 10,226, while the pro-Lecompton showing reached only 6,143.[20] A second vote on Lecompton, after Congress attempted to sweeten the deal in favor of the proslavery constitution, was even more decisive: 11,812 against, and only 1,926 in favor.[21] Kansas then went on to hold another convention, resulting in a Free State constitution, and afterward regular elections under that constitution.[22]

Governor Walker's repudiation of the fraud in October 1857 was thus a decisive step toward bringing a measure of peace to Kansas. It is ironic, and perhaps symbolic of the circumstances that prevailed in the territory, that his heroic move was to defy a court decree. Normally, a chief executive's defiance of a court order, particularly one concerning the counting of ballots, is cause for alarm. It certainly was the opposite of heroism when Governor Barstow of Wisconsin, in an effort to cling to power based on fraudulent returns, contemplated defiance of the Wisconsin Supreme Court in *Bashford v. Barstow*. The heroism of 1856 in Wisconsin belonged to the court, not the governor. But in Kansas the following year it was the opposite, a sign that the rule of law really had not yet fully taken hold in the territory. Walker's lawlessness in disobeying the court order was a necessary step to move Kansas closer to the point where regular government under a democratic constitution could prevail. Although Kansas was starting to achieve that orderly status by the end of the decade, its turmoil in the 1850s was propelling the nation to the all-encompassing Civil War.

Democracy During the Civil War

Constitutional republicanism, the idea of popular sovereignty controlled by and exercised through constitutional law, undoubtedly suffered severely as a result of the Civil War. Secession itself was, of course, the ultimate breach of the federal constitutional order, and to preserve the Union Lincoln imprisoned war critics and suspended the writ of habeas corpus.[23] But although fundamental constitutional freedoms were denied due to the exigencies of war, the prevailing impression has been that in the North democracy itself endured the Civil War. The great belief, in other words, is that free elections persisted throughout the war, at least on the Union side, and that the military did not undermine the authentic choices of the Union electorate. Lincoln was on the side of democracy, not dictatorship; that is what the nation has wanted to believe of its most beloved president.

There has been notable scholarly dissent to this national mythology. Focusing on the 1862 congressional elections, in which the Republican Party lost 23 House seats because of Lincoln's unpopularity at that point in the war—while the Democrats made "huge gains"[24]—several distinguished historians have maintained that military coercion at the polls in Border States prevented Democrats from taking over control of the House. If the Union Army had not subverted free elections in this way, the argument goes, congressional hostility to Lincoln's war efforts, including his Emancipation Proclamation, might have changed the course of the war significantly, perhaps causing the Union to seek peace terms with the Confederacy that would have permitted slavery to continue.[25]

Writing a century after the election in question, for example, University of Wisconsin historian William Hesseltine bluntly declared: "In 1862 it was the army-controlled votes of the Border States that overcame Democratic victories in the Northern states and enabled the Republicans to retain control over the House of Representatives."[26] More recently, Cornell historian Richard Bensel has expanded upon the point. Relying upon the reports of several contested congressional seats arising from the 1862 election, Bensel depicts the horrifically disenfranchising tactics employed by some Union Army officers and their state militia allies at polling places in Missouri and Kentucky.[27] Would-be voters suspected of disloyalty to the Union cause were not permitted to vote, and in some instances no voter was permitted to cast a ballot for candidates deemed sympathetic to the Confederacy.[28] Summing up the evidence, Bensel concluded: "Military intervention at the polls may very well have made a difference in the outcome of the war."[29]

The disputed congressional elections that Bensel described, however, tell a different story when examined from another perspective. There is no doubt about the egregiously improper disenfranchising practices that occurred at the polls, which Bensel detailed extensively. But whether this military interference with the ballot box affected the outcome of enough congressional seats to keep the House in Republican hands is another matter, more complicated and ultimately more momentous.

The Democrats of course wanted to take control of the House. In fact, after their strong showing in the 1862 elections, they organized a scheme to do so. Because the new Congress would not convene until December 7, 1863, they had plenty of time to work up their plan, which centered on the outgoing Clerk of the House, Emerson Etheridge, who had the responsibility to declare the properly credentialed members of the new House at the start of the session.[30]

The Republicans had installed Etheridge, a Tennessee politician, as Clerk in 1861 because at the time he was thoroughly pro-Union.[31] In fact, it was the Republicans who, fearful of losing control of the House after the 1862 elections, gave the Clerk unusually broad powers to determine who would be entitled to take seats at the very beginning of the new session. The lesson these Republicans apparently learned from the Broad Seal War was not to constrain the Clerk, but rather to expand his exclusionary powers.

On March 3, 1863, at the close of the previous lame-duck session, when they were still in power, the Republicans enacted a statute that in its entirety provided:

> That before the first meeting of the next Congress, and of every subsequent Congress, the clerk of the next preceding House of Representatives shall make a roll of the representatives elect, and place thereon the names of all persons *and of such persons only*, whose credentials show that they were regularly elected in accordance with the laws of their states respectively, or the laws of the United States.[32]

The key language of this short statute was the italicized clause, which gave the Clerk the authority to keep off the roll any claimant whose credentials he deemed improper. The Republicans thought that Etheridge could use this power to prevent from being seated Democrats or their allies, primarily from Border States, whom the Republicans considered disloyal—candidates who, in their view, were not entitled to have been elected in the first place. (Republicans also accused Confederate sympathizers in Border States of coercion at polling places under their, rather than loyalist, control.) If Republicans could knock out enough of their opponents through Etheridge's use of this new statute, then retaining their control of the House would be assured.[33]

Between March and December of 1863, however, Etheridge apparently had switched his allegiance from the Republicans to the Democrats. He soured on Lincoln's policies, including the Emancipation Proclamation (even though it exempted Border States like Tennessee). Consequently, he let it be known to the leader of the House Democrats, Samuel S. Cox of Ohio, that he would be willing to use his power as Clerk to their advantage, and not in favor of the Republicans. Etheridge ultimately identified for exclusion sixteen credentialed claimants whom the Republicans desperately wanted seated: five from Maryland (the state's entire delegation), six from Missouri (two-thirds of that state's delegation), one from Oregon (the state's sole representative), one from Kansas (another sole seat), and three from West Virginia (that new state's whole delegation). Etheridge was willing to be selective in his use of this power; he did not exclude three representatives from Missouri who were aligned with the Democrats. He also indicated that he would seat three representatives from Louisiana who also were on the Democratic side and whose seating the Republicans strenuously opposed. Heading into the December

7 opening of the House session, Democrats were cautiously confident that Etheridge's calculations were enough for them to prevail.[34]

Republicans, conversely, were increasingly anxious as December 7 approached. They considered ways that they might now prevent Etheridge's use of the credential-recognition power that they had given him. One option would be to have their most senior member, Elihu Washburne of Illinois, assert authority over the House for the purposes of correcting the Clerk's roll as necessary. Republicans called this option the "John Quincy Adams precedent,"[35] learning another lesson from the Broad Seal War (although Washburne's assertion of himself as chair of the House arguably would have been specifically partisan, in order that Republicans would prevail, whereas Adams had acted more neutrally to break the logjam in 1839).

Another option, which Republicans seriously considered with President Lincoln's active involvement, was to forcibly remove Etheridge from the floor of the House, so that they could seat the sixteen members whom he was prepared to exclude. Lincoln "was not inclined to rely exclusively upon moral force," his trusted advisers Nicolay and Hay wrote in their monumental biography of him.[36] Citing Nicolay's diary from the eve of the December 7 opening session, they quote Lincoln as saying: "If Mr. Etheridge undertakes revolutionary proceedings, let him be carried out on a chip, and let our men organize the House."[37] The distinguished historian David Donald, in his prizewinning biography of Lincoln, adds that Lincoln "promised to have a troop of soldiers ready to assist."[38] That Lincoln was prepared to use military force upon the US Capitol to maintain Republican control of the House when it met to organize itself on December 7, 1863, is not generally well known. Nonetheless, Lincoln's willingness to have the military interfere with the internal workings of Congress was much more significant—and dangerous to democracy—than the military interference at particular polling places, as problematic as that also was.[39]

Ultimately, however, this contingency along with the rest of the Republican strategizing proved unnecessary, because Etheridge and the Democrats had miscalculated. When December 7 finally arrived, Etheridge attempted to carry out the plan. He did exclude the sixteen claimants that the Republicans wanted seated, and he did seat the Louisiana claimants that the Republicans wanted excluded. But after he did so, the Republicans immediately moved to add the sixteen claimants to the rolls, and they succeeded based on a vote of the members—and only the members—whom Etheridge had recognized. Etheridge is to be credited for allowing a vote on the Republican resolution. The Democrats had hoped that he would rule it out of order altogether—a decision that might well have provoked Lincoln's planned show of force.[40] But when the Democrats asked for this ruling, Etheridge instead announced that his opinion was that the resolution was "in order, as being pertinent to the organization of the House."[41] Etheridge's handling of the matter indicates that he may not have moved all the way to the side of the Democrats, and certainly not as far as the Democrats had hoped—or needed.

The vote was 94–74 in favor of the Republicans.[42] At the moment when Democrats were relying on the power of the Clerk to keep dubious Republicans off the roll, they could not muster a majority of the House. This fact shows that military interference at the polls is not what kept the Democrats from gaining control of the House. The Democrats had their chance to organize the House based on a vote that excluded Republicans they believed had won as a result of military improprieties. Yet even with this crucial vote on their terms, the Democrats could not prevail; instead, there still was "a majority of twenty for the Government."[43]

Afterward, moreover, the Democrats could have attempted to unseat enough Republicans through the mechanism of contested elections. They did file three such contests, and indeed it is those contest proceedings that provide the evidence of the military coercion at the polls that the historian Bensel

Figure 4.2 Emerson Etheridge, Clerk of the House of Representatives, rejected the election certificates of pro-Lincoln candidates whose victories in 1862 the Democrats disputed, but the undisputed members overruled Etheridge and thus foiled the Democrats' efforts to take control of the House. Library of Congress.

described. But the Democrats did not file nearly enough contests to put control of the House potentially in play.[44]

Subsequently contesting only three of the sixteen initially excluded seats on grounds of military misconduct was no way for the Democrats to attempt to show that this military misbehavior deprived them of a controlling majority in the House. They did add one additional contest of a Kentucky member whom Etheridge had seated.[45] But even assuming that four members who were part of the Republican majority won their seats because of military interference with the elections, that number was hardly enough to affect the balance of power in the House. To be sure, there may have been other, uncontested seats affected by military improprieties. But the cardinal rule of disputed elections is that unless a defeated candidate formally puts to the test a claim that the defeat was wrongful, there is no way to evaluate the merits of that claim. Democrats undoubtedly had the opportunity to claim that their candidates were wrongly defeated because of military misconduct; they did so in four instances. That they did not do so in more must be taken as skepticism of the broader allegation that they were deprived of a majority in the House because of that military misconduct.

A more detailed examination of the contests themselves confirms this point. In the lead case from Missouri, which served as a precedent for the others, the Democrats did not even ask that their candidate be seated, only that the Republican be unseated.[46] In the Kentucky case, Democrats as well as Republicans ultimately concluded that the evidence of military impropriety was not widespread enough to undermine the Unionist candidate's large margin of victory in that particular district.[47] And in another of the contested cases from Missouri, the contestant was more pro-Government than the certified winner he was seeking to replace.[48] In short, while military misconduct at the polls was deplorable—as Henry Dawes, the Republican chair of the House Elections Committee emphatically and passionately declared at the time[49]—the available evidence does not sustain the claim that this military misconduct enabled Republicans to steal the House from the Democrats at that vital juncture of the Civil War.

What remains more disturbing is that some Republican leaders, including Lincoln himself, were prepared to use military force if Etheridge's rulings had deprived them of control over the chamber. Whether or not Etheridge was justified in his exclusion of the sixteen claimants, there needs to be some designated officer at the opening of the session to declare the initial roll of the House so that the body can begin to organize itself. It would be best if that officer could be impartial between the two main parties competing for control of the chamber. But in 1863 the Republicans had no basis for arguing that Etheridge's purported allegiance with the Democrats was justification for ousting him with military force. The Republicans, after all, had installed him as Clerk and given him the exact power he was exercising. That an individual official, originally believed to be trustworthy, is no longer trusted is not adequate justification for forcible ejection of that official by military means. Instead, if the Republicans had lost the crucial vote on December 7—and the sixteen had remained off the rolls, and the Democrats had proceeded to elect a Speaker and organize the House under their control—then the lawful and appropriate response of Republicans, including Lincoln, would have been to use the available procedures in the House for petitioning that their claimants be seated. If the Democrats had then been partisan in wrongly keeping out members who on the merits should have been seated, that would have generated a severe crisis—perhaps even justifying extraordinary measures at that point, given the exigencies of war, but not before. As Dawes himself said, Lincoln and the Republicans would have been justified in using military force only "to assert the freedom of elections" and "not to secure the election of particular men."[50] If Lincoln instead had insisted on Republican control of the House, regardless of what the certified returns provided, and regardless of what an honest assessment of all disputed seats would show, that insistence would have been worthy of condemnation.

Figure 4.3 Henry Dawes, chair of the House Elections Committee, deplored the efforts of fellow Republicans to secure a partisan advantage during the Civil War from military presence at the polls. Library of Congress.

Fortunately, however, this circumstance did not come to pass. December 7, 1863 came and went without any kind of coup d'etat, and the Republicans retained control of the House pursuant to the procedures established in advance for recognizing elected members. Their legitimate control continued as proceedings on specific contested seats worked their way through the system, with none of those contests affecting that legitimate control. Thus in this crucial respect, American-style representative democracy as it had come to be developed by the mid-nineteenth century was not subverted in the 1862 congressional elections, notwithstanding the military improprieties that occurred at some of the polls that year.[51]

The Unraveling of Reconstruction

The Civil War and Reconstruction undoubtedly put great strains on America's election procedures, including those used to resolve disputed elections. As has been well documented, the number of contested elections in Congress spiked during this period, particularly as a result of Republicans willing to contest Democratic victories in the South.[52] Reconstruction-related electoral disputes in former Confederate states at times had significant major national repercussions, as in 1872 when ballot-counting controversies in Alabama were severe enough to provoke two rival legislatures into organizing themselves separately, each purporting to elect its own US Senator (as state legislatures did before the adoption of the Seventeenth Amendment). 1872 was the year that Republican control in the South began seriously slipping away, as a result of concerted efforts by the Democrats to "redeem" the South according to their vision of white supremacy.[53]

In response to the fight waging in Alabama in 1872 between forces for and against Reconstruction, the US Senate, controlled by Republicans, seated the Senator sent by the Republican legislature in Alabama. This move departed from the usual rule that in the initial organization of a legislative chamber those holding official certificates of election have the right to be seated at least until their elections are subsequently challenged within the chamber.[54] In this respect, the Senate Republicans were acting in the same manner as Clerk Etheridge in the House had a decade earlier, much to the objection of Republicans then (and, unlike Etheridge, in 1872 the Senate Republicans had no statute or rule to justify their deviation from ordinary practice). In Alabama it was the Democratic claimants to the disputed seats who held the official certificates of election, but Republicans both in the state and in the US Senate considered those certificates to be resting on election fraud.[55] The crisis of the dueling legislatures in the state, including the significant civil disorder that it entailed, was not resolved without the intervention of the Grant administration backed by the threat of federal troops.[56]

As dire as the situation was in Alabama in 1872, much worse occurred that year in Louisiana and Arkansas, where vote-counting disputes subverted the gubernatorial elections and caused major outbreaks of violence. They also caused Congress to reject the Electoral College votes from both states in the presidential election that year, thus foreshadowing the Great Crisis of 1876.[57] Most disturbingly, as had happened in Bleeding Kansas, they demonstrated that sometimes elections held on American soil have failed to identify a winning candidate who reasonably can be perceived as the choice of the state's electorate.

The 1872 election in Louisiana could not have been much uglier or more chaotic. There was pervasive fraud, intimidation, and brutality as anti-Reconstruction whites attempted to take back control of their state's government—by whatever means available—from what they viewed as the forces of Northern occupation. The pro-Reconstructionists were almost equally determined to maintain power so that they could vindicate the rights of the freed slaves and others under their protection. As one historian has characterized it, "the actual returns mattered little" to both sides "for this was an extraordinary affair, even by the standards of Reconstruction."[58]

After the ballots were cast, two different groups claimed to be the official canvassing board for the state, and these in turn declared victorious two different gubernatorial candidates. William Kellogg was the pro-Reconstruction candidate, while John McEnery was the anti-Reconstruction candidate. Which side would control the state legislature was also at stake.

As the two sides struggled for power, the violence became extreme. One particularly gruesome episode, known as the Colfax Massacre, was the bloodiest confrontation during all of Reconstruction. Pro-Reconstructionists held possession of the Colfax courthouse, which the anti-Reconstructionists attacked on Easter Sunday. Many African Americans had taken refuge inside and around the courthouse, as it had become a kind of fortified armed encampment. When over 300 anti-Reconstruction ruffians stormed the grounds, the African Americans attempted to surrender. Scores, perhaps more than a hundred, were slaughtered in cold blood.[59]

The Grant administration supported the pro-Reconstruction Kellogg government, sending in additional federal troops to prop it up. They prevailed in the sense that the Kellogg government became the official regime in the state until the next election in 1876. But the use of increased military means to maintain pro-Reconstruction power only intensified anti-Reconstruction resentment. The opponents of Reconstruction would soon take over state

Figure 4.4 In its May 10, 1873 edition, *Harper's Weekly* contained this depiction of the Colfax Massacre, the most horrific component of the fight over the outcome of the 1872 election in Louisiana. The Ohio State University Billy Ireland Cartoon Library & Museum.

governments throughout the South, with Louisiana falling to the Redeemers as part of the accommodation necessary to end the dispute over the 1876 election.

There was an effort to use nonviolent judicial means to resolve the 1872 dispute in Louisiana. Indeed, pro-Reconstructionists even secured an order from the local federal district judge, Edward Henry Durell, who granted them possession of the statehouse and further ordered the anti-Reconstructionists to refrain from attempting to oust their opponents from the building. As authority for this order, Judge Durell relied upon the newly adopted Fifteenth Amendment.[60] This decree is the first—indeed, a virtually contemporaneous—judicial use of the Reconstruction Amendments to vindicate voting rights. Moreover, Judge Durell relied upon the creative argument that votes could be credited to individuals who attempted to cast ballots but were wrongly denied the right to do so.[61] But rather than setting a favorable precedent for the kind of rulings that would become routine a century later in the Civil Rights Era of the 1960s and 1970s, this initial decree was widely condemned at the time as an inappropriate exercise of federal judicial authority.

Figure 4.5 Edward Henry Durell in 1872 was the first federal judge to invoke the Fifteenth Amendment as authority for ordering that the outcome of a state election be free from the effect of wrongful disenfranchisement. *Harper's Weekly* (June 6, 1868).

Even many pro-Reconstructionists, including members of Congress, viewed the federal judiciary as an improper instrument for settling a dispute over the counting of ballots cast in an election operated by state officials pursuant to state law. The US Supreme Court avoided addressing the merits of the order because the anti-Reconstructionists failed to take a proper appeal to the intermediate federal appellate court.[62]

The events of the same year in Arkansas may have been even more bizarre. There the anti-Reconstruction candidate for governor was Joseph Brooks, while the pro-Reconstruction candidate was Elisha Baxter. Known as the Brooks-Baxter War, the episode had some of the same features as the Louisiana dispute, including a basic inability to conduct the vote-casting-and-counting process in a way consistent with minimally democratic standards.[63]

In Arkansas, the pro-Reconstructionists controlled the vote-counting process, including the state legislature. The state judiciary, however, turned out to be the wild card. Initially, the state supreme court declined to take jurisdiction over a petition filed by the anti-Reconstructionists. The court pointed to a provision of the state's constitution that expressly gave exclusive authority to the legislature to resolve disputes over which candidate won a gubernatorial election.[64]

Even after this supreme court decision, Brooks took his case to a sympathetic—and renegade—local state judge, who was willing to ignore the constitutional provision and rule that Brooks had won the election. Brooks then used that order in an effort to obtain political control. He was sworn into office by the chief justice, who supported him and who had dissented in the earlier ruling.[65]

President Grant initially tried to stay out of the controversy because he had been criticized for taking sides in Louisiana's disputed gubernatorial election. But with federal troops standing aside, the battle between opposing forces in the state escalated into armed conflict. In all, twenty were killed and many times that number were wounded.[66]

One question was whether the state supreme court would adhere to its original decision or instead affirm the ruling of the renegade lower-court judge. That depended in part on whether any of potentially wavering justices could be won over—and whether it would be possible to replace justices in the interim. Pro-Baxter militia kidnapped two justices thought sympathetic to Brooks, but they managed to escape. They joined forces with other pro-Brooks justices, and, purporting to be the supreme court, issued a new ruling that Brooks was the governor. They did not attempt to square their decision with the court's earlier contrary ruling.[67]

Baxter went back to the legislature to vindicate his claim to be governor. Grant was unable to broker a deal. Grant's attorney general sided with Baxter on the ground that the legislature supported him, and Arkansas's constitution gave the legislature this authority. After Grant intervened, the pro-Brooks justices on the court either resigned or were impeached and removed from office. In its third decision on the matter, the new supreme court reverted to its first decision holding that it lacked jurisdiction over the disputed election, because the constitution placed that authority in the legislature.[68]

The response of Congress to the events of 1872 in Louisiana and Arkansas is instructive. As part of the presidential election that year, Congress received and examined the Electoral College submissions from each state. Since the voting for presidential electors involved the same electoral procedures as the voting for governor—and thus especially in Louisiana was also plagued by fraud, intimidation, and violence—Congress ultimately concluded that it would not count the 1872 Electoral College votes from either Louisiana or Arkansas. In essence, the electoral system was so dysfunctional and undemocratic that it was unable to produce an outcome that was worthy of crediting as valid.[69] But this congressional disqualification of Louisiana and Arkansas in the 1872 presidential election did not affect the determination of the overall Electoral College majority: in his reelection bid that year Grant won an overwhelming victory of 286 Electoral College votes to only 42 undisputed Electoral College votes for his opponent, Horace Greeley. Even if one were to put Arkansas and Louisiana's combined 14 Electoral College votes in Greeley's column, they would not come close to making a difference.[70]

The situation, however, raised the obvious question of what would happen if the kind of dysfunctional and undemocratic electoral process that had occurred in Louisiana and Arkansas would actually affect the outcome of a presidential election. Would Congress continue to disqualify the Electoral College votes from such dysfunctional and undemocratic states? Or instead, would Congress be unwilling to deprive a state of its role in electing a president no matter how dysfunctional and undemocratic the state's own voting might be? Although the nation should have adopted a plan to deal with these contingencies in light of what happened in 1872, the nation seemed unwilling or unable to prepare for the predicament it would soon face.[71]

5

Hayes v. Tilden

To the Edge of the Constitutional Cliff

The 1876 presidential election instigated the nation's most perilous ballot-counting dispute, much more alarming than its counterpart in 2000. The dispute in 2000 ended 39 days before Inauguration Day, when on December 13 Al Gore publicly announced that he would not challenge the US Supreme Court's decision against him in *Bush v. Gore*, rendered the previous day. By contrast, the dispute over the 1876 election did not end until March 2, 1877, just two days before Inauguration Day, when Congress finally declared Rutherford B. Hayes, the Republican, winner over Samuel Tilden, the Democrat, and Tilden signaled that he did not wish to challenge this declaration by holding his own separate inauguration ceremony.

Historians debate just how precarious the circumstances were in the final days before March 4, 1877, when President Grant's term was scheduled to end and the newly elected president, either Hayes or Tilden, was supposed to take office. Some historians point to the compromise that was reached between Southern Democrats and Republicans, which called for the withdrawal of federal troops in the South—and thus the end of Reconstruction—in exchange for Southern acceptance of Hayes's inauguration.[1] On this view, Hayes's victory had become inevitable weeks before, as a result of certain proceedings established by Congress for the resolution of the dispute, and any lingering uncertainty before this outcome became official was only due to Democrats attempting to extract the best bargain they could before the March 4 deadline arrived. Other historians emphasize the precipitousness of the last-minute proceedings, the willingness of many Democrats to fight on even by military force if necessary, and the unpredictability of key political figures, including Tilden's own vacillation up to the end. From this alternative perspective, the nation came much closer to the ultimate constitutional crisis of two separate inauguration ceremonies, with two individuals purporting to assert the authority of commander in chief, than most Americans now realize.[2]

Figure 5.1 In December 1876, the German-American magazine *Puck* depicted the Hayes-Tilden election as a potential train wreck (with Tilden heading the train on the left, and Hayes on the right). The Ohio State University Billy Ireland Cartoon Library & Museum.

The danger in 1876 was caused in large part by the absence of any institution established in advance for handling the dispute. A similar danger was averted in 2000 by the US Supreme Court inserting itself into the controversy and then, most crucially, Gore's willingness to accept its decision as final. If either the Court declines to intervene next time, or if the candidate that loses in the Court decides (unlike Gore) to continue the fight in Congress, the next disputed presidential election could end up looking more like 1876 than 2000.[3]

Although an outgrowth of Reconstruction's demise, the Hayes-Tilden dispute exposed structural frailties in the nation's constitutional order that still exist—the ones that James Madison, James Kent, and Joseph Story had already recognized by the 1830s, but which were unchanged in 1876 and remain unchanged today. The ambiguity of the Twelfth Amendment, which engenders the uncertainty of what institution of government is supposed to resolve a disputed presidential election, is the heart of the problem, and that same ambiguity and its accompanying uncertainty still plague the system.

It is noteworthy also that the key state in the Hayes-Tilden dispute was Florida, just as it was in 2000. Perhaps a coincidence; perhaps not. Florida historically has been a state with a political culture that lends itself to deficiencies in the operation of the voting process and intense disputation if those deficiencies are potentially outcome-determinative in an important election. Consequently, it is conceivable that Florida could have another outcome-determinative controversy over the counting of ballots in a future presidential election. If so, how the Hayes-Tilden dispute was handled could prove to be precedent as relevant as *Bush v. Gore*. That possibility is cause for concern, because the nation came close to falling into a constitutional abyss in the Hayes-Tilden dispute. While just how close remains debatable, it was close enough that the nation should hope never to come that near to the edge of the precipice again. Because it was the statesmanship of individual politicians that pulled the nation back from the brink in the Hayes-Tilden crisis—particularly the resolute leadership of Samuel Randall, Speaker of the House of Representatives—and not the safeguards of the constitutional institutions in which those individuals operated, there is no guarantee that America will have similarly virtuous politicians capable of averting a plunge into the constitutional chasm if the nation again finds itself in a equivalent situation.

Thus, civic-minded Americans should review the story of the Hayes-Tilden dispute to develop the collective capacity of instituting a structural solution that would ward against the possibility of a similar crisis occurring again.

The Controversy Presented to Congress

Election Day in 1876 was Tuesday, November 7. As returns arrived that night, it appeared that Tilden had won. Early reports from the Southern states of Florida, Louisiana, and South Carolina indicated that Tilden was carrying those three states. Any of the three would do, as without them Tilden was just one electoral vote shy of the 185 needed to win a majority in the Electoral College.[4] Tilden also was well on his way to winning the overall popular vote nationwide, which he would do by over a quarter-million votes, about three percent of the total ballots cast.[5]

But Republicans still controlled the machinery of government in the three pivotal Reconstructed states, and leaders of the national party immediately dispatched the message to local Republicans: "With your state sure for Hayes, he is elected. Hold your state."[6] Thus began the effort to exploit the vote-counting process to yield a Hayes victory. Republicans would need to prevail in all three Southern states to reach an Electoral College majority.

What happened in Florida is illustrative of all three and also the most important, because Congress considered Florida first (taking the states in alphabetical order), and it thereby set a precedent for the other two. Florida's canvassing board had three members: its two Republicans were Samuel B. McLin, the secretary of state, and Clayton A. Cowgill, the comptroller; its sole Democrat was William A. Cocke, attorney general. A series of 2–1 partisan rulings produced the result that Hayes won all four of the state's electoral votes by a margin of 924 popular votes out of almost 50,000 (23,843 to 22,919).[7]

The result was manufactured by a deliberate manipulation of the count. If the canvassing board had simply accepted all the local returns, Tilden would have prevailed by 94 votes.[8] But the board acted on the view that it was entitled to invalidate local returns because of improprieties. Had the board consistently applied this view to all the local returns, it still would have ended up with a Tilden victory. In its decisive 2–1 rulings, however, the board selectively invalidated Tilden-favoring returns because of technicalities, while refusing to invalidate Hayes-favoring returns despite clear evidence of actual fraud.

For example, the board invalidated two precincts with a combined 354-vote margin for Tilden "because the election inspectors, rather than counting the votes immediately after the poll closed, took a dinner break and left the boxes unattended while doing so." Similarly, the board voided a third precinct with a 342-vote margin for Tilden "because the election inspectors had waited until the day after the election to count the votes and then had failed to do so in public view."[9] By contrast, the board refused to disqualify a precinct despite "proof" that "219 names had been fraudulently put upon the polling-list and the same number of votes added to the Republican majority." Likewise, in another precinct 73 "little joker" ballots "had been smuggled into the ballot-box" to inflate the Republican margin there, "while to cover up the trick the poll-list had been correspondingly increased."[10] Yet the board did not negate that fraud, nor invalidate precincts with technical deficiencies comparable to those that caused the invalidation of pro-Tilden precincts. One early historian called the board's behavior "tails I win and heads you lose."[11] A more recent study has estimated that, if the board had acted consistently in invalidating local returns because of improprieties, Tilden's margin of victory would have been at least 100 votes—and more than 1,000 if the board's most permissive evidentiary standard for invalidating returns had been uniformly applied.[12]

The board's result-driven inconsistency was apparent at the time. Francis Barlow, a Civil War hero (rising all the way from private to general) and former attorney general of New York, was a Republican sent by President Grant to observe the Florida count. Barlow reported back that, striving to emulate an "impartial court," his analysis of the local returns would yield "Tilden's majority" as 55 votes.[13] Although excoriated by fellow Republicans for this betrayal to his party, Barlow held his ground. "With the application of the same rules, either strict or lax, to the Democratic and Republican side of the question," he later testified to Congress, "I did not see how, fairly, the State could be given to the Hayes electors."[14] Writing in 1906, the historian Paul Haworth deemed Barlow "the least partisan man who witnessed the count." Reviewing all the evidence, Haworth confirmed Barlow's conclusion that "the board did its work in an unpardonably partisan manner." As Haworth summed it up: "In every important instance in which votes were thrown out the advantage inured to the Republicans, [while] the majority of the board refused to eliminate other returns, the validity of which was questioned, when by so doing they would have seriously diminished the Republican vote."[15]

Barlow even attempted to convince one of the Republican canvassers, Cowgill the comptroller, to rule fairly and not based on partisanship. Cowgill, however, did not heed Barlow's advice. In response to the public dissemination of Barlow's report to Grant, Cowgill attempted to defended his rulings as nonpartisan: "If I have acted wrongfully, I have erred in judgment only."[16] But this defense rang hollow in light of the facts. Even Cowgill's fellow Republican on the Florida canvassing board, Secretary of State McLin, was willing to

Figure 5.2 Francis Barlow, a former Civil War hero, was sent by President Grant to observe the Florida canvass and, resisting partisan pressure from fellow Republicans, reported that a fair count would yield a Tilden victory. R. F. Welch, *The Boy General.*

admit in congressional testimony that "the Florida canvass was not [an] honest, unbiased decision." Rather, "partisan feeling," McLin continued, "usurped the place of reason and sound judgment, and political expediency ruled the hour." As for himself, McLin acknowledged that he conducted the canvass "as a very active partisan." He explained that he never endeavored to treat the local returns consistently, but instead considered it "fairly allowable in politics that I should always lean to my own party, and give my decision in its favor, even at the hazard of straining a point."[17]

The upshot of McLin's confession to Congress was that an honest count of the ballots cast in Florida would have produced a victory for Tilden. The removal of the clearly fraudulent ballots alone would have yielded that result. "The conclusion, therefore, is irresistible that Mr. Tilden was entitled to the electoral vote of Florida, and not Mr. Hayes," McLin belatedly conceded.[18]

Yet the circumstances are complicated by the fact that African Americans suffered widespread intimidation and other forms of disenfranchisement in the casting of ballots in Florida that year. Hayes undoubtedly would have won Florida if African Americans had been permitted to exercise the equal voting rights that the Fifteenth Amendment to the US Constitution purportedly guaranteed.[19] But improperly suppressed votes cannot be counted. Thus, as the historian Haworth explained, Democrats were denied a *fair count* of valid ballots actually cast, but Republicans were denied a *fair election* by the systematically discriminatory disenfranchisement of eligible African Americans. Whether the two Republicans on Florida's canvassing board were justified in manipulating the count of ballots actually cast to achieve a Hayes victory, therefore, turns on whether, at least in this instance, two wrongs can make a right. Haworth ultimately thought not: "Wrong should not be met by wrong but by recourse to law, and free institutions are in grave danger when citizens, however good their intentions, endeavor to correct one wrong by another."[20]

Morally justified or not, the two Republicans on Florida's canvassing board consistently outvoted the sole Democrat and consequently awarded the state's electoral votes to Hayes. They did so on December 5, the day before the presidential electors themselves were required to meet to cast their official votes for president. This delay left no time for Democrats to challenge the lawfulness of the board's determination before the electors cast their votes the next day. Nonetheless, the Democrats refused to give up, and so on December 6 Tilden's electors met and cast their own votes for Tilden to be president. They sent these votes to Congress with a certification from Florida's Attorney General Cocke, the sole Democrat on the state's canvassing board, that they (rather than the Hayes electors) were the ones that the electorate had voted for back on November 7. Thus Congress received from Florida two separate certificates of electoral votes dated December 6, the date that all presidential electors throughout the country were constitutionally required to meet.[21] The other certificate was the one from the Hayes electors bearing a certificate from Florida's incumbent Republican governor, Marcellus Sterns, that they were the duly chosen electors as authoritatively determined by the canvassing board in its ruling on the previous day.

Nor was the submission to Congress of these two separate certificates the end of the matter in Florida. The Democrats filed suit in state court, seeking a judicial declaration that the Tilden electors rather than the Hayes electors were the valid ones under state law. On January 25, a Democratic judge sustained this claim.[22]

Meanwhile, Democrats filed a second suit directly in the Florida Supreme Court concerning the gubernatorial election that was also before the voters on November 7. Governor Stearns had been up for reelection, and the canvassing board's rulings that caused Hayes to win also had yielded a victory for him. The Florida Supreme Court, however, nullified that victory, ruling that a proper count of the ballots produced a win for his Democratic challenger, George Drew. On January 2 Drew took office, replacing Stearns. Then, on January 17, Florida's newly elected legislature, also in Democratic hands, ordered a recanvassing of the ballots in the presidential election. Two days later, the newly constituted canvassing board complied. With all three members of the board now Democrats, the board freshly determined that proper count of the ballots cast on November 7 showed that the Tilden electors rather than the Hayes electors had won. On January 26, Governor Drew certified this new determination, which also invoked the previous day's judicial ruling as a basis for declaring that when the Tilden electors had met on December 6 they were ones entitled under Florida law to cast the state's four electoral votes. With this third certification sent to Congress, there were now two on behalf of the Tilden electors, one dated December 6 and signed by the attorney general, the other dated January 26 and signed by the new governor; conversely, there was only one certificate on behalf of the Hayes electors, also dated December 6 but signed by the then-incumbent Governor Stearns.[23]

Louisiana and South Carolina also sent dueling certificates of electoral votes to Congress, although for each state there were only two rather than three certificates, and in each both certificates were dated December 6. In both states, the certificate for the Hayes electors was signed by the state's incumbent Republican governor, based on the determination of the state's Republican-controlled canvassing board. In Louisiana, the certificate for the Tilden electors bore the signature of a Democrat who claimed to be governor, but who exercised no powers of the office, as the Grant administration had used military force to uphold the Republican incumbent's authority. In South Carolina, the Tilden electors simply certified themselves.[24]

In Louisiana, the Democrats had an argument for invalidating the Hayes certificate not available in Florida. Louisiana law required that its canvassing board have at least one member from a political party different from the party to which the board's other members belonged. In 1876, however, the board had only four Republicans when it determined that the Hayes electors had won the state; the sole Democrat on the board had resigned and had not been replaced.[25] In South Carolina, the Democrats argued that the November 7 vote of the electorate must be declared void because the state's legislature had not enacted a voter registration law as the state's constitution required.[26] Invalidating either Louisiana's or South Carolina's electoral votes would not have given the state to Tilden, but it still would have worked to make him president—either on the theory that he had a majority of all electoral votes deemed valid or, if neither he nor Hayes had a majority, then the US House of Representatives, being controlled by Democrats, would proceed to elect Tilden under the special procedures set forth in the Twelfth Amendment.[27]

In addition to the disputes involving the three Southern states, the Democrats manufactured a dispute over just one of Oregon's three electoral votes. Even if Hayes were credited as winning all three of the Southern states, Tilden would reach the constitutionally required majority if he received just one more electoral vote from somewhere, and Oregon presented an opportunity. The federal Constitution prohibits presidential electors from "holding an office of Trust or Profit under the United States," and one of the three Hayes electors had been a local postmaster on November 7. There was no doubt that Oregon's citizenry had voted for the three Hayes electors, but Democrats now argued that this one of them was ineligible. The state's governor, a Democrat, was willing to go along with this plan, and he certified that the state's three electors were two for Hayes and one for Tilden. (On the theory that the third Hayes elector was ineligible, the slot must be filled by an elector receiving the next highest number of votes cast by the citizenry on November 7.)[28]

Oregon law, however, specified a method for correcting the defect of an ineligible elector prior to the meeting of the electors on December 6: the ineligible elector could resign and be replaced with someone chosen by the two indisputably eligible electors. In mid-November the ineligible elector resigned his position as postmaster, and thus the two other electors simply reappointed him since he was now eligible to serve. These three Hayes electors then met on December 6 to cast their electoral votes for Hayes. Although the governor refused to certify them as valid, the secretary of state was willing to certify that these three Hayes electors indeed had been chosen by the citizenry on November 7.[29]

The Democrats saw Oregon as their trump card. If the Republicans were correct in their claim that Congress must accept the Hayes certificates from all three Southern states just because those certificates bore the then-governor's signature on (or before) December 6, the date of the Electoral College meetings, then so too must Congress accept the Oregon governor's certificate dated December 6 showing one Tilden elector, along with two Hayes electors, to be the state's valid electors. Conversely, if Congress must honor the choice that Oregon's voters made on November 7 when they cast more ballots for Hayes than Tilden, then so too must Congress honor the choice of Florida's voters who, by a proper count, cast more valid ballots for Tilden than Hayes.[30]

Whether or not the Democrats were correct in their argument about Oregon, the fact remained that by mid-December it was evident that the electoral votes from four states would be seriously disputed when Congress convened in the new year to conduct its official count of all the electoral votes.

The Creation of the Electoral Commission

The Hayes-Tilden dispute was the nightmare scenario that Madison, Kent, and Story had feared because of the vulnerabilities inherent in the original constitutional design. The Twelfth Amendment, as well as the rest of the Constitution, was entirely silent on what to do in the event that two or more conflicting certificates of electoral votes came from a state—as was now the case with four states. As we saw in Chapter 2, the amendment said only that the electors of each state would send their certificates to the president of the Senate, who "shall, in the presence of the Senate and the House of Representatives, open all the certificates and the votes shall then be counted." Given its passive voice, the amendment is unclear on who exactly does the counting and, more crucially, did not resolve any disputes over which of the competing certificates from a single state is the one entitled "to be counted."

An argument could be made that the most natural reading of this ambiguous language was that the president of the Senate was the officer entrusted with the constitutional responsibility of counting the electoral votes from the states, with the Senate and House serving only as witnesses to that officer's counting. On this view, the further inference could be drawn that in the event of a dispute over which of competing certificates to count, it was this officer's responsibility—and thus authority—to make the determination of which certificate was the correct one. To be sure, giving the president of the Senate this authority is awkward, since that officer is often one of the candidates for the US presidency, as John Adams was in 1796 and Thomas Jefferson was in 1800 (and as Richard Nixon would be in 1960 and Al Gore in 2000). But the authors of the Twelfth Amendment were well aware of what had happened in 1796

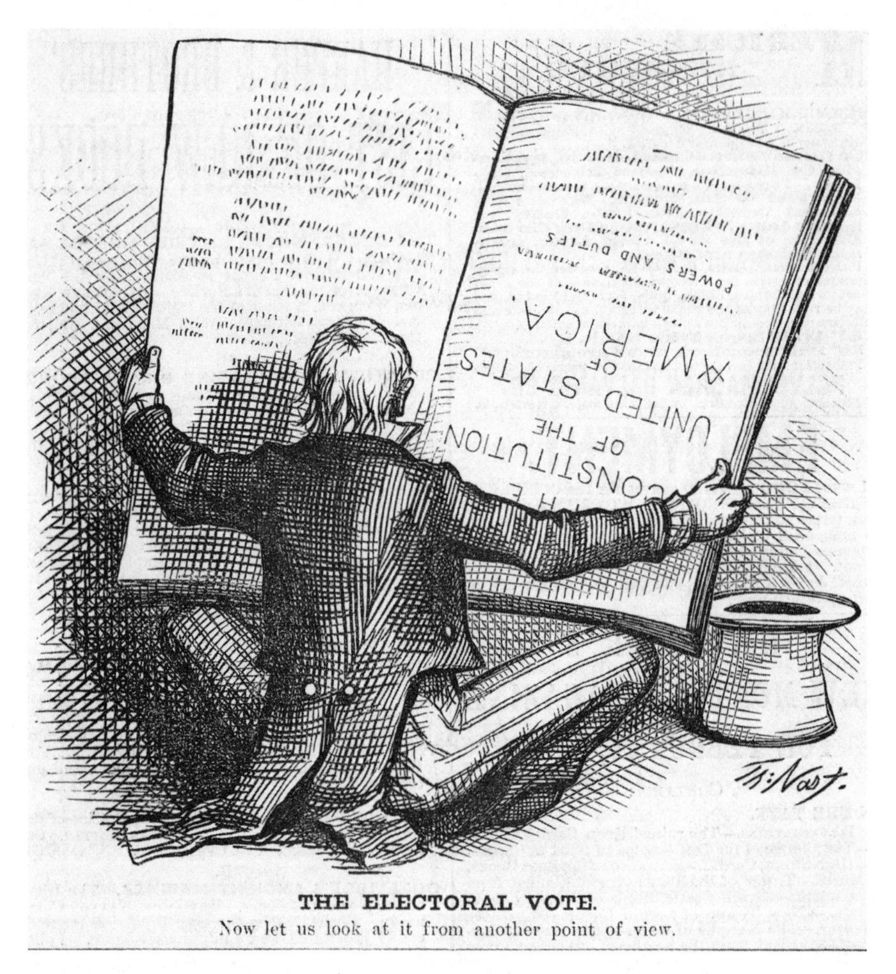

Figure 5.3 In *Harper's Weekly* (January 27, 1877), Thomas Nast depicted the constitutional confusion that Congress, and the country as a whole, faced over how to count the electoral votes. The Ohio State University Billy Ireland Cartoon Library & Museum.

and 1800, and yet did not change this feature of counting the electoral votes. And since the authority to resolve a dispute over competing certificates ultimately must lie somewhere, the president of the Senate is an easily identifiable individual for the public to blame if the counting is conducted dishonorably.[31] Whatever the merits of this constitutional argument, it was widely held among leading Republicans in the midst of the Hayes-Tilden dispute.[32] Conveniently, the president of the Senate at the time was a loyal Republican, Senator Thomas Ferry of Michigan. (Normally, the vice president of the United States is the president of the Senate, but Grant's vice president, Henry Wilson, had died, and at the time there was no mechanism for appointing a new vice president.

Ferry was president pro tempore of the Senate and thus its presiding officer throughout the Hayes-Tilden dispute.)

But this constitutional argument, however meritorious, was not the only one that could be made. Democrats, including Tilden, contended that no electoral votes from a state were eligible for counting without the consent of the House of Representatives. The Twelfth Amendment explicitly gave the House the power to pick the president in the absence of an electoral vote majority. This much at least was unambiguous. The implication of this power, the Democrats argued, was that the House must agree that an electoral vote majority exists in order for it to decline to exercise its authority to elect the president itself under the terms of the Twelfth Amendment. This counterargument, valid or not, was convenient for the Democrats since they then controlled the House.[33]

As the competing certificates arrived from four states, Congress and the nation were at a constitutional impasse. Republicans were asserting that Ferry, as president of the Senate, had the unilateral authority to declare Hayes elected. Democrats, conversely, were asserting that the House had unilateral authority to elect Tilden. The prospects of competing inauguration ceremonies loomed, after which the two different men would be giving orders to the military as putative commander in chief. The nation clearly could not tolerate the prospect of two sitting presidents simultaneously. Yet neither side was backing down.

Back before the electorate had cast ballots in November, Congress had been well aware of this potential impasse. The controversy over the electoral votes from Arkansas and Louisiana in 1872, although inconsequential to the ultimate result that year, made Congress realize that a similar controversy could affect a state whose electoral votes would determine whether or not a candidate received the majority necessary to avoid having the election go to the House under the Twelfth Amendment. Despite this realization, Congress permitted the November 1876 election to occur without enacting any kind of legislation designed to avert the constitutional impasse inherently at risk in this situation.[34] Now that the December 6 meetings of presidential electors had occurred and this constitutional impasse had arrived, the question was whether Congress (albeit belatedly) could still do something to the prevent simultaneous separate inaugurations of both Hayes and Tilden along with all the civil unrest that would occur in that intrinsically unstable scenario.

The problem, however, was that Congress itself was deadlocked. While Democrats controlled the House, Republicans controlled the Senate (thus giving them their ability to make Ferry its president pro tempore). Although hardliners on both sides seemed willing to take the dispute all the way to the brink, thinking that the other side would be the one to yield in the end, moderates from both parties worked to forge a compromise with the view of settling the dispute in a way that would avoid such brinksmanship.

Figure 5.4 Invoking the allegory of "Buridan's ass" (the donkey that cannot decide which pile of hay to eat and thus dies of starvation), Joseph Keppler portrays "Congr-ass" as unable to choose between Tilden and Hayes; one of the donkey's huge ears (labeled "the House of Representatives") points to Tilden, while the other (labeled "Senate") points to Hayes. *Puck* (December 1876), The Ohio State University Billy Ireland Cartoon Library & Museum.

CIVIL SERVICE REFORM
J. KEPPLER

On December 7, the day after all the constitutionally specified meetings of the presidential electors in the states, George McCrary, a Republican representative in the House (and author of the nation's preeminent treatise on election law), proposed the creation of a special joint congressional committee to craft "a tribunal whose authority none can question and whose decision all will accept as final."[35] McCrary's proposal was adopted, and a joint committee of seven Senators (four Republicans and three Democrats) and seven Representatives (four Democrats and three Republicans, including McCrary) convened to come up with a plan. Eventually, they settled on a special Electoral Commission that resembled to a considerable extent the joint committee itself.

This commission would consist of fifteen members: five senators, five representatives, and five justices of the Supreme Court. The commission's architects knew that the ten members of Congress would be evenly split among Democrats and Republicans, and they had in mind the five justices

Figure 5.5 George McCrary, representative from Iowa and author of a treatise on American election law, proposed the compromise that led to the creation of the Electoral Commission to adjudicate the dispute. Portrait by Henry Ulke; Center for Military History, US Army.

who would serve, with the expectation that two justices would lean toward the Democrats, two would lean toward the Republicans, and one—David Davis—would be as close to independent and impartial as possible. Rather than directly naming Davis to the commission, however, they provided that the first four justices, whom they specified in the legislation by the judicial circuits for which they were responsible, should select the fifth justice for the commission. They fully expected that the four justices would pick Davis as the obvious choice.

Once the joint committee hammered out this plan, which included the requirement that the Electoral Commission's rulings be final unless overturned by *both* houses of Congress, the plan went to the floor of both houses for enactment as legislation. In an effort to meet potential constitutional objections, the drafted legislation gave the Electoral Commission only such powers as the two houses of Congress themselves had, "acting separately or together," in the context of counting electoral votes pursuant to the Twelfth Amendment. Recognizing the dangers of delay, the proposed law limited debate in each house to two hours on the Electoral Commission's rulings with respect to each disputed state's electoral votes.[36]

Specifically designed to handle the four states in dispute, the commission's role was limited to states having two or more certificates purporting to be the electoral votes from any one state. For states having only one certificate of electoral votes, the statute specified that these electoral votes would count unless rejected by both houses of Congress, acting separately. Thus, the statute set up a bifurcated process, depending on whether a state had one or more certificates of electoral votes.[37] This bifurcation would unexpectedly prove crucial at the very end of the entire proceedings, shortly before Inauguration Day.

Both the Senate and the House passed the compromise statute, with roughly 70% support in both chambers. In the Senate, the vote was 47 to 17, or 73% in favor.[38] In the House, it was 191–86, amounting to 69% in support.[39] But an examination of the party breakdown of the vote in each chamber reveals that Democrats were more supportive than Republicans. Democrats in the Senate were virtually unanimous in support, 26–1, and close to it in the House, 160–17. Republicans in the Senate were close to evenly split, with 21 in favor and 16 against. In the House, Republicans were more than two-to-one *against* the bill: 69 to 31.[40]

The reason for this partisan discrepancy is that the Democrats thought they had a greater chance of Tilden reaching the White House if the bill was adopted than if it was not. They figured that Justice Davis would rule for their side on at least one of the four disputes destined to reach the commission: he would at least accept their argument about Oregon if he did not agree with their position on any of the three Southern states. Putting their fate in Davis's hands seemed better than going to the brink, since Grant was prepared to use military force in support of a unilateral declaration by Ferry of Hayes's election.[41]

Republicans, of course, saw the same situation from the opposite perspective. They seemed better off with Grant backing Ferry than making Justice Davis the arbiter. Still, the congressional adoption of the Electoral Commission bill was ultimately a bipartisan compromise. It could not have passed the Senate without Republican as well as Democratic support. Moreover, the 47 Senators who approved the plan came almost equally from both parties: 26 Democrats and 21 Republicans. Senator George Edmunds, a Republican from Vermont, was one of the commission's primary sponsors. When Congress enacted the bill in January of 1877, this legislative compromise was widely heralded as an act of statesmanship in an effort to save the Republic from a potential catastrophe.

The Commission's Deliberations

The strategic calculations that both parties made over the creation of the commission became moot when Justice Davis declined to serve as its fifteenth member. Illinois's legislature had picked Davis to be US Senator (as state legislatures did before ratification of the Seventeenth Amendment in 1913). Davis considered the role of commission tiebreaker incompatible with his new Senate appointment.[42]

With Davis unavailable, the four justices already designated for the commission by the compromise statute turned to Justice Joseph Bradley, the least objectionable of the remaining justices available. By the terms of the statute, the fifteenth commissioner was required to be a Supreme Court justice. But none had the same reputation for nonpartisan independence as Davis. Bradley, although moderate, was clearly a Republican.[43] Democrats were thus doomed by the statute's failure to permit looking beyond the Supreme Court to replace Davis as the nonpartisan fifteenth member of the commission.

As it turned out, Bradley played the decisive, tiebreaking role in the commission's consideration of all four disputed states. We of course can never know whether or not Davis, if he had served instead of Bradley, would have broken the series of 7–7 ties in the same way that Bradley did.[44] All we can do is examine the reasoning that Bradley offered for his rulings, to see if they appear tainted by partisanship (whether deliberate or not) or, rather, stand up as exercises of impartial analysis of the relevant issues. Again, of the four states, Florida is the primary one for consideration, with Oregon as secondary, to see if Democrats were justified in attacking Bradley as being inconsistent insofar as he ruled for Hayes in both cases.[45]

Figure 5.6 Justice Joseph Bradley became the pivotal member of the Electoral Commission after Justice David Davis declined to serve. Library of Congress.

Florida

Justice Bradley's opinion on Florida rested on two key points. First, Congress—and therefore the commission, which pursuant to its enabling statute had no more authority than Congress—had no power under the Constitution to question or revise electoral votes officially submitted by a state. Because Article Two of the Constitution gives each state legislature the authority to determine the manner of appointing the state's electors, Congress must accept whatever the state submits pursuant to this legislative authority, even if error or fraud occurred in whatever method of appointment was established by the state's legislature. As Bradley succinctly put this point: "It is the business and the jurisdiction of the State to prevent frauds from being perpetrated in the appointment of its electors, and not the business or jurisdiction of the Congress."[46] (In the parlance of the times, Bradley's ruling on this point meant that Congress was not entitled to "go behind the returns" to assess their underlying accuracy.)

The question remained how Congress or the commission was able to ascertain which is the official submission of the state when two or more submissions claim this status. On this question, Bradley made his second key point. Invoking the constitutional provision that requires that the "Day" on which the presidential electors "shall give their Votes . . . shall be the same throughout the United States," Bradley declared that each state is constitutionally constrained to settle the appointment of its electors by that nationally uniform date. "To allow a State legislature in any way to change the appointment of electors after they have been elected and given their votes, would . . . subvert the design of the Constitution in requiring all the electoral votes to be given on the same day."[47] This key point led to a corollary. Because not even a state's legislature can make a change regarding the appointment of its electors after the constitutionally uniform date, the officially authoritative submission of electoral votes to Congress is the one that conforms to the procedure for appointing electors established by the state's legislature prior to that date.

Given this reasoning, Bradley immediately rejected the third certificate from Florida, the one dated January 26, which invoked judicial and legislative proceedings in Florida that had occurred after the December 6 date for the casting of electoral votes. Although Tilden's lawyers argued that these subsequent proceedings merely confirmed what the attorney general had recognized to be the proper outcome under state law as of that date, Bradley refused to give these subsequent events any significance: "I think no importance is to be attached to the acts performed by the board of canvassers after the 6th day of December, nor to the acts of the Florida legislature in reference to the canvass. In my judgment, they are all unconstitutional and void."[48]

But what about, then, the certificate from the attorney general himself, which he had executed on the constitutionally crucial date of December 6? This certificate, the Democrats argued, was the correct representation of Florida law as of that key date, whereas the governor's certificate of that same date was based on a usurpation of the canvassing board's lawful authority. Bradley, however, rejected the underlying premise of this argument.

The state's canvassing board may have erred in its conduct of the canvass, but Florida's legislature had expressly given it the authority to review the local returns, invalidating those it found improper, and to declare which candidates for the office of presidential elector had received the most valid votes. Bradley quoted the relevant Florida statute, emphasizing and repeating the clause that explicitly provided that the "board of State canvassers [shall] proceed to canvass the returns of said elections and *determine and declare who shall have been elected to any such office*."[49] Given this statutory language, Bradley had no doubt that the canvassing board was entitled to speak for the state authoritatively on who its presidential electors were: "They certainly acted within the scope of their power, though they may have acted erroneously."[50] Therefore, according to Bradley, whatever the canvassing board had declared regarding the electors as of December 6th, Congress must recognize that declaration as the official position of the state on the appointment of its presidential electors: "It seems to me that the two Houses of Congress, in proceeding with the count, are bound to recognize the determination of the State board of canvassers as the act of the State, and as the most authentic evidence of the appointment made by the State."[51]

Bradley acknowledged that a state's legislature had the power to permit the state's judiciary to revise the canvassing board's determination, so long as the judiciary did so by the constitutionally uniform date for the casting of electoral votes: "The State may, undoubtedly, provide by law for reviewing the action of the board of canvassers at any time before the electors have executed their functions." The state's legislature, Bradley elaborated, "may provide any safeguard it pleases to prevent or counteract fraud, mistake, or illegality on the part of the canvassers." For example, it "may pass a law requiring the attendance of the supreme court or any other tribunal to supervise the action of the board, and to reverse it, if wrong." If the state's legislature had given a court this jurisdiction, and if the court "rendered its decision before the votes of the electors were cast," then "its judgment, instead of that of the returning-board, would have been the final declaration of the result of the election." But Bradley's acknowledgment of this point was no use to Tilden, since Florida's judicial pronouncements on the counting of the electorate's November ballots came too late: "I am entirely clear that the judicial proceedings in this case were destitute of validity to affect the votes given by the electors."[52]

Ultimately, the fact that then-incumbent Governor Stearns had certified the canvassing board's ruling in favor of the Hayes electors played virtually no role in Justice Bradley's analysis. He acknowledged that since 1792 Congress had required each state's governor to certify that the state's electoral votes were cast by duly appointed electors, and he was willing to say that a governor's certificate was "at least *prima facie* evidence of a very high character" that the electors so certified were in fact the duly appointed ones.[53] Bradley, however, was willing to let the governor's certificate be impeached on the ground that it did not accurately reflect the method of appointment established by the state's legislature. For example, if Florida's judiciary had overturned the canvassing board's decision before December 6th, and had done so pursuant to a state statute giving it this jurisdiction, then Bradley would have accepted as authoritative a certificate reflecting this result, even if this certificate lacked the governor's endorsement—and, indeed, even if there had been a contrary certificate from the governor purporting that the state's duly appointed electors were the ones identified by the canvassing board rather than the judiciary. Bradley undoubtedly had the upcoming Oregon dispute in mind when he explained the essentially inconsequential role that the governor's signature played in his Florida analysis.

Oregon

Regarding Oregon, Justice Bradley declared that the Democratic governor's certification of one Tilden elector, along with the two for Hayes, had no legal effect whatsoever because it was beyond the scope of the governor's authority under state law: "In my judgment, it was a clear act of usurpation. It was tampering with an election which the law had declared to be closed and ascertained." Oregon law had given its secretary of state the authority to declare which presidential electors had received the most votes cast by citizens on November 7. The secretary of state had made the necessary declaration that it had been the three Hayes electors who had achieved this victory. This declaration, as the state's authoritative pronouncement, was thus binding on Congress and the commission: "By [the secretary of state's] act and by this record of his act, the ascertainment of the election in Oregon was closed."[54]

Oregon law, moreover, provided a cure for the potential problem of the one Hayes elector being a postmaster on November 7. The two indisputably eligible Hayes electors had taken advantage of this available cure. Bradley found that there was no constitutional impediment to the reappointment of this elector pursuant to that Oregon procedure after having resigned the position of postmaster, and the state's governor had no warrant under state law to interfere with the permissible use of the procedure. Thus Justice Bradley concluded that the three Hayes electors "were the true electors for the State of Oregon on the 6th day of December, and that their votes ought to be counted," notwithstanding the contrary certification from the state's governor.[55]

Bradley endeavored to explain that his Florida and Oregon rulings were consistent because they both flowed from the same principle that the state's statutory law, as it stood on December 6, determined which institution of state government was entitled to the last word on who its presidential electors were. For Florida, "the final determination of the result of the [November 7] election was to be made by a board of canvassers invested with power to judge the local returns and to reject them for certain causes assigned." In Oregon, the "canvass for the State is directed to be made by the secretary of state." In neither case was the governor's certification consequential. It just happened that in Florida the canvassing board's determinative authority was echoed by the then-incumbent governor's certificate, whereas in Oregon the secretary of state's official pronouncement was not. In both cases, state law—not the governor's signature—was controlling.[56]

Louisiana and South Carolina

Justice Bradley treated Louisiana and South Carolina as essentially the same as Florida. State law in both states, like Florida, gave the canvassing board the authority to determine which presidential electors had won more votes cast by citizens on November 7. As for the wrinkle in Louisiana that state law required the canvassing board to have one member from a different political party than the other members, Justice Bradley found that noncompliance with this requirement was no basis for nullification of the canvassing board's determination that the Hayes electors had prevailed in the state. Invoking the general rule that a vacancy on a multimember body does not deprive it of jurisdiction as long as a quorum remains, Bradley added that the requirement of representation from more than one party could not be considered essential to the board's functioning: "Suppose, instead of dying or resigning, the [fifth] member changes his party affiliations; is there a vacancy then?"[57] Bradley thought the obvious answer to his rhetorical question was no. While a member from another party should be appointed to the board as soon as practicable, in the meantime the board was still empowered to canvass the returns of the November 7 election.

South Carolina was only slightly more complicated for Justice Bradley. He easily dismissed the Democrats' contention that the November election there was void because the state lacked a voter registration law as required by the state's constitution. None of the elections held for other offices also on November 7, including for governor, had been voided because of this defect. Thus Justice Bradley concluded, "in my opinion, the clause of the constitution in question is only directory, and cannot affect the validity of elections in the State, much less the official acts of the officers elected."[58]

After dispensing with this specific question, Justice Bradley went on to consider the broader claim that conditions in South Carolina might have been so chaotic as to require invalidation of the state's electoral votes. This broader claim proved somewhat more challenging. Bradley acknowledged that if conditions of anarchy were "of such a public character as to be within the judicial knowledge of the two Houses, of course they may take notice of it and act accordingly, as was done in the times of secession and the late civil war."[59] In that extreme situation, it would be appropriate for Congress to disregard electoral votes purportedly submitted on behalf of the state. But short of that extreme situation, Congress constitutionally under Article Two must accept what the state, pursuant to its own statutory laws, officially submits.

Moreover, Justice Bradley was emphatic in declaring that Congress, and therefore the Electoral Commission, was constitutionally barred, as part of its counting of the electoral votes from the states, from undertaking any evidentiary inquiry on whether such a condition of anarchy prevailed in a particular state. As Bradley construed the procedure set forth in the Twelfth Amendment, Congress can examine only the certificates accompanying the electoral votes submitted from a state, together with that state's laws, to determine whether the submitted electoral votes "can be regarded as expressing the will of the State."[60] No extrinsic evidence may be considered at that point (and none was in any of the previous disputes, including the one from Oregon, which was determined solely on the basis of the certificates and the state's laws).

Justice Bradley allowed that "Congress, in its legislative capacity, with the President concurring, or by a two-thirds vote after his veto, could pass a law by which investigation might be had in advance, under proper regulations as to notice and evidence and the cross-examination of witnesses; the results of which could be laid before the two Houses at their meeting for the count of votes, and could be used by them as a basis for deciding whether such a condition of anarchy, disturbance, and intimidation existed in a State at a time of the election of its electors as to render its vote nugatory and liable to be rejected." But no such law then existed, and in its absence Justice Bradley repeated his view that it would be "unconstitutional for the two Houses to enter upon such an inquiry."[61]

Because the two Houses could not take evidence on the disturbances in South Carolina, neither could the Electoral Commission, and in the absence of such evidence Justice Bradley did not think that the conditions there were so plainly anarchical as to permit "judicial notice" of the point ("judicial notice" meaning that the fact could be established without need of an evidentiary proceeding). As bad as conditions apparently were in South Carolina at the time of the casting and counting of ballots for presidential electors, there was in place a state government recognized by the United States, and that state government had submitted electoral votes pursuant to state law. Accordingly, Justice Bradley said he was constrained to hold that the electoral votes submitted by the Hayes electors from South Carolina should count.

Justice Bradley may have been confident in the conclusion he reached based on the standard he applied, but others were entitled to have their doubts. Different jurists, applying the same standard, reasonably could have reached the opposite conclusion—that conditions in South Carolina on November 7 were such that no valid election took place and thus no genuine will of the state had been expressed, and that the Electoral Commission was entitled to take "judicial notice" of this plain fact. To make this point is not to say that this alternative position would have been correct, only that a reasonable jurist could have viewed it so.[62]

The same point applies to Justice Bradley's rulings in general. On the fundamental principle that a state must settle the status of its presidential electors by the nationally uniform date for them to cast their electoral votes, Justice Bradley surely rested on solid ground. But with respect to the subsidiary question of whether Florida's canvassing board strayed so far from the conduct of the canvass that the attorney general better represented the authority of Florida law on that crucial date, or whether Louisiana's canvassing board was powerless to act because it lacked bipartisan representation, a different jurist sitting in his tiebreaking seat reasonably might have reached the opposite conclusion. Bradley's answers to these questions, while perhaps not unprincipled, were also not inevitable. And thus even if he sincerely strove to answer these questions without regard to partisanship, the answers that he gave demonstrated that they depended ultimately, not on the ineluctable logic of his reasoning, but instead on his identity as the individual entitled to break the 7–7 tie. That he happened to be a Republican and, for all four states, broke the tie in favor of Hayes, was too much for Democrats to accept as an exercise of impartial adjudication. Ultimately, however, everything came back to the fact that the Democrats had participated in the enactment of a statute that put Justice Bradley in that tiebreaking role after Justice Davis, the intended designee, declined to serve in that capacity.[63]

The End Game

Once the Democrats in the House of Representatives understood that the Electoral Commission was to rule against them 8–7 in all four states, some of them began to contemplate a strategy of delay that they hoped would deny any candidate a majority of Electoral College votes before Inauguration Day on March 4 and, therefore, permit the House of Representatives itself to elect a president pursuant to the Twelfth Amendment. But the Speaker of the House, Samuel Randall, refused to permit his fellow Democrats to be successful in this filibuster strategy. He ruled out of order any motion that would prevent the electoral vote from moving forward at a sufficiently timely pace to permit inauguration of the new president on March 4. Randall blocked one effort at obstruction after the commission's Oregon ruling and another after its South Carolina determination.[64]

Thus at 6 o'clock on February 28, the Senate and the House joined to open the certificates of electoral votes submitted from the states at the end of the alphabet. Having finished with all the states from Alabama through South Carolina, Congress was now up to Tennessee and Texas, and those two proceeded without incident. But then, when Congress got to Vermont, there was a surprise and "dangerous" development.[65]

Senator Ferry, presiding over the joint session under the terms of the Twelfth Amendment, asked if there was any objection to the single certificate received from Vermont, which had awarded its five electoral votes to Hayes. One representative, a Democrat, asked whether there were any "other returns, or papers purporting to be returns, received from the State of Vermont." Ferry replied: "There have been none received except the one submitted."[66]

At that point Representative Abram Hewitt of New York, who chaired the Democratic National Committee and managed Tilden's campaign, rose to speak. He declared: "I hold in my hand a package which purports to contain electoral votes from the State of Vermont." He said that he assumed that Ferry had already received another copy of the same Vermont submission and was surprised to learn that Ferry had not. He said that "the seals" of his Vermont package were "unbroken" and he wished to "tender this package" to Ferry for him to open pursuant to the process set forth in the compromise statute enacted in January.[67]

A Republican representative immediately objected to the receipt of this package, and Ferry declared that he could not receive it "after the first Thursday in February," which was the date that Congress had set for the submission of electoral votes from the states to the president of the Senate.[68] The Democrats knew that they could never get the commission to accept such an unorthodox submission of an alternative certification of electoral votes from Vermont, especially after much more plausible claims concerning Florida and the other disputed states had been rejected. But some of them wanted to put two certificates from Vermont before the commission simply for purposes of running out the clock, since March 4 was now only four days away. Reconvening the commission for each state in which there were two or more certificates consumed much more time than simply dealing with states from which only one certificate had been received, as the commission's experience thus far had shown. (Most of February had been consumed in the commission's, rather than purely congressional, proceedings.) Therefore, the obstructionist wing of the Democrats in the House pressed Ferry to accept Hewitt's package for the purpose of submitting it, along with the original certificate from Vermont, to the commission.

Ferry, however, refused to do so. One Democrat, Representative Springer from Illinois, persisted. Ferry ruled him out of order. Springer would not back down. According to one account, he "shrieked wildly, threw his arms about, and for a time refused to come to order."[69] There was general commotion in the hall, as Republicans repeatedly shouted cries of "Order! Order!" and "Object! Object!"[70]

Springer argued that he was raising a question under the statute that created the commission and that he was entitled to do so. Ferry responded: "The Chair decides that he will not entertain anything except objections to the [single timely] certificate [that had been received from Vermont]." Springer demanded an "appeal from the decision of the Chair." Ferry replied: "The Chair cannot entertain an appeal."[71]

Springer continued to protest: "The electoral vote of the State of Vermont now goes to the Commission, and cannot be considered separately by the two Houses."[72] Ferry continued to rule Springer out of order. Ferry permitted Springer to state an objection to the certificate from Vermont authenticating the Hayes electors, but he steadfastly refused any consideration of the purported second certificate that had been tendered by Hewitt. At Ferry's direction, the Senate simply walked out of the House's chamber, where the joint session was held, and went to conduct its own separate consideration of the single Vermont certificate, which it promptly accepted as valid.

On the next day—Thursday, March 1—the House met without the Senate. Immediately, there was a confrontation on what exactly was before the House. One side argued that, under the terms of the compromise statute enacted in January, the House must immediately deliberate and vote on the sole Vermont certificate that Ferry had ruled permissible to consider. If this was correct, the counting of the electoral votes would move quickly from Vermont to Virginia and on to the end, since the statute limited debate on each state to two hours. Furthermore, Vermont's votes for Hayes would count since the Senate already had accepted them (and, again, the statute require *both* houses of Congress to reject the electoral votes from a state with a *single* certificate, as Ferry had ruled Vermont to be).

But the obstructionists in the House, including Springer, continued to claim that the House could not begin to debate the single certificate because Ferry had improperly prevented plural returns from Vermont from going before the Electoral Commission. The obstructionists therefore wanted the House to send the matter back to the joint session under the Twelfth Amendment with a demand that Ferry, or the joint body, rectify Ferry's mistake.

If the obstructionists prevailed on this point, it would cause an increasingly treacherous delay. Ferry most certainly would not have acquiesced in a demand from the House to send Vermont to the commission. Nor is it likely that Ferry would have permitted the joint session of the two houses, as a single body, to vote on whether to overrule his previous determination that there was but one valid certificate from Vermont. If the obstructionists prevailed in the House on March 1, the whole electoral count would have come to a halt with no apparent way to end the stalemate before March 4. From their hard-line perspective, this stalemate was even better than sending Vermont to the commission, since an unresolved stalemate would permit the House to assert its prerogative under the Twelfth Amendment to elect Tilden directly itself. Yet if this unresolved stalemate occurred so close to the end of the counting process, it would defeat the whole purpose of the compromise statute, which had been to avoid the prospect of two separate inaugurations—one pursuant to the House's own direct election of Tilden, and the other pursuant to Ferry's unilateral declaration that Hayes had received a majority of electoral votes. Despite the good intentions underlying the enactment of the compromise statute, it appeared as the House began its deliberations on March 1 that the compromise was unraveling (or being derailed) and that the nation was on the verge of the dreaded constitutional impasse concerning which institution had the ultimate authority to resolve the disputed presidential election.

The ensuing session has been deemed "probably the stormiest ever witnessed in any House of Representatives."[73] One of the obstructionists, climbing across four desks, hurled himself at Speaker Randall in an effort to force the Speaker to adopt their position. "Some of the members grasped their revolvers," and "ladies, fearing a free fight was about to [occur], left the galleries."[74] Randall had to call for the sergeant-at-arms to maintain order.

Randall managed to get through the situation by refusing to delay the beginning of the two hours of debate on the single certificate (under the terms of the compromise statute in light of Ferry's ruling on Vermont), while at the same time permitting the House to vote on whether to take back to the joint session a protest on Ferry's refusal to entertain the second certificate. This way of proceeding did not satisfy the obstructionists because they knew it would permit Ferry to move on to Virginia and continue the rest of the count, and for this reason they tried to impede the House's proceedings as much as they could. As one of them argued, "you cannot proceed now to consider the objections to the electoral vote of the State of Vermont predicated upon the idea that there is but one single return from that State." Because Vermont is "a State with dual electoral returns," this hardliner continued, it must "be submitted under the law to the electoral commission" and this submission "must be preliminarily considered before you proceed" any further.[75] Another one of them objected to voting "as if there was only an objection to a single return," because then "how shall we ever get a vote on the second return?"[76]

But Randall would not budge. Ruling from the chair, and not permitting an appeal of his ruling, he started the clock on the single certificate debate. A hardliner asked incredulously, "Do I understand the Chair to rule that the two hours' debate is now to commence?" "The Chair so rules," Randall responded definitively. "Well, sir, I appeal from that decision," another filibusterer asserted. "The Chair declines to entertain the appeal," Randall replied amidst outcries and applause.[77]

Springer, who had made such a disturbance the day before in the joint session, exclaimed:

> I hope the Chair will not insist upon that position. This is one of the most important questions that ever came before this House. [Cries of "Regular order!"] I insist that this appeal must be entertained and that we must know whether this is a case that has gone to the commission or whether it is now to be considered by the separate Houses. This is not a dilatory motion, but one that arises upon a vital provision of the electoral law. . . . If this case under the law has gone to the commission, it is there now by the operation of the law and we have nothing before us.

Still, Speaker Randall refused to put the issue to a vote: "The Chair will entertain no [such] motion." "Will the Chair state the reason for his ruling?" "The Chair decides according to his conscience and the law," Randall answered.[78] After much commotion, the House eventually quieted down, and the two-hour debate proceeded as Randall had insisted.

As the debate unfolded, Representative William Levy, a Democrat from Louisiana, signaled that a significant development had occurred. Levy had participated in conversations between Southern Democrats and Hayes confidants, including a meeting at the Wormley Hotel, concerning how Hayes might treat the South, especially Louisiana and South Carolina, which were seeking withdrawal of the federal troops that had been propping up Reconstructionist governors there.[79] Appearing on the floor of the House in the midst of the debate, Levy announced that he now would "throw no obstacle, by any action or vote of mine in the way of the completion of the electoral count." Even more significantly, he urged others to do the same: "I . . . call upon those of my

Figure 5.7 Samuel Randall, Speaker of the House, blocked efforts by fellow Democrats to derail the counting of electoral votes. Portrait by William A. Graves; Collection of the US House of Representatives.

fellow-members who have been influenced in their action on this question by a desire to protect Louisiana and South Carolina to join me in the course which I feel called upon and justified in pursuing." He explicitly based his justification on the "assurances" that he had received from Hayes's associates: "The people of Louisiana have solemn, earnest, and, I believe, truthful assurances from prominent members of the republican party, high in the confidence of Mr. Hayes, that in the event of his elevation to the Presidency he will be guided by a policy of conciliation toward the Southern States, that he will not use the Federal authority or the Army to force upon those State governments not of their choice."[80]

Levy's speech doomed whatever chance the hardliners had left to derail the count and throw the election to the House under the Twelfth Amendment. In fact, at the end of the two-hour debate, when Randall permitted a vote on the obstructionists' resolution that Vermont should go to the Election Commission as a dual-certificate state—which by this point was a purely symbolic protest (since there also was the required vote on the single certificate, thereby enabling the count to proceed unobstructed)—the hardline position went down to defeat: 116 in favor to 148 against, and 26 recorded abstentions.[81] Instead, the House only sent back to the joint session its futile objection to Vermont's single certificate.

One might question the importance of Randall's refusal to permit a vote on the obstructionists' resolution *before* the two-hour debate, since the resolution failed afterward. Perhaps it would have been defeated beforehand if Randall had allowed the House to vote on it then. Any conjecture in this regard depends on assessing the significance of Levy's speech. We know that after his speech, 23 Southern Democrats refused to support the hardliner resolution, just as Levy urged (13 voting no and 10, including Levy himself, abstaining).[82] If these 23 had supported the resolution instead, it would have prevailed by a vote of 139 to 135 (assuming no other vote changes).[83] Thus, if we were to credit Levy with causing these 23 Southerners to change from supporting to opposing obstruction of the electoral count, the timing of the vote would indeed be critical. On that hypothesis, Randall's insistence that the vote occur after, not before, the two-hour debate saved the count from derailing, as it would have if the House had returned to the joint session refusing to proceed unless Vermont went to the commission.

Some accounts seemingly ascribe such significance to Levy's speech. A historian of the House and its Speakers described the obstructionists as believing "victory already won" before Levy's speech but deflated with the "gloom of defeat" after Levy spoke.[84] A Hayes biographer agreed: "That speech was accepted as the signal for ending the stalemate on Vermont."[85] And C. Vann Woodward, in his famous (albeit controverted) book on the "bargain" between Hayes and the Southern Democrats, described "the strength of the filibuster," which had been "reinforced with new recruits" on the morning of March 1, as plummeting—indeed essentially dissipating—as a result of Levy's speech.[86]

Yet there are reasons not to overstate Levy's role. The conversations between the Southerners and Hayes's representatives had been occurring for weeks. The Southerners and their allies arguably were using the threat of derailing the count as a bargaining ploy to see if they could exact greater concessions; but, on this view, they were bluffing and would not have actually derailed the count if the vote had occurred before the two-hour debate. And the numbers make it difficult to think that Levy's speech was decisive: he would have had to sway virtually all 23 Southerners who ended up refusing to support the hardline position; if just two of them would have voted against the hardliners before Levy's speech, the hardliners still would have failed.[87]

Discounting Levy's role, however, does not negate the significance of Randall's refusal to hold the vote earlier. Even if the hardliner position would have been defeated in advance of the debate, Randall could not have been entirely sure of that outcome. Otherwise, why not just let the House vote, and avoid all the "pandemonium" that his refusal instigated among the hardliners?[88] But Randall could not take this risk. The situation was fluid enough that there was a real chance, even if small, that the hardliners might prevail, and if that happened before the two-hour debate occurred, then the genuine constitutional crisis would have materialized. Given the absence of greater certainty at the time, Randall's insistence on proceeding with the two-hour debate must be credited with preventing the possibility of a national calamity that might have arisen had he acted differently.[89]

Randall's role in averting a potential disaster has been significantly unappreciated, especially in accounts of the Hayes-Tilden dispute written after 2000, which have tended to focus on the Electoral Commission for the purpose of comparing its 8–7 rulings to the Supreme Court's 5–4 rulings in *Bush v. Gore*. To be sure, in his definitive study of Reconstruction written in 1988, Eric Foner recognized: "No one played a more critical part in resolving the crisis than Speaker Randall."[90] But Chief Justice Rehnquist's book *Centennial Crisis* (2004) hardly mentions Randall at all and completely omits his decisive handling of the Vermont controversy on March 1. Likewise, Michael Holt's otherwise valuable 2008 synopsis of the Hayes-Tilden election makes no mention of the climatic insurrection over Vermont or Randall's firm steadfast suppression of it.[91] One must go back to much earlier accounts to find appreciation, comparable to Foner's, of Randall's "skillful and resolute guidance" of the House on March 1, for which he deserved "the respect and admiration of the country and of the world."[92] A Republican member of the House that day, who later became a political scientist at Oberlin College, credited Randall's "firmness and conscience" as potentially saving the nation from the "calamity" of an unfinished count of the electoral votes.[93] "Randall reached a sublime height on that day when he put before himself the good of the country," extolled a historian of the House in 1914, adding that Randall acted "in defiance of many in his own party" when "he cleared the way for the completion of the count."[94] A few years later, another House historian stated simply that Randall "saved the situation" with his "bold use of the enormous powers of the speakership."[95]

Randall had some sense of the role he was called upon to play. Shortly before becoming Speaker in December of 1876, and knowing then that the resolution of the Hayes-Tilden dispute must be his highest priority, he wrote to himself some notes outlining the creed he would follow while presiding over the House. Part of his commitment, sketched out on the back of a telegram he had received, was this pledge: "Absolute fairness to both sides and all portions of each side [i]n exercising the parliamentary powers of the chair."[96]

Yet there is not a high school student in America today who learns of Samuel Randall and what he did to save the nation from "anarchy and [another] civil war."[97] If any single individual is remembered for playing a decisive role in the resolution of the Hayes-Tilden dispute, it is Justice Bradley. But he is remembered for ruling in accordance with the interests of his party. It is forgotten that Randall, whose role was of comparable importance to Bradley's, acted contrary to the partisan pressures he faced. In a nation that needs reminders that sometimes politicians resist partisanship and instead, rising to the occasion, act in the interest of the entire public, this collective historical amnesia about Randall is regrettable and worth rectifying.

In any event, once Randall successfully broke the unexpected logjam over Vermont and the joint session resumed, there were no objections to the electoral votes from Virginia and West Virginia, both states going for Tilden. The Democrats did object to the single certificate from Wisconsin, but there was no pretense of a second certificate, as there had been with Vermont. When the House took up its separate debate on Wisconsin, the rhetoric from the remaining hardliners ran hot, and the session lasted until 4 o'clock in the morning on Friday, March 2. But sometime after midnight, while the House was still discussing Wisconsin, Randall received a telegram from Tilden saying that the candidate acquiesced in the completion of the count.[98] With the hardliners thus now utterly deflated, the House let the Senate back in for the final joint session. Ferry announced that Hayes, having received Wisconsin's electoral votes, had attained the 185 votes necessary for a majority. Accordingly, exercising his authority under the Twelfth Amendment as president pro tempore of

(a)

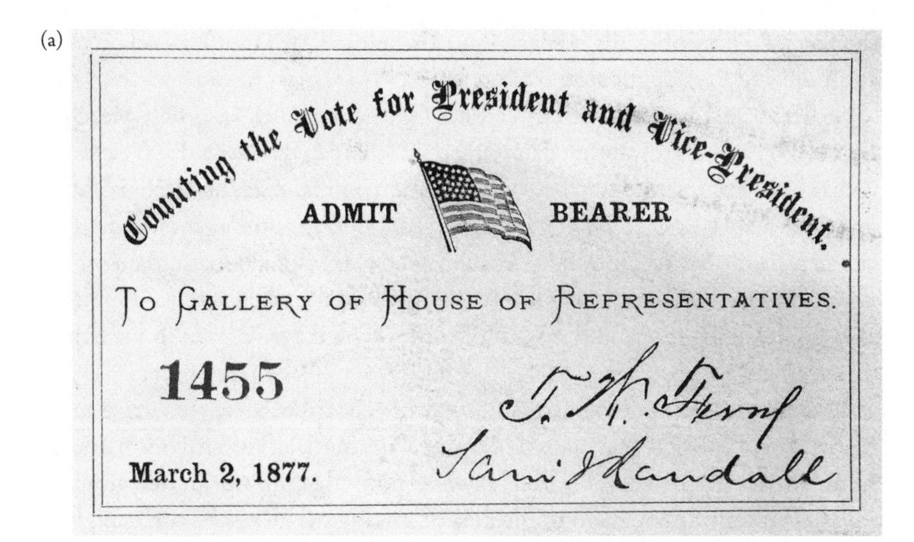

Figure 5.8a Samuel Randall kept, as a memento of his key role in bringing the electoral count to a successful completion, this ticket granting admission to the final joint session of Congress, when the winner of the presidency was announced. Historical Society of Pennsylvania.

(b)

THE PRESIDENCY—MR. FERRY ANNOUNCING THE RESULT OF THE COUNT.—From a Sketch by Theo. R. Davis.—[See Page 203.]

Figure 5.8b Senator Ferry on March 2 declared Hayes the official winner based on a majority of electoral votes, as rendered in *Harper's Weekly* (March 17, 1877). The Ohio State University Billy Ireland Cartoon Library & Museum.

the Senate, Ferry officially declared shortly before dawn that Hayes had been "duly elected President of the United States."[99]

Still, the dust had not entirely settled. On the next day, Saturday, March 3, the House passed a resolution declaring that Tilden had "received 196 electoral votes . . . in conformity with the Constitution and laws of the United States" and thus "he was thereby duly elected President." Although one member characterized this resolution as "revolutionary, treasonable, and damnable," everyone—including its supporters—understood it as entirely inoperable as a legal matter. It was just a way for disappointed Democrats to vent their frustration.[100]

Despite being ineffectual, the resolution contributed to the tension of that weekend. Grant was prepared to declare martial law in New York on rumors, entirely inaccurate, that Tilden (notwithstanding his telegram to Randall) might still be open to the idea of staging his own separate inauguration there.[101] Meanwhile, Hayes arrived in Washington on Friday, March 2, amid fears of an assassination attempt. Because March 4 was a Sunday, Grant decided to hold a private swearing-in ceremony for Hayes while he was having a dinner at the White House on Saturday night. Thus the public inauguration on Monday, March 5, was just for show.[102] Nonetheless, it was an important show, displaying as it did the nonviolent transition of power in even the most trying of circumstances.

A Final Thought

As one reflects on all the lessons to be learned from this debacle, one can sympathize with the plight of the Republicans as they confronted the prospects of losing the presidency solely because of rampant disenfranchisement of freedmen in violation of the Fifteenth Amendment. Even if the circumstance did not justify their intentional distortion of the counting of ballots actually cast, it is hard to see how they should have acted instead given the institutional arrangements that then existed. With no federal court remedy available at the time to rectify the Fifteenth Amendment violation, and no prospects of relief in a state legislature or judiciary controlled by Democrats, their own recourse was to exercise the power they held over the state's canvassing board. They undoubtedly abused this power, but they did so in service of the right to vote.

Perhaps then the ultimate lesson of the Hayes-Tilden dispute is the institutional inadequacy that put Republicans in the position of having to act immorally (deceitfully counting the valid ballots cast) in order to vindicate a fundamental moral principle (the equal right of all citizens, regardless of race, to participate in the election of the president). Consider how the Hayes-Tilden dispute might have unfolded if, instead, there had been an impartial institution, either state or federal, with the capacity to adjudicate the conflict fairly based on the merits of the contentions presented by both sides. The Republicans then would have presented to that impartial institution the evidence of the systematic disenfranchisement of African Americans, enough to undermine the validity of counting only those ballots actually cast. Based on the strength of that evidence, the impartial institution would have awarded the election to the Republicans (the merits of the case requiring that result, given the impossibility of holding an entirely new election for the presidency). In this way, a well-designed impartial institution for the adjudication of the controversy would have enabled the Republicans to prevail fair and square—rather than having their victory sullied by their need to dishonestly manipulate the count of valid ballots, as their only way to win in the absence of an appropriate adjudicatory tribunal.

6

The Gilded Age

An Era of Hypercompetitive Elections

The quarter-century between 1876 and 1900 was a uniquely unsettling period in the history of American politics, particularly with regard to the topic of this book.[1] In the 1880s, on the heels of the Hayes-Tilden dispute, the country faced a succession of three exceptionally close presidential elections (1880, 1884, and 1888). It is something of a miracle that none of the three devolved into a drawn-out controversy comparable to 1876—especially 1884, which was the closest of the three—but the nation escaped an immediate repetition of that kind of calamity. This narrow escape, however, was no thanks to Congress, which took a decade to enact any procedural reforms in response to Hayes-Tilden. Even then, the statute that Congress managed to enact in 1887 was exceedingly weak, as recognized by both its sponsors and critics at the time.[2]

Although the nation did not suffer a second significantly disputed presidential election in this period, the states experienced more ferocious and consequential ballot-counting disputes than in any other era in American history. In the North and the South, state legislatures used their power over counting ballots in gubernatorial elections to capture the governorship for the benefit of a political party without regard to the merits of the underlying vote-counting dispute. And when vote-counting disputes over seats in the state legislatures themselves affected which party would control a legislative chamber, those disputes triggered all-out legislative warfare with rival bodies pronouncing themselves the official law-making institution in the state. In some instances, control of both the governorship and the legislature became ensnared in the same underlying ballot-counting battle, in which case the fighting was especially intense.

Although the term "war" was used somewhat metaphorically in the press to describe these disputes, in an alarming number of cases its use verged on the literal. In multiple states (Maine, Montana, Colorado, Kansas, and Kentucky), incumbent governors called out the militia in an effort to influence which side prevailed.[3] One of the two candidates for governor in Kentucky's 1899 election was assassinated in the midst of the fight over who won the most votes. This assassination, coming at the end of this tumultuous quarter-century, was undoubtedly the lowest moment of the whole period, indeed of America's entire experience with ballot-counting controversies.

After Hayes-Tilden: Poor Preparation and Narrow Escapes

Senator George Edmunds, Republican of Vermont, had been one of the principal authors of the compromise that created the Electoral Commission of 1877 and had served as one of its members. In the course of the next decade, he was the leader of the effort in Congress to develop a permanent solution to the problem of an inadequate mechanism for resolving a disputed presidential election. The great tragedy is that the product of his strenuous efforts, the Electoral Count Act of 1887, did not match his own ideas for what the optimal solution would be.

In his thoughtful article of October 1877, reflecting on the ordeal he and the nation had just survived, Edmunds closed by observing:

> If it were possible to find or to constitute one single tribunal, having final power to count the votes and declare the result after the States had, through their tribunals, disposed of disputes, being the farthest possible removed from the heat of political prejudice, and possessing from its character and constitution the general confidence of the country, the best method of ascertaining who had been elected President would be reached.

He explained that "such questions" on counting ballots, "as they affect the right of the people at large, as well as private rights, and depend exclusively upon pre-existing laws and events," are "judicial in their nature." They "contain no element for the discretion of the legislator or the policy of the statesman." Therefore, "the decision of such questions" should be "withdrawn entirely from the political department of the government, and lodged where, according to the philosophy of free governments, it ought to be—with the judiciary."[4]

But as chair of the Senate's special committee to propose permanent reforms to the procedures for counting Electoral College votes, Edmunds did not craft a bill containing any such judicial tribunal. Rather, in December of 1878, on behalf of the committee, he reported a bill that eschewed the creation of a new institution, impartial or otherwise, and instead left the counting of Electoral College votes entirely in the hands of the two houses of Congress.[5] The only innovative procedure in this bill is one that purported to bind both houses of Congress to a conclusive and timely judgment of an authoritative state tribunal as to who its presidential electors were—a procedure that became part of the final version of the Electoral Count Act as adopted by Congress and came to be known in 2000 as its "safe harbor deadline." In the event that two returns from a state claimed this authoritative status, the bill provided that neither would count unless both houses of Congress agreed on which one. As Edmunds explained to his Senate colleagues, "if there happen to be two supreme courts in that state, one of them a constitutional and legal one, and the other not, but each claiming that character, . . . then this decision of the supreme court . . . will not govern in the count unless the two Houses concur."[6]

Edmunds undoubtedly abandoned his own preference for an adjudicatory tribunal because of the political realities at the time. Before the 1876 election, he had proposed a constitutional amendment that would have given the US Supreme Court jurisdiction over disputed presidential elections.[7] But, as he lamented in his October 1877 article, this proposal "was lately defeated in the Senate by a large majority."[8] Similar proposals reintroduced in 1877, after the Hayes-Tilden crisis was resolved, went nowhere in either house of Congress.[9] Evidently, there was sufficient residual distaste for the 8–7 split of the Electoral Commission, or more specifically the 3–2 split among the five justices on the commission, that few wanted to undertake the effort to craft a better judicial body for the task of resolving a presidential vote-counting dispute.

Edmunds gauged his senatorial colleagues well enough. His bill passed the Senate by a vote of 35–26 (with 15 absent).[10] But the House refused to take it up, focusing instead on a plan to amend the Electoral College by requiring district-based presidential elections. That alternative effort, however, also failed.[11]

The nation thus went into the 1880 presidential election as it had in 1876, without any procedure in the event that the election was disputed. Fortunately, it was not. But it came quite close to being so.

New York was the pivotal state that year, as it would be again in 1884 and 1888. The election was between two Civil War generals in the Union army, James Garfield for the Republicans and Winfield Scott Hancock for the Democrats. Initial returns showed Garfield ahead of Hancock in New York by 20,000 votes.[12] But Democrats were claiming that there were "at least 20,000 illegal Republican votes cast in New York."[13] They specifically claimed that Republicans had orchestrated a plan to have thousands of residents of neighboring states—Vermont, Massachusetts, and Pennsylvania—travel to New York to vote instead. They made similar allegations about Canadians crossing the border to vote in New York. There was even a story that 5,000 Democratic ballots had been dumped into the Hudson River.[14]

Hancock did not concede for almost a full week, waiting six days after Election Day. He conceded then not because he believed he genuinely lost New York. He thought that fraud had made the difference. The national chairman of the Democratic Party at the time and also the head of Hancock's campaign in New York were pushing him to contest the result, as payback for what had happened to Tilden four years earlier. But Hancock, fearing serious upheaval and maybe even civil war if the country was forced to face another fight like that one, declined to pursue that confrontational course.[15]

The Democrats, moreover, still controlled both houses of Congress in the lame-duck session that would count the electoral votes from the 1880 election. There was briefly some concern that they could try to use this power to overturn Garfield's victory. But they did not. Still, the scare of 1880 coming immediately after the ordeal of 1876 was a signal that the nation needed an established procedure in case another presidential election did end up disputed.[16]

Even so, and despite Edmunds's efforts, the nation still did not have a procedure in place in time for the 1884 election, which was even more perilously close than 1880. Twenty times closer: with the Electoral College outcome again hinging on New York, the margin there this time was only 1,047 votes.[17]

This time, however, the Democrat came out ahead. He was Grover Cleveland and New York's governor. His Republican opponent was James Blaine, former senator from Maine and Garfield's secretary of state. Garfield had been assassinated less than a year after taking office. Chester Arthur, who had ascended to the presidency, was denied the Republican nomination in 1884.

The result in New York—and thus in the nation—was in doubt for two weeks, until the official canvass was completed. During that period, the New York bar was pressed into service for both sides to scrutinize the returns for any signs of fraud or irregularity. There certainly were allegations of improprieties, but they did not pan out. Republicans focused on claims of inflated totals for Cleveland in New York City and Long Island. Invalidating the returns from two of the targeted precincts, which gave Cleveland margins of 727 and 372 (or 1,099, combined) would have been enough to erase his statewide margin of 1,047.[18] But after observing the canvass there, as elsewhere, the Republicans abandoned their threats to sue over the outcome of the election.

Ultimately, the fact that each side had top-notch lawyers watching every step of the canvass with eagle eyes gave legitimacy to the certification of Cleveland's victory. Once the canvass was over, the *New York Tribune*, which spoke for Republicans in the state, proclaimed: "The canvass of the returns has been thorough, careful and honest, and leaves no room for doubt as to the result."[19]

Blaine conceded the next day. He did so, his biographer explained, not out of fear or charity, but because he knew he had not been wronged.[20] Although a few partisans would continue to claim that Blaine had been cheated out of the White House, the prevailing view of Republicans—as well as the candidate himself—was that "a lack of votes, not a theft of votes" caused Blaine's defeat.[21]

New York's ability to resolve the 1884 presidential election peacefully, through law, was undoubtedly a major success. Not every presidential swing state could handle a 1,000-vote margin, then or later, as both 1876 and 2000 separately have shown. Nonetheless, 1884 also underscored the need for congressional procedures in case New York, or another state, would not be as successful the next time. Congress had flirted with disaster now twice in a row, even after the Hayes-Tilden calamity. If New York's 1884 election had been litigated, as the Republicans warned that it would have been if they had uncovered grounds for a suit, another nightmare would have unfolded. Congress was once again divided, with the Republicans controlling the Senate and the Democrats the House, just like for the 1876 election. Thus, still lacking any established procedure to handle a conflict over a state's Electoral College votes, Congress would have had to reinvent the Electoral Commission or some other ad hoc mechanism. But with partisanship intensifying in the 1880s, there would have been no guarantee that Congress could have managed an ad hoc compromise for the Cleveland-Blaine election in the same way that it had for Hayes-Tilden. Simply put, would the Democrats in the House have insisted upon electing Cleveland, and with what consequences? As one Democrat in the House warned before the election, "we may have a deadlock again next winter," and therefore "a bad law would be better than no law at all."[22]

This philosophy is what finally prevailed before the 1888 election. Senator George Hoar, Republican of Massachusetts and Edmunds's friend and colleague on the Electoral Commission of 1877, took the lead in getting passage of a bill. Hoar's version contained an additional provision, not part of Edmunds's original formulation, but essential to securing approval in the Democrat-dominated House. This additional provision concerned the situation in which Congress received two or more conflicting submissions each purporting to be the same state's authentic Electoral College votes. The additional provision declared that the submission certified by the state's governor as the true Electoral College votes of the states would be counted unless rejected by both houses of Congress. This provision differed significantly from Edmunds's version, which would have rejected all multiple submissions unless both houses of Congress agreed upon one. By contrast, in the event that the Senate and the House diverged on which of two or more submissions to accept, Hoar's version, rather than rejecting all, would make the state's governor the tiebreaker.[23]

When Hoar unveiled his version in the Senate, it met with immediate and stiff resistance. Senator John Sherman, Republican from Ohio and president pro tempore of the Senate at the time, was especially critical. As Sherman was a preeminent figure in his party (he had been Treasury secretary in the Hayes administration and a contender for the Republican presidential nomination in 1880 and 1884), his criticism was especially significant.[24] Sherman thought it wholly inappropriate to designate as the "final arbiter" the governor of a state, who "naturally belongs to one of the two parties represented by the two opposing colleges of electors."[25] Suppose "the governor has usurped authority and has falsely certified returns or manufactured them,"[26] Sherman asserted, drawing no doubt on the memory of the troubles that plagued Louisiana in 1872. Did Hoar really mean to make the governor's usurpation "final and conclusive," at least when the two house of Congress were deadlocked because of party conflict? Sherman called instead for "fixing upon a tribunal" to serve as the tiebreaker between the Senate and House in the case of their disagreement over multiple Electoral College submissions from a state: "It may be the Supreme Court; it may be an electoral commission organized under law; it may be a tribunal pointed out by the law beforehand in the nature of a judicial tribunal or some other kind of tribunal; but to leave the question in dispute to be decided by the governor of a State, it seems to me only involves this matter in greater difficulty."[27]

Figure 6.1 The two New England senators named George, Edmunds from Vermont and Hoar from Massachusetts, both Republicans, had served on the Electoral Commission of 1877 and led the effort in Congress to enact a new procedure for handling disputed presidential elections. (a) Library of Congress. (b) Portrait by Frederic Porter Vinton; Harvard Art Museums.

Hoar, like Edmunds, agreed with Sherman that the creation of a tribunal to arbitrate a partisan division between the two houses of Congress would be preferable. "A perfect bill," Hoar acknowledged, "would provide for a common arbiter between these two bodies." He, too, "would prefer to take the senior justice of the Supreme Court" to be this tiebreaker, rather than the governor of the state with the competing Electoral College submissions. But he did not think Congress could devise any federal arbiter that would be politically feasible. "There never has assembled," Hoar noted, "a Congress whose two Houses would agree as to the person who should be the suitable common arbiter between these two bodies"—apart from the emergency circumstances that engendered the ad hoc Electoral Commission of 1877. As for employing the chief justice for this purpose, "it would be impossible to expect an agreement on that official as an arbiter between the two branches in the present state of political and public sentiment in this country."[28] (The chief justice at the time was Morrison Waite, a Republican who had been specifically excluded from the Electoral Commission because Democrats perceived him as antagonistic to Tilden.[29]) When Sherman persisted in his attack, Hoar simply repeated the point: "I should unite with the Senator in agreeing to have either the Supreme Court or the senior justice of the court come in as an arbiter between the two bodies, but the Senator knows as well as I do that it is perfectly hopeless to expect to get any legislation to that effect."[30] Democrats in the House would block it.

Senator John Ingalls of Kansas, another Republican, also attacked Hoar's plan to rely on a state's governor as the tiebreaker. He was "amazed" that Hoar would do so given the conduct of Oregon's governor in 1876. Hoar's proposal, if it had been applicable in the Hayes-Tilden dispute, "would have resulted inevitably in giving the result of that election in favor of the Democratic candidate" because the "certificate of the governor of Oregon was that two of those electors were chosen by the Republicans and one was chosen by the Democrats," and Tilden only needed that one to have an Electoral College majority. Notwithstanding that the Oregon governor's certification was entirely contrary to the will of the electorate there, as well as to the law of the state, it would have prevailed under Hoar's proposal, because the Democrats in the House refused to reject it in favor of the legitimate certificate from Oregon's secretary of state. Ingalls wanted no part of a proposal that would let the governor's mendacity triumph in this circumstance.[31]

Ingalls's objections went further. He saw no way that a statute could fix the defect inherent in the constitutional procedures set forth in the Twelfth Amendment:

> Careful consideration of this subject will convince any thoughtful student of the Constitution that the scheme which has been devised

> and which now remains in our organic law is fatally defective, and that nothing can be done by way of legislation to cure the inevitable evils by which it is surrounded, and the more we proceed by legislation to patch, to bridge over apparent difficulties, to abbreviate the number of perils which surround it, by so much we retard and delay the exercise of the power which the people must ultimately be called upon to perform in adopting some system that shall remove the perils in which it is now environed.[32]

In other words, according to Ingalls, a constitutional amendment was required to create the mechanism that would avoid the risk of taking the nation "to the very verge and brink of revolution," as in 1877.[33]

As with Sherman, so too with Ingalls; Hoar did not disagree with the premise of his fellow Republican's critique. Hoar readily admitted that the defect was in the original constitutional design: "I say that what is not satisfactory is the condition of the constitutional provision on this subject, which commits a question to the decision of two bodies politic and does not provide for any common arbiter. That is the unsatisfactory thing."[34] But Hoar believed that the Necessary and Proper Clause of the Constitution gave Congress the power to enact a statute to fill the gap as best as possible. While he made clear that he would prefer to fill the gap with a neutral federal arbiter, be it the Supreme Court or otherwise, he was proposing to let the state's governor be the tiebreaker in order to have a bill palatable to the Democrats in charge of the House.[35]

Although Sherman and Ingalls were sound in their reasons why the state's governor was an entirely unsuitable tiebreaker, Hoar was accurate in his political calculus that this provision was necessary for a bill to pass the House. When the Senate sent to the House Edmund's original bill without Hoar's amendment, the House refused to assent, and the conference committee of which both Edmunds and Hoar were members ultimately acquiesced in the House's insistence on the gubernatorial tiebreaker. With that provision agreed to in conference, the bill became law as the Electoral Count Act of 1887.[36]

The problem with the law, however, was not just the substance of the gubernatorial tiebreaker; the Act also was, and remains, frustratingly ambiguous, including even as to the scope of its gubernatorial tiebreaker. For a statute whose conference committee report claimed "to clear up any ambiguity" concerning "the meaning of Congress as to the decision of all questions as to counting the votes of the States from which there are more than one return,"[37] it was laughably—but dangerously—obtuse. As John Burgess, a leading political scientist of the time, wrote shortly after the statute's enactment, its "language" is "very confused, almost unintelligible."[38]

One view of the gubernatorial tiebreaker is that it applies only when none of the multiple Electoral College returns from a single state purport to carry the imprimatur of the state's highest adjudicatory authority. On this view, if any of the multiple returns claims this authoritative status, but the two houses of Congress cannot agree on the matter, then none of the returns can count regardless of which one carries the governor's certificate. "If the Houses cannot agree on the authoritative determination," then (according to this view) "no vote from the state in question is counted. This result follows regardless of the governor's action."[39] In support of this interpretation, some commentators offer this reasoning: "If the decision of the authorized tribunal cannot be made out, then there is no valid return for the governor to certify."[40] This view certainly would go a long way to address the objections of Senators Sherman and Ingalls, but is it faithful to the agreement reached in the conference committee? Not according to a different interpretation of the statute, which holds instead that the gubernatorial tiebreaker applies any time the two houses of Congress cannot agree which one of several returns to accept.[41]

Regardless of which interpretation is the better one, it is fatal to the very purpose of the statute that there is such radical uncertainty about the meaning of its core provision. The whole aim of the Electoral Count Act was to provide clear guidance as to what must happen when a dispute arises over two or more Electoral College returns from a single state. Yet imagine the situation in which the state supreme court has timely determined that one slate of presidential electors is the proper one, while the governor certifies a different slate. Assuming that the two houses of Congress disagree, one interpretation of the statute holds that neither slate can count, while the other interpretation holds that the one certified by the governor does. This irreducible ambiguity in the statute is a recipe for disaster: the two candidates, their parties, and the nation as a whole anxiously await a rapidly approaching Inauguration Day, with two dueling interpretations of the statute in play.[42]

Nor is that the statute's only ambiguity. As Burgess and others have asked, what if two different individuals purport to be the state's lawful governor and each certifies a separate return?[43] (Hoar assumed that neither would count,[44] but that was before the final language of the conference committee was hammered out, and that final language does not actually speak to the situation.) Or what if Congress has on hand two different returns certified by the same governor, but at different times, perhaps because the state's supreme court has ordered the second certification after the governor already sent the first to Congress?[45] Or what if there is a debate about whether Congress has received one or two certificates, as occurred over Vermont at the very end of the Hayes-Tilden dispute until Samuel Randall broke that impasse? Imagine a governor submitting a second return that the president of the Senate refuses to accept, deeming it untimely (in the way that Ferry did in 1877), but the first return lacks the governor's certification. What happens then? Does the first return prevail as the only one (since the statute says a single return must count unless rejected by both houses of Congress), or does the governor's return prevail because it qualifies as a second return despite the president of the Senate's rejection of it and then trumps the first return because it carries the governor's certification? The 1887 statute does not begin to attempt to address this contingency, even though it is a variation of one that actually arose in—and nearly derailed—the Hayes-Tilden dispute.

Despite all this, the most glaring omission of the Electoral Count Act of 1887 concerns the consequence of a determination, if and when applicable, that neither of two competing Electoral College returns from a state will count. Does this invalidation change the denominator for the purpose of calculating whether a candidate has obtained an Electoral College majority? To illustrate with a hypothetical example: suppose a state with 20 Electoral College votes has all these votes invalidated. Assume also that the leading candidate has 260 undisputed Electoral College votes. If the denominator is unaffected, then (using the current total of 538 Electoral College votes) the candidate remains 10 below the necessary majority, 270, and the election falls to the House of Representatives under the Twentieth Amendment. But if the denominator is reduced by 20, then 260 suffices as a majority of 518. Hoar argued this point with Senator William Evarts, Republican from New York, but the two disagreed.[46] "When two such able lawyers as Senators Evarts and Hoar disagree," Burgess wryly observed at the time, "it certainly is to be concluded that there is necessity for greater clearness and exactness upon this point."[47]

Evidently, the goal was to enact any law they could before 1888, even if they knew it was woefully inadequate in many crucial respects. And the 1888 election proved that they were right to do so, as it was another close one in New York, which again determined the outcome. This time New York was more like 1880: a margin of 14,372 (not barely more than one thousand as it had been in 1884).[48] Grover Cleveland ran for reelection, but he lost his home state—and the White House—to the Republican challenger, Senator Benjamin Harrison of Indiana.[49]

Once again, there were allegations of improprieties. Some have called the 1888 presidential election the most corrupt in US history, particularly in the misuse of campaign cash to purchase votes.[50] Republican operatives purportedly purchased as many as 40,000 votes in New York, by putting political money on the street, through a secret million-dollar fund.[51] One high-ranking Republican was quoted as saying that Harrison would never know "how close a number of men were compelled to approach the gates of the penitentiary to make him President."[52] But Democrats were accused of similar tactics as well, and some historians have questioned whether the actual corruption that year was as extensive as its perception.[53]

In any event, Cleveland did not attempt to challenge the outcome. Instead, he ran again in 1892 and clobbered Harrison in a rematch. Thus the procedures of the Electoral Count Act were not tested in 1888—although they easily could have been if that year had been as close as 1884, given the extent of the alleged improprieties. Nonetheless, Congress did not return to the task of eliminating the imperfections it knew to exist in its stopgap statute, which was better than nothing but hardly more than that.

It remains regrettable that Congress was unable to redress these deficiencies. One certainly cannot second-guess Hoar's judgment that political feasibility precluded anything more ambitious. A decade had passed since the Hayes-Tilden dispute without adoption of Edmunds's bill as originally introduced, much less any new constitutional amendment to cure the defects of the Twelfth Amendment. To say now that Congress in the 1880s should have enacted such an amendment, or at least a better statute, would be historical naïveté. Yet one can still wish that the political conditions had permitted achievement of what the leading participants knew was required. It is remarkable that Edmunds, Hoar, Sherman, Ingalls—among many others—all explicitly acknowledged that (in Hoar's words) "the failure of the Constitution, the *casus omissus*, is the failure to provide an arbiter when [the Senate and House] disagree."[54] But they were incapable of supplying the missing institution. As Sherman said, it need not have been the Supreme Court; any tribunal would be better than letting the governor of a disputed state have the last word. But they could not begin to craft a tribunal acceptable to both political parties.

The nation simply had not yet reached sufficient political maturity. After the Hayes-Tilden dispute, Senator Edmunds had hoped that "the time is not far distant" for the adoption of such a "judicial" tribunal to adjudicate a disputed presidential election.[55] But a decade later was still too soon.

Turmoil in the States

When one considers the overall political conditions that existed in the Gilded Age, it is not surprising that Republicans and Democrats in Congress at the time could not create a neutral arbiter for disputed presidential elections. Polarization between the two parties reached new extremes in this era, a level rivaled again only recently. In Congress, this polarization yielded political divisiveness, partisan distrust, and legislative deadlock.

In the states, the same polarization produced a "veritable epidemic" of destabilizing vote-counting disputes.[56] In West Virginia (1888) and Tennessee

(1894), the state legislature under control of the Democrats used technicalities to essentially steal the governorship for their party's candidate.[57] In West Virginia, the Republican candidate held his own inauguration ceremony and marched toward the statehouse with 400 armed supporters only to back down at the last minute to avoid bloodshed.[58] The next Democrat to serve as governor of the state conceded in his memoirs that his predecessor had been installed in office only as a result of partisan fraud.[59] Likewise, in Tennessee honorable Democrats acknowledged that their fellow partisans in the legislature perpetrated outright theft of the gubernatorial election, a "steal" they saw as comparable to "the Tilden-Hayes affair."[60]

Up north, circumstances were no better. In utter defeats of the democratic process, Connecticut (1890) and Rhode Island (1893) were unable to resolve disputes over gubernatorial elections for the entire term of office for which the elections had been held. Consequently, in each case, the previous incumbent held over for the whole new term. In Connecticut, the holdover was not on the ballot, and thus in no way the electorate's choice for the new term. Furthermore, the holdover was a Republican, whereas the returns showed the Democratic candidate for the new term as winning a majority. Nonetheless, Republicans in the state legislature used a pretext of disqualifying enough ballots to deprive the Democrat of a majority, and the holdover Republican used a crowbar to keep the Democrat out of office (thus earning the appellation of "the crowbar governor"). In a mirror image of what had occurred in West Virginia only two years earlier, the Democrat marched with supporters to claim his right to the governor's office, only to back down in order to avoid a violent confrontation.[61] In Rhode Island the holdover was a Republican running for reelection, and he used deadlock in the state's legislature to stay in office for the full term whether or not he was actually the preferred choice of the voters; the returns showed his opponent as having 183 more votes.[62] In neither of these two New England elections did democracy work: the holdover could claim no electoral pedigree for staying in office, but instead did so because the state was incapable of declaring a winner of the election.

As tumultuous as these disputed gubernatorial elections were, even more so were the situations in which rival legislatures purported to possess a state's lawmaking power. This situation occurred in Montana in 1890, Colorado in 1891, Kansas in 1893, and New Jersey in 1894. The triggering condition was enough legislative seats in dispute to affect which party was able to assert majority control. Each party would attempt to claim the disputed seats for itself, and on this basis begin to assert its right to legislate. But of course a state can have only one authoritative legislature, and thus the situation of rival legislatures is inherently unstable. Even so, Montana managed to lose its entire legislative session (its very first upon attaining statehood), because of its inability to

SEE HON. MICHAEL D. HARTER'S ARTICLE, "STOP THE PURCHASE OF SILVER," ON EDITORIAL PAGE.
THE FOURTH ARTICLE OF THE SERIES ON "NEW YORK SOCIETY" WILL BE PUBLISHED IN OUR NEXT NUMBER.

FRANK LESLIE'S
ILLUSTRATED
WEEKLY

Vol. LXXVI.—No. 1955.
Copyright, 1893, by Arkell Weekly Co.
All Rights Reserved.

NEW YORK, MARCH 2, 1893.

[Price, 10 Cents.

SPEAKER DOUGLASS BREAKING IN THE DOOR OF THE HALL OF REPRESENTATIVES.

REPUBLICANS FORCING THEIR WAY UP THE STAIRS TO THE LEGISLATIVE HALL.

POPULISTS RESCUING THE CLERK OF THEIR HOUSE FROM REPUBLICAN OFFICIALS.

FIGHTING FOR THE CONTROL OF A STATE.

THE REVOLUTIONARY PROCEEDINGS IN THE KANSAS LEGISLATURE—ATTEMPT OF THE POPULISTS TO DISPOSSESS THE LAWFUL REPUBLICAN HOUSE OF REPRESENTATIVES.—Drawn by Miss G. A. Davis and E. J. Meeker, from Sketches by G. M. Stone.—[See Page 135.]

Figure 6.2 The Legislative War of 1893 in Kansas commanded national attention—as evidenced by this cover of *Frank Leslie's Illustrated*, a popular magazine of the era; in addition to showing the confrontation of the two rival legislatures on the stairs, the cover (in its upper-left corner) pictures one side battering the door to the legislative chamber. The Ohio State University Billy Ireland Cartoon Library & Museum.

resolve this kind of impasse.[63] In Colorado, there were "actual riots on the floor of the House," as each faction attempted to assert control, and in the midst of the confrontation two police officers were shot, one fatally.[64] Kansas narrowly averted similar bloodshed in its "Legislative War of 1893," but only because a severe blizzard descended on the statehouse during the night in which military confrontation between the two sides seemed most imminent.[65]

A common theme that emerges from all these disputes is the role that the state's judiciary played—or did not play—in diffusing the crisis. In West Virginia, Connecticut, and Rhode Island, the disputes became as ugly as they did because the state supreme court refused to intervene.[66] In Montana, the dispute lasted the full legislative session because the state supreme court's attempt at intervention came too late to be useful for that session (but at least it prevented a repeat of the same problem subsequently).[67] By contrast, in Colorado, Kansas, and New Jersey, the crisis quickly resolved as soon as the state supreme court issued a ruling on the merits in favor of one side or the other.[68]

The involvement of the state supreme court, however, was not by itself a guarantee that the crisis would end. There needed to be a willingness of the losing side to acquiesce in the court's ruling. This point was vividly illustrated by Maine's disputed election of 1879, when the state almost suffered its own internal civil war because of its incumbent governor's refusal to abide by a ruling of the state's supreme court.

Joshua Chamberlain to the Rescue: Maine, 1879

Emblematic of how precarious politics had become in the Gilded Age was Maine's armed conflict over its elections of 1879, both gubernatorial and legislative, which became intertwined in an especially ugly power struggle between opposing parties and their leaders. Maine is a state that at other times, before and since, has been exemplary in handling vote-counting disputes in high-stakes elections. Four decades earlier, in 1837, Maine led the nation by being the first state to turn to its supreme court successfully to diffuse a potential crisis over a disputed gubernatorial election. On that occasion, the legislature had sought an advisory opinion from the Maine Supreme Court on whether local returns should be disqualified because of formal defects (the same kind of issue that had occurred in New York in 1792 and Massachusetts in 1806). When the court unanimously declared no, the legislature immediately accepted this judicial pronouncement, and the fight for the governorship ceased.[69]

In the twentieth century, Maine would become something of a model on how to handle recounts in gubernatorial elections quickly and smoothly.

In 1962 and again in 1970, the state would have gubernatorial elections with margins of 500 votes or less, and yet would have little difficulty in decisively declaring a winner well before Inauguration Day two months later.[70] The state's success in 1970 would be particularly impressive because there had been some fear then that Republicans would use their control of the state's senate to block the inauguration of the apparently winning Democrat. But nothing like that materialized. Instead, Maine in 1970 provided a civics lesson on how to handle a close gubernatorial election with transparency and integrity in order to implement the will of the eligible electorate as reflected in the ballots they cast.[71]

Not so a century earlier, in 1879. On the contrary, far from being a civics education on the proper operation of democracy, Maine's experience that year was a lesson in the evil to avoid: incumbent politicians clinging to power regardless of what the voters want, and even in defiance of the state's highest court and the rule of law. This attempted usurpation of authority provoked resistance, and soon opposing military forces amassed armaments and descended upon the capitol prepared for battle. Only the mediation of Joshua Chamberlain, legendary hero at Gettysburg—again facing great risk to his own personal safety, but now within his home state—prevented shots from being fired. Eventually, he persuaded the incumbent governor to accept, rather than defy, the verdict of the state supreme court, and then the conflict became capable of resolution.[72]

The crisis, known in the state as "The Twelve Days that Shook Maine," had its roots in the particular procedures the state then used to elect its legislature and governor. Under Maine's constitution and laws, local officials sent their election returns to the governor and executive council, which collectively had the power to declare the result. This power applied to elections for the state's legislature as well as for other offices. The legislature, in turn, had the power to pick the governor when no candidate won a majority of ballots cast. This constitutional arrangement precipitated the crisis, as the incumbent governor with the support of the council attempted to manipulate the results of enough legislative elections to produce a legislature sufficiently congenial to reinstall him into office even though he was far from popular at the ballot box.

The incumbent governor was Alonzo Garcelon, a Democrat. The political situation in Maine at the time was complicated by a robust Greenback party, which opposed a requirement that currency be backed by gold. The Greenbacks ran their own candidate for governor in 1879, a lumberman named Joseph L. Smith. In the state's legislature, the Democrats and Greenbacks were united as Fusionists in their opposition to Republicans, whose gubernatorial candidate that year was Daniel F. Davis.

When the ballots were counted, Garcelon was a distant third, with 21,851 votes compared to Davis with 68,967 and Smith with 47,643.[73] Indeed, Davis came very close to a majority of all ballots cast. But not quite. Therefore, the legislature would need to choose the governor. Moreover, the legislature was not required to choose among the top two vote-getters. Rather, the procedure was more complicated: the House picked two among the top four finishers, with the Senate selecting one of the two sent over by the House. Thus, Garcelon still had a chance.

Based on the initial returns of the legislative elections, however, it did not look like much of a chance. These returns showed both chambers being controlled by Republicans, narrowly but decisively. The Republicans, of course, would vote to give the governorship to Davis, a result that would not have seemed inappropriate given how close Davis had come to a majority and thus to outright possession of the office.

Yet Garcelon began conniving with the council to invalidate enough Republican legislative victories to put control of the legislature in the hands of the Fusionists.[74] To be sure, these Fusionists might pick Smith instead of him, since Smith outpolled him two-to-one. But Garcelon had the advantage of incumbency, which might cause the Fusionists to settle upon keeping him in office. (Moreover, even if he would not remain governor, Garcelon may have hoped to ingratiate himself with the Fusionist coalition as the best way to promote the remainder of his political career.[75]) Democrats in Maine also saw an opportunity to exact some revenge for what they still saw as the theft of the presidency only three years earlier. "You cheated us in the count for the President, but we have the returning board here in Maine," one Democrat leader in the state purportedly told a Republican.[76]

Garcelon and the council trumped up a variety of pretexts for disqualifying Republican ballots.[77] But they were all technicalities, including the age-old technique of invalidating a ballot because a candidate's name was spelled differently on different ballots even when it was obvious that they were all intended to be cast for the same candidate. For example, the council would not credit a vote for "G. S. Hill" as belonging to the same legislative candidate as a vote for "George S. Hill" (or, similarly, a vote for "F. W. Hill" as a vote for "Francis W. Hill").[78] The council also threw out votes from towns where the returns had been signed by only three aldermen instead of four—despite the fact that the form contained spaces for only three signatures.[79] Outraged, Republicans went to the state's supreme court to stop this electoral theft.

The court unanimously sided with the Republicans, ruling that ballots could not be invalidated based on the technicalities identified by the governor and council.[80] The court was not a balanced institution, having six Republicans on the bench and only one Democrat.[81] Still, the unanimous

Figure 6.3 Governor Alonzo Garcelon of Maine manipulated the state's 1879 election returns in an effort to keep him and his partisan allies in power, thereby precipitating "The Twelve Days That Shook Maine." *New England Magazine* (1895).

ruling was an indication that a lawful resolution of the dispute would recognize the Republican majorities in both chambers of the legislature, and thus the legislature in turn would be free to award the governorship to Davis.

But Garcelon refused to obey the court's ruling. Instead, he went ahead with awarding certificates of election to enough Fusionist legislative candidates to give the Fusionists control of both chambers.[82] At this point, the dispute began to move precipitously toward violent confrontation. Both sides were mobilizing for a military-style showdown. The editor of a Republican newspaper in Bangor was explicit in his call for insurrection:

> This gross outrage is not against Daniel F. Davis, but against the will of the people who are the sovereignty in this state. The people alone have the power to right it and they must right it. They must rise like the heroes of Bunker Hill and say this must not be![83]

His words were echoed by other Republicans, including Hannibal Hamlin, who returned to the US Senate after serving as Lincoln's vice president.[84] Here is another vivid example:

> I thank God that I am not too old to carry a musket. . . . I have a right that my vote should be counted, and I shall not submit to having this

> right wrested from me. There are thousands of old soldiers in our state who will lead the men of our state to maintain their rights, even if they thus have to shed their life's blood for it.[85]

Meanwhile, Fusionists were organizing their own paramilitary troops.

One good move that Garcelon made was to put Joshua Chamberlain in charge of the state's militia, in an effort to keep the peace in the state. Chamberlain was revered throughout the state—and the nation—for his heroism during the Civil War, especially at Gettysburg. Although he had been a Republican governor in the state, he was one man capable of standing above the partisan fray. Once in charge he ordered the militia to reposition itself in a way that would reduce the risk of an inadvertent conflagration, and in his remarks he made clear that he would permit neither side to prevail through force. At one point a band of thugs associated with the Fusionists appeared at Chamberlain's office, and, brandishing their weapons, threatened to assassinate him unless he let their side prevail.[86] Reportedly, Chamberlain in response to this threat opened his shirt and, pointing to his Civil War scars, said that they could do to him what the South had failed to do, but he was not going to let them take Maine's government by violence. Chamberlain's show of courage embarrassed his attackers, and they receded without harming him.[87]

Both sides purported to organize the state's legislature according to their respective claims. The Fusionists met pursuant to certificates that Garcelon had awarded them in defiance of the supreme court's decision. The Republicans in turn organized their own legislative bodies based on the supreme court decision itself. Thus, Maine simultaneously confronted the problem of rival legislatures and a battle over who would serve as governor.[88]

Both sides wanted Chamberlain to accept their claims of legitimacy. But Chamberlain refused to take sides, requiring instead that the matter to go back before the state's supreme court. The court, again unanimously, ruled in favor of the legislature organized according to the principles of its previous decision—in other words, the Republican-majority legislature.[89] The court did not mince words:

> By their action in granting certificates to men not appearing to be elected, or refusing to grant certificates to men clearly elected, they [referring to "the governor and council," explicitly identified in the court's previous sentence] may constitute each house with a majority to suit their own purposes, thus strangling and overthrowing the popular will as honestly expressed by the ballot.[90]

For almost two weeks, the Fusionists defied this second supreme court opinion, continuing to hold their own legislative sessions. But based on the supreme court ruling, Chamberlain recognized the lawful authority of the Republican-majority legislature, which indeed proceeded to install Davis as governor. Chamberlain turned over the authority of the militia to Davis. Ultimately, twelve days after the court's definitive pronouncement, the Fusionists finally backed down, acquiescing in Davis's claim to the office and disbanding their separate legislature.[91]

After this ordeal, the state eliminated the requirement that a gubernatorial candidate win a majority in order to win the office outright; instead, a plurality would suffice. Interestingly, in the very next election, in 1880, the result was close enough that there might have been a dispute as to which candidate was winner. The Fusionist candidate, Harris Plaisted, was ahead of Republican Davis, now the incumbent, by only 169 votes. Although Republicans continued to control the legislature, and might have tried to use this power to keep Davis in office another term, they declined to hold onto the governorship through an exercise of raw political power. Not wanting to treat their

Figure 6.4 Joshua Chamberlain, hero at Gettysburg, diffused the crisis over the 1879 election by insisting, in his role as commander of the state militia, that Governor Garcelon and his allies obey the judgment of the Maine Supreme Court. Bowdoin College.

opponents the way their opponents had treated them only one year earlier, the Republicans purported to act pursuant to a higher principle: if the opposing gubernatorial candidate appeared to be the people's choice based on the vote, even a close one, then that candidate should be seated in office regardless of which party happened to hold the reins of power at the time. In this way, then, Maine seemed to learn from its earlier mistake, becoming more virtuous as a result of the near-disaster of 1879. But it was a hard way to learn the lesson, and one misstep—perhaps a bullet in Chamberlain's heart—might instead have thrown the entire state into convulsive violence.[92]

The Maine dispute, moreover, reverberated nationally. The Democratic Party dispatched its top legal talent from around the country to advise Garcelon.[93] James Blaine, then US senator from Maine and soon-to-be Republican presidential candidate in 1884, desperately wanted Republicans to maintain control of Maine's legislature so that he could maintain as much political influence as possible. Indeed, Blaine himself had been one of the Republicans urging "a great and popular uprising" if necessary to protect their electoral victory.[94] Other national Republicans also rallied to the cause as the dispute raged on. In the end, though, it was not outsiders who resolved the crisis. Chamberlain and the justices of the state's supreme court were local heroes, even while Chamberlain was nationally prominent.

The US Supreme Court Refuses Involvement: Kentucky, 1899

Twenty years later, Kentucky confronted a crisis similar to Maine's: a disputed gubernatorial election that split the state and its legislature into two belligerent camps. Kentucky, however, lacked a heroic figure like Joshua Chamberlain, capable of transcending partisanship to diffuse the conflict for the sake of the state as whole. As a result, Kentucky was unable to avoid bloodshed in the way that Maine had managed. On the contrary, in the only instance of a gubernatorial candidate being assassinated in the midst of a ballot-counting battle throughout all of American history, the Democratic candidate in Kentucky that year, William Goebel, was fatally shot while the electoral dispute was raging. The bullet was fired from the secretary of state's office; the secretary of state, Caleb Powers, was a Republican "and an outspoken Goebel critic."[95] Although Powers's conviction was overturned on appeal, the weight of historical evidence suggests that partisan Republicans were responsible for the premeditated murder of Goebel in the hope that his death would help them keep control of the governor's office away from the Democrats.[96]

Kentucky's disputed gubernatorial election of 1899 also ended up in the US Supreme Court, in a case called *Taylor v. Beckham*, and is important for the precedent it set there.[97] The Court refused to take jurisdiction over a claim that the state's procedures for resolving the vote-counting dispute violated the Fourteenth Amendment—a claim directly analogous to the one that the Court sustained a century later in *Bush v. Gore*. The Court's rejection of the Fourteenth Amendment claim prompted an impassioned dissent from Justice John Marshall Harlan, most famous for his dissent in *Plessy v. Ferguson*, the case that upheld racial segregation in the South. Harlan's dissent in *Plessy* was subsequently vindicated in *Brown v. Board of Education*, the school desegregation case.[98]

Harlan's dissent in *Taylor v. Beckham* received similar vindication in the US Supreme Court's Fourteenth Amendment ruling in *Bush v. Gore*. But this vindication took almost twice as long, with *Bush v. Gore* coming a full century after *Taylor v. Beckham* (compared to the six decades it took for the Court to repudiate *Plessy* in *Brown*).[99] Meanwhile, as a result of *Taylor v. Beckham*, for the entire twentieth century the federal judiciary was impotent to protect electoral democracy from the kind of partisan power grab that triggered the civil unrest in Kentucky. While nothing as extreme as assassination of a candidate occurred in a twentieth-century dispute over ballots, the US Supreme Court's insistence on staying out of these disputes had profound consequences for the development of American politics, as we shall see. States were left to fend for themselves, for better or worse, and in Kentucky at the turn of the century it was definitely for the worse.

In 1899, conditions were ripe for the outbreak of political violence: "A kind of class warfare seemed to be occurring."[100] There had been conflagrations over toll roads in the state, with the incumbent Republican governor, William O'Connell Bradley, backing the affluent companies that owned the roads, while the Democratic majority in the state legislature sided with lower-income citizens who objected to the tolls.

Bradley was term-limited, and the Republicans nominated the incumbent attorney general, William S. Taylor, in their effort to keep the governorship in their hands. His opponent was William Goebel, then the leader of the Democrats in the state's senate. From that perch, and preparing for his gubernatorial run, Goebel orchestrated the enactment of a controversial election law that bore his name. This Goebel Election Law created a three-member Board of Election Commissioners, to be dominated by two Democrats, which would appoint local election officials and adjudicate all election disputes.[101]

Anticipating violence after an ugly campaign, both sides prepared for Election Day with a show of force. The Democratic mayor in Louisville added 500 private police officers—ostensibly to keep the peace, but perhaps to intimidate Republicans. Governor Bradley responded by calling out the militia.[102]

Unofficial initial returns showed Taylor winning by about 2,000 votes, but Goebel immediately cried fraud, claiming that Republicans used fake "tissue paper ballots" to fabricate Taylor's lead.[103] Democrats also wanted to invalidate 1,200 ballots inadvertently printed "W. P." instead of "W. S." Taylor. Nor were Democrats above arguing that all of Louisville's returns, which favored Taylor by more than 3,000 votes, should be tossed out on the ground that Bradley's invocation of the militia was intimidating—an argument that conveniently overlooked what the Louisville mayor had done.[104]

As in Tennessee five years earlier, some Democratic-leaning newspapers urged acceptance of the Republican gubernatorial victory. They did not want their party to be guilty of the kind of electoral theft that they felt had been committed against Tilden. As one paper put it, "better that a Republican should hold the office forever than that the Democratic party should dishonor itself by Hayesing it to Goebel."[105] Republicans meanwhile were fearful that they would be counted out of their victory, as they just had been in Tennessee. They proclaimed their determination not to let it happen again, vowing to hold on to the office by force of arms if necessary.

As the Goebel-created Board of Election Commissioners was preparing to issue its official ruling, a Republican force of about 500 armed "mountain men" descended upon Frankfort, the state capital. The board, however, surprised everyone by ruling 2–1 that it would accept the election returns on their face, rather than attempting to adjust them in Goebel's favor. Thus, the board declared that Taylor had won by 2,383 votes. The board's decision set the stage for the next phase of the dispute, since the board said that only the state legislature had the power to go behind the returns.[106] In hindsight, it would have been far better if the board's evidently nonpartisan result had been final, with the state's legislature powerless to review it.

As the fight moved to the legislature, the risk of armed conflict sharply escalated. The Republicans inaugurated Taylor on the strength of the board's ruling, and Taylor amassed a militia of over a thousand soldiers. The Democrats countered with their own equally large battalion.

In the legislature, the Democrats appeared to rig the results so that Goebel would win. They formed an investigatory committee that was supposed to be selected at random, but when the names were picked out of a box, there were ten Democrats and only one Republican—perhaps a statistical fluke, but a highly suspicious one. Moreover, the committee's conduct fueled the Republicans' fears: all of its procedural and evidentiary rulings favored Goebel's position.[107]

Amidst this toxic atmosphere, on January 30 Goebel was shot—but not immediately killed—when he was walking across the statehouse grounds toward the senate's chamber. Vowing revenge, the Democrats on the legislative committee quickly announced its decision that Goebel had won the election. Taylor, purporting to be governor, ordered the legislature to remove itself from Frankfort, to the town of London, a Republican "stronghold." The Democrats in the legislature, however, defied this order and, instead, met secretly in a Frankfort hotel (the statehouse having been rendered off-limits by the strength of Taylor's troops), without any Republican members of the legislature joining them. There, proclaiming themselves a sufficient legislative quorum, the Democrats voted to accept the committee's decision and thus declared Goebel governor. On his deathbed, Goebel took the oath of office.[108]

With the two partisan armies arrayed against each other in Frankfort, civil war in the state was a real risk. Taylor asked President McKinley to send in federal troops, but McKinley refused. No matter how dangerous the conditions, he did not want to be the first Republican president since Reconstruction to send in the US Army to prop up a Republican governor at odds with a state legislature controlled by Democrats. On February 3, Goebel died and instantly became a martyr. His running mate, J.C.W. Beckham, was sworn in as Goebel's successor, thus directly vying with Taylor's claim to the same office. Without McKinley's backing, Taylor realized he needed to deescalate

Figure 6.5 The February 10, 1900 edition of *Harper's Weekly* illustrated the assassination of Kentucky gubernatorial candidate William Goebel; as Goebel slumps, armed bystanders look up at the secretary of state's windows from where the bullet was fired. The Ohio State University Billy Ireland Cartoon Library & Museum.

the tension and made it known that he would accept the determination of the courts as to which of the two was entitled to serve as governor.[109]

On April 6, 1900, the state's highest court ruled against Taylor by a vote of 6–1, with two Republican jurists joining four Democrats in concluding that the judiciary had no power to review a declaration bearing the legislature's official seal of which candidate has been elected governor.[110] As to Taylor's claim that the secret meeting of the Democrats could not constitute a legitimate official decision of the legislature, the majority of the Kentucky court responded that when the official journal of the legislature contains an entry asserting that the legislature had voted to declare Goebel the winner, the courts must accept that journal entry as final and conclusive: "The courts are without jurisdiction to go behind the record made by the legislature under the constitution."[111] Recognizing that this principle could permit the majority in the legislature to perpetrate a fraud or commit another form of "great injustice," the court observed:

> Public authority and political power must, of necessity, be confided to officers, who, being human, may violate the trust reposed in them. This perhaps cannot be avoided absolutely, but it applies also to all human agencies. It is not fit that the judiciary should claim for itself a purity beyond others; nor has it been able at all times with truth to say that its high places have not been disgraced.[112]

The court allowed that the state's constitution might explicitly grant the judiciary power to overturn the legislature's certification of a gubernatorial election on grounds of fraud or error, but absent any such explicit authorization, the judiciary would decline to become embroiled in the quintessentially political question of which gubernatorial candidate won the election.

The state supreme court also addressed, and rejected, the novel claim that the state had violated the Fourteenth Amendment in its handling of this particular election: "In determining merely the result of the election according to its own laws the state deprives no one of life, liberty, or property." The court added that what procedures should determine who won the election was "wholly a matter of state policy."[113] But by considering and rejecting this Fourteenth Amendment claim, the Kentucky court procedurally put the case in a posture by which Taylor could make an appeal to the US Supreme Court on this question of federal law.[114]

The US Supreme Court, in an 8–1 decision, also ruled against Taylor. Six of the eight technically voted to dismiss Taylor's appeal on the ground that the political question doctrine jurisdictionally precluded the federal judiciary's consideration of the Fourteenth Amendment claim raised by Taylor. The two other justices in the majority would have affirmed the Kentucky court's decision on the simple ground that Taylor's Fourteenth Amendment claim lacked merit for essentially the reason stated by the state court.[115]

Invoking the precedent of *Luther v. Borden*, the progenitor of the political question doctrine in the US Supreme Court, Chief Justice Fuller wrote for the Court:

> The commonwealth of Kentucky is in full possession of its faculties as a member of the Union, and no exigency has arisen requiring the interference of the general government to enforce the guaranties of the Constitution, or to repel invasion, or to put down domestic violence.[116]

Aware of the facts on the ground, Fuller found it necessary to add: "In the eye of the Constitution, the legislative, executive, and judicial departments of the state are peacefully operating by the orderly and settled methods prescribed by its fundamental law, *notwithstanding there may be difficulties and disturbances arising from the pendency and determination of these contests*."[117] The fact that the state judiciary refused to second-guess the state legislature's declaration of the gubernatorial winner, based on the state judiciary's interpretation of the state's constitution, created no Fourteenth Amendment violation entitled to be remedied by the US Supreme Court: "It is clear that the judgment of the [state court], in declining to go behind the decision of the [legislature, being] vested by the state Constitution and laws with the ultimate determination of the right to these offices, denied no right secured by the 14th Amendment."[118] If the consequence of this arrangement under state constitutional law was a fundamental breach of democracy, in usurping the electorate's right to have their valid ballots counted fairly, then—according to the US Supreme Court—the "remedy" must "be found in" the legislature itself, which the Court called "the august tribunal of the people, which is continually sitting, and over whose judgments on the conduct of public functionaries the courts exercise no control." Accordingly, Fuller pronounced: "We must decline to take jurisdiction on the ground of deprivation of rights embraced by the 14th Amendment, without due process of law."[119]

Justice Harlan was the only member of the US Supreme Court who would have sustained Taylor's Fourteenth Amendment claim. Harlan was fully prepared to order the state's judiciary—and legislature—to uphold Taylor's title to the office of governor. Perhaps because he was a Republican from Kentucky, he felt especially wronged by what happened in his home state. In any event, he was livid: "No such farce under the guise of formal proceedings was ever enacted in the presence of a free people who take pride in the fact that our

American governments are governments of laws and not men." He knew he was getting personal about colleagues he grew up with: "It is not a pleasant thing to say—but after a thorough examination of the record a sense of duty constrains me to say—that the declaration by that body of men that Goebel was legally elected ought not to be respected in any court as a determination of the question in issue, *but should be regarded only as action taken outside of law, in utter contempt of the constitutional right of freemen to select their rulers.*"[120]

Getting more specific, Harlan added: "There was a fixed purpose on their part, whatever the facts might be, to put Goebel into office and to oust Taylor." The pretense that Goebel "had received the highest number of legal votes cast was in total disregard of the facts—a declaration as extravagant as one adjudging that white was black, or that black was white." Harlan reminded his readers that the secret hotel meeting of the Democrats acted without even bothering to review the evidence gathered by the legislature's investigative committee; they "shut their eyes against the proof for fear that it would compel them to respect the popular will as expressed at the polls." Harlan acknowledged that Democrats were entitled to be outraged at Goebel's murder, but that did not justify the crime that they then committed against democracy itself: "Indignant as naturally they were and should have been, at the assassination of their leader, they proceeded in defiance of all the forms of law and in contempt of the principles upon which free governments rest, to avenge that terrible crime by committing another crime, namely, the destruction by arbitrary methods of the right of the people to choose their chief magistrate."[121]

Connecting the egregious facts with the new federal constitutional law of the Fourteenth Amendment, Harlan "grant[ed] that it is competent for a state to provide for the determination of contested election cases by the legislature," but simultaneously insisted that the legislature must obey "due process of law" when exercising this competency. What was the specific violation of due process here? At this juncture, Harlan made his most analytically significant—and rhetorically powerful—point: "The overturning of the public will, as expressed at the ballot box, without evidence or against evidence . . . is a crime against free government, and deserves the execration of all lovers of liberty." Due process, in other words, necessarily entails the fundamentals of democracy. Moreover, because the Court must enforce the Fourteenth Amendment's protection of due process, the Court must safeguard democracy: "I cannot believe that the judiciary is helpless in the presence of such a crime. The person elected, as well as the people who elect him, have rights that the courts may protect."[122]

Justice Harlan put all of his energy and ability into his *Taylor v. Beckham* dissent, and his effort was worthy of the case's importance. The historical significance of the US Supreme Court's decision in *Taylor v. Beckham* is much greater than its name recognition. It set the precedent, lasting a century, that the US Supreme Court would not involve itself in a state's vote-counting dispute. The Court cited *Taylor v. Beckham* as its leading precedent on this point in the subsequent case of *Snowden v. Hughes*, decided in 1944, which came to eclipse the earlier case (the latter one being a product of the new era of constitutional jurisprudence at the Court that arose after 1937).[123]

Justice Harlan's dissent in *Taylor* also holds a much more significant place in his own judicial career than has been recognized in recent years.[124] It is the defining statement of Harlan's view on the federal judiciary as the ultimate protector of the voting process at the core of self-government. From *Plessy*, we have come to know Justice Harlan as the protector of minority rights from majoritarian tyranny. But we have forgotten Harlan's role in heralding the federal judiciary as the protector of majority rule itself, in the form of the electorate's right to have its will—as expressed by the majority of valid votes—prevail. In overlooking this second strand of Justice Harlan's

Figure 6.6 Justice John Marshall Harlan dissented in *Taylor v. Beckham*, the Supreme Court decision denying federal courts the power to review the counting of ballots by a state; Harlan's position prevailed 100 years later in *Bush v. Gore*. Library of Congress.

jurisprudence, the United States has not yet recognized just how much it owes to this great justice.[125]

As for the case at hand, *Taylor v. Beckham* managed to diffuse the conflict over Kentucky's gubernatorial election of 1899. Beckham assumed undeniable authority of the office based on the decision, and Taylor fled to Indiana to avoid prosecution as part of a conspiracy to assassinate Goebel. The end of this power struggle, however, did not signal an end to controversies over Kentucky's ability to conduct democratic elections fairly. On the contrary, just a few years later, in 1905, the race for mayor of Louisville was so tainted with fraud that the state's judiciary had to void the election entirely.[126]

The larger legacy of *Taylor v. Beckham,* however, was the adamant and categorical unwillingness of the federal judiciary to intervene, no matter how egregious a state's vote-counting practices. This refusal would be put to the test in 1948, when ballot-box stuffing was shown to have contributed more fake votes than the certified margin of victory in Lyndon Johnson's crucial election that served as the steppingstone to his momentous career in the Senate and then the presidency. But the US Supreme Court would let that subversion of electoral democracy go unremedied, as it had a half-century earlier in the Kentucky case.

The Court knew full well the implications of its jurisdictional ruling in *Taylor v. Beckham.* By 1899, the Justices had seen ample proof that what unfolded in Kentucky, while especially intense, was hardly unique or aberrational in American politics. Merely by reading the newspapers of the previous decade, the justices knew what had transpired in Connecticut and Montana in 1890, in Colorado in 1891, in Kansas and Rhode Island in 1893, in New Jersey and Tennessee in 1894, and all the other accumulated electoral ugliness of the decade. The country seemingly had gone crazy with vote-counting disputes that engendered civil unrest as well as negated the will of the eligible electorate, contrary to the very purpose of holding the elections. Still, as the nineteenth century gave way to the twentieth, the US Supreme Court made emphatically clear that any cure for these deficiencies in the functioning of democracy would need to come from elsewhere in America's political system and culture.

7

The Progressive Era

Missed Opportunities at a Time of Reform

The Progressive Era brought profound changes to American democracy. Women's suffrage. Direct election of US senators. Primary elections. Ballot initiatives and referenda. Campaign finance regulation.[1]

But not significant alteration of the procedures for resolving disputed elections. Although the topic received some attention from Progressive leaders, it was not a top priority on the reform agenda. Equal suffrage for women was undoubtedly a more pressing matter, as was the right of citizens to choose their senators themselves (rather than have senators selected by state legislatures). The consequence was that when political forces derailed efforts to improve ballot-counting procedures, the lack of a sustained reform effort on this particular topic prevented getting the adoption of new procedures back on track.

This frustration of ballot-counting reforms occurred around the country, especially in New York. In 1891, the state was shocked by a momentous ballot-counting scandal. Three years later, a constitutional convention took up the subject of ballot-counting reform. Its attention to the topic was limited, diverted by other priorities, and its reform measures incomplete. A decade later, the progressive governor Charles Evans Hughes pushed a new recount law through the state's legislature. But when the state's highest court declared the recount reform unconstitutional in an unnecessary and dubious ruling that reflected outdated views of civil procedure, there was no attempt to resurrect the reform by other means.

Hughes himself is symbolic of the incompleteness of the Progressive Era on the subject of ballot-counting reform. Despite his sincere and fervent belief that the law must guarantee a fair count, he did not see his vision fulfilled. Moreover, after he himself was a candidate in the exceptionally close presidential election of 1916—one that easily could have tailspinned into another Hayes-Tilden—he did not champion procedural reform of the method for adjudicating a presidential ballot-counting dispute.

Still, despite the failure of the Progressive Era to adopt major concrete measures for improving ballot-counting procedures, it would be a mistake to think that the Progressive Era had little positive effect on the counting of votes. The cultural conditions that enabled all the other improvements in democracy during the Progressive Era, especially women's suffrage, transformed social expectations concerning what was appropriate and inappropriate behavior in the context of counting votes. With women and men coming to the polls to cast their ballots on equal terms, it became more difficult to think of electoral competition in militaristic terms, with the two parties operating like two armies waging war against each other.[2] Thus the type of violence that plagued major vote-counting disputes in the 1890s, leading to the especially ugly assassination of a gubernatorial candidate in Kentucky at the end of that turbulent decade, became socially taboo once the ethos of the Progressive Era became firmly rooted.

The social understanding of democracy and what it entailed in terms of counting ballots fairly changed subtly and significantly as a result of the Progressive Era. The idea of a party winning at all cost, regardless of law and the basic bonds of a civil society, diminished in its social acceptability. Consequently, as we shall now examine, the kind of brazenly lawless conduct that occurred in New York in 1891 would become culturally off-limits as the Progressive Era unfolded, even though New York was unable to instantiate its invigorated commitment to a fair count in new legislation.

We start, then, with a tale that might seem more suited to the Gilded Age. But where the Gilded Age ends and the Progressive Era begins is hazy and open to debate. In any event, illustrating the difficulty of the transformation from a condition of chronic electoral corruption to a commitment, even if not fully realized, to electoral integrity requires starting the story in the depths of depravity. That something as ugly as New York's "Stolen Senate" episode could occur as late as 1891, when supposedly the Progressive Era was already underway, indicates just how far it would be necessary to progress in order to achieve a political system in which subversion of the electorate's will was no longer a serious threat.

New York's Stolen Senate of 1891

In 1891, Democrats in New York demonstrated the extremes to which partisans were willing to go in the pursuit of political power. Under the leadership of outgoing governor David Hill, who was becoming US senator for the state, the Democrats were not content simply to concoct pretexts for disqualifying Republican ballots in the hopes that partisan allies on the bench would go along with their scheme. Rather, when the judiciary balked, the Democrats simply defied the judiciary.[3]

Unlike in Maine in 1879, the Democrats in New York would not proclaim this defiance openly. Instead, through subterfuge, they lied to the courts about crucial details of the vote-counting process. Only afterward was the nature of their mendacity revealed. Although it was then resoundingly condemned, the condemnation came too late to undo the electoral theft that Hill and his partisan henchmen successfully had perpetrated.

The key fact about the elections of November 1891 in New York was that the Democrats unquestionably won the governorship and the state assembly (the lower house of the state's legislature), but not the state senate. Counting the ballots as cast, the local returns showed the Republican candidates winning 17 senate seats, the Democrats winning 14, and an independent candidate winning one. These returns, if they stood, would let the Republicans keep a narrow but decisive grip on the senate, thereby depriving Democrats of complete control of the state's lawmaking powers.[4]

Looking at those returns, however, Democrats desperately wanted to capture total control, which they saw tantalizingly within reach. For Hill's entire eight years as governor, since 1885, Republicans had been able to block his policies in the legislature. Hill harbored presidential ambitions, and he wanted to show that as boss of the Empire State's Democrats, he could still manage to deliver the entire state to his party. If he could flip the results of just a few senate seats, Democrats would be assured of having the power to enact Hill's legislative agenda. Even more crucially, they would also be able to dictate the next round of reapportionment—enabling them to gerrymander districts in their favor—as well as determine the method of choosing delegates to the state's upcoming constitutional convention, which was already behind schedule because of the persistent legislative gridlock.

Consequently, Hill orchestrated a plan by which the Democrats were able to deprive Republicans of their apparent victories in three senate seats and convert these three seats to the Democratic candidates, even though those three Democrats had won fewer votes than their Republican opponents. No wonder it was called the Stolen Senate, since the conversion of these three seats—contrary to the will of the voters in each district—achieved its objective of putting the Democrats in control of the chamber. In two cases, this scheme involved the concurrence of the state's highest court, the Court of Appeals, which was also dominated by Democrats. In the third case, Hill's argument for undoing the eligible electorate's choice was so preposterous that the judicial Democrats were unwilling to go along. But the court's refusal did not stop Hill; instead, acting through subordinates, he willfully disobeyed the court's decree and, by means of a false and unlawful count of

Figure 7.1 Governor David Hill of New York in 1891 orchestrated the "Steal of the Senate" in order to obtain full legislative power for his party in the state. Portrait by Morton Bly; N.Y. Hall of Governors.

ballots, caused the Democrat to receive the official certification as winner of the election.

First Targeted Seat

One of the three converted seats was the twenty-seventh senate district, which encompassed the western upstate counties of Chemung, where Elmira is, and Steuben, home of Corning and its well-known glassworks. The Democrats claimed that the winning Republican candidate, Franklin Sherwood, was ineligible to serve in the senate because he held the position of park commissioner in a local town. The members of the State Canvassing Board were Democrats, and Republicans feared that the board would refuse to certify Sherwood's election based on this claim of ineligibility. The Republicans thus went to state court asking for a writ of mandamus that would order the State Canvassing Board to give Sherwood his certificate of election. By a 5–2 vote, the New York Court of Appeals—the state's highest court—denied the Republicans this writ. All five judges in the majority were Democrats, and the two dissenters were Republicans. Even the majority agreed with Sherwood that the State Canvassing Board, as a merely ministerial body, was not entitled to pass judgment on whether Sherwood was ineligible to serve in the senate.[5] Only the senate itself could do that, in keeping with the longstanding tradition of legislative chambers having the sole power to judge the qualifications of their own members. Thus the only role for the State Canvassing Board was to certify the count of the ballots cast in the election, and there was no disputing that Sherwood received the most votes. Still, the Democratic majority of the court said that there could be no writ of mandamus in this context. Even though the senate itself was to be the ultimate judge of Sherwood's eligibility, the majority of the court deemed him ineligible based on its own reading of the state's constitution. The majority then ruled that mandamus is unavailable to anyone seeking to act contrary to the constitution: "A party can demand a *mandamus* only to secure or protect a clear legal right, never to accomplish a wrong."[6] The Republican dissenters reasoned that Sherwood had an unambiguous right to the certificate of election—since he undeniably won the most votes—and that was all that should have mattered to the court.[7] But without this writ of mandamus, the State Canvassing Board was free to refuse Sherwood his certificate, and that is exactly what it did.

One can argue that Sherwood was in a weak position to complain if indeed he was ineligible. Nonetheless, there is no escaping the fact that two Democrat-dominated bodies, the State Canvassing Board and the Court of Appeals, deprived the district's voters of their choice on who should represent them in the senate. There is little doubt that if a Democrat had been the candidate seeking the certificate of election based on the ballots actually cast and counted, Hill's allies on the canvassing board would have given the candidate that certificate and (if the Republican opponent had litigated the matter) the court would have left the issue of eligibility to the senate to consider. Thus, the process for resolving the dispute over this seat was hardly evenhanded in how it treated the two contending parties.

Second Targeted Seat

The second senate seat that the Democrats captured from the Republicans was an even more troubling outcome from the perspective of electoral fairness and legitimacy. This seat was for the twenty-fifth district, which included Onondaga County, where Syracuse is located. Stealing the seat turned on an error made by local election officials: they sent the official ballots designated for one precinct to another precinct by mistake.

The 1891 election was one of the first in New York involving the use of so-called Australian ballots, which the officials were responsible for printing and distributing.[8] It seemed as if the officials had trouble implementing the new law.[9] As a practical matter, the error did not prevent voters from making a choice in their local senate election: even though these voters received the ballot for the wrong precinct, the correct candidate for their twenty-fifth district was on the ballot, and they were thus able to use the faulty ballot to make an authentic electoral choice. There was no doubt, in other words, which candidate the eligible voters actually wanted.

The returns showed that the Republican candidate would win if these ballots were counted, but not otherwise.[10] The Democrats challenged these ballots on the ground that they were improper under the state's new election law adopting the Australian ballot. In a 4–3 vote of the state's highest court, the Democrats prevailed on this argument. Recognizing the importance of the case, not only to the particular political fight before them, but also as a major precedent for future similar disputes, the judges on both sides of the issue wrote at great length.

The judges in the majority were all Democrats, and they explicitly adopted a "strict compliance" standard for the new Australian ballot statute.[11] The majority opinion refused to protect the voters from the wrongdoing of the local election officials:

> It may be . . . a hardship that the result should operate to render null so many votes, and to alter what may have been an honest expression of popular will; but it would be an evil, in comparison with which the hardship complained of is as nothing, if a law, which the people of this state through their legislature so deliberately framed and have solemnly adopted, should be so construed as to render fraudulent evasion possible.[12]

In other words, even though there was no showing that the Republicans acted fraudulently with respect to these ballots, the majority seemed to believe that the mere theoretical risk of fraud in general was enough to throw out the ballots (or that enforcement of the law for its own sake was more important than protecting voters from erroneous disenfranchisement).

A concurring opinion by Judge O'Brien, one of the Democrats in the majority, added:

> But it is said that this result will disenfranchise the electors who cast these ballots in good faith, believing that they were the proper official ballots. The answer is that when an elector attempts to express his will

> at an election by the use, through either design or accident, of ballots which the law declares shall not be counted, the courts have no power to help him.[13]

Judge O'Brien, rather hardheartedly and unrealistically, asserted that it was the voter's fault for accepting from the poll worker a defective ballot: "The law contemplates that the elector will not blindly rely upon anyone, not even the election officers, in the preparation of the ballot."[14] Yet even a faultless voter would get no relief from Judge O'Brien: "Even if . . . those electors had no knowledge or means of knowing" of the official mistake, and even if "they could not without some inconvenience provide themselves with ballots such as the law required, we would still be obliged to hold that it would be far better that their votes should be deemed ineffectual than that the fundamental purpose of an important public statute be subverted."[15]

The dissenters, two Republicans and one Democrat, argued vociferously for an interpretation of the statute that would prevent the disenfranchisement of innocent voters as a result of official error. The Democrat in dissent was Judge Rufus Peckham, who would later serve on the US Supreme Court (and most famously write the Court's *Lochner* opinion on economic liberty).[16] In this electoral dispute, Peckham did not hide his disgust with his colleagues in the majority: "To utterly disenfranchise hundreds of innocent legal voters because the employe[e] or messenger of some public officer made a mistake like the one in question, seems to me to work a burlesque on the ballot act and its construction."[17]

Peckham explained that the statute's goal was ballot secrecy, and there was absolutely no evidence of any breach of ballot secrecy in this case: "The ballots were voted in fact without any objection or challenge in a single instance by any human being, and were counted by inspectors of election without a protest from any source."[18] Indeed, Peckham found it hard to imagine even theoretically how the swapping of two precincts' ballots could be undertaken for nefarious purposes: "It would be highly improbable that any official would intentionally and corruptly perform the act which forms the mistake in this case." There was no reason to fear that anyone could tell from this mistake how a particular voter had voted. To construe the statute as requiring the disqualification of these ballots was "a gross injustice," one that "no fair reading of any ballot law would permit." In addition to its "disenfranchisement on innocent electors," this "unreasonable and unnecessary" construction of the statute negated the "will of the majority" by denying victory to the candidate whom the voters had actually chosen and awarding the office instead "to one who in fact was never elected."[19]

One of the dissenting Republicans, Judge Charles Andrews, added his own opinion, and it echoed Peckham's outrage at the "injustice" of the court's "narrow, technical, harsh, and unnecessary construction of the law."[20] Taking on the argument advanced in Judge O'Brien's concurrence, Judge Andrews asked rhetorically: "Is it conceivable that it was the intention of the legislature in enacting [the new Australian ballot law] to place upon the voter the responsibility of ascertaining whether an official ballot delivered to him corresponds in every particular, in form, size, and indorsement, with the description in the statute, at the peril, in case of misjudgment, of a forfeiture of his vote?"[21] He answered his own question:

> The legislature must be supposed to have known that the great majority of voters are plain men, who would not be familiar with the details of a complicated statute. . . . The law obligates them to receive the ballot furnished them by the election officers. . . . The misstating on the ballot of the proper number of the election district would not be likely to attract their attention, and in the case in question it was known neither to the inspectors nor the voters.[22]

Consequently, like Judge Peckham, Judge Andrews concluded that the court's "decision defeats the will of the majority and subverts, in the particular case, the foundation principle of republican government." Invoking New York's narrow presidential election of 1884, Judge Andrews observed that the statewide margin there was fewer than the number of ballots invalidated in this state senate race by the court's ruling. "Corrupt officials," therefore, can use this kind of pretext to manipulate the outcome of an election. "In place of protecting the right of suffrage," the court's decision actually "destroys it."[23]

The dissenting opinions expressed what over a century later would be called "the Democracy Canon," namely the idea that election statutes should be construed wherever possible to favor counting ballots cast by eligible voters.[24] Judge Andrews was especially explicit on this point: "Assuming that [the statute] is capable of two constructions—one preserving the right of the voter, and the other forfeiting it—can it be doubtful which construction ought to prevail?"[25] But the Democracy Canon did not prevail in this case. The reason, it would seem, was the rank partisanship of the four judges who controlled the court's outcome. To be sure, those judges offered an explanation why they felt obligated to invalidate the ballots. From the perspective of the twenty-first century, however, that explanation does not withstand the withering attack of the dissents, including the one penned by Judge Peckham, a fellow Democrat. If the proverbial shoe had been on the other foot, and the invalidation of these ballots would have caused the defeat of the Democrat rather than the Republican candidate for this senate seat, one has little confidence that the court would have reached the same result. As a historian of New York's Court of Appeals has put it, "the perspective of more than ninety years later" has shown the court's decision in this case to have been "particularly troublesome."[26] More bluntly, the court majority seemed complicit in Governor Hill's machinations to give the Democrats control of the senate.

Third Targeted Seat

Hill, however, had more maneuvers in mind, ones that even these four Democrats on the Court of Appeals could not stomach or condone. As troubling as was the 4–3 ruling on the misdelivered Onondaga ballots, most disturbing of all was the way the Democrats took the third senate seat from the Republicans. Moreover, arithmetic showed that Hill did not need this additional seat in order to capture control of the senate.[27] But Hill was greedy and wanted an extra seat as insurance.[28]

This seat was for the fifteenth district, which included Dutchess County, where Poughkeepsie and other Hudson River Valley communities are located. The fight began with another dispute over the new Australian ballots, but one involving a different type of problem. Here, the problem was essentially a smudge that the printing process had left on the ballots. The Democrats claimed that these smudges were identifying marks that invalidated the ballots.[29] If these ballots were invalidated, the Democratic candidate again would prevail; otherwise, the Republican would win. But this argument was too much for any of the Democrats on the Court of Appeals, which unanimously ordered that the State Canvassing Board refrain from certifying a result that excluded these ballots.[30]

Instead, as the Court of Appeals explained, the State Canvassing Board should certify a corrected return from the county that included these ballots—assuming such a corrected return arrived by the board's deadline for certifying the result of the election. But Hill and his henchmen conspired to prevent the State Canvassing Board's timely receipt of the corrected return. The key figure in the conspiracy was Isaac Maynard, the state's deputy attorney general, who was specifically serving as the State Canvassing Board's counsel, a role that included arguing its cases in the Court of Appeals. After the county clerk delivered three copies of the corrected return to the appropriate state offices, as required by state law, Maynard managed to remove them from all three offices, so that they would be unavailable to the State Canvassing Board before the all-important certification deadline.

When the board met on the evening of December 29, several hours after the Court of Appeals had issued its ruling, the board had before it only the uncorrected return—called the "Mylod return" after the local official who had prepared it—that the Court of Appeals specifically had instructed it to

Figure 7.2 Isaac Maynard, deputy attorney general of New York, implemented the "Steal of the Senate" by mendaciously suppressing the corrected election returns, in defiance of a decree from the state's highest court. Florida Center for Instructional Technology, University of South Florida.

ignore. As investigations would later show, members of the State Canvassing Board undoubtedly knew that Maynard had purloined the copies of the corrected return. They were loyal Hill Democrats, and one, the attorney general, was Maynard's direct boss.[31] In any event, in direct defiance of the Court of Appeals, they proceeded to canvass the Mylod return and, with it, certify the Democrat as the winner of the seat.

Having secured this additional seat for the Democrats, Hill was assured that his party would control the senate come January. Mission accomplished. Afterward, the Court of Appeals held the members of the State Canvassing Board in contempt for their acceptance of the Mylod return in contravention of the court's order. This opinion, written by a Democrat (Judge John Clinton Gray), said that there was no room for any other conclusion:

> There was neither uncertainty nor ambiguity in the direction by this court . . . commanding the defendants to disregard the so-called

> Mylod return in issuing their certificate of election, and, instead thereof, to consider only such return as might thereafter be filed.[32]

Putting it bluntly, the court wrote: "What constitutes the contempt here is that the defendants, knowing of the order for the issuance of a preemptory writ of mandamus, have done the very thing which the issuance of the writ was intended absolutely to prevent."[33]

A Summation of the Stolen Senate

One history of New York, published in 1922, offered this assessment: "No such striking abuse of the election machinery had occurred in New York State since 1792, when John Jay was deprived of the governorship by the throwing out of votes of three counties on pretexts of the most extreme technicality in clear denial of substantial justice and the rights of voters."[34] While that comparison has validity as far as it goes, it does not go far enough. Yes, the Stolen Senate was similar to 1792 insofar as it involved ballots invalidated on overly technical grounds, with the consequence that the eligible electorate was denied the candidate of its choice. But the Stolen Senate also involved two egregious elements not present in 1792.

First was the State Canvassing Board's deliberate disobedience of the Court of Appeals decree, for which the board's members earned the court's official contempt. That flouting of a direct judicial order, in addition to subverting the choice of the eligible electorate in the particular election at issue, was entirely incompatible with the rule of law in a constitutional democracy. The hallmark of constitutional democracy—at least as practiced in America—is the power of the judiciary to require the executive branch's compliance with the court's interpretation of the state's laws. When that interpretation concerns the operation of the electoral process, executive branch defiance of the court's decree undermines democracy as well as the rule of law. Not even Governor Barstow of Wisconsin was willing to be that brazen in 1856. Like Governor Garcelon of Maine in 1879, however, Governor Hill and his cronies were willing to take that ultimately defiant and despotic step. New York in 1891, alas, lacked a Joshua Chamberlain to frustrate Hill's subversion of democracy and law.

Second, and even more disconcerting, was the intentional fraud perpetrated by Maynard and any member of the State Canvassing Board who knew of his misconduct. Above and beyond the defiance of the Court of Appeals' decree, which did not require knowing what had happened to the corrected return, were Maynard's deliberately deceitful moves to prevent that corrected return from reaching the board. Although this extra measure of deceit was not essential to the success of the Stolen Senate plot, it was especially heinous. Garcelon at least was open in refusing to obey his state's highest court. Maynard, as Hill's agent, was clandestine in disobeying the decree of his state's highest court.

After Maynard's treachery, the condemnation from leading lawyers—including prominent Democrats—was loud and clear. By then, Maynard already had been rewarded for his party loyalty with an appointment to the very court whose decree he had disobeyed. But the furious reaction to the truth, once exposed, left him in disgrace. The New York Bar Association issued an unequivocal report signed by Elihu Root, among other luminaries of seven Democrats and two Republicans:[35]

> Our conclusion, then, is that no justification of the removal of the corrected election returns from the offices of [the state's canvassers] on the morning of December twenty-second can be found.... [Furthermore, Maynard] saw the Board of State Canvassers violating the law and issuing a false certificate upon a false return, and making his act in removing the true return the pretext for their action.... The only way in which [the Democratic candidate] could be counted in was by suppressing the corrected return and counting the illegal one. As matter of fact, the illegal one was counted. As matter of fact, the corrected return was suppressed. [Maynard's conduct,] it seems very clear to us, could have possibly had no other end in view except the one that was actually accomplished.... The offence committed by Judge Maynard is one of the gravest known to the law.[36]

A historian of the state's highest court has observed: "No such public castigation has ever touched a judge of the Court of Appeals as that directed to Maynard."[37]

In short, partly because of Maynard's intentionally deceitful misconduct as New York's deputy attorney general and counsel for the State Canvassing Board, this Stolen Senate episode must be seen as a particularly low moment in the history of American democracy. But by no means is Maynard alone to blame for this disgraceful episode. The members of State Canvassing Board deserved being held in contempt for their willful disobedience of the Court of Appeals, and Hill is properly condemned for orchestrating the entire plot. Nor can the Court of Appeals escape criticism. Even if it refused to go along with the most extreme of Hill's maneuverings, and appropriately punished the flagrant flouting of its decree, the majority of that court sullied its judicial reputation by facilitating Hill's plan with respect to two of the three seats in contention. In both those instances, the court majority took dubious legal positions, apparently based on partisan motivations, that contradicted what the eligible voters wanted. If the court had been genuinely impartial in its rulings in all three cases, it is highly doubtful that Hill and Maynard would have been able to steal the senate, no matter to what lengths they were willing to go as part of their plot.

New York's Constitution of 1894

Three years after the Steal of the Senate, New York held a constitutional convention. Since 1886, when the electorate of the state had voted overwhelmingly in favor of calling a constitutional convention, the state had been under a legal obligation to hold one. But a deadlock between Governor Hill, arch-Democrat that he was, and the legislature, in Republican hands, had prevented the state from holding elections to select the delegates to a constitutional convention. Once Hill had accomplished his theft of the senate, Democrats controlled both chambers of the legislature as well as the governorship, and they proceeded with their plan to elect delegates to a constitutional convention based on a map that they had gerrymandered.[38]

The plan backfired. The elections were held in 1893, after the public had become thoroughly disgusted with the Democrats—in part because of the Stolen Senate (and especially Maynard's receipt of a high court judgeship in reward), in part because of other unethical conduct by Democrats, and in large part because of the economic collapse that year, for which the Democrats as the party in power were blamed. Accordingly, when the constitutional convention met in 1894, it was dominated by Republicans.[39]

The convention adopted several Republican-friendly electoral changes. One required that newly naturalized citizens wait 90 days before becoming eligible to vote. Another required that residents of towns with populations over 5,000 register in person in order to be able to vote; in other words, no registration by mail, except for residents of less populous localities. A third required that voting be by secret ballot only and permitted the use of new voting machines for this purpose. A fourth required that municipal elections be held at different times than statewide or federal elections—so that the influence of machine politics in the cities, which increased turnout among Democrats for municipal elections, would not extend to statewide or federal elections, in which Republicans had a fighting chance.[40]

The convention also adopted a rule that required local boards of elections, except again for some smaller town and village elections, to have "equal representation" of both major political parties. This provision is important because it is the first time that there was explicit recognition in the state's constitution that democratic politics in the state consisted of ongoing electoral competition between two main political parties. Although some form of a two-party system had existed since the Clinton-Jay election of 1792, and had become obviously permanent since at least the Whigs-Democrats battles of the 1830s, the state constitution had never before recognized the necessity of structural fairness between the two competing parties in the operation of the electoral process. But now, in the words of the sponsor of this measure, the constitution would "secure purity and absolute impartiality in the conduct of elections" with the adoption of this equal representation requirement.[41] As the principal chronicler of the convention put it, the delegates "seized the opportunity to intrench [*sic*] in the Constitution itself the important principle that under a government by party, election machinery should be under the [evenly bilateral] control of the two principal political parties."[42]

It is perplexing, however, that the delegates did not extend the principle of equal representation to the State Canvassing Board. It was, after all, the State Canvassing Board that had perpetrated the Stolen Senate just three years earlier (albeit at Governor Hill's request). And, of course, it was the State Canvassing Board that had acted on partisan impulse to deprive John Jay of his gubernatorial victory in 1792. Indeed, it was the lopsided partisan split of the State Canvassing Board in 1792 that had provoked James Kent to cry out for "an equally biassed" tribunal. Thus, if the delegates wanted to entrench the principle of equal representation for both political parties in the situation where it mattered most—when partisan control of a branch of state government hinged on the counting of disputed ballots—then they should have extended the principle beyond the local election boards to the State Canvassing Board itself. Yet the sponsor of the equal representation provision explicitly disclaimed any such intent:

> I will say that there is no effort to regulate the canvassing of votes after election. The law in that respect remains unaltered. This simply covers the case of registration, of the distribution of ballots and the voting as it occurs on election day. The matter of canvassing is, of course, unaffected.[43]

And again: "There is nothing in the constitutional amendment that refers to canvassing at all."[44] And yet again: "It refers only to the conduct of the election at the election, and not to proceedings after the election. It has no reference to canvassing."[45]

Why? It is not as if the delegates to the constitutional convention had forgotten the Stolen Senate episode. The president of the convention, Joseph Choate, had been the attorney for Republicans who sought and obtained the writ of mandamus that the State Canvassing Board had flouted. Choate, moreover, was no figurehead; rather, he took primary responsibility for the issues the convention addressed.[46] And Elihu Root, who had signed the report of the New York City Bar Association condemning Maynard for his participation in the senate theft, was the second most influential member of the convention. With these two men leading the convention, it was impossible that the body overlooked the Stolen Senate episode. Indeed, passing reference was made to it during debate.[47] Thus the only conclusion is that the delegates chose not to alter the structure of the State Canvassing Board, despite their desire to adopt the equal representation principle in the context of the authority of local election boards over the process of registering to vote and the casting of ballots.

There remains the vexing question of *why* did they not wish to apply their self-described important principle of equal representation to the State Canvassing Board. There can be no satisfactory definitive answer, but it is possible to offer some speculative explanations. One possibility is that the Republicans believed that they had adequately defeated Maynard. After his condemnation by the bar, the electorate thoroughly repudiated him in his bid to earn a seat on the state's highest court by means of election. Moreover, because the members of the State Canvassing Board had been held in contempt of court, Republicans may have felt that they had inflicted enough punishment to deter another attempt at such seriously egregious misconduct.

Also, as much as they could not have forgotten the Stolen Senate misdeeds, by the time the constitutional convention was underway the Republicans may have been focused on what they believed were more urgent electoral problems. There had been significant ballot-casting fraud in the election of 1893, and the equal representation provision was in large part designed to prevent that kind of misconduct.[48] On this view, the limitation of the equal representation provision to local election boards (in cities of a certain size) was not so much a rejection of applying the same idea to the State Canvassing Board as targeting this provision to a different kind of concern.

The delegates, too, may have viewed the State Canvassing Board as a merely ministerial body. It was not supposed to be a body on which partisan affiliation could make a difference. All it was supposed to do was arithmetically add up the local returns it received; it exceeded its power if it attempted to evaluate the validity of those local returns. Therefore, the delegates may have seen no reason to require that the equal representation principle apply to it. To the contrary, requiring equal representation of both political parties on the State Canvassing Board might have invited speculation that the board had more discretionary powers than was intended; in other words, that it was not merely ministerial after all.

Another factor may have been at work as well. The convention was well aware that the equal representation principle ran the risk of tie votes. The delegates explicitly discussed this risk.[49] Ultimately, they thought this risk worth taking at the local level with respect to the ballot-casting process. They reasoned (rightly or wrongly) that the implementation of election rules at the polls was an administrative matter, for which some flexible accommodation among members of opposing parties might be possible. In any event, they thought that one-party domination of the ballot-casting process was worse than the possibility of bipartisan deadlocks.[50] But a tie vote of the State Canvassing Board would be a different matter: election results had to be certified in order for the winning candidate to take office, and tie votes that prevented the certification of elections risked decapitating the entire state government. To be sure, the recognition that evenly divided partisans might end up with a tie vote, when applied specifically to the State Canvassing Board, is an idea somewhat in tension with the notion that this board is merely ministerial. Nevertheless, the fear of a deadlocked State Canvassing Board easily may have played a role in the convention's decision not to apply the equal representation principle to that body. Evidently, the convention did not consider the possibility of a nonpartisan, tiebreaking member of the body.

Finally, insofar as the Stolen Senate episode was so outrageous precisely because it involved high-level officials willing to disobey a direct court order and to intentionally lie about their conduct as part of their partisan power-grab, the convention delegates may have thought that no written constitutional provision ultimately could be effective against such power-hungry mendacity. They had to hope instead that future officeholders would exercise at least a bit more self-restraint. If so, and especially if the State Canvassing Board would truly confine itself to its purely ministerial role, then perhaps existing arrangements regarding its composition were adequate. And if not, perhaps no new arrangement could curtail a State Canvassing Board willing to go to the lengths that the one in 1891 did.

In any event, for whatever reason, the constitutional convention did not touch the composition or structure of the State Canvassing Board. It left in place the institution that had done such damage in the two worst instances of disputed elections in the state's history. Consequently, it left the state vulnerable to the possibility that another instance of the same sort might afflict the state in the future. And if the convention did not touch the State Canvassing Board because it could think of no reform that might be useful, then the convention failed to imagine the possibility of designing an institution with equal representation of the two major parties yet without the risk of deadlocking in tie votes. In the hyperpolarized political environment of the 1890s, even enlightened statesmen like Elihu Root could not imagine a figure worthy of sitting on the State Canvassing Board who would serve as a nonpartisan and neutral tiebreaker.

The New York City Mayoral Election of 1905

Although no bright line divides the Gilded Age from the Progressive Era, the one morphed into the other around the turn of the century. Thus, by 1905 the Progressive Era was well underway. Teddy Roosevelt had served out the bulk of McKinley's presidential term and in doing so had pursued his own progressive agenda.[51] Then, in November of 1904, after campaigning on his Square Deal platform, Roosevelt had won the presidency in his own right, achieving the largest landslide victory up to that point in American history. In New York, Roosevelt's home state, 1905 was the year that reform-minded Charles Evans Hughes earned widespread acclaim by exposing corruption, including campaign finance improprieties, in the life insurance and utilities industries.[52] The following year, Hughes would ride that wave of popularity to become New York's governor, a position Roosevelt had held before becoming vice president and then, upon McKinley's assassination, president.

Consequently, when New York City experienced an especially close mayoral election in 1905, it was a test of how well the leading city—in both the Empire State and the nation as a whole—could perform the basic democratic task of counting votes in this new Progressive Era. Sadly, the electoral system did not perform especially well. Marred by serious allegations of significant fraud at the outset, this election is noteworthy as a demonstration of just how confused and uncertain the legal regime was concerning how to handle a situation of this kind. Here, early in the twentieth century, participants in the drama sought a sensible method for counting ballots to choose the leader of a modern metropolis, but they were confounded by an antiquated and perplexing legal system that required them to rely on an ancient and outmoded method for challenging an election's apparent winner. Hughes led the effort to develop a fair and rational method for recounting the mayoral votes, but he was stymied by the Court of Appeals, which insisted upon a narrow-minded and misinformed interpretation of the state's new 1894 constitution.[53]

The cast of characters for the 1905 election was colorful. The incumbent mayor running for reelection was George McClellan, son of the Civil War general. McClellan was a Democrat who had the support of the Tammany machine.[54] His principal opponent was not a Republican, but rather the newspaper mogul William Randolph Hearst, who was running as an independent on a pledge to clean up city politics (although some questioned the sincerity of this pledge). The Republicans ran a relative nonentity, William Ivins.[55]

Election Day saw widespread reports of hideous misconduct, including "Hearst's poll watchers being beaten and shot at" and ballot boxes ending up in the East or Hudson Rivers.[56] There were also allegations of "floaters" and "repeaters" casting multiple ballots throughout the day.[57] When the initial returns the next morning showed McClellan ahead of Hearst by only 3,485 votes, Hearst vowed to fight on.[58]

The authority to canvass the returns lay initially with the city's Board of Aldermen, a body which Hearst did not trust, as it was dominated by Democrats. Therefore, Hearst filed suit in state court asking for a recount of ballots in precincts where, according to the tally sheets used in those precincts, the number of votes counted exceeded the number of ballots cast. Hearst cited section 84 of the state's election law, which appeared to provide that "the ballots must be recounted" where there was a discrepancy of this kind.[59]

The New York Court of Appeals, however, by a 5–2 vote, interpreted this statute as giving the local canvassing officials the sole discretion on whether to conduct a recount in this situation.[60] The justices in the majority were three Democrats and two Republicans. Two other Republicans were the dissenters. Thus the court was not as evidently partisan as it had been during the Stolen Senate debacle, but its fractured decision was a sign of weakness in the state's election law and jurisprudence.

The reasoning of the majority opinion was that a court-ordered recount is available only in a *quo warranto* proceeding, *after* the election result has been certified, with the defeated candidate bearing the burden of proving that the winning candidate is not entitled to the office. Hearst, by contrast, was seeking a precertification recount, and the majority did not believe that the judiciary could order such a procedure. The majority explained that the fear of court-imposed delay in the issuance of the certification motivated its statutory interpretation: "A good reason may be found for the noninterference of the court with the ministerial work of the election officers in the higher necessity that the result of a public election shall promptly be made known."[61] The court thus construed section 84 as "a guide to the inspectors of elections," telling them that "they must at once go over again and recanvass the ballots" if they find that they themselves made a mistake: "The section does not say, nor imply, that the court may, at some time subsequent to the closing of the election, order a recount."[62] The court also observed that the state's statutory law required that upon completion of the canvass, ballot boxes remain preserved "inviolate" for the benefit of a subsequent *quo warranto* proceeding. A court-ordered recount before certification of the election's result had the potential for undermining this statutory policy.

The majority acknowledged that its refusal to permit a precertification recount under section 84 ran contrary to several previous decisions from the same court. But the majority expressly disavowed those precedents in favor of its new policy-driven interpretation of the statute. The dissenters, not surprisingly, chastised the majority for repudiating the relevant precedents. The dissenters also took issue with the majority's policy views. The dissenters observed that the whole point of preserving the ballots—in contrast to permitting them to be destroyed after the initial count on election night, as the state's law previously had allowed—was to enable the possibility of achieving an accurate result: "It will certainly be a great disappointment to the citizens of the city of New York to be assured that they are in little or no better position in case of an alleged fraudulent count than under the old election law, when the burning ballots and memoranda formed a part of the bonfire which celebrated the current victory." The dissenters also viewed *quo warranto* as an inadequate remedy: "If it is to be the settled construction of the election law that the ballots, locked and sealed in the ballot boxes for six months after an election, cannot be recounted save in an action of *quo warranto*, which may drag for years through the courts, a new election law cannot be too soon drafted and enacted."[63]

This judicial call for a new election law was heeded by Hughes, once he became governor in January of 1907. Interestingly, Hughes's opponent in the 1906 gubernatorial election was William Randolph Hearst, who used his strong showing in the mayor's race (even if he had been "counted out," as he claimed) to propel his candidacy for even higher office. Hughes, however, wanted Hearst to have a recount of the 1905 mayoral election, albeit a much belated one. Yet the matter was not moot, as litigious skirmishes over the possibility of a *quo warranto* proceeding were still dragging their way through the state's judicial system. Whatever Hughes's motivation—most charitably, a pure desire to have the system achieve an accurate result; more cynically, a strategic ploy to help a political rival obtain a nonthreatening office—Hughes vigorously lobbied the legislature to enact a new recount law that would not depend on the vagaries of *quo warranto*.[64] "Our entire system of government depends on honest elections and a fair count," Hughes told the legislature in one of his first official acts as a governor.[65]

The legislature did what Hughes requested. But when Hearst attempted to take advantage of the new law, the Court of Appeals rebuffed him again—this time by ruling the new law unconstitutional. The court was now unanimous in this opinion, saying that the law violated at least one of two propositions. First, insofar as the law required the state's judiciary to recount the ballots, the law violated the state's constitutional requirement that all "counting votes" be done by "bipartisan" bodies on which both major parties are "equally represented"—as stated in the 1894 constitution. The court observed, perhaps somewhat ironically, that it was "apparent" that "the courts by whom the recanvass is to be made are not bi-partisan bodies." Second, insofar as the new law was a substitute for a *quo warranto* proceeding, as a "judicial determination of the title to office," then it violated the constitutional requirement that a jury determine any disputed issues of fact in a *quo warranto* proceeding.[66]

Figure 7.3 Charles Evans Hughes, as governor of New York, fought for passage of legislation to provide a fair recount of New York City's mayoral election of 1905. Portrait by Thomas Corner; N.Y. Hall of Governors.

The court's reasoning was rather dubious since, as we have seen, the authors of the 1894 constitution expressly disavowed any intent to have the requirement of bipartisan representation apply to the canvassing of ballots, as distinct from the conduct of election officials at precincts on Election Day. Nor did Hughes and the legislature view their new recount law as directly interfering with *quo warranto* itself; rather, they viewed it as precisely the kind of separate procedure that the Court of Appeals, in its prior ruling, had distinguished from *quo warranto* but had said that the legislature had not made available. Nonetheless, the court's latest decision was the final word on the validity of the new statute, and thus the statute was null and void.[67]

The court made clear that Hearst could still pursue a recount through a conventional *quo warranto* proceeding ("in that suit everything that is authorized or directed by the statute before us, opening the boxes, recount and the like, can be had"[68]), and that is exactly what Hearst did. In fact, he had filed for *quo warranto* back in 1905, but the attorney general of the state at the time had blocked the proceeding from going forward. One of the problems with the ancient writ of *quo warranto*—and thus one of the reasons why Hughes had pushed so hard for a more modern form of recount proceeding—is that *quo warranto* historically was a public action, initiated on behalf of the citizenry as a whole. Accordingly, the attorney general of a state, as the primary lawyer for the public, possessed the power to control a *quo warranto* proceeding.

In 1907, New York's new attorney general now permitted Hearst's *quo warranto* proceeding to go forward. McClellan, who held office as the city's mayor pursuant to the certification of election in December of 1905, objected to the renewal of the *quo warranto* proceeding. He argued that a new attorney general could not reinstate what the previous attorney general had vetoed. The judiciary, however, rejected McClellan's argument, permitting the case to proceed.

McClellan then argued that the attorney general was required to itemize with specificity how the count of the ballots would change if the case were to go to trial. The judiciary also rejected this argument, but this time in a 4–3 decision by the state's highest court. Two Democrats and two Republicans were in the majority, two Republicans and one Democrat in dissent: another deeply fractured ruling, but at least not along party lines.[69] The majority opinion agreed with the attorney general that it would be impossible to show with specificity how the count of ballots would change unless and until the ballot boxes were opened and the ballots recounted: "[The law] cannot require a plaintiff to furnish the particulars of evidence which is not within his power to furnish or preclude him from giving lawful and proper evidence upon the trial, by reason of his inability to specify in advance what such evidence will disclose."[70] As for some preliminary mini-trial on whether there was reason to think that election officials acted improperly, the majority thought it more efficient simply to move quickly to the main trial of what the ballots themselves showed concerning which candidate actually won the election: "Whether there were errors in the returns or an omission to count the ballots for the candidate for whom they were cast are questions which can be determined from the ballots themselves when the boxes are opened and the ballots are counted."[71]

The dissent countered that the attorney general "should be made to state with particularity such facts as justified his claim."[72] McClellan, the dissent continued, "was entitled to know what facts in each election district had affected the result of the balloting therein and the particular respects in which the law had been violated."[73] The dissent saw an important policy at stake:

> It would be intolerable if the Attorney General . . . or if any defeated candidate . . . may maintain such an action upon a general averment that a candidate other than the certified incumbent of the office had been elected. . . . [Otherwise,] it becomes possible to throw the result

of any election, state or local, in doubt upon vague and wholesale assertions.[74]

Like the majority, the dissent was making a valid point about the practical aspects of litigating this kind of case. But the issue of how much factual specificity to require at the start of the litigation has no easy solution, as subsequent cases would confirm.[75] The majority was on solid ground in observing that the request for a recount cannot be put to an impossible burden of demonstrating in advance what the recount itself will show.

In any event, the *quo warranto* action was permitted to go to trial, where Hearst's longstanding claims of fraud fizzled for lack of sufficient evidence. In the end the recount showed Hearst gaining only 863 votes, far from enough to overturn McClellan's victory.[76] The wait for this result, moreover, was excessively long. It came in June of 1908, almost three full years after the election itself.

While Hearst finally was given a chance to prove who really had won, the whole process showed a system in need of major repair. Whether or not a recount was available was unclear at the moment when clarity was most needed—right after Election Day, when the race was so close, and the cries of fraud so loud—and the judges themselves could not agree on most key points. Moreover, the unconstitutionality of Hughes's recount law, according to the state's highest court, meant that a recount could not occur without the approval of the attorney general, a discretion that might be exercised capriciously for partisan purposes. The Empire State clearly deserved better.

No Further Reform in Progressive New York

Nonetheless, little of significance changed in the aftermath of the Hearst recount mess. In 1915 New York had another constitutional convention, with an especially distinguished group of delegates, but its focus was on issues other than the counting of ballots.[77] One goal was to reorganize state government, including reducing the number of elective offices, giving the governor greater appointment powers. Another was to increase home rule for municipalities. The delegates also proposed enfranchising women. The convention considered, but did not adopt, the idea of making all election officials nonpartisan civil servants who would be required to pass a competitive exam. In any event, the draft constitution that the convention submitted to the state's electorate was overwhelmingly rejected, by more than two to one: 910,462 to 400,423.[78]

Nor was there meaningful improvement in New York's statutory law applicable to the counting and recounting of ballots. In 1911, Governor John Dix astutely remarked to the legislature that New York's election laws still suffered from being susceptible to excessive partisanship.[79] But his words produced no legislative change. A 1913 treatise on the state's election laws, written by a prominent attorney (who indeed had been Mayor McClellan's lawyer during the Hearst recount litigation), lamented that "the provisions of the laws as to these official canvasses are complex and unsystematic."[80]

Such was the state of affairs when, in 1918, New York's gubernatorial election was close enough that one of the candidates—in fact, the incumbent seeking reelection—wanted a recount, but was unanimously denied one by the state's highest court. The incumbent was Charles Whitman, a Republican, and the challenger was Al Smith (who would run unsuccessfully for president in 1928). The initial count showed Smith ahead by only about 12,000 votes out of almost two million cast.[81] Whitman went to court claiming at least a right to examine the ballots, even if this examination would not technically be a recount. The state judiciary, however, rejected this request as unnecessary and unduly burdensome prior to certification.[82] The Court of Appeals would not require even a reexamination of those ballots that had been protested at the time of the original canvass, because Whitman could not show that the original decisions of the election inspectors would be overturned.[83]

Whitman did not attempt a *quo warranto* proceeding. He was too far behind for that. Thus, New York escaped having its antiquated procedures being tested in a situation they could not handle. But that escape only forestalled the impetus for the kind of changes the state really needed. The Progressive Era ended with New York's leading reformers, including Charles Evans Hughes, unable to provide the state with a modern recount law.

The 1916 Presidential Election

Hughes is a leading protagonist in another Progressive Era saga of a missed opportunity for reform in the context of counting ballots. He is joined in this story by his progressive counterpart Woodrow Wilson, who had become New Jersey's reform-minded governor in 1911, the same year that Hughes had moved from New York's governorship to the US Supreme Court. In 1916 the two former chief executives of neighboring states, despite their shared commitment to progressive policies (including a shared record of supporting electoral reforms), were opposing candidates for the presidency. Wilson was the incumbent, having won the White House in 1912, when Roosevelt split the Republican Party by running his Bull Moose campaign against his protégé William Howard Taft. Hughes agreed to step down from the Court in an effort to reunite Republicans as their nominee.[84]

The views of the two candidates were close. Roosevelt quipped that Hughes was a "whiskered Wilson" and that they were separated only by a shave.[85] The result of the election itself turned out even closer. These two titans of the Progressive Era—Wilson had been president of Princeton University and, as a leading political scientist of his generation, the author of major books on American government, while Hughes would be reappointed to the Court as chief justice—must have realized how close their own election came to devolving into a repetition of the Hayes-Tilden debacle. Nonetheless, they did nothing (either together or separately) to provide the nation with a better mechanism for handling the kind of situation that, through sheer good fortune, they narrowly averted.[86]

California, with its thirteen electoral votes in 1916, ended up being pivotal to determining the Electoral College winner. Hughes did not concede defeat until November 22, when certification of California's canvass was essentially complete, with Wilson ending up winning the state by only 3,420 votes out of a total of just under a million (999,250).[87] Both sides lawyered up for a fight on an even more momentous scale than in the 1880s. Moreover, if Hughes had contested California, Wilson would have contested Minnesota, which had twelve electoral votes, and which Hughes won by only 389 votes out of 387,367 (one-tenth of one percent). Without either California or Minnesota, Wilson stood at 264 electoral votes, two short of the necessary majority at the time. Either California's thirteen or Minnesota's twelve would put Wilson over the top, with some room to spare. Hughes, on the other hand, needed both states, which would have given him 267 electoral votes, just barely enough.[88]

If the fight to win the White House had gone all the way to Congress, it is unclear what would have happened. The Democrats controlled the Senate; neither party had a majority in the House of Representatives. Applying the Electoral Count Act of 1887 would have been especially precarious in 1916. Invalidating California's votes would have raised the major interpretative uncertainty exposed by Senators Evarts and Hoar (as discussed in the previous chapter): would Wilson still have had a majority of electoral votes (on the theory that the denominator as well as numerator was reduced by invalidating California's thirteen), or would the House of Representatives have been entitled to elect Hughes using the special procedure of the Twelfth Amendment, in which each state had one vote (and which would have favored the Republicans, since they controlled a majority of state delegations in the House)? Fortunately for the nation, the inadequacies of the Electoral Count Act were never tested in 1916, as the election never came close to needing any method of congressional resolution.[89]

In the first few days after Election Day, there was loose talk on both sides about fraud and vote-buying in California. Nothing significant, however, materialized. While scrutiny of the returns revealed vote-tallying errors, they affected both sides equally and appeared random.

Some suggest that Hughes would not have fought the result regardless of what evidence turned up.[90] They argue that he was a reluctant candidate, who had really loved being on the Supreme Court, and he did not want to rock the boat given the growing international crisis involving the Great War in Europe. But newspaper accounts indicate that this assessment, while accurately capturing some of his sentiments, is insufficiently nuanced. There were at least some signals that Hughes was prepared for the possibility of a legal battle to win the presidency. As the *Washington Post* observed at the time, Hughes took a "judicial view [of] the matter," reflecting his background, and he was going to let his decision about what course of action to pursue be determined by the evidence.[91]

If the evidence had shown enough grounds for judicially contesting the result in California, Hughes likely would have acquiesced in the Republican Party's desire to wage that fight. Indicating the strength of their intent to go to court over California if necessary, Republicans retained former US attorney general George Wickersham to lead their legal team. That move was not dissimilar to the enlistment of James Baker to supervise the Republican legal effort in 2000.

For several days after the polls had closed, and while results were still uncertain, the chairman of the Republican Party, William Willcox, spoke to the press about his party's "demand [for] a recount in every State where the result was so close that ignorance or the mistake of election officials might change it."[92] Hughes had to restrain this litigious enthusiasm by publicly announcing that "in the absence of absolute proof of fraud no such cry should be raised to becloud the title of the next President of the United States."[93] But this announcement was careful not to foreswear any possibility of recounts; rather, they would be limited to instances in which scrutiny of the canvass "had disclosed good reasons for such action."[94]

Moreover, it was Willcox who prevailed upon Hughes to refrain from conceding until the official canvass was complete. If Wickersham and his team had uncovered significant problems in California, Hughes would have been hard-pressed to resist Willcox and the party in taking the next steps toward obtaining an accurate count. California's great success in 1916 was that despite a margin of less than 4,000 votes, it offered no ammunition with which to fight that kind of battle.

Yet California's success led to a larger missed opportunity. After Hughes conceded, he did not take up the cause of improving procedures to prepare for the next time a presidential candidate refused to concede until completion of the canvass in a pivotal state. Next time that pivotal state might not have the same success as California; instead, it might be more like Florida in 1876 (or Louisiana or South Carolina that same year). Nor did Wilson press upon the nation the necessity of improved procedures to resolve a disputed presidential election, even though as a professor he had written a book lamenting the failure of the justices serving on the Electoral Commission of 1877 to rise above partisanship.[95]

The Great War in Europe pushed aside any possibility of reforming the procedures for a disputed presidential election. Wilson and Hughes clearly were capable of bipartisan cooperation, but not to deal with the remote risk of another Hayes-Tilden fiasco—not when the war was an immediate reality. Before the November election, Wilson planned to let Hughes become president immediately, rather than waiting until March 4, if the returns had shown that Hughes had won. Pursuant to the plan, Wilson would have made Hughes his secretary of state, and then Wilson and his vice president would have resigned, so that Hughes would have become president in advance of his own inauguration.[96] But Wilson's bipartisan ingenuity was limited to the context of the crisis over the war in Europe. Neither he nor Hughes contemplated anything similar regarding the possibility of a constitutional crisis over the counting of electoral votes, despite their own experience of coming as close as any presidential candidates since Hayes and Tilden to a repetition of that kind of crisis.

Although one can understand why the 1916 presidential election did not produce a reform of the inadequate Twelfth Amendment, and its accompanying Electoral Count Act of 1887, this missed opportunity poignantly symbolizes the overall failure of the Progressive Era to develop innovative procedures for the adjudication of major ballot-counting disputes.[97]

8

America in the Middle of Its Century

A Tarnished Ideal

The 1920s and 1930s experienced something of a lull in the nation's encounters with major disputed elections. The US Senate, new to the task of reviewing ballots cast by voters as a consequence of the Seventeenth Amendment (ratified in 1913), had a less-than-stellar start. It conflated the question of whether a candidate had won more valid votes with the question of whether the candidate had engaged in campaign finance improprieties that might justify excluding an election winner from serving in the body. Thus, in denying a seat to the winner of Pennsylvania's 1926 election, the Senate invoked both the fact that considerable voting fraud had occurred, especially in Philadelphia, and also the fact that the winner had spent exorbitant sums in both the primary and general elections.[1] The problem, however, was that the amount of voting fraud, although disturbingly large, was not nearly enough to account for the winner's 170,000-vote margin of victory.[2] Insofar as the Senate fudged its reasons for excluding the winner—was it the voting fraud, or the campaign spending, or some combination of both?—the Senate lacked a coherent case for depriving Pennsylvania voters of representation by the candidate they had decisively chosen when considering the valid ballots cast in the election.[3] But if the Senate's verdict was a frustration of Pennsylvania's democratic choice, at least this impairment of democracy was confined to just one of the 96 seats then in the body. It did not undermine the democratic character of the popularly elected Senate as a whole.[4]

In 1931, the Senate came close to experiencing a ballot-counting dispute that threatened the functioning of the whole chamber. But like an asteroid that comes close to colliding with Earth but ultimately passes without leaving any trace of the near miss whatsoever, the Senate's flirtation with disaster in 1931 left no mark. What happened was that the 1930 elections produced an essentially even split between Democrats and Republicans in the Senate, with Hoover's vice president (Charles Curtis) being able to break ties in favor of the Republicans as necessary. But potentially disputable seats threatened to give the Democrats a chance to capture outright control of the chamber. This threat evaporated, however, once it became clear that any challenge mounted by the Democrats would have been meritless.[5] It is fortunate that the Senate did not confront a serious vote-counting dispute in 1931—like the one it would face from New Hampshire in 1974 (discussed in Chapter 9)—because then an all-out partisan fight over even just one seat could have paralyzed the entire body, preventing it from organizing itself at the beginning of its new term and preventing it from conducting any legislative business. That kind of legislative paralysis would have been especially problematic at a time when the nation was suffering the onslaught of the Great Depression. But, in actuality, the Senate's 1931 brush with a vote-counting disaster did no damage at all.

The nation continued to experience sporadic disputes over gubernatorial elections in the 1920s and 1930s, but none were especially earth-shattering—not even in the states in which they occurred—and there was nothing like the paroxysms of upheaval that had afflicted gubernatorial elections in the Gilded Age. New Jersey's 1937 election was the most disturbing of the period, because it showed that the state offered no forum for a candidate to get a fair hearing on a claim of serious electoral improprieties. This procedural deficiency occurred, moreover, in the state where Woodrow Wilson, as its progressive governor in 1911, had shepherded into law major electoral reform—thereby confirming that Progressive Era electoral reform largely ignored the problem of inadequate procedures for ballot-counting disputes. But the margin of victory in New Jersey's 1937 gubernatorial election was some 45,000 votes, more than the likely scope of the alleged electoral improprieties. The lack of a forum for considering the claim, although highly problematic in principle, most probably in this instance did not lead to the inauguration of a governor whom the voters had not chosen.[6]

As the 1940s approached, America had in place the electoral system that would define its character as a twentieth-century democracy. That system included the adoption of the Australian (government-generated) ballot as the principal mechanism for averting voter fraud. It was undoubtedly an improvement over what America had experienced even as late as the end of the nineteenth century. But it was a system that still left the nation vulnerable to close elections becoming ensnared by ballot-related mischief. The nation would receive unwelcome reminders of this unfortunate truth just as it was establishing its dominance as the preeminent global superpower.[7]

The two decades from America's entry into World War Two in 1941 to the inauguration of John F. Kennedy in 1961 are the centerpiece of the American century, both temporally and symbolically. In the forties, America helped save the world from Hitler and the totalitarian Axis. The fifties produced the quintessential American culture of suburbia, big cars, fast food, rock-and-roll, and Hollywood—all captured afterward by Hollywood itself in such iconic films as *Bye Bye Birdie* and *Grease*.[8]

It was a time when America was supposed to be at its best and do things right: "the greatest generation."[9] Having made the tanks that won the war, it would make the cars to rule the road.[10] America, the world's marquee democracy, surely could run elections properly and count votes correctly—or so that was the image that the nation wished to project both at home and abroad. After all, America was promising to bring democracy to all corners of the globe and to protect freedom from communism, as it had defeated fascism. The confidence, even (in hindsight) cockiness, of the country was evident in Kennedy's inaugural address: "We shall pay any price, bear any burden . . . to assure the survival and the success of liberty."[11]

Therefore, it tarnishes that national self-image to realize that some of America's most significant elections in this era were far from models of a well-functioning democracy. On the contrary, these important elections were examples of that most insidious pestilence to inflict a democracy: the deliberate stuffing of the ballot box in an effort to subvert the electorate's choice. What is more, when that ballot-box stuffing was detected and might prove the difference in the outcome of a major race, America's electoral system was unable to provide a remedy to undo or counteract the apparent electoral theft. America's failure to live up to its ideal of a well-functioning democracy, at the time when it was reaching the apex of its global ascendency, specifically concerned its continuing lack of satisfactory procedures to handle a dispute over potentially outcome-determinative invalid ballots. This incapacity was especially ironic insofar as the major elections it affected included Kennedy's own presidential election of 1960, as well as the critical career-elevating election in 1948 of his running-mate and successor, Lyndon Johnson.

The Battle Over Ballot Box 13

Americans who have heard the phrase "Ballot Box 13," especially in light of Robert Caro's multivolume biography of Lyndon Johnson, may know that this phrase relates to Johnson's rise to national prominence.[12] They might even know that Ballot Box 13 became the focal point of Johnson's questionable 87-vote victory over Coke Stevenson, the former Texas governor, in the runoff that was part of the primary to determine the Democratic Party's candidate for US Senator in 1948. But most Americans do not realize that Ballot Box 13, in addition to propelling Johnson into the Senate and toward the presidency, played a crucial role in the development of election law in the United

States. The litigation over Ballot Box 13 confirmed for another half-century, until *Bush v. Gore*, what *Taylor v. Beckham* had established a half-century earlier during the hideous fight over Kentucky's gubernatorial election of 1899: no matter how fraudulent or nefarious a state's vote-counting process, it was not susceptible to federal court intervention pursuant to the Fourteenth Amendment of the US Constitution. This purely jurisdictional doctrine would permit undemocratic features of Texas vote-counting procedures to continue without abatement, a fact that would have even greater national repercussions a dozen years later when Kennedy chose Johnson as his running mate because of Johnson's capacity to deliver Texas.

In 1948, Texas exemplified the worst features of representative government in the United States at the midpoint of the twentieth century. Texas was effectively a one-party state, and that party persistently engaged in race discrimination in the conduct of its primary elections. To say that Texas was operating a political system that qualified as a genuine democracy would be an inaccurate use of the term.[13]

Moreover, Texas law did not leave enough time between the primary process and the general election. The primary process included the possibility of a runoff if no candidate won a majority of the votes in the primary itself, and that is what happened in 1948. The runoff was on August 28, and although the general election was not until November 2, Texas law essentially required the general election ballot to be ready—with the name of the primary winner on it—by October 2, a full month earlier.[14] That meant there were only five weeks from the date the runoff ballots were cast to the practical deadline for when any disputes over those ballots must be finished. (Five weeks also happens to be the amount of time available for resolving any disputed presidential election under the Electoral Count Act; as the nation learned in 2000, five weeks does not guarantee enough time to complete litigation over a closely fought statewide race.)

There can be no doubt that "Landslide Lyndon's" 87-vote victory in the runoff was procured by fraudulent means. The two leading biographies of Johnson, Robert Dallek's as well as Caro's, both describe the addition of 202 extra votes for Johnson at the end of the tally sheet for Precinct 13 in Jim Wells County.[15] The fraud was perpetrated by taking the names of individuals who in fact had *not* voted, and, after the polls had closed, adding them at the end of the list of the voters who had actually cast ballots.[16] So brazen was this fraud that the perpetrators added the extra names in alphabetical order, as they appeared on a poll tax list, and they used a different color of ink than had been used to record the names of the actual voters.[17] Indeed, Caro's account, which is especially vivid, includes the confession of Luis Salas, who ordered and supervised the writing of the fraudulent names. Salas, during Caro's interview of him, produced a confessional memoir that Salas had written about the episode.[18]

There is some debate about whether Stevenson's campaign also engaged in ballot-box stuffing in this 1948 election. Dallek portrays Johnson's campaign as "fighting fire with fire"[19] and seems inclined to credit accounts that both sides were "stealin' votes."[20] But only Stevenson came forward with credible evidence of actual fraud, including testimony introduced in court—as Josiah Daniel's indispensible analysis of the judicial proceedings over this election observes.[21] Johnson neither rebutted Stevenson's evidence nor offered any evidence of wrongdoing on the other side. Dallek, too, ultimately embraces the consensus view that "the additional votes from South Texas [including Ballot Box 13] gave Johnson his narrow, last-minute victory."[22] Statistical analysis suggesting that Stevenson's vote totals, like Johnson's, may have been improperly inflated is not the equivalent of the eyewitness accounts—and even a documented confession—of the fabricated votes that were added to Ballot Box 13.[23]

Had court proceedings been completed on Stevenson's claim that Johnson's 87-vote margin of victory was a consequence of fraud, the inescapable

Figure 8.1 Luis Salas, who confessed to perpetrating the stuffing of Ballot Box 13, kept a copy of this photo memorializing the event and later gave the photo to journalist Ronnie Dugger; Lyndon Johnson also kept his own copy of the same photo, showing it to Dugger during an interview at the White House in 1967. LBJ Presidential Library.

conclusion is that Stevenson would have established the merits of that claim with judicially admissible evidence concerning the 202 fraudulent votes in Ballot Box 13; in contrast, from all that is known, Johnson had no comparable evidence with which to defeat Stevenson's claim in court. Indeed, the court-appointed special master who presided over Stevenson's case subsequently said that, based on the evidence he had heard, he would have sustained Stevenson's claim on the merits.[24] The special master, however, was divested of jurisdiction pursuant to the doctrine of *Taylor v. Beckham* before having a chance to render his ruling on the merits. The question inevitably arises: was Stevenson's failure to obtain a judicial ruling on his claim a consequence of a mistake he and his attorneys made in filing their claim in federal rather than state court, or instead was Stevenson forced to file suit in federal court because he had no opportunity for a fair hearing of his claim in state court? To answer this question, one must review what actually transpired.

The 202 extra votes in Precinct 13 were not reported until Friday, September 3, almost a full week after Election Day, on Saturday, August 28.[25] The initial returns from Precinct 13 on Election Night already were suspiciously lopsided: 765 for Johnson, 60 for Stevenson. Now they were much more so. As Johnson's large lead in Precinct 13 jumped considerably, only one extra vote was added for Stevenson.[26]

Stevenson sent three lawyers to Jim Wells County to investigate. They arrived on Tuesday, September 7, the day after Labor Day.[27] When they asked to examine the election records, as they were entitled to do under state law, the chair of the county Democrats refused. So Stevenson decided to go there himself, and he brought with him the legendary Texas Ranger, Frank Hamer, who among other feats had brought down Bonnie and Clyde. In a scene out of the Wild West, Stevenson and Hamer—with Hamer's hand ready to reach for his gun—marched down to the bank where the election records were, as a gang of local *pistoleros* (with their guns also in view) moved out of their way to let them proceed.[28]

Stevenson did get to inspect the election records, although he was not permitted to copy them. But his aides got enough of a look to see the 202 extra names added for Johnson (plus the one more name added for Stevenson) at the end of the voter list, in different ink and handwriting from all the previous votes, but in the same ink and handwriting as each other. They also noticed that these extra names were in alphabetical order, going through the alphabet multiple times: "When the end of the alphabet was reached then the A's began again—as if whoever had been writing the names had miscalculated and gotten to the end of the alphabet too fast, and had thereupon simply gone back to the A's and started over."[29] Even more tellingly, one of Stevenson's aides saw the tally sheet for Ballot Box 13 and saw that the "7" in Johnson's initially reported total of "765" votes had been changed to a "9"—"an additional loop [had been] added to the 7 to make a nine out of it."[30]

After examining these records, and while still in Jim Wells County, Stevenson secured affidavits from some of the individuals whose names were listed at the end of the voter list. All of these individuals swore they had not voted. There were also three dead persons listed among the extra voters. Furthermore, the last person named before the switch in ink signed an affidavit swearing that he voted shortly before the polls closed, adding credence to Stevenson's theory that the extra names were simply added fraudulently after the polls closed to give Johnson enough extra votes at the end of the canvass to put him over the top.[31]

But Stevenson did not secure this evidence until Friday, September 10,[32] a full week after the extra 202 votes had been reported—and almost two full weeks after Election Day, when speed was absolutely crucial to having any chance of overturning Johnson's putative 87-vote victory. In hindsight, when Stevenson's attorneys were denied access to the records on Tuesday, September 7, they should have filed suit immediately in state court seeking an order to produce them. Taking justice into his own hands even with the aid of Frank Hamer, while a dramatic move, was not a wise litigation strategy.

Stevenson also hoped that he could convince the executive committee of the Jim Wells County Democrats, which was undergoing a change in leadership, to correct the county's returns. The committee was planning to meet on Saturday, September 11, to consider Stevenson's request. But late at night on Friday, September 10, Johnson's attorneys went to a friendly state judge in Austin and got an injunction stopping the committee from amending the returns from Jim Wells County.

Simply put, Johnson beat Stevenson to the courthouse. If Stevenson had filed first, with a state judge potentially friendly to him, he might have been able to block Johnson's injunction. Not only might Stevenson earlier that week have gotten his own order to examine the election records from Jim Wells County, but on the strength of the evidence shown in those records (or based on the ongoing refusal to turn over those records), he might also have gotten a court order requiring the executive committee of the local Democrats to amend its return to delete the apparently fraudulent 202 extra votes added six days after the polls closed. Had Stevenson obtained that kind of court order by Friday, September 10, he would have changed the entire posture of the litigation.

It is true that the local state judges in Jim Wells County would not have been receptive to a Stevenson petition of this kind. Because of local politics, dominated by George Parr (the so-called Duke of Duval), they were predisposed to be more favorable to Johnson. But Johnson had gotten his injunction from a judge in Austin, and it seems implausible that Stevenson—the popular former governor—could not have found his own potentially receptive judge in the state capital. In any event, even if he had been denied relief in state trial court, there was precedent for going straight to the Texas Supreme Court in a case involving a high-stakes vote-counting dispute when time is of the essence.[33]

On Monday, September 13, the State Executive Committee of the Texas Democratic Party met to certify the statewide results of the party's primary. During a dramatic meeting that night, the State Executive Committee voted 29–28 to accept the county's submission containing the 202 extra votes and, as a result, certified Johnson's 87-vote victory.[34] The party's convention ratified the State Executive Committee's certification the next day. Because of the party's control over the primary election under Texas law, this certification was tantamount to one from the state's authoritative canvassing board.

Stevenson immediately decided to contest the certification. He did so, not by filing an action in any state court, but instead seeking an injunction in federal court. That move was ultimately unsuccessful. Whether or not it was the wrong move depends on whether he had alternatives. Although it would have been better to bring a precertification claim in state court (along the lines just discussed), it still was not too late to start a postcertification proceeding in state court. Although the Jim Wells County courthouse would not have been a hospitable venue for such a lawsuit, Stevenson could have filed suit in Austin or even in Fort Worth, where the Texas Democratic Party held its convention that year—and thus where the party's certification of Johnson's 87-vote victory had occurred.

Stevenson also could have considered a *quo warranto* petition directly in the Texas Supreme Court. Because Johnson had been certified for a spot on the general election ballot, he was technically holding the "office" of a certified candidate under state law, and *quo warranto* could have been used to try Johnson's title to that public office. Alternatively, the emergency procedure of "certiorari before judgment" could have been used to get the case in the Texas Supreme Court when otherwise there would be no time to appeal an adverse judgment from a lower court.[35]

Stevenson, however, tried none of that. Instead, he rolled the dice—a big gamble—and filed suit in federal court on the theory that the fraudulent fabrication of extra votes in Precinct 13 of Jim Wells County violated the Fourteenth Amendment of the US Constitution. It was a theory directly contradicted by the controlling *Taylor v. Beckham* precedent. If the fraudulent fabrication of extra votes in the Kentucky gubernatorial election of 1899 was not a Fourteenth Amendment violation cognizable in federal court, as the US Supreme Court had expressly held in *Taylor v. Beckham*, then neither was the fraudulent fabrication of extra votes in a Texas primary election for US Senator.

Taylor v. Beckham had never been overturned. On the contrary, just four years before Stevenson's battle with Johnson, in *Snowden v. Hughes* the US Supreme Court explicitly reaffirmed the jurisprudential principle of *Taylor v. Beckham.*[36] *Snowden* involved a state canvassing board's failure to certify a candidate's primary election victory despite having won enough votes under state law to earn a spot on the general election ballot. Notwithstanding the board's flagrant frustration of the primary electorate's will, the US Supreme Court in *Snowden* refused to permit the federal judiciary to offer any relief. "The unlawful administration by state officers of a state statute fair on its face, resulting in its unequal application to those who are entitled to be treated alike, is not a denial of equal protection," the Court elaborated in its reaffirmation of *Taylor v. Beckham,* "unless there is shown to be an element of intentional or purposeful discrimination between persons or classes."[37] By this caveat, the Court had in mind racial discrimination, as the Court made clear from the other precedents it cited. Absent such discrimination, however, the doctrine of *Taylor v. Beckham* precluded federal court consideration of the case.

Stevenson was not claiming that race discrimination motivated the stuffing of Ballot Box 13. Thus, his case was comparable to *Snowden.* Given how recent and emphatic a ruling *Snowden* was, Stevenson's lawyers must have realized that they had virtually no chance of success in federal court. Consequently, they must have thought that they had absolutely no chance whatsoever of succeeding in state court.

Stevenson's attorneys may have hoped that they could make some use out of *United States v. Classic,* a 1941 criminal case in which the Supreme Court had sustained the theory of a federal indictment for ballot-counting fraud in a congressional primary election. The Court's reasoning in *Classic,* however, did not rest on the Fourteenth Amendment—the Court made that explicitly clear.[38] Instead, the Court there relied upon the power of Congress under Article One of the Constitution to regulate congressional elections, including by the enactment of criminal laws to protect the purity of those elections. Pursuant to that same Article One power, Congress *could* enact rules for recounts in US Senate elections or authorize federal court proceedings to contest the certification of US Senate elections, including primary elections. (Any such congressional statutes under Article One would only displace *state* procedures otherwise applicable to Senate elections, so that they would not interfere with *the Senate's* ultimate constitutional authority as "the Judge of the Elections, Returns, and Qualifications of Its own Members.") But Congress had not yet enacted those kinds of laws—in sharp contrast to the criminal statutes that Congress had enacted. At the time Stevenson filed his federal lawsuit, there was no federal statutory basis for a civil action in federal court to contest the certification of a US Senate election. Resting on Article One grounds, *Classic* consequently held no hope for Stevenson. The only federal statutes available to Stevenson in 1948 existed to protect Fourteenth Amendment rights, not Article One powers. But three years after *Classic, Snowden* confirmed that (absent race discrimination) the Fourteenth Amendment provided no federal court basis to complain of improprieties in state procedures used to certify the results of an election.

Stevenson, at least, found himself a sympathetic federal trial judge, T. Whitfield Davidson, who sat in Fort Worth (not Austin, thus underscoring the point that Stevenson might have filed in *state* court in Fort Worth).[39] As soon as he received Stevenson's papers on Wednesday, September 15, Judge Davidson issued a temporary restraining order to block Johnson's name from going on the ballot. He set a hearing for six days later, Tuesday, September 21. With the clock ticking, Stevenson should have asked for the hearing to be scheduled sooner.

Meanwhile, Johnson went to the Texas Supreme Court seeking a writ of mandamus to require the secretary of state to place his name on the ballot. The court declined based on an affidavit from the secretary of state saying that he indeed would put Johnson on the ballot, given the certification of the Texas Democratic Party, unless judicially ordered otherwise.[40] This delphic pronouncement from the Texas Supreme Court, refusing to give Johnson exactly what wanted but rather adopting a wait-and-see posture, suggests that Stevenson at least had some chance of fair hearing in that body, if he had endeavored to plead his case there.

On September 21, Judge Davidson rejected Johnson's motion to dismiss Stevenson's case for lack of jurisdiction. In open court, Judge Davidson announced that Stevenson "would still have an equitable hearing in this court" even "if there was no statute on the books" applicable to the situation.[41] As he stated later in his memoirs, repeating a point he made at the hearing, his overarching judicial philosophy was: "There shall be no wrong without a remedy."[42] Consequently, he began to hear Stevenson's evidence concerning the fraudulent addition of the extra 202 votes for Johnson in Precinct 13 of Jim Wells County. Stevenson's witnesses were able to get on the record their unrebutted testimony concerning the change in ink, and the listing of the additional names in alphabetical order. There was also the testimony of individuals listed among the extra names of voters, who swore in federal court that they had not voted that day. Johnson's attorneys offered no evidence of their own to contradict Stevenson's account of the fraud.[43]

After hearing this evidence Judge Davidson announced on Wednesday, September 22, that he was appointing a special master to go to Jim Wells County and examine the election records for Precinct 13. He did not require the special master to act with any particular haste. His only instruction was that the master report back by October 2, the effective deadline for putting a candidate's name on the ballot.[44]

The master scheduled a hearing in Jim Wells County for Monday, September 27. The tally sheet at the bank, which Stevenson had seen, had been lost, or at least that is what one witness claimed. (This witness was Luis Salas, the one who later confessed that he had intentionally committed perjury and indeed had perpetrated the fraud).[45] The master then ordered that Ballot Box 13 itself be opened, as it should contain another copy of the tally sheet.[46] But first Ballot Box 13 would need to be found among the other ballot boxes from Jim Wells County. On Tuesday, September 28, the master began examining ballot boxes one at a time because many of them were not marked with their precinct number. Because of delays the hearing was adjourned until the following day. On Wednesday, September 29, it was necessary to get a locksmith, because keys for many of the padlocks were missing.[47] As the master was progressing through the boxes (after the locksmith had opened them), word came that Justice Hugo Black of the US Supreme Court had enjoined any further proceedings in the case and had lifted Judge Davidson's temporary injunction against Johnson's name going on the ballot. Box 13 would never be opened, thus never providing direct confirmation of the ample unrebutted evidence already in the record of the federal court proceeding of the fraud that had been committed.[48]

Johnson's attorneys, with Abe Fortas in the lead, had devised a strategy for getting the case to Justice Black as quickly as possible. The plan called for an immediate appeal of Judge Davidson's temporary injunction to the US Court of Appeals for the Fifth Circuit, with the goal of losing quickly there, so as to get the case faster to Justice Black, who had responsibility for reviewing emergency petitions from the Fifth Circuit. On Wednesday, September 22, the same day that Judge Stevenson appointed the special master and extended his temporary injunction, Johnson's lawyers filed their Fifth Circuit appeal. Two days later, on Friday, September 24, Johnson had his Fifth Circuit order refusing to nullify Judge Davidson's rulings.[49]

On Saturday, September 25, Fortas presented his emergency application for a stay of the proceedings. On Sunday, Black said he would entertain the application, setting an unusual in-chambers hearing for Tuesday, September 28. At the hearing, Fortas argued that, plain and simple, the federal judiciary lacked jurisdiction over the matter; it was an issue for state courts.[50] Justice Black agreed with that position: "The legal principle involved was not complicated: federal courts are supposed to stay out of state elections"[51]—exactly the holding of *Taylor v. Beckham* five decades earlier. As much as Stevenson's lawyer tried to get Justice Black to focus on the fraud, those facts were simply not cognizable in this federal court case.

Black orally announced his decision after lunch on Tuesday, but it was not put in writing until the next day.[52] Thus down in Jim Wells County, the special master continued to search among the ballot boxes for the telltale one from Precinct 13. Black's written order, however, arrived before he found the right box.

By that date—Wednesday, September 29—it was, as a practical matter, too late for Stevenson to seek relief in state court, with the October 2 deadline just three days away. He did not even bother to try. Instead, there were merely some mopping-up proceedings back in the Fifth Circuit to confirm Justice Black's ruling.

Because Stevenson never attempted to seek relief in state court, no one can determine conclusively whether or not the Texas judiciary as a system was incapable of treating his claim fairly. One can, of course, be suspicious of a state judiciary whose members are themselves elected, as was the case in Texas. But because the dispute concerned a primary election, it is not enough to know whether the justices of the Texas Supreme Court were Democrats or Republicans to assess the extent to which that body might have been biased toward one side or the other. And, as for Democrats on the Texas Supreme Court at the time, it would be foolish to speculate whether they would have come to a hypothetical case as Johnson Democrats or Stevenson Democrats.[53]

The Texas electoral system itself was riddled with fraud. The stuffing of Ballot Box 13 was just one particularly glaring instance of practices that had occurred in the state before 1948 and would occur again afterward.[54] But that fact is not the same as saying that the Texas judiciary was utterly incapable of removing the taint of fraud in a high-stakes statewide election when the margin was exceptionally close. One can harbor suspicions, but they must remain inconclusive. This much, however, is clear: in 1948 Texas did not provide a procedure capable of inspiring public confidence that it would achieve an accurate and fair determination of which candidate, Johnson or Stevenson, actually received more valid votes. That failure alone, at a time when postwar America was proclaiming itself as a model of democracy to the world, is a stark indication that Texas was unable to practice what the nation preached.

Stevenson asked the US Senate to investigate the Texas primary. But it being a primary, rather than a general election, the Senate had little incentive to dig deeply. There was no doubt, after all, that Johnson had won the general election once he was on the ballot as the Democratic Party's nominee. There was even less incentive for the Senate to investigate after the Democrats became the majority party in the chamber, as they did in January of 1949.[55] Nonetheless, the seating of Johnson in the Senate that January, and all the subsequent electoral victories in his remarkable career, could never erase the stain of the flagrant fraud that launched "Landslide Lyndon" on his way.

Figure 8.2 "Landside Lyndon" was indelibly tainted by the ballot-box stuffing that clinched his 1948 US Senate victory, as portrayed in this cartoon three decades later. Bob Englehart Collection, The Ohio State University Billy Ireland Cartoon Library & Museum.

If Lyndon Johnson's rise to the Senate in 1948 was emblematic of American representative government in the middle of the twentieth century, it was a poor showing. Regardless of doubts about the capacity of the Texas courts to provide impartial justice to Coke Stevenson, and regardless of Stevenson's mistaken calculation not to give the Texas courts even a try, the glaring shortcoming from the perspective of the twenty-first century is Hugo Black's refusal to let the federal judiciary guarantee the sanctity of the ballot box. Black's decision was undoubtedly correct as a matter of precedent, given the Supreme Court's decision in the Kentucky case of *Taylor v Beckham*. But that precedent, dubious from the start, was no longer suited to the nation that America had become, or at least professed to be, after World War Two.

As a matter of constitutional principle, Justice John Marshall Harlan's dissent in that turn-of-the-century Kentucky case had the better of the argument, just as Harlan's dissent in *Plessy v. Ferguson* did.[56] Harlan, however, was ahead of his time. A half-century later, the times were catching up. By the middle of the twentieth century, the separate-but-equal doctrine of *Plessy* was ripe for overruling. So too was the self-negating jurisdictional limitation of

Taylor v. Beckham, that the federal courts had no power to protect the voting rights of citizens from even blatant ballot-box stuffing. In just a few short years, the US Supreme Court would eviscerate the rationale for *Taylor v. Beckham* with its 1962 pronouncement in *Baker v. Carr* that the political question doctrine (upon which *Taylor v. Beckham* rested) had no applicability to the protection of voting rights under the Fourteenth Amendment.[57]

Baker v. Carr would be a vindication of Justice Harlan's magisterial dissent in *Taylor v. Beckham*, just as *Brown v. Board of Education* would vindicate his *Plessy* dissent.[58] But this vindication would come too late to benefit Coke Stevenson. In 1948 the overruling of *Taylor v. Beckham* was not quite ripe enough—at least not in the context of an emergency stay application presented to a single justice on the Court.

1960: No Procedure for a Fair Fight

The 1960 presidential election was not disputed in the way that the elections of 1876 and 2000 were. Richard Nixon publicly conceded that he had lost to John Kennedy on the morning after Election Day, and in the days that followed he rejected the repeated urging of fellow Republicans (including President Eisenhower) that he pursue recounts in Illinois and Texas, which if both successful would have given him an Electoral College majority and thus the presidency.[59]

Nixon knew he could not win a presidential recount in 1960. He needed to prevail in *both* Illinois *and* Texas. Neither alone would be enough. Even if he could prove that Mayor Daley of Chicago had stolen Illinois for Kennedy, he would also need to prove that Lyndon Johnson's machine had stolen Texas for the Kennedy-Johnson ticket. But the Johnson machine controlled all of Texas government at the time, including the state's judiciary as well as legislature. Whatever the reality of the situation, Nixon had no prayer of proving in a Texas court that a legitimate count of valid ballots in the state would show him, rather than Kennedy, winning.[60] And Coke Stevenson's case against Johnson of only a dozen years earlier, by going all the way to the Supreme Court and ending with Justice Black's emphatic denial of federal court jurisdiction, demonstrated conclusively that Nixon had no recourse in federal court to show that he, not Kennedy, really had more valid votes there. Consequently, Nixon, the pragmatic politician, saw no reason to demand a recount in Illinois, even assuming he could get a fair one there, when it was utterly pointless to pursue one in Texas.

To be sure, given available evidence, it is impossible to say that Nixon would have prevailed if fair recount procedures had been available to challenge the outcome in both Illinois and Texas (and assuming, with such procedures available, Nixon the pragmatist would then have pursued them). Kennedy's reported lead in both states, while narrow, was not nearly so narrow as the Florida leads that either Hayes had in 1876 or Bush would have in 2000. It would have been a daunting litigation challenge for Nixon to reach an Electoral College majority in 1960 even supposing the presence of impartial tribunals for adjudicating the two cases.

Still, the available evidence suggests that the two cases, if adjudicated impartially, would have been much closer than many realize or might care to admit. Indeed, the best historical judgment to be made is that one cannot be at all confident how litigating the results in Illinois and Texas would have turned out if conducted with procedures fully fair to both sides. This conclusion is disconcerting. It shows that the 1960 presidential election was not "beyond the margin of litigation," to use post-2000 terminology.[61] Rather, it was not susceptible to litigation because there was no adequate procedure with which to litigate potentially winning claims.

This analysis of 1960 is inevitably, if regrettably, yet another indictment of the electoral system that America had at the time. It means that America, despite then claiming to be the world's preeminent democracy, continued to lack a vote-counting mechanism for accurately determining which candidate won an especially competitive presidential election. Given this analysis, moreover, 1960 must be seen as similar to 1876 and 2000 even though Nixon never contested the outcome. If the problem with both 1876 and 2000 was that nation's vote-counting system could not produce an accurate count of the valid ballots in a presidential election (a judgment that must await Chapter 11), then 1960 is another example of a presidential election revealing the same problem. The implication is significant: it is much easier to dismiss two such instances as aberrational, especially when spaced a century apart; it is much harder to do when the same problem appears in triplicate, with two of the three instances occurring recently and only forty years apart—and thus within the space of just ten presidential elections.[62]

Given the sobering implications of this analysis, it merits some elaboration of its component premises.

Texas

Initial returns showed Kennedy ahead of Nixon in Texas by about 40,000 votes, an apparently insurmountable lead.[63] (Official returns later would pin Kennedy's victory at 46,257.[64]) It certainly was vastly larger than Landslide Lyndon's 87-vote margin in 1948. Any recount lawyer would immediately tell a client candidate that overcoming a 40,000-vote deficit would be extraordinarily difficult even if the fairest of procedures were available to challenge it.

One might think, moreover, that a lead that large was immune from the taint of fraud. In other words, even if Johnson's allies in Texas engaged in some ballot-box stuffing in 1960, as they had in 1948, presumably it would not have occurred on a scale to account for Kennedy's margin of victory in the state. On this presumption, Kennedy's Electoral College majority would be fair and square—and thus his title to the presidency free and clear—whatever may have happened in Chicago.

Yet despite the size of the margin, recent retrospectives on the 1960 election cast doubt on the validity of Kennedy's Texas victory. They suggest that the pro-Johnson machine might have been capable of perpetrating enough vote-rigging to account for all of Kennedy's margin of victory—and more. The historian W. J. Rorabaugh in his book *The Real Making of the President*, timed to commemorate the half-century anniversary of the election, reviews the available evidence and concludes: "By comparing poll books to the vote count, it was clear that 100,000 votes had been counted that simply did not exist."[65]

Although Rorabaugh is careful not to claim that all these extra votes were tallied for Kennedy rather than Nixon, he goes on to consider an additional and relevant "oddity" in Texas's voting process that year. Many localities in the state used "negative ballots" that required voters to cross out the names of all the candidates whom they did *not* want to win, leaving unblemished the name of the single candidate they favored. In 1960, there were four presidential candidates on the ballot, and thus voters were required to cross out three names. There was evidence to indicate that Democrats in control of the counting process invalidated ballots if only Kennedy's name was crossed out (not counting those ballots for Nixon because two other names were also unblemished) but counted as votes for Kennedy ballots with only Nixon's name crossed out (even though these ballots also had two other unblemished names). At the time, "Republicans charged that more than 100,000 Republican ballots had been disallowed in Texas, and thousands of Democratic ballots with the same type of error had been added in."[66]

Although finding the evidence ultimately inconclusive, Rorabaugh cites several specific examples that tend to substantiate this charge. For instance, in Fort Bend Precinct 1, which favored Nixon, 182 ballots were disqualified, while in Fort Bend Precinct 2, which went overwhelmingly for Kennedy, none were invalidated. Based on Rorabaugh's analysis, it is plausible to conjecture that the combination of over 100,000 fabricated votes statewide and a possibly similar number of inconsistently treated "negative ballots" (Nixon's voided, Kennedy's counted) might have been what gave Kennedy his victory in the state. In any event, Rorabaugh at least makes the case that the validity of Kennedy's victory in the state, despite its superficially large margin, is not entirely free from doubt.[67]

Robert Caro, in *The Passage of Power* (volume four of his LBJ biography), corroborates Rorabaugh's disquietude about the 1960 vote in Texas. In addition to echoing the point about the "negative ballots," Caro claims that pro-Johnson fraud in areas controlled by George Parr, the Duke of Duval, was essentially as prevalent in 1960 as 1948. Caro quotes Ed Clark, a Texas secretary of state known as the "secret boss" of the state: "Down on the border . . . the leaders did it all. They could vote 'em or count 'em, either one." Caro then bluntly asserts that in 1960 just as in 1948 "George Parr counted them for Lyndon Johnson." After examining "the nine counties controlled by Parr and his allies," Caro concludes that Kennedy "came out of these counties with a plurality of 21,691"—not enough to account for all of his statewide margin by any means, but enough to account for almost half of it.[68] Caro, like Rorabaugh, stops short of asserting that Kennedy owed his Texas victory to vote-counting fraud. But also like Rorabaugh, Caro clearly wishes to leave his readers thinking that vote-counting fraud might have been the decisive factor in Texas in 1960. If Caro and Rorabaugh are correct, no one should be confident that Kennedy's victory in the state would have survived had it been subjected to the scrutiny of an impartial recount process.

Illinois

With Texas open to doubt, it becomes necessary to consider Illinois. If Illinois also is open to doubt, then by virtue of simple arithmetic so is the entirety of Kennedy's Electoral College victory.[69] It matters, then, whether there is substance to the allegations that Daley stole Illinois for Kennedy. Without an unimpeachable Texas victory to depend on, Kennedy's legacy requires his Illinois win to be irrefutable for his presidential victory as a whole to be unclouded.

Kennedy won Illinois by 8,858 votes, according to the officially certified results.[70] A partial court-supervised recount of another race on the ballot in Cook County that year, the office of the state's attorney in Cook County, showed that that the officially certified result of *that* election undercounted the total for the Republican candidate, Benjamin Adamowski, by 8,875 votes—or roughly the same amount as Kennedy's margin of victory.[71] A sophisticated analysis of that partial recount by the historian Edmund Kallina in *Courthouse over White House* offers reasons to believe that Nixon would not have gained as much as Adamowski from an equivalent court-ordered recount. (There was no such court-supervised recount of the presidential race in Illinois.) In an earlier administrative recount of the paper ballots in Cook County, which looked at the votes for both of these races, Adamowski gained significantly more votes than Nixon. Therefore, Kallina reasons, Adamowski's gain in the subsequent court-ordered recount should be discounted proportionally in order to estimate how much Nixon might have gained from a court-supervised recount.[72]

Kallina's analysis, while meticulous and tenable, still leaves the matter subject to some uncertainty. First of all, the administrative recount had been conducted by Chicago's board of elections, which was under control of the Democrats and not known for its electoral impartiality. Second, as the subsequent court-supervised recount demonstrated, the earlier administrative recount had been wildly inaccurate even with respect to the amount of Adamowski's gain—and, as Kallina himself recognizes, these severe inaccuracies cannot be attributed to honest mistakes but instead must be deemed an intentional manipulation of the count.[73] Might not Chicago's election officials have been intentionally undercounting Nixon's vote even more during the earlier administrative recount, since the national spotlight in November and December of 1960 was so intently focused on the presidential election? Presumably the Daley machine did not want the administrative recount to suggest that Illinois indeed may have been stolen for Kennedy. Ultimately, as Kallina explicitly acknowledges, the court-supervised recount demonstrated "that the results of the [earlier administrative] recount cannot be taken literally for either the state's attorney race or, by implication, for the presidential race."[74] One is left with the admittedly inconclusive, but nonetheless unsettling, fact that the partial court-supervised recount showed that a Republican candidate on the 1960 ballot in Cook County had been deprived of essentially the same amount of votes as Kennedy's margin of victory in the state.

Moreover, the court-supervised recount was partial in that, like the administrative recount, it only covered precincts that used paper ballots rather than voting machines. It was also incomplete, even with respect to these paper ballots, insofar as it did not attempt to disqualify ballots on grounds of voter ineligibility or other improprieties. It was, in other words, simply a recount of the paper ballots as cast. Thus the partial court-supervised recount did not address what were viewed as the most serious allegations concerning the efforts of the Daley machine to win the presidential election for Kennedy: the fabrication of invalid votes whether cast on paper or machine.[75]

There undoubtedly was some significant amount of vote fabrication by Chicago Democrats in the 1960 election. As Kallina himself concludes in a subsequent book, *Kennedy v. Nixon*, "Democrats committed a massive amount of vote fraud in Chicago in 1960."[76] But the question remains whether there was enough of it to be the cause of Kennedy's victory in the state. Kallina observes that a special prosecutor's report released in April of 1961 casts doubt on many of the most sensationalistic claims made by Republicans in the immediate aftermath of Election Day.[77] Based on his own extensive review of the evidence, Kallina thinks that "tens of thousands" of votes is the amount "stolen" by Democrats "in the state's attorney's election,"[78] and the special prosecutor himself estimated that 10,000 votes was the amount by which Adamowski had been wronged.[79] But Kallina does not believe that Chicago Democrats also stole as many votes on behalf of Kennedy, and the special prosecutor was careful not to venture an opinion about what an honest count of the presidential election in Chicago would have shown.

Does it make sense that the Daley machine would steal tens of thousands of votes in a local race, but not in the presidential election on the same ballot? Perhaps. "All politics is local," after all. Moreover, Chicago Democrats were particularly fearful of a local prosecutor's power to indict them for improprieties and thus had particularly powerful reasons for wanting to keep this local office out of Republican hands.[80]

There are reasons to be skeptical, however, that the Daley machine would have been effective in stealing the local prosecutor's race but not the presidential election at the top of the ticket. For one thing, the mechanics of a disproportionately down-ballot theft seem odd. As Kallina also explains, the vast majority of precincts in Chicago used voting machines rather than paper ballots, and examination of these voting-machine precincts (both immediately after the election and in the subsequent special prosecutor's investigation) did *not* reveal a significant discrepancy between the number of votes recorded on the machines and the number of votes reported on the tally sheets for those precincts.[81] Thus, if there was fraud in these precincts, it must have been in the casting of votes on the machines, not in the counting of these votes afterward. (In theory, this vote-casting fraud might have been committed by ineligible voters, or the rigging of the machines to produce more votes than actual voters—although the special prosecutor's report indicated that, in fact, there may not have been an extensive amount of these improprieties.[82]) But why would a Democrat who agreed to cast a fraudulent vote on a voting machine be willing to pull the lever for the Democrat running in the down-ballot race but not for Kennedy at the top of the ticket—especially when the voting machines in use made it easy to vote a straight party ticket?[83]

Kallina's theory of disproportionately massive down-ballot fraud also requires one to discredit the boast that Daley apparently made to Kennedy about delivering Illinois. In his book *Conversations with Kennedy*, Ben Bradlee quoted Kennedy on Election Night as jovially recounting that Daley had told him earlier that evening, "with a little bit of luck and the help of a few close friends, you're going to carry Illinois"—the implication being that Daley was doing his best to pad Kennedy's total with some extra votes.[84] But maybe Daley never made that remark. Bradlee's quoting of it was double hearsay, clearly inadmissible in any judicial proceeding that might have attempted to

Figure 8.3 This photo and accompanying *Chicago Tribune* article (Nov. 6, 1960) instructed readers on how they could vote a straight-ticket ballot on the voting machines then in use.

get at the truth of the matter. Or, maybe even if Daley did say it, it was just puffery—that he wanted to ingratiate himself with Kennedy, but he had not actually attempted to rig the election in Kennedy's favor. Or maybe the "help of a few close friends" was purely legitimate get-out-the-vote efforts. But suppose that Daley did attempt to deliver Illinois to Kennedy, including by impermissible vote-counting means, as Kallina himself seems to assume.[85] Are we then to believe that Daley's machine was capable of fabricating tens of thousands of illicit extra votes for a down-ballot race, but incompetent in manufacturing the same number of votes for the party's candidate at the top of the ticket? To believe Kallina's theory of disproportionately massive down-ballot vote-rigging, one must simultaneously assume that Daley wanted to rig the election for Kennedy but was incapable of doing so, even as he was capable of stealing tens of thousands of votes in the very same election. It is a hard combination of propositions to square with common sense, and one that is inconsistent with this statement that Kallina makes about Daley: "Although the big-city machines in 1960 were not what they had been, the Chicago Democratic Party of Mayor Richard J. Daley remained a model of efficiency when it came to getting out the vote and making sure that it came out correctly."[86]

There is also the oft-repeated contention that even if Daley did steal more votes for Kennedy than Kennedy's margin of victory, there was more than enough downstate vote-stealing by Republicans on behalf of Nixon to offset whatever illicit vote-rigging Daley's machine did for Kennedy. According to this contention, the illegalities on both sides are a wash, and Kennedy's victory in Illinois remains valid as an honest reflection of the electorate's will. The problem with this contention, however, is that the evidence is unavailable to back it up. Kallina, who has studied this topic more extensively than anyone else, puts the point succinctly: "To my knowledge, no one has produced a single documented example of Republican vote fraud in Illinois in 1960."[87] Moreover, it is unsavory to say "the other side cheated more than we did"; it is hardly the model for how to conduct elections in what was supposed to be the world's leading democracy at the height of the Cold War.

Ultimately, it is impossible to say whether an honest and accurate count of valid, and only valid, ballots in Illinois would have resulted in a victory in that state for Nixon rather than Kennedy. Kallina has said the same:

> No final resolution of the controversy over the presidential contest is possible. . . . It appeared that in Chicago, Nixon was cheated out of several thousand votes, at a minimum, but this estimate was not so overwhelming that one can assert with confidence that Nixon was swindled out of Illinois's electoral votes. . . . The fact is that no one can say with certainty who "really" carried Illinois in 1960. The available evidence is too fragmentary and inconclusive to permit a final judgment. The debate over Illinois's electoral votes in 1960 will likely pass into history alongside the outcomes of 1876 in Florida, Louisiana, and South Carolina.[88]

This assessment, then, leaves the outcome in Illinois very much in doubt. Add to this the doubt that one must have about the result in Texas, and the consequence is unavoidable: Kennedy's entire Electoral College victory over Nixon in 1960 might have been contestable. If impartial tribunals had conducted complete recounts of the presidential election in both states, the result might have ended up either way.

Nixon's Concession and Its Significance

Nixon, however, never requested a recount in either state. On Election Night itself, the networks and newspapers erroneously were projecting a decisive

Figure 8.4 Nixon, with his wife Pat, making his Election Night statement that Kennedy would win "if the present trend continues." Photograph by Hank Walker, *Life Magazine* (November 21, 1960; pp. 34–35), Getty Images.

Kennedy win.[89] California was being called for Kennedy, even though Nixon correctly knew that he would eventually win it on the strength of absentee ballots.[90] Nixon faced great pressure to concede, including from key members of his own party. Nixon resisted this pressure enough to make a carefully calibrated statement, just after midnight Pacific time, that stopped short of an outright concession: "If the present trend continues, Senator Kennedy will be the next President of the United States."[91] But Nixon's words were perceived as all-but-conceding, rather than taking a more neutral "let's wait and see" posture.

When Nixon awoke the next morning, he reevaluated the situation. Even if he could turn Illinois around, he considered Texas completely out of reach. Instead, he temporarily pinned his hopes on Minnesota, although it along with Illinois still would not have been enough to reach an Electoral College majority. But when told that Minnesota was hopeless, he was willing to telegraph Kennedy a more formal concession statement upon which Kennedy could rely to declare victory.[92]

The following week, after a trip to Florida where Nixon met with Kennedy in a symbolic gesture to confirm his acceptance of Kennedy's win, Nixon took another look at the possibility of overturning the apparent result. His supporters in both Illinois and Texas were alleging widespread fraud on Kennedy's behalf and raising the idea of seeking recounts in both states. Urged by national as well as local leaders in the Republican Party to support these efforts, Nixon specifically considered the possibility of pursuing recounts in both Illinois and Texas. But he quickly concluded that the idea of a recount in Texas was an utter nonstarter. As he bluntly recalled in his 1962 memoir *Six Crises*, "there was no procedure whatever for a losing candidate to get a recount in Texas"[93]—a judgment confirmed by historians.[94] Even if there had been a formal procedure available for Nixon to invoke, it would have been biased against him by the Texas Democrats, loyal to Johnson, who thoroughly controlled its operation. "Lyndon Johnson was not about to tolerate a loss in his state," Kallina has succinctly observed. "With a powerful political machine at their disposal and virtually no organized Republican opposition, Democrats could do whatever they pleased with the election returns."[95] With zero chance of prevailing in a Texas recount, regardless of the merits, Nixon was not going to pursue an Illinois recount just for show.

Would Nixon have sought recounts in both Illinois and Texas if fair procedures had been available in both states for doing so? Nixon himself gave us reasons to think not. He acknowledges the fear of being labeled a "sore loser," thereby destroying "any possibility of a further political career," if he had "demanded a recount and it turned out that despite the vote fraud Kennedy had still won."[96] This same fear would have applied even if, contrary to Coke Stevenson's experience, the federal courts in 1960 had been ready and willing to overturn elections tainted by proven vote fraud. Facing that 40,000-vote deficit in Texas, Nixon would have had no guarantee whatsoever of convincing an impartial federal court to erase all of it because of fraud.

Nixon also tells us of his concern for the harm to the country that a recount fight would cause: "If I were to demand a recount, the organization of the new Administration and the orderly transfer of responsibility from the old to the new might be delayed for months."[97] Here Nixon seems to assume that Congress would have permitted any recount dispute to extend beyond January 20, 1961—a dubious proposition given that both houses of Congress were controlled by Democrats at the time and thus had the power under the Electoral Count Act of 1887 to jointly reject any challenges to Kennedy's electoral vote certifications that Nixon might have made. But even if the legal premise of Nixon's political concern was shaky, the concern remained genuine. Whether a recount battle lasted weeks or months, Nixon perceived the risk that it would seriously divide a nation that needed a measure of unity to fight the Cold War: "The bitterness that would be engendered by such a [recount] maneuver . . . would, in my opinion, have done incalculable and lasting damage throughout the country."[98]

Politicians are not required to seek recounts simply because there is a chance of winning them. Rather, it is the responsibility of politicians in exercising statesmanship to decide whether, on balance, it is more in the public interest to pursue a fair count or instead graciously concede. If Nixon had declined to pursue a recount in a situation where a fair process for one was available to him, then lingering allegations of vote fraud should not be permitted to cloud Kennedy's victory. In such a situation, Nixon would have had his chance to prove his claims but would have disavowed that opportunity as was his right.

But it remains the stubborn fact that Nixon never had a chance for a fair recount. This complicates the inquiry. A politician who concedes defeat when the electoral system is rigged against him cannot confer legitimacy on his opponent's victory. To be sure, the politician wisely might decline to pursue a futile fight, if only to maintain civil peace in the society. But refusing to challenge a count of ballots that has been fabricated and has no chance of changing does not make the count, or the election it determines, the outcome of a democratic process. Rather, it remains the product of a corrupt regime, with the politician resigned to live in the system as it exists rather than instigating civil strife. Insofar as Nixon never attempted a recount in Texas because the state at the time did not operate a process capable of counting ballots fairly, the validity of Kennedy's Electoral College victory as an exercise of democratic choice must remain in doubt.

Interestingly, but ironically, one of the reasons that Nixon gave for not seeking recounts in 1960 was the negative image of America it would display to the world in the midst of the Cold War:

> I could think of no worse example for nations abroad, who for the first time were trying to put free electoral procedures into effect, than that of the United States wrangling over the results of our presidential election, and even suggesting that the presidency itself could be stolen by thievery at the ballot box.[99]

Nixon continued with this explanation:

> It is difficult enough to get defeated candidates in some of the newly independent countries to abide by the verdict of the electorate. If we could not continue to set a good example in this respect in the United States, I could see that there would be open-season for shooting at the validity of free elections throughout the world.[100]

The validity of Nixon's logic on this point, however, ultimately hangs on whether the vote-counting process in America is capable of identifying "the verdict of the electorate." If so, then walking away from available recount procedures does not undercut the democratic validity of that verdict. But if not, then declining to pursue a recount confirms, rather than rebuts, the suspicion that the reported vote total may reflect nothing more than "thievery at the ballot box."

Thus, Nixon's own account of his concession reveals for us the disturbing truth about mid-century America that he says he was attempting to shield from the world. He tells us that the primary reason he did not seek a recount in Texas was the utter impossibility of obtaining it. Yet that reason is the one that undercuts the pretense that the United States was using an exemplary system to conduct its 1960 presidential election. Perhaps back then Nixon was successful in concealing from the world the fact that America could not count ballots fairly and accurately in a closely competitive presidential election. A half-century later, however, with the benefit of historical analysis and reflection, that fact no longer is hidden.

In sum, we cannot be confident that the result in 1960 was the product of a vote-counting process aimed identifying the choice made by the ballots the electorate cast. Instead, the result may have been nothing more than the product of a process manipulated by those who controlled it, to produce a desired outcome regardless of the electorate's choice, with no means to challenge that manipulation. Given this unsettling but unavoidable possibility, the 1960 presidential election must be viewed as a failure of American government to operate a well-functioning democracy. That failure puts 1960 alongside 1876—and, as we shall later consider, 2000—in a disturbing series of instances in which the nation has lacked the institutional capacity to identify accurately the winner of the presidency.

American Democracy in the Forties and Fifties

Johnson's victory over Stevenson in 1948 and Kennedy's over Nixon in 1960, when taken together, might simply be viewed as revealing a particular problem with Texas, rather than with America more generally, during this period in the nation's history. It is true that not every example of a ballot-counting battle in this era amounted to the kind of failure as in these two momentous Texas examples. There were successes along with the failures. Still, it would be wrong to conclude that the Lone Star State was unique in its democratic deficiencies at this time.

One shining example of success—an instance of what America wanted to display proudly to the world—occurred at the threshold of this period, on the eve of America's entry into World War Two. While Germany blitzed the British skies, Missouri demonstrated how to use its judiciary and the rule of law to safeguard democracy from a threat of usurpation instigated through a ballot-counting dispute. In the state's 1940 gubernatorial election, initial returns showed the Democrat trailing by less than 4,000 votes. Democrats controlled the state's legislature, and they thought they could challenge enough ballots to prevent the Republican candidate from becoming governor. But the Democrats lacked the evidence to sustain their plot. Questionable ballots numbered only in the hundreds, not thousands. The Missouri Supreme Court, even though all-Democrat, unanimously refused to permit the legislature to delay the Republican's inauguration. Local newspapers hailed the court's rebuff of the "governor steal."[101]

After World War Two was over, America was not always able to replicate this kind of success even though the nation self-consciously wanted to put its best face forward during the Cold War. In 1954, the US Senate made this goal explicit while it was still fighting over the outcome of New Mexico's US Senate election from two years earlier.[102] The state had suffered a systemic breakdown of the voting process on Election Day, including widespread violation of the right to a secret ballot. Ultimately, enough senators from both parties concluded that the problems, while egregious, were not sufficient to void the outcome and declare the seat vacant. But along the way, senators rhetorically asked: "How can we demand free elections and the secrecy of the ballot for other nations and tolerate such conditions within the confines of our own Nation?"[103]

Nor was this New Mexico mishap unique. Just a few years later, New Mexico had two gubernatorial elections in a row, 1958 and 1960, where the incumbent governor at the time (a Democrat in one, a Republican in the other) attempted to manipulate the procedures of the state's canvassing board in an effort to cling to power, displaying behavior more typical of nineteenth-century governors.[104] Michigan, in its 1948 US Senate election, suffered severe breakdowns in its voting procedures, including systematic miscounting of split-ticket ballots.[105] The Senate condemned the state's administrative malfeasance for "depriving [the state's] voters of their civil right to cast their ballot for the candidate of their choice" as well as "the civil right to have their vote counted after it has been cast."[106] It was sadly ironic that Michigan, the home of America's quintessential automobile industry and thus the leading embodiment of the nation's technological prowess, was incapable of operating an electoral system that counted ballots fairly and accurately.[107]

Nor were the nation's electoral ills limited to administrative incompetence. There were other instances of flagrant ballot-box stuffing; not just the most notorious examples emanating from Texas. West Virginia's 1946 US Senate election suffered from substantial electoral fraud, including the organized used of ineligible "floaters" escorted to the polls by local police.[108] Two years later, one of the most promising protégés of Justice Felix Frankfurter,

Figure 8.5 Daniel R. Fitzpatrick, cartoonist for the *St. Louis Post-Dispatch* and twice winner of the Pulitzer Prize, lauded the Missouri Supreme Court for thwarting the partisan theft of the governorship, characterizing the court's ruling as "The Majesty of the Law." Historical Society of Missouri.

Edward Prichard—a man viewed by many as having the potential to become president—destroyed his career by adding 254 fake votes to a ballot box in a ham-handed effort to swing Kentucky's 1948 US Senate election for the Democrats.[109]

One particularly glaring instance of vote-counting manipulation that negated the electorate's choice was Rhode Island's 1956 gubernatorial election. There, in sharp contrast to Missouri's 1940 success, it was the state supreme court that perpetrated the denial of what a majority of eligible voters wanted. The instrument of the court's frustration of democracy was the invalidation of absentee ballots through a "strained" and unnecessarily technical interpretation of the state's constitution.[110] The majority of the court, three Democrats with one Republican dissenting (and the remaining justice recused), ruled that the state's constitution required nonmilitary absentee ballots to be cast on Election Day rather than beforehand.[111] Since absentee ballots by definition are not cast at polling places on Election Day, what the court majority meant was that civilian absentee voters needed to sign and notarize their ballots on Election Day and could not do so any earlier.

The court's decision contradicted common sense as well as the most directly relevant provisions of state law. A state statute enacted only three years previously, and supported by the incumbent Democrat who was running for reelection, specifically gave nonmilitary absentee voters the right to sign and notarize their ballots before Election Day.[112] The most recent constitutional amendment, in 1948, was an expansion of nonmilitary absentee voting to disabled voters (not just travelers) and expressly gave the legislature the right to enact implementing statutes. An earlier constitutional amendment, from 1930, also addressed absentee voting in general terms and gave the legislature implementing authority. A third constitutional amendment concerned only military absentee voting, but none of these constitutional amendments expressly precluded civilian absentee voters from signing and notarizing their ballots before Election Day.[113]

Nothing in the constitution needed to be read as voiding the 1953 statute that, at the incumbent governor's urging, gave civilian voters this right and upon which these voters relied in the 1956 election. Yet the three Democrats on the court claimed that the state's constitution compelled them to nullify 4,954 ballots of innocent voters who were just complying with the state statute, as their absentee voting instructions had told them to do. Invalidation of these ballots turned the incumbent Democrat's defeat into victory; whereas the Republican challenger had been certified the winner based on a count that included the disputed ballots because of their lawfulness under the state statute, the court's order to expunge them from the count put the Democrat on top. As the leading text on Rhode Island constitutional law bluntly explains, the court's decree "offended the general public's sense of fair play and hurt the image of the court as an impartial tribunal."[114]

Rhode Island's Republicans briefly considered attempting to take the case to federal court on the ground that the state supreme court's disenfranchisement of innocent voters violated the US Constitution. It is a claim that would have won had it been presented two decades later, as a 1978 case from Rhode Island, *Griffin v. Burns*, would subsequently show. And it is a claim that would receive a sympathetic hearing from the Supreme Court that decided *Bush v. Gore* at the end of the twentieth century. But in 1956 it was not a winning claim. Rather it would have met the same jurisdictional barrier as Coke Stevenson's federal claim in 1948. In the middle of the twentieth century, the precedent of *Taylor v. Beckham* emphatically precluded federal court review of a state's manipulative disenfranchisement of innocent voters that undermined the electoral choice the voters made and delivered the election to the candidate that the participating voters did not want. That this manipulation in Rhode Island in 1956 occurred at the hands of the state's judiciary, rather than some other organ of state government, made no difference to the jurisdictional barrier imposed by *Taylor v. Beckham*. It only showed that state supreme courts could not always be trusted to set aside partisanship and to count votes fairly, contrary to such successes achieved by other state supreme courts, including Missouri's in 1940 and extending back to Wisconsin's in *Bashford v. Barstow* in 1856.

9

The Sixties and Their Legacy

The Rise of Democratic Expectations

The 1960s were a time of major transformation in the basic prerequisites for the operation of American democracy. The Voting Rights Act of 1965 finally provided the procedural mechanisms necessary to secure the franchise for US citizens of African ancestry. The Act fulfilled a promise made in 1870 with the adoption of the Fifteenth Amendment, which ostensibly barred states from denying voting rights based on race.[1] But it had been a promise mocked by a century of nonenforcement, including by the US Supreme Court, which in 1903 had pronounced itself powerless to remedy Alabama's systematic defiance of the Amendment's simple command to treat blacks and whites equally with respect to voting.[2] It is ironic that the 1965 Act was spearheaded so effectively by Lyndon Johnson, who had benefited from the blatant denial of equal voting rights in the form of ballot-box stuffing. Nonetheless, passage of the Act was an epic national achievement and would reap its intended benefits for decades: increased electoral participation by previously disenfranchised Americans.

Another transformative development of the 1960s, of comparable significance to the Voting Rights Act, was the new constitutional law of one-person-one-vote. This revolution in the Supreme Court's constitutional jurisprudence, energetically pursued by Chief Justice Earl Warren, came in stages. First, in the 1962 case *Baker v. Carr*, the Court abandoned its longstanding barrier to the consideration of election-related issues under the so-called political question doctrine, which had emanated from the Court's refusal to get involved in Rhode Island's Dorr War of 1842, and which had led directly to the Court's unwillingness in 1900 to protect against ballot-box stuffing in *Taylor v. Beckham*.[3] The Court's opinion in *Baker v. Carr* did not explicitly overrule *Taylor v. Beckham*. It did not need to, since *Baker* specifically concerned legislative apportionment and not the counting of ballots. Still, the reasoning of *Baker v. Carr*, that the Equal Protection Clause of the US Constitution provides an enforceable standard for the federal judiciary to apply to safeguard the equality of voters in the conduct of elections, inevitably undermined the judicial self-abnegation in *Taylor v. Beckham.*[4]

The second stage in the one-person-one-vote revolution came two years later in *Reynolds v. Sims,* which was the case to declare explicitly that the US Constitution embodied a one-person-one-vote requirement. Like *Baker v. Carr,* the specific context of *Reynolds v. Sims* was legislative apportionment—the drawing of lines on a map to differentiate the districts that would elect the representatives to the state's legislature. In this particular context, the federal constitutional requirement of one-person-one-vote entailed that each member of the legislature be elected by equally populous constituencies. The consequence of the Court's ruling in *Reynolds v. Sims* was immediate and profound, requiring all states to redraw their legislative maps to give more populous parts of states, especially urban areas, more legislative representation than they had received for decades. Chief Justice Warren considered it the "most significant" decision of his tenure, because it implemented the fundamental democratic norm of majority rule.[5]

As revolutionary as *Reynolds v. Sims* was, the Warren Court soon made clear that its new constitutional requirement of one-person-one-vote was not limited to the arena of legislative apportionment. Rather, in 1966, in a case from Virginia, the Court invoked its fresh precedent from *Reynolds v. Sims* to invalidate the obligation to pay a poll tax as a prerequisite to casting a ballot.[6] Three years later, the Warren Court extended the logic of this poll tax decision to invalidate a New York law that limited the right to vote in school board elections to those who either owned or rented a dwelling in the school district or had children attending the district's schools. The Court insisted that the Constitution's fundamental guarantee of political equality of one-person-one-vote meant that any adult citizen residing in the school district, who would be entitled to vote for members of the state's legislature, must also be entitled to vote for the district's school board members.[7]

Early Precursors to *Bush v. Gore*

It would be decades before the Supreme Court had occasion to apply its new one-person-one-vote principle to the counting of ballots. That development would not occur until *Bush v. Gore,* when the Court stopped the recount in the 2000 presidential election because Florida's recounting procedures could not guarantee the equal treatment of identical ballots. Many observers would express surprise that the Court viewed the constitutional requirement of one-person-one-vote as germane to recount rules. But they should not have been surprised. One-person-one-vote, as *Reynolds v. Sims* itself had explained, was the Court's effort to operationalize what it saw as the essential elements of a democracy. Thus, one-person-one-vote ineluctably applied to any aspect of elections that could conceivably be essential to their democratic character. The equal counting of identical ballots, all cast by eligible voters, easily could be so conceived. To disqualify one ballot but not another, when both were the same, would seem a direct—indeed literal—contradiction of one-person-one-vote.[8] Thus, it was only a matter of time before the precedent of *Reynolds v. Sims* would be applied to the counting of ballots. The only surprise would be that the first Supreme Court case to do so would involve a presidential election.[9]

One case from the sixties serves as a particular harbinger of *Bush v. Gore*, signaling how after *Reynolds v. Sims* the Court easily could become embroiled in a major ballot-counting fight. The case is *Fortson v. Morris*, from 1966, the same year as the Court's poll-tax decision. The issue in the case was not the counting of ballots, but whether a runoff election had to be put back to the vote of the electorate or instead could be given over to the state's legislature. Georgia had a law that if no candidate for governor received over 50% of the vote in the general election, then the state's legislature—and not the electorate in another round of voting—would choose among the top finishers. Civil rights groups challenged Georgia's law as a violation of one-person-one-vote. In a 5–4 ruling, the Supreme Court disagreed. In an opinion by Justice Hugo Black, the Court explained that Georgia was not required to hold an election to fill the office of governor; rather, its governor could be appointed by the legislature, as had been the case until 1825 and as in many other states in the early nineteenth century. Nor did a two-stage process, where the electorate had the opportunity to vote for governor at the initial stage, require that the electorate also make the selection at the second stage. The doctrine of one-person-one-vote governed the initial stage, because the state had chosen to involve the electorate at that stage; but the doctrine no longer applied when the electorate's involvement ended and thus did not preclude the use of legislative appointment for the second stage. "A method which would have been valid if initially employed is equally valid when employed as an alternative," Justice Black explained.[10]

The four dissenters in *Fortson v. Morris*—the four liberals on the Court at the time (Douglas, Brennan, and Fortas, as well as Warren)—would have extended *Reynolds v. Sims* to require that once the voters are initially involved in the selection of the state's governor, the runoff must be theirs to determine as well. Justice Fortas wrote for his dissenting brethren: "The integrity of the vote is undermined and destroyed by any scheme which can result in the selection of a person for Governor who receives the lesser number of popular votes."[11] In light of *Bush v. Gore* at the end of the century, what is significant about *Fortson v. Morris* is not the particular issue in the case, but its illustration of how the Court can split 5–4 when adjudicating a dispute over the procedure that will determine the outcome of a pending high-stakes election, like this one for Georgia's governor at the height of that state's debate over racial desegregation. Once one sees the justices disagreeing so sharply over whether one-person-one-vote obligates the state to hold a runoff election, then it is easy to imagine the justices also diverging sharply over the particular procedures that one-person-one-vote requires a state to employ when counting ballots in a runoff—or a recount. And if that kind of disagreement can occur on the Court in the context of a Georgia gubernatorial election, it can just as easily occur in the context of a Florida presidential election. In this way, *Fortson v. Morris* was an obvious harbinger of *Bush v. Gore*; circumstances, however, did not cause the Court to confront that more momentous case for another thirty-four years.

It also took time for the lower federal courts to apply the precedent of *Reynolds v. Sims* to a ballot-counting dispute. A leading case in 1978, *Griffin v. Burns* concerned absentee ballots in Rhode Island, just as the litigation over the state's 1956 gubernatorial election had. This time, however, the election was not for governor. Rather, it was a primary election for a seat on Providence's city council. Nonetheless, in *Griffin*, the Rhode Island Supreme Court replicated its inappropriately strained reading of state law in order to invalidate absentee ballots cast by voters in reliance on instructions from the state's election officials. Here, the state supreme court ruled that state law permitted absentee voting in general elections only, and thus not primaries, even though Rhode Island's secretary of state had implemented absentee voting in primaries for the previous seven years and had advertised its availability for this particular election. Pursuant to established procedures, election officials had counted the absentee ballots in the particular city council primary election and had declared a winner based on that count. The state supreme court subsequently overturned that result, ordering all the absentee ballots disqualified, with the consequence of yielding a different winning candidate.[12]

In *Griffin v. Burns*, the United States Court of Appeals for the First Circuit (with jurisdiction over Rhode Island) refused to tolerate this disenfranchisement of innocent, eligible voters. "When a group of voters are handed ballots by election officials that, unsuspected by all, are invalid," the federal circuit court declared, "the election itself becomes a flawed process."[13] The court specifically invoked *Reynolds v. Sims* as authority for its ruling. To remedy the unconstitutional disenfranchisement of these absentee voters, the federal court ruled that if the state itself would not reinstate their votes (together with the certification of the original winner based on the inclusion of those votes), then the US Constitution required voiding the flawed election and holding a new one.

Griffin v. Burns did not reach the US Supreme Court. Rhode Island did not attempt to defend its own supreme court's decision in that forum. Consequently, the nation's highest court did not then get the chance to consider the applicability of *Reynolds v. Sims* to this kind of ballot-counting dispute. Instead, the lower federal courts continued to sow the seeds of *Griffin v. Burns* and similar cases. These seeds would blossom in Alabama's 1994 election for chief justice, discussed in the next chapter, and then reach fruition six years later in *Bush v. Gore*.

Meanwhile, as this jurisprudential doctrine developed over several decades, the states continued to confront the occasional high-stakes disputed election. Sometimes these would occur in a governor's election, sometimes in a US Senate race. Although these disputes in the sixties and seventies did not directly involve the precedent of *Reynolds v. Sims*, they nonetheless arose in the same atmosphere that yielded that precedent and its principle of one-person-one-vote. The rise of democratic expectations reflected in both the jurisprudence of one-person-one-vote and the enactment of the Voting Rights Act also played an increasing role in how states handled vote-counting disputes in major elections. The increased demand that politics operate consistently with democratic ideals and standards was a cultural component of the 1960s and ensuing decades. This cultural development produced a noticeable improvement in the ability of states to settle major disputed elections in ways that accorded with the public's perception of electoral fairness. The prime example was Minnesota's gubernatorial election of 1962.

Minnesota Sets the Standard for a Successful Recount

No year in US history has produced more recounts in gubernatorial elections than 1962.[14] There were five that year, four in New England and one in Minnesota. The New England quartet produced little turmoil, even in Rhode Island, which had suffered such difficulty in a disputed gubernatorial election only six years earlier.[15] Only Massachusetts experienced a bit of a dustup, when a court ordered a second reexamination of ballots in Springfield after the incumbent Republican questioned the propriety of voting practices there. But the judicial inquiry found no significant problems, and the incumbent conceded defeat on December 20.[16] The three other New England recounts were also complete by then, in plenty of time for the winners to be inaugurated in January. Not so in Minnesota, where inauguration of the new governor was delayed until March. But while it took longer than desirable, Minnesota developed a procedure for resolving its disputed election that continues to serve as a model of fairness.[17]

This Minnesota election was exceptionally close, much closer than any of the New England races that year, which helps explain why it remained unsettled for so long. The final margin of victory in Minnesota was only 91 votes.[18] Measured as a percentage of total votes (1,246,948), this margin was the narrowest of any gubernatorial election in the entire twentieth century: 0.0073%.[19] Fifty years earlier, Kansas had a governor's race with a tighter absolute margin (29), but that margin was larger in percentage terms: 0.0087%.[20] A half-century later, Minnesota's 1962 margin would be eclipsed by Washington's 2004 gubernatorial election, where the final 133-vote margin of victory was only 0.0047% of all votes counted there. Still, Minnesota's 1962 gubernatorial election was closer even than the state's 2008 US Senate election, which had a final margin of 312 votes out of not quite three million total (and thus slightly more than one-hundredth of one percent).[21]

The 1962 governor's race in Minnesota was between the Republican incumbent Elmer Andersen and challenger Karl Rolvaag of Minnesota's Democratic-Farmer-Labor Party, which is essentially Minnesota's version of the Democrats (and will be labeled such here). Local circumstances combined with national conditions to make the race extraordinarily close. Like the New England quartet, this Minnesota election was affected by the ultimate "October surprise" of the Cuban Missile Crisis. Kennedy's successful handling of it gave a last-minute boost to Democrats, who had been lagging because of the otherwise rocky start to Kennedy's presidency (especially the Bay of Pigs debacle).[22] Beyond this, Minnesota had its own October surprise: in the last week of the campaign, Andersen's administration was accused of negligently substandard work on a major interstate highway construction project.[23]

As returns came in on Election Night and over the next few days, the lead bounced back and forth like a ping-pong game. The final precincts did not report until Friday of that week, November 9. These came from remote islands in the north that were accessible only by boat and air. The difficulties of communicating with them were compounded by a major snowstorm. Normally, their handful of votes would not make a difference in the outcome. But in this instance they might. Thus, in a scene more suited to the previous century, the whole state waited for these late-arriving returns.

At the same time, other localities around the state had been canvassing and thus correcting errors in their initial returns. These corrections contributed to the ping-pong ball going back and forth across the net some more. When the "canoe vote" arrived Friday night, Andersen held the lead by a few dozen votes, but by the next morning Rolvaag was ahead by 139 as a result of more error corrections.[24]

The State Canvassing Board was due to certify the election on Tuesday, November 20, two weeks after Election Day. Before then, the local boards

Figure 9.1 The Cuban Missile Crisis was still on everyone's mind as Minnesotans contemplated their 1962 gubernatorial election, still very much unsettled on December 21, when this cartoon appeared in the *Minneapolis Star*—and it would remain unresolved for three more months. By permission of Roy Justus and the *Minneapolis Star* (now *Star Tribune*).

of elections were required to submit to the secretary of state the results of the canvass. During the ten days between Saturday, November 10 and the deadline for certifying the election, the county canvassing boards continued their process of error correction. Rolvaag maintained the lead through most of that period. Indeed, based on all the completed canvasses submitted to the secretary of the state by November 20, Rolvaag was on top by 58 votes.[25]

With Rolvaag ahead, the Republicans developed the strategy of asking counties to take another look and, if they uncovered additional errors, to submit amended canvasses to the secretary of state. The Democrats argued that the local elections boards were not permitted to reopen their canvasses once submitted to the secretary of state, and the Democrats took this issue to court. A state judge agreed with the Democrats and ordered the counties to refrain from amending their canvass reports. The Minnesota Supreme Court, however, voided this lower court order on the ground that the state judiciary must wait until after the State Canvassing Board had acted.[26]

The State Canvassing Board, in turn, decided to delay its certification. This delay gave the counties the chance to grant the Republican request for a recanvass. Ten counties took advantage of this chance. Their amended submissions, if accepted, would flip the result of the race yet again, this time with Andersen prevailing by 142 votes. When the five-member State Canvassing Board reconvened on Monday, November 26, it announced after much deliberation that it was unable to reach a final decision certifying the gubernatorial election. The two Democrats on the board announced that they would reject the amended submissions and certify Rolvaag the winner. Two of the three Republicans declared that they would reach the opposite conclusion, accepting the amended reports and certifying Andersen reelected. The third Republican announced that he was inclined to agree that the amended reports should be accepted as long as they showed that there had been "substantial compliance" with the state's election laws, but that the issue was a legal one that only the state supreme court could resolve.[27]

With neither the Minnesota Supreme Court nor the State Canvassing Board wishing to decide the matter, the election looked like a hot potato that no one wanted to touch. Nonetheless, back it went to the court, where two justices recused themselves because of their service on the State Canvassing Board, leaving five justices to hear the case: three Republicans and two Democrats. These five split along party lines. The three Republicans ruled that the amended submissions must be accepted. The two Democrats contended that they must be rejected. The result was to require the State Canvassing Board to certify Anderson the winner. The court announced this order on Tuesday, November 29, with the written majority and dissenting opinions following two weeks later, on December 11.[28]

The disagreement between the majority and dissent was couched in the language of the age-old debate between flexibility and strictness in the interpretation of election laws. The majority acknowledged that a "literal reading of the statute would justify the conclusion that in elections involving state offices the corrective action must be taken before the county board certifies its result to the secretary of state." The majority, however, believed that this literal reading should be rejected in favor of an interpretation imbued with the "purpose" of the law, which was to achieve "the true result" reflecting "the vote actually cast." The majority expounded: "Procedural statutes governing elections are intended to safeguard the right of the people to express their preference in a free election by secret ballot and to have the results of the election governed by the votes so cast."[29] Applying that principle, the majority observed that there was no argument with the proposition that "the amended returns from the ten counties involved reflect the true vote of the people." Accordingly: "To now hold that the results of this election must be based on the return that everyone concedes is erroneous would be a perversion of our whole election process in the pursuit of strict adherence to statutes that need not be so strictly construed." The majority considered it unconscionable "to permit the outcome of the election to rest on an admitted mistake rather than on known fact" and thus "to declare the loser to have won the election."[30]

The dissent defended a literal reading of the statute on grounds of fairness and uniformity. The majority's approach permitted amended returns coming from some, not all, counties, and the participating counties might be skewed in terms of partisanship. The dissent countered that it agreed with the "contention that all the votes should be counted" but believed that the majority's approach did not implement this principle. On the contrary:

> A selective recount may now be secured in certain counties by grace of the voluntary act of canvassing boards. In other counties where the accuracy of the vote may be equally suspect the boards may arbitrarily deny a recount.[31]

Far from achieving an accurate result, the majority's interpretation of the statute merely "permits the party with the most active and persuasive partisans to prematurely gain the advantage of a selective recount."[32] In taking this position, the dissent anticipated the equal protection principle embraced by the US Supreme Court four decades later in *Bush v. Gore*. Moreover, the dissent echoed Aaron Burr and Edmund Randolph from 1792 almost verbatim when it asserted: "It should be an elementary principle of construction of election laws that they should not be given an interpretation which will invite abuse."[33]

Thus, the basic jurisprudential divide present since the eighteenth century reappeared in this closest of twentieth-century gubernatorial elections. The Minnesota Supreme Court was no more capable of resolving this fundamental philosophical debate than was the New York canvassing board in 1792. What was most regrettable about the Minnesota Supreme Court's decision was that it, like the New York canvassing board's, split along partisan lines. Indeed, this Minnesota Supreme Court ruling was the low point in the state's handling of the 1962 election.

But this nadir of partisan division prompted some self-reflection on the part of key leaders in the state, particularly the chief justice: "The court system in Minnesota was being shaken to its timbers by the political tempest of the recount." Accordingly, the chief justice was looking for a way to restore the Minnesota judiciary's "positive image and to retain the confidence of the citizens in the courts."[34] For all the ugliness of this 3–2 partisan split, it contained the seeds for a new nonpartisan approach to take hold in the next phase of this disputed election.

The 3–2 ruling had determined only which candidate was certified the winner after completion of the canvass, an important step to be sure but hardly the end of the whole process. Minnesota law permitted the losing candidate to contest the certification and, significantly, this contest would take place in court and not in the state legislature. Thus, as soon as the 3–2 ruling was announced, the prospect arose that the election would come back to the Minnesota Supreme Court in the form of a contest. The immediate question was what trial court would hear the contest and thus shape the case before the possibility of an eventual appeal back to the state supreme court?

The chief justice let it be known that he wanted the two sides to "agree on a neutral judge to handle the [contest]."[35] The attorneys for the two candidates then developed a plan whereby the contest would be considered by a three-judge trial court. The attorneys picked the three judges they wanted for this panel: one appointed by a Democrat (Sidney Kaner), another appointed by a Republican (J. H. Sylvester), and third who had been originally appointed by a Democrat but who had been elevated to a higher court by a Republican (Leonard Keyes). By choosing these three judges, both sides thought that they had adequate representation on the panel and, at the same time, that the panel was evenhanded and balanced despite having an odd number of members. The chief justice readily signed an order giving jurisdiction over the contest case to the three-judge panel the two sides had selected.[36]

By early December, Minnesota had in place a mechanism agreeable to both candidates by which to adjudicate the contest. It would take until March 19 for this three-judge court to reach its final decision. During that time, Andersen remained in the governor's office, but not by virtue of having been certified the election's winner. Instead, Minnesota's constitution specifically provided that the incumbent governor shall hold over until the new governor is finally "chosen and qualified," and this provision was interpreted as applying until the termination of the postcertification judicial contest (and not just the completion of all precertification administrative proceedings).[37] In any event, the holdover provision did not matter in the particular instance, because the incumbent Andersen also held the certification. Nor was this a situation, as Missouri had suffered in 1940, in which a partisan legislature was attempting to manipulate the rules and procedures concerning who was to sit in the governor's office during the pendency of a contest. Instead, because the contest was to be heard in court—and before a three-judge panel carefully chosen to be evenly balanced to both sides—the citizens of Minnesota were willing to wait patiently for the court's deliberations to take place. (As the state would learn in 2008, the circumstances are different if the certified winner is not the incumbent, and the state must wait until a lengthy contest ends before that certified winner can take office.)

In filing his contest, Rolvaag decided to ask for a statewide recount of all ballots, rather than to select specific precincts to recount. It was a wise decision, one that Al Gore should have emulated four decades later, because it—together with the identity of the court empaneled—gave the public confidence that the purpose of the contest was to seek the correct result. "The people of Minnesota would never be firmly convinced that Rolvaag really won if only selected precincts were chosen, as compared to a state-wide recount."[38] So said the leading contemporaneous account of this election, in words equally transferable to the American people in 2000.

The practical consequence of this decision was the need to assemble the individuals who would conduct the statewide recount. The parties replicated on a local level the same structure of the three-member court that was supervising the entire process. They created one hundred local recount teams, each comprised of a Democrat picked by the Rolvaag campaign, a Republican picked by Andersen's campaign, and a neutral member mutually agreeable to both sides. The two sides also jointly hammered out the rules and procedures to govern the local recount teams. These rules essentially permitted either side to challenge a ballot, in which case it would go to the three-judge court for resolution; the neutral member of each local recount acted as a referee rather than as a tiebreaking decision-maker.[39]

There was never any doubt that there would be a statewide recount once Rolvaag asked for one. Since Rolvaag had not alleged fraud, but only counting errors, Andersen might have argued that, without some reason to believe that the errors skewed to the Democrats' disfavor, Rolvaag as contestant had not met his burden of requiring a statewide inspection of all ballots.[40] After all, randomly distributed errors could be expected to cancel each other out. But in the aftermath of the canvass-stage litigation, where just ten counties had decided to take another look and had uncovered enough errors to flip the result, the prevailing sentiment in the state was that it was necessary to take another look for errors in all counties and that the contest lawsuit was now the appropriate procedure for doing so.

The statewide recount started on December 19, 1962. It ended on February 5, 1963, with Rolvaag ahead by 138, but having produced 97,000 challenged ballots necessary to review (plus an additional 7,000 absentee ballot envelopes). Ten bipartisan teams, each with one Democrat and one Republican, began a process of screening the challenged ballots to reduce the number necessary to submit to the court. Because there had been many overzealous challenges, the first round of screening reduced the number of challenged ballots to 22,000. A second phase of the screening process, in addition to reducing the number even further to 1,192, organized disputed ballots into twenty-four categories. These categories concerned the way in which voters had marked their ballots and whether those marks evinced a clear enough indication of which candidate the voters wished to cast their ballots for. Several categories concerned various types of ballot markings that could void a ballot regardless of a voter's intent, such as a clearly unlawful distinguishing mark like the voter's name or initials.[41]

Starting on February 25, the three-judge panel began to examine each category of disputed ballots. The category with the most ballots, and thus the most significant one, concerned ballots on which voters had made two different types of marks to indicate their preferences for candidates. For example, a voter might use an "X" in some places and a checkmark ("✓") in other places. Based on a precedent from the Minnesota Supreme Court, which involved a local election and which was decided while the gubernatorial contest was pending, these mix-marked ballots were void under Minnesota law.[42] The three-judge panel in the gubernatorial contest had no choice but to follow this precedent and in doing so essentially buttoned up a victory for Rolvaag. Although his 138-vote lead was eaten away by the panel's rulings regarding several other categories, the ruling on this one—by invalidating more Anderson votes than Rolvaag votes—netted the Democrat enough of a margin to withstand reductions in other categories.

The contest trial included some issues that did not involve ballot markings, but these proved inconsequential. Rolvaag had considered challenging thousands of absentee ballots based on various grounds of alleged ineligibility. In the end, however, he mostly abandoned these challenges. (Minnesota would have the opportunity to consider similar issues involving absentee ballots in 2008.) The three-judge court did rule that 31 absentee ballots were ineligible because they had been hand-delivered rather than mailed, as required by Minnesota law. As these 31 ballots had not yet been irretrievably mingled into the entire statewide count, the court ruled that they must be deducted from the count. The court did permit the counting of another group of 22 absentee ballots that had been improperly rejected despite compliance with the relevant rules and an adequate chain of custody.[43]

In the entire statewide contest, there were remarkably few claims of mismanagement of the voting process by local election officials. With respect to a single precinct, Rolvaag claimed a series of administrative failures, including failure to secure the ballots and other voting materials against the risk of tampering, significant enough to warrant invalidating the entire precinct's vote. But without any evidence—or even allegation—that actual tampering had occurred, the three-judge panel ruled that "the facts do not justify the disenfranchisement of the voters of the precinct."[44] Thus, it was a fair assessment that this statewide recount revealed "no fraud in Minnesota's election and in its system."[45] Late in the proceedings, when it became clear to the Republicans that they could not prevail, they attempted to challenge the entire recount on the ground that local officials had not sufficiently secured the integrity of the ballots. The court, however, easily dismissed this claim.

On March 15, the three-judge panel ultimately determined that Rolvaag had won the election by 91 votes. All of the court's rulings had been unanimous.[46] They were also perceived by both sides—and the public as a whole—as fair: "During the [entire] three and one-half months [of the contest], both Republicans and DFL-ers found no grounds on which to criticize adversely the procedures and actions of the judges."[47] The judges themselves, as one of them said subsequently, were certainly concerned about the need to adjudicate the case impartially: "The preservation of the integrity of the judicial process in the State of Minnesota was the most important function that we had."[48]

Andersen briefly considered the possibility of an appeal to the Minnesota Supreme Court, but on March 22 announced that he would not appeal. As one of his advisers told him, "the Supreme Court will never reverse the three-judge

Figure 9.2 *Recount*, the book on Minnesota's 1962 election, aptly captioned this photo (photographer unknown): "The formation of this three-judge panel, Judges Sidney E. Kaner, J. H. Sylvester and Leonard Keyes, proved to be the prime factor in bringing about an orderly and just decision of the highly explosive recount."

panel which it set up itself to handle this whole recount problem." On March 25, 76 days after the originally scheduled date for the gubernatorial inauguration (January 9), Rolvaag took office.[49]

It was a ceremony that should have occurred sooner. Although the judges who presided over the contest said in a subsequent interview that they did not see how the case could have been adjudicated more quickly, 139 days from Election Day to Inauguration is excessive even in a statewide race as close as this one was. As the *Washington Post* opined, "the delay was embarrassing."[50] The state could have started its recount immediately, making it an administrative procedure auxiliary to the certification of the canvass rather than part of a judicial contest. Minnesota indeed would reform its process in this way; still, in 2008 the state found it even more difficult to resolve a disputed election speedily.

Although it took too long to settle the 1962 election, it was a process that ended well. As the *Washington Post* observed: "The calm and orderly demeanor of Minnesotans in a difficult and trying situation is a tribute to their political stability and maturity and to their faith in democratic government."[51] Yet it did not start out auspiciously. The partisan 3–2 decision of the Minnesota Supreme Court over the power of local election boards to amend their returns after submission to the secretary of state threatened to make Minnesota in 1962 seem just like Rhode Island six years earlier: a state where the judiciary, by manipulating the rules for counting ballots, is simply an instrument of a partisan power grab to perpetuate an incumbent whom the electorate actually voted out of office. But, unlike in Rhode Island, the Minnesota judiciary in 1962 saved itself. With creativity motivated by a striving for impartiality, it invented an eminently fair institution to handle the dispute. Consequently, when the election was finally over, even professional observers like the *Washington Post* would forget the initial misstep and pronounce that "the courts performed their duties without reproach."[52] Of course, it was not just any court that had acted this way. It was the special three-judge panel designed for the occasion by the lawyers for the two candidates. It is to the creation of this evenly balanced tribunal that the entire success of the experience should be attributed: "If anything acted as a regulator making Minnesota's recount orderly, accurate, and fair, it was the formation of this three-judge panel."[53]

The New Normal: Placid Gubernatorial Recounts

Minnesota stands out as exemplary in the way it resolved its 1962 election, in part because of its special tribunal and in part because of the election's exceptionally close margin. But in this new era of heightened democratic expectations, reflected in the one-person-one-vote principle of *Reynolds v. Sims*, Minnesota was hardly the only state to achieve success in the resolution of disputed gubernatorial elections. Indeed, as already noted, 1962 involved the New England quartet of four other successful gubernatorial recounts. Two of these four states, Maine and Rhode Island, repeated this success in 1970. When one recalls the great difficulties these two states previously had with disputed gubernatorial elections—Maine in 1879, Rhode Island in 1893, and then again as recently as 1956—the successes of these two states in 1962 and 1970 signaled a change in political culture. Attempting to win through procedural manipulation had become no longer acceptable. Instead, recounts became the routine in order to determine the genuine choice of the participating and eligible electorate, and the recount procedures had to be followed faithfully and honorably to yield this democratic outcome.

Emblematic of Maine's commitment to this process in 1970 was its secretary of state's order that all ballots be secured in a room with a 24-hour television camera, so that the public could continuously monitor their integrity.[54] This transparency helped to diffuse the threat of litigation aimed at delaying the inauguration of the new governor.[55] Under the public's watchful eye, it turned out that there were no problems susceptible to litigation. Notwithstanding a 500-vote margin (0.15%), the election was settled by mid-December, in plenty of time for January's inauguration ceremony.[56]

Nor was New England the only part of the country to have this sort of success. Despite some hiccups, both Ohio and Alaska in 1974 conducted gubernatorial recounts that validated the initial results and quickly produced concessions from the losing candidate.[57] New Jersey had a similar experience in 1981. Indeed, New Jersey borrowed successful practices from the past. Like Maine in 1970, New Jersey immediately secured the custody of all votes statewide, thereby assuring the public that they would not be tampered with. Moreover, emulating Minnesota, New Jersey used recount rules jointly drafted by attorneys from both campaigns. Although New Jersey's 1981 election included some ugly tactics aimed at suppressing African American turnout, the losing candidate expressly disavowed any suggestion that they affected the outcome of the race. And although New Jersey's recount exposed inconsistencies in the counting of absentee ballots—the kind of inconsistencies that would trigger equal protection litigation after *Bush v. Gore*—this problem also did not affect the outcome, as the losing candidate publicly acknowledged. Thus, despite these flaws, New Jersey showed that it had transformed itself from earlier eras, when because of procedural manipulations the state had failed to yield results that reflected the electorate's will. This transformation was another instance of the change wrought by the elevation of democratic expectations in the 1960s.[58]

Not every gubernatorial election conformed to the new pattern. In 1982, Illinois suffered a dispute suggesting that it had yet to transform itself. Official returns showed the Republican incumbent, Jim Thompson, defeating challenger Adlai Stevenson III by 5,074.[59] A subsequent investigation by the local federal prosecutor, however, "estimated the vote fraud in Chicago to be approximately 10 percent or 100,000 votes"—a staggering amount.[60] Stevenson had sought a statewide recount (on issues separate from the fraud), but he was denied one by a 4–3 decision of the Illinois Supreme Court.[61] The judicial split was largely, but not entirely, on partisan lines: one Democrat joined three Republicans in the majority, with three Democrats dissenting. The majority's reasons for rejecting a recount were odd: the court claimed that the law providing for a recount was unconstitutional even though no party to the case had argued the constitutional point, and the majority needed to stretch the constitutional text to reach its conclusion. The majority also said that, even if a recount were permissible, the candidate seeking the recount would have to show beforehand each vote-counting mistake the recount would correct: a kind of Catch-22 standard that defeats the purpose of conducting the recount.[62] The sole Democrat in the majority did not write separately to explain why he was joining such an odd opinion. Perhaps he thought a recount futile given the large amount of Chicago-based fraud, which if rectified would have increased Thompson's margin. In any event, the lack of a recount and the failure of the court to offer a cogent explanation left Illinois open to the charge leveled in the dissenting opinion: "It may be that a recount would not have changed the announced results, but it will always be uncertain what was the will of the people in the gubernatorial election of 1982."[63]

Illinois was aberrational in its failure to conduct a successful gubernatorial recount. The clear trend since the sixties was in the opposite direction. Especially emblematic of the new era, wrought by the Voting Rights Act and one-person-one-vote, was Virginia in 1989. The recount in that state that year confirmed Douglas Wilder as the state's first African American governor since Reconstruction. Upon completion of the recount, Wilder's Republican opponent graciously declared him to be the "true winner."[64] That public confirmation of democracy's successful operation could not have occurred in the state a century or half-century earlier. A transformation indeed had arisen.

US Senate: Legislative Partisanship Endures

The success of the states in resolving disputed gubernatorial elections was not replicated for US Senate elections. The problem was not the states, but the Senate itself. In 1972 the US Supreme Court made clear that states were entitled to conduct their own recounts in US Senate races, as long as the Senate retained the ultimate authority to determine which candidate (if any) to seat as the winner.[65] In the aftermath of the Court's decision, one can compare two categories of disputed Senate races: (1) those settled in the states without the Senate's involvement; and (2) those reaching the Senate, requiring its determination. When one makes this comparison, it becomes evident that the first category fared much better, and this is true even when one directly compares disputes of comparable magnitude. Simply put, the step of taking a dispute to the Senate escalated the contentiousness and prolonged the controversy, as the Senate lacked procedures well-suited for these cases.

Even as late as the 1970s, the Senate had experienced relatively few ballot-counting disputes compared to the House of Representatives. Citizens had been casting ballots for senators only since 1914, after adoption of the Seventeenth Amendment. In the first six decades thereafter, only a handful of significant ballot-counting disputes had required the Senate's resolution, and in those cases the Senate's record was inconsistent. For example (as touched on briefly at the outset of the previous chapter), the Senate refused to seat the winning candidate in Pennsylvania's 1926 election, William Vare. The Senate reached this decision, not because he had secured fewer valid votes than his opponent, but essentially because Vare had spent too much money in support of his campaign. Although there had been allegations of ballot-box stuffing on Vare's behalf, there was not enough fraud to account for his victory margin, which was over 170,000 votes. Nonetheless, by a 58–22 vote, the Senate deemed Vare too corrupt to be worthy of a seat in the chamber.[66]

By contrast, the Senate let the certified winner of New Mexico's 1952 election keep his seat even though the certified margin was only 5,375 and a systemic breakdown of polling place operations had caused a myriad of problems, including over 50,000 ballots that were cast in violation of ballot secrecy rules.[67] In addition, during the state's recount of the race, a local judge had hastily burned 13,000 ballots in direct violation of applicable ballot-custody rules in order to prevent the ballots from being recounted.[68] When the Senate threatened to stalemate over this election, five Republicans joined all the Democrats (as well as one independent) to reject a Republican-led effort to declare the election void on the ground of improprieties large enough to undermine the narrow margin of victory.[69] While the result can be lauded as a display of modest bipartisanship, it is difficult to square with the unseating of Vare.

Moreover, the Senate never attempted to institutionalize any impartial procedure, in the spirit of the Grenville Act, to adjudicate this sort of dispute. Given that the Seventeenth Amendment itself was adopted as a reform measure, it would have been consonant with that reform to develop a novel procedure to handle ballot-counting disputes that reached the Senate. But no such new procedure was pursued. That left the Senate to resolve disputes over the elections of its members with its normal political processes, which were designed to slow down the consideration of legislation in an effort to enhance deliberation. Whatever the merits of the Senate's procedures for considering the enactment of new laws, their built-in delaying mechanisms are entirely inappropriate when the issue is which candidate won more votes in a close race where a significant number of votes are disputable.

In 1974, four US Senate seats ended up in dispute. Two of these disputes were settled without need of the Senate's involvement. The other two went to the Senate, where they became mired in ugly partisanship. This single year, therefore, offers something of a small-scale natural experiment on the effect of adding the Senate's involvement into the mix. Far from improving the process, the Senate only made matters worse.

The four states with these disputes were North Dakota, Nevada, New Hampshire, and Oklahoma. In all four, the Republican candidate was ahead after the canvass and still ahead after a recount. In two of the four, North Dakota and Nevada, the Democrat then graciously accepted defeat (even though there were matters that easily could have been pursued further by a candidate so inclined), and the dispute was resolved by mid-December. In both cases, the Republican winner was seated in the Senate without incident.[70]

By contrast, in the other two, New Hampshire and Oklahoma, the Democrat challenged the Republican's victory in the US Senate, where at the time the Democrats predominated 61–37 (not counting these two seats). As a result, the two disputes raged on for months. In the case of New Hampshire, the Senate kept the seat vacant and, after much deliberation and deadlock, on June 30, 1975, ordered a new election between the two candidates. With respect to Oklahoma, the Senate did seat the Republican provisionally, but did not dismiss the Democrat's contest—and thus left the election in doubt—until March 4, 1976, sixteen months after the ballots had been cast.[71]

To be sure, the New Hampshire election was extraordinarily, indeed uniquely, close. The Republican's victory, as certified by the state, was by a mere two votes, out of over 200,000 cast (for a margin, in percentage terms, of 0.0009%, or less than one thousandth of a percent). Moreover, the procedures that New Hampshire itself used were suspect in that a three-member ballot board consisting of two Republicans and one Democrat split 2–1 in enough instances to account for the Republican candidate's two-vote victory. But the Senate Democrats did not rectify this procedural defect by putting in place a neutral body along the lines of Minnesota's three-judge court in 1962—even though one senator, Claiborne Pell (a Democrat), recommended just such a procedure. Instead, it appeared as if most Senate Democrats wished to use their power to add the New Hampshire seat to their column, and this impulse was resisted by Senate Republicans (as well as some sympathetic Southern Democrats) by using their ability to filibuster to achieve a deadlock that could be broken only by calling a new election.[72]

A jump ball is the best one can do when one cannot figure out who deserves possession. In this case, however, the inability to figure it out was not the judgment of an impartial referee trying to make the right call. Instead, it was the consequence of the two teams' mutually giving up after neither one could rip the ball out of the other side's hands.

Here are the ugly details.

New Hampshire

Election Day in 1974 was Tuesday, November 5. The seat had become open after being held for twenty years by Norris Cotton, a Republican. Louis Wyman, a congressman, was trying to keep the seat for the GOP. John Durkin, recently the state's insurance commissioner, was trying to win it for the Democrats. On Friday, November 8, the secretary of state announced an official count, with Wyman ahead by 355 votes.

The recount, conducted under the supervision of the Republican secretary of State, was completed on November 27, with the result showing a Durkin victory by a mere ten votes. The turnabout in the result was attributed to human error by the secretary of state. The recount discovered 947 votes that had not been part of the November 8 official tally, and Durkin outpaced Wyman almost 3 to 1 among these previously missing votes. Wyman promptly appealed to the state's Ballot Law Commission (BLC), a three-member board with plenary authority over any issues arising in the recount. At the time, the BLC had two Republicans: its chair, Ronald Snow, and Warren Rudman, the state's future US senator. Even the BLC's lone Democrat, Roger Crowley, was viewed by other Democrats in the state as lacking sufficient party loyalty, being too closely tied to both the Republican governor and candidate Wyman. (Crowley's son had briefly worked part-time for Wyman.)[73]

The BLC was indeed unanimous in most of its rulings. But it did split 2–1, with Crowley dissenting, over enough ballots to make a difference in the outcome.[74] In one instance, what the secretary of state had ruled a "no vote," the two Republicans on the BLC ruled was a vote for Wyman. In another instance, a ballot that the secretary of state had counted for Durkin was ruled a no vote by the two BLC Republicans. There were others like these. In a race that ended up with a two-vote margin, these split decisions by the BLC were what flipped the result from a Durkin victory to a Wyman win.[75]

When Wyman presented his certificate of election, the Senate on January 28 in "a straight party line vote" declined to accept it, even provisionally.[76] One Republican protested, "You don't seem to care if Mr. Wyman's certificate is valid!" Howard Cannon, the Democrat in charge of his party's handling of the matter in the Senate, retorted, "You're absolutely right!"[77]

Cannon's committee, with five Democrats and three Republicans, then undertook the task of endeavoring to determine which candidate had won.[78] At this point, Wyman was willing to stand for a new election, but Durkin thought he could prevail in the Democrat-dominated committee and then the Senate. Durkin's plan, however, was stymied when one of the Democrats, James Allen of Alabama, began to vote consistently with the Republicans. The committee, thus deadlocked 4–4 on enough ballots and issues to leave the election unresolved, sent the matter back to the full Senate on May 22. At the time, one of the committee members, Senator Pell, argued that "the actual counting of the N. H. ballots, and as much as possible of the procedural decision-making relative to the N. H. Senate election contest, should not be done by elected individuals, but should have been delegated to a neutral body chosen from a panel recommended by the American Arbitration Association or other impartial source agreed upon by the contestants."[79] But this wise suggestion, reflecting the same principle successfully employed by Minnesota in 1962 (and harkening all the way back to James Kent's exhortation in 1792), was never acted upon.

In the full Senate, 57 Democrats were prepared to support Durkin's position that he had won the race, but 60 votes were necessary to break a filibuster, and four Southern Democrats including Allen refused to go along with what the rest of their party wanted.[80] On June 29, the *Washington Post* editorialized that "partisan tempers and suspicions" were preventing the "stalemate" from ending. "What is increasingly in doubt is the Senate's capacity to deal with this contest in an orderly and reasonable way," the editorial lamented, pointing to the "disgraceful mess."[81] Two weeks later, another *Post* editorial reiterated: "The Senate looks increasingly petty and partisan."[82] Another week passed, with the *Post* commenting that it would be "easy—almost embarrassingly easy—for disinterested observers" to find an impartial method to make the necessary ballot-specific and related procedural rulings to conclusively identify a winning candidate.[83] But such a solution was elusive, the *Post* observed, because "the contest has become a test of partisan power, loyalty, and stamina."[84] After yet another two more weeks, the *Post* fumed that it would be "incredible" if "partisan stubbornness" caused the Senate to take a recess until September with the election still unresolved.[85] A neutral "mediator" was needed, but the two sides could not manage to bring themselves to agree on one.[86]

Finally, the stalemate ended when Durkin agreed to submit to a new election. It is perhaps ironic that Durkin waited so long to reach this agreement since he won the subsequent election, held on September 16, 1975, by a decisively uncontestable margin of over 27,000 votes.[87] And although holding this election was obviously preferable to letting the impasse drag on even longer, it did not acquit the Senate of the charge that it had mishandled the whole matter. As the *Post* put it:

> The Senate did not make a positive finding that the November results were too close or too confused to call. Instead, the Senate found itself immobilized and unable to carry out at all its constitutional responsibility to judge Senate returns. This failure, caused and compounded by partisanship and pettiness on every side, has made this debacle one of the worst Senate performances in recent memory.[88]

Especially after New Hampshire's own partisan handling of the ballot-counting process, it could have been a great civics lesson if the Senate had shown both the state and the nation as a whole how to conduct an impartial recount. Not only was that opportunity squandered, but the nation received the opposite lesson: self-interested politicians are almost always incapable of counting ballots fairly.

Oklahoma

The Senate's inadequacy in handling a disputed election was illustrated even more clearly with the Oklahoma election of 1974. That election was nowhere near as close as New Hampshire's. Initial returns showed Henry Bellmon, the incumbent Republican, beating his Democrat challenger, Edmond Edmondson, by about 4,000 votes (or 0.5% of the almost 800,000 ballots cast).[89] Edmondson immediately claimed that there had been problems with Tulsa's voting machines. His main complaint was that the machines had not been programmed to permit straight-party voting, as required by state law, and even though many of those machines contained instructions as if they enabled a straight-party vote. He also complained that the US Senate race had been listed in the wrong spot on the ballot, after state races rather than before. Edmondson sued in state court to have the entire Tulsa vote invalidated, a remedy that would give him the election since he had prevailed over Bellmon by 18,000 votes in the rest of the state.[90]

Using a procedure reminiscent of Minnesota's in 1962, Oklahoma law required the two candidates to agree upon a judge to adjudicate the dispute. The judge they selected, Knox Byrum, happened to be a Democrat.[91] Judge Byrum, however, dismissed Edmondson's claim after hearing Edmondson's own expert, on cross-examination, admit that he could not testify that the asserted problems actually caused enough lost votes in Tulsa to make a difference in the outcome of the race. Judge Byrum rejected the idea that all of Tulsa should be disenfranchised based on speculation on how the ballot's design might have affected some unknown number of Tulsa's voters.

On December 21, 1974, the Oklahoma Supreme Court unanimously affirmed Judge Byrum's ruling. The court declared that, with respect to the Tulsa votes that Bellmon received, "Edmondson failed to establish and there is no competent evidence to support a finding that . . . Bellmon would not have received [these] votes . . . if the voting machines had been properly programmed with proper instructions."[92] Moreover, with respect to ballots cast in Tulsa that did not record any vote for US senator, the Oklahoma Supreme Court ruled that it could not presume that the asserted problems caused this undervote: "No competent evidence establishes why all the voters did not vote in all the races, [and] this Court may not speculate on the voters' reasons for voting as they did."[93] The court observed that a higher percentage of Tulsa voters recorded votes in the US Senate race (97%) than in the rest of the state (96%), thus contradicting the notion that the Tulsa machines caused a falloff in the US Senate election. In short, all nine justices of the Oklahoma Supreme Court agreed with Judge Byrum that Edmondson had failed to prove that he lost the election because of the machine problems he identified. Eight of these nine justices were, like Edmondson and Judge Byrum, Democrats.

Not willing to give up, Edmondson took his case to the Senate. Given the fairness of Oklahoma's proceedings, as well as the reasonableness of the result those proceedings reached, it should have been any easy case for the Senate to dismiss. After all, Edmondson had picked the trial judge who had ruled against him, and he could not have asked for a friendlier tribunal than the Oklahoma Supreme Court that had unanimously affirmed the trial judge's ruling. The basic facts, too, were against him: the votes actually recorded in Tulsa were unimpeachable, as the state supreme court had explained, and the missing votes could not be attributed to machine defects in Tulsa—especially since there were more missing votes elsewhere in the state.

Despite all of this, the Senate did not quickly dismiss the case. Instead, the Democrat-dominated Senate sent the case to committee, where it languished while the Senate was mired in the Durkin-Wyman mess from New Hampshire. Even after the Senate was finished with the Durkin-Wyman contest, it took another six months to resolve the Oklahoma race. The committee purported to find new evidence—not considered by the Oklahoma judiciary—on why the bad design of the Tulsa ballots might have made a difference in the Senate race. But the additional evidenced consisted of expert witnesses who, quite clearly, had been hired to make a case for Edmondson's position. By a 5–3 partisan vote, the committee recommended that the Senate declare the seat vacant.[94]

The Republicans understandably were livid. Among other arguments, they cited the 1952 New Mexico election: if the massive administrative problems in New Mexico then were not enough to void that election, then the comparatively minor problems in Tulsa should not be a basis for voiding Bellmon's victory based on the actual ballots cast and counted.[95]

The committee majority had overplayed its hand. When the issue reached the Senate floor, nine Southern Democrats balked and joined all the Republicans to defeat the committee's recommendation. (Seven other Democrats did not vote.) Thus, on March 4, 1976, the Senate finally declared Bellmon the winner of his race, an issue no nonpartisan tribunal ever would have considered in doubt after the Oklahoma Supreme Court's ruling back in December of 1974.[96]

Claiborne Pell, while the case was still in committee, had reiterated his call for such a nonpartisan tribunal:

> The Senate should consider a change in its procedures to provide for a review of challenged elections by an impartial, independent arbiter or panel of arbiters, whose sole responsibility would be to provide an advisory report to the Senate, with findings of fact and a recommendation as to whether it is reasonably possible to determine the will of the electorate and, if so, a recommendation on the course the Senate should follow in resolving the dispute.

This advisory panel, Pell understood, "could not substitute for the constitutionally-required judgment of the Senate." Nevertheless, he insisted, "it would assist measurably . . . in the formation of that judgment." Pell was honest enough to acknowledge that Senators, including himself, had succumbed "in the New Hampshire election dispute" to the "natural inclination" for "party-line voting."[97] The impartial advisory panel would be a tool to help Senators resist that temptation. As before, Pell's call went unheeded.

The unavoidable conclusion from the Senate's handling of the 1974 elections in New Hampshire and Oklahoma is that the Senate egregiously mishandled both. While New Hampshire had not acquitted itself well in its own procedures, the US Senate did nothing to improve the situation, only wasting many months before declaring itself incapable of conducting a review of the count. As for Oklahoma, the state was a model of fairness in the procedures it used, and the Senate only prevented these procedures from having their effect until finally the partisans in the Senate relented in the face of a filibuster. Especially when compared with the two disputed elections from 1974 that never reached the Senate, it would have been better if the Senate had never become involved with any of them.

Figure 9.3 Senator Claiborne Pell of Rhode Island unsuccessfully urged his colleagues to use an impartial tribunal to adjudicate the disputed elections in 1974 from New Hampshire and Oklahoma. AP Photo/Harvey Georges.

In contrast to how Minnesota resolved its 1962 gubernatorial election, the handling of New Hampshire's 1974 US Senate election seems particularly poor. If the revote had been the product of a mutual agreement between the two candidates as an outgrowth of fair procedures employed by the state, the situation would have looked more like Minnesota's. As extraordinarily close as that gubernatorial election was, with its 91-vote margin, New Hampshire's two-vote margin is something else again. One can imagine a handpicked, evenly balanced tribunal of the kind used in Minnesota coming to the conclusion that rather than declaring a victory based on a two-vote differential, the only fair disposition would be a revote. But that is not what happened. Instead, a tribunal dominated by one party attempted to declare the candidate of the same party the winner by a mere two votes, and then the opposing candidate took the fight to the Senate, which stalemated instead of attempting to handle it fairly.

In 2008 (as we shall see in Chapter 12), Minnesota would have its own disputed US Senate election and would replicate a version of the balanced three-judge panel that it used for its 1962 gubernatorial election—thereby avoiding the unfairness that New Hampshire exhibited in 1974. Furthermore, Minnesota would be fortunate that its fair procedures, unlike Oklahoma's in 1974, would not be subjected to Senate review and thus not mired in the quicksand of a Senate rendered dysfunctional by partisan quarrelsomeness.

10

The Eighties and Nineties

Reemergence of Intensified Partisanship

Ronald Reagan's election signaled a new period of American politics, as conservative forces within the Republican Party ascended. Gone were the days when the social programs of the New Deal and Great Society were taken for granted. As Bill Clinton famously conceded in his 1996 State of the Union address, "the era of big Government is over."[1]

The transformation that Reagan represented was not, however, a conversion to the hegemony of one-party domination. As Clinton's election itself showed, Democrats were capable of remaining competitive, given the right candidate and circumstances. In fact, the increased competitiveness of national politics after 1980, in which both Republicans and Democrats had good chances of winning control of all three elected branches of the federal government (the two houses of Congress as well as the presidency), caused the fight for power between the two parties to intensify.[2] Battles over policy in Congress became more acrimonious, and correspondingly the struggle to win seats there became more hard-edged. Although the hyperpolarization and concomitant divisiveness in Congress would not become so readily apparent until after 2000, the signs of its emergence were appearing by the 1980s.[3]

The new competitiveness between the two parties was also having an effect in the South. Long the bastion of one-party rule by the Democrats, Republicans were making rapidly accelerating inroads. In 1965, the year of the Voting Rights Act, not a single state of the former Confederacy had a Republican governor. Twenty years later, in 1985, only two did (North Carolina and Tennessee). But in just two more years that number jumped to five (Alabama, Florida, North and South Carolina, and Texas). And a decade after that, in 1997, eight out of the eleven ex-Confederate states—a majority for the first time since Reconstruction—had Republican governors (Alabama, Arkansas, Louisiana, Mississippi, South Carolina, Tennessee, Texas, and Virginia; only Florida, Georgia, and North Carolina did not).[4]

Inevitably, this intensification of electoral competition between the two parties, both nationally and regionally, spilled over into vote-counting disputes when and where they occurred. Both a symbol and catalyst of the new hyperpartisanship in Congress was the so-called Bloody Eighth, the battle over the 1984 election for Indiana's Eighth Congressional District. Although a fight for just one seat in the House of Representatives, at a time when Democrats already held 70-seat advantage (252–182), the leadership of the Democrats in the House was nervous that President Reagan could peel off the support of conservative Democrats from the South (the so-called Boll Weevils) to form his own functioning majority in the chamber.[5] Thus Democrats fought for this single Indiana seat as if the stakes could not have been higher, and their ferocity spawned even greater antipathy among House Republicans, who used the Bloody Eighth as a rallying cry to lay the foundation for their takeover of the chamber a decade later in the Gingrich Revolution of 1994.[6]

1994 was also the year of a monumental vote-counting dispute in the South, one that both symbolized the accelerating rise of Republicans in the region and generated the most important judicial precedent prior to *Bush v. Gore* on the role that the transformative one-person-one-vote doctrine of *Reynolds v. Sims* has in the context of counting ballots. This major dispute concerned the election that year for Alabama's chief justice, an office that no Republican had held since Reconstruction. But the same political forces that were giving Gingrich the ability to turn the US House of Representatives Republican for the first time in four decades were also enabling Republicans to pull ahead for the first time in over a century in the race for chief justice of Alabama. Only if Democrats could convince a court to count apparently invalid absentee ballots would they be able to keep the seat for another term. Although one might think that the Alabama Supreme Court would be incapable of adjudicating the validity of ballots cast in an election for its chief justice—each member of the court being directly affected by the choice of its chief justice and thus having an obvious conflict of interest—several of the court's members were willing to opine on the validity of the pivotal absentee ballots. These renegade jurists even had the chutzpah to proclaim the ballots valid despite the explicit language of state law that provided otherwise. This audacious ruling prompted Republicans to seek relief in federal court, which laid down the trailblazing precedent that *Reynolds v. Sims* and its doctrine of one-person-one-vote gives the federal judiciary the authority to prevent a state court from subverting the result of an election by changing the rules for counting ballots after they have been cast.

Whether viewed separately or together, both the Bloody Eighth and the Alabama chief justice election were harbingers of what would happen in 2000. The Bloody Eighth showed how vitriolic a vote-counting dispute could become when the national parties saw the battle as significant. Indeed, some of the key players involved in *Bush v. Gore* cut their proverbial teeth in the Bloody Eighth episode. Likewise, the 1994 Alabama chief justice election served as a model of how the federal judiciary could repudiate a state-court ruling perceived as antithetical to the proper operation of democracy.

For anyone wishing to understand how *Bush v. Gore* emerged from antecedents in the eighties and nineties, it pays to take a closer look at both the Bloody Eighth and the 1994 election for Alabama's chief justice. It is worth noting also that problems with absentee ballots provided the fodder for each of these two major conflagrations. Along with Miami's mayoral election of 1997, for which a Florida appeals court nullified all of the absentee ballots because of rampant fraud, these episodes signaled that absentee ballots are a particularly vulnerable component of the voting process.[7] Based on the track record of the eighties and nineties, one would predict that in the early part of the twentieth-first century absentee ballots would continue to provide an attractive target of opportunity for any candidate wishing to challenge a close election result. Absentee ballots indeed threatened to become a major focal point of the disputed presidential election in 2000, until the Gore campaign for political reasons abandoned its willingness to challenge procedurally deficient absentee ballots. But the prediction would prove true in 2008, in Minnesota's disputed US Senate election, where litigation over absentee ballots became the main event.

The Bloody Eighth

In the 1984 election for Indiana's Eighth Congressional District, Frank McCloskey was a one-term incumbent Democrat in a seat previously held by Republicans. McCloskey was vulnerable in a year that would be very good for Republicans, with Ronald Reagan on his way to a monumental reelection landslide over Walter Mondale. McCloskey's Republican challenger was Rick McIntyre, a two-term state representative.[8]

Initial returns showed McCloskey leading by 190 votes, then dropping in early December to just 72.[9] Amidst calls for a recount, it emerged that Gibson County had submitted erroneous initial returns to the secretary of state, Republican Ed Simcox, and that corrected returns would put McIntyre ahead by 34 votes.[10] Once Gibson County corrected this error, Simcox certified McIntyre the winner of the election even though fourteen other counties in the district had not yet completed their own recounting of ballots. The Democrats had tried to get a federal judge to order Simcox to certify McCloskey the winner before he received Gibson County's amended return, but the federal judge had refused to intervene.[11]

McCloskey then went to the US House of Representatives in an effort to block McIntyre from assuming office. On January 3, 1985, as other Representatives took their seats in the new Congress, the House voted along straight-party lines, 238 to 177, to keep the Indiana Eighth vacant while its Administration Committee examined the election.[12] Meanwhile, on February 4, the fourteen other counties finally finished their recounts, with McIntyre's margin of victory expanding to 418 votes.[13]

The House Administration Committee had a dozen Democrats and only seven Republicans. It created a three-member task force to investigate the vote count in the Indiana Eighth. The task force had two Democrats, Leon Panetta of California and Bill Clay of Missouri. The one Republican was Bill Thomas, also of California, indeed from a district adjacent to Panetta's.[14] The task force's chair, Panetta would later become Bill Clinton's chief of staff and then CIA director and secretary of defense in the Obama Administration. But Panetta had started his political career as a Republican, working in the Nixon administration.[15] In 1985, still fairly junior among Democrats in the House, he had the chance to prove his loyalty (and usefulness) to his new party by winning this battle for the Democrats.

The fight involved virtually every type of ballot-counting problem conceivable, including the same type of hanging chads on punch-card ballots that would become the focal point of the 2000 presidential election. But the main issue that made the Bloody Eighth so combative, provoking apoplectic fury among Republicans, was the task force's treatment of absentee ballots that had not been properly notarized or witnessed according to Indiana law. This same issue would feature prominently a quarter-century later, in Minnesota's disputed US Senate election of 2008.

The problem was that although Indiana law strictly maintained that nonconforming ballots were ineligible to be counted, at least five of the fifteen counties in the congressional districts had failed to comply with the law and wrongfully counted absentee ballots that lacked the required notarization or witnessing. County clerks had sent these ballots to local precincts in violation of a state-law requirement that these ballots be retained at the county's offices, so that they would *not* be counted at local precincts.[16] Nonetheless, they had been sent and counted there, and now they were irretrievably commingled with all other counted ballots, so that it was physically impossible for the task force to uncount them.

The task force's challenge was how to handle absentee ballots that were equally nonconforming as the ones improperly counted (equally lacking the requisite notarization or witnessing) but thus far had been excluded from the count in compliance with state law. All three members of the task force accepted the general principle that it should "treat like ballots the same."[17]

When Thomas, the Republican, stated, "I think we have to handle like ballots in a similar way," Panetta replied, "Well, I would not disagree with that."[18] In *Bush v. Gore*, the US Supreme Court would recognize this principle as an element of equal protection, guaranteed by the federal Constitution. But in the eighties the task force saw it more as a value to respect rather than a requirement to obey.

The task force's difficulties were compounded by the fact that there were two types of equally nonconforming absentee ballots that had not yet been counted. One type had also been sent to the local precincts in violation of state law, but had been caught there to prevent the further violation of being counted. The other type had been retained by the county clerks, never sent to the local precincts, in full compliance with state law.[19]

The task force grappled with the problem at its meeting on April 10, 1985. By that point, the task force's recount of the entire district was nearing completion, and McCloskey (the Democrat) had pulled even with McIntyre (the Republican). Over Thomas's objection, the task force had decided to deviate from Indiana's strict ballot-counting rules to deal with another discrepancy that emerged. With respect to ballots cast in polling places on Election Day, state law required their disqualification unless they contained the initials of two poll workers, one from each party, as well as the precinct number penciled on the ballot. Many counties refused to enforce these strict requirements on the ground that doing so would disenfranchise innocent voters, since the failure to comply with these rules was poll worker error. (There was no allegation that fraud had caused the noncompliance with these requirements.) But other counties had complied, causing some 5,000 otherwise valid ballots to be disqualified solely on this basis, many of them coming from predominantly African American precincts.[20] The task force had decided to count all of these irregular ballots, to maintain equivalence with those already counted elsewhere in disobedience to state law. Thomas, the Republican member of the task force, had proposed that ballots lacking all three required elements—the two sets of initials and the precinct number—remain uncounted on the ground that these ballots lacked any indicia of reliability. But the two Democrats on the task force let them all in, and as a result McIntyre's 418-vote lead had entirely evaporated.

Now, on April 10, it was time to confront what to do about the nonconforming absentee ballots, which—in contrast to those cast in polling places—were thought generally to favor Republicans. The topic prompted an extended discussion between Panetta and Thomas, with Clay (the other Democrat) remaining silent. Panetta and Thomas were able to agree that the first type of nonconforming absentee ballots, those that had been sent to the local precincts but had remained uncounted, should be counted in accordance with the principle of treating "like ballots" alike. As Thomas put it, "those nonnotarized absentee ballots that were sent to the precinct and opened and already counted has to be, I think, the standard that we apply to those other nonnotarized ballots that were sent to the precinct, because you cannot count some and not others that are in the same category."[21] Panetta concurred: "We will count all of the absentee ballots that went to the precinct" pursuant to the task force's "basic approach"—"because they are like ballots."[22]

But Panetta and Thomas struggled over how to handle the second type of nonconforming absentee ballots, those that had never been sent to the precincts at all. At the April 10 meeting, Panetta repeatedly expressed the view, albeit somewhat tentatively, that these ballots might deserve different treatment simply because they had been retained by the county clerks. Early in the discussion, Panetta posited: "There could be a distinction drawn between like ballots and unlike ballots in the sense that the ones that were retained by the county clerk as unnotarized were never reviewed, never looked at, basically set aside, never referred back to a precinct at all, so that in essence they were treated very differently from the ones that actually went back to the precinct then and were evaluated along with other ballots in some instances." As the discussion progressed, Panetta's position became firmer:

> It seems to me, that we can draw a distinction based on those within the precinct level, and the question then becomes, can you then say that the ones that are back in the County then ought not to be counted? My view is that they ought not to be counted because the county clerks basically made their judgment at that time, set those aside.[23]

Thomas, conversely, hardened his view in the opposite direction over the course of the deliberations. Initially, he stated his openness to the distinction that Panetta was proposing, based on the possibility that ballots kept by the county clerk (after being disqualified) might have been kept in a less secure condition than those sent to the precincts:

> I think the question is, were the ballots that were retained by the county clerks as being nonnotarized under Indiana law, were they treated differently or not exactly the same as those that were out in the precinct. If they were not, then I think we can honor those in the precinct without honoring those in the clerk's office.[24]

Later on, however, Thomas emphasized the flip side of the same coin: if the county clerks kept the nonconforming ballots in equally secure conditions as those in the precincts, then both groups should be counted equally along with the nonconforming ballots already counted in the precincts. He called it "the most perverted thing I can think of" to reject absentee ballots kept by the county clerk if "they were treated exactly like" the ballots sent to the precincts in terms of "identical security." As long as the security conditions "are identical," Thomas repeatedly asserted, "I don't see how we can't count them."[25]

The hardening of the positions on both sides in the course of the deliberations may have reflected the increasing awareness, on the part of both Panetta and Thomas, that this second category of nonconforming absentee ballots might well determine the result of the entire race. In any event, the two sides agreed to defer final consideration of how to handle the category until they received further factual information from the counties on the key point, at least for Thomas, concerning the security conditions for these ballots retained by the county clerks. Panetta was careful to announce that, for him, this additional information might not matter: "It may very well be that despite [these additional] statements, I think there is a difference just by virtue of the fact that some are forwarded to the precinct, and the others are retained."[26] But Panetta was willing to go along with the collection of "additional evidence from the clerks" to see if it would shed any light on "how [these ballots] were treated."[27]

The task force next met on April 18. Meanwhile, with the recount virtually complete except for a final decision on what to do with the nonconforming absentee ballots kept at the clerk's offices, McCloskey had finally managed to eke ahead of McIntyre by a mere three votes. A fourth would later be added to his infinitesimal lead, making it the closest House race of the century.[28]

At the April 18 meeting, the task force heard a report on the additional evidence they had requested the previous week. They learned that several counties in fact had kept the disqualified absentee ballots completely secure. Even so, Panetta announced that he would adhere to his previously stated view that these ballots were in a "different class" from nonconforming ballots sent to the precincts simply because "they were kept at the county clerk's level" and thus "were never counted by anyone—the county clerk or anybody else—nor attempted to be counted by anyone because they basically abided by Indiana law by essentially voiding those ballots."[29] Clay, the other Democrat, said it had been wrong for the task force to count even those nonconforming absentee ballots sent to the precincts (although Clay had not stated that position at the April 10 meeting). Clay did not want to "compound the error" by now counting the nonconforming ballots retained by the clerks.[30]

Once Thomas saw that both Democrats were definitely against counting this batch of absentee ballots—there were 32 of them, more than enough to make a difference in the outcome of the election—he became furious.[31] "I cannot believe this," he exclaimed, directly accusing Panetta of "hypocrisy."[32]

Thomas thought it was particularly two-faced that Panetta "didn't care about Indiana law" when considering the nonconforming ballots cast at polling places, but now that absentee ballots were at issue "what I hear piously stated is that we had better talk about upholding the Indiana law." Thomas thought it "ironic," too, that the previous week Panetta was willing "to count those ballots that sent to the precincts," but now, even though the task force had learned that the ones retained by the clerks were kept securely—"so we know they are not tainted, we know they have not been contaminated"—Panetta refused to treat them the same. Furthermore, Thomas blasted, Panetta was taking this position although the retained ballots were no more nonconforming under Indiana law than the ones sent to the precincts (in fact less so, since they were supposed to be retained there, rather than sent to the precincts). Thomas repeated his charge: "To hide behind Indiana law saying they held them at the courthouse and therefore we don't count them is the absolute height of hypocrisy and I am surprised that the gentleman from California is willing to go that far in terms of being inconsistent under his own rules."[33]

Panetta retorted by saying that Thomas himself was inconsistent in his newfound eagerness to "trash Indiana law" by counting "the unnotarized, unwitnessed absentee ballots that were retained by the clerks," when previously Thomas had insisted upon compliance with Indiana law to "eliminate about 4,800 to 5,000 ballots" cast at polling places because they "had no initials [or] precinct numbers."[34] Panetta further defended his own distinction between the two groups of nonconforming absentee ballots, depending on whether they were sent to the precincts or retained by the clerk: "There is no question in my mind that these ballots were isolated by the clerks because they were not to be counted" and thus "are very different from the other ballots that we counted," which had been "forwarded to the precincts" and needed to be treated the same as equally nonconforming ballots already counted at the precincts: "We made the decision where those ballots were forwarded to the precinct they would all be counted" and so "there is a legitimate basis on which to make the decision that those retained by the county clerks ought not to be counted."[35]

Thomas, however, would not back down. He parried Panetta's charge that he was at least equally inconsistent, and riposted that Panetta was changing the rules just because McCloskey had pulled ahead:

> My argument is don't hide behind Indiana law at this date. My gosh, the rules you shoved down my throat didn't give much credence to Indiana law at the time. And now you are arguing that Indiana law will protect you from having some votes count that may change the outcome that you feel you already know.

Lest anyone miss his point, Thomas repeated that he was entitled to rely on Panetta's own rules once they had been made: "Yes, you crammed those rules down [my] throat by a straight partisan vote, but once we are under those rules let's at least try to be consistent under those rules and not game play the rules for one or the other's advantage."[36]

Thomas and Panetta continued to exchange heated words. But it did not change the result. Later in the proceeding, Thomas said he had felt as if he had been "raped" by the majority of the task force—a comment that drew considerable media attention.[37] Thomas defended the charge: "I use that word purposefully, because rapists try to conquer and dominate and humiliate their victims."[38]

Thomas, however, was hardly alone among Republicans in the vehemence with which he expressed his ire. In their official Minority statement accompanying the House Administration Committee's ratification of the task force, the Republicans on the committee echoed Thomas's basic accusation: "If McCloskey had been behind at that time, the Minority is confident that the Majority would have opened and counted those votes in hopes of reviving their candidate."[39] In their conclusion, the Republicans captured the essence

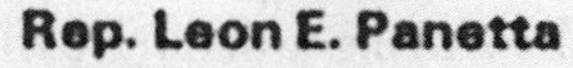

Figure 10.1 On May 5, 1985, the *Los Angeles Times* ran a story featuring the two congressmen from California dueling over the Bloody Eighth on behalf of their respective parties; accompanying the story were these photos supplied by their congressional offices.

of their complaint: "The Majority's total disregard of fair play magnifies the abuses of partisanship and rends the basic fabric of the House."[40]

As the matter moved to the House floor, Republicans escalated their rhetoric. Newt Gingrich condemned the "lesson in thug rule."[41] Dick Cheney proclaimed, "it's time to go to war."[42] Republicans attempted to bring the House to a halt, calling for a new election of the kind that occurred to resolve the 1974 New Hampshire Senate election.[43] But Republicans lacked the power of the filibuster in the House, and on May 1, 1985, the Democrats prevailed in voting to seat McCloskey. The Republicans walked out in protest, and they kept their rancor with them for decades, into the twenty-first century.[44]

Republicans also tried to overturn the outcome in federal court, raising equal protection and due process claims of the kind that they would present again in *Bush v. Gore*. But the federal judiciary ruled the claims nonjusticiable on the ground that under the Constitution the House, like the Senate, held final authority to judge the election of its own members. Then-judge (and soon-to-be Justice) Antonin Scalia wrote the lead opinion, declaring it "difficult to imagine a clearer case" of the court's "lack [of] jurisdiction to proceed."[45] The Republicans were left only with their sense that Democrats did not play fair and that there was no tribunal from which they could receive an impartial adjudication of the ballot-counting dispute. Investigative reporting later would show that McIntyre indeed would have prevailed by at least nine votes if the 32 disputed absentee ballots had been counted.[46]

Ultimately it matters little whether Panetta or Thomas had the better view on the disposition of the ballots, to count them or not. Rather, the crucial point is one of procedure and perception. Because the task force had two Democrats and one Republican, and because the key ruling was a 2–1 partisan split, Democrats could not refute the charge that they were manipulating the ballot-counting rules midstream to achieve the desired result. Of course, the Bloody Eighth was hardly the first instance of this kind of 2–1 partisan split by an authoritative ballot-counting body. In 1876, the Florida Canvassing Board had done exactly the same, with far greater repercussions.

But the Bloody Eighth earned its appellation—although no actual blood was shed—because ethical expectations had risen in the century since Hayes-Tilden. Although one of the Florida canvassers had confessed to "straining the rules" to "favor" his "own party," that sin was not one that congressional Democrats were willing to acknowledge in their handling of this Indiana election. The morality of ballot-counting had come to insist that the party in power treat the other party as it would insist on being treated if the roles were reversed. Perhaps this ethical injunction was nothing more than the ancient Golden Rule applied to the particular context, but it was a requirement now considered essential to the proper functioning of two-party competition in an electoral democracy. And it was a requirement that Republicans believed that Democrats had breached in this instance.

In his memoirs Leon Panetta devotes less than a page to the Bloody Eighth episode, but in that short space he attempts to defend his conduct. He glosses over some key details—as, for example, when he asserts that "Thomas had agreed to the rules and process for the recount," despite the fact that Thomas clearly dissented on key rulings. Panetta also frames the crux of his defense in terms of an assertion that he acted consistently with the Golden Rule: "Republicans would have done the same if one of theirs had won by four votes."[47] Since he does not elaborate, it is unclear exactly what Panetta means. He could be claiming that Republicans would have been just as self-serving in manipulating the recount process to their own advantage if they had been in the position to do so. But that seems the weaker reading of his sentence. Instead, in context it appears that Panetta claims that it was perfectly fair to act as he did, because both parties would consider the task force's conduct appropriate for whichever party happened to be in control of ballot-counting in similar circumstances.

Whether or not Panetta advances a normatively sound understanding of the Golden Rule, the record shows that he is factually inaccurate in his characterization of how Republicans would behave if given the opportunity in similar circumstances. Ten years later, after the Gingrich revolution of 1994 put the Republicans in control of the House, Connecticut had an exceptionally close race for its Second Congressional District. Republicans could have used this Connecticut election as payback for the Bloody Eighth. But they chose not to, exercising laudable self-restraint. Bill Thomas was on the task force for this election, and he was determined not to do unto Democrats what they had done unto Republicans a decade earlier. When the House Republicans awarded the Democratic candidate the Connecticut seat, the winning Democrat acknowledged that he had been treated more fairly than had his Republican candidate in the Bloody Eighth episode.[48]

The 1994 Alabama Chief Justice Election

Absentee ballots were also the centerpiece of the most doctrinally significant disputed election of the era between *Reynolds v. Sims* and *Bush v. Gore*. This statewide election was neither for governor nor US senator, but instead for chief justice on the Alabama Supreme Court. Regardless of whether or not judges should be elected, the symbolism of a vote-counting dispute in an election for chief justice is acutely poignant. The office of chief justice is the highest embodiment in a state of its commitment to the rule of law and the fairness of the legal system. If counting the ballots in a chief justice election is corrupt, then what hope is there for democracy in that state? Although there were no allegations of fraud in the *casting* of absentee ballots in Alabama's 1994 chief justice election, there were serious and strenuous allegations that the *counting* of those absentee ballots was, if not outright fraudulent, at least highly corrupt.

These allegations were raised in federal court, even briefly appearing in the US Supreme Court for a ruling by Justice Anthony Kennedy on an emergency stay petition. The case created a major Fourteenth Amendment precedent that, at least in retrospect, serves as a strong signal of exactly the kind of claim that would prevail in *Bush v. Gore*. Thus, in understanding the evolution from *Reynolds v. Sims* to *Bush v. Gore*—both doctrinally under the Fourteenth Amendment, and institutionally in terms of federal court involvement—this particular disputed election is undoubtedly the most important of the entire 35-year period.

The incumbent chief justice was a Democrat, Ernest Hornsby, who before his judicial service had been president of the state bar as well as the state's trial lawyers association. The Republican challenger was Perry Hooper, a lower-court state judge and one-time Republican nominee for US senator from the state. Although Alabama had not elected a Republican as chief justice since Reconstruction, by 1994 the state had been trending sufficiently Republican to make this campaign ferocious and expensive. Business interests invested hitherto unimaginable sums on behalf of Hooper, while trial lawyers spent profusely in an effort to help Hornsby keep his seat.[49]

On Election Night, November 8, Hooper was ahead by several thousand votes, but a quarter of the state's precincts still had not reported, and absentee ballots had not yet been included.[50] By Thursday, Hornsby had pulled ahead but by the tiny margin of only 304 votes (out of more than one million cast). He declared victory, but Hooper immediately went to a favorable state judge to secure a temporary restraining order to preserve all the records from the election.

Meanwhile, over the next few days during the canvass, the correcting of errors caused the count to flip back in favor of Hooper. A voting machine "glitch" had deprived Hooper of 295 votes, and a 100-vote tabulation mistake in Hornsby's favor meant that Hooper was now ahead by at least 91 votes. More mistakes required adding another 170 votes to Hooper's total.[51]

Now that Hornsby was behind, it was his turn to seek a friendly judge. His allies found one in Montgomery County, where Judge Joseph Phelps enjoined official certification of the election until after an examination of uncounted absentee ballots.[52] The Democrats claimed that as many as two thousand rejected absentee ballots were entitled to be counted. The issue was a classic one pitting the claims of "strict compliance" and "substantial compliance" against each other. Alabama's statute said that an absentee ballot must either be notarized or have two witnesses, and the principle of "strict compliance" would demand that a ballot satisfy this explicit statutory requirement in order to be counted. The Democrats, however, argued that Alabama law had adopted the contrary principle of substantial compliance. In support, they cited two recent Alabama Supreme Court decisions: *Williams v. Lide* and *Wells v. Ellis*.[53] Thus, the Democrats contended, an absentee ballot should be counted even if lacking notarization or any witness as long as it has the voter's own signature and address. Judge Eugene Reese, who had taken over the case from Judge Phelps, agreed with the Democrats and on November 17 ordered the counting of rejected absentee ballots according to this substantial compliance standard.[54]

The Republicans then went to federal court and the next day, November 18, secured another temporary order, this one prohibiting the counting of previously uncounted absentee ballots. The issue of how to handle the disputed absentee ballots under Alabama law was complicated by the state's obligation under the federal Voting Rights Act to obtain approval for any change in the state's voting rules.[55] Republicans argued that Judge Reese's order to count absentee ballots according to the substantial compliance standard, rather than adhering strictly to the explicit statutory requirements, was such a change in the state's voting rules. The US Department of Justice (DOJ), however, exercising its authority under the Voting Rights Act, quickly gave its approval for Judge Reese's substantial compliance standard. In a letter to Secretary of State Jim Bennett, a Democrat who later converted to the Republican Party, US DOJ wrote that the Alabama Supreme Court had previously approved the substantial compliance standard (as Hornsby's supporters had claimed). Moreover, the DOJ letter added, some Alabama counties apparently had already adopted the substantial compliance standard as their own local practice, and thus it would be a change in the law to switch back to strict compliance. The federal court then dismissed the Republican lawsuit on the authority of the DOJ "preclearance" letter.[56]

November 23 was the date on which the secretary of state was supposed to certify the results of the elections, but back in federal court the Republicans secured another order prohibiting certification prior to further consideration of the uncounted absentee ballots. A Reagan appointee, Judge Alex Howard of the federal district court in Mobile, issued this order. The Republicans, having lost their Voting Rights Act argument, focused on the Fourteenth Amendment of the federal Constitution as a basis for relief. They continued to claim that Judge Reese's adoption of the substantial compliance standard was a change in Alabama law. They now contended that this change—coming after the ballots already had been cast in the election—was a retroactive alteration of the voting rules in violation of the Fourteenth Amendment's Due Process Clause. In their filings with Judge Howard, the Republicans argued: "To now treat as legal, ballots which were void, invalid and illegal at the time purportedly cast prior to the election, is the functional equivalent of altering ballots or stuffing the ballot box."[57]

On December 5, Judge Howard ruled that it would be "abominable under the US Constitution" to count the disputed absentee ballots. Agreeing entirely with the Republicans, Judge Howard proclaimed succinctly: "You cannot change the rules of the election after the election is held."[58] On appeal, in a 2–1 decision issued a month later (on January 4), the Eleventh Circuit wholeheartedly endorsed that statement of principle but stopped short of ruling that it had been violated in this case. Instead, the federal appeals court certified to the Alabama Supreme Court the question of whether the rejected ballots were entitled to be counted under state law even though they lacked the statutory requirements of notarization or two witnesses. Invoking *Reynolds v. Sims* and *Griffin v. Burns* as the leading relevant cases, the Eleventh Circuit's majority opinion said that (1) "fundamental unfairness" violates due process, (2) "failing to exclude the contested absentee ballots will constitute a postelection departure from previous practice in Alabama," and (3) "this departure would . . . implicate fundamental fairness."[59] The circuit court majority thus gave the Alabama Supreme Court a chance to say that despite its earlier substantial compliance precedents, a proper understanding of Alabama law in this instance demanded strict compliance with the statutory requirement of notarization or two witnesses.

Judge Edmondson, in dissent, complained that federal judiciary was improperly interfering in a state election. Edmondson thus essentially invoked the longstanding principle underlying the *Taylor v. Beckham* precedent, from Kentucky's gubernatorial election of 1899, which had been confirmed in many cases, including by Justice Hugo Black's stay in the Ballot Box 13 litigation. But Judge Edmondson did not cite these venerable precedents, and neither did the majority. It was as if the Eleventh Circuit judges knew, or at least assumed, that the old jurisprudence was no longer relevant after the revolution wrought by *Reynolds v. Sims*. (All three of the Eleventh Circuit judges were appointed by Republican presidents.)

The Alabama Supreme Court did not accept the invitation offered by the Eleventh Circuit majority. Nor did the court turn the case over to temporary justices, as Hooper suggested, on the grounds that the election of the court's chief justice was a matter "too close to home" for any of them to be impartial. The state's new attorney general, Jeff Sessions (who later would become the state's US senator), proposed the creation of a special bipartisan court to hear the case, and the governor concurred with that recommendation. Yet three of the court's nine justices insisted on staying on the case even though they had given money to Hornsby's reelection campaign.[60] They were joined by a fourth who also had close ties to Hornsby, including receiving campaign contributions from Hornsby's son.[61] These four released an opinion in direct defiance of the Eleventh Circuit, arguing first that the federal judiciary did not have proper jurisdiction in the case (essentially agreeing with Judge Edmondson's dissent) and, second, that Alabama law embraced the substantial compliance doctrine prior to this election and thus the disputed ballots should be counted in accordance with that doctrine. Indeed, this four-justice opinion protested: "For this Court or any court to now hold that the ballots that met the three-pronged test of *Williams v. Lide* are not to be counted, would, in and of itself, work a change in Alabama law."[62] These four justices also observed that at least some absentee ballots in this very election already had been counted even though they lacked notarization or two witnesses, and therefore to refuse to count other "absentee ballots, legally and materially indistinguishable from those that were counted" would be discriminatory and unlawful.

One justice who chose to participate in the case dissented. Four other justices had the decency to sit the case out, including Hornsby himself (who was entitled to stay on the court until the winner of the election was finally determined).[63] None of the five justices who participated explained how they were entitled to act as the court when six were necessary for a quorum. The dissenting opinion focused on arguing that under a proper interpretation of the relevant Alabama Supreme Court precedents, the substantial compliance doctrine did not extend as far as the four-justice majority opinion said and therefore did not justify the counting of absentee ballots that lacked either notarization or two witnesses. The attorney general then filed a rehearing petition, which raised the issue of a quorum and argued the necessity of appointing a special court to hear the case. The four justices in the original majority issued an order striking the rehearing petition. This time the dissenting justice also argued that the court lacked jurisdiction for absence of a quorum.[64]

The case then went back to the Eleventh Circuit, which on April 26 remanded the case to Judge Howard for an evidentiary trial of the factual issue whether prior to this particular election Alabama election officials actually ever counted absentee ballots that lacked either notarization or two witnesses. The Eleventh Circuit gave Judge Howard seventeen specific factual questions to answer, but as the appellate court itself summarized "the purpose of this court's remand [is] to determine the practice in Alabama regarding the counting of the contested absentee ballots prior to the November 8 election, to determine the extent to which such practice was known to reasonable absentee voters in Alabama, and to determine what effect, if any, the contested absentee ballots had on the outcome of the election for Chief Justice."[65] As the preliminary step of this fact-finding process, Alabamans officially learned for the first time on May 14 that Hooper indeed would win the election by 123 votes if the roughly two thousand disputed ballots remained uncounted.[66] Over a month later, 139 more votes were added to Hooper's official lead, for a total of 262, when one locality discovered and corrected a tabulation error in its returns.

The fact-finding trial in Judge Howard's courtroom finally started on September 18. The evidence quickly became clear that "election officials in all but one Alabama county—Washington—have said in written answers or in testimony in Howard's court that ballots lacking the signatures of two witnesses or a notary public as required by state law have been thrown out in the past."[67] Nonetheless, Democratic partisans, including Don Siegelman, continued pressing to get the ballots counted. At the time Siegelman was lieutenant governor. Previously, he had been Alabama's secretary of state and attorney general and later he would become governor, thereby being the only person elected to all four of the state's top executive branch positions. (His own bid for reelection as governor in 2002 would become disputed when one county

Figure 10.2 This cartoon, by Mark Cullum, appeared in the *Birmingham News* on May 2, 1995, reflecting dismay that the 1994 Alabama chief justice election was still mired in litigation six months after ballots had been cast (and would remain litigated for another six months). Permission of Mark Cullum.

reported a voting machine malfunction that once corrected swung the election to his Republican opponent. Later, Siegelman's career would become tarnished when he was convicted of federal bribery charges for doing favors for campaign contributors.) On September 20, 1995, Siegelman testified before Judge Howard that the disputed absentee ballots in the chief justice election should count. Siegelman's testimony caused Judge Howard to become livid. "With his face turning red and his voice growing loud," Judge Howard accused Siegelman of contradicting his own explicit instructions to local election officials in 1980 when he was secretary of state.[68] Siegelman's instructions had stated:

> If, upon examination, the affidavit obviously does not comply with Alabama law, that is, if it is not properly witnessed or notarized, is not signed by the voter, or does not otherwise contain sufficient information to determine that the person is a qualified elector and is entitled to vote absentee, the ballot should not be counted.[69]

Siegelman said that he understood this instruction to mean that "election workers should count ballots without witness signatures if they can determine by other means, including 'by calling people in the courthouse' that the person is entitled to vote absentee."[70] Judge Howard clearly found Siegelman's statement disingenuous at best. In his written opinion issued on September 29, Judge Howard all but directly accused Siegelman of dissembling:

> The Court FINDS his testimony to be diametrically opposed to the instructions he issued to election officials while he was Secretary of State and there is no credible evidence he ever communicated his current position to anyone while he was Secretary of State. *He failed to provide a rational explanation of his present position and the Court found his testimony to be unworthy of belief.*[71]

Judge Howard also noted that the 1980 instructions had been cosigned by the state's attorney general at the time, Charles Graddick, and Graddick testified before Judge Howard "that it was his understanding that ballots such as the contested absentee ballots should not be counted."[72]

Judge Howard's written opinion also confirmed, as the evidence had shown, that "the rules for counting absentee ballots have been consistently applied by every county, except one, in the State of Alabama." Specifically: "The practice of the State of Alabama with regard to absentee ballots contained in affidavit envelopes signed by the voter, but without proper notarization or proper witnessing by two adult witnesses, since at least 1980, has been to exclude the ballot from the vote count." In a footnote to this sentence, Judge Howard acknowledged that "the Court does not mean that some such ballots have not slipped through and been counted." But "those votes would be subject to challenge through the state election contest process" as being contrary to the well-established practice of not counting them. Judge Howard emphasized that the secretary of state has always told local election officials "that such ballots **ARE NOT** to be counted."[73] Moreover, even in Washington County, "no officials charged with running the elections . . . instructed voters that unwitnessed or unnotarized ballots would or might be counted." Thus, "no voting official in any of the sixty-seven counties of Alabama ever instructed any prospective voter that a ballot such as the contested absentee ballots might be counted." For this reason, no "reasonable voter" could have understood the explicitly "mandatory" instructions in the ballot materials that "your signature must be notarized, OR you must have two persons witness and sign the bottom of the envelope" to be anything other than that "a ballot is improper unless it is witnessed or notarized." Based on all this, Judge Howard concluded that to count such ballots would be a "change" in the state's vote-counting law, "applied retroactively," that (as the Republicans had argued) "amounts to ballot-box stuffing" and thus violates due process. Putting in writing what he earlier had said in open court, Judge Howard characterized this "post-election change of practice" as "abominable under the Constitution of the United States." Judge Howard's words were essentially the same as those of Justice Harlan's *Taylor v. Beckham* dissent from a century earlier.[74]

Judge Howard also quickly dismissed the claim that to leave these ballots uncounted, when other indistinguishable ones had already been counted in the same election, would violate equal protection. This claim was premised on a point raised by the Alabama Supreme Court's four-member majority opinion: some ballots in the chief justice election had been counted although lacking notarization or two signatures. But Judge Howard put this problem in the category of an inadvertent mistake, which he said would not justify counting additional ballots in violation of the same state law. Any voter who had cast a noncompliant absentee ballot "had no right to have his vote counted" and thus the refusal to count it could not, in Judge Howard's view, violate the Fourteenth Amendment.[75] (Judge Howard's position on this equal protection point would be the same one adopted by the Minnesota Supreme Court in 2009 in the *Coleman v. Franken* lawsuit involving the US Senate election.) Accordingly, Judge Howard ordered the certification of Hooper's victory based on the count as it stood without the disputed ballots.

The Democrats allied with Hornsby did not give up. Instead, they took the case back to the Eleventh Circuit, where it was a foregone conclusion that they would lose based on the factual record that Judge Howard had assembled. On

October 13, the Eleventh Circuit indeed affirmed Judge Howard's ruling.[76] It was a different three-judge panel, and this time it was unanimous. The Eleventh Circuit's opinion observed that Judge Howard's factual determinations were "supported overwhelmingly by the evidence": only one county strayed from the otherwise "uniform" practice to "exclude ballots enclosed in envelopes that did not bear the signature of either a notary public or two witnesses." Like Judge Howard, the Eleventh Circuit recognized "that a small number" of ballots indistinguishable from the disputed ones "slipped through" and were already counted in the chief justice election itself. But there were only 49 of these slipped-through ballots, much less than Hooper's 262-vote margin of victory. Thus the Eleventh Circuit considered the slipped-through ballots to be "of no consequence." They surely did not establish the basis for a Fourteenth Amendment claim that additional noncompliant ballots should be counted.[77]

The Eleventh Circuit then confirmed that, based on these facts, it would violate due process to count the disputed ballots. The due process "principle of law" that the Eleventh Circuit's previous opinion had articulated "was clear," the new panel pronounced: "The facts established on remand in the district court were stronger in favor of [Hooper's position] than the prior panel could have expected." It followed then that Hooper "has presented a claim for relief" under the federal Constitution and that the state's officials, including the state's judiciary, must be enjoined from counting the disputed ballots. On this basis, Judge Howard's injunction that Hooper be permitted finally to assume the office of chief justice must be obeyed "forthwith," and the Eleventh Circuit made this ruling effective immediately. Once again, there was no mention of *Taylor v. Beckham* or its progeny in the Eleventh Circuit's opinion.

The litigation still was not finished. There was one more court the Democrats could go to—the US Supreme Court—and go there they did. They sought an emergency stay of Judge Howard's order, as affirmed by the Eleventh Circuit, on the ground that it was an incorrect interpretation of the Fourteenth Amendment. In essence, Hornsby's supporters in this case were filing the same type of emergency application that Lyndon Johnson had filed almost a half-century earlier in his battle with Coke Stevenson. Hornsby's supporters were making the same argument that Abe Fortas had made on Johnson's behalf: that the Fourteenth Amendment provided no basis for federal court supervision of ballot-counting in a state election. Yes, Judge Howard's intervention was predicated on the proposition that Alabama's change of law was tantamount to ballot-box stuffing, but Coke Stevenson's case had been based on actual ballot-box stuffing—and still Justice Black had ordered that there was no role for the federal judiciary to play under the Fourteenth Amendment. In the first case of its type in the US Supreme Court since Justice Black's order, Hornsby's Democrats were asking for a repeat of that decree.

The emergency application was assigned to Justice Anthony Kennedy, who was the circuit justice responsible for handling emergency matters coming out of the Eleventh Circuit. On October 14, one day after the Eleventh Circuit's decision in the case, Justice Kennedy granted a temporary stay, to give him or the full Supreme Court additional time to consider the matter before the final certification of the election took effect pursuant to Judge Howard's ruling.[78] Justice Kennedy's stay, even if only temporary, looked like he might indeed be taking a position equivalent to Justice Black's in the Stevenson-Johnson dispute. The next day, however, Justice Kennedy referred the emergency application to the full Court, as he was entitled to do. Four days later, on October 19, in a one-line order without any accompanying opinion, the full Court vacated Justice Kennedy's temporary stay and denied the emergency application.[79]

The full Court thus obviously did not take the same position as Justice Black had on his own in 1948, but until the papers of the justices on the Court at the time become public, we cannot know the reasoning behind the Court's denial of a stay in this case.[80] Was it disagreement with Justice Black's view that there is no role for the federal judiciary under the Fourteenth Amendment in a vote-counting dispute of this nature? Was it acceptance of Judge Howard's view, and the Eleventh Circuit's, that a due process violation had occurred on the facts of this case? Or was it something about the procedural position of the litigation that caused the Court to decline to weigh in? Also, was there any consideration of *Taylor v. Beckham* and its relationship to *Reynolds v. Sims*? For now at least, we cannot know. But we do know that this case put before the Court, and Justice Kennedy specifically, the kind of Fourteenth Amendment issues that would arise in the 2000 presidential election only five years later.

On the same day that the full US Supreme Court vacated Justice Kennedy's temporary stay, October 19, Alabama's secretary of state finally and unconditionally certified Hooper as the election's winner.[81] The next day he was sworn in as chief justice, almost a year after the voters had cast their ballots. It seemed bizarre to many observers that it took eleven months after the Montgomery County state judge first ordered the disputed absentee ballots to be counted based on the substantial compliance doctrine, which had occurred back on November 17, for the entire judicial system—state and federal—to bring the controversy to an end.

Moreover, with the benefit of hindsight, the argument for counting the disputed absentee ballots in this chief justice election looks exceptionally weak. To be sure, the Alabama Supreme Court had articulated the substantial compliance doctrine with respect to absentee ballots in two precedents before 1994. But as Hooper and his allies claimed all along, neither of those precedents had applied the substantial compliance doctrine specifically to the issue of absentee ballots lacking either notarization or two witnesses. Instead, the first of the two precedents, *Wells v. Ellis* (1989), merely adopted the substantial compliance doctrine generally and remanded that case for an application of the doctrine to a variety of deficiencies (such as "no reason marked for voting absentee").[82] The second of the two precedents, *Williams v. Lide* (1993), affirmed a lower-court decision that certain ballots were ineligible to be counted even under the substantial compliance doctrine.[83] That opinion stated that there were outer limits to how "lenient" the substantial compliance doctrine could be and that the ballots in question there had exceeded those limits. "Accordingly," for example, "the trial court acted properly in refusing to admit into evidence absentee ballots lacking an address."[84] But that case did not require specific consideration of ballots lacking notarization or two witnesses.

It was a big leap for the four-justice majority of the Alabama Supreme Court to claim that its prior adoption of the substantial compliance doctrine had established a baseline from which refusal to count the disputed ballots in the chief justice election would be improper under state law. And once the evidence at trial established that only one county deviated from the doctrine of strict compliance with respect to the specific requirement of notarization or two witnesses, it became impossible to assert that the prevailing practice had been to count such ballots in accordance with the substantial compliance doctrine. It really would have been a change in state law to count them now for the first time and to announce this change after the ballots had been cast, applying the new rule retroactively. Whether or not the change was a due process violation justifying federal court intervention in the state's vote-counting process, it was a situation that appeared like an unfair partisan attempt to capture a major election through an after-the-fact adjustment of the vote-counting rules.

As early as 1974, a just decade after *Reynolds v. Sims,* a young attorney named Kenneth Starr wrote a law review article explaining how *Reynolds* already had generated a substantial body of judicial precedents justifying federal court invalidation of state electoral results in cases involving voting rights abuses serious enough to violate the Fourteenth Amendment.[85] Starr, of course, would go on to become a DC Circuit judge and US solicitor general, often mentioned as a potential Supreme Court nominee, before gaining widespread notoriety as the Whitewater special prosecutor who went after President Clinton for his misconduct in the Monica Lewinsky scandal. But at the very beginning of his career, Starr was prescient in writing that the federal judicial power to intervene in a state election was, according to the theory of *Reynolds,* derived from the court's basic "equitable power" to fashion a remedy suitable to the protection of the relevant constitutional rights at stake.

Starr's forecast was confirmed only a few years later in the 1978 case of *Griffin v. Burns*, and then solidified two decades later with the Eleventh Circuit's decision in *Roe v. Alabama*. That precedent, moreover, was but a preview of the fruit that *Reynolds* would bear in *Bush v. Gore*. By reaching the US Supreme Court, even if only on an emergency stay application, *Roe v. Alabama* put both the Court and the country on notice that similar constitutional claims could arise in a presidential election.

11

Florida 2000

Avoiding a Return to the Constitutional Brink

Bush v. Gore is the US Supreme Court decision that has been credited with—or blamed for—ending the 2000 presidential election with its interrupted recount still unfinished. Bush and Gore, of course, were the two candidates: George W. Bush, the governor of Texas and son of the forty-first president, challenging the incumbent vice president, Al Gore. *Bush v. Gore,* the court case, is often used interchangeably as shorthand for Bush-versus-Gore, the entirety of the dispute over the outcome of the election.[1]

But that dispute encompassed much more than just the US Supreme Court's decision, which in truth did not even end the fight. Rather, the end came the next day, December 13, when Gore announced he would not attempt to renew the recount through additional proceedings in Florida's courts. Had he done so, he and Bush conceivably might have pursued their fight all the way to Congress, as Hayes and Tilden had over the 1876 election. If Bush-versus-Gore had reached Congress it would have been the first real test of the impenetrably ambiguous Electoral Count Act of 1887, with unpredictable consequences.[2] Thus it was Gore's concession of December 13, and not the Court's ruling of the previous day, that truly ended the fight for the presidency as a practical matter.

Bush v. Gore, the court case, moreover, concerned only one aspect of the overall vote-counting dispute: the so-called dimpled or hanging chads produced by incomplete puncturing of punch-card ballots.[3] *Bush v. Gore* did not concern issues that had arisen over absentee ballots, which the Gore campaign abandoned in the wake of public criticism. Much more significantly, *Bush v. Gore* did not address the problem of the so-called butterfly ballot, which apparently caused thousands of Gore supporters to mistakenly cast their ballots instead for Pat Buchanan, the conservative pundit running as a minor-party candidate. Even Buchanan acknowledged, both then and subsequently, that Gore would have been president but for the butterfly ballot.

Nor did *Bush v. Gore*, as presented to the US Supreme Court, involve all the issues concerning dimpled and hanging chads. The US Supreme Court was not in a posture to decide what would have been a fair process for the counting of these chads, from the standpoint of *either* Florida's legislature setting up that process in advance of the election *or* Florida's judiciary attempting to make the best of the situation once confronted with the challenge of how to handle these chads given the state's existing statutory framework. Instead, the US Supreme Court's role was limited to considering whether the Florida Supreme Court had acted improperly in its treatment of the chads, and, if so, what to do about the impropriety at that juncture and given the date by which Florida's recount procedures needed to end.

When considering the entirety of Bush-versus-Gore, it is worth disentangling three distinct lines of inquiry. First, did Florida's electoral system accurately identify the aggregate preference of the eligible voters who attempted to record their preferences through that system, and, if not, why was Florida unable to remedy this inaccuracy? Second, what would have been a fair procedure for handling the chads that became the focus of the litigation, and insofar as the procedure used fell short, who is responsible for that failure and with what consequence? Third, insofar as the US Supreme Court did become involved in the dispute, did it act appropriately, and if not, what effect did its involvement ultimately have?

A Fair Count Does Not Guarantee an Accurate Result

Regarding the first line of inquiry, there can be little doubt that more Florida voters who cast ballots in the 2000 presidential election preferred Gore to Bush and that a well-functioning electoral system would have accurately captured this preference, thus making Gore the winner of the presidency.[4] As already indicated, Palm Beach County's infamous "butterfly ballot" alone sufficed to frustrate the aggregate preference of the participating and eligible electorate. Bush's certified margin of victory ended up only 537 votes.[5] But in Palm Beach County, Pat Buchanan received some 3,400 votes, over two thousand more than anywhere else in the state.[6] Statistical analysis confirmed the common sense conclusion that the faulty ballot design caused this discrepancy, as would-be Gore voters inadvertently miscast their ballots for Buchanan.[7] Although Gore's name was the second listed on the left, the holes for voters to punch ran down the middle of the ballot, and the second hole was the one for Buchanan (whose name was the first on the right). As Buchanan himself explained, "My name right beside his on the butterfly ballot cost Al Gore thousands of votes—and the presidency."[8]

Gore's lawyers understandably concluded that Florida law provided no judicial remedy for a mistaken electoral outcome caused by the butterfly ballot. In a suit filed on behalf of affected voters, the Florida Supreme Court unanimously concluded the ballot's design, however problematic and consequential it was, did not violate state law.[9] Even if it had, it is unclear what remedy the state court should have provided. There was insufficient time to hold a whole new election in Florida, since the state's presidential electors were constitutionally required to cast their official Electoral College votes on the same day as the electors in all other states, which Congress had specified as Monday, December 18. Limiting a revote to just Palm Beach County would have raised grave constitutional questions, especially if Palm Beach voters who had not participated in the initial election were permitted to participate in the revote, but Florida voters elsewhere were not similarly given a second chance to cast a ballot.[10]

Although statistics showed that the butterfly ballot deprived Gore of enough votes to cost him the election, it was difficult to see how a court could order a statistical adjustment to the actual count of the ballots as cast. Statistics, by nature, are probabilistic. Was a court to declare that but for the butterfly ballot, Gore maybe would have won by 1,500 votes, or maybe by only 1,000 votes, or maybe even by only 500, when the actual count of the votes recorded on the ballots themselves showed Bush, not Gore, winning by 537?[11]

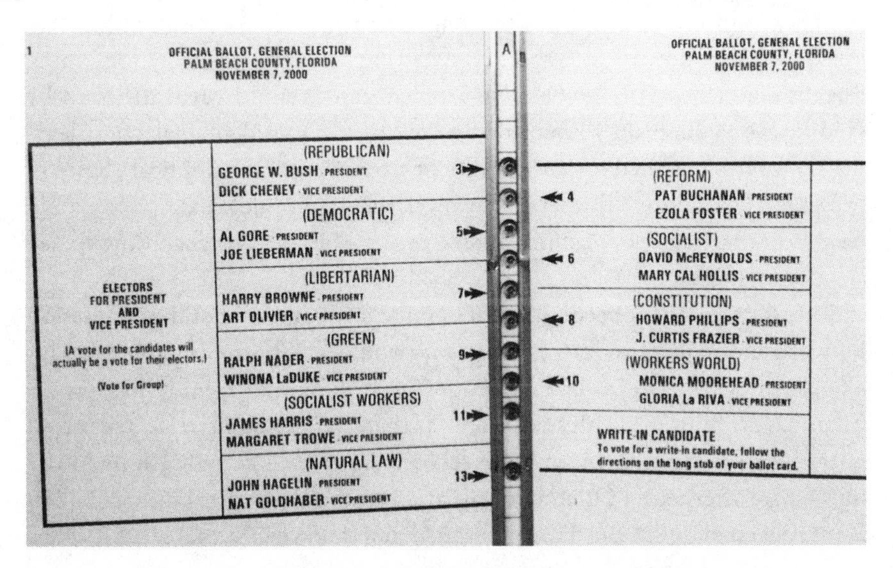
OFFICIAL BALLOT, GENERAL ELECTION
PALM BEACH COUNTY, FLORIDA
NOVEMBER 7, 2000

ELECTORS FOR PRESIDENT AND VICE PRESIDENT
(A vote for the candidates will actually be a vote for their electors.)
(Vote for Group)

(REPUBLICAN) GEORGE W. BUSH PRESIDENT, DICK CHENEY VICE PRESIDENT 3
(DEMOCRATIC) AL GORE PRESIDENT, JOE LIEBERMAN VICE PRESIDENT 5
(LIBERTARIAN) HARRY BROWNE PRESIDENT, ART OLIVIER VICE PRESIDENT 7
(GREEN) RALPH NADER PRESIDENT, WINONA LaDUKE VICE PRESIDENT 9
(SOCIALIST WORKERS) JAMES HARRIS PRESIDENT, MARGARET TROWE VICE PRESIDENT 11
(NATURAL LAW) JOHN HAGELIN PRESIDENT, NAT GOLDHABER VICE PRESIDENT 13

OFFICIAL BALLOT, GENERAL ELECTION
PALM BEACH COUNTY, FLORIDA
NOVEMBER 7, 2000

4 (REFORM) PAT BUCHANAN PRESIDENT, EZOLA FOSTER VICE PRESIDENT
6 (SOCIALIST) DAVID McREYNOLDS PRESIDENT, MARY CAL HOLLIS VICE PRESIDENT
8 (CONSTITUTION) HOWARD PHILLIPS PRESIDENT, J. CURTIS FRAZIER VICE PRESIDENT
10 (WORKERS WORLD) MONICA MOOREHEAD PRESIDENT, GLORIA La RIVA VICE PRESIDENT
WRITE-IN CANDIDATE
To vote for a write-in candidate, follow the directions on the long stub of your ballot card.

Figure 11.1 The infamous butterfly ballot, which confused enough voters to affect the outcome of the 2000 presidential election, but for which there was no remedy. Wikimedia.

The Florida Supreme Court might have simply voided the election on account of the faulty butterfly ballot as well as myriad of other problems that undermined the outcome as an accurate reflection of the electorate's aggregate preference. But as the court itself observed, voiding the election without a revote "would result in the disfranchisement of [all the state's] voters."[12] While Florida's legislature would be entitled to appoint the state's presidential electors directly (to fill the gap left by voiding all the votes of the citizenry), there was no guarantee that electors chosen by the legislature would match the aggregate preference of the voters who dutifully cast their own ballots to choose the state's presidential electors. Indeed, because Florida's legislature was in Republican hands, the Gore campaign fully understood that voiding the election was worse than useless from its perspective. That judicial remedy would guarantee Bush's receipt of Florida's electoral votes by legislative fiat—and, with them, the presidency.

Whatever one thinks of the Florida Supreme Court's decision regarding the butterfly ballot, this much is clear: a correct count of the ballots as cast is not necessarily the same as an accurate recording of the preferences that the voters wished to make. Even assuming for the moment that a full and fair recount of the votes on the eligible ballots actually cast would confirm Bush's narrow margin over Gore, this assumption is not the same as saying that Bush would have won if Florida had employed a sound system for recording the preferences of the eligible voters who endeavored to participate in the presidential election. As was also true in 1876, an unbridgeable gap can sometimes exist between a fair *counting* and a fair *casting* of ballots. A fair recount of the votes on the ballots cannot undo the kind of casting problem caused by something like the butterfly ballot. That kind of problem can be cured—if at all—only by voiding the election altogether, and, in the case of a presidential election, leaving the void to be filled not by a revote of citizens, but by a political choice of the state's legislature. Ultimately, however, whether or not that option would have been desirable, it was unavailable under Florida's law according to the state's supreme court.[13]

Turning then to the second line of inquiry, and cognizant of the distinction between fair *counting* and fair *casting*, what would have been the procedures for a fair recount of Florida's ballots in 2000 and what result would those procedures have produced? Bush's position was that a fair recount, in fact, occurred pursuant to Florida law: it was the recounting of ballots by machine in the immediate aftermath of Election Day, and it confirmed Bush's victory (albeit by a reduced margin). Bush's team argued, not implausibly, that machines are inherently fairer than humans in counting ballots because machines, unlike humans, harbor no psychological preference for one candidate over the other. In any event, Bush's team further contended, Florida law at the time required a machine recount but contained no provisions designed for a manual recount, by humans, of all ballots in a statewide election. Whatever might be suitable provisions for a manual recount if adopted legislatively in advance of an election, once the ballots had been cast in this particular election the only fair recount was the machine recount provided for by law.[14]

Putting aside this powerful point, suppose for the moment that Florida's judiciary had been explicitly empowered in advance to order a complete manual recount of all ballots cast in the state's 2000 presidential election. A model for that kind of recount had occurred in Minnesota's 1962 gubernatorial election, and Minnesota would repeat a similar version for its 2008 US Senate election. Thus we can imagine Florida having conducted a Minnesota-style recount in 2000, but ultimately we can make no confident judgment on whether that kind of recount would have yielded a result with Bush or Gore ahead.

There never was a manual inspection of all Florida ballots cast in 2000. The closest approximation was an examination by a media consortium of just the ballots that the machines classified as either "overvotes" (those improperly voted for two or more candidates in the same presidential race) or "undervotes" (those showing no choice of any presidential candidate).[15] But this limited examination could not detect any ballots in which a voter wrote on a ballot in an effort to undo a mark for a candidate (where the machine picked up the mark, and recorded the ballot as cast for that candidate, while failing to detect the voter's intent to nullify that mark). Moreover, although the media consortium's review was an effort to encompass all overvotes and undervotes, localities were unable to deliver to the media consortium 1,345 ballots that the machines originally had classified as overvotes or undervotes and thus should have been part of the consortium's review. These ballots had simply disappeared—but, had they still existed, might have made the difference.[16]

The consortium's limited review produced a result with Gore ahead by a miniscule margin of 107, as long as both overvotes and undervotes were included in its analysis.[17] But overvotes were never part of the recount actually requested by Gore or ordered by the Florida Supreme Court—the problem of dimpled and hanging chads, the focus of the actual litigation in Florida, being a problem of undervotes and not overvotes. Conversely, the media consortium's review did not replicate the conditions of real-world recount procedures, with lawyers for both sides being able to observe and potentially challenge ballot-specific determinations made by the humans conducting the recount. Moreover, being human, the individuals employed by the media consortium were unable to set aside their own partisan affiliations when evaluating ballots. For example, Democratic reviewers "were 25 percent more likely to deny a mark was for Bush" than Republican reviewers.[18] In a real-world recount, these determinations would have been subject to judicial oversight and potentially reversed. The media consortium's review cannot be considered to replicate a fair recount, and its results cannot be taken as evidence that either Gore or Bush would have prevailed if a fair manual recount, like those in Minnesota, had occurred in Florida.

Turning to the third line of inquiry, what should be said of the US Supreme Court's involvement in this disputed presidential election? To appraise the Court's role requires understanding the specific circumstances of the dispute in which it eventually occurred. For that understanding, one must consider how the dispute chaotically unfolded during the five weeks from Election Night, as the polls were closing, to the Court's decision in *Bush v. Gore.*

Election Night

The evening got off to a bad start when the networks, based on faulty exit polling, prematurely declared that Gore was going to win Florida. NBC, CBS, and ABC all made this announcement about ten minutes before the polls had even closed in the western Panhandle—an irresponsible mistake that made Republicans appropriately livid.[19] Although it seems doubtful that Bush lost votes because of this snafu, CNN already had been announcing that the polls would close in Florida at 7:00 p.m. Eastern time, overlooking the fact that the Panhandle would continue voting until 8:00 p.m. Eastern, and in an election that ultimately came down to only a few hundred votes, it is not inconceivable that this earlier misreporting may have suppressed last-minute turnout in that part of the state. Of course, once the Bush campaign discovered CNN's errors, it activated an emergency get-out-the-vote phone operation, making "tens of thousands of calls into Republican households in the Panhandle," and thus may have boosted Republican turnout there as a result.[20]

The media's overall irresponsibility on Election Night 2000, however, ran much deeper than its initial miscall of Florida for Gore. The networks had accustomed themselves to being the pronouncers of presidential victory, as if they—and not government authorities at a later date—made the official declaration of which candidate won the White House. Even worse, in an era of enhanced competition between the traditional broadcast networks and the more recent cable news rivals, there had developed an intense frenzy to be the quickest to call a state for a candidate. Such was the environment when at 7:08 p.m. Eastern time, Dan Rather touted for CBS: "Let's get one thing straight from the get go. . . . If we say somebody has carried a state, you can pretty much take it to the bank, book it, that that's true."[21] With the networks conveying that kind of attitude, it is no wonder that the public was bewildered when later that same night the networks retracted their call of Florida for Gore, then gave the state—and the presidency—to Bush, and still later retracted that second call, leaving the impression that the election was somehow inappropriately up in the air.[22]

But it was not only the networks that were caught by surprise on Election Night in 2000. The candidates, too, were unprepared for an election close enough to need a recount. They were unprepared both logistically and psychologically. Not only did they not have recount teams preassembled to fly to a state where they might be needed (as would occur in subsequent cycles); more significantly, they did not know how to handle themselves in the circumstance where there was no obvious winner on Election Night.

Gore never should have put himself in the situation where he needed to telephone Bush a second time to retract the concession that he had made to Bush in his first call. When the networks declared Florida for Bush (shortly after 2:15 a.m. Eastern), Gore told his advisers, "I want to concede," and he proceeded to do so by phoning Bush.[23] Gore's mistake was not merely failing to check in with his own campaign staffers, who had very different numbers from the networks at that moment. His more fundamental mistake was thinking there needed to be a concession speech, from one candidate or the other, on Election Night based on whatever inevitably incomplete and uncertain numbers were then available, from whatever source. Instead, Gore could have taken the position, as Charles Evans Hughes did in 1916, that there was an official canvassing process to occur before a winner of the state was certified; unless he could be reasonably certain that the canvassing process would not alter the outcome, there was no reason not to let the process unfold before any candidate conceded that the election was over.

In his memoirs, Bush acknowledges getting "hot" as a result of Gore's retraction. He also reveals that he was tempted to "go out and declare victory" anyway, until his brother Jeb persuaded him otherwise.[24] The candor of Bush's memoirs in these respects is commendable, but his attitude at the time shows that he, too, was not emotionally prepared for a razor-thin (and thus indeterminate) result on Election Night. Like Gore, he believed that the election should be finished on Election Night, with winner and loser conclusively determined based on whichever way the networks added up the best numbers available at the end of the night. He was not oriented to the view, as any candidate should be, that the outcome of an especially competitive election may require waiting for the official result at the end of the canvass.

But for Bush this misimpression was not consequential, as it was for Gore. After all, Gore was the one who had conceded that he had lost the election. Even though that concession had no official status in Florida's canvassing procedure, it automatically put Gore on the defensive throughout the entire subsequent vote-counting process. In retracting the concession, Gore tried to claim that Florida was "too close to call," but he himself already had made Bush the presumptive winner whose presumptive victory Gore was attempting to undo. It was an entirely self-inflicted wound.

A Hand Recount or Not? That Was the Question

On Wednesday morning, November 8, the Florida secretary of state's numbers showed a gap of only 1,784 votes between the two candidates, with Bush in the lead.[25] Almost 6 million ballots had been cast, making the lead about 0.03% of the total—an order of magnitude far smaller than the 0.5% trigger of a mandatory machine recount as set forth in Florida's election code at the time. By the next day, as a result of that machine recount, Bush's lead had narrowed to only 327 ballots. It grew again to 930 votes once overseas and military absentee ballots were added eight days later (on Friday, November 17).[26]

The competing strategic imperatives of the two campaigns were clear. For Bush, the objective was to stay ahead by avoiding any additional recounting of ballots. Gore, being behind, had exactly the opposite goal: to figure out a way to have another recount, a manual one to supplement the one that already had occurred by machine.

The relevant Florida statutes were maddeningly unclear on whether or not a manual recount should occur in a statewide election. The statutes provided two ways in which a candidate who was behind after the machine recount, like Gore, could challenge the result. The first, called a "protest," was an administrative procedure that occurred as part of the canvass before the outcome of the election was officially certified. The second, called a "contest," was a judicial lawsuit after certification to attack that official result as erroneous.[27]

Certification was a pivotal, and hugely important, point in the whole process. Unlike anything that occurred on Election Night, it was the official—and legally authoritative—declaration of the winner. After certification, the losing candidate truly would be attempting to take away a victory that the law had determined belonged to the opposing candidate. It is therefore understandable that Bush's team wanted to convert his lead, however small, into a certified victory as quickly as possible, whereas Gore's strategists wanted to prevent Bush from becoming the certified winner. In the first week of the vote-counting fight, Gore's advisers did not think that he could survive a certified Bush victory. Especially in the aftermath of Gore's retracted concession on Election Night, they thought that the public pressure for Gore to reinstate that concession after certification of a Bush victory would be too withering to withstand.

The protest statute provided that a candidate could request a manual recount, but said that those requests were to be directed to "the county canvassing board," as if it applied only to local and not statewide elections. Moreover, the statute said that the county canvassing board *may* choose to conduct a manual recount, but did not say that it must do so. The statute also seemed to suggest that a countywide manual recount might be appropriate only in the event of "an error in the vote tabulation," understood to mean a technological failure that prevented the voting machines from tabulating the ballots in the way that they were designed to do.[28]

Interpreted this way, the statute would not contemplate a countywide recount for the purpose of reviewing ballots for which the machines, operating as designed, failed to detect a vote. These were the undervotes, which were known and expected to occur in every election with machines operating exactly as designed. Undervotes regularly occurred using both optical scan or punch card ballots, although they were more prevalent with the latter, a more primitive form of voting technology. With an optical-scan ballot, on which voters filled in ovals (like standardized tests), sometimes the oval was not filled in well enough for the scanner to detect. With a punch-card ballot, voters were required to punch out small perforated pieces of their ballots—these pieces were called chads—so that the machine could detect the holes that the voters had created by dislodging the chads. With some frequency, however, voters would fail to dislodge their chads completely, causing the machines to miss votes that the voters had intended.[29]

The question, then, was whether it was appropriate in a statewide election to use the protest procedure to conduct a manual recount, where the machines were working as designed, for the purpose of discovering undervotes on either optical-scan or punch-card ballots that the machines had failed to detect. In furtherance of its strategic objective, the Bush campaign took the position that, no, to do so would not be a proper use of the protest procedure. The Gore campaign, by contrast, needed there to be a manual recount in search of undervotes undetected by the machines; otherwise, it was all over, and Gore had lost. Accordingly, the Gore campaign pressed for an interpretation of the protest statute that, not limited to errors in the functioning of the vote-tabulation machinery, would permit the manual retrieval of undervotes.

Another problem for the Gore campaign was that Secretary of State Katherine Harris, in partisan alliance with the Bush campaign, adopted the more restrictive interpretation of the statute. Even if this interpretation was the more natural reading of the statute's text, and thus would have been adopted by a neutral arbiter, Harris was no neutral. In what appeared to be a flagrant breach of professional ethics, she was consulting with the Bush campaign in deciding how to exercise her supervisory authority over the canvassing process.[30] When Gore asked four counties to look for undervotes, Harris told them that under the statute it was unlawful for them to do so.[31]

Figure 11.2 A pile of Palm Beach's punch-card ballots waiting to be recounted, with the first ballot in hand showing several hanging chads. AP Photo/*Palm Beach Post*; Lannis Waters.

Even worse from Gore's perspective was the deadline that the state's statutes set for completion and certification of the canvass. In two separate places, the statutes stated that the secretary of state must receive the returns from each county "by 5 p.m. on the seventh day following an election."[32] This same deadline applied whether or not a county chose to conduct a manual recount as part of a protest. Even if a county was willing to go ahead and search for undervotes during the canvass (in contravention of the secretary of state's instructions), the county needed to complete this search by close of business on November 14, one week after Election Day. That tight schedule did not leave much chance for a large urban county, like Miami-Dade, to complete a countywide manual recount, further suggesting that the protest procedure was not suited to a search for undervotes.

Furthermore, the statutes seemed to be quite strict about this deadline. One of the two relevant statutes said that the secretary of state "shall" ignore "all missing counties" and proceed forthwith to a statewide certification of the election based only on the county returns in compliance with the deadline.[33] The other statute was more lenient, saying that the secretary "may" ignore a county's late returns and proceed immediately with the statewide certification, leaving that county out of the final results.[34] Either way, the statutes did not require the secretary to wait past the deadline for a county to finish looking for undervotes in response to a protest.

In hindsight, Gore's strategic objective would have been better served by skipping the protest procedure and moving straight to a contest.[35] Although that alternative approach would have required Gore to acquiesce in the certification of Bush's victory, it would have permitted more time for the contest to unfold. More significantly, it would have avoided Gore's having to ask the Florida Supreme Court to adopt a strained and dubious interpretation of the relevant state statutes—an interpretation that cast the Florida Supreme Court in an extremely unfavorable light, especially in the eyes of the more powerful US Supreme Court. But Gore felt compelled to fight a certification of Bush's victory at all costs. To the extent that he did so because of his earlier retracted concession, then it was indeed that concession that put him in a posture from which he could not recover.[36]

Gore's Self-Defeating Use of the Protest Procedure

The three counties that Gore most cared about were Miami-Dade, Broward, and Palm Beach. Located at the southeastern end of the state, these were the three most populous of Florida's 67 counties, with Democratic-leaning constituencies that provided Gore the greatest potential to cut Bush's lead by uncovering undervotes. Gore was heavily criticized for seeking manual recounts in only four counties. (Volusia was included because of oddities in its fluctuating Election Night returns.[37]) His defense was that the protest statute required him to ask on a county-by-county basis.

None of Gore's three targeted counties came close to completing a manual recount by the statute's deadline of 5 p.m. on Tuesday, November 14. Miami-Dade and Broward had not even agreed to look for undervotes. Palm Beach, which had started, reversed course after learning of Secretary of State Harris's disapproval. When Secretary Harris announced the next day (Wednesday, November 15) that she would not accept any late-arriving amended returns based on manual recounts—and would instead certify the election on Saturday, November 18, once all the overseas and military ballots were in—Gore made the fateful decision to challenge her decision rather than proceeding directly to a judicial contest of that certification.[38]

Terry Lewis, the Tallahassee-based state judge to whom the case had been assigned, upheld Secretary Harris's decision to reject any late-arriving recounts. Earlier, he had required Harris to provide reasons for her decision, but since the relevant Florida statutes said that she either "shall" or "may" ignore late returns, Judge Lewis accepted the reasons that she gave. Her primary point was that, as long as the voting machines had functioned as designed, a manual search for undervotes was not a valid excuse for late returns.[39]

Gore's team appealed Judge Lewis's decision to the Florida Supreme Court, which extended the protest period by requiring Harris to accept any amended returns resulting from manual recounts as long as they were complete by Sunday, November 26.[40] This new deadline left little time for conducting a subsequent judicial contest, given that the state's presidential electors were constitutionally required to cast their official Electoral College votes on Monday, December 18 (only three weeks later). Moreover, the Electoral Count Act of 1887 gave states a safe harbor deadline of six days earlier: if Florida could resolve all disputes over the appointment of its presidential electors before Tuesday, December 12 (using rules and procedures the state had promulgated in advance of Election Day), then Congress promised to abide by the state's resolution of those disputes.[41] Everyone, including the Gore legal team, presumed that Florida would want to take advantage of this safe harbor deadline. Strategically, the Gore team stressed the safe harbor deadline's importance: they did not want the US House of Representatives, controlled by Republicans, to be entitled to disavow a Florida-based recount favorable to Gore. But the new protest-phase deadline of Sunday, November 26, then left only sixteen days to hold an entire judicial contest of the election, including appeals, before the safe harbor window slammed shut.

Extending the deadline turned out, for Gore, to be a waste of precious time. Broward County managed to finish a manual recount by then, but Palm Beach County did not (missing by a couple of hours). Most famously, Miami-Dade halted its manual recount after the so-called Brooks Brothers riot, in which Republican protesters—fearful that fraud was occurring in a process largely shielded from public view on the nineteenth floor of Miami's Clark Center office tower—vociferously demanded a stop to the recount.[42] On November 26, with no new numbers from either Miami-Dade or Palm Beach, Katherine Harris certified Bush's presidential electors as victorious. The certification that Gore's legal team had fought so hard to avoid happened eight days after it would have without the deadline's extension.[43]

Moreover, the Florida Supreme Court's opinion setting the new deadline was an exercise of judicial gymnastics that made the US Supreme Court suspicious of the state court's motives. The Florida Supreme Court more than doubled the explicit statutory deadline of "5 p.m. on the seventh day after the election" to the *nineteenth* day after the election. Whereas the statutory

Figure 11.3 Teresa LaPore, Palm Beach County's supervisor of elections, and Christie Whitman, governor of New Jersey, study a challenged ballot on November 25, 2000. AP Photo/Charles Rex Arbogast.

language said that the secretary either "shall" or "may" ignore local returns submitted more than a week after Election Day, the Florida Supreme Court now insisted the opposite: the secretary must *not* ignore local returns as long as they arrive within three weeks after Election Day.

The Florida Supreme Court claimed that it was eschewing a "hyper-technical" reading of the statutes in order to protect the constitutionally guaranteed right to vote.[44] But the court never explained how constitutional law required a manual search for undervotes as part of the protest phase of Florida's electoral process, to the point of necessitating such a drastic alteration of the statutory language. Was it *unconstitutional*, as distinct from bad policy, to confine the protest phase to a machine recount in those situations where the machines were working as designed? The Florida Supreme Court seemed to assume that the answer to this question was yes, although constitutional law had never been understood to require any recount at all.

James Baker, the chief of Bush's legal team, recommended that Bush take the case to the US Supreme Court. Other Bush lawyers were dubious about this move. "What's the federal question?" they essentially asked, knowing that the US Supreme Court is jurisdictionally limited to questions of federal rather than state law. The Florida Supreme Court's opinion, however aberrant it might be, was premised mostly on state rather than federal law. (The general references in its opinion to the constitutional right to vote could be construed to implicate federal as well as state constitutional principles, but otherwise it seemed to be an exegesis of state law.) Furthermore, even if there were a federal question for the US Supreme Court to consider, why would the Court take the case? The US Supreme Court has discretionary jurisdiction, meaning it is entirely free to accept or decline cases within its power to decide. Because the Court might wish not to ensnare itself in the process of picking the next president, most seasoned Court-watchers predicted the Court would decline to review the Florida Supreme Court's decision. But Bush took Baker's advice to go to the US Supreme Court, and Baker was correct.[45]

On Monday, December 4, the US Supreme Court issued a unanimous opinion vacating the Florida Supreme Court's decision and remanding it for clarification. The federal high Court diplomatically, but pointedly, observed that it could not discern the basis for the state court's decision. The federal Court, in particular, was concerned that the state court had ignored the federal constitutional provision in Article Two that gave the state legislature the authority to determine the method by which to appoint the state's presidential electors. If the state court had so distorted Florida's statutory deadline as to contradict the Florida legislature's chosen method for appointing the state's presidential electors, then the state court might have violated the state legislature's authority vested by Article Two.[46]

The US Supreme Court's opinion was a shot across the bow, warning the Florida court to avoid any further signs of inappropriate bias in favor of Gore (including by means of deviating from preestablished rules).

The Contest

The Law

Florida law was unclear on the circumstances that might justify a manual recount as part of a contest. The statute provided that "grounds for contesting an election" included "rejection of a number of legal votes sufficient to change or place in doubt the result of the election." To enforce this substantive standard, the statute gave the court wide-ranging powers: "The circuit judge to whom the contest is presented may fashion such orders as he or she deems necessary to ensure that each allegation in the complaint is investigated, examined, or checked, to prevent or correct any alleged wrong, and to provide any relief appropriate under such circumstances." Together, these statutory provisions appeared to grant the contest court the authority to require a manual recount in order to search for undervotes.[47]

Cutting the other way, however, was the fact that the contest statute provided no guidance for when a court-ordered manual recount would—or would not—be appropriate. In a statewide election, was a contestant automatically entitled to a statewide manual recount merely by filing the contest? Surely not. What if the number of apparent undervotes exceeded the certified winner's margin of victory; did that fact alone warrant a manual recount in a contest? Without any evidence on point, there was no reason to believe that the mere existence of undervotes would benefit one candidate or the other. Indeed, one might presume the undervotes randomly would be split 50–50 between two candidates.[48] Thus even with an estimated 60,000 undervotes, if Bush and Gore split the undervotes evenly, Gore would not overcome Bush's 537-vote victory.[49] Since Gore necessarily would bear the burden of proof in a contest (as he was seeking to overturn Bush's certified victory), was he entitled to a manual recount in a contest if all he showed was a large number of undervotes—*without any additional evidence that the undervotes would split more favorably in his direction, enough to overcome Bush's 537-vote advantage?* That question would prove crucial.

The Case

On Monday, November 27 (the day immediately after Sunday's certification), Gore filed the contest that his advisers had wrongly thought the public would not tolerate. It turned out that the public had much more patience than the pundits had predicted.[50] But Gore still did not seek a statewide manual recount. Instead, his contest asked only for a completion of Miami-Dade's manual recount as well as a revision of Palm Beach's recount using a more favorable standard for identifying undervotes on punch-card ballots.[51]

The contest was assigned to Judge Sanders Sauls, who held a two-day trial over the weekend of December 2 and 3.[52] Gore's expert witnesses testified to the existence of retrievable undervotes but did not establish a factual basis for believing that Gore rather than Bush would receive more of them. Bush's expert, conversely, testified to the expectation that these undervotes would be randomly—and thus evenly—distributed between the two candidates.[53]

On Monday, December 4, Judge Sauls rejected Gore's contest entirely. Invoking precedent, he declared that Gore as plaintiff was obligated to show "a reasonable probability that the results of the election would have been changed" as a consequence of the uncounted undervotes. Gore had failed this essential obligation: "In this case, there is no credible statistical evidence, and no other competent substantial evidence to establish by a preponderance of a reasonable probability that the results of the statewide election in the State of Florida would be different from the result which had been certified."[54]

Judge Sauls's interpretation of the statute was reasonable. Otherwise, a contestant could demand a recount just because there were more undervotes than the certified margin of victory. Nonetheless, the Florida Supreme Court repudiated it on December 8. This time, however, the Florida Supreme Court was not unanimous, but instead split 4–3.[55]

The majority opinion's interpretation of the contest statute permitted the contestant to plead selected uncounted votes that were enough "to place in doubt the result of the election." Moreover, the majority said that Gore was entitled to have the court assume—without any obligation to provide supporting evidence—that all of the targeted undervotes were cast for him rather than Bush:

> A person authorized to contest an election is required to demonstrate that there have been legal votes cast in the election that have not been counted (here characterized as "undervotes" or "no vote registered" ballots) and that available data shows that a number of legal votes would be recovered from the entire pool of the subject ballots which, *if cast for the unsuccessful candidate*, would change or place in doubt the result of the election.[56]

It was a huge assumption, and the majority gave no explanation for why it was appropriate, compared to the alternative assumption that undervotes might split evenly between the two candidates.[57]

The majority did say that it was necessary to examine all undervotes statewide, not just those in Miami-Dade, and thus remanded the case for a statewide recount. The majority, however, rejected the idea of redoing the recount in Palm Beach pursuant to a more lenient standard for recovering undervotes. This particular aspect of the majority's ruling would become all-important, because it indicated that different localities were entitled to conduct their recounts according to different standards for evaluating undervotes. According to the majority opinion, no statewide uniform standard was required.[58]

Justice Major Harding wrote the main dissent, agreeing with Judge Sauls that Gore had failed to meet his "obligation to show, by a preponderance of the evidence, that the outcome of the statewide election would likely be changed" by a recount of undervotes.[59] Chief Justice Wells added his own impassioned dissent, inviting the US Supreme Court to intervene again. Wells claimed that the majority opinion violated the US Constitution because it provided no standard for conducting the statewide recount that it ordered. Wells also argued that it was wrong for the majority's recount to exclude overvotes.[60] In short, Chief Justice Wells teed up the equal protection issue on which the US Supreme Court would rely to nullify the majority's recount.

The case went back to Judge Sauls, who immediately stepped aside, and it was reassigned to Judge Terry Lewis. Now the case needed to move at hyperspeed to meet the safe harbor deadline, just four days away. At 8:00 p.m. on Friday, December 8, just a few hours after the Florida Supreme Court's order requiring the statewide recount of undervotes, Judge Lewis held a hearing on what the standard for reviewing those undervotes should be. In particular, he wanted to know how the recount should handle the dimpled and hanging chads on the punch-card ballots.

Different localities had adopted different standards for these chads. A "two-corner rule," which required at least two corners of a chad to be dangling in order to count, was much stricter than the "sunshine standard," which would count any chad that let light show through. This sunshine standard in turn was stricter than one that was willing to count any dimpled chad where the "totality of the circumstances" indicated that it reflected the voter's intent to vote for that candidate. Broward County had changed standards in the middle of its recount, moving from the two-corner rule to the most lenient dimpled chad standard. Likewise, Palm Beach adjusted its standard in response to a state trial judge's ruling that it should use the most lenient standard, but it did not go back and review ballots previously evaluated under a stricter standard.[61]

In light of all this, Judge Lewis was asking a genuinely vexing question when he pressed the lawyers for what standard to apply. Gore's team wanted the most lenient standard. Bush's attorney argued that to adopt any specific standard now would be to change the law after Election Day, thereby depriving

Florida of safe harbor status. Judge Lewis decided against setting a specific standard, implying only "if in doubt, throw it out." He ordered all counties to complete their recounts by 2 p.m. Sunday. He said he was available to resolve any disputes, including on how to discern a voter's intent under the general standard that was left unspecified.[62]

The next morning, Saturday, December 9, the recount began. But Bush had already sought an emergency stay from the US Supreme Court, and at 2:40 p.m. on Saturday afternoon, the Court by a 5–4 vote granted the stay. As soon as Judge Lewis heard the news, he halted the recount. Although the recount had been underway for just a few hours, it was moving at a pace that gave it a reasonable prospect of meeting Judge Lewis's deadline the next afternoon. But the stay, as was its purpose, blocked that from happening.[63]

Although the US Supreme Court's decision on the merits would come three days later, it was the Court's stay order of December 9 that prevented completion of the recount by the safe harbor deadline.[64] If the Court had let the recount continue while deliberating its merits, the Court still could have nullified the recount (thus reinstating the certified result) before expiration of the deadline on Tuesday, December 12. But by stopping the recount while deliberating its merits, the Court precluded the possibility of reinstating the recount in time to meet the deadline even if the Court ended up validating the recount on the merits. In this way, the stay order predetermined the subsequent merits decision, even though stay orders are supposed to do the opposite (the purpose of a stay being to freeze a situation in place so that events while the case is pending do not overtake the significance of the subsequent decision on the merits).[65]

Despite being the decisive ruling in the case, the stay order contained no opinion from the Court to justify its imposition. Justice Stevens, on behalf of the four dissenters, captured the essence of the problem in saying the stay was "tantamount to a decision on the merits in favor of the applicants."[66] Justice Scalia, writing solely for himself, felt obligated to defend the stay: "The counting of votes that are of questionable legality does in my view threaten irreparable harm to [Bush], and to the country, by casting a cloud upon what he claims to be the legitimacy of his election." Justice Scalia's idea seems to be that if Gore took the lead based on an improper recount, the public wrongly would think Gore had a valid claim to the office, and that no subsequent judicial repudiation of the recount could erase the erroneous public perception—making it impossible to reinstate Bush's certified victory so that it would be equivalent to Gore never having taken the lead. "Count first, and rule upon legality afterwards," Justice Scalia quipped, "is not a recipe for producing election results that have the public acceptance that democratic stability requires."[67] But with the safe harbor deadline just three days away, "rule on the legality first, and count afterwards" was not an option.

The Decision

Although the merits appeared moot after the stay, there was a moment during the oral argument at the Court when suddenly it seemed as if Justice Kennedy, the pivotal member of the 5–4 tribunal, might have second thoughts.[68] This moment did not last long. When David Boies, Gore's celebrated attorney, took his turn at the podium, it quickly became clear that Boies had no answer for the equal protection concern that Justice Kennedy pressed him on. Indeed, Boies even conceded that "you might have an Equal Protection problem" given Kennedy's premise, which he emphasized repeatedly, that in evaluating the disputed chads Florida had been using at least "two objective standards and they were different."[69]

Thus, when the Court released its merits decision at 10:00 p.m. on Tuesday, December 12 (the date of the safe harbor deadline), it was not surprising that the Court ruled that Florida's recount procedures violated equal protection. The key to the Court's equal protection analysis, as Kennedy's questioning of Boies had anticipated, was that the inspection of chads "can be confined by specific rules designed to assure uniform treatment." Being "practicable," the Court concluded that this specification was "necessary" to "avoid the arbitrary and disparate treatment" of voters. Because the one-person-one-vote principle of *Reynolds v. Sims* required safeguarding the right to vote from "arbitrary and disparate treatment," it followed that this principle could not permit "the standards for accepting or rejecting contested ballots [to] vary not only from county to county but indeed within a single county from one recount team to another"—as Boies had conceded that they might. Indeed, on this point, the Court was 7–2, not 5–4, as Justices Souter and Breyer agreed with the five conservative Justices (including Kennedy) about the presence of an equal protection problem.[70]

Some have called the Court's equal protection analysis unprincipled and self-consciously so.[71] They point particularly to one sentence of the Court's opinion: "Our consideration is limited to the present circumstances, for the problem of equal protection in election processes generally presents many complexities."[72] On due reflection, however, that sentence is nothing more than an expression of the Court's conventional methodology, in the tradition of the common law, of taking cases one at a time, judging each on its own facts, and thus issuing binding pronouncements of precedent no broader than necessary to dispose of the particular case at hand. When one considers all the other areas of constitutional law in which the Court has rendered very fact-specific judgments—determining what searches or seizures are unreasonable, what official uses of religious symbolism amount to an establishment of religion, or what pornographic images cross the line into forbidden obscenity ("I know it when I see it")—one must recognize that there was nothing aberrant about the Court's caution in *Bush v. Gore* that equal protection analysis of a state's ballot-counting procedures would be highly fact-dependent.[73]

More controversial than its equal protection reasoning was the Court's remedy for the equal protection violation that it found. Rather than simply remanding the case for the Florida Supreme Court to determine whether a recount was possible notwithstanding the state's apparent desire to meet the safe harbor deadline, the US Supreme Court ordered that no more recounting occur.[74] But like its stay of three days earlier, this order was not the normal way to proceed. Typically, after identifying an error of federal constitutional law committed by a state supreme court, the US Supreme Court returns the case to the state court for further proceedings cleansed of the error. In *Bush v. Gore,* this conventional approach dictated giving the Florida Supreme Court a chance to decide whether under state law it was more important to meet the safe harbor deadline or to attempt another recount consistent with equal protection. But the US Supreme Court in *Bush v. Gore* refused to give the Florida Supreme Court another chance. On this point, as with the stay, the federal Court fractured 5–4.

The four dissenters cogently argued: "Whether there is time to conduct a recount prior to December 18, when the electors are scheduled to meet, is a matter for the state courts to decide."[75] The majority's only response was that the dissent's "proposed remedy—remanding to the Florida Supreme Court for its ordering of a constitutionally proper contest until December 18—contemplates action in violation of Florida Election Code," given Florida's own desire for safe harbor status.[76] But that meager response exposed that the majority was resting its remedial decree on a proposition of state law, which the federal Court had no authority to determine.

Behind the scenes, while the case was pending, the four dissenters had attempted to persuade Justice Kennedy to conform to the conventional practice of a remand on the state-law issue. But Kennedy would not be swayed. Kennedy "would later explain that the outcome had to do with bringing a renegade court to heel"—the renegade court clearly being the Florida Supreme Court in his view.[77] That renegade court could not have another opportunity to concoct a procedure, one previously unknown to state law, evidently aimed at manufacturing a victory for Gore.

The End

Despite the 5–4 directive against any new recount, Gore contemplated going back to the Florida Supreme Court for a ruling on the state-law question that was its prerogative to decide—namely (notwithstanding the fact that the safe harbor deadline was now past) whether Florida law allowed for a recount during the six days before the constitutionally mandated meeting of the

(a)

(b)

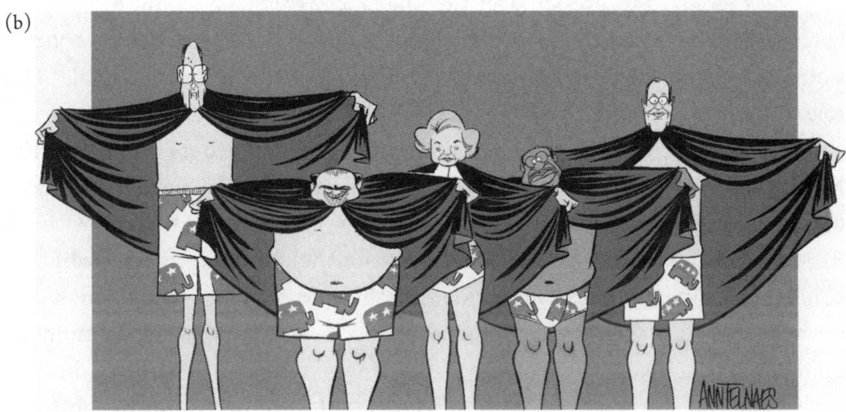

Figure 11.4 The fundamental problem in the 2000 recount was that neither the Florida nor the US Supreme Court appeared immune from partisanship. (a) Gary Varvel's cartoon illustrates the perception that the Florida Supreme Court was populated by Democrats, and thus an unfair forum for Bush as the Republican candidate. (b) Ann Telnaes, in this cartoon for which she won the Pulitzer Prize, portrays the *Bush v. Gore* majority as clad in GOP-imprinted underwear beneath their robes; with this image, she vividly captures the perception that these five justices were motivated by party politics rather than legal considerations in halting the recount. By permission of Gary Varvel and Creators Syndicate, Inc. By permission of Ann Telnaes and Cartoonist Group.

presidential electors on Monday, December 18. But the next morning Gore decided against taking that step, which undoubtedly would have escalated the entire controversy immensely, by necessarily challenging the authority of the US Supreme Court for its no-new-recount order and setting up the potential for an ultimate showdown in Congress.[78] Instead, Gore decided that now he would definitively and irrevocably concede. And so he did, in a pitch-perfect speech that began: "Just moments ago I spoke with George W. Bush and congratulated him on becoming the 43rd president of the United States. And I promised him that I wouldn't call him back this time."

Eloquent throughout, Gore's concession speech contained a passage encapsulating a theme of this book:

> History gives us many examples of contests as hotly debated, as fiercely fought, with their own challenges to the popular will. Other disputes have dragged on for weeks before reaching resolution, and each time both victor and vanquished have accepted the result peacefully and in a spirit of reconciliation. So let it be with us.

Gore closed, as he began, with a graceful touch of self-deprecating humor: "And now, my friends, in a phrase I once addressed to others, it's time for me to go."[79]

Gore's concession did not end the election officially. In fact, as vice president, Gore was required to preside over the official congressional count of electoral votes on January 6, 2001, pursuant to the Twelfth Amendment. But his concession made his official pronouncement of Bush's victory purely ceremonial.[80] His role on January 6 would have been entirely different, and altogether problematic, if he had been willing (and, with the aid of another recount ordered by the Florida Supreme Court, able) to sustain his fight until then. Imagine the national nightmare if, echoing the impasse of 1876, Gore had claimed that the Twelfth Amendment gave him, as president of the Senate, the authority to decide which of conflicting electoral votes from Florida were the ones to count—while simultaneously the House of Representatives, in Republican hands, propounded an interpretation of the Twelfth Amendment that empowered it to elect Bush directly itself. Gore's concession of December 13 put to rest fears that any such nightmare scenario might develop. Consequently, it was Gore's concession—not the official pronouncement of January 6, nor the Court's rulings in *Bush v. Gore*—that ended the dispute over the 2000 presidential election.

Absentee Ballots

Some have suggested that if Gore had opened up another front he could have won the vote-counting war. That other front would have concerned military absentee ballots. Florida law (as a result of a consent decree in a previous federal court lawsuit) permitted these ballots to arrive up to ten days after Election Day, but they needed to have been cast on or before Election Day. Florida law further required that as evidence of having been cast on time, they needed to be either postmarked or dated and signed by Election Day.[81]

Gore's attorneys initially had been inclined to challenge any military ballot that lacked either a postmark or a dated signature. But a memo outlining the approach leaked, and on *Meet the Press* Joe Lieberman (Gore's running mate) disavowed the idea. As a result, Bush's team was able to convince local canvassing boards in Republican territories to count military ballots that they otherwise would have rejected.[82]

There were not enough of these ballots, however, to account for Bush's ultimate victory. According to a *New York Times* analysis, there were only 294 ballots counted that lacked either a postmark or a dated signature—not nearly enough to erase Bush's 537-vote margin of victory through a disqualification of these, even assuming all had been cast for Bush, which of course would be an untenable assumption.[83] Taking account of all military and overseas ballots that were counted despite flaws under Florida law complicates the analysis a bit, but points to the same conclusion. There were 680 of these flawed ballots. Some were military ballots with a domestic rather than foreign postmark. Others lacked the signature of a witness. Still more had a variety of problems. Despite these defects, it is not at all clear that Florida law called for their rejection. Earlier, the Florida Supreme Court had adopted the substantial compliance standard in favor of leniency in the evaluating of such ballots.[84] Still, even if all 680 of these

Figure 11.5 Gore, standing, paper in hand, at the top dais, presided over the joint session of Congress on January 6, 2001, where he was required to declare Bush the winner of the presidential election. AP Photo/Kenneth Lampert.

ballots had been rejected, it is highly doubtful that Gore would have come out ahead. To be sure, 680 is more than 537. But 609 of these ballots would have had to have been cast for Bush in order for them to have been outcome-determinative, which would have amounted to a highly improbable 89.5% in Bush's favor.[85]

There was another issue that arose over absentee ballots. It turned out that some local election officials had acted improperly in how they handled *applications* for absentee ballots. They had wrongly favored Republican voters in fixing flaws in these applications. But the voters themselves had done nothing wrong, and there were no defects in their absentee ballot submissions as distinct from their antecedent applications. Thus it would have been unduly draconian to disqualify those ballots—and thereby disenfranchise the innocent voters—solely because the officials had acted improperly with respect to the applications.

Even so, some of Gore's attorneys, including David Boies, wanted to challenge those absentee ballots. Gore refused. There were more than enough of them that excluding them would have made a difference, but they never would have been excluded. Indeed, the courts rejected efforts by litigants unaffiliated with Gore's campaign to exclude these votes.[86]

Boies says he would have included a claim to disqualify these ballots in Gore's contest if only to force the courts to be consistent between accepting these ballots despite their defects and accepting uncounted chads that the machines could not read. Boies says the juxtaposition of the two kinds of ballots would show that Republicans could not have it both ways: accepting these absentee ballots while simultaneously rejecting the machine-unreadable chads.[87] (This strategy is reminiscent of the one that Democrats used in the Hayes-Tilden dispute, when they added Oregon into the mix in the hope that doing so would force the Electoral Commission to agree with their position on either Oregon or the other disputed states. But that strategy had not worked then, and Boies's updated version of it would not have worked in 2000.) Boies overlooks an obvious distinction: the problem with the absentee ballot applications did not involve any deficiency on the part of the voter, whereas the voters at least contributed in part to the failure to punch their chads all the way through. There seems little reason to think that including this absentee ballot issue in any way would have affected the equal protection decision of the US Supreme Court concerning the lack of an adequate standard for the evaluation of chads.

Thus the ancillary skirmishes over absentee ballots ultimately did not factor in the outcome of the 2000 presidential election. But disputes over absentee ballots would become significant in the decade that followed.

Bush v. Gore in Historical Perspective

With the story of Bush-versus-Gore now told, we can return to questions we raised at the outset. Was the counting of Florida's presidential ballots unfair, and, if so, is the US Supreme Court to be blamed (to any extent) for that unfairness? One certainly can fault the US Supreme Court for not letting Florida's judiciary decide whether Florida law permitted another attempt at a constitutionally acceptable recount during the six days between the safe harbor deadline and the meeting of the presidential electors. But even if another recount had occurred during that period, it might not have made any difference in the outcome (since, as we have seen, the media consortium's review must be considered ultimately inconclusive). In any event, it is hard to pin on the US Supreme Court primary responsibility for the recount process running out of time. For that, Gore's own litigation strategy seeking a futile extension of the protest phase, and the Florida Supreme Court's distortion of the applicable statutes granting an extension even beyond what Gore sought, are much more responsible.

Nor should the US Supreme Court's equal protection ruling be seen as contributing any unfairness to the counting process that occurred for Florida's presidential ballots in 2000. On the contrary, that equal protection ruling was a genuinely necessary corrective for unfairness inherent in the ballot-counting process authorized by the Florida Supreme Court. Had the shoe been on the other foot, no Democrat would have found acceptable a procedure that permitted the same ballot, with an identically dimpled chad, to be counted differently depending on whether it was counted by one local official rather than another. In that mirror-image situation, Democrats would have been the ones to contend that the disqualification of one dimpled chad, while simultaneously counting another in the very same election, was arbitrarily discriminatory disenfranchisement in violation of the fundamental one-person-one-vote principle enshrined in equal protection jurisprudence since *Reynolds v. Sims.*[88]

Indeed, that was the very essence of the Court's reasoning in *Bush v. Gore,* and *Reynolds v. Sims* was the key precedent that the Court cited to support its reasoning. *Bush v. Gore* was the logical outgrowth of the *Reynolds* revolution in equal protection jurisprudence applicable to elections. It took four decades for this logical extension to be made explicit, because there had not been a ballot-counting dispute significant and controversial enough to require the Court's intervention during that period. The Georgia gubernatorial election of 1966 showed that the Court would intervene if the stakes were high and a federal issue squarely presented. The 1994 Alabama chief justice election came close to needing a decision on the merits from the Court, and its refusal to grant an emergency stay in that case was a signal of where the jurisprudence was heading. By letting stand the Eleventh Circuit's reliance on the Fourteenth Amendment to invalidate Alabama's abusive manipulation of its own rules for counting absentee ballots, the Supreme Court indicated at the very least that it was open to the jurisprudential step it would take in *Bush v. Gore*.

That step, however, was contrary to *Taylor v. Beckham* and Justice Black's repudiation of the federal district court's proceedings in the Ballot Box 13 litigation of *Stevenson v. Johnson*. But no one cited those earlier precedents to the Court in *Bush v. Gore*. The case moved too quickly for even the best lawyers to reach back for those pre-*Reynolds* precedents. The Court never had to confront the conflict between two strands of its own jurisprudence. Instead, *Bush v. Gore* shows implicitly that the idea of the federal judiciary refraining from involvement in a state's ballot-counting controversy, which was the essence of both *Taylor v. Beckham* and Justice Black's decree in *Stevenson v. Johnson*, did not survive the *Reynolds* revolution.

One should not lament its passing. *Taylor v. Beckham* would have been a better decision if Justice Harlan's dissent had prevailed. Likewise, the battle over Ballot Box 13 would have been fairer if Justice Black had not prevented the federal district court from examining its contents. Insofar as the jurisprudence of *Taylor v. Beckham* and *Bush v. Gore* are diametrically at odds, the nation's ability to fulfill its commitment to democracy is much more secure as a result of the Court's decision at the close of the twentieth century, rather than the one rendered at the century's start.[89]

If any single institution is to blame for unfairness in the ballot-counting procedures used in the 2000 presidential election, it is Florida's legislature. It is the one that established recount rules that made no sense for a statewide election, especially a presidential one. It should have known better given Florida's role in 1876.

But Florida's failure in 2000 was more than just its procedures for counting ballots. That failure also included defects in its procedures for casting ballots—defects that no fair recount could have remedied. Moreover, the consequence of those defects was that in 2000 Florida was incapable of achieving even the rough justice that occurred in 1876. Back then the unfair manipulation of the state's counting rules had the effect of giving the election to Hayes, who would have won if the casting rules had been fair. Even though two wrongs don't make a right, and the wrongful disenfranchisement of African Americans in 1876 did not justify stuffing the ballot box with invalid votes (as well as the other egregious manipulations of the counting rules undertaken by Florida's canvassing board in 1876), the end result of a Hayes victory was what the eligible electorate actually wanted in 1876.

The same, however, cannot be said of Florida's failures in 2000. Its ballot-counting flaws did not erase its ballot-casting defects. Rather, this time the two types of deficiencies reinforced each other. The result was the inauguration of a president that the majority of the participating voters of Florida, and thus the nation as a whole, had not intended to elect.

12

After *Bush v. Gore*

Reinvigorated Demand for Electoral Fairness

Following the 2000 presidential election, there was a concerted national effort to fix the ballot-casting problems that had surfaced. With the enactment of the Help America Vote Act (HAVA) of 2002, Congress eliminated the punch-card voting machines that had produced the hanging chads at issue in *Bush v. Gore*. The Act also mandated the availability of provisional ballots so that no one wrongly purged from the voter rolls would be without a remedy. Federal law now required that these provisional ballots be counted if the voter in fact was entitled to participate in the particular election.[1]

But Congress made no effort to change—or even clarify—the procedures to be used in the event of another disputed presidential election. The safe harbor deadline remains exactly five weeks after Election Day, with the constitutionally required meeting of the presidential electors in all states six days later. The National Commission on Federal Election Reform, chaired by ex-presidents Carter and Ford and established to make recommendations in light of the 2000 fiasco, looked at the five-week length of the safe harbor deadline but advocated against any change: "Though we do not recommend pushing the 'safe harbor' deadline even earlier than December 12, we also do not recommend setting this date any later." The Carter-Ford Commission believed that "five weeks . . . allows enough time for counting and recounting ballots and some time for resolution of contests as well."[2] Yet the decade after 2000 yielded multiple disputed elections, including two major statewide ones, that cast serious doubt on the ability of even a well-run state to resolve a disputed presidential election fairly and accurately within five weeks.

The Carter-Ford Commission also observed that the most serious defect of the entire 35-day period during which the 2000 presidential election remained unsettled was the uncertainty of what procedures would be used to achieve a resolution: "Everyone who observed the 2000 election crisis was struck by the sheer unreadiness of every part of the system to deal with a close election."[3]

Yet a key element of that unpredictability remains unaddressed. It was a surprise to most that the US Supreme Court intervened in the 2000 dispute. Would it be a surprise if the Court did—or did not—intervene the next time?

The Court's jurisdiction in *Bush v. Gore* was entirely discretionary and that feature of the system has not changed at all. There is no requirement that the US Supreme Court get involved in the next disputed presidential election. Nor is there a requirement that the Court stay out of the fight. If one side or the other frames an issue of federal law for the Court to consider, then the Court can take the case—or not—as it chooses. This unbridled discretion is a severe defect when, as the Carter-Ford Commission explained, "to the maximum extent possible, partisans on both sides should be able to foresee, before a recount, how a vote will be [treated in that recount]."[4]

In the very next presidential election after 2000, the country came much closer than many realize to the possibility of having to confront this unsettling situation. In 2004, the outcome again turned on a single state, this time Ohio. On Election Night that year, it looked as if Ohio might be close enough to provoke another ballot-counting fight like the one that had occurred four years earlier. To be sure, the fight would not have been over punch cards. Instead, the provisional ballots that Congress in HAVA had just mandated as a form of voter protection would have been the obvious target of opportunity for eager litigators waiting to pounce at the direction of their respective candidates. Being inherently questionable in their status—if the provisional voter's eligibility had been indisputable, the voter would have cast a regular ballot instead—provisional ballots were an open invitation to fight over a tight finish.

But Ohio in 2004 did not end up quite close enough for this scenario to unfold. Although there were 158,642 provisional ballots cast in Ohio that year,[5] this number was not large enough in relationship to the lead that George Bush had over John Kerry, his Democratic challenger, at the end of Election Night: 121,012 votes.[6] Even if all the provisional ballots were determined to be eligible for counting, an obviously untenable proposition, Kerry would have needed to win almost 90% of them (88% to be exact), another untenable proposition. The math showed that a fight was not worth it. In the jargon coined at the time, Bush's margin of victory was "beyond the margin of litigation."[7] Kerry conceded at about 11:00 a.m. on Wednesday, the day after Election Day.[8]

To election professionals, 2004 in Ohio was a near-miss scare, akin to the doomsday asteroid that comes frighteningly close to hitting earth but ultimately passes safely by without a trace of damage.[9] Had the 2004 presidential election in Ohio resulted in a margin similar to the state's outcome in either 1976 (when Carter beat Ford by only 11,116 votes) or 1948 (when Truman bested Dewey by only 7,107), then Kerry undoubtedly would have pressed on, and the nation would have become engulfed in a Florida-like fight over the provisional ballots (and possibly others as well).[10] There would have been litigation in both state and federal courts over whether or not to count particular provisional ballots, and the US Supreme Court would have been asked to weigh in.

One need not concoct hypotheticals to realize what a nightmare it would have been. In 2008, an Ohio congressional election was tied up for weeks in litigation over provisional ballots, and if it had been a presidential election the safe harbor deadline easily might have been missed.[11] Two years later, an Ohio local judicial election was unresolved for over twenty months because of a lawsuit challenging the disqualification of provisional ballots.[12] The claim in that case, which prevailed in the federal court of appeals 2–1 (with the judges regrettably split along partisan lines), was an equal protection argument derived directly from *Bush v. Gore*.[13] Testimony in the case showed that poll workers had mistreated ballots because they could not tell the difference between odd and even street address numbers.[14] If a presidential election had hinged on these ballots, it is unclear how the lawsuit could have been completed within the five-week timeframe mandated by the safe harbor deadline.

Ohio is hardly alone in having its elections mired in lawsuits over provisional ballots. In 2004, for example, North Carolina had a statewide race (for office of superintendent of public instruction) go to its supreme court. At issue was the validity of provisional ballots cast in a precinct other than the one in which the voter resided. The all-Republican court ruled the ballots ineligible under the state law at the time, only to have the Democratic-controlled state legislature enact a new law to supersede this result.[15] Had a presidential election been at stake, the next move presumably would have been to federal court based on the due process precedent from the 1994 Alabama chief justice election.[16] But since the North Carolina Supreme Court did not issue its ruling until February 5 in the following year (2005) and the state legislature did not enact its superseding statute until March 2, one can only surmise how this same fight over North Carolina's provisional ballots would have played out under the compressed schedule imposed by the safe harbor deadline.

This litigation over provisional ballots proved that if a presidential election ended up close enough in a pivotal state, it would be easy, despite the elimination of punch-card machines and their hanging chads, to replicate the kind of fight that had occurred in 2000. But provisional ballots were not the only source of vulnerability after 2000. Other issues, especially those involving absentee ballots, could prove fruitful grounds of contention in a tight race. This point was most vividly made by the two most prominent disputed elections in the first decade of the new century: Washington's gubernatorial election of 2004 and Minnesota's US Senate race of 2008. While each of these disputes was certainly important in its own right, especially for the state in which it occurred, together they present an ominous warning about the nation's preparedness for another disputed presidential election. Neither of these disputes was resolved until June of the following year, well beyond the timeframe acceptable for a presidential election. Even more disturbingly, for both these disputes the candidate perceived as leading on the date of the safe harbor deadline that year (and even six days later, on the date that presidential electors met) was not the candidate who ultimately prevailed. Had either of these disputes involved presidential ballots, the question inevitably arises whether either state would have been able to identify the actual winner within the amount of time Congress allotted for doing so.[17]

Washington's 2004 Gubernatorial Election

It is well known in law, as in life, that the perception of fairness—or of unfairness—can be more important than whatever the reality of the situation may be.[18] That truism certainly applies to Washington State's experience with its gubernatorial election of 2004. While it can be argued that the ultimate result, in which the Democrats prevailed, reflected a valid application of the relevant rules, the process of getting there was so riddled with errors and surprises—and was administered in crucial respects by institutions controlled by Democrats—that Republicans in the state irredeemably felt cheated of the election. A decade later, Susan Hutchinson, the chair of the state's Republican Party (and former TV anchor), continued to repeat the charge that Democrats were "masters of election fraud as proven in 2004 when they stole the election."[19]

The 2004 election pitted Attorney General Christine Gregoire, the Democrat, against state senator Dino Rossi, the Republican, vying for an open seat.[20] On Election Night it became apparent that it would be impossible to identify a winner, even unofficially, until all the mailed ballots had arrived and been counted. In 2004, over two-thirds of the state's ballots—there were almost two million of them—were cast by mail. State law permitted them to be counted if they arrived up to a week after Election Day as long as they were postmarked by Election Day.[21]

From the beginning, the vote-counting process was afflicted by a dynamic in which Gregoire was searching for votes in heavily Democratic King County, which includes Seattle and by itself would account for almost one-third of the state's total votes, while Rossi wanted to keep the King County total as low as possible. Conversely, Rossi wanted to find extra votes in Republican-friendly areas elsewhere in the state, whereas Gregoire had no interest in harvesting ballots in these outlying regions. This stark geographic division bred mistrust between the two sides, which increasingly felt like warring camps attempting to gain ground in enemy terrain while tenaciously holding their own ground.

Washington law permitted absentee voters to correct clerical defects, like a missing or problematic signature, on their absentee ballot envelopes, as long as they did so by November 17, 2004. The Gregoire campaign almost immediately endeavored to help King County absentee voters fix these problems. Using publicly available lists of absentee voters whose ballots would be invalidated if not corrected, the Democrats began contacting these voters to encourage them to rectify the matter.[22]

The Democrats also wanted to do the same with 929 provisional ballots in King County that potentially would be rejected. But the law did not provide Democrats with the same access to the names of the provisional voters whose ballots were in this precarious situation. Indeed, a section of the federal Help America Vote Act of 2002 easily could have been construed as prohibiting the release of this information to anyone except the provisional voters themselves: "Access to information about an individual provisional ballot shall be restricted to the individual who cast the ballot."[23] Despite requests from local Democrats, and despite being run by Democrats, the King County Department of Elections declined to release this information. This decision might have signaled to Republicans that King County's election officials were not trying to sway the election for Gregoire, but as the process wore on this piece of evident impartiality would become washed away in a flood of suspicious recriminations.[24]

The Democrats then sued King County in local state court, which accepted their claim that the identity of provisional voters whose ballots were at risk of rejection was public information. The court construed the relevant section of HAVA as protecting only the secrecy of the votes made on the ballots themselves. In other words, the public could not know whether a provisional ballot was cast for Gregoire or Rossi, but the public—and thus the candidates and their partisan supporters—could know who cast the provisional ballot. The court said that any other interpretation of HAVA would be inconsistent with "the public's right to an open and transparent electoral process."[25] It was a laudable ruling in terms of public policy (the integrity of an election, after all, does depend on a public explanation of why ballots are rejected), but it was not the most straightforward reading of the relevant HAVA language. In any event, it was hugely consequential, as everyone involved understood. When discussing the ruling at a press conference, the chair of the state's Democratic Party wept openly with joy, "tears streaming down his face."[26]

As the November 17 deadline for completing the canvass approached, the media-reported lead seesawed back and forth. Here's how the newspapers reported the lead as it stood at the end of each day:

Friday, November 12	Rossi up by 1,920
Monday, November 15	Gregoire up by 158
Tuesday, November 16	Rossi up by 19

Gregoire's jump ahead on Monday, November 15, was a surprise based on a larger-than-expected number in King County of both returned absentee ballots and validated provisional ballots.[27] Although there was nothing to negate the eligibility of these extra ballots, they primed the Republican fear that King County was capable of discovering extra ballots for Gregoire whenever she needed them.[28]

Republicans intervened in the pending state-court lawsuit over provisional ballots, asking the judge to preclude counting provisional ballots for which the voters did not show up in person to validate the ballot (relying instead on campaign workers to do so). In most instances, the provisional ballot envelope was missing a signature or other item of information, and the campaign worker had gone to the voter's home to remedy the problem. Republicans wanted the court to require the voter to appear in person as a deterrent against potential fraud. The judge, however, dismissed this concern as unfounded and thus refused to block the counting of these challenged ballots.[29]

Still, when the canvass was complete on Wednesday, November 17, Rossi was ahead by 261 votes. That infinitesimal margin, less than one-thousandth of one percent (0.0093%, to be precise), triggered an automatic machine recount. Influenced by *Bush v. Gore*, and claiming a violation of equal protection, the Republicans filed suit in federal court against King County over the specific procedures used to conduct the recount there.[30] According to the county's rules, where the machine recount registered an undervote in the gubernatorial election, local officials would examine the ballot to see if it contained a clearly identified vote that the machine was unable to read; if so, the officials would remake the ballot so that the machine could read it. Fearful that the local officials would find and remake more Gregoire votes than a strictly impartial observer would, the Republicans asked the federal court to block the county's ballot-remaking practice. The federal court, however, declined to intervene, observing that if necessary the remade ballots could be compared to the originals in a subsequent lawsuit.[31] Although Republicans would file that subsequent lawsuit in January, they never raised an allegation about improper Gregoire votes as a result of this ballot-remaking process. Thus one can assume that this skirmish was another instance in which Republican fear of King County's procedures was unfounded, at least insofar as the fear was that those procedures would give Gregoire a victory to which she was not entitled. Nonetheless, it contributed to the habitual posture of the Republican Party fighting over the vote-counting process against the Democratic-controlled King County administration.

The machine recount ended on November 24, with Rossi still ahead, but this time by only 42 votes. At this point, Gregoire was entitled to a manual recount if she was willing to pay for it, and she was. She could have asked for only county-specific recounts, but after Gore's mistake along those lines in 2000, she wisely opted for a statewide recount.[32]

More litigation occurred over the scope of the manual recount. The Democrats sued directly in the state supreme court in an effort to have the recount include review of 15,000 absentee and provisional ballots that had been rejected during the canvass. On December 14, the Washington Supreme Court unanimously rejected the Democrats' petition. As the court put it, "under Washington's statutory scheme, ballots are to be 'retabulated' only if they have been previously counted or tallied."[33] In this respect, Washington was like other states (including Minnesota and Virginia) in defining a recount to exclude a "recanvass" of ballot-eligibility determinations.

The Washington Supreme Court's opinion, however, cited a state statute that permitted a local canvassing board to recanvass ballots if the board "finds that there is an apparent discrepancy or inconsistency in the returns."[34] This citation would prove important because the previous day, December 13, King County announced that it had discovered 561 absentee ballots that had been improperly rejected because of an administrative failure to upload voter registration cards into the county's computerized voter registration database. At the time of this discovery, both sides knew that these ballots easily could determine the outcome of the election. Although there never would be any evidence that anything but administrative incompetence caused this surprise, it was one surprise too many for the Republicans to withstand (having already been burned by the unexpectedly large number of extra King County votes arriving late during the canvass)—and there would still be more disconcerting surprises to come. The chair of the state Republican Party, Chris Vance, exclaimed that Republicans were "absolutely convinced that King County is trying to steal this election" and warned of "mass protests [in] the streets."[35]

On December 15, the King County Canvassing Board split 2–1, along party lines, on whether or not to recanvass these absentee ballots, which had already grown in number from 561 to 573.[36] The two Democrats on the board voted to permit inclusion of the ballots, stating that the voters should not be disenfranchised because of administrative error. The lone Republican on the board voted to postpone consideration of the issue. The Democrats on the board had the more equitable position. The *Seattle Times*, which had endorsed Rossi's candidacy, editorialized in favor of counting these ballots.[37] But it certainly would have helped the situation if the body making this decision was an impartial one and not dominated by the party whose position it favored. From the Republican perspective, it looked something like a repeat of the Task Force's 2–1 ruling in the Bloody Eighth (as described in Chapter 10).

Vance and other Republicans supporting Rossi's campaign then sued to prevent these ballots from being included as a part of the hand recount. Their theory was that under the Washington Supreme Court's December 14 opinion, these ballots should not be recounted because they were not counted initially; as that opinion had stated, a recount does not include a recanvass of ballots originally rejected for lack of eligibility. These ballots had been rejected (albeit erroneously) on the ground that their voters were not registered, since the voters were not found in the computerized database. If Gregoire was still behind at the end of the hand recount, Republicans argued, she could bring a separate contest claim in an effort to have these ballots added as having been wrongly excluded.

The Republicans filed this lawsuit in Pierce County (where Tacoma is located), a more hospitable location than King County. On December 17, they were successful in securing an order preventing the recounting of absentee ballots that had been rejected initially. The judge agreed with the Republicans that any reconsideration of these ballots must be confined to a postrecount contest of result.[38] By this point, the number of these mistakenly rejected absentee ballots had jumped from 573 to 735, as unprocessed voters with last names at the beginning of the alphabet had been overlooked.[39]

The Democrats appealed the Pierce County judge's order. Sam Reed, the Republican secretary of state, supported the Democrats on this issue, arguing that King County had authority under the relevant statute to include in the manual recount the erroneously rejected absentee ballots. On December 22, the Washington Supreme Court unanimously agreed with this position. In essence, the high court updated its December 14 decision, either clarifying or revising it (depending on one's point of view) to give local canvassing boards the discretion to decide whether or not to recanvass initially rejected ballots as part of the manual recount. The local boards were under no obligation to do so (as the December 14 decision had pronounced), but now they were entitled to do if they believed that they had made a clear mistake in rejecting the ballots initially.[40]

As it turned out, these 735 disputed ballots did not determine which candidate was ahead at the end of the manual recount. On the same day as the state supreme court's new ruling, Gregoire pulled ahead of Rossi by a mere ten votes.[41] She did so based on the manual examination of the ovals and other ballot-markings that the machines had miscounted. Still, the 735 extra absentee ballots made a big difference. After reviewing these ballots, the King County Canvassing Board determined that 566 were eligible to be counted, and counting these ballots extended Gregoire's lead to 129 votes, the officially certified result announced on December 30.[42] Although a 129-vote margin is miniscule, especially in the context of almost 3 million cast, it is a whole order of magnitude larger than only ten votes.

Immediately after the state supreme court's December 22 decision, Rossi tried to have recanvassed about 500 more rejected ballots from around the state. But the secretary of state ruled that this request came too late since all other counties beside King had already certified their final postrecount results. In King County itself, the canvassing board refused to take up additional previously rejected ballots that the Republicans wanted reconsidered.[43] The board distinguished these from the 735 that they were willing to review on the ground that the Republican-proffered ballots had problems identified during the initial canvass and the voters failed to take the opportunity given them to correct those problems, whereas the Democrats' 735 were initially rejected solely because of the county's mistake.

The only recourse for the Republicans at this point was a judicial contest of the election, which they pursued. Meanwhile, Gregoire was inaugurated on January 12, as scheduled.[44] Among the claims Republicans included in their contest was the allegation that many ballots had been rejected that, under state law, should have been counted. The contest further alleged an equal protection violation stemming from the rejection of some ballots equivalent to others that were counted. The trial court, however, early in pretrial proceedings dismissed the equal protection claim concerning previously rejected ballots.[45] The trial court in essence ruled that it lacked jurisdiction to consider whether some ballots were mistreated in relationship to others; it only had jurisdiction to decide whether ballots, on their own terms and not in relation to others, were treated properly under state law. This ruling left open the possibility that Republicans would continue to claim that some absentee ballots that were entitled to be counted on their own terms had been improperly rejected. But the Republicans abandoned this claim, instead focusing at trial on what they then perceived to be the larger problem of ballots that *were* counted but should *not* have been.

During the trial, the Republicans identified major problems concerning the handling of absentee ballots, especially in King County. Hundreds more absentee ballots surfaced that never had been reviewed during the canvassing process, but pursuant to the court's earlier order it was now too late to consider them. Even worse, in King County alone the court credited evidence showing that 875 more absentee votes were counted than absentee ballots were cast. But the trial court ultimately ruled that state law did not provide any available remedy for this problem. If a candidate cannot stop the wrongful counting of absentee ballots before they are commingled with the rest of the state's tally, a judicial contest of the election is unable to undo the mistake.[46]

In total, the trial court found that 1,678 ineligible ballots were included in the result, a number dwarfing by far Gregoire's 129-vote certified margin of victory at the end of the manual recount. Of these invalid ballots, 1,401 had been cast by felons whose right to vote had not been restored. Another 252 were provisional ballots for which no registered voter could be found.[47] Nineteen were cast in the name of dead voters and thus obviously unlawful, and the final six were the second of two ballots illegally cast by double-voters.

Because all of these 1,678 invalid ballots had long been commingled with the entirety of the counted ballots in the election, it was impossible to identify for which gubernatorial candidate each had been voted or, indeed, whether a vote for governor had been cast on the particular ballot. Only by contacting each and every one of the 1,678 individuals who had cast the ineligible ballots, including whoever anonymously had cast the nineteen ballots in the names of deceased voters—and then asking all these individuals how they voted—would there be any possibility of attributing each invalid ballot to a particular candidate for the purpose of deducting that vote from the candidate's total. (In other words, if a person who cast an invalid ballot testified that the ballot had been cast for Rossi, then one vote could be deducted from Rossi's total.) But even assuming that tracking down these 1,678 individuals would be feasible, requiring them to testify for which candidate these ballots were cast would violate the secrecy of the ballot, and one could not be sure that their testimony would be trustworthy given the ineligibility of the ballots that they cast. For example, a felon who wanted Gregoire to win and had cast his unlawful ballot for her could dishonestly testify that he had voted for Rossi, and if this testimony were credited, then Rossi's total rather than Gregoire's would be deducted by a single vote.

Rossi argued that either of two remedies should be adopted in light of the 1,678 invalid ballots. First, on the basis that Gregoire's 129-vote advantage was unreliable, Rossi argued in favor of a revote. As the trial court observed, however, a state statute expressly prohibited that remedy absent proof that enough of the invalid ballots had been cast for Gregoire.[48] The demonstrated presence of unlawful votes substantially greater than the certified margin of victory did not suffice under state law to void the certification and require holding a new election. Given the explicitness of the relevant statutory language, this point was true no matter how much larger the number of invalid ballots than the certified margin.

Second, Rossi argued that the court should use the methodology of "proportional deduction" to identify the precincts in which the unlawful ballots were cast and deduct from each candidate's statewide total the number equal to the percentage of unlawful ballots in each precinct that is the same percentage as the candidate's votes in that precinct. To illustrate with an example, suppose there were 10 invalid ballots in a particular precinct and Gregoire won that precinct 60% to 40%; the methodology of proportional deduction would deduct six votes from Gregoire's statewide total and four from Rossi's.[49]

The trial court rejected Rossi's contention that proportional deduction would be appropriate in this case. Based on expert testimony submitted by Gregoire's attorneys, the trial court found that proportional deduction rested on a statistically fallacious assumption insofar as it presumed that unlawful ballots in a precinct were distributed between the two candidates in the same ratio as all the ballots in the precinct: "Felons and others who vote illegally are not necessarily the same as others in the precinct." As the expert testimony further explained, factors other than precinct of residency may be a more important predictor of which candidates the unlawful ballots were cast for. For example, especially in light of the fact that Gregoire was female, while Rossi was male, "gender may be as significant or a more significant factor than others."[50] The evidence at trial also showed that more unlawful ballots were cast by male rather than female voters. If Rossi did better among men than women overall, then perhaps a greater proportion of the unlawful ballots should be allocated to Rossi, on the hypothesis that more of them were cast by men than women.

Because Rossi as the contestant bore the burden of proof, the trial court ruled that his evidence, including his own expert testimony, was not enough to overcome the doubts about proportional deduction established by Gregoire's experts. The trial court concluded that whatever the difficulty, Rossi was required to introduce the testimony of voters who cast unlawful ballots to establish that they cast enough of those ballots for Gregoire to account for her 129-vote margin of victory. But Rossi offered no evidence of this kind. Accordingly, the trial court ruled that Gregoire's victory must stand. The trial judge did adjust the final margin to 133 upon unrebutted evidence that four invalid votes had been cast for Rossi.[51]

The trial court's decision came on June 6, 2005, seven months after Election Day. Some Republicans urged Rossi to fight on by appealing the decision to the Washington Supreme Court. But he decided against doing so. His concession speech was less than fully gracious. He said that "because of the political makeup of the Washington Supreme Court, which makes it almost impossible to overturn this ruling, I am ending the election contest."[52] True or not, it certainly was not equivalent to saying that he had lost as a result of a fair

Figure 12.1 Doug Chayka's illustration in *Seattle Weekly* depicted the utterly chaotic nature of Washington State's 2004 gubernatorial recount. With permission of Doug Chayka, www.dougchayka.com.

and impartial process even if he disagreed with the substance of the decision reached by that process. Consequently, his speech made it all the more difficult for Republicans to believe in the legitimacy of Gregoire's victory.

Yes, the State of Washington had survived the ordeal. In percentage terms (0.0047%) it was the closest gubernatorial election in over a century, even closer than Minnesota's in 1962 (0.0073%). There had never been any serious risk of civil unrest, despite some of the escalated rhetoric along the way. Secretary of State Sam Reed had behaved impartially, and admirably, throughout. Moreover, despite insinuations to the contrary, there was no evidence that the Washington Supreme Court had been biased toward the Democrats in its rulings. Although there were more Democrats than Republicans on the court, its two key rulings were unanimous, and one of the two (the first) went against Gregoire's position. Even King County had not been proven biased against Rossi, just inept.

Still, the episode could hardly be considered a success. The administrative errors were too numerous, unexpected, and significant for one to believe that the process had worked properly. Some counting rules were strictly followed (no reconsideration of mistakenly counted ballots), while others were not (no recanvassing of mistakenly uncounted ballots). The answer to a counting question often depended on the identity of which particular state official answered it (which trial or appellate court, or which discretionary election administrator). It was not a rational, orderly, predictable process designed to foster a voter's confidence in the integrity of the outcome regardless of that voter's partisan affiliation.

Furthermore, the end result was a margin of victory swamped by a tenfold larger number of admittedly invalid ballots included in the count. As with the 2000 presidential election, there could be no assurance that the inaugurated officeholder was the candidate who received the most valid votes from the eligible voters who cast them. If the nation's goal after *Bush v. Gore*, as reflected in the Help America Vote Act of 2002, was to conduct elections so that the results matched the eligible electorate's choices, Washington's 2004 election was a severe disappointment and an immediate indication that more improvements were urgently needed.

Minnesota's 2008 US Senate Election: *Coleman v. Franken*

Four years later Minnesota showed that an exceptionally close statewide election, even one with significant problems in the administration of the voting process, need not end up with the same bitter aftertaste as Washington's did.[53] To be sure, there were incorrigible Republicans who refused to believe the result in Minnesota was fair. But they were noticeably fewer than those in Washington with the same feeling. The two major newspapers in Minnesota, both of which had endorsed the Republican candidate's bid for reelection, embraced the ultimate victory for the Democrat as the result of a scrupulously fair process.[54] Even the Republican candidate's own lawyer acknowledged afterward that the process could not have been more impartial toward both sides.[55]

The key to Minnesota's success in 2008 was essentially the same as what had made the resolution of the state's 1962 gubernatorial election so commendable: the use of a specially empaneled three-judge court designed to be evenly balanced between both sides. The particular method of selecting the three-judge panel differed in the two cases. In 1962 the chief justice had forced the two candidates to pick the three judges, and they each chose one seen as associated with one of the two sides with the third being a genuine neutral. In 2008 the Minnesota Supreme Court as a whole picked the three judges, choosing two with backgrounds affiliated with each of the two contending parties and the third associated with neither but instead with the state's Independence Party. Despite these differences in details, the upshot was the same: a tribunal that the public could, and did, trust to dispense justice fairly to both candidates.[56]

Had Minnesota not used a structurally evenhanded tribunal to adjudicate the dispute, but instead a tribunal whose majority shared the same partisan affiliation as the candidate whom that tribunal determined to be the winner, then the election would have ended in extreme acrimony—and might even have gone all the way to the US Senate for even more bitterly partisan disputation. Indeed, before Minnesota put its evenhanded tribunal in place to resolve the 2008 election, it was on track to end up in that kind of ugly situation. Just as in 1962, at a preliminary stage of the process the Minnesota Supreme Court had issued a divisive 3–2 decision that prompted fears that partisanship, not fairness, would determine the outcome of the dispute. But also just like in 1962, backlash against that distasteful 3–2 ruling helped precipitate the creation of the evenly balanced tribunal to handle the remainder of the process. Thus, as was true four decades before, once the transparently impartial tribunal was in place, Minnesota could bury the 3–2 ruling as ultimately inconsequential and go about assuring that the final resolution would satisfy an appropriate standard of fairness.[57]

In Minnesota's 2008 US Senate race, the Republican candidate was one-term incumbent Norm Coleman, who previously had been mayor of St. Paul. Coleman had narrowly won in 2002 after his opponent, Senator Paul Wellstone, died in a plane crash only eleven days before the election that year. Coleman's Democratic challenger in 2008 was Al Franken, the prominent comedian previously best known for his fifteen years with *Saturday Night Live*.

On November 18, two weeks after Election Day, the State Canvassing Board certified Coleman the winner by only 215 votes, out of 2.9 million counted. State law provided that any margin less than a half-percent triggered an automatic recount. Coleman's margin, less than a hundredth of a percent, was obviously far below that threshold. During the canvass, some Republicans grumbled because Coleman's margin had been 725 on the morning after Election Day, before dropping as local officials corrected errors. But this complaint became moot, since the automatic recount essentially erased the result of the canvass and began the counting process all over again with the candidates tied zero-zero.[58]

Minnesota's automatic recount, an innovation since 1962, displayed several positive features in 2008. First, because the recount was conducted under the authority and supervision of the State Canvassing Board, there was no risk of inconsistent or variable standards applied at the local level that would affect a ballot's ultimate treatment in the recount. Each candidate could challenge any ballot disposition made at the local level, and all such challenges would be reviewed by the State Canvassing Board. Both sides initially were a bit overzealous in their challenges (although not nearly as much as had been the case in the judicial recount for the 1962 election). Of the 6,655 challenges initially, both sides whittled the number down to 1,337 for the board to review.

Second, the board permitted its review of the challenged ballots to be televised over the Internet, with a screen that enabled citizens watching the proceedings to see each ballot that the board was evaluating. This transparency engendered public trust in the board's rulings. Citizens could see for themselves that the board was reviewing each ballot deliberately and fairly.

Third, Minnesota law had well-defined rules for determining when ballot markings counted, or did not count, as a vote. The secretary of state even had published a recount guide containing pictures with examples of how different types of ballot markings should be treated. The State Canvassing Board scrupulously followed these rules as well as its own ballot-by-ballot precedents as it implemented these rules. Thus the Minnesota recount was the opposite of what had occurred in Florida in 2000, where vague and unspecified standards created a system of arbitrary lawlessness as different local recount teams treated identical ballots differently. In 2008 Minnesota's State Canvassing Board clearly was acting pursuant to the rule of law, applying lucid and precise rules in a uniform manner.[59]

Fourth, the board's law-abiding behavior was fostered by the fact that four of board's five members were judges, including Chief Justice Eric Magnuson and a second justice from the state's supreme court. The four jurists were joined by the secretary of state, Mark Ritchie. Chief Justice Magnuson helped to set a judicial tone for the board's proceedings. He was the one who, by drawing a series of ballot markings as they arose, developed a system of precedent to use while evaluating each ballot under the rules. Ritchie, who nominally chaired the board's meeting, was visibly willing to let Chief Justice Magnuson share in a leadership role during the board's deliberations.[60]

Moreover, although not planned, it was fortuitous that the membership of the board was also visibly balanced in partisan backgrounds. Magnuson and Ritchie, as the board's leaders, were from opposite parties. One of the judges had been appointed by Jesse Ventura, the former governor who had won as the candidate of the state's Independence Party. Another judge had no obvious partisan affiliations. The board was unanimous in virtually all of its rulings, and this unanimity confirmed that the board was conducting itself impartially and not favoring one party or the other.

One feature of the board's role in the recount, however, turned out to be problematic. By law, in conducting the automatic recount, the board was

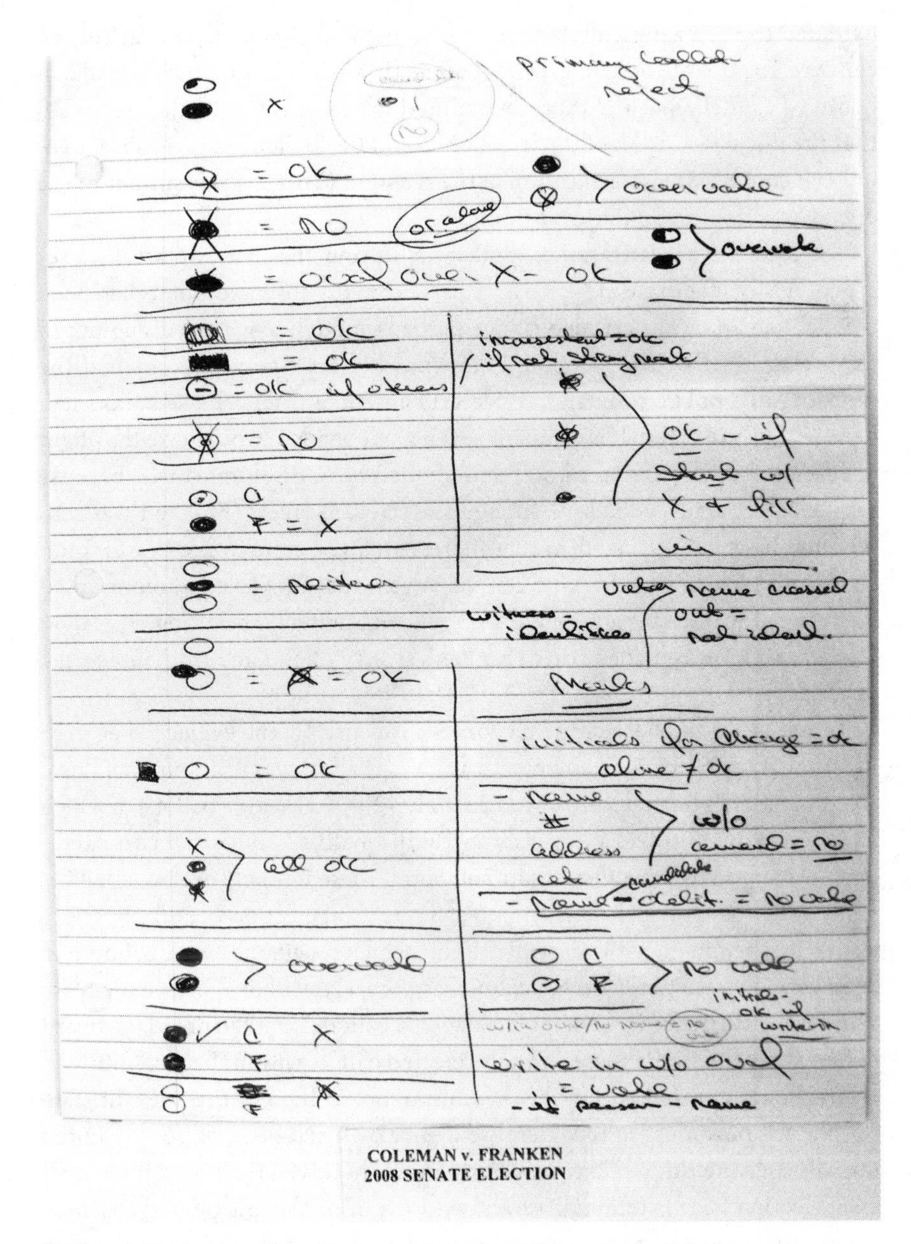

Figure 12.2 Chief Justice Magnuson created this "hieroglyphic" sheet to serve a system of precedent in the 2008 recount; widely recognized within the state as a key factor in the recount's fairness, it was further invoked as precedent two years later when the state faced another recount in its gubernatorial election. Courtesy of Eric Magnuson.

confined to reviewing ballots that had been counted initially as part of the canvass. The board could not review ballots that local election boards had disqualified as ineligible and thus not counted in the canvass. The law provided that the disqualification of those ballots could be challenged in a subsequent judicial contest, after certification of the recount. (This law was similar to the one in Washington on the same point.)

Yet even as the canvass was underway during the first two weeks after Election Day, it became increasingly clear that many absentee ballots had been disqualified and some erroneously so, perhaps enough to make a difference in this exceptionally close election. Franken, who was trailing Coleman at the time, began a public campaign to identify absentee voters whose ballots had been wrongly rejected. His campaign even made a video to publicize the plight of several absentee voters who seemingly had been disenfranchised because local election officials had misapplied the relevant rules. (Franken was represented by the same law firm that represented Gregoire in the Washington battle four years earlier, Perkins Coie, a powerhouse firm that has represented many leading Democrats in election-related matters, including President Obama, and it was evident that Franken's strategy benefited from Gregoire's experience.)

While the local phase of the recount was occurring, the evidence began to mount that the problem of uncounted absentee ballots was a serious one. Local election officials had rejected approximately 12,000 absentee ballots, of which an estimated 1,600 had been improperly disqualified. With the two candidates separated by little more than 200 votes, these wrongly excluded ballots easily could be outcome-determinative. Some local election boards conscientiously had begun the process of identifying which specific absentee ballots had been wrongly rejected. As the recount was preparing to come before the State Canvassing Board for its review of challenged ballots, Franken urged the board to find a way to include these wrongly rejected ballots within the recount.[61]

The board considered Franken's petition, but in light of the relevant state statute, felt powerless to recount absentee ballots that had not been counted initially. In something of a compromise move, however, the board invited all local election boards to identify, on their own initiative, uncounted absentee ballots that upon further review these local boards believed were wrongly rejected. Exactly what would happen to these new piles of wrongly rejected ballots, the State Canvassing Board did not know. Maybe the board could find some statutory authority to include in the recount at least those ballots that the local boards now believed were entitled to be counted. The board at least could defer consideration of this issue until the end of the recount, and in the meantime there presumably was no harm if the local boards conducted their own further review of the uncounted absentee ballots.

Coleman, still in the lead, did not want to open up the possibility of additional ballots being included in the recount. On December 12, the same day that the State Canvassing Board made its request of the local officials to search for and set aside wrongly rejected ballots, Coleman asked the Minnesota Supreme Court to keep all uncounted ballots out of the recount. With two justices recused because of their service on the State Canvassing Board (Chief Justice Magnuson being one of them), five justices heard the case. They split 3–2. Of the three in the majority, two were judicial conservatives appointed by Governor Tim Pawlenty, a Republican, and one by Ventura, the Independent. The two dissenters were widely known as the court's most liberal members. Thus the 3–2 split seemed at least ideological, if not partisan. Superficially, it looked like the five justices were letting politics influence their judgment on the rules for counting ballots, just as it had appeared after the court's similar 3–2 split in 1962.

In fairness to the court in 2008, the majority opinion most likely was an effort at compromise undertaken by Justice Helen Meyer, the Ventura appointee and a moderate. Although the majority agreed with Coleman that the relevant state statutes did not authorize recounting ballots not initially counted, the opinion went on to say that a ballot ought to count if both candidates as well as the relevant local election board all agreed that the ballot was wrongly rejected. Thus the majority ordered the attorneys for both candidates to examine ballots that the local boards had identified as wrongly rejected. If in good faith both attorneys agreed with the local board's admission of error—and the majority admonished the attorneys that they were required to conduct this examination in good faith—then these ballots could be delivered to the State Canvassing Board for inclusion in the recount.[62]

The idea of counting ballots that everyone agreed were entitled to be counted seemed consistent with common sense. The problem, however, was that it created a procedure not enacted by the legislature and one which gave each candidate a veto over ballots to be counted. In any event, it was not a consensus solution, as the two liberal justices on the court vehemently dissented. They argued that if it was permissible under Minnesota law to count these ballots without waiting for a subsequent judicial contest, then they should be counted solely on the ground that the local officials now believed them entitled to be counted, regardless of what either candidate's attorney thought about the particular ballot. If Justice Meyer had been able to secure the assent of all five Justices for her creative compromise, it might have worked better; then it would have had the veneer of nonpartisan unanimity, necessarily causing both sides to be more cooperative in implementing the procedure. As it was, neither candidate's legal team had proposed the novel procedure, and thus both sides could balk at its implementation. In the absence of unanimity at the Minnesota

Supreme Court, it would have been better if the category of wrongly rejected absentee ballots had been ruled definitely either in or out of the recount, but Justice Meyer's compromise left them in a legal limbo that subjected them to further disputation before the recount could be certified as complete.

While the issue of absentee ballots was pending in the Minnesota Supreme Court, the State Canvassing Board was undertaking its review of the ballots challenged during the local phase of the recount (these ballots having been among those originally counted and thus indisputably appropriate for consideration as part of the recount). Ironically enough, almost as soon as the Minnesota Supreme Court had issued its 3–2 "candidate veto" order, the strategic interests of the two candidates flipped. Franken had overtaken Coleman in the recount by 49 votes. Consequently, although Franken previously had been the one fighting for the inclusion of as many previously uncounted absentee ballots as possible, now it was in his interest to close down the process and keep out any additional ballots. Conversely, whereas Coleman had gone to the Minnesota Supreme Court to stop the inclusion of previously uncounted ballots, now he was the one arguing in favor of counting more absentee votes. Recount lawyers affiliated with one party or the other jokingly observe that they are able to argue either side of an issue depending solely on whether in the particular case their candidate is ahead or behind; the goal to win trumps any ideological considerations at the moment. In 2008, Minnesota proved this point within the context of a single recount, as the two sides traded positions midstream.[63]

With some difficulty, including a return visit to the Minnesota Supreme Court that refused to let Coleman expand the pile of absentee ballots for review, the attorneys for Franken and Coleman managed to agree upon 933 of the 1,346 ballots that the local officials identified as wrongly rejected. When these 933 ballots were added to the recount, Franken's lead increased to 225. On January 5, 2009, the State Canvassing Board certified Franken as winning the election by this amount.[64]

The next day Coleman filed a judicial contest, focusing on the issue of absentee ballots. He argued that thousands more absentee ballot should be counted. He made this claim on two distinct grounds. First, he argued that Minnesota law embraced the substantial compliance doctrine and thus should be interpreted leniently to permit the counting of absentee ballots even if they were technically deficient in some minor respect. This argument was similar to the ones that Democrats had invoked in Alabama's 1994 chief justice election. Second, relying on *Bush v. Gore*, Coleman argued that equal protection required counting ballots that were identical to ballots already counted. In other words, because some local election boards had been willing to count absentee ballots despite certain technical defects—for example, if the ballot's witness was not a registered voter—Coleman argued that it would violate equal protection to disqualify other ballots whose only problem was the same technical defect. This argument was essentially the same as the one that Republicans made in the Bloody Eighth episode, although now with the backing of the *Bush v. Gore* precedent.[65] Coleman also argued that if counting more technically deficient ballots was not the proper remedy, then both Minnesota law and equal protection required voiding the result of the election on the ground that thousands of equally deficient ballots were irretrievably polluting the count as it currently stood. This last argument was equivalent to the one that Rossi had made in Washington's 2004 gubernatorial election.

Under Minnesota law, Coleman's contest had the effect of suspending the certification of Franken's election. Unlike in 1962, the consequence was not to leave Coleman in the US Senate seat as a holdover. Instead, the seat would remain vacant until the contest was concluded, even though the seat happened to be an important one at a crucial moment for the nation's government and economy. In the aftermath of the 2008 elections, with this seat vacant, there were 59 Democrats in the Senate, one shy of the number necessary to break a filibuster. If Franken were seated even just provisionally, he would give the Democrats in Congress the power to enact the new Obama administration's agenda without the ability of Republicans to block it. (The Democrats already controlled the House.) President Obama was inaugurated in January 2009 during the darkest days of the Great Recession, and regardless of whether one agreed with his policies, the new president was claiming a mandate to address the severe crisis. With Minnesota's empty Senate seat pivotal in this way, Franken went to the Minnesota Supreme Court in an effort to obtain at least a temporary certificate while Coleman's contest was pending. The Minnesota Supreme Court unanimously denied this request.[66]

Meanwhile, Minnesota law obligated the chief justice to appoint a three-judge panel to adjudicate Coleman's contest. Because the chief justice was still recused on account of his participation on the State Canvassing Board, this duty devolved to the next most senior justice, Alan Page (who had been a star football player with the Minnesota Vikings). Justice Page had been one of the two dissenters in the court's 3–2 candidate veto order. Consequently, he was not predisposed to using the method employed in 1962 of forcing the two candidates to pick the three judges. That method had worked well back then, but the contentiousness surrounding the consideration of absentee ballots thus far suggested that it would be better simply to supply the two candidates with an evenly balanced and impartial three-judge panel.

In any event, Justice Page astutely decided not to pick the three judges by himself, although he had the authority to do so. Instead, he conferred intensely with the four other justices who were not recused, and after two weeks of internal deliberations on the composition of the panel, Justice Page announced the appointment of "an experienced, geographically and politically diverse three-judge panel."[67] The panel had one judge appointed by a Democratic governor (Elizabeth Hayden), one appointed by a Republican governor (Denise Reilly), and one appointed by Ventura, the Independent (Kurt Marben). It was a transparently "tripartisan" panel, as politically balanced as feasible.

Even more significant, the geographic diversity on the panel meant that the three judges did not know each other. Consequently, they were on best behavior with each other throughout their deliberations. "It was like being on a little boat with two strangers at the very beginning," one of them said afterward.[68] The three of them knew the value of unanimity, having seen the adverse reaction to the Minnesota Supreme Court's 3–2 split. Thus they worked hard to maintain their own unanimity. They were successful. Not one of their many decisions throughout the entire contest resulted in a publicly recorded dissent. This unanimity was key to their rulings being accepted as impartial and fair. As in 1962, it was the selection of the three-judge panel that was the most important factor in the state's successful resolution of the election.

Figure 12.3 The tripartisan panel of Denise Reilly, Kurt Marben, and Elizabeth Hayden was instrumental to the perception that Minnesota used a fair procedure to resolve its disputed 2008 US Senate election. This photo appeared in *MinnPost*, an online news journal that covered the dispute extensively. Photographer: Richard Sennott. Courtesy of *MinnPost*.

Coleman identified 5,467 previously uncounted absentee ballots that he wanted the three-judge court to count. In urging the court to accept these ballots, Coleman heavily relied on the substantial compliance doctrine. For example, Minnesota's law on absentee voting still contained the archaic requirement that an absentee voter have a witness sign the ballot envelope to vouch for the voter's identity and attest that the voter was not improperly influenced in casting the ballot. Minnesota's law required that this witness be either a notary public or a registered voter in the state. (At least Minnesota did not require two witnesses, as Alabama had in 1994.) As part of his submission, Coleman had identified 318 ballots that had been rejected for lacking a valid witness and another 131 with an incomplete address listed for the witness. These were among the many specific types of absentee ballots that Coleman conceded were technically deficient under the statute but which the doctrine of substantial compliance should protect.[69]

In a series of pretrial rulings, however, the three-judge court rejected the applicability of the substantial compliance doctrine to absentee voting, which the court characterized as a privilege rather than a right under Minnesota law. Instead, the three-judge panel ruled that it would accept a previously uncounted ballot only if Coleman submitted evidence that the ballot actually complied with all the specified requirements of Minnesota law regarding absentee voting. The media reported, and Coleman treated, the court's rulings as if they prevented Coleman from prevailing on any of the ballots he wanted counted. In fact, the three-judge court ultimately showed itself to be quite permissive in its evaluation of ballots. For example, in the end the court accepted as valid any witness who "has *ever* been registered to vote in Minnesota," even if not registered at the specific time of serving as the ballot's witness.[70] Similarly, if the witness supplied a Minnesota address and there was no evidence to the contrary, the court presumed the witness to be registered voter in the state without need for further proof of this fact. Likewise, as for incomplete witness addresses, if the address could be ascertained from the face of the ballot (as in the case of one spouse witnessing for another but failing to write their address twice), or if enough of the address was present (like a street name or P.O. box number) to permit verification of the address in the state's voter registration database, then the court considered the ballot to be in compliance with the statutory requirement. But Coleman failed to take advantage of the court's permissiveness. After perceiving the court's pretrial rulings as crippling, Coleman essentially gave up on trying to provide ballot-specific evidence that might comply with the court's interpretation of Minnesota law. When it turned out that the court was willing to be lenient in its consideration of such evidence, Coleman failed to provide the kind of evidence that would work to validate specific ballots.

Coleman also failed to articulate a distinction within the substantial compliance doctrine that might have proved advantageous. Since the nineteenth century American election law has distinguished between official errors and voter errors when considering whether to count a technically deficient ballot.[71] Generally wishing to protect voters from disenfranchisement caused by mistakes made by government workers rather than by the voters themselves, courts historically have been much more willing to apply a doctrine of leniency in the former circumstance even when they are unwilling to do so in the latter. On this view, voters can be held responsible for their own errors that have the regrettable effect of disqualifying their ballots, but they should not suffer for the sins of faulty functionaries. This distinction is so well-ingrained in American law that one can even label it as the doctrine of "constructive compliance," insofar as the voters themselves have done all that they can to comply with the relevant rules and only official maladministration has frustrated technically complete compliance.[72] Some 1,500 of the ballots that Coleman wanted the court to count were amenable to an argument rooted in the narrower principle of constructive compliance rather than the undifferentiated and more ambitious claim that even voter error is protected under the substantial compliance doctrine. But Coleman made no effort to tailor his contest in this way, even as a fallback position.

Instead, Coleman's primary alternative to his substantial compliance argument was his reliance on equal protection. He was able to show that some local boards had counted ballots despite flaws whereas other local boards had rejected ballots for having identical flaws. For example, some localities were willing to count a ballot whose witness was neither a notary nor registered voter, while other localities disqualified ballots for this reason. Coleman argued that this opposite treatment of equivalent ballots violated *Bush v. Gore*, and he claimed that the proper remedy was to count the previously uncounted ballots that were identical to those already counted.

The three-judge panel unanimously rejected Coleman's *Bush v. Gore* argument. The court repeatedly emphasized that Minnesota's requirements concerning absentee voting were clear and specific, in contrast to Florida's law concerning the identification of a voter's intent in the context of hanging or dimpled chads. But was this distinction—even if true—a sufficient reason to reject Coleman's equal protection claim? The court seemed to think so based on the idea that just because one locality had let slip through ballots that were ineligible to be counted, it did not follow that equal protection required the counting of equally ineligible ballots that other localities successfully had managed to disqualify. The court had in mind the hypothetical, raised during the trial, of some ballots cast by felons or noncitizens slipping through the cracks; surely, their inclusion in the count did not require on equal protection grounds the counting of other ballots cast by felons or noncitizens that had been properly caught and rejected. Yet this hypothetical, as cogent as it was on its own facts, was not a strong analogy for all the circumstances to which Coleman was claiming that equal protection applied.[73]

For example, one large category of ballots that Coleman was pursuing involved voters who had received the wrong form of ballot because local officials had made a mistake. There was nothing about the voters themselves that was intrinsically disqualifying. They were neither felons nor noncitizens nor belonging to any other category of inherently ineligible voters. Instead, if they had received the correct form of ballot from the government in response to their entirely appropriate application, and cast their ballots for the same candidates, their ballots would have been completely eligible to be counted. It was a simple administrative mistake that had caused these voters to receive the wrong form, and Coleman had identified 637 of these ballots as having been rejected because of this particular technical noncompliance. Minnesota law may have been crystal clear in requiring these ballots to be cast on the correct form, but even if so, did that clarity end the equal protection inquiry? Insofar as similarly defective ballots had been counted elsewhere in the state despite technical noncompliance in this same respect, did equal protection permit rejection of these 637 ballots whose defect was due entirely to the government's own error and not at all the fault of these otherwise perfectly eligible voters? Arguably, these 637 wrongfully disenfranchised voters had a much more sympathetic equal protection claim than the Florida voters whose dimpled or hanging chads had been treated differently than similarly dimpled or hanging chads elsewhere in the state. After all, the Florida voters could have protected themselves from discriminatory disenfranchisement by making sure to dislodge their chads completely. These 637 Minnesota voters, by contrast, could have done nothing to protect themselves from wrongful and discriminatory disenfranchisement as a consequence of negligent government workers.

If Coleman had developed the constructive compliance distinction between official and voter error, he could have pursued it not solely in the context of what Minnesota law required in the circumstances, but also as part of his equal protection claim. Doing so would have made his equal protection argument much more forceful and compelling, at least with respect to a significant portion of the ballots he was striving to get counted. But he never developed his equal protection argument in this way. Instead, he merely presented it in generic form, asserting that any noncompliant ballot should be counted as long as one identically noncompliant ballot had been counted anywhere else in the state. Presented this way, it was easily dismissed by the three-judge court.

The trial court therefore accepted neither substantial compliance nor equal protection as a reason to count any ballots that, in its view, did not actually comply with Minnesota's absentee voting rules. The trial court also rejected Coleman's argument for voiding the election on the ground that the certified count contained thousands of absentee ballots that were not entitled to be counted according to these same Minnesota rules. The court's rejection of this argument was procedural and essentially the same as the Washington court's rejection of the equivalent argument in the contest of that state's 2004 gubernatorial election. The time to challenge an absentee ballot as ineligible was on or before Election Night, not after that absentee ballot already had been counted and commingled with all the other counted ballots in the election. In Minnesota there was even a 1976 state supreme court precedent to support that proposition, *Bell v. Gannaway*, and the three-judge panel readily employed it to deny Coleman's request for an order invalidating the certification of Franken's victory.[74]

Once the court rendered its legal judgments, all that was left was to implement its determination of whether any additional ballots met its understanding of the statutory standards. The court identified 351 that did, many of which had been proffered during the trial by Franken rather than Coleman. When these were counted, they increased Franken's lead to 312.[75]

The three-judge court's final orders were released on April 13, over five months after Election Day, and over three months after a US senator should have taken office. Coleman could have declined to take an appeal, just as Governor Andersen had declined an appeal in the contest over the 1962 gubernatorial election. Dino Rossi had also declined an appeal in the contest over Washington's 2004 gubernatorial election. But Coleman decided to fight on and reiterate his legal claims in the Minnesota Supreme Court.

Coleman, however, was no more successful there than he had been in the trial court. On June 30, the Minnesota Supreme Court affirmed the three-judge panel on all grounds, and this time the state supreme court's ruling was unanimous, thereby emulating the three-judge panel in this salutary respect. The supreme court's reasoning, however, was noticeably different from the three-judge panel's in one important feature. Although Coleman never argued the point, the supreme court itself drew the distinction between voter error and official error as the reason for a ballot's technical noncompliance with statutory rules. In the context of absentee voting, the supreme court agreed with Franken that the substantial compliance doctrine could not excuse a voter's own errors. But the supreme court indicated that it would not tolerate disqualification of an absentee ballot if noncompliance was attributable solely to the government's own mistake. "The distinction between errors by voters and errors by election officials is an important one," the high court declared. Ballots, the court added, "should not be rejected because of irregularities, ignorance, inadvertence, or mistake, or even intentional wrong on the part of election officers."[76] But the court did not need to apply this principle in this case, since Coleman never offered any argument or evidence specifically designed to protect voters from official error.

In rejecting Coleman's equal protection claim, the supreme court largely relied on the three-judge panel's reason for distinguishing *Bush v. Gore*—the clarity of Minnesota's law compared to Florida's—and included an additional twist. The supreme court observed that in *Bush v. Gore* the officials examining the dimpled and hanging chads knew from "the face of the ballot" how their determinations would affect the relative position of the two candidates, Bush and Gore, and thus the situation created "opportunities for manipulation of the decision for political purposes." By contrast, in Minnesota "the decision at issue was whether to accept or reject absentee ballot return envelopes before they were opened, meaning that the actual votes on the ballot contained in the return envelope were not known to the election officials applying the standards."[77]

This observation was insightful. Surely one of the concerns animating *Bush v. Gore* was the fear that local recount officials might have manipulated the standards for counting dimpled and hanging chads in order to help elect their preferred candidate. Still, it seems difficult to believe that the equal protection principle of *Bush v. Gore* is completely inapplicable to absentee ballots that remain hidden in sealed envelopes. If local officials are entirely arbitrary in their consideration of identical absentee ballots, accepting some and rejecting others even though identical in all relevant respects, surely the US Supreme Court would apply the *Bush v. Gore* precedent to invalidate that arbitrariness notwithstanding the fact that absentee ballots, rather than chads, are involved. Especially if that arbitrary discrimination of absentee voters resulted in the disenfranchisement of voters solely because of the government's own mishandling of the ballots, then the federal constitutional claim would be particularly strong. But the Minnesota Supreme Court did not dwell on this point, perhaps because it had already indicated that as a matter of state law it would protect voters from disenfranchisement caused by official error. Thus the equal protection claim as the Minnesota Supreme Court envisioned it would concern only absentee ballots invalidated because of the voter's own mistake, a much less sympathetic situation. In any event, because Coleman had not refined his equal protection argument on appeal but continued to present the claim in entirely generic terms, the Minnesota Supreme Court saw no need to elaborate its own equal protection analysis much beyond what the three-judge court already had provided.

The Minnesota Supreme Court likewise relied on the *Bell v. Gannaway* precedent, much as the three-judge court had, as the basis for refusing to void the election. The supreme court candidly acknowledged that it might seem anomalous to apply *Bell v. Gannaway* in a situation where a candidate had no opportunity to challenge an absentee ballot's eligibility before it was counted. But the supreme court observed that the state's legislature had intended to preclude any challenges to absentee ballots once commingled into the total count, and thus any policy objection to that rule needed a statutory amendment. The supreme court clearly had no interest in voiding the election just because thousands of absentee ballots had been improperly counted in violation of Minnesota law.[78]

On appeal, Coleman added a due process argument to his other claims. He argued that the three-judge trial court had retroactively changed Minnesota law, in violation of due process, by rejecting the substantial compliance doctrine when many administrative officials had embraced that doctrine on Election Day. Coleman was trying to rely on the due process precedent that had emerged in the 1994 Alabama chief justice election. The problem, however, was that he was on the wrong side of the facts for purposes of this theory. Alabama had violated due process because it had moved from a prevailing rule of strict compliance applicable to the counting of absentee ballots on Election Day to the more relaxed doctrine of substantial compliance for the first time in the context of a review of ballots after they had already been cast and rejected. Coleman, conversely, was trying to say that a move from substantial to strict compliance was equally objectionable under due process. Whether or not that could ever be true—after all, enforcing strict compliance is just enforcing the law as written and thus never a deviation from the law in the way that a retroactive move to substantial compliance is—the Minnesota Supreme Court held that the factual predicate for Coleman's claim was lacking. According to the court, the prevailing law in Minnesota on Election Day in 2008 regarding the counting of absentee ballots was strict, not substantial, compliance. Insofar as some local officials applied substantial, not strict, compliance on Election Law, they were violating the prevailing state law, not following it. In the eyes of the Minnesota Supreme Court, the three-judge panel's reiteration of strict compliance was not a change in state law but a reinforcement of it. There being no change in state law, there was no due process problem.[79]

With that, Coleman's contest was over. He did not pursue his fight any further, neither attempting to take his federal constitutional arguments to federal court, nor attempting to contest the election in the US Senate. (The latter audience obviously would have been inhospitable, since the chamber was dominated by 59 Democrats.) Instead, this time Coleman conceded, and he did so on the same day that the Minnesota Supreme Court ruled, June 30. Moreover, when his concession came, it was appropriately gracious—unlike Rossi's four years earlier in Washington. While acknowledging that he had "wanted to win," he called upon his supporters, along with all citizens of the state, to accept the outcome as the legitimate product of a democratic process.[80] A week later, on July 7, eight months after Election Day, Franken took the seat as Minnesota's junior US Senator.

Once the election was finally resolved, there was considerable praise for the means that Minnesota had employed to resolve it. The state's two leading newspapers, despite both having endorsed Coleman's reelection, embraced the outcome as "fair," "legitimate," and thus worthy of respect. The *Minneapolis Star Tribune* editorialized that the judicial unanimity, which included Republican jurists, proved that the result "was determined according to impartial law, not partisan favor." The *St. Paul Pioneer Press* echoed that sentiment with accolades for the "impartial, competent, and independent judiciary" that produced the result. Although some disgruntled Republicans could not stomach the result, the legitimacy of an impartial process cannot be undercut by the obstinacy of a few unreasonable zealots. There was widespread public acceptance of the view that Minnesota, unlike Florida in 2000, had managed to handle a close election in a way worthy of a democracy endeavoring, in fairness to the voters and both candidates, to follow the rules as laid down in advance of the election.[81]

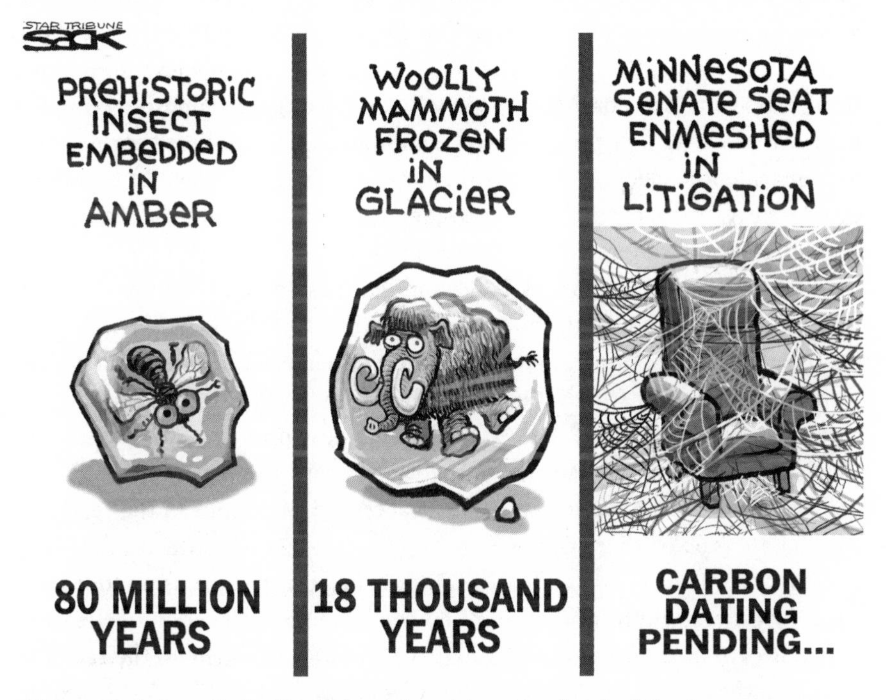

Figure 12.4 Steve Sack effectively rendered the point that the litigation over Minnesota's 2008 US Senate election took far too long to resolve—and ended up leaving the seat vacant for six months. By permission of Steve Sack and Creators Syndicate, Inc.

Minnesota's successful resolution of its 2008 US Senate election was all the more impressive precisely because it came after *Bush v. Gore* rather than before. That equal protection precedent, as intentionally indeterminate as it was (which is not the same as saying it was deliberately unprincipled), had opened a Pandora's box of potential future equal protection claims regarding virtually every aspect of the voting process. Ambiguity invites litigation, and the meaning of the equal protection principle articulated in *Bush v. Gore* was as ambiguous as any constitutional principle the Court had ever articulated.[82] *Coleman v. Franken* itself involved an equal protection claim based on *Bush v. Gore,* but it was only one of dozens of cases in the decade after 2000 that relied on that precedent to challenge some aspect of a state's rules for casting or counting ballots. As already observed, since 2004 Ohio had become the battleground for many of these novel equal protection arguments, but it was not alone.[83] In the post-2000 environment Minnesota faced a greater challenge than it had in 1962, at least given a goal of resolving litigation in a way that both sides would perceive as fair. Washington had shown itself unable to meet that greater challenge, but Minnesota managed to handle it.

Still, Minnesota's success came at a considerable price. It took until eight months after Election Day to seat Franken as the winner. That amount of delay should be unacceptable for any election. The voters are entitled to have their chosen candidate take office at the beginning of the officeholder's term; anything else is a frustration of democracy that elections are supposed to implement. In any event, nothing like an eight-month delay is remotely feasible for a presidential election. Thus, if the nation wishes to achieve Minnesota's standard of fairness for a disputed presidential election, it will be necessary to develop a way to compress that fairness into a far shorter timeframe.

While both Washington in 2004 and Minnesota in 2008 reflected the increased litigiousness of the voting process after 2000, it would be wrong to think that all major statewide races that were similarly close ended up ensnared in protracted lawsuits. In 2006, Vermont had a recount of its election for state auditor. That recount showed the Democrat winning by 102 votes, even though the initial count had shown the Republican winning by 137. Still, on December 21, the Republican graciously accepted the results of the recount, and there was no further dispute.[84]

Similarly, in both 2005 and 2013, Virginia had recounts in its elections for attorney general. Both times, the initial count upon certification of the canvass was extremely close: 323 in 2005; 165 in 2013. Both times, the recount increased the margin of victory: to 360 votes in 2005; to 907 in 2013.[85] Both times, the recounts were relatively free of controversy, and neither time was there any litigation after completion of the recount. Consequently, both times the election was over in December (as in Vermont). Despite being a major

Figure 12.5 Brian Schoeneman, secretary of Fairfax County's Electoral Board, and David Wasserman, a political analyst at *The Cook Political Report*, were two of the most prolific and effective users of Twitter during the canvassing of returns in Virginia's 2013 attorney general election. Courtesy of Brian Schoeneman and David Wasserman.

battleground state, Virginia was able to avoid the kind of extended contest that afflicted Washington and Minnesota. Indeed, Virginia's 2013 election was widely heralded among election professionals as the first in which Twitter was used to dramatically increase the public transparency of the canvassing of the returns from the state's polling places, thereby significantly increasing the public's confidence in the accuracy of the outcome.[86]

In fact, shortly thereafter, Virginia repeated its great success in a special election held to fill a seat in the state's senate. The outcome would determine whether the Democrats would take control of the legislative chamber. After the canvass, the Democrat was ahead by only nine votes. A recount added two more, for a total margin of victory of just eleven.[87] Yet the Republican candidate's concession was immediate, and no litigation based on *Bush v. Gore* or otherwise ensued. When compared with the great difficulty Ohio experienced with its consequential legislative election in 2012, just a year earlier (the episode with which this book began), Virginia's handling of this legislative seat is especially impressive.

The goal for the future is to have more experiences like Virginia's, and fewer like Ohio's—or Washington State's in 2004. If a state must have extended litigation over the counting of ballots, then let it be fair like Minnesota's. But it would be better to avoid such lawsuits in the first place, if possible. Virginia proves that even after 2000, not all high-stakes recounts need to metastasize into six-month-long lawsuits. The challenge will be to develop methods for replicating Virginia's success even in states, like Ohio, that have shown themselves to be more prone to extensive ballot-counting disputation.

Conclusion

The Enduring Quest for a Fair Count

When Charles Evans Hughes insisted on a recount for New York City's disputed mayoral election of 1905, he proclaimed: "Our entire system of government depends on honest elections and a fair count."[1] It was a proclamation with which James Madison would agree. The Constitution and "right reason," Madison told his fellow members of Congress when debating the first congressional election tainted by ballot-box stuffing, required purging "corruption" from the counting of ballots and awarding the election to whichever candidate "had the greatest number of sound votes."[2]

The practice of popular sovereignty in Hughes's time differed significantly from Madison's and would change even further during the Progressive Era of which Hughes was such a major figure. Madison would have been surprised to see the direct election of US Senators and the enfranchisement of women, to mention just two of the Progressive Era's biggest changes. But he would have been entirely familiar with Hughes's demand for a fair count of valid votes, because it was exactly the same demand that he himself had made over a century earlier.

Through all the transformations in American democracy since Madison helped draft the Constitution—from the expansion of the franchise to virtually universal adult suffrage (with the notable exception of felon disenfranchisement), to the adoption of the so-called Australian ballot as a way to protect ballot secrecy, to the huge increases in the power of the federal government and especially the presidency—the idea of a fair count has been a constant component of how to conduct elections. When Governor Edward Everett of Massachusetts in 1838 refused to let his fellow partisans in the legislature install him into office for another term, it was because an honest tally of the votes "unquestionably" revealed "a majority" for his opponent, "although its admission costs my election."[3] When two decades later Governor William Barstow of Wisconsin refused to act as Everett did and instead attempted to cling to office despite the fact that an honest count of the ballots showed a victory for his opponent, the Wisconsin Supreme Court ordered Barstow's removal from office in order to vindicate the principle that (as George McCrary's leading election law treatise put it): "It matters not how high and important an office may be, an election to it must be by the majority or plurality of the legal votes cast."[4] And when Francis Barlow went to Florida as President Grant's "personal representative" to observe that state's counting of ballots in the presidential election of 1876, Barlow undertook his mission pursuant to Grant's directive "to see that the board of canvassers made a fair count of the votes actually cast."[5]

In the twentieth century no less than the nineteenth, the idea of a fair count was the standard to which elections were expected to adhere. In his fight over Ballot Box 13, all Coke Stevenson said he wanted was "an honest count" of the votes. The federal judge, until blocked by Justice Black for lack of jurisdiction, responded that his court was prepared to vindicate that principle: "If enough ballots were stuffed to have changed the result," that "wrong" would require "a remedy."[6] A half-century later, the federal judge in the case concerning Alabama's 1994 chief justice election invoked the same principle, ruling that he would not permit a manipulation of vote-counting rules that amounted to stuffing the ballot box.[7] And in the fight over the 2000 presidential elections, both sides professed that they were seeking a fair count of the ballots cast.[8]

The Obstacles to Achieving a Fair Count

As enduring as the idea of a fair count has been throughout American history, fully vindicating the idea in practice has had its challenges and limitations. Not least of the difficulties has been the many politicians throughout the decades who, while recognizing the ethical imperative of honesty in the counting of ballots, were willing to disobey this ethical imperative when doing so would advance their personal or partisan interests. No more poignant example exists than Edward Prichard, Felix Frankfurter's "most brilliant" protégé, who many believed might have been president one day if he had not been caught stuffing a ballot box in Kentucky's 1948 US Senate election. "I did it. It was wrong," Prichard later confessed, recognizing his abandonment of electoral morality when caught up in the competitive desire to help his party win the Senate seat.[9]

The shortcomings in the effort to achieve a fair count have not been caused solely by the mendacity of politicians. Rather, as the historian Paul Haworth observed in the context of the Hayes-Tilden dispute, a fair *count* does not guarantee a fair *election*. Or, as we developed the point more precisely in the context of the Bush-Gore dispute, fairness in the *counting* of ballots cannot always redress unfairness perpetrated that occurred in the *casting* of them.

Ballots never cast cannot be counted. If voters are improperly turned away from the polls without the opportunity to cast a ballot, as they were in both 1876 and (to a lesser, but still pernicious, extent) 2000, a fair count of ballots actually cast will never rectify the wrongful disenfranchisement. Likewise, if voters are coerced or duped into casting a ballot for a candidate who is not their choice, counting their ballots as cast will satisfy the standard of an accurate and honest count, but the result will not reflect the authentic will of the voters who cast those ballots. If there are enough of these inauthentic ballots, they could undermine the outcome of the election insofar as it purports to be an aggregation of the electorate's authentic choices. Some of the nation's earliest ballot-counting disputes involved problems of this kind, specifically in the form of claims (backed by considerable evidence) that military force improperly pressured voters at the polls. In 2000, a different form of this problem occurred when Florida's butterfly ballot inadvertently duped thousands of voters who wanted Gore into casting their ballots for Pat Buchanan instead.

When a fair count cannot rectify a problem of wrongful disenfranchisement—when the number of disenfranchised voters is larger than the lead shown by a fair count—then the only possible remedy is to void the election and either hold a revote or fill the office through some sort of substitute appointment process. But as George McCrary observed in his influential nineteenth-century treatise on election law, America always has had great difficulty in deciding when to void an election because of problems that occurred during the casting of ballots.[10] This was certainly true in 1876 and 2000, where there was overwhelming political pressure to count a disputed state's Electoral College votes in favor of one candidate or the other, rather than declaring those electoral votes uncountable because of wrongful disenfranchisement or other overriding ballot-casting problems.

Yet it is not only in presidential elections where this intense pressure is felt, as Washington's 2004 gubernatorial election demonstrates. There, the number of invalid ballots tainting the count (1,678) was over ten times the lead by which one candidate was ahead of the other (129), but still the court was unwilling to declare the result void. No doubt the fear that a revote might simply replicate a similar problem induces the desire to decide the initial election one way or the other, even if admittedly imperfect, rather than risking another problem in a revote.[11]

Yet it is not just reluctance to hold a revote that has exposed difficulties with the idea of a fair count. In some circumstances, it is simply unclear whether a fair count entails the inclusion or exclusion of disputed ballots. That was true in Minnesota's 2008 US Senate election: should nonconforming absentee ballots in some localities be counted because equivalently nonconforming absentee ballots in other localities already have been irretrievably counted? It was also true in the 2000 presidential election: should ballot markings unreadable by vote-tabulating machines operating as designed be examined for the possibility that they might contain an identifiable vote even if state law has not provided a specific standard by which to determine whether a marking in fact constitutes an identifiable vote? While cogent arguments could be made by both sides in both cases, candor requires acknowledging that the simple idea of a fair count—the enduring idea shared from Madison to Hughes to the present—does not logically dictate an answer one way or the other to these subsidiary issues in these specific circumstances.

The Persistent Value of Striving for a Fair Count

Despite all of its inherent limitations, the idea of a fair count remains a standard to uphold. Although in some situations it may be unclear what the standard requires, in other circumstances it will be perfectly obvious what misconduct flagrantly breaches the standard. Prichard knew it was wrong to pad the count with fake ballots in Kentucky's 1948 US Senate race, but he did it anyway. The same was true that year for Luis Salas and Ballot Box 13.[12] Whenever blatant misconduct like that occurs, and is caught, it should be remedied.

Simply put, elections should not be stolen. That is the fundamental point that Hughes was endeavoring to vindicate in New York City's mayoral election of 1905. It is not a fancy or sophisticated idea. But it is an essential one. As George McCrary wrote in his treatise, America must aspire to remain true to this proposition: "An adequate remedy will always be found either at law or in equity for frauds perpetrated against the purity of elections."[13]

As imperative as it is that elections not be actually stolen, it is also important that they not be perceived to be stolen. Ballot counting is something for which appearances truly matter. A review of the history chronicled in this book shows that the most persistently troublesome ballot-counting disputes experienced in America have been those where the losing side believes itself to have been the victim of electoral theft. This was true in 1792, when John Jay and his supporters thought they had been robbed of the governorship. It was true of 1876, when Democrats thought Hayes procured the presidency through fraud and thus persisted in calling him "His Fraudulency" or "Rutherfraud" Hayes. It was true of that ugliest of disputed elections, Kentucky's in 1899, where Republicans thought they had been defrauded on the governorship and retaliated by assassinating the Democratic candidate.

More recently, it was true of the Bloody Eighth (the 1984 election for Indiana's Eighth Congressional District), where Republicans thought they had been robbed by Democrats in Congress, sowing seeds of enmity that have produced poisonous congressional relations persisting to the present. And it was true in 2000, when many Democrats thought that the US Supreme Court stole the election for Bush. "We Wuz Robbed" is the title that Spike Lee gave to the short film he made about the 2000 election, succinctly capturing how he and many others felt. Whether or not this perception of electoral theft correctly matched the reality of the situation, "We Wuz Robbed" is a sentiment best avoided about the counting of ballots in a presidential election.

Conversely, some of the greatest success stories in America's experience with ballot-counting controversies are those instances in which a court, embodying the rule of law, stepped forward to thwart the theft of an election. The Wisconsin Supreme Court's intervention in 1856 in *Bashford v. Barstow* is certainly a leading example. Equally meritorious was the Missouri Supreme Court's similar decision in 1940. Even the about-face of the Massachusetts legislature in 1806 qualifies as a major success precisely because the legislature, on sober second thought, refused to follow through with the electoral theft that had been put into motion.

The Need for a Neutral Arbiter

Comparing these historical examples, some successful and others not, underscores the importance of an institution that can be perceived as trustworthy by both sides. Many of the instances in which one side believes itself to be the victim of a stolen election are situations that involve not outright ballot-box stuffing, but instead the perception that the other side has been able to distort the counting rules in its favor: "As American political parties discovered long ago, changing the rules is one way to win."[14] Changing the rules, however, provokes particular outrage when it happens after the ballots have been cast and the change appears designed to harvest enough extra votes to flip the outcome of the election. This kind of outrage at the apparent manipulation of counting rules was particularly powerful in the Bloody Eighth episode and was responsible for its special vehemence.

All of these instances of perceived electoral theft would have benefited from the existence of an institution that the losing side could not have considered as rigged against it, dominated by partisans loyal to the opposing side. The problem of the Bloody Eighth was that the decisive vote-counting was conducted by a body split 2–1 along partisan lines, fueling the suspicion that the decision

Figure C.1 A fundamental truth about vote-counting disputes, as reflected in this Steve Sack cartoon, is that the position each party takes in a recount is controlled by its overriding desire to win—thereby necessitating a neutral arbiter, so that neither side can dictate the outcome through a strategic manipulation of the vote-counting rules. By permission of Steve Sack and Creators Syndicate, Inc.

to count some ballots but not others was purely pretextual and unprincipled, driven solely to achieve the desired partisan result. It was exactly the same problem that afflicted the 2–1 determinations of the Florida Canvassing Board in 1876 (made worse when the suspicion of deliberately partisan manipulation of the vote-counting rules was confirmed by the confession of one of the two Republicans on the board).

It was the same sort of problem that caused the perception in 2000, on the part of many Democrats, that "We Wuz Robbed." It did not matter that there might be reasonable arguments to support the 5–4 rulings of the US Supreme Court in *Bush v. Gore*. (If what the Florida Supreme Court was doing was tantamount to stuffing the ballot box with invalid votes, as Bush supporters believed—making the Florida Supreme Court in 2000 equivalent of the Alabama Supreme Court in 1994—then it becomes at least understandable, if not necessarily correct, that the five-member majority of the US Supreme Court would want to enjoin the Florida Supreme Court from distorting the count with the addition of the invalid ballots.) Instead, it mattered only that the five conservative Republican appointees on the Court, over the strenuous objection of the four liberal members (including the only two Democratic appointees) had halted, and then precluded, the recounting of ballots that might have shown Gore to have won more votes. From the perspective of Democrats, it was the situation of the other side robbing them of the election (or at least robbing them of the chance to prove who had won the election).

The same problem had surfaced in Philadelphia, even before the Constitution was written there, when in 1781 one side walked out in protest, after feeling robbed by the other side, just as Republicans two centuries later would walk out in protest over the Bloody Eighth. Similarly, in 1792, it was the identical us-versus-them dynamic between Jay's Federalists and Clinton's Jeffersonian Democratic-Republicans. The Jay side definitely thought that the Clinton side, *the other side*, had *stolen* the election by using its dominance of the canvassing committee to perpetrate a 7–4 partisan disqualification of ballots that should have been counted.

As James Kent recognized at the time, the only way to avoid this perception (other than clearer counting rules in advance that would have given the canvassers no interpretative discretion whatsoever) would be an authoritative vote-counting tribunal with an equal number of both *us* and *them* on it. The immediate objection to Kent's proposal, of course, is that a vote-counting tribunal cannot have the same number of members from each of the two sides, because then the body most likely would just deadlock in tie votes. But Minnesota solved this problem for its 1962 gubernatorial election and its 2008 US Senate election. Minnesota found ways to add a potential tiebreaking member who was from neither one side nor the other. For 1962, Minnesota did it by forcing the two sides to pick the members of the tribunal, and after they picked one from each side, they settled on a third whom both sides perceived as genuinely neutral. For 2008, Minnesota did it by picking a tripartisan panel with the third member coming from the state's Independence Party to provide neutral balance to the two other members, one from each side.

Congress tried something like this for the Hayes-Tilden dispute. They wanted two Republican and two Democratic appointees on the US Supreme Court to jointly choose a fifth justice who, like the third Minnesota judge for both 1962 and 2008, was genuinely seen as coming from neither side. The problem, however, was that intended fifth justice declined to serve, and they were left with the fifth justice having to be a third Republican. Thus the intention of a having a neutral tiebreaker immediately devolved into a situation of us-versus-them. When the Electoral Commission repeatedly ruled 8–7 on all four disputed states submitted to it, with all eight Republicans outvoting all seven of the Democrats, the unavoidable perception among Democrats was that the *other side* prevailed solely by outnumbering *us* on the decisive vote-counting tribunal. Regardless of the original intent behind the creation of the Electoral Commission, it turned out to be the same problem that Jay and his Federalists faced in 1792 all over again. The result had been rigged by the other side's overrepresentation on the relevant body.

At least Congress tried to create a neutral tiebreaking mechanism for the Hayes-Tilden dispute. So many of the nation's most serious ballot-counting battles have suffered precisely because there was no such attempt to put in place a neutral institution of any kind—no effort to constrain a partisan power-grab by whichever side happened to control the existing vote-counting authority at the time. There was no pretense of neutrality for the Bloody Eighth. Nor had there been in the whole series of destabilizing Gilded Age vote-counting disputes, of which Kentucky's in 1899 was the most severe. Rhode Island's 1956 gubernatorial election was reminiscent of that disappointing earlier era precisely because its supreme court decision was such a transparently partisan interpretation of the relevant constitutional provisions concerning absentee ballots. Likewise, New Hampshire's 1974 US Senate election ended up in such a mess because, first, the state's ballot-counting board made its decisive 2–1 partisan rulings and then, second, the Senate itself became mired in its own purely partisan divide. Even worse was the Senate's handling of the Oklahoma election that same year, when the state had actually used a Minnesota-style method of having the two sides choose a neutral judge, only to have the Senate—along purely partisan lines—consider at length the feasibility of overturning that neutral decision. In both the New Hampshire and Oklahoma cases, the Senate as a whole ignored Claiborne Pell's wise and repeated call for some sort of Minnesota-style "impartial, independent arbiter or panel of arbiters" to help the Senate avoid "party-line voting" in these cases.

The Importance of Individuals

In the absence of a neutral institution, the resolution of a vote-counting dispute often depends on the personality of key individuals involved and the particular choices they make at key moments in the disputes. Generally, it is wise to be wary of the so-called "great men" view of history, which overemphasizes the role that the character and choices of specific individuals play in what happens to a society as it moves through time.[15] Instead, the contrary view of history stresses the larger social forces that constrain and shape the conduct of specific individuals. But whatever the appropriate balance between these two contending perspectives in other contexts of historical inquiry, how ballot-counting disputes are handled is one area in which the character and choices of particular individuals have played decisive roles.

It is partly a matter of the choices that the losing candidates make about whether or how far to push a fight. There is the example that Jay set, on Hamilton's advice, when he decided to accept defeat this time and run again in the next election. It is an example that Nixon followed in 1960, with similar success when he ran again in 1968. Although it occurred much further down the road of his particular disputed election, there is also Al Gore's decision to accept the 5–4 decision in *Bush v. Gore* rather than attempting to take the fight all the way to Congress. And there shall always be the especially impressive example of Edward Everett's refusal to disqualify ballots to gain another term as governor of Massachusetts, even though his party controlled the state's legislature and had the power to give it to him. (Just consider the different attitudes to the use of the power over the vote-counting process exhibited by Edward Everett, on the one hand, and by Lyndon Johnson's supporters in the Ballot Box 13 episode, on the other.)

Also important have been the choices that other individuals have made in an effort to defuse, or in some instances intensify, a vote-counting controversy. During Pennsylvania's Buckshot War of 1838, it was General Robert Patterson, the commander of the state militia, who prevented the outbreak of major violence by refusing the incumbent governor's call for military force to support the governor's pretextual claim to have won reelection. Joshua Chamberlain, the Civil War hero, played a similar role as commander of Maine's militia, when in 1879 he refused to support the incumbent governor's manipulation of election returns in an attempt to stay in power. Indeed, Chamberlain's role in 1879 can be seen as a kind of ad hoc effort to have him act as a neutral arbiter for the dispute, given his transcendent political reputation in the state at the time. Although not officially asked to serve as a neutral arbiter when appointed to command the state's militia, Chamberlain (with public support) took it upon himself to perform as a neutral broker, thereby averting a clash of arms over the election.

Other individuals have played equally significant roles in the midst of major vote-counting disputes. John Quincy Adams, without any legal authority, stepped forward to lead the US House of Representatives when it was deadlocked in electing a Speaker in 1839 as a result of the Broad Seal War over New Jersey's entire congressional delegation. His unique stature as an ex-president permitted him to fill the institutional and legal vacuum that existed in the situation, as there needed to be some way to move forward for the sake of the nation, and he was suited to be the statesman that the occasion required. Even more significantly, Samuel Randall served as the statesman of the hour when he resisted the last-minute efforts of fellow partisans in the House to derail the counting of electoral votes in the Hayes-Tilden dispute. (The necessity of Randall's statesmanship, we recall from Chapter 5, became apparent only after a surprise maneuver over Vermont's electoral votes exposed a flaw in the special congressional statute enacted to adjudicate the Hayes-Tilden dispute.) Once again, a legal and institutional void created a deadlock in Congress—an even more precarious deadlock given the fast-approaching date for the inauguration of the new president—and Randall filled that void by acting in accordance with the overriding interest of the nation as a whole, rather than succumbing to the intense partisan pressure he faced from fellow Democrats.

A central lesson of such episodes is that it would be better to have sound rules and institutions, rather than having to rely on individual statesmanship to fill a legal and institutional void. But in the absence of such rules and institutions, better to have individual politicians act like statesmen in the overall public interest, rather than risk further confrontation and potential major unrest by attempting to pursue narrow partisan advantage. Of course, no set of rules and institutions can stop avaricious politicians determined to steal an election, as New York's Stolen Senate debacle of 1891 illustrates. But history shows that partisan mendacity to that extreme degree has been rare, and instead improvements in both the rules and institutions for handling vote-counting disputes can reduce the degree to which the public is at risk from major confrontations provoked by rapacious politicians.

The Overall Trend: More Peaceful and Fairer Outcomes

Although the United States hardly has achieved perfection regarding the resolution of disputed elections, the full sweep of American history shows considerable progress in handling these disputes. A comparison of the nineteenth and twentieth centuries reveals an absence of the kinds of violence and civil unrest in twentieth-century disputes that plagued many of the ones that occurred in the nineteenth century. It is not just that the nineteenth century suffered systemic breakdowns in democracy caused by the particular pathologies of the Civil War era, including Bleeding Kansas beforehand and Reconstruction afterwards. The Buckshot War of 1838 in Pennsylvania and Maine's bellicose contretemps of 1879 are episodes of civil disorder not attributable to those pathologies. Instead, they reflect a culture more prone to political violence, a condition that essentially disappears in twentieth-century vote-counting disputes.

What explains this dramatic reduction in the risk of violence in the context of vote-counting disputes? One factor may be a general reduction of violence in society, as discussed by Steven Pinker in *The Better Angels of Our Nature.*[16] Another factor directly relating to the voting process is the enfranchisement of women by the Nineteenth Amendment in 1920. With elections no longer male-only, they could no longer be associated principally with martial values and practices. The competition of electoral politics needed to be more like sport and less like battle. More broadly, the general transformation of democracy that occurred in the Progressive Era had a positive influence on expectations concerning the resolution of disputed elections. In this respect, Hughes's insistence on a recount for New York City's mayoral election of 1905 symbolizes the heightened demand for electoral fairness ushered in by the Progressive Era.[17]

It was not merely the elimination of violence in which the twentieth century was more successful than the nineteenth in terms of vote-counting disputes. In general, twentieth-century America saw fewer incidents in which the democratic will of the electorate was thwarted by incumbent officeholders abusing their power. Relatedly, there were on average fewer attempts—whether successful or unsuccessful—by incumbent officeholders to subvert the democratic will in this way.

The increased use of a state's judiciary, rather than its legislature, as the institution for resolving a major ballot-counting dispute contributed to this comparative success of the twentieth century. To be sure, the use of a court is no guarantee of avoiding partisan manipulation of vote-counting rules, as many examples in this book demonstrate, including the egregious decision of Rhode Island's supreme court in 1956. Even so, on average, courts are better at handling these cases than legislatures, and this truth became particularly evident once the federal judiciary began to police a state's vote-counting procedures for violations of due process, as in *Griffin v. Burns* (another Rhode Island case involving the egregious distortion of absentee-voting rules) and *Roe v. Alabama* (still another distortion of absentee-voting rules, but this time in a different part of the country). A head-to-head comparison of the performance of the Alabama Supreme Court and the federal judiciary in the 1994 election for Alabama's chief justice shows the relative superiority of the federal judiciary's ability to deliver unbiased rulings in this sort of case.[18] Nevertheless, the institutional innovations that the state courts in Minnesota and Oklahoma developed to deliver evenhandedly impartial rulings in the major vote-counting disputes they faced were achieved without any supervision from the federal courts. Likewise, entirely on its own initiative, the Missouri Supreme Court in 1940 set aside partisanship to protect the electorate's choice for governor from being subverted by a trumped-up vote-counting ruse in the legislature.

The twentieth century was also more successful than the nineteenth in avoiding major vote-counting disputes in the first place. Through the use of the Australian ballot and lever-style voting machines, states employed procedural and technological innovations that made their election results less prone to disputation. By the middle of the century, the rapidly increased use of administrative recounts to double-check the accuracy of election results reduced the necessity to pursue litigation over those results. While an administrative recount takes an election into overtime, by itself an orderly recount process established in advance (and thus expected in close races) does not instigate controversy or contentiousness. Indeed, in the second half of the twentieth century many states experienced routine recounts, even in close gubernatorial and US Senate elections, where the losing candidate graciously accepted the results of the recount without further protest—and occasionally even called off the completion of the recount before it was finished.

Virginia, in particular, demonstrated an especially impressive track record of major statewide recounts without significant controversy, a record it has continued into the twenty-first century with its successful recounts of attorney general races in 2005 and 2013. With Twitter enabling even greater transparency of the counting process than was previously feasible, Virginia's 2013 experience suggests that the future holds the promise of managing the vote-counting process even more fully in accordance with fundamental democratic values than has been possible in the past. Transparency could claim to be democracy's most basic value, if only because it permits monitoring compliance with democracy's other fundamental commitments.[19]

Reducing the Risk of Major Vote-Counting Disputes

The avoidance of vote-counting disputes is a worthwhile goal. It is much better not to have a fight over the counting of ballots than to be put to the test of whether the fight can be fair. It is thus ironic that in the twenty-first century, since the presidential election of 2000, the nation has taken steps that have the potential for increasing the chance of major vote-counting disputes, reversing some of the positive trends of the twentieth century.

Despite the hanging chads of *Bush v. Gore*, the nation has increased rather than decreased its reliance on paper ballots. The expectation was that with funds provided by the Help America Vote Act of 2002, the nation would replace punch-card ballots, as well as antiquated lever machines, with touchscreen computerized voting machines. But the 2004 presidential election produced fears that those touchscreen machines, if they lacked a paper record, could be susceptible to undetected hacking and manipulation of the count. Many localities that purchased these touchscreen machines have since replaced them with optical-scan paper ballots. Although these optical scan ballots have the virtue of being unhackable paper records, they present opportunities for uncertainty and mischief associated with any paper ballots: fights over ambiguous ballot markings and the stuffing of ballot boxes with extra fabricated ballots if adequate chain-of-custody precautions are not maintained.

Moreover, since 2000, there has been a rapid rise in absentee voting, as states look for low-cost ways to eliminate long lines at polling places on Election Day. Not only are absentee ballots a paper-based technology even in jurisdictions that use touchscreen machines in their polling places, but absentee ballots are also well-known to be particularly vulnerable to disputation and abuse. It is no accident that many of the most significant vote-counting disputes of recent decades have focused on issues associated with absentee ballots. These include the Bloody Eighth, Alabama's chief justice election of 1994, Miami's mayoral election of 1997, and Minnesota's US Senate election of 2008. Were it not for political choices made within the Gore campaign, absentee ballots easily could have become another focal point of dispute in the 2000 presidential election.

It is possible that new forms of voting technologies can reduce some of the risks associated with the currently prevailing reliance on absentee and other paper-based ballots. For example, one innovative idea is to cast ballots on smartphones or iPad-like tablets, which would then be scanned at polling places to produce a paper record.[20] This technology would eliminate the interpretive issues associated with markings on paper ballots, and by requiring voters to appear in person to scan their ballot even if filled out at home, would curtail some of the potential abuses associated with absentee voting (like unscrupulous party operatives fraudulently applying for, and mailing back, absentee ballots in the name of unsuspecting registered voters). A digital time stamp on the scanned ballot, matched to a time stamp on the paper record, would counteract the possibility of adding fake ballots to the count after the polls close.[21]

No electoral system, no matter how well designed and administered, can completely eliminate the risk of a vote-counting dispute. Nonetheless, a state can reduce this risk through careful drafting of its rules for the casting and counting of ballots. The main cause of serious vote-counting litigation is ambiguity, imprecision, or other forms of uncertainty in the content of the relevant rules and how they apply to particular situations. This uncertainty concerns not only the first-order rules regarding casting and counting procedures, but also the second-order rules regarding the consequences of failure to follow the first-order rules. Throughout US history, when there have been breaches of the first-order rules for conducting elections, but no legislative specification of the consequences of these breaches, courts have asked whether the first-order rules should be treated as mandatory, meaning that a ballot cast in violation of the rule cannot count because of the breach, or merely "directory," meaning the ballot is still potentially countable notwithstanding the breach. This same issue has surfaced in case after case (e.g., Pennsylvania, 1781; New York, 1792 and 1891; Maine, 1837; Alabama, 1994; Minnesota, 2008). The treatise writers of the nineteenth century understood this issue as the most prevalent and significant that courts must face in vote-counting cases.[22] The law-review literature of the early twenty-first century addressed the exact same issue, seeing that it had yet to be definitively resolved.[23]

Guided by their own sense of the values underlying the electoral system (as well as the specific first-order rule at issue), courts have had to decide for themselves whether to treat particular first-order rules as mandatory or directory. But the fundamental values underlying the electoral system can point in opposite directions, as particular cases have shown from the very beginning, including New York's gubernatorial election of 1792. The value of protecting eligible voters from disenfranchisement can point to considering a first-order rule directory, but the value of protecting the integrity of election can point to making the same rule mandatory. When courts have the discretion to determine where the balance of these competing considerations lie, their decisions are subject to potential biases, whether conscious or not, as Frederick Brightly so cogently documented in his treatise of 1871.[24] Moreover, as Brightly also observed, judicial precedents on whether primary rules are mandatory or directory are easily distinguished from one case to the next. A large degree of uncertainty—and thus disputability—would be eliminated by legislatures making clear not only the first-order rules but also the second-order rules on which first-order rules should be treated as mandatory or directory.

One source of ambiguity that is not so easy to eliminate is the equal protection doctrine of *Bush v. Gore*. Even assuming that the Court did not intend its equal protection holding to be unprincipled (with no precedential value in equivalent cases), the scope of that holding is notoriously unclear.[25] Nonetheless, the equal protection jurisprudence that emanates from *Bush v. Gore* will most likely improve the accuracy and fairness of ballot-counting in the states, as lower court rulings over the past decade have started to show.[26] Most importantly, now that *Bush v. Gore* has repudiated the hands-off posture of the federal judiciary announced in *Taylor v. Beckham* and reinforced by Justice Black in the Ballot Box 13 litigation, there can no longer be blatant electoral thefts of this kind. The federal judiciary will no longer tolerate ballot-box stuffing or its near equivalents, as the federal court's intervention in Alabama's 1994 chief justice election demonstrated, thereby anticipating *Bush v. Gore* in this respect.

The upshot is that no state, regardless of what region of the country it is in, can deviate from the fundamental national commitment to an honest count of the eligible ballots actually cast according to the rules established in advance of the election. This new guarantee of the federal judiciary's enforcement of this fundamental national principle, called for by Justice John Marshall Harlan in 1900 but not realized as Supreme Court precedent until 2000, promises to be as significant a development in the law applicable to vote-counting disputes as any in the nation's entire history. By 2100—a century after *Bush v. Gore,* two centuries after *Taylor v. Beckham,* and three centuries since the Founding Generation—there likely will be a robust new body of federal constitutional law on the specific subject of ballot-counting, enforceable by federal courts, that will be seen as the twenty-first century's distinctive contribution to the field (and all attributable to the confirmation in *Bush v. Gore* of the federal judiciary's appropriate role in this area).

In the meantime, however, the equal protection holding of *Bush v. Gore* will be a source of considerable uncertainty and thus will invite, not discourage, litigation over close electoral outcomes. Any plausible equal protection claim in light of *Bush v. Gore* will be pursued if a trailing candidate believes it offers a chance for a victory. Over time, a body of precedent adjudicating these plausible *Bush v. Gore* claims will reduce the uncertainty of this new equal protection jurisprudence. But this process has just begun. The best the states can do in the interim is to adopt clear and consistent rules that minimize exposure to plausible *Bush v. Gore* claims, which likely will center on imprecision and inconsistency in a state's vote-counting procedures, as *Bush v. Gore* itself did. Moreover, if states monitor the ongoing development of equal protection jurisprudence and update their election codes accordingly, they will further protect themselves from serious equal protection challenges to their vote-counting practices.[27]

These are the various ways, therefore, that a state can do its best to avoid a major vote-counting dispute. Still, the question remains how well-equipped a state is to handle one if it does occur. To return to the metaphor invoked in the introduction, it would be better never to need to use a ship's lifeboats, but if the need arises, has the ship been adequately prepared in this respect?

One clear lesson of this book is that ballot-counting disputes inevitably will occur despite a state's best efforts to avoid them. After Hayes-Tilden, they occurred in gubernatorial and state legislative elections with even greater frequency and ferocity during the hyperpolarized period of the Gilded Age. And after Bush-Gore, they have occurred in gubernatorial, US Senate, and other types of elections during another era of hyperpolarized politics. But even in periods of relatively normal political competition, as in America from the 1940s through the 1970s, they will occur episodically. To what extent, then, has the nation's previous experience with these volatile controversies caused it to be better prepared for the next occasions in which they unexpectedly arise?

The Institutional Capacity for a Major Vote-Counting Dispute

Gubernatorial Elections

Consider Texas. Although hardly unique in its vulnerability to an acute vote-counting dispute, Texas is noticeably so and thus worth focusing on as illustrative of the problem. The governorship there is a position of high visibility nationally and a potential stepping-stone to the presidency, as it was for George W. Bush. Although statewide elections have not been especially competitive in Texas recently, demographic shifts suggest that the state may become more purple and less red in the future. Thus the state could be caught unprepared for a gubernatorial election in which a Democratic challenger ends up surprisingly close to a Republican incumbent, and the resolution of a ballot-counting dispute might well make the difference.[28]

One worries how well Texas would handle this situation. The concern stems not merely from the state's experiences in 1948 and 1960. Contemporary political culture in Texas is notoriously sharp-elbowed and perhaps increasingly so. The fight over redistricting in 2003 produced a breakdown in the basic functioning of the state's legislature, with Democrats fleeing to neighboring states to prevent a quorum.[29] The weapon of criminal prosecution has been employed as part of political contestation in the state, first against Tom DeLay and then against Rick Perry.[30] It is difficult to discern in this particular state a reservoir of good will towards one's political opponents adequate to withstand an intense vote-counting controversy. As US history repeatedly has shown, a willingness of partisans to treat each other honorably—even magnanimously—is necessary for a fair resolution of a high-stakes vote-counting dispute, and this is particularly true when the existing institution empowered to adjudicate the dispute is less than ideal.

In Texas, the institution currently empowered to adjudicate a disputed gubernatorial election is its legislature, far from the ideal institution for the dispute.[31] If Texas experiences a ballot-counting dispute in a close gubernatorial election it is hard to imagine the state's legislature resolving that dispute fairly, according to the merits of the case, rather than purely as an exercise of political power by whichever party happens to be dominant in the legislature at the time. It is not clear that in the political culture of twenty-first-century Texas a gubernatorial candidate who felt robbed of a rightful victory would be as willing to wait for the next election as John Jay was in 1792. Rather, the candidate's supporters might demand immediate justice, and the candidate might encourage that demand.[32]

A future dispute over ballots in a Texas gubernatorial election is likely to end up in federal court under some sort of claim based on the precedents of

Bush v. Gore and *Roe v. Alabama*. Moreover, unlike in 1948, the federal judiciary now has jurisdiction to decide the merits of the claim. The federal court would demand that the state's vote-counting meet federal constitutional standards for fairness, assuming that the state's legislature would fall short of this standard. In this way, Texas might end up contributing significantly to the development of the equal protection jurisprudence pursuant to *Bush v. Gore*, a legacy that would please Coke Stevenson, however belatedly.

US Senate Elections

Even after *Bush v. Gore*, the federal judiciary has only a limited capacity to affect the outcome of a vote-counting dispute in a US Senate election. The federal courts could take jurisdiction over Fourteenth Amendment claims arising in the context of a state's canvassing or recount procedures, which would occur before the ultimate issuance of the state's certificate of election. Once that certificate has been issued, however, and a subsequent contest is filed in the Senate itself, then further federal court review would be precluded given the Senate's exclusive authority under the Constitution to judge the election of its members. Even if there were a plausible argument that the Senate was violating basic constitutional principles of due process or equal protection in its treatment of ballots, there would be no power in the federal courts to second-guess or otherwise supervise the Senate's determinations regarding the counting of those ballots.

If a federal court already had spoken on the treatment of those ballots in the context of a lawsuit arising out of the state's earlier canvassing or recount proceedings, and especially if the federal court already had said that fundamental fairness as guaranteed by due process and equal protection required that these ballots be counted in a certain way, one might hope that the Senate would give appropriate regard to the federal court's reasoning. But partisan politics could take over in the Senate and negate a fair count of the ballots achieved by a federal court.

Electoral injustice perpetrated by a partisan Senate, however, is unlikely to cause major trauma to the nation as a whole. As long as this partisan injustice is confined to a single Senate seat, the consequence is to deny the electorate of that particular state its right to fair representation with respect to that one senator. That injustice, while not to be ignored, is not the same as the denial of fair representation with respect to the state's chief executive or with respect to a legislative chamber as a whole.

From a national perspective, the scenario to worry about is where the outcome of the single seat has the potential to determine which party is able to assert majority control in the chamber. The Senate had difficulty with this kind of situation in the dispute over New Mexico's 1952 election, with the temptations of partisan conquest almost getting the better of the institution. Ultimately, however, six Republicans crossed party lines to settle the dispute on the ground that the state's problems with administering the election, while severe, were not enough to require voiding the election.[33] The 1950s, however, were a time of much greater bipartisan cooperation in the Senate and much less polarization in America's politics. If in the foreseeable future partisan control of the Senate turned on a disputed seat, would there be similar crossing of party lines to settle the dispute and thus permit the Senate to turn to legislative business? In an era when the dominant party has been willing to exercise the nuclear option to prevent filibusters of presidential nominees, there is reason to fear a lack of sufficient comity to enable the Senate to function in the case of a dispute over a seat that would determine which party has that dominant status.[34]

The Senate would do well to embrace Claiborne Pell's suggestion of establishing an "impartial, independent arbiter or panel of arbiters" to assist in this kind of situation.[35] By rule, the Senate could provide that the arbitral decision would prevail unless overturned by the Senate itself. But a Senate deadlocked by partisanship would not be able to muster the necessary votes to break a filibuster and overturn the arbitral decision. In this way, the determination of which party has majority status in the Senate could be resolved quickly and fairly, with the Senate then able to move on to other matters.[36]

Presidential Elections

As each presidential election since 2000 has approached, there has been a fear that it, like 2000 itself, would remain unresolved on the morning after Election Day and thus extend into overtime—as if an overtime election by itself would be a crisis.[37] It is worth remembering, however, that a presidential election that remains undecided for a week or two after Election Day is *not* by itself a crisis and need not metastasize into one. The presidential elections of 1884 and 1916 were unsettled in this way while waiting for the official canvassing of returns to be complete in the pivotal states (New York in 1884, California in 1916). Each time the canvass proceeded smoothly, and no litigation occurred. Similarly, in the future, if it takes two weeks to determine the winner in a pivotal state while the verification of provisional and absentee ballots occurs along with the other normal functions of the canvass, there is (at least in principle) no reason why there needs to be any litigation or controversy over the outcome of the presidential election. Ideally, in other words, an overtime presidential election in the future would proceed no differently than the two overtime attorney general elections that Virginia experienced in 2005 and 2013.

Realistically, however, it is easy to foresee an overtime presidential election quickly becoming embroiled in litigation before the completion of the canvass. The nation then would face another ballot-counting contestation like the one in 2000, only with the fight over hanging chads replaced by one over provisional or absentee ballots, for example. The US Supreme Court might become involved again, as in *Bush v. Gore*. Whether or not it does, perhaps next time the fight might continue all the way to Congress. If so, the convoluted, essentially incomprehensible, and utterly inadequate procedures of the Electoral Count Act of 1887 would come into play, whereas they did not (apart from the safe harbor deadline) in 2000.

Consequently, Congress should forestall that possibility by replacing the antiquated 1887 Act—which its own authors knew to be an insufficient stopgap measure—with a simple procedure that empowers an impartial Electoral Count Tribunal to adjudicate any dispute that arises when the joint session of Congress convenes under the Twelfth Amendment to receive the electoral votes from the states. It would be preferable to amend the Twelfth Amendment itself to eliminate the inherently awkward joint session of Congress, and instead make the impartial Electoral Count Tribunal the sole national body involved in the process of tallying the states' electoral votes. But a constitutional amendment is much more difficult to achieve than statutory reform, and a well-crafted new statute would suffice to fix the most glaring flaws of the 1887 Act. The new statute would put all disputes over a state's electoral votes before the tribunal (not just some of them, as was the case in the compromise statute for the Hayes-Tilden dispute) and would make the tribunal's decision controlling unless overturned by both houses of Congress (thereby providing a measure of accountability, but permitting the tribunal to prevail in the event of partisan deadlock).

As part of this reform, Congress should also consider adjusting the dates of the Electoral College calendar to give the states two additional weeks for their own procedures to adjudicate ballot-counting disputes that arise in a presidential election. Currently, the safe harbor deadline is exactly five weeks after Election Day, with the meeting of the Electoral College the following week. Congress should eliminate the current six-day gap between the safe harbor deadline and the Electoral College meeting. This gap is a relic of the nineteenth century and its slower methods of official communication. As long as a state conclusively resolves a dispute by the end of the day before the Electoral College meets, that brief interval of time should suffice to permit the state to achieve safe harbor status. If in the future the Electoral College meets at noon on January 1, then a state should receive safe harbor status if it completes its adjudication of a presidential vote-counting dispute before midnight on December 31.

Moreover, moving the Electoral College meeting from mid-December to January 1 would give states enough time to complete a fair recount of presidential ballots, if they used this additional time wisely. Washington in 2004 completed its gubernatorial recount by the end of December, and Minnesota in 2008 came close to doing so in its senatorial recount (certifying the result on January 5, and this certification could have occurred earlier with a minor acceleration of its overall recount timetable). To be sure, both states subsequently experienced postrecount contests that lasted until June of the following year. But for a presidential election, canvassing and recount procedures could be modified to require that any issues that might be raised in a subsequent judicial contest to be litigated either in or alongside the canvass and the recount.[38]

Some might object that holding the Electoral College meeting on January 1, rather than mid-December, would delay and disrupt the transition from one presidential administration to the next. Even when America knows who will be its next president on Election Night, there is preciously little time for the appointment of the cabinet and key White House officials. Waiting until January 1 to know which candidate won would only exacerbate this problem considerably, or so the argument goes.

But in the context of a disputed election, the relevant comparison is not between early November and January 1. Rather, it is between mid-December and January 1. The presidential transition inevitably will be disrupted by the uncertainty of a ballot-counting dispute. The question is whether two more weeks in an effort to achieve a fair count of those ballots is worth the two additional weeks of delay in starting the official transition from one administration to the next. (While the dispute is pending, the public would understand the need for both sides quietly to begin preparations for a transition, and indeed such preparations occurred on both sides in 2000.[39]) When evaluating marginal benefit and marginal cost in this way, there is a strong argument in favor of permitting two additional weeks for the resolution of ballot-counting disputes. If Congress requires a calendar that makes it virtually impossible for a state to achieve a fair count by the date the Electoral College meets—and both Washington and Minnesota were unable to complete their statewide recounts by this date—then the nation faces the prospect of having a president it did not choose. The apparent winners of the disputed elections in Washington and Minnesota on the date of the Electoral College meetings in 2004 and 2008 were *not* the candidates that ultimately won both elections. Moving the date of the Electoral College meeting from mid-December to January 1 would make no difference in the normal situation of an undisputed outcome, as will almost always be the case; the election would have been long since settled on Election Night with the usual concession speech from the losing candidate. But in the rare circumstance in which the two extra weeks would provide a chance to inaugurate the candidate whom the electorate actually chose, rather than having to inaugurate the candidate whom the electorate rejected, that difference is worth the price of two additional weeks of uncertainty during the transition period.

Even if Congress decides to leave the Electoral College calendar unchanged, with its five short weeks between Election Day and the safe harbor deadline, Congress still should adopt the more pressing reform of an impartial Electoral Count Tribunal. Whatever the uniform date for Electoral College meetings in all states, Congress needs a mechanism in the event that a dispute over the outcome in a pivotal state heads to Congress after that date. An impartial Electoral Count Tribunal would be the best mechanism to handle that contingency, far preferable to the impenetrable ambiguities of the 1887 Act.[40]

The Optimal Design of an Impartial Tribunal

There are alternative ways to design a genuinely neutral Electoral Count Tribunal. The simplest, and thus most transparently comprehensible to the American people, would be to have all nine justices of the US Supreme Court unanimously agree upon the individuals to serve on a three-member tribunal. The reason to empanel a three-member tribunal is to have the potential tiebreaking neutral member flanked by two copanelists, each of whom is seen as representative of the two parties to the conflict.[41] This way, in the internal deliberations of the tribunal, the neutral member is able to engage back-and-forth with the arguments on both sides. If the three-member tribunal ends up unanimous in its rulings—as did Minnesota's three-judge panels appointed to adjudicate its 1962 and 2008 disputed elections—so much the better for the nation. But a 2–1 ruling of this body, after all the evidence and arguments have been considered, is the most evenly impartial means by which to settle the controversy.

One could consider a larger tribunal. For example, five members, with two Democrats, two Republicans, and one neutral. But one of the lessons of Hayes-Tilden is that it is dangerous to have a single tiebreaker outnumbered by partisans on both sides. When there is more than one member from each party on the panel, the tendency will be for two teams to form within the body itself, with each side exerting pressure to sway the tiebreaker. Within the internal dynamics of the body, the sole tiebreaker would be outnumbered two to one when facing pressure from each of the two teams. It is much better to establish an equilateral triangle in which the neutral tiebreaker has one-on-one relations with each of the two other sides. That perfect equality in the relations among all three members is more conducive to genuine deliberation on the merits of the case among all three members. Without bloc voting by both sides competing for allegiance of the single tiebreaker, this equilateral triangle of three members is more likely to achieve unanimity than a 2–2–1 arrangement. Greater trust, including respect for the confidentiality of the tribunal's internal deliberations, is also more likely in a three-member format rather than a larger one.

One could also consider the possibility of a five-member tribunal, designed to have three neutrals along with one member from each of the two parties.[42] This vision is attractive insofar as the three neutrals always would outnumber both partisans. The difficulty with this approach lies in the extra challenge of identifying three neutrals, rather than one, as well as backups for each of the three neutral positions in the event that one or more declines to serve, like Justice Davis in the Hayes-Tilden dispute. Especially in a disputed presidential election, when presumably every citizen of stature who might be thought qualified to serve on the tribunal would be presumed to have an opinion on which candidate would make a better president, there will be the task of identifying someone whom the two parties and the public perceive as genuinely neutral and not already predisposed to one side or the other. It will be hard enough to find one such person as well as the necessary backup. Thus it is preferable not to compound the challenge by having to identify triple the number of neutrals.[43]

One might argue that it would be impossible to find even a single neutral person of sufficient stature to be worthy of serving as the decisive tiebreaker in a disputed presidential election. Colin Powell? One side or the other might object.

But to dispel doubt about the possibility of finding anyone to serve as the neutral tiebreaker for a disputed presidential election, consider this experiment conducted in 2008. A group of scholars organized a simulated adjudication of a hypothetical disputed presidential election that turned on provisional ballots cast in Colorado. The three-judge panel for this adjudication was designed to be evenly balanced. Thomas Phillips, former chief justice of Texas, was a prominent and widely respected jurist with a visibly Republican background. Patricia Wald, former chief judge of the US Court of the Appeals for the DC Circuit, was similarly well-regarded but with a Democratic pedigree. The two of them were asked to agree upon a third panelist, and without any prompting they chose David Levi, a former federal trial judge who was dean of Duke University's law school (and son of former US attorney general Edward Levi).[44] Dean Levi exemplifies the kind of person who could be called upon to act with utmost integrity and impartiality in the event that an actual disputed presidential election needs to be resolved. If all nine justices of the US Supreme Court called upon him to play this role in the same way that Phillips and Wald did as part of the simulation, the nation could be confident that it had used the fairest possible method for the resolution of the disputed presidential election—and that whatever judgment Levi actually reached in this role (whether or not agreed upon by his two copanelists) would be the most fair-minded, impartial, and nonpartisan that could be humanly possible.

If this role envisioned for Levi seems similar to the one actually performed by Justice Bradley in 1877, it has some crucial differences. Bradley was picked to replace David Davis as the tiebreaker on the Electoral Commission of 1877 not because Bradley was viewed as the next most impartial jurist in America, but because the statute shortsightedly had limited the selection of the tiebreaker to sitting members of the Supreme Court. David Levi, or anyone else in the role of the tiebreaker for a disputed presidential election, need not be a current member of the Supreme Court—or even a sitting judge on any court for that matter. Instead, Levi himself illustrates that an individual may be especially well-suited to serve as a neutral arbiter despite being currently employed in a capacity other than full-time adjudicator. As long as that individual is unanimously chosen by all nine justices of the Court, then that individual can undertake the role of the tiebreaker with the nation's confidence that the

Figure C.2 Patricia Wald, David Levi, and Thomas Phillips—all distinguished former judges—formed a politically balanced panel to adjudicate a hypothetical case of a disputed presidential election in 2008; after a "moot court" argument by two leading Supreme Court litigators, this three-judge panel rendered a unanimous opinion resolving issues of the kind that could arise based on the precedent of *Bush v. Gore*. Courtesy of Georgetown Law School.

individual is indeed the best person for the job. Moreover, on the assumption that Levi (or someone like him) agrees in advance of the election to serve in this capacity should the need arise afterwards, then there is no reason to think that Levi would back out if and when that contingency actually occurs. But if illness or other unexpected circumstances prevented Levi from fulfilling the role, the same statutory mechanism that authorizes the nine justices to select him could (and should) also require the justices to select an alternate in advance and, as with Levi himself, would permit the justices to choose any individual they deemed most suitable for the role—not necessarily a currently sitting jurist, either on the Supreme Court or otherwise.[45]

With the benefit of historical hindsight, we can see that the Electoral Commission of 1877 was not an inherently flawed idea. Instead, it was the particular details of the idea's implementation that caused the institution to perform more poorly than initially anticipated. For the next disputed presidential election, and surely there will be one sooner or later, it is possible for Congress to establish in advance a better structured tribunal, one without the flaws of the 1877 commission but which still incorporates James Kent's essential idea of an evenly balanced body that is equally fair to both sides.[46]

Minnesota's successes for its 1962 and 2008 elections show that it can be done. There is no guarantee, of course, that were Congress to adopt a Minnesota-style tribunal for disputed presidential elections it would work just as successfully in that higher-stakes context. A three-judge panel adjudicating a disputed presidential election might be more susceptible to a 2–1 split rather than the consistent 3–0 unanimity that Minnesota achieved for both 1962 and 2008—although, interestingly, the three-judge panel of Levi, Phillips, and Wald created for the simulated presidential election was also unanimous in the decision it rendered as part of the experiment.[47] If the presidential panel did split 2–1, inevitably there would be those looking to uncover hidden bias on the part of the purportedly neutral tiebreaker, despite the lengths to which the system was designed to make the tiebreaker as genuinely neutral as possible. Maybe the purported neutral really is a closet Democrat, or closet Republican (depending on which side the tiebreaker ends up agreeing with)—and thus predisposed to rule in favor of one side after all, just as Justice Bradley was.

A tribunal designed to be fair to both sides, however, does not need to work perfectly in every instance. It just needs to function better than a vote-counting tribunal that intentionally is structured to have more members from one side than the other. To be sure, a political party will always prefer the option of outnumbering the opposing party on the vote-counting tribunal, compared to an arrangement that gives each party an equal number with a neutral tiebreaker. The inherent desire to win causes a competitor to welcome a friendly referee, even though the competitor cannot countenance a referee favoring the opposition.

Yet if the tribunal is not designed to be fair to both sides, there is always the risk that the opposition will have the upper hand. In a competitive two-party system, given an institutional arrangement that enables one party to outnumber the other on the vote-counting tribunal, there is no guarantee that one's own party will always dominate that body. Because it is unpredictable when the next election close enough to generate a credible vote-counting controversy will occur, one's own party may be caught with the surprise of having the other side control the vote-counting tribunal just at the moment when the tribunal's role in the democratic process is most salient and consequential. In that case, the us-versus-them dynamic gives the other side the power to manipulate the counting of the ballots based on its sheer numerical advantage alone. When the other side exercises that power to award the disputed election to its own candidate, the perception of "We Wuz Robbed" is the inevitable consequence.

Ultimately, the health of a two-party system depends on the proposition that neither party controls the process for counting ballots. The core concept underlying the two-party system is that each side recognizes the other as a legitimate competitor in the recurrent quest to win the approval of the electorate at regularly scheduled intervals. Acceptance of the other side in this way requires, whenever a ballot-counting dispute materializes, that each party refrain from endeavoring to undermine the particular choice between the two parties that the electorate wished to make at the particular time. When one side holds a numerical advantage on the vote-counting tribunal, respect for the right of the electorate to choose the other party over one's own means forgoing the ability to use this numerical advantage to dictate the outcome in one's favor. Because it is unrealistic to expect partisans to exercise this kind of self-restraint in the heat of the competitive battle, it is necessary to adopt the institutional reform that gives neither side that numerical advantage.[48]

A national goal for the twenty-first century should be to implement the institutional reform first articulated in America by James Kent at the end of eighteenth century, and occasionally adopted in some places at some times, but not yet widespread or routine. Us-versus-them, with one side in control of the count, should become eclipsed as a general rule by a model of equal representation of both sides in the counting process, with a neutral referee to arbitrate otherwise irresolvable disputes between the two sides over the proper conduct of the count. No neutral referee will always be free of criticism from one side or the other over particular judgments that the referee must make. But that criticism does not automatically negate the referee's genuine neutrality. The critics deep down know this truth, regardless of whatever invective of bias they may hurl at the referee in the heat of the moment. In the end, a genuinely neutral referee with whom one disagrees is still far better than a system that is structurally biased by placing the counting of ballots in the control of the opposing political party.

If America can achieve the creation of a genuinely neutral referee for the resolution of its disputed elections, that accomplishment would be a major step forward in fulfilling the ideal of a fair count, shared from Madison to Hughes to the present. Madison, like other Founders, did not see the need for an institutional embodiment of a neutral referee. They overlooked this need because they did not anticipate the structural permanence of ongoing two-party competition, us-versus-them. But that dynamic quickly developed, and America has been endeavoring ever since to accommodate that reality. In the specific context of ballot-counting disputes, the best that can be achieved is the adoption of an evenly balanced tribunal with a neutral tiebreaker. As the history of disputed elections in America's first two-and-a-quarter centuries shows, achieving that much is plenty good enough. Demanding more than that would be to insist on a conception of vote-counting fairness that is humanly unattainable.

Appendix

DATA ON OVERTIME ELECTIONS

This appendix contains three tables of data concerning statewide elections for which the outcome remained unsettled for longer than the day immediately after Election Day—and thus extended into overtime. The first table concerns overtime gubernatorial elections since the momentous presidential election of 1876, the second concerns overtime US Senate elections since ratification of the Seventeenth Amendment, and the third concerns overtime statewide elections of any type since 2000. An explanation of each column of data follows.

Explanation of Tables

The sources from which these tables derive include official secretary of state records, well-known election information databases, and newspaper articles.

Initial Margin: This column expresses the gap, in absolute number of votes, between the two leading candidates at the beginning of the particular election's overtime period. The column aims to measure that gap on the day immediately after Election Day. To do that, the main source used is the *New York Times* Thursday-morning-after-the-election-edition, which often has detailed vote totals for US Senate and gubernatorial elections, reflecting the gap between the two candidates on the Wednesday night immediately after the election. Occasionally, however, the *Times* did not publish this data—particularly in the context of (1) older elections, especially in Western states, and (2) elections to offices other than US Senator or governor—in which instances the data comes from other newspapers.

Initial Margin (I.M.) %: This figure reflects the percentage that separated the two leading candidates immediately after Election Day, omitting third parties. This percentage usually was drawn from the same source that provided the "initial margin" expressed in absolute number of votes. Note also that the ~ symbol was used where the absence of complete totals made it necessary to estimate.

Final Margin: This column expresses the gap, in absolute number of votes, between the two leading candidates at the end of the overtime period. To calculate this number, the main source used is *Congressional Quarterly*'s *(CQ)* online database, which has comprehensive election statistics for most federal elections and state gubernatorial races dating back to 1824. Occasionally, the presence of (1) a recount, (2) a postcertification court decision invalidating ballots, or (3) a challenge before the relevant legislative body, would result in a change not reflected in *CQ*'s database. In those instances, secretary of state websites or newspaper sources provide the final margin of victory.

Final Margin (F.M.) %: This figure reflects the percentage that separated the two leading candidates when the overtime period ended. This percentage usually was drawn from the same source that provided the "final margin" expressed as absolute number of votes. The ~ symbol is also used to show estimated final margins when necessary.

Date Conceded: In the overwhelming majority of elections—particularly modern elections—the losing candidate delivered a public concession speech or otherwise manifested acquiescence in the election's results (for example, by sending a private letter or telegram to the winning candidate). More infrequently, a candidate did not publicly acknowledge defeat, and rumors of a forthcoming contest would swirl, casting doubt on the election's status. In such an instance, newspaper accounts and other published sources were used to determine when the election could truly be deemed settled.

# of Days: This number represents the number of days that passed between Election Day (typically, the first Tuesday in November) and the "Date Conceded."

Recount: In general, this category refers to administrative procedures that occur after the canvassing of returns is complete but before final certification of the result. Although recounts can occur pursuant to court order (and, when they do, they are included in this column), this category encompasses those recounts that took place without any need for litigation. The more cursory procedure of retallying returns, which regularly occurs in each canvass of the returns, is not included in this classification of recounts. Occasionally, candidates will obtain recounts in particular precincts, which the tables label a "partial" recount.

Litigation: If a candidate (or a surrogate) initiated a state or federal lawsuit in an attempt to bridge the vote gap (or otherwise to upset the results as they appear on the face of the returns), that fact is noted in this column.

Winning Party: The party affiliation of the candidate who took office following the election, unless otherwise noted.

Information concerning additional sources used to generate the data in these tables, particularly when necessary to supplement the main source for the type of data in question, can be found in "Information on Sources for Appendix in *Ballot Battles: The History of Disputed Elections in the United States*," available at The Ohio State University's Knowledge Bank: http://hdl.handle.net/1811/71168, also archived at http://perma.cc/WW5L-7EBF.

Also, the following anomalous entries in the tables deserve a brief explanation:

Table A.1 Overtime Gubernatorial Elections, 1878 to Present

1890 CT: The legislature was unable to resolve the dispute, so the incumbent governor held over.

1893 RI: The legislature was unable to resolve the dispute, so the incumbent governor held over.

1894 NV: *Winning Party:* Silver Party.

1896 SD: *Winning Party:* Populist Party.

1898 SD: *Winning Party:* Populist Party.

1962 RI: The symbol "Y*" reflects the fact that the postelection ballot-counting process in RI 1962—while nominally part of the canvass—functioned essentially like a recount insofar as it encompassed an examination of the ballots themselves and not solely a retallying of the returns.

Table A.2 Overtime US Senate Elections, 1914 to Present

1926 PA: *Date Conceded:* On December 6, 1929, the Senate voted to declare the seat vacant. See "Senate Bars Vare by Vote of 58 to 22; Rejects Wilson Too," *New York Times*, December 7, 1929.

1934 NM: Bronson Cutting (R) led in the certified total but was killed in a plane crash on the way back to New Mexico after Dennis Chavez (D) initiated contest proceedings in the Senate. A committee report absolved Cutting of wrongdoing. New Mexico's Democratic governor appointed Chavez to the vacant seat.

1974 NH: The US Senate declared the seat vacant, and a new election was held on September 16, 1975. The Democrat won the rematch.

1984 WV: Jay Rockefeller (D) was certified the winner pursuant to WV Code § 3-6-1, which required certification within 30 days of the election (December 5). His opponent—John Raese (R)—never sought a recount, which would have extended the deadline for certification under the state statute. Nor did Raese contest the election in the US Senate (the only available forum for doing so, given WV law). Nonetheless, Raese refused to concede defeat, telling a reporter in 2010 "I've never conceded that race. I'm still waiting after 26 years." *John Raese on Rockefeller Race*, YouTube Video, 1:32, posted by "observerwv," September 25, 2010, accessed on July, 14, 2015, www.youtube.com/watch?v=XEK0RCiE5Wc.

Table A.3 Overtime Statewide Elections, 2000 to Present

2011 WI Supreme Court: The election was technically a nonpartisan election, but Prosser received support from Republicans, while the Democratic Party backed Kloppenburg.

Table A.1 **Overtime Gubernatorial Elections, 1878 to Present**

Year	*State*	*Initial Margin*	*I.M.%*	*Final Margin*	*F.M.%*	*Date Conceded*	*# of Days*	*Recount*	*Litigation*	*Winning Party*
1878	OR	61	2.17	69	0.17	06/20	17	N	N	D
1879	ME	19,638	15.80	21,324	15.40	01/28/80	142	N	Y	R
1884	MI	1,409	4.26	3,953	1.01	11/23	19	N	N	R
1885	NY	10,823	8.46	11,134	1.12	11/14	11	N	N	D
1886	CA	999	3.40	659	0.34	11/20	18	N	N	D
1886	NH	249	0.37	458	0.67	06/01/87	211	N	N	R
1888	CT	1,418	0.96	1,415	0.96	01/10/89	65	N	N	R
1888	IN	598	1.73	2,200	0.42	11/15	9	N	N	R
1888	WV	47	0.20	237	0.07	02/04/90	455	Partial	Y	D
1890	CT	3,520	2.67	3,683	2.80	N/A	N/A	N	Y	N/A
1890	MN	1,672	0.96	2,267	0.94	12/17	43	N	N	R
1890	NE	2,330	5.15	1,144	0.81	02/06/91	94	N	Y	D
1890	NH	724	0.93	93	0.11	01/07/91	64	N	N	R
1892	MA	2,834	0.76	2,534	0.68	12/02	24	N	N	D
1893	RI	185	0.42	185	0.42	N/A	N/A	N	Y	N/A
1894	CA	2,133	0.90	1,206	0.54	01/10/95	65	N	Y	D
1894	NV	81	3.30	1,362	14.99	12/23	47	N	N	S
1894	TN	9,246	8.60	2,354	0.36	05/08/95	183	N	N	D

(*continued*)

Table A.1 **Continued**

Year	*State*	*Initial Margin*	*I.M.%*	*Final Margin*	*F.M.%*	*Date Conceded*	*# of Days*	*Recount*	*Litigation*	*Winning Party*
1896	SD	89	5.07	319	0.39	12/19	46	N	Y	P
1898	SD	1,200	0.46	339	0.46	12/16	38	N	N	P
1899	KY	5,277	8.23	2,383	0.62	05/21/00	195	N	Y	D
1900	KY	15,159	5.18	3,689	0.78	11/15	9	N	N	D
1900	MN	5,056	1.69	2,254	0.74	11/30	24	N	N	R
1900	NE	2,510	2.10	861	0.38	11/13	7	N	N	R
1902	CA	1,804	1.34	2,549	0.88	11/19	15	N	N	R
1902	NY	8,896	3.49	8,803	0.67	11/06	2	N	N	R
1902	OR	334	0.80	246	0.29	06/07	5	N	N	D
1906	KS	2,064	0.71	2,123	0.70	11/12	6	N	N	R
1910	ID	680	2.36	895	1.11	11/12	4	N	N	D
1912	IA	49	0.01	1,699	0.45	01/15/13	71	N	N	R
1912	ID	1,793	7.18	1,082	1.66	11/07	2	N	N	R
1912	KS	456	0.20	29	0.0087	12/10	35	N	Y	D
1912	WA	660	0.42	622	0.32	12/07	32	N	N	D
1915	KY	671	0.17	471	0.11	11/11	9	Partial	N	D
1916	AZ	175	2.09	43	0.07	05/02/17	176	Y	Y	D
1916	ID	1,772	2.79	572	0.45	11/18	11	Partial	N	D

1916	MO	3,952	0.55	2,263	0.30	01/16/17	70	N	N	D
1916	OH	11,987	1.40	6,616	0.59	01/02/17	56	N	N	D
1916	WV	179	0.08	2,766	0.99	12/06	29	N	N	D
1918	AZ	333	8.93	339	0.66	11/21	16	N	N	R
1918	NY	12,238	0.62	14,842	0.74	01/12/19	68	N	Y	D
1919	MD	327	0.15	165	0.07	11/10	6	N	N	D
1924	MO	12,274	1.08	5,872	0.46	12/19	46	N	N	R
1924	NM	2,473	3.46	199	0.18	09/21/25	321	N	Y	D
1926	AZ	366	0.46	399	0.50	12/10	38	N	N	D
1926	NE	2,943	0.75	3,432	0.84	11/22	20	N	N	R
1926	NM	1,842	4.36	3,771	3.46	11/04	2	N	N	R
1926	WY	1,168	15.44	1,365	1.96	11/04	2	N	N	R
1930	KS	427	0.07	251	0.06	11/24	20	N	Y	D
1932	ME	1,265	0.53	2,358	0.98	11/21	70	Partial	N	D
1937	NJ	44,630	3.09	45,266	3.00	01/28/38	87	Y	Y	D
1940	IN	12,120	0.70	3,478	0.20	03/06/41	121	Y	N	D
1940	KS	1,828	0.22	430	0.06	01/10/41	66	N	Y	R
1940	MA	9,217	0.46	5,588	0.28	12/14	39	Y	N	R
1940	MO	3,457	0.19	3,613	0.20	05/21/41	197	Y	Y	R
1940	WA	4,516	0.68	5,816	0.74	01/14/41	70	N	N	R

(continued)

Table A.1 **Continued**

Year	*State*	*Initial Margin*	*I.M.%*	*Final Margin*	*F.M.%*	*Date Conceded*	*# of Days*	*Recount*	*Litigation*	*Winning Party*
1944	UT	1,421	0.58	1,056	0.42	05/25/45	199	N	Y	D
1948	CT	2,285	0.27	2,225	0.26	01/05/49	64	N	Y	D
1950	MI	5,697	0.31	1,154	0.06	12/12	36	Y	N	D
1952	MI	4,989	0.18	8,618	0.30	12/16	42	Y	N	D
1956	IL	48,620	1.17	36,877	0.86	11/12	6	N	N	R
1956	RI	190	0.10	711	0.18	01/01/57	56	Partial	Y	D
1958	NE	3,262	0.79	1,640	0.38	02/26/59	114	Y	Y	D
1958	NM	2,626	1.37	1,914	0.94	11/23	19	N	Y	D
1958	VT	1,038	0.84	719	0.58	01/12/59	69	Y	N	R
1960	NM	3,100	1.18	1,988	0.66	12/23	45	N	Y	R
1962	MA	9,063	0.43	5,431	0.26	12/20	44	Y	Y	D
1962	ME	405	0.14	483	0.16	12/14	38	Y	N	R
1962	MN	115	0.01	91	0.0073	03/22/63	136	Y	Y	D
1962	RI	46	0.01	398	0.12	11/30	24	Y*	N	R
1962	VT	1,759	1.50	1,348	1.12	01/14/63	69	Y	N	D
1966	GA	1,769	0.19	3,039	0.34	01/10/67	63	N	Y	D
1966	HI	4,272	2.04	4,516	2.12	06/25/68	595	N	Y	D
1970	AK	2,796	4.73	5,045	6.34	11/05	2	N	N	D

1970	ME	702	0.22	500	0.15	12/15	42	Y	N	D
1970	MI	150,110	6.73	44,111	1.68	11/05	2	N	N	R
1970	OK	3,123	0.47	2,181	0.32	11/14	11	Y	Y	D
1970	RI	2,548	0.76	1,871	0.54	12/14	41	Partial	N	D
1974	AK	380	0.52	287	0.32	11/28	23	Y	N	R
1974	OH	10,178	0.34	11,488	0.38	12/13	38	Partial	N	R
1979	LA	10,402	0.76	9,557	0.70	12/13	5	N	Y	R
1981	NJ	1,158	0.05	1,797	0.08	11/30	27	Y	Y	R
1982	IL	2,952	0.08	5,074	0.14	01/07/83	66	Partial	Y	R
1989	VA	5,533	0.31	6,741	0.38	12/21	44	Y	N	D
1990	AZ	4,527	0.44	44,401	4.72	02/27/91	113	Runoff	Y	R
1990	MI	19,133	0.75	17,595	0.70	11/08	2	N	N	R
1990	NE	4,781	0.84	4,030	0.70	11/09	3	N	N	D
1993	NJ	33,051	1.39	26,093	1.06	11/29	27	N	Y	R
1994	AK	339	0.22	536	0.31	11/07/95	364	Y	Y	D
1994	MD	6,187	0.45	5,993	0.42	01/16/95	69	N	Y	D
2002	AL	3,195	0.24	3,120	0.24	11/17	12	Y	Y	R
2002	AZ	25,284	2.75	11,819	1.06	11/10	5	N	N	D
2004	WA	1,064	0.06	133	0.0047	06/06/05	216	Y	Y	D
2010	CT	8,424	0.76	6,404	0.56	11/08	6	N	N	D
2010	MN	9,057	0.50	9,080	0.50	12/08	36	Y	Y	D

Table A.2 **Overtime US Senate Elections, 1914 to Present**

Year	*State*	*Initial Margin*	*I.M.%*	*Final Margin*	*F.M.%*	*Date Conceded*	*# of Days*	*Recount*	*Litigation*	*Winning Party*
1922	TX	112,818	39.64	103,997	30.66	02/03/25	819	Y	N	D
1924	IA	4,327	0.49	1,420	0.16	04/12/26	524	Y	Y	D
1924	NM	3,009	3.89	2,897	2.59	04/30/26	542	N	Y	D
1926	PA	126,368	8.70	N/A	N/A	N/A	1,130	Partial	Y	Vacant
1934	NM	1,163	0.84	1,284	50.42	05/06/35	181	N	Y	R*
1938	IN	1,770	0.12	5,197	0.34	04/13/39	156	N	Y	D
1946	MD	16,941	7.01	1,624	0.35	05/20/48	562	Y	N	D
1946	WV	6,393	1.32	2,924	0.54	07/28/49	996	Partial	N	D
1948	MI	34,374	1.78	44,827	2.19	07/28/49	268	N	N	R
1952	NM	4,784	2.13	5,375	2.24	03/23/54	504	Y	Y	D
1962	AL	6,019	1.61	6,803	1.72	02/04/63	90	N	N	D
1962	SD	295	0.11	597	0.23	12/05	29	Y	N	D
1964	NV	2,843	2.54	48	0.04	12/10	37	Y	Y	D
1964	PA	25,904	0.58	70,635	1.48	11/19	16	N	N	R
1968	OR	2,516	0.32	3,293	0.40	12/30	55	Y	N	R
1970	IN	3,877	0.22	4,283	0.24	06/12/72	587	Y	Y	D
1972	CO	9,354	1.05	9,588	1.06	12/05	28	N	N	D
1974	NV	595	0.38	624	0.40	12/10	35	Y	N	R

1974	NH	588	0.27	2	0.0009	09/16/75	315	Y	Y	N/A
1974	ND	90	0.04	186	0.08	12/13	38	Y	N	R
1974	OK	3,990	0.52	3,835	0.50	03/04/76	485	N	Y	R
1978	TX	17,024	0.77	12,227	0.54	12/08	31	Partial	Y	R
1978	VA	3,796	0.31	4,721	0.38	12/17	40	N	Y	R
1980	GA	14,202	0.92	27,543	1.74	11/11	7	N	N	R
1980	VT	2,536	1.24	2,755	1.34	12/22	48	Y	N	D
1982	RI	8,723	2.64	8,212	2.40	11/10	8	N	N	R
1984	KY	4,037	0.32	5,269	0.42	11/27	21	N	N	R
1984	WV	30,891	4.35	29,553	4.12	*	N/A	N	N	D
1988	FL	4,936	0.12	34,518	0.84	11/16	8	N	N	R
1994	CA	123,610	1.69	162,127	2.08	02/07/95	91	N	Y	D
1996	LA	12,280	0.73	5,788	0.34	10/01/97	330	N	Y	D
1998	NV	459	0.11	428	0.10	12/10	37	Y	Y	D
2000	WA	3,197	0.18	2,229	0.10	12/01	24	Y	N	D
2002	SD	527	0.16	524	0.16	11/13	8	N	N	D
2004	AK	10,688	4.62	9,349	3.22	12/17	45	Y	N	R
2008	MN	477	0.02	312	0.01	06/30/09	238	Y	Y	D
2010	AK	13,588	6.70	10,252	4.00	12/31	59	N	Y	I

Table A.3 **Overtime Statewide Elections, 2000 to Present**

Year	*State*	*Election Type*	*Initial Margin*	*I.M. %*	*Final Margin*	*F.M.%*	*Date Conceded*	*# of Days*	*Recount*	*Litigation*	*Winning Party*
2000	CO	St. Educ. Bd.	510	0.03	90	0.005	11/28	21	Y	N	D
2000	FL	President	1,784	0.03	537	0.01	12/13	36	Y	Y	R
2000	WA	US Senate	3,197	0.18	2,229	0.10	12/01	24	Y	N	D
2000	WA	Sec'y of St.	11,841	0.72	10,222	0.45	12/01	24	Y	N	R
2002	AL	Governor	3,195	0.24	3,120	0.24	11/17	12	Y	Y	R
2002	AZ	Governor	25,284	2.75	11,819	1.06	11/10	5	N	N	D
2004	WA	Governor	1,064	0.06	133	0.0047	06/06/05	216	Y	Y	D
2004	AK	US Senate	10,688	4.62	9,349	3.22	12/17	45	Y	N	R
2004	NC	Sup. Pub. Instr.	13,810	0.50	8,535	0.26	08/23/05	294	Y	Y	D
2005	VA	A.G.	1,585	0.08	360	0.02	12/21	43	Y	Y	R
2006	CO	Sec'y of St.	31,940	1.92	23,871	1.56	11/14	7	N	N	R
2006	NC	Ct. of App.	3,552	0.23	3,466	0.22	11/28	21	Y	N	R

2006	OH	Auditor	76,592	2.14	48,791	1.28	12/18	41	N	N	R
2006	VT	Auditor	834	0.38	102	0.05	12/21	44	Y	Y	D
2008	MN	US Senate	477	0.02	312	0.01	06/30/09	238	Y	Y	D
2010	AK	US Senate	13,588	6.7	10,252	4.00	12/31	59	N	Y	I
2010	CT	Governor	8,424	0.76	6,404	0.56	11/08	6	N	N	D
2010	MN	Governor	9,057	0.50	9,080	0.50	12/08	36	Y	Y	D
2010	NC	Ct. of App.	N/A	N/A	6,655	0.60	12/20	48	Y	Y	R
2011	WI	Sup. Ct.	204	0.01	7,006	0.47	05/31	56	Y	N	R
2013	VA	A.G.	32	~0.003	907	0.04	12/18	43	Y	Y	D

NOTES

Prologue

1. Apryl Babarcik's experience formed part of *O'Farrell v. Landis*, a legal case brought to challenge a local election held in 2012, as described in this prologue. The main documents filed in the case can be found at the *Election Law @ Moritz* website: http://moritzlaw.osu.edu/electionlaw/litigation/OFarrell.v.Landis.php.

   For further information about provisional ballots, see Edward B. Foley, "Uncertain Insurance: The Ambiguities and Complexities of Provisional Voting," in *Voting in America: American Voting Systems in Flux—Debacles, Dangers, and Brave New Designs*, vol. 3, ed., Morgan E. Felchner (Westport, CT: Praeger, 2008), 75–89; Edward B. Foley, "The Promise and Problems of Provisional Voting," *George Washington Law Review* 73 (2005): 1193.
2. Ohio H. R. "Contest of the November 6, 2012 98th House District Election: Count the Votes: Minority Report," at 13 (May 6, 2013) (hereafter Count the Votes: Minority Report); see also Deposition of Apryl Babarcik, in Evidence of Contestor Joshua O'Farrell, vol. II, at 7–10, *O'Farrell v. Landis* (No. 2012–2151).
3. "Presidential General Election, Ohio, 2012 All Counties," *CQ Press* (Voting and Elections Collections), http://library.cqpress.com.proxy.lib.ohio-state.edu/elections/download-data.php?filetype=&office=1&areatype=2&year=2012&format=3&license=on&emailto=&emailfrom= accessed July 13, 2015.
4. "Official Results for 2012 General Election," Ohio Secretary of State, accessed March 30, 2015, www.sos.state.oh.us/elections/Research/electResultsMain/2012Results.aspx.
5. Catherine Candisky, "General Assembly Election Complaint to be Heard by House," *Columbus Dispatch*, Feb. 23, 2013, 4B.
6. "Count the Votes: Minority Report"; Contestor Joshua E. O'Farrell's Merit Brief in Support of Context of Election Petition, at 17–18, *O'Farrell v. Landis* (Feb. 11, 2013) (No. 2012–2151) (hereafter Contestor's Merit Brief).
7. See O'Farrell v. Landis, 985 N.E.2d 458, at ¶13 (Ohio S. Ct. 2013).
8. Catherine Candisky, "Ohio House Confirms Victory by GOP Lawmaker," *Columbus Dispatch*, May 23, 2013. See also "GOP Wins Final Contest for Total Control of House," *Columbus Dispatch*, Dec. 15, 2012; Jim Siegel, "Panel Validates Lawmaker's 8-Vote Win," *Columbus Dispatch*, May 8, 2013.
9. Pennsylvania's Buckshot War is discussed in Chapter 3, the 1890s in Chapter 6.
10. New York's Stolen Senate is discussed in Chapter 7.
11. In 2013, Virginia had a recount in a legislative race that would determine which party would control the state senate, as discussed in Chapter 12. That recount was handled peaceably and did not even cause the kind of litigation that occurred in Ohio the previous year. Likewise, Montana in 2004 had a ballot-counting dispute in a legislative seat that would

determine partisan control of the state's house of representatives. Jim Robbins, "Ruling Puts Democrats in Control in Montana," *New York Times*, Dec. 29, 2004. Although that dispute prompted litigation that required a ruling from the Montana Supreme Court, *Big Spring v. Jore*, 109 P.3d 219 (2005), it never provoked the civil unrest that plagued the state a century earlier, when in 1891 the legislature was incapable of meeting for an entire session because of ballot-counting disputes in enough seats to prevent the statehouse from organizing itself (see Chapter 6, note 63).

12. See Philip Lawson, *George Grenville: A Political Life* (New York: Oxford, 1984).
13. Quoted in Luther Stearns Cushing, *Lex Parliamentaria Americana: Elements of the Law and Practice of Legislative Assemblies in the United States of America* (1856), 58.
14. Caroline Morris, *Parliamentary Elections, Representation and the Law* (Oxford: Hart, 2012), 80.
15. Cushing, *Lex Parliamentaria Americana*, 58.
16. For a comprehensive analysis of the procedures that the fifty states currently use to adjudicate ballot-counting disputes, see Joshua A. Douglas, "Procedural Fairness in Election Contests," *Indiana Law Journal* 88 (2013): 1. For state legislative elections, all but two states (North Dakota and Hawaii) continue to give each legislative chamber the authority to determine the winners of elections for seats in that chamber. Ibid., 6. The legislative chambers are entitled to exercise this authority on an entirely partisan basis, as Ohio's did in Landis-O'Farrell dispute. Douglas observes that for gubernatorial elections in 1874 Pennsylvania adopted a complicated procedure that contains a random component to it, but it has never been tested. Ibid., 13–17. Iowa, too, uses a random lottery to select the members of its legislature to form a tribunal to adjudicate disputed gubernatorial elections. Ibid., 13. See also Chapter 7's discussion of Kentucky's 1899 disputed gubernatorial election, where a lottery was supposed to be used to select a legislative committee to adjudicate the dispute, but the resulting composition of the committee was highly improbable.
17. C. H. Rammelkamp, "Contested Congressional Elections," *Political Science Quarterly* 20, no. 3 (1905): 421.
18. John Franklin Jameson, "Review of James Bryce: The American Commonwealth," in *John Franklin Jameson and the Development of Humanistic Scholarship in America: Selected Essays*, vol. 1, eds. Morey Rothberg and Jacqueline Goggin (Athens: University of Georgia, 1993), 37. Henry Dawes, a leading figure in Congress during the nineteenth century, also lamented America's failure to adopt an equivalent of the Grenville Act: "What was said by Mr. Granville . . . is to-day as true of contests in the House of Representatives as it then was of those in the House of Commons." Henry L. Dawes, "The Mode of Procedure in Cases of Contested Elections," *Journal of Social Science* 2 (1870), 65.
19. "If any Sheriff, or deputy Sheriff, shall directly or indirectly, so interfere in the elections of senators or Delegates, as to shew partiality for any of the candidates, he shall forfeit and pay the sum of two hundred pounds . . . and moreover be deprived of his right of voting for two years." Virginia Law 1784, "An Act Altering the Time of the Annual Meeting of the General Assembly, and for other Purposes," chap. 20, sessions acts. See also Richard R. Beeman, *The Varieties of Political Experience in Eighteenth-Century America* (Philadelphia: University of Pennsylvania Press, 2004); Charles S. Sydnor, *Gentlemen Freeholders: Political Practices in Washington's Virginia* (Chapel Hill: University of North Carolina, 1952).
20. See St. George Tucker, *Blackstone's Commentaries: With Notes of Reference, to the Constitution and Laws, of the Federal Government of the United States; and of the Commonwealth of Virginia*, vol. 1 (Philadelphia: W.Y. Birch and A. Small, 1803), 179n62 (hereafter Tucker, Blackstone's Commentaries).
21. See Chapter 1 for further discussion of this disputed election, including Madison's role in it.
22. While regretting the Founders' oversight, we can be sympathetic to the circumstances that caused it. For a more severe critique, see Bruce Ackerman, *The Failure of the Founding Fathers* (Cambridge, MA: Harvard University Press, 2005).
23. *Boston University Law Journal* recently held an entire symposium devoted to this topic: see editors' foreword, "America's Political Dysfunction: Constitutional Connections,

Causes, and Cures" (Symposium), *Boston University Law Review* 94 (May 2014): 575. Rick Pildes has also delivered a characteristically insightful analysis of the ills that currently beset America's political system. See Richard Pildes, "Romanticing Democracy, Political Fragmentation, and the Decline of American Government," *Yale Law Journal* 124 (2014): 804.

24. For more on learning lessons from abroad in electoral dispute cases see Steven F. Huefner, "What Can the United States Learn From Abroad About Resolving Disputed Elections?," *New York University Journal of Legislation and Public Policy* 13 (2010): 523.
25. See Daniel P. Tokaji, "America's Top Model: The Wisconsin Government Accountability Board," *Election Law Journal* 3 (2013): 583; Tokaji, "The Future of Election Reform: From Rules to Institutions," *Yale Law and Policy Review* 28 (2009): 139 (describing Australia as exemplary); Morris, *Parliamentary Elections,* 88 (describing Britain's current Election Court for disputed seats in Parliament).
26. See Government of India, *The Constitution of India,* Art. 54 (Dec. 1, 2011) (English Consolidated Version): "The President shall be elected by the members of an electoral college consisting of—(a) the elected members of both Houses of Parliament; and (b) the elected members of the Legislative Assemblies of the States."
27. Despite their greater commitment to impartial election administration than the United States, the other Anglo-inheritance nations have not escaped the difficulties inherent in determining a fair count when violations of vote-casting rules occur at polling places. For example, the Supreme Court of Canada recently split 4–3 over whether to count ballots affected by administrative errors. The majority ruled in favor of counting them, in order to prevent the disenfranchisement of voters because of administrative mistakes, whereas the three dissenters would have strictly enforced the rules governing the voting process. See Opitz v. Wrzesnewskyj, [2012] S.C. C. 55 (Can.). This sharp division replicates a similar debate that has existed among American judges since the eighteenth century, as this book shall show. For an analysis of the judicial division on Canada concerning conceptions of democracy, see Yasmin Dawood, "Democracy and Dissent: Reconsidering the Judicial Review of the Political Sphere," *Supreme Court Law Review* 63 (2d) (2013): 59.
28. In this respect, resolving disputed elections resembles the decennial task of redistricting legislatures: it would better serve the public interest if there were an impartial institution to draw the new legislative districts, but rarely are political parties willing to embrace an impartial institution even knowing that it would protect them from gerrymanders perpetrated by the other side; the desire to have the chance to perpetrate one's own gerrymander on one's political enemies is strong enough to outweigh the incentive to accept a neutral compromise. In the arena of redistricting, however, there has been some recent progress toward the creation of neutral commissions (as, for example, in California), whereas the task of resolving dispute elections has been even more resistant to such institutional reform.
29. See Huefner, "What Can the United States Learn," 531–33; Tim Padgett and Mishelle Mitchell, "Dodging a Bullet in Costa Rica," *Time,* Mar. 8, 2006, available at http://content.time.com/time/world/article/0,8599,1170929,00.html.
30. Ana Paula Ambrosi, Alex M. Saragoza, and Silvia D. Zárate, eds., *Mexico Today: An Encyclopedia of Life in the Republic* (Santa Barbara: ABC-CLIO, 2012), 262.
31. America certainly would not wish to emulate the experience of Afghanistan in its disputed presidential election of 2014. That dispute ended only after the United States brokered a constitutionally dubious power-sharing agreement between the two candidates. Nor was there any certainty that this power-sharing would work to keep the peace between potentially warring factions within Afghanistan. See Carlotta Gall, "In Afghan Election, Signs of Systemic Fraud Case Doubt on Many Votes," *New York Times,* Aug. 23, 2014; Rod Norland, "After Rancor, Afghans Agree to Share Power," *New York Times,* Sept. 21, 2014.
32. See Noëlle Lenoir, "Constitutional Council Review of Presidential Elections in France and a French Perspective on *Bush v. Gore,*" in *The Longest Night: Polemics and Perspectives on Election 2000,* eds. Arthur J. Jacobson and Michel Rosenfeld (Berkeley: University of California Press, 2002), 295–317.

Introduction

1. See George Athan Billias, *Elbridge Gerry: Founding Father and Republican Statesman* (New York: McGraw-Hill, 1976). For an excellent current discussion of American democracy as a whole, focusing on the systemic challenges associated with reforming those facets in need of reform, see Bruce E. Cain, *Democracy More or Less: America's Political Reform Quandary* (New York: Cambridge University Press, 2014).
2. The literature on campaign finance is immense, especially after *Citizens United*. For historical perspectives, see Zephyr Teachout, *Corruption in America: From Ben Franklin's Snuffbox to Citizens United* (Cambridge, MA: Harvard University Press, 2014); Robert E. Mutch, *Buying the Vote: A History of Campaign Finance Reform* (New York: Oxford University Press, 2014); Robert C. Post, *Citizens Divided: Campaign Finance Reform and the Constitution* (Cambridge, MA: Harvard University Press, 2014), Chapter 1. See also Richard L. Hasen, *Plutocrats United: Campaign Money, the Supreme Court, and the Distortion of American Politics* (New Haven, CT: Yale University Press, forthcoming 2016).
3. Recent books addressing the current state of efforts to improve America's ballot-casting processes include Barry C. Burden and Charles Stewart III, eds., *The Measure of American Elections* (New York: Cambridge University Press, 2014); R. Michael Alvarez and Bernard Grofman, eds., *Election Administration in the United States: The State of Reform after* Bush v. Gore (New York: Cambridge University Press, 2014); Martha Kropf and David Kimball, *Helping America Vote: The Limits of Election Reform* (New York: Routledge, 2012). Improving polling place operations was also the focus of the Presidential Commission on Election Administration (PCEA), which in January 2014 released a 71-page report on the topic. See Nathaniel Persily (PCEA's senior research director) et al., *The American Voting Experience: Report and Recommendations of the Presidential Commission on Election Administration* (Washington, DC: PCEA, 2014).
4. Alexander Keyssar, *The Right to Vote: The Contested History of Democracy in the United States*, rev. ed (New York: Basic Books, 2009) is the canonical text on the changing scope of the franchise in American history. Keyssar's book, moreover, is a model for this one, which aims to provide for the specific topic of vote-counting disputes the kind of Founding-to-present account that *The Right to Vote* gives to rules governing the extension of the suffrage itself.
5. This important point is the theme of Tracy Campbell's valuable study *Deliver the Vote: A History of Election Fraud, an American Political Tradition—1742–2004* (New York: Carroll & Graf, 2005).
6. For a contemporary analysis of the difficult remedial issues that arise from breaches in vote-casting procedures, see Steven F. Huefner, "Remedying Election Wrongs," *Harvard Journal on Legislation* 44 (2007): 265.
7. For a detailed exploration of the value and design of an impartial adjudicatory tribunal for ballot-counting disputes, see Joshua A. Douglas, "Procedural Fairness in Election Contests," *Indiana Law Review* 88 (2013): 1.
8. Dennis Thompson expresses this view: "An election is legitimate to the extent that it is conducted in accordance with rules established through the appropriate legal and political process of a society." He adds: "This is not a high standard." Dennis F. Thompson, *Just Elections: Creating a Fair Electoral Process in the United States* (Chicago: University of Chicago Press, 2002), 2–3.
9. Pippa Norris offers a more robust conception of legitimacy, one tied to the idea of electoral integrity. While an election need not be perfectly fair to be legitimate in the eyes of the public, it must satisfy a threshold of integrity or else it will lack legitimacy (in other words, acceptability), and that is true even if it is conducted in accordance with the rules that exist in society at time. The rules themselves, in other words, may lack integrity. See Pippa Norris, *Why Electoral Integrity Matters* (New York: Cambridge University Press, 2014).
10. This book, like so many others, owes an intellectual debt to the work of Richard Hofstadter, especially *The Idea of a Party System: The Rise of Legitimate Opposition in the United States, 1780–1840* (Berkeley: University of California Press, 1969).
11. See J. Morgan Kousser, *Shaping of Southern Politics: Suffrage Restriction and the Establishment of the One-Party South, 1880–1910* (New Haven, CT: Yale University

Press, 1974); V. O. Key, *Southern Politics in State and Nation* (New York: Knopf, 1949); see also Matthew D. Lassiter and Joseph Crespino, *The Myth of Southern Exceptionalism* (New York: Oxford University Press, 2010).

12. Alex Keyssar's monumental study of America's regulation of the franchise chronicles "the spread of democratic values in the first half of the nineteenth century, and . . . a renewed commitment to them in the mid-twentieth century." Keyssar, *The Right to Vote*, 296.
13. Bush v. Gore, 531 U.S. 98 (2000).
14. On the evolution of elected state courts, see Jed Handelsman Shugerman, *The People's Court: Pursuing Judicial Independence in America* (Cambridge, MA: Harvard University Press, 2012).
15. Taylor v. Beckham, 178 U.S. 548 (1900).
16. Plessy v. Ferguson, 163 U.S. 537 (1896).
17. Brown v. Board of Education, 347 U.S. 483 (1954).
18. The institutional superiority of the federal judiciary in protecting voting rights has been a major theme of my colleague Dan Tokaji's scholarship. See, e.g., Daniel Tokaji and Owen Wolfe, "*Baker, Bush,* and Ballot Boards: The Federalization of Election Administration," *Case Western Reserve Law Review* 62 (2012): 969.
19. One of Keyssar's main points is that the expansion of the franchise, far from being uniformly forward-moving, has been subjected to considerable backsliding over the course of US history. See Keyssar, *The Right to Vote*, xxi–xxiii.
20. "Counted out" is the phrase used to convey the manipulation of the process to achieve the desired result. Or, as Joseph Stalin purportedly said, "it does not matter who votes; all that matters is who counts the votes." Del Dickson, *The People's Government: An Introduction to Democracy* (New York: Cambridge University Press, 2014), 173. Tom Stoppard put the point in his play *Jumpers*: "It's not the voting that's democracy. It's the counting." Both versions were quoted by the two dissenting opinions in the Minnesota Supreme Court's first, and controversial, foray into the state's disputed 2008 US Senate election. Coleman v. Ritchie, 758 N.W.2d 306, 309 (Minn. 2008) (Page, J., dissenting) (quoting Stalin); ibid., 311 (Anderson, Paul H., J., dissenting) (quoting Stoppard).

Chapter 1

1. On the intellectual foundations of the new American constitutions, state and federal, see Gordon S. Wood, *The Creation of the American Republic, 1776–1787* (Chapel Hill, NC: University of North Carolina Press, 1969). Although discussing the franchise and some particular rules to protect the ballot-casting process (ibid., 169–70), that book does not examine the specific issue of ballot-counting disputes. Likewise, Keyssar limits his discussion of the Founding era, as he does for the rest of his superlative study, to the rules governing the eligibility to cast ballots. Alexander Keyssar, *The Right to Vote: The Contested History of Democracy in the United States*, rev. ed (New York: Basic Books, 2009); see also Alec C. Ewald, *The Way We Vote: The Local Dimension of American Suffrage* (Nashville, TN: Vanderbilt University Press, 2009), 24–26 (describing voting practices in the Founding Era, but not the processes for resolving disputed elections); Willi Paul Adams, *The First American Constitutions: Republican Ideology and the Making of State Constitutions in the Revolutionary Era* (Chapel Hill: University of North Carolina Press, 1980).
2. See Mary Patterson Clarke, *Parliamentary Privilege in the American Colonies* (New Haven, CT: Yale University Press, 1943), 145. "It is clear, then, that throughout British America, with varying degrees of promptness, the colonies, one by one, assumed the right of deciding in assembly their own election contests." Ibid., 145; see also Cortlandt F. Bishop, *History of Elections in the American Colonies* (New York: Columbia College, 1893), 187–88.
3. Clarke, *Parliamentary Privilege*, 149.
4. Philip S. Klein and Ari A. Hoogenboom, *A History of Pennsylvania*, 2nd ed. (University Park: Pennsylvania State University Press, 1980), 92; Robert L. Brunhouse, *Counter-Revolution in Pennsylvania, 1776–1790* (Harrisburg: Pennsylvania Historical Commission, 1942), 114. Even before this major 1781 dispute arose, there had been some disputes over the counting of ballots for seats in the new legislature created by Pennsylvania's constitution of 1776. See ibid., 8, 54–55. In fact, the organization of the

first legislature under the new constitution was a tumultuous affair because of disputes over the qualifications of those elected, but those disputes tended to concern eligibility requirements and not the counting of votes. Ibid., 21–22.

5. Harry Marlin Tinkcom, *The Republicans and Federalists in Pennsylvania, 1790–1801: A Study in National Stimulus and Local Response* (Harrisburg: Pennsylvania Historical and Museum Commission, 1950), 4.
6. For further information on Pennsylvania's egalitarian constitution of 1776 and the intense fight over its adoption, as well as the turbulence of politics in Pennsylvania during the Founding period between 1776 and 1790, see J. Paul Selsam, *The Pennsylvania Constitution of 1776: A Study in Revolutionary Democracy* (Philadelphia: University of Pennsylvania Press, 1936); see also E. Bruce Thomas, "Political Tendencies in Pennsylvania, 1783–1794" (PhD diss., Temple University, 1938).
7. See James Grant Wilson, "Colonel John Bayard (1738–1807) and the Bayard Family of America: The Anniversary Address Before the New York Genealogical and Biographical Society, February 27, 1885," *New York Genealogical and Biographical Record* 16, no. 1 (April 1885).
8. For a bibliographical account of John Dickinson's political life, see generally Milton E. Flower, *John Dickinson: Conservative Revolutionary* (Charlottesville: University Press of Virginia, 1983).
9. See Kenneth R. Rossman, *Thomas Mifflin and the Politics of the American Revolution* (Chapel Hill: University of North Carolina Press, 1952).
10. Brunhouse, *Counter-Revolution in Pennsylvania*, 262n53.
11. *Minutes of the Supreme Executive Council of Pennsylvania: From Its Organization to the Termination of the Revolution*, vol. XIII (Harrisburg: Theo Penn & Co, 1853), 191–92 (hereafter *Minutes*, vol. XIII).
12. Brunhouse, *Counter-Revolution in Pennsylvania*, 105–06. See also *Minutes*, vol. XIII, 188–90.
13. Specifically, two days before the election, Lacey attended a meeting of officers at his headquarters organized by his aide-de-camp. At the meeting, the officers agreed which candidates to support at this election, which included several Assembly seats as well as the disputed seat on the Supreme Executive Council. After the meeting, Lacey's aide-de-camp and others prepared tickets with the names of the designated candidates, with the plan that these tickets would be distributed to the soldiers at the polling places for them to use as their ballots. On Election Day, the officers marched their soldiers to the polls, gave them these tickets, and "with their swords drawn" would not let them leave until these ballots had been cast. *Minutes*, vol. XIII, 190. The petition particularly complained that the soldiers had no opportunity for deliberating, or "consulting with their friends," about which candidates to support—or, in general, for "acting and judging like freemen, as they ought to have done." Ibid.
14. *Minutes*, vol. XIII, 191.
15. Ibid., 192. The petition even alleged that this same officer, Colonel Anthony Bitting, when ordering his men to cast the tickets given to them, "said every man who refused was a tory and he would whip them." Ibid., 191. Later, however, the lawyers for the petitioners would withdraw this particular allegation during the Council's deliberations on the petition.
16. *Minutes*, vol. XIII, 191.
17. Ibid., 118, 188, 192, 226.
18. *Minutes*, vol. XIII, 188 (Council date: Feb. 11, 1782).
19. See Alyn Brodsky, *Benjamin Rush: Patriot and Physician* (New York: St. Martin's, 2004).
20. See Louis Richards, "Hon. Jacob Rush, of the Pennsylvania Judiciary," *Pennsylvania Magazine of History and Biography* 39, no. 1 (1915): 53–68.
21. See Esther Ann McFarland and Mickey Herr, *William Lewis, Esquire: Enlightened Statesman, Profound Lawyer, and Useful Citizen* (Darby, PA: Diane, 2012).
22. See Edwid F. Halfield, Jonathan Dickinson Sergeant, *Pennsylvania Magazine of History and Biography* 3, no. 4 (1878): 438–42.

23. See Lawrence Henry Gipson, *Jared Ingersoll; A Study of American Loyalism in Relation to British Colonial Government* (New Haven, CT: Yale University Press, 1920).
24. Brunhouse, *Counter-Revolution in Pennsylvania* at 106–07. Based on information provided by Brunhouse (page numbers in parentheses), the following is the partisan identification of the Council's members:

1.	William Moore, Pres.	City of Philadelphia	moderate Radical (104)
2.	John Bayard	County of Philadelphia	Radical (105)
3.	Dr. Joseph Gardner	Chester	Radical (165)
4.	Gen. John Lacey Jr.	Bucks	Radical (105)
5.	James Cunningham	Lancaster	
6.	James Ewing	York	mild Radical (107)
7.	John Byers	Cumberland	mild Radical (107)
8.	Sebastian Levan	Berks	
9.	John Van Campen	Northampton	mild Radical (107)
10.	John Piper	Bedford	Radical (107)
11.	James Potter, VP	Northumberland	Radical (105)
12.	Christopher Hayes	Westmoreland	
13.	Dorsey Pentecost	Washington	mild Radical (107)

25. Brunhouse, *Counter-Revolution in Pennsylvania*, 106–107; *Minutes*, vol. XIII, 221 (Council date: Mar. 11, 1782).
26. *Minutes*, vol. XIII, 224–25 (Council Date: Mar. 12).
27. Ibid., 226.
28. They viewed these "facts" as "incontestible":

    > It is in clear proof that the tickets were formed by the officers without the consent of the privates; . . . that the militia in general had no opportunity of consulting with their friends, or such of them as they might have chosen to consult, with regard to the propriety or impropriety of the tickets put into their hands; that the greatest part of the militia who voted at the election voted under the orders of General Lacey.

    Ibid., 225.
29. Ibid., 226. "All elections, whether by the people or in general assembly, shall be by ballot, free and voluntary" was the exact language of the constitution, § 32. Constitution of Pennsylvania (1776).
30. The moderates elaborated upon their robust conception of electoral freedom:

    > When we speak of a free election, if we wish to apply a constitutional and legal sense to the epithet, we mean to comprehend under it, not only a freedom from force, *but also a freedom from any undue influence whatever.* Even the request of a man in power, tho' made in the most humble manner, must always imply a threat, if denied; a promise, if complied with. This will naturally have great influence upon elections.

    Ibid., 226–27 (emphasis added). They then "applied" this principle "to the circumstances proved to have attended the formation, the writing, and the distribution of the tickets," as well as "to the manner of giving in the tickets" (as the casting of ballots). The conclusion "undeniably" followed "that the election was not free." Ibid., 227.

The moderates went even further in discussing the constitutional right to a secret ballot:

> Of such essential importance is the freedom of elections in every free government, that a positive regulation calculated for protecting and securing it, becomes of indispensible obligation; such is the regulation in the Constitution for voting by ballot. The true reason of it is, as we conceive, *to secure elections from undue influence.*

Ibid. (emphasis added). Moreover, they exhibited a sophisticated understanding of this right to a secret ballot. They knew it was just as important to electoral freedom that a citizen be permitted to decline to vote for an disfavored candidate as to be able to cast a ballot for a favored one: "It is directed that the elector shall vote by ballot, that he may have the power of concealing, if he chooses to conceal, from all the world, not only the persons for whom he votes, but those also for whom he doth not vote." Ibid. It was on this specific point that the moderates thought the conduct of Lacey and his officers most objectionable:

> A militia man had no opportunity of altering the tickets put into his hand, but in the presence of his fellow soldiers, and probably of his officers too. By taking the pen or paper into his hand, he was obliged to disclose that he meant either to alter or to totally reject the ticket . . . recommended to him by military superiority. Consequently to disclose, either in whole or in part, for whom he did not vote. This shews that this election cannot, according to the true reason and spirit of the regulation [in the Constitution], be called an election by ballot.

Ibid. An election without a secret ballot, they emphatically concluded, is not a "free" election "in the sense and degree intended by the Constitution." Ibid.

31. Chief Justice McKean had been a Conservative previously, but he had since switched sides. Brunhouse, *Counter-Revolution in Pennsylvania,* 35. Bryan, no moderate, was a leader of the Radicals. Ibid., 51–52.
32. *Minutes,* vol. XIII, 230.
33. Ibid. (emphasis added).
34. Ibid.
35. Ibid., 229–30.
36. Ibid., 230. As for other allegations of misconduct by the military officers, the two Supreme Court judges punted because they had not heard the evidence in support of them. If the overall claim of the petition was that "the private men in the militia were prevented from 'acting and judging like freemen,'" then these two judges asked:

> How many were thus prevented? By whom were they prevented? In what manner were they prevented? Were they restrained from voting or compelled to vote through violence or fear? Without these answered, no opinion can be given to this part of the [petition].

Ibid., 229. In this way, their opinion left the heart of the matter unaddressed.

37. Ibid., 231.
38. Ibid.
39. Ibid., 225. The most thorough historical examination of this period in Pennsylvania history concludes: "From the evidence available it appears that the election was very irregular." Brunhouse, *Counter-Revolution in Pennsylvania,* 107.
40. *Minutes,* vol. XIII, 228, 231; Brunhouse, *Counter-Revolution in Pennsylvania,* 107.
41. Charles Pettit to Nathaniel Greene, February 14, 1782, in *Letters of Nathaniel Greene,* ed. Dennis M. Conrad, vol. X (Chapel Hill: University of North Carolina Press, 1998), 365–66, 514.
42. Ibid., 366.
43. U.S. Const., art. I, § 5, cl. 1; Josh Chafetz, *Democracy's Privileged Few: Legislative Privilege and Democratic Norms in the British and American Constitutions* (New Haven, CT: Yale University, 2007), 287.
44. See Gordon Wood, "Experiment in Republicanism," chap. 1 in *Empire of Liberty: A History of the Early Republic, 1789–1815* (Oxford: Oxford University Press, 2009), 5–52. The

Framers of the Constitution were trusting that the overall design of the document would keep partisanship and political self-interest in check. They hoped for sufficient virtue in the men who would be sent to Congress to prevent undue abuses of this unchecked power. It is important to understand, as Gordon Wood has explained, that the Founders did *not* think that separation of powers, and the architecture of the Constitution more generally, would enable the system to work to secure the public interest even if the politicians were entirely lacking in virtue (meaning that politicians were entirely self-serving without regard to the public interest). The key point was that a well-designed Constitution would enable the system to economize on the relatively meager, but not entirely nonexistent, degree of virtue that could be expected of politicians (men not being angels, as Madison put it in *Federalist 51*). But like even a fuel-efficient engine without any gas at all, the constitutional machinery of checks and balances would not work if the politicians were entirely lacking in virtue. As Gordon Wood has consistently maintained, "in the 1780s James Madison had his doubts about th[e] moral capacity of the people stretched to the limit, but even he admitted that ordinary people had to have sufficient 'virtue and intelligence to select men of virtue and wisdom' or 'no theoretical checks, no form of government, can render us secure.'" Ibid, 9; see also Wood, *Creation of the American Republic*, 534. I am indebted to Bruce Cain for emphasizing this important point in our discussions. See also Bruce E. Cain, *Democracy More or Less: America's Political Reform Quandry* (New York: Cambridge University Press, 2015).

45. R. B. Bernstein, "Parliamentary Principles, American Realities: The Continental Confederation Congresses, 1774–89," in *Inventing Congress: Origins and Establishment of the First Federal Congress*, eds. Kenneth R. Bowling and Donald R. Kennon (Athens: Ohio University Press, 1999), 123. The use of the terms "Federalists" and "Antifederalists" here refers to the two sides to the debate over the ratification of the new Constitution. See Pauline Meier, *Ratification: The People Debate the Constitution, 1787–1788* (New York: Simon & Schuster, 2010), xiv–xv, 92–95 (discussing the limits of the conventional "Antifederalist" term). At the risk of some confusion, the term "Federalist" also describes one of the two political parties that emerged in the United States, both nationally and regionally, by 1792. But before this political party achieved its full development in the 1790s as one of the two contenders of America's "first party system," scholars sometimes refer to the emerging entity as the "proto-Federalists." Adding to the potential confusion is the fact that there is considerable overlap between the individuals who were the Federalists during the ratification debate and the proto-Federalists as they coalesced into the Federalist party of the 1790s. Richard Hofstader provides an excellent guide by which to navigate through these transitions as America's two-party politics begins to take root. Richard Hofstadter, *The Idea of a Party System: The Rise of Legitimate Opposition in the United States, 1780–1840* (Berkeley: University of California Press, 1969). See also Wood, *Empire of Liberty*; Stanley Elkins and Eric McKitrick, "The Emergence of Partisan Politics: The 'Republican Interest,'" chap. VII in *The Age of Federalism: The Early American Republic, 1788–1800* (New York: Oxford University Press, 1993), 257–302; John F. Hoadley, *The Origins of American Political Parties, 1789–1803* (Lexington: University Press of Kentucky, 1986); William Nisbet Chambers, *The First Party System: Federalists and Republicans* (New York: Wiley, 1972).

46. Merrill Jensen and Robert A. Becker, eds., *The Documentary History of the First Federal Elections, 1788–1790*, vol. I (Madison: University of Wisconsin Press, 1976), x–xi; see also Ralph Louis Ketchham, *James Madison: A Biography* (Charlottesville: University of Virginia Press, 1971), 275. But see Thomas Rogers Hunder, "The First Gerrymander? Patrick Henry, James Monroe, and Virginia's 1788 Congressional Districting," *Early American Studies* 9, no. 3 (Fall 2011): 781–820 (arguing that Henry did not distort the boundaries by drawing artificially strange shapes, but acknowledging the evidence that Henry did choose boundaries in an effort to defeat Madison); Irving Brant, *James Madison: Father of the Constitution, 1787–1800* (Indianapolis: Bobbs-Merrill, 1950), 238 (while recognizing that the district "was not misshapen," explaining that it "was fashioned to control the election" and thus "took the form of what should have become known as the Henrymander instead of the Gerrymander").

47. See Richard P. McCormick, "New Jersey's First Congressional Election, 1789: A Case Study of Political Skulduggery," *William & Mary Quarterly* 6, no. 2 (April 1949); see also Richard P. McCormick, *Experiment in Independence: New Jersey in the Critical Period, 1781–1789* (New Brunswick, NJ: Rutgers University Press, 1950); Gordon DenBoer, Lucy Trumbell Brown, and Charles D. Hagermann, ed., "The Elections in New Jersey," chap. XII in *The Documentary History of the First Federal Elections, 1788–1790*, vol. III (Madison: University of Wisconsin Press, 1986), 1–189.
48. See McCormick "New Jersey's First Congressional Election, 1789," 239–40.
49. Ibid., 239, 245. See also *First Federal Elections*, vol. III, 82–106 (in particular, p. 91).
50. DenBoer, *First Federal Elections*, vol. III, 106 (text of proclamation by Governor William Livingston, March 19, 1989).
51. Linda Grant De Pauw, ed., *Documentary History of the First Federal Congress of the United States of America*, vol. III (Baltimore: Johns Hopkins University Press, 1977), 26 (text of House journal from Saturday, April 18, 1789); see ibid., 3–7, 19–20 (March 5, 1789–April 2, 1789 & April 13, 1789).
52. DenBoer, *First Federal Elections*, vol. III, 149.
53. Ibid., 106.
54. Ibid., 107.
55. Ibid. Madison was not alone in recognizing the significance of this first brewing dispute over ballot-counting in a congressional election. On March 24, Alexander White, his fellow member of Virginia's delegation to the House, wrote to another Virginian back home: "It is somewhat remarkable that Circumstances should so soon arise, to prove the propriety of that part of the Constitution which gives to Congress the power of regulating Elections." White was glad that the new federal House had this power; otherwise, the "state faction" exhibited in New Jersey to "keep open the polls in some counties" showed "that without it, the general government might, and probably would be, done away by the machinations of wicked men in the particular States." (This sentiment, expressed in the *Virginia Gazette* on the day the House attained its quorum, was undoubtedly White's, given its echo of his letter of a few days earlier.) Ibid., 431n1. White was expressing the common Federalist view, advanced by Madison among others, that the structure of the new federal Constitution would cause more virtuous conduct among the politicians of the federal government than in the states, and White was applying that idea specifically to ballot-counting disputes. A question to consider is whether the House, throughout American history, has been able to live up to White's expectations in this regard. (The so-called Bloody Eighth episode arising from the 1984 congressional elections, as discussed in Chapter 10, would be one example to the contrary.)
56. The full letter is contained in Charles F. Hobson et al., eds., *The Papers of James Madison*, vol. 12 (Charlottesville: University Press of Virginia, 1979), 22–23.
57. The ratification debate was particularly contentious—and consequential—in New York. See Meier, *Ratification*, 320–400 (in particular: "On to Poughkeepsie," chap. 11; "The New York Convention I," chap. 12; and "The New York Convention II," chap. 13).
58. DenBoer, *First Federal Elections*, vol. III, 143 (letter from Erkuries Beatty to Josiah Harmar, March 31, 1789).
59. Ibid., 138–39 (text of *Brunswick Gazette*, Mar. 24).
60. McCormick, *Experiment at Independence*, 302.
61. DenBoer, *First Federal Elections*, vol. III, 143 (Alexander Hamilton to Jonathan Dayton, March 26, 1789).
62. Ibid., 144 (Abraham Clark to Jonathan Dayton, March 1789).
63. De Pauw, *First Federal Congress*, vol. III, 69 (House Journal: May 21, 1789). Digests of the first contested elections in the US House of Representatives are contained in M. St. Clair Clarke and David Hall, *Cases of Contested Elections in Congress, 1789–1834* (Washington, DC: Gales & Seaton, 1834); Chester H. Rowell, *A Historical and Legal Digest of All the Contested Election Cases in the [US] House of Representatives from the First to the Fifty-Sixth Congress, 1789–1901* (Westport, CT: Greenwood Press, 1976). See also Jeffrey A. Jenkins, "Partisanship and Contested Election Cases in the House of Representatives, 1789–2002," *Studies in American Political Development* 18, no. 2 (2004): 112–35.

64. DenBoer, *First Federal Elections*, vol. III, 153, 156–57. One must remember that given the nature of transportation in the late eighteenth century, the idea that Congress (based in Manhattan) might conduct its own investigation of an election in a far-flung state was even more daunting than the idea, in the twenty-first century that the United Nations (also based in Manhattan) might investigate allegations of electoral irregularities in Africa or Asia.
65. Ibid., 158, 161–62 (reprinting two different accounts of the House debate).
66. Ibid., 162–64 (*Daily Advertiser*: July 31, 1789).
67. "If there was any limitation, the Time was past" as of March 18, and "if there was none, the Time was not come." Ibid., 164–65.
68. There is some suggestion in the committee's report that the governor and his council had received returns from Essex in their first meeting on March 3. Ibid., 167. But this assertion is contradicted by the rest of the available record. Regrettably, many original documents are missing, presumably destroyed during the fire at the Capitol set by British troops during the War of 1812. See Steve Vogel, *Through the Perilous Fight: Six Weeks That Saved the Nation* (New York: Random House, 2013).
69. DenBoer, *First Federal Elections*, vol. III, 170.
70. The veil-of-ignorance idea is the foundation of John Rawls's deservedly famous *A Theory of Justice* (Cambridge, MA: Belknap Press of Harvard University Press, 1971).
71. The usual spelling is "Laurence," although occasionally it appears as "Lawrence."
72. DenBoer, *First Federal Elections*, vol. III, 170–71.
73. Ibid., 172–73.
74. Ibid., 174 (Elias Boudinot to Elisha Boudinot, September 2, 1789).
75. Ibid. (Fisher Ames to George Richards Minot, September 3, 1789) (emphasis in original).
76. Ibid.
77. 3 Annals of Cong. 479 (March 21, 1792).
78. See George R. Lamplugh, *Politics on the Periphery: Factions and Parties in Georgia, 1783–1806* (Cranbury, NJ: University of Delaware Press, 1986), 91–95; Lisle A. Rose, *Prologue to Democracy: Federalists in the South, 1789–1800* (Lexington: University of Kentucky Press, 1968), 60–68; see also William Omer Foster Sr., *James Jackson: Duelist and Militant Statesman, 1757–1806* (Athens: University of Georgia Press, 1960); Harry Emerson Wildes, *Anthony Wayne: Trouble Shooter of the American Revolution* (New York: Harcourt Brace, 1941).
79. Foster, *James Jackson*, 92–93: "The first official report in 1791 had given Wayne 266 and Jackson 245."
80. 3 Annals of Cong. 464–65 (March 13, 1792).
81. Ibid., 464.
82. Ibid., 467.
83. Ibid.
84. Ibid., 460, 462.
85. Ibid., 459.
86. *Proceedings in the House of Representatives of the United States of America Respecting the Contested Election for the Eastern District of Georgia* (Philadelphia: Parry Hall, 1792), 49 (hereafter *Proceedings for E. D. of Georgia*).
87. Ibid., 50.
88. 3 Annals of Cong. 472 (March 16, 1792).
89. "Jackson already had become a prominent critic of national policy." Rose, *Prologue to Democracy*, 60.
90. This table of the congressional vote (minus the Speaker's vote) may help:

Proto-Party	**Seat Jackson**	**Keep Seat Vacant**	**Total**
Federalist (pro-admin)	6	27	33
Jeffersonian (anti-admin)	23	2	25
Total	29	29	58

Kenneth C. Martis, *The Historical Atlas of Political Parties in the United States Congress, 1789–1989* (New York: MacMillan, 1989), 71; *Proceedings for E. D. of Georgia*, 58–59 (reporting the yeas and nays); compare with 3 Annals of Cong. 479 (March 21, 1792) (reporting the yeas and nays but omitting the name of Israel Smith, an anti-administration member from Vermont). See also Rose, *Prologue to Democracy*, 67–68 (similarly analyzes the partisan nature of this vote).

91. The Speaker of the House from Oct 24, 1791, until March 3, 1793, was Jonathan Trumbull and was pro-administration. Martis, *Historical Atlas*, 71; Charlie Rose, chairman, *History of the United States House of Representatives, 1789–1994* (Washington, DC: Government Printing Office, 1994), 401 (Appendix Table A-1).
92. 3 Annals of Cong. 476 (March 20, 1792).
93. Ibid., 478.
94. *Proceedings for E. D. of Georgia*, 52.
95. Robert A. Rutland et al., eds., *The Papers of James Madison*, vol. 14 (Charlottesville: University Press of Virginia, 1983), 254–56.
96. 3 Annals of Cong. 476–77 (March 20, 1792).
97. *Proceedings for E. D. of Georgia*, 57.
98. The state had an unusual law: it required voters to cast ballots having, not one, but two names of preferred candidates for this single seat. In one county, however, 77 ballots contained only one candidate's name. The local election officials counted these ballots, despite the state statute, and these disputed ballots made the difference in John Patten's margin of victory. The House, however, agreed with its election committee's report that these ballots were unlawful and should not have been counted. Since removing these ballots reversed the result, the House unseated Patten and awarded the election to Henry Latimer, Patten's opponent. (Patten is sometimes spelled Patton.) See, e.g., M. St. Clair Clarke and David Hall, *Cases of Contested Elections in Congress, 1789–1834* (Washington, DC: Gales & Seaton, 1834), 69.
99. 4 Annals of Cong. 454 (Feb. 14, 1794).
100. Martis, *Historical Atlas*, 24. In this case, the opposing position was not to keep the seat vacant, but instead to award the seat to the certified winner, who was also anti-administration.
101. See Hofstadter, *The Idea of a Party System*, 80–86; see also Wood, *Empire of Liberty*, 161–62.
102. 4 Annals of Cong. 454 (Feb. 14, 1794) (testimony of John Page, representative from Virginia).
103. Clarke and Hall, *Contested Elections*, 78–84. The illustrious historian Edmund S. Morgan discussed this case in his book *Inventing the People: The Rise of Popular Sovereignty in England and America* (New York: Norton, 1988), 186–89. According to Morgan, "in none of these eighteenth-century elections . . . did the contest depend much on principle." Ibid., 189.
104. Thomas A. Mason, Jeanne K. Sisson, and Robert A. Rutland, eds., *The Papers of James Madison*, vol. 15 (Charlottesville: University Press of Virginia, 1985), 125 (letter from Abram Trigg to James Madison, Oct. 1, 1793). Trigg also complained that the polls had been kept open an extra day in a pro-Preston part of the district but not in parts favorable to him. This secondary allegation was similar to the New Jersey case, and since it had not been successful there, was not the main basis for challenging this Virginia election in the House.
105. 4 Annals of Cong. 599 (April 17, 1794). In addition, "three soldiers stood at the door of the court-house, and refused to admit a voter because he declared that he would vote for the petitioner." Ibid. A melee ensued because "many of the country people were dissatisfied with the conduct of the soldiers." Ibid. But the damage had been done, according to the committee report.
106. Ibid.
107. One congressman, Thomas Scott of Pennsylvania (another proto-Federalist), "saw no harm in" the military presence at the polls: "They [the soldiers] had a right to be there, for they were equally entitled with other American citizens to give their votes in the choice

of a Representative." 4 Annals of Cong. 609 (April 29, 1794). Scott had not been involved in the dispute over the Supreme Executive Council seat in 1781.

108. Ibid., 612.
109. Ibid., 613. Smith himself had been subject to the very first contested election in Congress, on the ground that he had not been a citizen for the requisite number of years. He survived that challenge to his eligibility. For the case of David Ramsay v. William Smith, see Clarke and Hall, *Contested Elections*, 23–37.
110. 4 Annals of Cong. 611 (April 29, 1794).
111. Ibid., 613.
112. Ibid.
113. *Papers of James Madison*, vol. 15, 6–7 (James Madison to Thomas Jefferson, April 12, 1793).
114. Ibid., 124–25 (letter from Abram Trigg to James Madison, Oct. 1, 1793).
115. Henry L. Dawes, "The Mode of Procedure in Cases of Contested Elections," *Journal of Social Science* 2 (1870): 6–7.

Chapter 2

1. See Joseph E. Kallenbach, *The American Chief Executive: The Presidency and the Governorship* (New York: Harper & Row, 1966), 4, 11. When the federal Constitution was drafted in 1789, seven of the original thirteen states had a legislatively appointed governor, and Pennsylvania still had its Supreme Executive Council rather than a single governor at all (as we saw in Chapter 1). The seven were New Jersey, Delaware, Maryland, Virginia, North Carolina, South Carolina, and Georgia. Delaware would be the first to switch to an elected governor, in 1792. Michael J. Dubin, *United States Gubernatorial Elections, 1776–1860: The Official Results by State and County* (Jefferson, NC: McFarland, 2003), 26. Maryland would not make this move until 1838, New Jersey not until 1844, and Virginia in 1851. Ibid., 96, 158, 283. South Carolina would be the last to make the switch, after the Civil War in 1865. Ibid., 238.
2. Kallenbach, *The American Chief Executive*, 15. In New York the governor exercised this veto power as a member of the state's Council of Revision, whereas in Massachusetts "the governor alone exercised this power." Ibid., 24.
3. An election also needed to be close enough that disputing particular ballots might make a difference; however, the first few elections in both states tended to be rather uncompetitive affairs. In New York, George Clinton won the first five gubernatorial elections (held triennially), sometimes unopposed. Then, in 1792, John Jay mounted a powerful challenge on behalf of the nascent Federalist Party, thereby triggering the nation's first vote-counting dispute in a statewide race. See Dubin, *Gubernatorial Elections*, 160. Similarly, in Massachusetts, John Hancock won twelve of the first fourteen gubernatorial elections (held annually), also often unopposed, suffering only a temporary setback because of Shay's Rebellion. From 1800 to 1805, Caleb Strong had his own impressive string of five gubernatorial victories, until in 1806 the Jeffersonian Republicans thought they could defeat Strong's bid for reelection by disqualifying enough local returns that he had won. See ibid., 103–105. For the politics of Massachusetts during the Founding Period, see Ronald P. Formisano, *The Transformation of Political Culture: Massachusetts Parties, 1790s–1840s* (Oxford: Oxford University Press, 1983); Paul Goodman, *The Democratic Republicans of Massachusetts* (Cambridge, MA: Harvard University Press, 1964); James M. Banner Jr., *To the Hartford Convention: The Federalists and the Origins of Politics in Massachusetts* (New York: Knopf, 1970).
4. On Jay's leading role in drafting New York's 1776 Constitution, see Walter Stahr, *John Jay: Founding Father* (New York: Hambledon & London, 2005), 73–75; see also Frank Monaghan, *John Jay: Defender of Liberty* (New York: Bobbs-Merrill, 1935), 93–94.
5. See Ronald M. Peters Jr., *The Massachusetts Constitution of 1780: A Social Compact* (Amherst: University of Massachusetts Press, 1978), 13–14. The constitution said only that "the Secretary of the Commonwealth . . . shall lay [the returns of the gubernatorial election] before the Senate and the House of Representatives, to be by them examined;

And in the case of an election by a majority of all the votes returned, the choice shall be by them declared and published: But if no person shall have a majority of votes" then the legislature itself, by a set procedure, shall elect the governor. Ibid., 210. The constitution did not say what would happen if the House and Senate disagreed on whether a candidate received a majority of the votes returned.

The adoption of the 1780 constitution in Massachusetts might have generated its own form of a vote-counting controversy, but a serious dispute did not materialize. The constitutional convention had declared that ratification by a supermajority of towns was necessary for the constitution to take effect. As the returns came in, it appeared that support for the constitution as drafted failed to reach the specified supermajority level. Some towns had declared that they would approve the constitution only on condition that certain amendments would be made. But the convention ignored these qualifications and treated these towns as an affirmative vote in favor of the constitution for the purpose of meeting the required supermajority threshold. Because the previous attempt to adopt a constitution for the commonwealth in 1778 had been rejected by the voters, the leaders of the subsequent effort in 1780 were unwilling to accept a second defeat. Thus, they "simply declared that the draft had been accepted." Willi Paul Adams, *The First American Constitutions: Republican Ideology and the Making of the State Constitutions in the Revolutionary Era* (Chapel Hill: University of North Carolina Press, 1980), 90. Consequently, as the eminent historian Samuel Elliot Morison observed, it is debatable whether the 1780 constitution "was ever legally ratified." Samuel Elliot Morison, "Struggle Over the Adoption of the Constitution, 1780," in *Proceedings of the Massachusetts Historical Society*, vol. 50 (Cambridge, MA: Harvard University Press, 1917), 354. Nonetheless, it was quickly accepted as if it were, and its dubious method of ratification did not generate a precedent in Massachusetts on how to handle a controversy over the counting of ballots. Still, one wonders whether this willingness to cut corners on such a momentous matter as the adoption of the commonwealth's first constitution contributed to an atmosphere in which, a quarter-century later, partisan politicians in the legislature convinced themselves that they were entitled to manipulate election returns in order to win the governorship.

6. Hofstadter's Chapter 2, "A Constitution against Parties," is the canonical statement of this point. See Richard Hofstadter, "A Constitution against Parties," in *The Idea of a Party System: The Rise of Legitimate Opposition in the United States, 1780–1840* (Berkeley: University of California Press, 1969), 40–73.
7. See Hofstadter, *The Idea of a Party System*, 260–63 (discussing the early historian Jabez Hammond on the rise of political parties in New York). The Madisonian-Jeffersonian opponents to Federalists were sometimes called Democrats, Republicans, or Democratic-Republicans, but for sake of simplicity will be called Republicans in this first stage of the development of political parties under the new federal Constitution. For their role in New York, see Alfred F. Young, *The Democratic Republicans of New York: The Origins, 1763–1797* (Chapel Hill: University of North Carolina Press, 1967); see also John L. Brooke, *Columbia Rising: Civil Life on the Upper Hudson from the Revolution to the Age of Jackson* (Chapel Hill: University of North Carolina Press, 2010). I have written previously on New York's disputed election of 1792. See Edward B. Foley, "The Founders' *Bush v. Gore:* The 1792 Election Dispute and Its Continuing Relevance," *Indiana Law Review* 44 (2010): 23.
8. Robert Allen Rutland et al., eds., *Papers of James Madison*, vol. 14 (Charlottesville: University Press of Virginia, 1983), 197–98.
9. Ibid., 370–72.
10. Monaghan, *John Jay*, 325.
11. Jabez Hammond, *The History of Political Parties in the State of New York* (Albany, NY: C. Van Benthuysen, 1842), 54.
12. Monaghan, *John Jay*, 326; see also Stahr, *Jay*, 283.
13. "An Act for regulating Elections," in *Laws of the State of New York: Comprising the Constitution and the Acts of the Legislature* (New York: Thomas Greenleaf, 1792), chap. XV, § XIX. The statute provided that the polls would open on the last Tuesday in April

and stay open for no more than five days, the time of closing to be determined by each municipality's authorities. The statute referred to these local authorities as "election inspectors," requiring them to administer the election "faithfully, honestly, and impartially." Ibid., 327.

Voting at the polls was by a paper ballot "so folded or rolled up, and tied or otherwise closed as to conceal the writing thereon." The ballots were "to be put in a box . . . with a sufficient lock thereto . . . and a small hole shall be made in the lid or cover of the box, sufficient only to receive each ballot, and through which all ballots shall be put into the box." Each night the inspectors were to seal the boxes, "so as to cover the holes in the lids thereof," until used again the next day. Ibid., 322.

Upon closing of the polls, the inspectors were to package the ballots, together with the lists of voters who had cast the ballots, in a container "bound with tape and sealed in such a manner as to prevent its being opened without discovery." After signing and sealing these containers, each municipality's inspectors were to deliver them "without delay" to the sheriff of their county. Ibid.

14. Ibid., 324. Indeed, the statute specified that "immediately upon making such determination as aforesaid, all the poll books or lists and ballots or tickets for governor . . . shall be destroyed by the said joint committee."
15. Alan Taylor, *William Cooper's Town: Power and Persuasion on the Frontier of the Early American Republic* (New York: Knopf, 1995), 180.
16. No one will ever know Jay's exact margin of victory, as the canvassers immediately burned the ballots, as called for by the statute. But everyone involved believed that Otsego, a heavily pro-Federalist part of the state, would have put Jay ahead of Clinton, and modern analysis confirms that contemporaneous belief. See Young, *Democratic Republicans of New York*, 308. James Kent gave his brother a contemporaneous calculation of the relevant numbers, with this conclusion: "Mr. Jay had the majority of the votes of the people of this state. Indeed this fact is conceded by all sides. No hesitation on that ground. If all the votes had been canvassed, Jay would have been elected by a majority of at least 400." James Kent to Moss Kent Jr., June 15, 1792, in *James Kent Papers*, Library of Congress. The 1898 edited collection of Kent's papers contains only the last sentence of this passage. William Kent and James Kent, *Memoirs and Letters of James Kent* (Boston: Little, Brown, 1898), 44.

    The canvassers also voided the ballots from two other counties, but they were much smaller and, unlike Otsego, would not have made a difference to the outcome one way or the other. See Young, *Democratic Republicans in New York*, 307–308.
17. Robert Troup to Jay, New York, May 30, 1792, in *Correspondence and Public Papers of John Jay, 1782–1793*, vol. 3, ed. Henry P. Johnston (New York: G. P. Putnam's Son), 1891, 424; see also James Kent to Moss Kent Jr. June 15, 1792 ("law quibbles"); the "law quibbles" passage is omitted from the 1898 edited collection *Memoirs and Letters of James Kent*.
18. Rufus King, "Opinion to the Canvassers," in *An Impartial Statement of the Controversy, Respecting the Decision of the Late Canvassers* (New York: Thomas Greenleaf, 1792), 10. Despite its name this pamphlet was not impartial, but rather a collection put together to favor Clinton's side of the case. Nonetheless, it included King's argument on behalf of Jay.
19. Trumbull's statement is contained in *An Appendix to the Impartial Statement of the Controversy Respecting the Decision of the Late Committee of Canvassers* (New York: Childs & Swaine, 1792), 12. The pamphlet was created by Federalist supporters of Jay published in response to the misnamed *Impartial Statement* on behalf of Clinton.

    The constitution of 1776 specified that "every male inhabitant of full age . . . shall be entitled to vote" for governor if "possessed of freeholds of the value of one hundred pounds." Trumbull explained that the legislature was not entitled to enact any law that defeated this all-important constitutional right to vote. "The Legislature have undoubtedly authority to pass laws to guard this right, but not to destroy it." More specifically, the legislature may "point out the proper mode in which returns shall be made, but not to devise modes that may be impracticable." And just to be clear: "What the Legislature cannot do by direct statute, they certainly cannot do by construction and implication." Ibid.

20. Ibid. Two centuries later, Professor Richard Hasen would celebrate the subsequent development of this canon of statutory construction. See Richard L. Hasen, "The Democracy Canon," *Stanford Law Review* 62 (2009): 69.
21. *Appendix to Impartial Statement*, 12.
22. Written pseudonymously by "Plain Sense," it subsequently has been attributed to Joshua Sands, one of the four dissenters on the canvassing committee. A wide-ranging exegesis touching on Roman and British law, only to reject those "precedents" as "below the dignity of man" insofar as they deviate from "republican principles," this essay pointedly invoked the "more serious" and most recent "precedent of the corrupt election in Georgia," which required "the removal of General Wayne from his seat in Congress." The same remedy ought to apply in this case, the essay concluded. New York's legislature, "by a concurrent resolution of both houses, [should] declare what the constitution has already done, the acts of the majority of the canvassers null and void, so far as they relate to the election of governor." Joshua Sands, *The Rights of Suffrage* (Hudson, NY: Ashbel Stoddard, 1792), 3, 14–15. Doing so would be "tantamount to declaring" a "vacancy" in the governorship, and "the president pro tempore of the senate would, according to the constitution, act as governor and lieutenant governor until a new election could be had." Ibid., 19.
23. Jay's supporters in Lansingburgh, north of Albany, issued a public proclamation to deplore "the palpable prostitution of those principles of virtue, patriotism, and duty, which has been displayed by a majority of the canvassing committee, in the wonton violation of our most sacred and inestimable privileges, in arbitrarily disenfranchising whole towns and counties of their suffrages." John P. Kaminski, *George Clinton: Yeoman Politician of the New Republic* (Madison, WI: Madison House, 1993), 220. Jay's followers elsewhere rallied to the cause with similar denunciations.
24. James Kent to Moss Kent Jr., June 15, 1792, 44.
25. The fourth was Joshua Sands, who had been put on the committee as a Republican "friend of Clinton," but who soon would become a Federalist. Ibid.
26. Robert Troup to Hamilton, August 24, 1792, in *The Papers of Alexander Hamilton*, vol. XII, ed. Harold C. Syrett (New York: Columbia University Press, 1967), 272.
27. Foley, "Founders' *Bush v. Gore*," 55 (quoting Jay's papers). A similar Dutchess County group likewise condemned the state assembly for "electing a totally partisan list of canvassers, all six of whom were announced supporters of the incumbent." Kaminski, *Clinton*, 219–20.
28. Taylor, *William Cooper's Town*, 177.
29. Sarah Jay to John Jay, New York, June 10, 1792, 431–42.
30. Kaminski, *Clinton*, 213. These Clintonian canvassers complained that if they ruled "for Jay it will be ascribed to our being duped by the multiplicity of their Law opinions." Ibid. This concern seems rather weak: that they might be persuaded by the arguments of the Federalists on their merits is hardly a sign of being "duped" or improperly swayed. Ibid.
31. Ibid., 222.
32. Jefferson to James Madison, June 21, 1792, in *The Works of Thomas Jefferson*, vol. 7, ed. Paul Leicester Ford (New York: G. P. Putnam's Sons, 1904), 123–24. On the same day, Jefferson wrote to James Monroe: "To retain the Office when it is probable the majority was against him is dishonorable." Jefferson to Monroe, Philadelphia, June 23, 1792, 128.
33. Madison to Jefferson, June 29, 1792, in Rutland, *Papers of James Madison*, 331–32.
34. See, e.g., John Theodore Horton, *James Kent: A Study in Conservatism, 1763–1847* (New York: D. Appleton-Century, 1939), chap. 7. See also John H. Langbein, "Chancellor Kent and the History of Legal Literature," *Columbia Law Review* 93 (1993): 547; Judith S. Kaye, "Commentaries on Chancellor Kent," *Chicago-Kent Law Review* 74 (1993): 11.
35. James Kent to Moss Kent Jr., June 15, 1792, 44–45 (emphasis in the original handwritten letter; "a court" and "without appeal" are underlined).
36. I have kept the original spelling of "biassed," which in the handwritten manuscript appears as "biafed," where the eighteenth-century convention of a "long s" (which looks like an "f")

is used instead of a double "ss." The 1898 collection *Memoirs and Letters of James Kent* prints the phrase as "equally biassed." Kent, *Memoirs and Letters of James Kent*, 45.

37. Hammond, *History of Political Parties*, 68.
38. See, e.g., Monaghan, *John Jay*, 335–36; Monaghan titles the relevant chapter "Clinton Filches the Governorship." See also Sean Wilentz, *The Rise of American Democracy: Jefferson to Lincoln* (New York: Norton, 2005), 52 (attributing Clinton's victory to "flagrant voter fraud").
39. My account of Cooper's behavior is taken primarily from Alan Taylor's Pulitzer Prize winning *William Cooper's Town* supplemented by Hammond, *History of Political Parties in the State of New York* and Young, *Democratic Republicans in New York*, as well as the other sources from Foley, "The Founders' *Bush v. Gore.*"
40. Taylor details Cooper's specific acts of intimidation, "giv[ing] ballots to several men, taking them by the arm, and dragging them to the polls." Taylor, *William Cooper's Town*, 174 (quoting eyewitness account).
41. "Cooper's activity turned out virtually every male eligible to vote—and many who were not." Ibid., 175.
42. While the administration of the first congressional election in New Jersey had certainly been questionable, Cooper's practices were more egregious. Thomas Jefferson characterized Cooper as the "Bashaw of Otsego, furious partisan of Jay," understanding why Clinton's supporters would not trust Cooper to run a fair election in his county. Jefferson to Monroe, Philadelphia, June 23, 1792, in *The Works of Thomas Jefferson*, ed. Paul Leicester Ford, vol. 7 (New York: G. P. Putnam's Sons, 1904). Cooper's conduct, moreover, supports the thesis that tyrants manipulate elections not merely to win them, but also to send a message to their subjects of the full extent of their domination. See Alberto Simpser, *Why Governments and Parties Manipulate Elections: Theory, Practice, and Implications* (New York: Cambridge University Press, 2013).
43. Taylor, *William Cooper's Town*, 178–79.
44. "Pray detain the Commission until Smith has deputed some faithful person to deliver the box to the Secretary." Ibid., 179.
45. Ibid.
46. Taylor considers it "very unlikely that Cooper, Smith or Goes tampered with the ballots, given their confidence that Otsego had produced a near unanimity for Jay." Ibid. But he agrees that the behavior of these Federalists was inherently suspicious: "What was the messenger of a candidate for lieutenant governor doing handling the official box of ballots that would probably determine the election?" Ibid.
47. Jefferson to Madison, Philadelphia, June 21, 1792, 123.
48. "Reasons Assigned by the Majority of the Canvassers, in Vindication of their Conduct," in *Impartial Statement*, 18.
49. Here the canvassers echoed an argument that Aaron Burr had made to them (to counter, as the state's other US Senator, the Federalist argument from Rufus King). "Opinion to the Canvassers," in *Impartial Statement*, 7.
50. "Reasons Assigned," in *Impartial Statement*, 17. Although all this was enough, the majority made clear their awareness of more: "But had the question been doubtful it was attended by other circumstances which would have determined the committee against canvassing those ballots." Ibid., 19. Pointedly contrasting Otsego with other instances where technical violations of the ballot-custody rules raised "no suspicion" about "the fairness of those elections," the majority identified Otsego as exemplifying why "general principles . . . touching the freedom of elections and security against frauds . . . compelled them to reject the votes." Ibid., 20. In sum, the specifically enumerated facts, together "with other suggestions of unfair practices, rendered the conduct of the Otsego election justly liable to suspicion; and the committee was constrained to conclude that the usurpation of authority by Richard R. Smith was wanton and unnecessary, and proceeded from no motive connected with the preservation of the rights of the people, or the freedom *and purity of elections.*" Ibid., 19 (emphasis in original).
51. "Act for Regulating Elections § X" in *Laws of the State of New York*, 324. All the Federalist lawyers accepted that this statute negated, at least for this gubernatorial election, the

ancient common law writ of *quo warranto*, which permitted a court to try an officeholder's title to the office. One Federalist lawyer briefly suggested having the legislature enact a new statute specifically authorizing a writ of *quo warranto* in this case. (For details, see Foley, "The Founders' *Bush v. Gore*," 31n54.) But that suggestion seemed no better than the one made by Joshua Sands, writing as Plain Sense in *The Right of Suffrage*, that the legislature simply declare the election void as unconstitutional. Either way, the suggestion was impractical, since the Clintonians had a lock on the legislature, as evidenced by the composition of the canvassing committee, and Clinton himself held the gubernatorial veto power.

52. Monaghan, *John Jay*, 336; Hamilton to King, Philadelphia, July 25, 1792, 99.
53. Taylor, *William Cooper's Town*, 181.
54. Young, *Democratic Republicans of New York*, 311.
55. King to Hamilton, New York, July 10, 1792, 20–21.
56. Hammond, *History of Political Parties*, 70; Kaminski, *Clinton*, 217.
57. Hamilton to Rufus King, Philadelphia, June 28, 1792, (emphasis in the original), in *Hamilton Papers*, vol. XI, 588–89; Hamilton to King, Philadelphia, July 25, 1792, 99.
58. See Foley, "Founders' *Bush v. Gore*," 74.
59. Ibid., 75.
60. James Monroe to Madison, Albemarle, June 27, 1792, 330–31.
61. Hamilton to King, June 28, 1792, 588. Hamilton himself confessed to King that, for him, the legal question presented to the canvassers concerning the Otsego ballots, was "not absolutely free from difficulty." Hamilton to King, Philadelphia, July 25, 1972, 99. For Hamilton, however, this uncertainty was all the more reason to seek political revenge in the next election, rather than to seek a legal remedy for the arguably wrongful vote-counting in this one.
62. Kent reinforced his commitment to this view once he had settled on the idea of a single-purpose constitutional convention. Previously, while he thought there ought to be an immediate remedy, he did not perceive one as existing. But now he saw that the single-purpose constitutional convention could provide the immediate "redress" that was so urgently warranted. James Kent to Moss Kent Jr., July 11, 1792, 46.
63. Samuel Eliot Morison, *Harrison Gray Otis, The Urbane Federalist: 1765–1848* (Boston: Houghton Mifflin, 1969), 275.
64. The single best source on this gubernatorial dispute remains Edward Stanwood, "The Massachusetts Election in 1806," in *Proceedings of the Massachusetts Historical Society*, vol. XX (1906), 12.
65. "Election of Governor," *New England Palladium*, June 10, 1806.
66. "We understand Mr. Story did not vote with the majority of the Committee on all questions." *Columbian Centinel*, June 11, 1806.
67. Stanwood, "Massachusetts Election," 17 (the committee "retained all votes for Sullivan which were returned for Sulivan, or Sullivon"). Many pointed out as well that what might look like "Stoon" to some, was also "Stron" with the "r" smudged into an "o" as a result of "accidental blotting of the ink." *Columbian Centinel*, June 7, 1806. One representative reported that "a magnifying glass" made "plain that the word intended was Stron." "Election of Governor," *New England Palladium*, June 13, 1806 (remarks of Rep. Upham during debate of June 10). This observation made the invocation of the supposed phonetic rule even more suspicious in this particular case.
68. "If I can't make a phonetic understanding of the name, I say no." Kim Murphy, "Counting of write-in ballots underway in Alaska Senate election," *Los Angeles Times*, Nov. 10, 2010 (quoting the chief of Alaska's Division of Elections). See also Chad Flanders, "How Do You Spell M-U-R-K-O-W-S-K-I?," *Alaska Law Review* 28 (2011): 1; Justin Levitt, "Fault and the Murkowski Voter: A Reply to Flanders," *Alaska Law Review* 28 (2011): 41.
69. "An Appeal: To the People of Massachusetts on the Report of The Elections," *Boston Gazette*, June 9, 1806.
70. "Election of Governor," *New England Palladium*, June 13, 1806 (remarks of Rep. Upham during debate of June 10).

71. Stanwood, "Massachusetts Election," 17.
72. "An Appeal," *Boston Gazette*, June 9, 1806.
73. The third issue concerned town of Troy, which submitted two genuinely conflicting returns, one showing Strong receiving 59 votes and the other with Sullivan obtaining 68 votes. Each return showed zero votes for the other candidate. Apparently, there had been a conflict within this town as to which party controlled the relevant local offices, and thus each party claiming official authority submitted separate returns, but reporting only the votes cast for its candidate. The committee neither disqualified nor counted both returns from Troy. Instead, it chose to count only the return containing the 68 votes for Sullivan (and none for Strong), and it did so without even conducting a formal evidentiary inquiry of its own as to what the truth in Troy actually was. See Stanwood, "Massachusetts Election," 16–17.

    The final issue involved the return from the town of Parsonfield, which contained a notation that that it had not been properly sealed by the town's clerk, as required by the state's constitution. Although the canvassing committee had rejected the returns from other towns because of similar defects, the committee decided to accept this return despite the notation. The Jeffersonians on the committee argued that the notation might have been a subsequent addition fraudulently designed to invalidate the return. But the Jeffersonians had no evidence to support this conjecture, and indeed refused to consider evidence proffered by the Federalists that would have corroborated the validity of the notation. This move netted Sullivan 145 votes. See Commonwealth of M.A. S. Comm., *Report on Votes for Governor and the Protest* (June 5, 1806).
74. The June 9 *Boston Gazette* editorial called the committee report a breach of "the first duty of a Legislator in a republican form of government," which was to act as "a servant of their people" and follow "their will":

    > The Report of the Committee of the Elections, bears, upon the face of it, the most fragrant violation of the will of the people, the most daring inconsistency in itself, the utmost breach of faith, and an outrageous stretch of prerogative. For by it, the free electors of this Commonwealth, have their rights wrestled from their grasp.

    "An Appeal," *Boston Gazette*, June 9, 1806. An editorial in the *Centinel* on June 11 condemned the "striking partiality of the report," a consequence "of the strides which men will take who '*feeling power forget right.*'" (Emphasis in the original.) *Columbian Centinel*, June 11, 1806.
75. "State Legislature," *Repertory*, June 10, 1806, 2.
76. Ibid. Apparently, the blotting of the "r" made it look like an "o"—thus making "Stron" look like "Stoon."
77. Stanwood, "Massachusetts Election," 18.
78. *Repertory*, June 6, 1806.
79. "Proceedings," *Repertory*, June 13, 1806.
80. "Returns for Governor," *Columbian Centinel*, June 7, 1806, 2.
81. "Debate on the Report of the Committee of Elections," *Boston Gazette*, June 12, 1806 (remarks of Mr. Whitman).
82. "Election of Governor," *New England Palladium*, June 13, 1806 (reporting house proceedings on June 10), 1. See also *Journal of House of Representatives of Commonwealth of Massachusetts, commencing on* Tuesday, June 10, 1806.
83. "Election of Governor," *Centinel*, June 11, 1806 (reporting house proceedings of June 10).
84. Ibid.
85. Ibid.
86. "Election of Governor," *New England Palladium*, June 13, 1806.
87. "State Legislature," *Repertory*, June 17, 1806.
88. Stanwood, "Massachusetts Election," 18–19.
89. "Legislature of Massachusetts," *Columbian Centinel* June 14, 1806, 1 (reporting proceedings of June 11). It is possible, too, that the death of John Avery, Massachusetts's first (and, until then, only) secretary of state, who had served since 1780, might have helped to dampen the partisan divide. He died on Saturday, June 7, and the House of

Representatives on Tuesday, June 10, suspended debate on the disputed gubernatorial election in order to attend his funeral.

90. Sullivan's nineteenth-century biographer, Thomas Amory, suggests that Sullivan may have signaled to his supporters that he did not wish to become governor based on such dubious manipulation of the canvassing of returns. Thomas Coffin Amory, *Life of James Sullivan* (Boston: Phillips, Sampson, 1859), 159. First, Amory argues that the Republicans could have gotten away with their plan if they had wanted to: "The republicans had full power to carry out their triumph, had they not be restrained by a sense of its injustice." Ibid. Amory observes that Sullivan "was undoubtedly consulted, in respect to their course, by the republican leaders." Amory also contends that Sullivan would not have wanted the job under the circumstances: "Elevation to a post for which another had received a fuller expression of popular will would have afforded him no gratification, and been at variance with all his political principles." Ibid. Amory, finally, asserts that the party's overnight reversal could not have come so quickly unless it was the candidate himself who decided to take this position: "There is greater probability of this having originated with the candidate than with his supporters." Ibid., 160.
91. "Proceedings," *Repertory*, June 13, 1806, 2; see also "State Legislature," *Repertory*, June 10, 1806 (remarks of Mr. Otis).
92. This point relates to the question whether Clinton, like Sullivan, should have refrained from using available reins of power, to seize the governor's office. This question vexed and divided the Virginians who were attempting to be impartial in evaluating from afar what was the right and honorable thing for Clinton to do in New York. Jefferson, as we have seen, thought that virtue compelled Clinton to "decline the office," but Madison agreed only if it were "*clear* that a majority of legal honest votes were given ag'st him." Madison to Jefferson, June 29, 1792, 331–32. In other words, Madison believed that Clinton should not "force himself upon the people" only if his situation were the same as what Sullivan's would be fourteen years later. Ibid. As long as it was at least *plausible* that Clinton, rather than Jay, had the "majority of legal honest votes," then Madison believed that Clinton actually owed it to "his party" to fight for his claim to the office. And, as Madison explicitly noted, the plausibility of that claim "may depend I think on the question of substance involved in the conduct of the Otsego election." Ibid. Thus party loyalty displaced virtue as the relevant consideration if, as Clinton and his followers surely believed, it was plausible that Cooper and his cronies in Otsego had corrupted the ballot box arriving from there.
93. Worthington Chauncey Ford, ed., *Writings of John Quincy Adams*, vol. III (New York: McMillan, 1914), 145–46.
94. Virtue, especially the self-conscious need to live up to his own standard of political virtue, is a theme of Fred Kaplan, *John Quincy Adams: An American Visionary* (New York: Harper Collins, 2014).
95. There has been a suggestion that Story was called upon to "mediate [the] disputed Massachusetts election [of] 1806" because of his "reputation for sensitivity and statesmanlike discretion." Herbert A. Johnson, *The Chief Justiceship of John Marshall, 1801–1835* (Columbia: University of South Carolina Press, 1998), 40. But research for this book has uncovered no evidence that Story played any such mediating role, only that he did not go as far as other Republicans in his willingness to invalidate local returns when doing so would favor the opposing party (but also fell short of the impartiality exhibited by his Republican colleague, David Goodwin)—and that Story was sensitive to criticism that his position appeared tainted by a degree of partisanship. Kent Newmyer, Story's biographer, without claiming that Story mediated the 1806 dispute (or was asked to do so), does credit Story with "nonpartisan conduct" during the proceedings. R. Kent Newmyer, *Supreme Court Justice Joseph Story: Statesman of the Old Republic* (Chapel Hill: University of North Carolina Press, 1986), 56. To a point, this credit is fair, for the reasons and according to the account set forth in this book. But it seems an overstatement to suggest that Story's conduct in the matter was entirely nonpartisan, especially when one contrasts it with Goodwin. Ultimately, based on all the available evidence, Story at this stage of his career comes up short of the ideal of impartiality that one might wish to ascribe to him, particularly with respect to such a momentous matter

as the counting of ballots in the election for chief executive of the polity. (I am grateful for correspondence with Professor Newmyer on this point.)

96. Joseph Story, *Commentaries of the Constitution of the United States*, vol. 3 (Boston: Hilliard, Gray, 1833), 327.
97. James Kent, *Commentaries of American Law* (New York: O. Halsted, 1826), 256.
98. In between New York's election in 1792 and Massachusetts's in 1806, Delaware had two disputed gubernatorial elections of its own. The first, in 1801, was the much closer one. The returns showed that the Jeffersonian candidate, David Hall, had defeated the Federalist, Nathaniel Mitchell, by a mere 18 votes statewide. The vote was very lopsided geographically: Hall's support came from the northern part of the state, while Mitchell was overwhelmingly preferred in the south. The Federalists claimed that Hall's victory was invalid because unqualified voters had been permitted to cast ballots. "Delaware 1801 Governor," American Antiquity Society, accessed July 14, 2015, http://elections.lib.tufts.edu/catalog/tufts:de.governor.1801.

    Delaware's new constitution of 1792 gave the authority to adjudicate any disputed gubernatorial election to a "joint committee, consisting of one-third of all the members of each branch of the Legislature, to be selected by ballot of the Houses respectively." (Signed the same day as New York's canvassers awarded that state's disputed election to Clinton, Delaware's constitution had no opportunity to benefit from that experience.) D.E. Const. of 1792, art. 3, § 2. The Federalists, who controlled the state's House of Representatives, wanted to set up a joint committee to investigate these allegations, as called for in the constitution. The Jeffersonian minority, by contrast, opposed this effort on the grounds that the allegations of wrongdoing were insufficiently specific to trigger this investigatory process. David Peltier, "Party Development and Voter Participation in Delaware," in *Delaware History*, vol. XIV (Wilmington: The Historical Society of Delaware, 1970), 90. Interestingly, they cited the disputed Georgia congressional election of 1791, between Jackson and Wayne, as an example of a case where the allegations were appropriately specific. The Jeffersonians in the House, however, were solidly outvoted by the Federalist majority. Roger Martin, *A History of Delaware Through Its Governors, 1776–1984* (Wilmington: McClafferty Print, 1984), 98–99.

    The proceedings in the state senate are more difficult to understand. It was a small body, with only 9 members. There was a 4–3 vote (2 apparently not present) to reject any pursuit of an investigation. It appears that six of these seven votes were along party lines, but that John Vining's was not. He was a Federalist who had served in the US House of Representatives and the US Senate and had returned to the state senate at the end of his life. (Indeed, he was to die in office just a few weeks after this vote.) With the senate refusing to investigate, Hall was seated. Peltier, "Party Development," 90.

    Four years later, Mitchell, the Federalist, beat a different Jeffersonian opponent, Joseph Haslet, by 341 votes. The Republicans now complained that they had been robbed by fraud on behalf of the Federalists, but the Federalists in control of the legislature refused to pursue any investigation. Mitchell, like John Jay, benefited from the Hamiltonian precept of simply running stronger next time. "Delaware 1804 Governor," American Antiquity Society, accessed March 24, 2015, http://elections.lib.tufts.edu/catalog/tufts:de.governor.1804; Peltier, "Party Development," 95.
99. On the election of 1800, see James Roger Sharp, *The Deadlocked Election of 1800: Jefferson, Burr, and the Union in the Balance* (Lawrence: University Press of Kansas, 2010); Edward J. Larson, *A Magnificent Catastrophe: The Tumultuous Election of 1800, America's First Presidential Campaign* (New York: Free Press, 2007); John Ferling, *Adams vs. Jefferson: The Tumultuous Election of 1800* (Oxford: Oxford University Press, 2004); Susan Dunn, *Jefferson's Second Revolution: The Election Crisis of 1800 and the Triumph of Republicanism* (Boston: Houghton Mifflin, 2004); Bernard A. Weisberger, *America Afire: Jefferson, Adams and the Revolutionary Election of 1800* (New York: William Morrow, 2000).
100. See Bruce Ackerman, *The Failure of the Founding Fathers: Jefferson, Marshall, and the Rise of Presidential Democracy* (Cambridge, MA: Belknap Press of Harvard University Press, 2005); see also Bruce Ackerman and David Fontana, "Thomas Jefferson Counts

Himself Into the Presidency," *University of Virginia Law Review* 90 (2004): 551. Ackerman describes how the Electoral College tie in 1800 depended on counting Georgia's Electoral College votes even though they were technically deficient. But there was no doubt about whom Georgia's electors voted for (Jefferson and Burr), or that these electors were the correct individuals from Georgia to hold the office of presidential elector. The deficiency was simply a clerical error in the formalities with which the electoral vote was transmitted from Georgia to Congress. Although such formal defects in the transmission of votes from more local to more central authorities clearly could cause major vote-counting disputes, as in New York's gubernatorial election of 1792, they did not do so in this case. They did not spark an objection from Federalists, despite the fervor with which they were opposing Jefferson—and insofar as they were concocting other plots by which they might hold onto the presidency. Had the Federalists latched on to this issue, the saga of 1800 might have taken another, perhaps even more precarious turn. But they did not, and in the overall context of what actually transpired, the formal defect in Georgia's Electoral College papers turned out to be a nonissue. Ibid.

Ackerman suggests that Jefferson, as presiding officer, acted speedily to count Georgia's votes in his (and Burr's) favor. But, as Ackerman acknowledges, the formal defect was noted in the joint session of Congress, and the issue was reported in the papers. The Federalists could have objected if they wanted to. But attempting to invalidate Georgia's participation in the presidential election on such flimsy grounds was too much, even in the midst of this intense partisan competition. Some may even have remembered how Jay and his New York Federalists felt after being counted out on such formalistic—and disenfranchising grounds—in 1792. In any event, in 1800, the Federalists preferred to make their fight by trying to break the Electoral College tie in Burr's favor, rather than attempting to pretend that one of their own candidates was constitutionally entitled to win the presidency.

It is worth noting also, as does Ackerman, that Vermont had a similar formal defect in its Electoral College transmission in 1796, but Jefferson (who then would have benefited from invalidating of Vermont's votes) did not want to press the point: "Surely in so great a case, substance & not form should prevail." The presidency, Jefferson added in a letter to Madison, should be based on "the choice of the people substantially expressed," rather than letting a technical defect result in the "phaenomenon of a Pseudo-president." Ackerman, *The Failure of the Founding Fathers*, 72; Ackerman and Fontana, "Thomas Jefferson Counts Himself," 577.

101. See, e.g., Sharp, *Deadlocked Election*, 158–62.
102. See Tadahisa Kuroda, *The Origins of the Twelfth Amendment: The Electoral College if the Early Republic, 1787–1804* (Westport, CT: Greenwood Press, 1994).
103. US Const. amend. XII (emphasis added).
104. Story, *Commentaries on the Constitution*, 303.
105. A copy of the Ross Bill is contained in *Counting Electoral Votes*, H.R. Misc. Doc. No. 13, 44th Cong., 2d Sess. (Washington, DC: Government Printing Office, 1877), 16. The exemption for disputes over ballots cast by citizens for presidential elections is in section 8. Ibid., 18. The Ross Bill is discussed in J. Hampden Dougherty, *The Electoral System of the United States* (New York: G. P. Putnam's Sons, 1906), 63–73.
106. A proposed constitutional amendment in 1798, offered by Senator Humphrey Marshall of Kentucky, would have "provided that in case any contest should arise relative to any vote for President, the same should be determined by the Senate, and for Vice-President, it should be decided by the House of Representatives." Herman Ames, *The Proposed Amendments to the Constitution of the United States During the First Century of Its History*, vol. II (Washington, DC: Government Printing Office, 1897), 117. This provision, in addition to being prescient about the possibility of such contests, gestured toward impartiality by allocating to the opposite chamber the adjudicatory authority over disputes arising from the election for which the counterpart chamber was responsible. In other words, since the House potentially played a decisive role in presidential elections, the Senate would adjudicate disputes (and vice versa). This amendment, alas, did not

adequately account for the fact that partisanship could compromise the judgment of either chamber.

107. Story, *Commentaries on the Constitution*, 303.

108. The 1800 election exposed another problem that could arise in the context of a dispute over counting ballots in a presidential election. One of the dangers of the stalemate over the tie between Jefferson and Burr was the possibility that the date for the inauguration of the new president, March 4, might arrive without a choice having been made. The Constitution did not clearly specify what would happen in this situation, although the Federalists claimed that they could invoke at least by analogy its provision that "Congress may by Law provide for the Case of Removal, Death, Resignation, or Inability, both of the President and Vice President, declaring what Officer shall then act as President, and such Officer shall act accordingly, until the Disability be removed, or a President shall be elected." U.S. Const. art. II, § 1, cl. 6. "Inability" does not exactly describe the failure to elect a new president and vice president—it seems more like the incapacitation of president and vice president already inaugurated into office, especially residing next to "Removal, Death, [and] Resignation"—but it was close enough, and thus the Federalists considered Congress empowered to designate a "president pro tempore" of the Senate to serve as acting president for as long as the House remained deadlocked between Jefferson and Burr. With Federalists still controlling Congress until March 4, 1801 (apart from the special procedure in the House of one-vote-per-state to break Electoral College ties), there was serious consideration of using this control to keep the presidency in Federalist hands indefinitely even though the election had shown that the nation wanted to transfer power to Jefferson and the Republicans. Without even having to acquiesce in Burr as better than Jefferson, the Federalists instead could simply select one of their own. See Ackerman, *The Failure of the Founding Fathers*, chap. 2.

    Had the Federalists carried out this plan to exploit a presidential vacancy resulting from a failure to end the stalemate by March 4 (a stalemate that the Federalists themselves were prolonging by blocking a ninth state in the House from choosing Jefferson), a constitutional crisis of utmost proportions would have erupted. Jefferson and Republicans would not have accepted the Federalists' holding on to the presidency in this fabricated way, signaling their willingness to use military means if necessary to prevent this Federalist "usurpation." See Sharpe, *Deadlocked Election*, 140, 153. While the House remained deadlocked over Jefferson and Burr, James Monroe and Thomas McKean, as Republican governors of Virginia and Pennsylvania, were considering contingency plans in the event that their state militias would be needed to break the Federalist stranglehold over Jefferson's rightful election. Ibid., 154–55.

    Bayard's acquiescence in Jefferson's election defused the increasing risk of military confrontation, even all-out civil war, over the outcome of the 1800 election. The Twelfth Amendment, as part of its alteration of Electoral College procedures, also addressed the risk that the House might fail to elect a president when called upon to do so; in that case, the Senate's separate election of the vice president, pursuant to the new procedures, would serve to fill the presidential vacancy temporarily: "If the House of Representatives shall not choose a President whenever the right of choice shall devolve upon them, before the fourth day of March next following, then the Vice-President shall act as President, as in the case of the death or other constitutional disability of the President." U.S. Const. amend. XII.

109. The difficulties associated with the Twelfth Amendment are explored in Nathan L. Colvin and Edward B. Foley, "The Twelfth Amendment: A Constitutional Ticking Time Bomb," *University of Miami Law Review* 64 (2010): 475.

110. Madison to George Hay, Montpellier, August 23, 1823, letter, National Archives, accessed March 24, 2015, http://founders.archives.gov/volumes/Madison/99-02.

111. Two other candidates, one of which was Henry Clay, had siphoned off enough Electoral College votes to prevent Jackson from reaching a majority. This multiplicity of candidates occurred because the nation was transitioning from its first two-party system to the second, with Whigs replacing Federalists as the opponents of the Democratic-Republicans.

See Daniel Walker Howe, *What Hath God Wrought: The Transformation of America, 1815–1848* (New York: Oxford University Press, 2007), 208–11.

112. Donald O. Dewey, "Madison's Views on Electoral Reform," *Western Political Quarterly* 15 (1962): 140–45.
113. Madison to George McDuffie, Montpellier, January 3, 1824, letter, National Archives, accessed March 25, 2015, http://founders.archives.gov/volumes/Madison/99-02. By "viciating," Madison means what today we would call "vitiating."
114. Madison to Robert Taylor, Montpellier, January 30, 1826, letter, National Archives, accessed July 10, 2015, http://founders.archives.gov/volumes/Madison/99-02.

Chapter 3

1. On the political violence of this era, see David Grimsted, *American Mobbing, 1828–1861: Toward Civil War* (New York: Oxford University Press, 1998), esp. chapters 6 and 7 for the interrelationship of partisan competition and election-related violence in the North. See also Paul O. Weinbaum, *Mobs and Demagogues: The New York Response to Collective Violence in the Early Nineteenth Century* (Ann Arbor: UMI Research Press, 1979); Paul A. Gilje, *The Road to Mobocracy: Popular Disorder in New York City, 1763–1834* (Chapel Hill: University of North Carolina Press, 1987); Michael Feldberg, *The Turbulent Era: Riot and Disorder in Jacksonian America* (New York: Oxford University Press, 1980).
2. See Joel H. Silbey, *The American Political Nation, 1838–1893* (Redwood City, CA: Stanford University Press, 1991); Joel H. Silbey, *The Partisan Imperative: The Dynamics of American Politics Before the Civil War* (Oxford: Oxford University Press, 1985), chapters 3 and 4; Richard L. McCormick, *The Party Period and Public Policy: American Politics from the Age of Jackson to the Progressive Era.* (New York: Oxford University Press, 1986), chapters 4 and 5; Richard P. McCormick, *The Second American Party System: Party Formation in the Jacksonian Era* (New York: Norton, 1966), chap. 7. On the period generally, see Daniel Walker Howe, *What Hath God Wrought: The Transformation of America, 1815–1848* (New York: Oxford University Press, 2007).
3. See Richard Hofstadter, *The Idea of a Party System: The Rise of Legitimate Opposition in the United States, 1780–1840* (Berkeley: University of California Press, 1969), chap. 6; Silbey, *The American Political Nation*, 42–45.
4. The presidential election of 1844 might have triggered a major ballot-counting dispute, but it did not. Historians credit allegations that widespread election fraud in New York may have accounted for Polk's 5,106-vote victory over Clay in the state. See, e.g., Howe, *What Hath God Wrought*, 688–89; Tracy Campbell, *Deliver the Vote: A History of Election Fraud, an American Political Tradition, 1742–2004* (New York: Carroll & Graf, 2005), 24; see also Michael F. Holt, *The Rise and Fall of the American Whig Party* (New York: Oxford University Press, 1999), 198–206 (expressing a more tentative view). If New York had gone for Clay, he rather than Polk would have won the presidency; it was the swing state of this era, as it would be in the 1880s (see Chapter 6).

   But Clay and his Whig party did not press a major challenge to the outcome in New York. Horace Greeley, the influential editor of the *New York Tribune*, "vowed he would risk his life to sift through ballots and throw out every illegal vote if it would give New York to Clay." Gregory A. Borchard, "The New York Tribune and the 1844 Election," *Journalism History* 33, no. 1 (2007): 55. But Greeley's talk produced little action, perhaps because voiding invalid votes would not necessarily yield a Clay victory. Throwing out New York's electoral votes, rather than awarding them to Clay, still would have resulted in a Polk victory, since the Democrats overwhelmingly controlled the House of Representatives, which would have had the power to elect Polk under the Twelfth Amendment in the absence of an Electoral College majority: "The Central Clay Committee in New York City spent $5000 investigating the matter, but nothing came of it." David S. Heidler and Jeanne T. Heidler, *Henry Clay: The Essential American* (New York: Random House, 2010), 394. See also John Bicknell, *America 1844: Religious Fervor, Westward Expansion, and the Presidential Election that Transformed the Nation* (Chicago: Chicago Review, 2015), 221.

If litigation over this presidential election had arisen, it certainly would have been the principal electoral dispute of America's Second Party System and would have provided something of a preview of the constitutional crisis that occurred in 1876. One question, which would benefit from further inquiry, is whether the failure of the Whigs to contest the outcome of the 1844 presidential election in New York was due primarily to lack of sufficient evidence, or instead, the inadequacy of the procedural mechanism available for pursuing a remedy for the alleged electoral theft. In this respect, the 1844 election potentially raises interesting parallels to 1960 (discussed in Chapter 8).

5. Some have argued that New York's election riot of 1834 needs to be understood in the context of widespread social violence throughout the nation that year. Carl E. Prince, "The Great 'Riot Year': Jacksonian Democracy and Patterns of Violence in 1834," *Journal of the Early Republic* 5, no. 1 (1985): 8 (identifying twenty-four nationally significant episodes of social violence). See also Weinbaum, *Mobs and Demagogues*, 1: "Mob violence moved to the forefront of the American consciousness during 1834."
6. Edwin G. Burrows and Mike Wallace, *Gotham: A History of New York City to 1898* (New York: Oxford University Press, 1999), 574.
7. Ibid.
8. The secondary sources dispute whether one person was killed or instead recovered after near-death injuries. See Gilje, *The Road to Mobocracy*, 139–40; Weinbaum, *Mobs and Demagogues*, 5; Howe, *What Hath God Wrought*, 431. These authors agree that only one was killed.; cf. Grimsted, *American Mobbing*, 333n4: "Weinbaum and Paul Gilje say one policeman was killed, but I think this is the victim, long unconscious and expected to die, who eventually recovered." See also Joanne Reitano, *The Restless City: A Short History of New York from Colonial Times to the Present* (New York: Routledge, 2006) (and sources cited therein).
9. Burrows and Wallace, *Gotham*, 575.
10. Prince, "The Great Riot Year," 12. Prince describes the military as "federal troops"; Reitano says that the governor called in the state militia. Reitano, *The Restless City*, 44. Headley suggests that both were brought in to quell the unrest. J.T. Headley, *The Great Riots of New York, 1712–1873* (New York: Dover Publications, 1971), 75–76.
11. Prince, "The Great Riot Year," 12. Among their specific concerns were that some immigrants had been fraudulently naturalized on the eve of the election, just for the purposes of voting in this election. Headley, *Great Riots of New York*, 66–67.
12. "When the polls were closed at evening, the ballot-box of the Sixth Ward [the Democratic neighborhood where much of the violence had occurred] was taken under a strong guard to the City Hall, and locked up for the night. It was followed by four or five thousand excited men, but no violence [at that point] was attempted." Ibid., 76–77.
13. Headley numbers the crowd at "ten to fifteen thousand." Ibid.
14. Gilje, *The Road to Mobocracy*, 140. Another historian has added: "In no [other] antebellum riot did so many police suffer such serious injury as in the spring New York political riot." Grimsted, *American Mobbing*, 204.
15. Gilje, *The Road to Mobocracy*, 140.
16. Ibid.
17. Grimsted characterizes Philadelphia's election riot as "marking that city's rites of passage to the new two-party system." Grimsted, *American Mobbing*, 203.
18. Frederick C. Brightly, *A Collection of Leading Cases on the Law of Elections in the United States* (Philadelphia: Kay & Bro., 1871), 641. Brightly, a prominent attorney and politician in Philadelphia in the middle of the nineteenth century, wrote his election law book because he lamented the increasing partisanship of the judiciary in adjudicating election cases. Attributing "this great evil" to the rise of "an elective Judiciary," he hoped that his book would help to thwart "the growing tendency in our country, to disregard all law but that of power." Ibid., 581, 666, 752.
19. In Pennsylvania at this time, the Whigs were associated with the Anti-Mason Party. For sake of simplicity, I will just refer to them as the Whigs. See Alexander Kelly McLure, *Old Time Notes of Pennsylvania* (Philadelphia: J. C. Winston,

1905); see also Philip S. Klein and Ari Hoogenboom, *A History of Pennsylvania*, 2nd ed. (New York: McGraw-Hill, 1973), 149–50; Henry Richard Mueller, *The Whig Party in Pennsylvania* (New York: Columbia University Press, 1922), chap. 1; Alexander Harris, *A Review of the Political Conflict in America* (New York: T. H. Pollock, 1876), chap. 4; William Henry Egle and Joseph Ritner, "The Buckshot War," *Pennsylvania Magazine of History and Biography*, no. 1 (1899).

20. Brightly, *Leading Cases*, 641.
21. On the nineteenth century's difficulty with the phenomenon of rival legislatures, see Paul Samuel Reinsch, *American Legislatures and Legislative Methods* (New York: Century, 1907), 217. Reinsch describes the "serious political danger" that can arise in this situation.
22. Alexander Kelly McClure, *Old Time Notes of Pennsylvania*, vol. 1 (Philadelphia: J. C. Winston, 1905), 50.
23. Ibid.
24. A subsequent committee empaneled to investigate, which was controlled by Democrats, found that fraud had occurred and even had been perpetrated "with the advice and cooperation of William B. Reed, the attorney-general of the commonwealth, and John G. Watmough, the sheriff of the city and county of Philadelphia." Brightly, *Leading Cases*, 641, 645.
25. Harris, *Political Conflict in America*, 44–45.
26. In Pennsylvania, the secretary of state is also known as the "Secretary of the Commonwealth," because officially the state is called the Commonwealth of Pennsylvania.
27. Ibid., 45–46. See also Thomas Frederick Woodley, *The Great Leveler* (New York: Stackpole Sons, 1937), 87. Although some sources spell "Burrowes" as "Burrows," the former appears more prevalent and preferred.
28. See Mueller, *Whig Party of Pennsylvania*, 49: "The Whig judges, incensed at [the rejection of the Northern Liberties returns,] made out returns, which were based on the districts carried by the Whigs and which showed that the Whig candidates to the state senate and house had been elected."
29. Harris, *Political Conflict in America*, 45–46. In making this argument, the Democrats repeatedly observed that their exclusion of the Northern Liberty votes alone made no difference in the result of these eight seats. In other words, had they just added the Northern Liberties votes to the Philadelphia County returns that their ten Board members certified, the result for these eight house seats would be the same (which was not true for the congressional seat in play). The Whigs countered that after the Democrats had opened the door to throwing out returns based on allegations of local fraud, the issue no longer was solely the inclusion or exclusion of the Northern Liberties votes. Rather weakly, or at least self-interestedly, the Whigs claimed that the only returns that they could authenticate in Philadelphia County were from the districts in which they were in control. Ibid., 47.
30. Ibid., 49. See also James Ross Snowden, *Report of the Committee Appointed to Enquire Into the Causes of the Disturbances at the Seat of Government* (Harrisburg, PA: Boas & Coplan, 1839), 13; Ralph Korngold, *Thaddeus Stevens: A Being Darkly Wise and Rudely Great* (New York: Harcourt, Brace, 1955), 56–58.
31. Egle and Ritner, "The Buckshot War," 142.
32. Klein and Hoogenboom, *A History of Pennsylvania*, 149.
33. Harris, *Political Conflict in America*, 47. Harris characterized Burrowes's comments, "as a threat of revolution . . . arousing partisan passion to its highest pitch of intensity."
34. See Hans L. Trefousse, *Thaddeus Stevens: Nineteenth Century Egalitarian* (Chapel Hill: University of North Carolina, 1997), 58. This book has an account of the Buckshot War that is decidedly favorable to the Whig point of view. But it is factually misleading in at least one detail. It asserts that in Philadelphia, "the Whig judges counted the returns from all but the disputed ward." Ibid. While it is true that the Whig judges counted almost all of the votes from the Northern Liberties, they excluded returns from many other districts, a key fact that this account omits.
35. "The speaker . . . escaped through the window behind the chamber. Stevens and Burrowes, threatened by the mob, followed, jumping six to seven feet to the ground and eventually arriving at the governor's residence." Ibid.

36. Egle and Ritner, "Buckshot War," 151–52.
37. Harris, *Political Conflict in America*, 57.
38. Ibid.
39. Klein and Hoogenboom, *History of Pennsylvania*, 150; Egle and Ritner, "The Buckshot War," 153.
40. Paul Revere Frothingham, *Edward Everett: Orator and Statesman* (Boston: Houghton Mifflin, 1925), 149. See also Paul A. Varg, *Edward Everett: The Intellectual in the Turmoil of Politics* (Selinsgrove, PA: Susquehanna University Press, 1992).
41. Frothingham, *Everett*, 153.
42. *Boston Courier*, January 20, 1840 (emphasis added).
43. Ibid.
44. Frothingham, *Everett*, 154.
45. Ibid., 153–55.
46. Ibid., 153.
47. Ibid., 154.
48. See Richard P. McCormick, *The History of Voting in New Jersey: A Study of the Development of Election Machinery, 1664–1911* (New Brunswick, NJ: Rutgers University Press, 1953), 116.
49. Ibid., 118.
50. See U.S. Const., art. I, § 5, cl. 1.
51. Jeffrey A. Jenkins and Charles Stewart III, *Fighting for the Speakership: The House and the Rise of Party Government* (Princeton, NJ: Princeton University Press, 2013), 111, 113.
52. McCrary takes the position that the conduct of the clerk was improper:

    > In the twenty-sixth Congress, the clerk of the House undertook to omit from the roll both the claimants for each of the several contested seats, and by this action the organization was delayed for some ten days. In this he was clearly wrong, for it was his duty to place upon the roll the names of the persons holding proper certificates of election, without regard to the question whether the seats of any such persons were to be contested.

    George W. McCrary, *A Treatise on the American Law of Elections* (Keokuk, IA: R.B. Ogden, 1875), 380.
53. Jenkins and Stewart, *Fighting for the Speakership*, 114.
54. Cong. Globe, 26th Cong., 1st Sess. 19 (1839).
55. See, e.g., Herbert Bruce Fuller, *The Speakers of the House* (Boston: Little, Brown, 1909), 75; see also Jenkins and Stewart, *Fighting for the Speakership*, 115n11.
56. Cong. Globe, 26th Cong., 1st Sess. 20 (1839).
57. Ibid., 35.
58. Ibid., 39.
59. Ibid.
60. Jenkins and Stewart, *Fighting for the Speakership*, 115.
61. Ibid., 115–25.
62. McCormick, *History of Voting in New Jersey*, 119.
63. In his diary for Dec. 6, 1839, Adams notes that there were concerns that he would not act as Chair with sufficient "impartiality." Charles Francis Adams, ed., *Memoirs of John Quincy Adams*, vol. 10 (Philadelphia: J. B. Lippincott, 1876), 149. Adams undoubtedly intended to act honorably in undertaking the unorthodox role of Chair in order to resolve the impasse. As Fred Kaplan's recent and fine biography of Adams makes clear, Adams conducted his political career with a high sense of moral rectitude, and although he was a partisan Whig, he would have deemed it dishonorable to abuse the position of Chair that he undertook for the sake of the nation. Fred Kaplan, *John Quincy Adams: American Visionary* (New York: Harper, 2014). See also Harlow Giles Unger, *John Quincy Adams* (Boston: De Capo, 2012), 286: "Congress turned to" Adams because he was the "the only man every member trusted."
64. W. A. Robinson and Louis Clinton Hatch, *Maine: A History* 1919; reprint (New York: American Law Society, 1974), 227–29; John E. Godfrey, *Memoir of Hon. Edward*

Kent, LL.D. (1879), 456, available in *Making of Modern Law* (Farmington Hills, MI: Gale, 2015).

65. On the prohibition against advisory opinions, see Erwin Chemerinsky, *Federal Jurisdiction*, 6th ed. (New York: Wolters Kluwer Law & Business, 2012), 46–54.
66. 48 U.S. 1 (1849).
67. One constitution allowed more citizens to vote than the other; different governors had been elected in separate votes held pursuant to each of the two constitutions, and subsequently both winners were claiming the right to exercise the inherently exclusive powers of the state's chief executive. See Erik J. Chaput, *The People's Martyr: Thomas Wilson Dorr and His 1842 Rhode Island Rebellion* (Lawrence: University of Kansas Press, 2013).
68. The three leading nineteenth-century texts on disputed elections all discuss the use of *quo warranto* for this purpose. See McCrary, *American Law of Elections*, 196–200, 240; Brightly, *Leading Cases*, 663–64; Thomas M. Cooley, *A Treatise on the Constitutional Limitations Which Rest Upon the Legislative Power of the States of the American Union*, 1st ed. (Boston: Little, Brown, 1868), 623–33. See also Stephen A. Siegel, "A Conscientious Congressman's Guide to the Electoral Count Act of 1887," *Florida Law Review* 56 (2004): 570–71.
69. 4 Wisc. 567 (1856). A precursor arose a few years earlier in New York, in the context of the statewide election for the state's treasurer. People v. Cook, 8 N.Y. 67 (1853). Brightly includes this New York case in his book and adds a lengthy discussion on it. Brightly, *Leading Cases*, 423–54.
70. Joseph A. Ranney, *Trusting Nothing to Providence: A History of Wisconsin's Legal System* (Madison: University of Wisconsin Law School, 1999), 84. See also Richard N. Current, *The History of Wisconsin: The Civil War Era, 1848–1873* (Madison: Wisconsin Historical Society Press, 2013), 227; Jack Start, *The Wisconsin State Constitution* (New York: Oxford University Press, 2011), 13–14.
71. John Bradley Winslow, *The Story of a Great Court* (Chicago: T. H. Flood, 1912), 101. See also Campbell, *Deliver the Vote*, 44.
72. Ranney, *Trusting Nothing to Providence*, 84.
73. *Bashford*, 658.
74. Ibid., 662: "It was contended by the counsel for the respondent, that the question arising in this case is a political one, and not properly cognizable before a judicial tribunal. We cannot view the question in that light." The invocation by Governor Barstow's counsel of *Luther v. Borden* and its "political question doctrine" appears at page 608 of the official report of the case. Barstow's counsel was Matt Carpenter, "who would go to the United States Senate and become one of the greatest advocates ever to appear before the U.S. Supreme Court." Ranney, *Trusting Nothing to Providence*, 84.
75. In a concurring opinion, Justice Smith—the Democrat on the Wisconsin Supreme Court—was much stronger in denouncing the position of his fellow Democrat, incumbent Governor Barstow:

    > The counsel for the respondent (Mr. Barstow) had chosen to put the motion on the supposition of a bald, naked, successful usurpation of the office of governor. The counsel had claimed that the individual now exercising the functions of governor, although a usurper, by succeeding, had acquired such a position, that no other department of the government possessed the power or the right to inquire by what authority he held it.

    Ibid., 662. This argument, Justice Smith explained, was plainly unconstitutional:

    > The constitution admitted of no usurper. . . . If an individual could usurp the executive office, and hold and exercise it in defiance of the constitution, he was not coequal with the other departments; he was above the other departments, and above the constitution itself; and, if successful, he destroyed the constitution and all the departments it had ordained.

Ibid., 663. For a fellow Democrat to so boldly reject the governor's position was especially significant, an important display of the nonpartisan unity of the Wisconsin Supreme Court on this crucial point.

76. Winslow, *The Story of a Great Court*, 104; Ranney, *Trusting Nothing to Providence*, 86.
77. *Bashford*, 800.
78. Winslow, *The Story of a Great Court*, 105.
79. Ibid., 106.
80. Ranney, *Trusting Nothing to Providence*, 84.
81. Ibid., 80.
82. On this aspect of *Marbury*, see Gordon Wood, *The Empire of Liberty: A History of the Early Republic: 1789–1915* (Oxford: Oxford University Press, 2009), 441: "Marshall was able to make his point [about the power of the Court to interpret the Constitution] without having to suffer the consequences." Wood adds: "Certainly most Republicans were not troubled by [*Marbury*]. If Marshall wanted to circumscribe the power of his Court, as he did in the Marbury decision, then he had every right to do so." Ibid., 442.
83. Campbell, *Deliver the Vote*, 45.
84. Winslow, *The Story of a Great Court*, 107.
85. See Robert Carrington Nesbit, *Wisconsin: A History* (Madison: University of Wisconsin Press, 1973), 233 (summarizing the view that "the prestige of the court prevented a threatened resort to violence by Democratic hotheads.") See also Clark S. Matteson, *The History of Wisconsin* (Milwaukee: Wisconsin Historical Publishing, 1893), 300 (detailing how the court's decision ultimately diffused the incipient crisis); Reuben Gold Thwaites, *Stories of the Badger State* (New York: American Book Company, 1900), 219–21 (describing the acceptance of Bashford's claim to the governor's office in response to the court's decision); L. B. Hills and J. C. Snow, "Meeting at Waupun-Rejoicing of the People," *Milwaukee Daily Sentinel*, March 31, 1856.
86. Cooley, *Constitutional Limitations*, 624n1.
87. McCrary, *American Law of Elections*, 283–84.
88. Campbell, *Deliver the Vote*, 45.

Chapter 4

1. See, e.g., Samuel Issacharoff, "Beyond the Discrimination Model on Voting," *Harvard Law Review* 127 (2013): 95; Michael J. Pitts, "Redistricting and Discriminatory Purpose," *American University Law Review* 59 (2010): 1575; Guy-Uriel E. Charles, "Race, Redistricting, and Representation," *Ohio State Law Journal* 68 (2007): 1185; Richard H. Pildes, "The Decline of Legally Mandated Minority Representation," *Ohio State Law Journal* 68 (2007): 1139; Nathaniel Persily, "Promises and Pitfalls of the New Voting Rights Act," *Yale Law Journal* 117 (2007): 174; Daniel Tokaji, "The New Vote Denial: Where Election Reform Meets the Voting Rights Act," *South Carolina Law Review* 57 (2006): 689; Heather Gerken, "Understanding the Right to an Undiluted Vote," *Harvard Law Review* 114 (2001): 1663.
2. See, e.g., J. Morgan Kousser, *The Shaping of Southern Politics: Suffrage Restriction and the Establishment of the One-Party South, 1880–1910* (New Haven, CT: Yale, 1974); V. O. Key Jr., *Southern Politics: in State and Nation* (New York: Vintage Books, 1949); See also C. Vann Woodward, *The Origins of the New South, 1877–1913* (Baton Rouge: Louisiana State University Press, 1951); Matthew D. Lassiter and Joseph Crespino, eds., *The Myth of Southern Exceptionalism* (New York: Oxford University Press, 2010); Edward L. Gibson, *Boundary Control: Subnational Authoritarianism in Federal Democracies* (New York: Cambridge University Press, 2012) (in particular chap. 3, "Subnational Authoritarianism in the United States: Boundary Control and the 'Solid South'").
3. The literature on Bloody Kansas is extensive. For background, see James McPherson, *Battle Cry of Freedom* (New York: Oxford University Press, 1988) (in particular, chap. 5, "The Crime Against Kansas"). Particularly useful for this book has been Nicole Etcheson, *Bleeding Kansas: Contested Liberty in the Civil War Era* (Lawrence: University

Press of Kansas, 2004). See also David M. Potter, *The Impending Crisis, 1848–1861* (New York: Harper & Row, 1963); James A. Rawley, *Race & Politics: "Bleeding Kansas" and the Coming of the Civil War* (Philadelphia: Lippincott, 1969).

4. "Kansas Affairs," H.R. Rep. No. 34–200, at 30 (1856). The House Committee reported 6,307 total votes, but the sum of the legal (1,410) and illegal (4,908) votes that the committee reported equals 6,318. Also, in November of the previous year, the territory had held an election to send a delegate to Congress, and that election had been flooded with imposter ballots (although not enough to affect the outcome of the race). See John D. Bright, *Kansas: The First Century*, vol. 1 (New York: Lewis Historical Publishing, 1956), 99; Etcheson, *Bleeding Kansas*, 59.
5. "Kansas Affairs," 41.
6. A. T. Andreas, *History of the State of Kansas* (Chicago: Atchison County Historical Society, 1883), 99.
7. Sherman was a member of the coalition, opposed to the Democrats, that was emerging as the new Republican Party, although they were then still called simply the "Opposition" in Congress. See Kenneth C. Martis, et al., *The Historical Atlas of Political Parties in the United States Congress, 1789–1989* (New York: Macmillan, 1989), 32–34.
8. The other northerner was William Howard of Michigan, who chaired the committee and after whom its report has been named. Mordecai Oliver was the dissenter.
9. "Kansas Affairs," 34.
10. Ibid., 70.
11. Ibid., 73.
12. "There is no argument as to the illegal and unjustifiable acts of the Missouri voters in March, but not enough protests had been filed to invalidate the decisions in the voting precincts; so the governor had no choice but to issue the certificates of election." Charles M. Correll, "The Kansas Territory May 30, 1854–January 29, 1861," in Bright, *Kansas: The First Century*, 102. See also Andreas, *History of the State of Kansas*, 97 (praising Reeder given the situation).
13. In his congressional testimony, Reeder claimed that he "was not then aware of the frauds perpetrated in the other districts." Andreas, *History of the State of Kansas*, 97 (quoting testimony). But this claim is belied by Reeder's other assertion that he was facing death threats from the proslavery forces if he "persisted in taking cognizance of the complaints made against the legality of the elections." Ibid. Andreas also reports: "The general facts concerning the Missouri invasion of the ballot boxes at the election were known throughout Kansas from the day after the election." Ibid.
14. The majority congressional committee, as one of its formal conclusions, asserted: "That in the present condition of the Territory a fair election cannot be held without a new census, a stringent and well-guarded election law, the selection of impartial judges, and the presence of United States troops at every place of election." "Kansas Affairs," 67. On this point, the dissent did not disagree. Finding impartial judges, however, would have proved an extraordinary challenge.
15. Professor Nicole Etcheson writes that Governor Reeder, a month after certifying the unopposed seats, traveled to Washington for consultations with President Franklin Pierce, during which Reeder "requested a new election for the legislature—with sufficient military force to ensure fairness." Etcheson, *Bleeding Kansas*, 61; See also "Kansas Prospects," *New York Times*, May 4, 1855, 4; Pierce, however, never granted any such request, but instead dismissed Reeder and appointed a replacement more sympathetic to the proslavery cause. McPherson, *Battle Cry of Freedom*, 147. With this decision, the opportunity was lost to test whether a new legislative election under strong military intervention might have made a difference in diminishing the degree of violence about to break out.
16. McPherson, *Battle Cry of Freedom*, 169; Etcheson, *Bleeding Kansas*, 192–93.
17. The nine, from Reeder to Medary, includes three acting governors, one of whom (Daniel Woodson) exacerbated the crisis while another (Frederick Stanton) took steps that eventually helped to diffuse it. See Kenneth M. Stampp, *America in 1857: A Nation on the Brink* (New York: Oxford University Press, 1990), 160–64. At the October 6, 1856 election for territorial delegate to Congress, "illegal voting by Missourians at accessible points was

as scandalously and openly carried on as at previous elections" but the Free Soilers were boycotting this election anyway. Andreas, *History of the State of Kansas,* 154.

18. Etcheson, *Bleeding Kansas,* 147.
19. Ibid., 153.
20. John N. Holloway, *History of Kansas: From the First Exploration of the Mississippi Valley to its Admission into the Union* (Lafayette, IN: James, Emmons, 1868), 477; Geo. W. Martin, ed., *Transactions of the Kansas State Historical Society, 1907–08,* vol. 10 (Topeka, KS: State Printing Office, 1908), 216.
21. Noble L. Prentis, *A History of Kansas* (Topeka, KS: Caroline Prentis, 1899), 72.
22. Etcheson, *Bleeding Kansas,* 75–76, 155, 206.
23. See Mark E. Neely Jr., *The Fate of Liberty: Abraham Lincoln and Civil Liberties* (New York: Oxford University Press, 1991). One of the most prominent war critics arrested was Clement Vallandigham, an ex-Congressman and former newspaper editor in Ohio. Ibid., 65; See also McPherson, *Battle Cry of Freedom,* 56; David Herbert Donald, *Lincoln* (New York: Simon & Schuster, 1995), 419–21.
24. Donald, *Lincoln,* 382; See Carson et al., "The Impact of National Tides and District-Level Effects on Electoral Outcomes: The US Congressional Elections of 1862–63," *American Journal of Political Science* 45, no. 4 (2001). Donald, like others before and since, characterizes the losses as a "severe rebuff." Donald, *Lincoln,* 382; James McPherson "challenges this conclusion," observing that Republicans experienced "the *smallest* net loss of congressional seats in an off-year election in twenty years." *Battle Cry of Freedom,* 561–62; The prevailing view is more line with Donald than McPherson.
25. I am indebted to Richard Pildes for drawing this particular topic to my attention. He raised it in a series of posts on *Richard Hasen's Election Law blog,* http://electionlawblog.org/?p=54144 (and links therein), accessed July 10, 2015.
26. William B. Hesseltine, *Lincoln's Plan of Reconstruction* (Gloucester, MA: Confederate Publishing, 1963), 43–44.
27. It is not anachronistic to deplore the military disenfranchisement that occurred in the Border States in the election of 1863. Henry Dawes, a leading Republican from Massachusetts and chair of the House Elections Committee, voted *against* seating a pro-administration candidate whose victory was tainted by military coercion. In doing so, he contradicted the wishes of most members of his party, and in a major speech on the floor of the House he strenuously and eloquently defended his position. "I uphold the Government," he readily acknowledged, in its "bounden duty to keep every traitor from the ballot-box." But the military had crossed the line by having "gone to the extent not only of keeping treason away from the polls, but also of giving direction to the election, of dictating, of directing, of controlling, more or less, the results of an election." Cong. Globe, 34th Cong., 2167 (May 10, 1864). The military abuse in this situation was unmistakably flagrant: "It was known to a whole city that the entrance to the polls was guarded by crossed bayonets, and that no man could approach them unless the ballot he carried bore the right name!" Ibid., 2168. It was imperative, Dawes maintained, not to squander the opportunity to show that "the purpose of the Administration in all this interference with elections was, not to secure men upon this floor to vote as we wanted them, but that it was solely and simply to keep treason from reaching the Government through the ballot-box." Ibid., 2167. (For emphasis, Dawes repeated even more succinctly that the Union Army's proper mission in the Border States "was not to carry an election, but to secure the freedom of elections.") Moreover, Dawes recognized that his principled position might cost his party some seats in the House. Still, it was more important to uphold the fundamental principle of free elections, even at a time of civil war: "It is no justification that the men who are put into seats here without the free choice of those they assume to represent are with us and concur with us in the measures we hold most dear, and in the efforts we are making on this floor to protect and save the nation." Ibid. For more details on this particular dispute and Dawes's role in it, see Bruce Tap, "'Union Men to the Polls, and Rebels to Their Holes': The Contested Election Between John P. Bruce and Benjamin F. Loan, 1862": 24–40. Although a Republican, Dawes "was fiercely independent on some issues and was not afraid to challenge others within the Republican party." Ibid., 33.

28. Richard Franklin Bensel, *The American Ballot Box in the Mid-Nineteenth Century* (New York: Cambridge University Press, 2004), 260–61. To take one particularly vivid occurrence, Thomas Price was the incumbent Democrat from Missouri's Fifth Congressional District and running for reelection, but Unconditional Unionists—who were Border State allies of Republicans—did not consider Price sufficiently loyal. At one polling place, when Captain Murphy, a Union loyalist, heard that Price was "running ahead," Murphy exclaimed, "I will be damned if I don't put a stop to it" and proceeded to organize a militia effort to intimidate anyone else from voting there for Price, including by threatening to shoot them. Ibid., 250–51.
29. Ibid., 261.
30. The leading account of this episode is Herman Belz, "The Etheridge Conspiracy of 1863: A Projected Conservative Coup," *Journal of Southern History* 36, no. 4 (1970), 549–67. It is also discussed in Jeffery A. Jenkins and Charles Stewart III, *Fighting for the Speakership: The House and the Rise of Party Government* (Princeton, NJ: Princeton University Press, 2013), 244–47; See also Donald, *Lincoln*, 468; John G. Nicolay and John Hay, *Abraham Lincoln: A History*, vol. 7 (New York: Century, 1909), 389–94.
31. Belz, *Etheridge Conspiracy*, 554.
32. 12 Stat. 804 (emphasis added) (March 3, 1863).
33. Belz, *Etheridge Conspiracy*, 552–53. Republicans were also concerned about potentially disloyal members of Congress sent from Louisiana and other occupied Confederate states. Ibid., 553. As Belz observes, however, the statute was not limited to that particular problem; instead, it was written broadly "in the event that votes were needed to keep the House in administration hands." Ibid.
34. Belz, *Etheridge Conspiracy*, 557–58.
35. Ibid., 560n55.
36. Nicolay and Hay, *Lincoln*, 391.
37. Ibid.
38. Donald, *Lincoln*, 468.
39. See also Michael Burlingame, *Abraham Lincoln: A Life*, vol. 1 (Baltimore: Johns Hopkins University Press, 2008), 592; Michael Burlingame and John R. Turner Ettlinger, eds., *Inside Lincoln's White House: The Complete Civil War Diary of John Hay* (Carbondale: Southern Illinois University Press, 1997), 101, 115, 120–21.
40. Belz, *Etheridge Conspiracy*, 566.
41. Cong. Globe, 34th Cong., 5 (December 7, 1863).
42. Belz, *Etheridge Conspiracy*, 562; Jenkins and Stewart, *Fighting for the Speakership*, 246–47. Because of the Civil War, party affiliation was not as rigid at the time as other moments of American history. There were 83 or 84 Republicans, depending on how one member—Rufus Spalding of Ohio—is classified. All of them, including Spalding, voted against the crucial motion, which was to table the Republican resolution to add the names of those that Etheridge excluded. These 84 were joined by six Unionists (five from Border States as well as, ironically, one of the Louisianans that the Republicans wanted to exclude) and four Democrats who defected from their party's position on this critical vote. Against the Republican position were 67 Democrats and seven Unionists.

    The Democrats could have prevailed on this key vote only by holding all 71 of their members together, as well as securing the support of thirteen Unionists, along with Spalding (who some classify as a Democrat; see Belz, *Etheridge Conspiracy*, 562n64; Jenkins and Stewart, *Fighting for the Speakership*, 247n10). If the Democrats had prevailed in this way, by the narrowest of 85–83 margins, then (with the sixteen claimants still excluded) they could have proceeded to elect Sam Cox, the Democrat, as Speaker and organize the House under their control. But that is not what happened, and not because of Republican machinations. Instead, Democrats lost the decisive vote at the time the sixteen were still excluded, and that is because they did not all stick together on the crucial vote. Even if all thirteen Unionists had voted with the 67 Democrats who supported tabling the Republican resolution to seat the claimants whom Etheridge had excluded, the motion would have failed 80–88 *because four Democrats were unwilling to go along with their party's plan to keep these claimants out of the House.* Therefore, Republicans prevailed in their ability to keep the

House under their control through the exercise of ordinary parliamentary procedure, conducted democratically, and not through any coercion of the process. Insofar as Bensel suggests that Republicans achieved "a working majority" through undemocratic means, his analysis does not focus on the pivotal nature of the defeated motion to table, which is what let the Republicans achieve their control of the House. See Bensel, *American Ballot Box*, 261. Bensel conjectures that "the Democrats would probably have organized the House" if all the Unionists had been aligned with them. Ibid., 261–62. But this conjecture is belied by the fact that the Democrats would have come up short on the pivotal motion to table because of the four defections from their ranks—a point appropriately emphasized by both Belz and Jenkins & Stewart.

After prevailing on the crucial motion, the Republicans proceeded to add the excluded sixteen members to the rolls in batches, by state. First came the five Marylanders, then the six Missourians, followed by the single Oregonian and lone Kansan, and then finally the three West Virginians. The Republicans then moved to exclude the two Louisianans that the Clerk had recognized, but Etheridge ruled that motion out of order until after the election of a Speaker. Once the Republicans elected Schuyler Colfax as Speaker, they then proceeded to unseat the two Louisianans.

43. Nicolay and Hay, *Lincoln*, 394.
44. On December 7 itself, the Republicans specifically asked Etheridge whether he had competing "contestants" for any of the sixteen seats in dispute that day. Etheridge's answer was that "three or four of the Missouri members have contestants," as well as one from West Virginia. Cong. Globe, 34 Cong., 4. Contests did materialize for three of the six Missouri claimants that the Republicans wanted seated, but none from West Virginia. These three were the seats held by Benjamin F. Loan, Joseph W. McClurg, and Francis P. Blair Jr. Two contests for members whom Etheridge put on the rolls—King and Scott—also occurred. But these two members were Democrats, and thus these contests would not have helped the Democrats win control of the House. Chester H. Rowell, *A Historical and Legal Digest of all the Contested Cases in the House of Representatives of the United States, 1791–1901* (Westport, CT: Greenwood Press, 1901), 186; see also D.W. Bartlett, *Cases of Contested Elections in Congress* (Washington, DC: Government Printing Office, 1865), 505. Moreover, even though Bensel suggested (p. 261) that improper military interference may have occurred in Maryland, none of the five Marylanders whom the Republicans wanted seated—but Etheridge initially excluded—were ever challenged in a subsequent contest. Nor was the Kansan or the Oregonian.
45. *McHenry v. Yeaman*, H.R. Rep. No. 38–70 (1864); See also Rowell, *Contested Cases*, 193.
46. See Bartlett, *Contested Cases*, 506.
47. *McHenry v. Yeaman*, 2 ("by no possible contingency could the majority actually received by the sitting member have been overcome").
48. *Knox v. Blair* in Rowell, *Contested Election Cases*, 190. See William E. Parrish, *Frank Blair: Lincoln's Conservative* (Columbia: University of Missouri Press, 1998), 151; Allan G. Bogue, *The Congressman's Civil War* (Cambridge: Cambridge University Press, 1989), 93.
49. See note 27 for details on Dawes.
50. Cong. Globe, 34th Cong., 2167 (May 6, 1864).
51. The military was employed for electoral purposes again in 1864, but there is no allegation Lincoln won reelection that year because of military improprieties at the polls. Nor are there claims that in 1864 the Republicans retained control of the House because of military pressure at the polls. That year the Republicans made huge gains in Congress relative to 1862, picking up 46 seats. The much-improved status of the Union Army's fight against the Confederacy accounts for the Republican Party's increased popularity among voters. See Leonard Newman, "Opposition to Lincoln in the Elections of 1864," *Science & Society* 8, no. 4 (1944): 305; Donald, *Lincoln*, 542–45.
52. Jeffery A. Jenkins, "Partisanship and Contested Election Cases in the House of Representatives, 1789–2002," *Studies in American Political Development* 18, no. 2 (2004): 112, 127; See also Jeffery A. Jenkins, *Partisanship and Contested Election Cases in the Senate, 1789–2002, Studies in American Political Development* 19, no. 1 (2005): 53.

53. See William Gillette, *Retreat from Reconstruction, 1869–1879* (Baton Rouge: Louisiana State University Press, 1982): 96–103; See also Douglas R. Egerton, *The Wars of Reconstruction: The Brief, Violent History of America's Most Progressive Era* (New York: Bloomsbury Press, 2014), 293–98.
54. See Anne M. Butler and Wendy Wolff, *United States Senate: Election, Expulsion and Censure Cases, 1793–1990* (Washington, DC: Government Printing Office, 1995), 178–81; See *also* Paul Samuel Reinsch, *American Legislatures and Legislative Methods* (New York: Century, 1907), 218. Alabama's troubles began in 1870 with rival claimants to the governorship that year, but that unrest was only a prelude to the "anarchy" that unfolded two years later. See Gillette, *Retreat from Reconstruction*, 95–98.
55. See Gillette, *Retreat from Reconstruction*, 95–96; See also S. Rep. No. 43-291 (April 20, 1874).
56. The issue of rival legislatures is discussed more extensively in Chapter 6.
57. Nathan L. Colvin and Edward B. Foley, "The Twelfth Amendment: A Constitutional Ticking Time Bomb," *University of Miami Law Review* 64 (2010): 475, 498.
58. Ted Tunnell, *Crucible of Reconstruction: War, Radicalism and Race in Louisiana* (Baton Rouge: Louisiana State University Press, 1984), 171. See also Gillette, *Retreat from Reconstruction*, 110–16; Joe Gray Taylor, *Louisiana Reconstructed, 1863–1877* (Baton Rouge: Louisiana State University, 1974) 241–49; Ella Lonn, *Reconstruction in Louisiana after 1868* (Gloucester, MA: G.P. Putnam's, 1918).
59. Scholars diverge in their assessments of how many were murdered in the massacre. See LeeAnna Keith, *The Colfax Massacre: The Untold Story of Black Power, White Terror, and the Death of Reconstruction* (New York: Oxford University Press, 2008), 109 (acknowledging that estimates of the carnage vary from 70 to 165, but crediting the plausibility of the higher number); Charles Lane, *The Day Freedom Died: The Colfax Massacre, the Supreme Court, and the Betrayal of Reconstruction* (New York: Henry Holt, 2008), 265–66 (acknowledging that "a precise accounting of the number of blacks killed has proved elusive" and concluding that the best estimate is in 60–80 range).
60. Charles Lane, "Edward Henry Durell: A Study in Reputation," *Greenbag* 2d 13 (2010) 161–62, 167 (lauding Durell's decision as an attempt to "preserve the liberty of many citizens in Louisiana, [which it] probably did"); Everette Swinney, "Enforcing the Fifteenth Amendment 1870–1877," *Journal of Southern History* 28, no. 2 (1962): 207–08; *Compilation of Senate Election Cases from 1789 to 1913* (Washington, DC: Government Printing Office), 494–95.
61. Gillette, *Retreat from Reconstruction*, 111.
62. Ex Parte *Warmouth*, 84 U.S. 64 (1872).
63. See Logan Scott Stafford, "Judicial Coup D'Etat: Mandamus, Quo Warranto, and the Original Jurisdiction of the Arkansas Supreme Court," *University of Arkansas at Little Rock Law Journal* 20 (1998): 891. See *also* James H. Atkinson, "The Arkansas Gubernatorial Campaign and Election of 1872," *Arkansas Historical Quarterly* 1, no. 4 (1942): 307; Earl F. Woodward, "The Brooks and Baxter War in Arkansas, 1872–1874," *Arkansas Historical Quarterly* 30, no. 4 (1971): 315; Thomas Cooley discussed the episode in his essay, "The Guarantee of Order and Republican Government in the States," *International Review* 2, no. 1 (1875): 57–87.
64. Stafford, "Judicial Coup D'Etat," 940–41. See *Brooks v. Baxter*, 28 Ark. 129 (1873).
65. Atkinson, *Election of 1872*, 321.
66. Stafford, "Judicial Coup D'Etat," 972.
67. Ibid., 964–65.
68. Ibid., 980. See *Baxter v. Brooks*, 28 Ark. 173 (1873).
69. See Stephen A. Siegel, "The Conscientious Congressman's Guide to the Electoral Count Act of 1887," *Florida Law Review* 56 (2004): 553–54. The presidential election in Louisiana was entangled in the pervasive problems there, while in Arkansas the Brooks-Baxter War was somewhat more confined to the gubernatorial election. As a result, Louisiana sent two competing slates of electoral votes to Congress, whereas Arkansas sent only one. Consequently, some commentators have contended that Congress treated Arkansas unjustly insofar as it rejected its single certificate of electoral votes. See J. Hampden

Dougherty, *The Electoral System of the United States* (New York: G. P. Putnam's Sons, 1906), 86–88; Edward Stanwood, *A History of Presidential Elections* (Boston: Houghton, Mifflin, 1892), 301. Siegel, however, maintains that Congress appropriately disqualified Arkansas on the ground that "there had been no lawful election" in the state, and that subsequent condemnation of Congress on this point amounts to revisionist history. See Siegel, *Conscientious Congressman's Guide*, 554 & n66.

70. *Presidential Elections, 1789–2000* (Washington, DC: CQ Press, 2002), 195.
71. In 1875 the Senate considered various proposals for how to handle the kind of problem that had occurred in 1872, but was unable to settle upon any of them. In March of 1876, the Senate did pass a measure in a vote that divided along party lines, but the partisan nature of this division caused the Senate to reconsider the issue. Then, having set aside the matter, the Senate failed to take it up again, and consequently the nation headed into the 1876 election without any measure in place. See Colvin and Foley, "The Twelfth Amendment," 500–01; Dougherty, "The Electoral System," 91–103; Charles Fairman, *Five Justices and the Electoral Commission of 1877* (New York: Macmillan, 1988) (supplement to *History of the Supreme Court of the United States*, the Oliver Wendell Holmes Devise), 35–37.

Chapter 5

1. As Eric Foner clarifies, the federal troops did not immediately leave the South, but instead were withdrawn to their barracks under orders not to interfere with the installation of new regimes under Democratic control in Louisiana and South Carolina. This move caused the collapse of the Republican claimants to power in those two states, whose hopes had depended upon being backed by federal force. Thus the order for the federal troops to stand down had the effect, as Foner puts it, of demonstrating that federal "soldiers would no longer play a role in [Southern] political affairs" and thereby symbolized "the abandonment of Reconstruction," defined as the "decisive retreat from the idea, born during the Civil War, of a powerful national state protecting the fundamental rights of American citizens." Eric Foner, *Reconstruction: America's Unfinished Revolution, 1863–1877* (New York: Harper & Row, 1988), 582.
2. Eric Foner, widely recognized as his generation's leading historian of the Reconstruction, is himself somewhat mixed in his own assessment. On the one hand, he says that the basic deal—Hayes's inauguration in exchange for Republican recognition of Democratic control in the South—was a "foregone conclusion," at least "by February 1877." On the other hand, Foner acknowledges that Samuel Randall, as Speaker of the House, made crucial rulings on March 1 that prevented Democrats from "obstruct[ing] the count" and sending the "crisis" into dangerously unknown territory. Foner, *Reconstruction*, 581. (Randall's crucial role will be detailed toward the end of this chapter.) Paul Leland Haworth, the early twentieth-century historian whose book on the Hayes-Tilden election still stands as the best single source on the subject, credits the view that a civil war easily could have erupted over the dispute if the nation had not so recently suffered so much carnage in the Civil War:

> Few of the generation which has grown up since then will ever have any but the faintest conception of the gravity of the situation existing during the winter of 1876–77. . . At the time probably more people dreaded an armed conflict than had anticipated a like outcome to the secession movement of 1860–61.

Paul Leland Haworth, "Compromise or Civil War?," chap. 10 in *The Hayes-Tilden Disputed Presidential Election of 1876* (New York: Russell & Russell, 1906), 168–219. Haworth adds, quoting Senator George Hoar of Massachusetts (who helped create and served on the Electoral Commission, which helped to diffuse the crisis), that "in his opinion there would have been a resort to arms had it not been 'for the bitter experience of a few years before.'" Ibid., n1.

Another prominent participant in the ordeal, Senator George Edmunds of Vermont, also thought that "the very stability of the Union" had been at stake. In an article written shortly after the disaster had been averted, Edmunds wrote that the nation had been at a real risk that both Hayes and Tilden "would have take the oaths of office" and "each would have called upon the army and the people to sustain him against the usurpations of the other." The "awful tragedy of anarchy and civil war" that would have ensued, Edmunds maintained, might have caused the demise of democratic governance in America, with "some other system of government . . . established upon the ruins of our national structure." George Edmunds, "Presidential Elections," *American Law Review* XII (1877): 3–4.

3. See Nathan L. Colvin and Edward B. Foley, "The Twelfth Amendment: A Constitutional Ticking Time Bomb," *University of Miami Law Review* 64 (2010): 475.
4. My narrative of the Hayes-Tilden dispute draws on Haworth supplemented by original sources as well as more recent accounts, the best single volume of which is Holt, *By One Vote: The Disputed Presidential Election of 1876* (Lawrence: University Press of Kansas, 2008). Also especially valuable is Keith Ian Polakoff, *The Politics of Inertia: The Election of 1876 and the End of Reconstruction* (Baton Rouge: Louisiana State University Press, 1973). After the 2000 election Chief Justice Rehnquist wrote his own *Centennial Crisis: The Disputed Election of 1876* (New York: Knopf, 2004), a useful introduction but without the depth or perspective of other available sources. Cf. Roy Morris Jr., *Fraud of the Century: Rutherford B. Hayes, Samuel Tilden, and the Stolen Election of 1876* (New York: Simon & Schuster, 2004) (a decidedly one-sided account).
5. *Presidential Elections, 1789–2000* (Washington, DC: CQ Press, 2002), 125.
6. Rehnquist, *Centennial Crisis*, 97; Polakoff, *Politics of Inertia*, 202. A similar telegram, although somewhat more inquiring and less commanding, was sent by other party leaders a few hours later: "Hayes is elected if we have carried South Carolina, Florida, and Louisiana. Can you hold your State? Answer immediately." Polakoff, *Politics of Inertia*, 203. The intent behind both versions of the telegram was the same. As Polakoff put it, even in these early hours after the polls closed, national Republican leaders "were clearly contemplating use of the returning boards in three of the Republican states of the South to nullify Democratic majorities which might appear on the face of the returns." Ibid.
7. Jerrell H. Shofner, *Nor Is It Over Yet: Florida in the Era of Reconstruction, 1863–1877* (Gainesville: The University Presses of Florida, 1974), 325. See also Haworth, *Hayes-Tilden*, 68.
8. See Shofner, *Nor Is It Over Yet*, 325; See also Jerrell H. Shofner, "Florida in the Balance: The Electoral Count of 1876," *Florida Historical Quarterly* 47, no. 2 (1968): 146. Shofner derives the figure of 94 by including the authentic return from Baker County rather than the fraudulent one that the canvassing board discarded. See also Polakoff, *Politics of Inertia*, 218. Haworth (at page 74) puts the number at 93.
9. Holt, *By One Vote*, 192.
10. Haworth, *Hayes-Tilden*, 73–74.
11. William Watson Davis, *The Civil War and Reconstruction in Florida* (New York: Columbia University/Longmans, Green, 1913), 727.
12. Shofner, "Florida in the Balance," 148.
13. A copy of Barlow's report to Grant appeared in a December 15, 1876, *New York Times* article entitled "The Vote of Florida." Barlow also wrote a subsequent letter, summarizing his findings, in the *New York Herald* (dated December 15, published December 18). Both documents are discussed in Richard F. Welch, *The Boy General: The Life and Careers of Francis Channing Barlow* (Madison, NJ: Farleigh Dickinson University Press, 2003), 230–31.
14. H.R. Misc. Doc. No. 45-31, pt. 1, at 1363 (1878).
15. Haworth, *Hayes-Tilden*, 67, 73, 75.
16. Cowgill's response is appended to Barlow's report in the copy printed in "The Vote of Florida," *New York Times*, 6.
17. H.R. Misc. Doc. No. 45-31, pt. 2, at 98–99 (1888). McLin's statement, part of his congressional testimony, was evidently prepared by another (the written statement was not in his own handwriting), but in response to questioning, he embraced it as "correct," as bearing his signature, and "part of [his] evidence" in the proceeding. Ibid., 98.
18. Ibid., 99.
19. See Holt, *By One Vote*, 181:

Had blacks been allowed to vote freely, Hayes easily would have carried all three states in dispute, Mississippi, and perhaps Alabama as well. Democrats at the time and later pro-Democratic historians who cried that the election had been stolen by Republicans, that it was the 'fraud of the century' conveniently ignored the clear evidence of the force, intimidation, and fraud used by Democrats to keep blacks from the polls.

20. Haworth, *Hayes-Tilden*, 331. It would not have served the strategic interests of Republicans simply to invalidate Florida's electoral votes for the presidency on the ground of improper and consequential disenfranchisement of African Americans, because with Florida removed from the count Tilden would have prevailed pursuant to the Twelfth Amendment. Nor was a remedy in federal court available for the egregious Fifteenth Amendment violation—especially not after the reversal and widespread repudiation of the federal judge in Louisiana who had attempted to rectify the wrongful disenfranchisement of black voters there in 1872 by adjusting the count based on ballots that had never been cast.

    Perhaps the morally responsible course for Republicans in Florida would have been to demand that the state's legislature repudiate the November vote as irredeemably tainted by Fifteenth Amendment violations, thereby requiring the legislature to award the state's electoral votes directly. But that course would have been a nonstarter politically, as the Democrats had gained control of the state's legislature in the 1874 elections. See Foner, *Reconstruction*, 549–50. Alternatively, perhaps the two Republicans on Florida's canvassing board, rather than purporting to count the returns in Hayes's favor, could have announced instead that they were taking it upon themselves to *adjust* the returns to compensate for the wrongful disenfranchisement of eligible African American voters in violation of the Fifteenth Amendment. Although that move would have been beyond the canvassing board's power under state law, it would arguably have been no more so than what the board actually did and would have had the virtue of forthright honesty (rather than the vice of manipulative deception). But that honesty would have made the board's action more vulnerable in a state-court challenge filed by the Democrats. Moreover, if the Republicans on the canvassing board had simply counted the ballots as cast and then had Republican voters sue the board in state court because of the wrongful disenfranchisement, the state court likely would have been unwilling to provide a remedy that would have awarded the state's electoral votes to Hayes.

21. Article Two, Section One of the Constitution provides: "The Congress may determine the Time of chusing the Electors, and the Day on which they shall give their Votes; which Day shall be the same throughout the United States." U.S. Const. art. II, § 2.
22. Haworth, *Hayes-Tilden*, 79.
23. Ibid., 77–79. The three Florida certificates are set forth in *Electoral Count of 1877: Proceedings of the Electoral Commission and of the Two Houses of Congress in Joint Meeting Relative to the Count of Electoral Votes Cast December 6, 1876* (Washington, DC: Government Printing Office, 1877), 11–14.
24. Haworth, *Hayes-Tilden*, 155–56; Holt, *By One Vote*, 189.
25. Haworth, *Hayes-Tilden*, 238–40; Holt, *By One Vote*, 195. The Democrat on Louisiana's canvassing board had resigned on December 24, 1874, leaving almost two full years to find and appoint a replacement. Ella Lonn, *Reconstruction in Louisiana After 1868* (New York: G. P. Putnam's Sons, 1918), 287, 447–48.
26. Haworth, *Hayes-Tilden*, 153–54; Holt, *By One Vote*, 186; Polakoff, *Politics of Inertia*, 310–11.
27. One of acute ambiguities of the Twelfth Amendment is the uncertainty whether disqualification of a state's electoral votes changes the denominator for determining whether a candidate has won a majority of electoral votes (by reducing the total number of electoral votes so that fewer electoral votes are required for a majority). If the denominator remains unchanged, then invalidating the electoral votes of a pivotal state will throw the election to the House of Representatives. But if invalidating a state's electoral votes reduces the denominator by the number of electoral votes invalidated, then the candidate who has more electoral votes will have a majority and thus win the presidency outright. As

discussed in Chapter 6, even after the Hayes-Tilden dispute Congress failed to remedy this ambiguity despite being thoroughly aware of its existence and its potential for great mischief.

28. Haworth, *Hayes-Tilden*, 163; Holt, *By One Vote*, 203; Polakoff, *Politics of Inertia*, 222–24.
29. Haworth, *Hayes-Tilden*, 164–65; Holt, *By One Vote*, 203; Polakoff, *Politics of Inertia*, 227.
30. If the Oregon governor had simply certified two electoral votes for Hayes, leaving the state's third electoral vote void, the posture before Congress would have been essentially the same, since the separate certificate from the secretary of state would have contained three electoral votes for Hayes. If Congress counted all three Oregon votes for Hayes based on this secretary of state certificate, then Hayes would receive an Electoral College majority (although just barely) if he also received all the electoral votes from the three disputed Southern states.
31. See Bruce Ackerman, *The Failure of the Founding Fathers: Jefferson, Marshall, and the Rise of Presidential Democracy* (Cambridge, MA: Harvard University Press, 2005), 58; see also Colvin and Foley, "The Twelfth Amendment," 1048n25, 1070, 1086.
32. Haworth, *Hayes-Tilden*, 177, 208. William Maxwell Evarts, former attorney general and Hayes's lead lawyer in the dispute, "was one of the number that believed in the right of the president of the Senate to count" the electoral votes from the states, thereby also implicitly having the constitutional authority to decide which among disputed certificates should be counted. J. Hampden Dougherty, *The Electoral System of the United States* (New York: G. P. Putnam's Sons, 1906), 222.
33. Haworth, *Hayes-Tilden*, 177:

    > If, as the Democrats asserted, the counting was to be done under the direction of the two houses, then a deadlock seemed likely to ensue. Such a deadlock, they contended, would throw the election into the Democratic House.

    Senator George Edmunds afterward reflected on the fear that the Democrats might force a confrontation based on this interpretation:

    > What *might* have followed was a declaration of a majority of the House that there had been no election at all, after which Mr. Tilden (according to the law in case of a failure to elect) could have been elected by the House,—as against the inevitable claim of Mr. Hayes that the returns as made to the president of the Senate in accordance with the requirements of the Constitution, showed that he had been elected President of the United States.

    George F. Edmunds, "Another View of 'The Hayes-Tilden Contest,'" *The Century*, May 1913, 192. Edmunds then commented on what would have happened if this conflict in constitutional interpretation persisted: "In the then state of public feeling I think there can be little, if any, doubt that an armed collision of the supporters of the respective claimants would have taken place." Ibid., 200.
34. For the failed attempt by the Senate, before the 1876 election, to adopt a measure to handle this situation, see Chapter 4, note 72.
35. Haworth, *Hayes-Tilden*, 190.
36. A copy of the Electoral Count Act of 1877 is contained in *Proceedings of the Electoral Commission*, 4–5. Interestingly, too, the bill provided: "Nothing in this act shall be held to impair or affect any right now existing under the Constitution and laws to question, by proceeding in the judicial courts of the United States, the right or title of the person who shall be declared elected, or who shall claim to be President or Vice-President of the United States, if any such right exists." Evidently the drafters of this legislation, including presumably George McCrary (as one of its main authors), contemplated the possibility that the writ of *quo warranto* might exist to test the legitimacy of a president's claim to having been duly elected; at the very least, the statute was not negating the availability of such *quo warranto* procedures that conceivably might exist.
37. In short, if a state submitted *only one* certificate, its electoral votes would count unless rejected by both houses; if a state submitted *two or more* certificates, the Electoral Commission's determination would prevail unless overruled by both houses.

38. 5 Cong. Rec. 913 (1877).
39. 5 Cong. Rec. 1050 (1877).
40. Haworth, *Hayes-Tilden*, 217; De Alva Stanwood Alexander, *A Political History of the State of New York*, vol. III (New York: Henry Holt, 1909), 356.
41. Haworth, *Hayes-Tilden*, 208. On Grant's willingness to use military force during the Hayes-Tilden dispute, see Holt, *By One Vote*, 184; Polakoff, *Politics of Inertia*, 299–300; H. W. Brands, *The Man Who Saved the Union: Ulysses Grant in War and Peace* (New York: Doubleday, 2012), 570–72; Lonn, *Reconstruction in Louisiana After 1868*, 440; see also Brooks D. Simpson, "Ulysses S. Grant and the Electoral Crisis of 1876–77," *Hayes Historical Journal* 11, no. 2 (1992): 5, 17–19.
42. Davis was chosen senator in Illinois shortly before the vote in Congress on the compromise bill to create the Electoral Commission, but by this time it was too late for the Democrats to repudiate the compromise that they had embraced. See Haworth, *Hayes-Tilden*, 218–19. Holt (at 220–21) writes: "When the House and Senate voted on January 26, however, many congressmen did not know of Davis's decision." They might have hoped that Davis could still serve on the commission before stepping down from the Court to become a senator.
43. Bradley had been appointed to the Court by Grant in 1870, having served as a corporate lawyer representing insurance and railroad companies in particular. Almost immediately upon joining the Court, his was one of the key votes to sustain the constitutionality of paper money, thereby overruling a decision just two years earlier to the contrary. This repudiation of precedent had been one of President Grant's goals in making Bradley's appointment, and Bradley's compliance was perceived by many as injecting too much politics into the Court's adjudication of constitutional controversies. Charles Fairman, "The Education of a Justice: Justice Bradley and Some of His Colleagues," *Stanford Law Review* 1 (1949): 217–20.
44. Davis's biographer indicates that Davis believed the commission "unnecessary and unconstitutional" because, in his view, Congress "had no authority to pass on the question" of the validity of a state's electoral votes. Apparently, instead, Davis thought that "the Democrats . . . should file a *quo warranto* proceeding, present all their evidence, and let the Supreme Court decide it." Willard L. King, *Lincoln's Manager: David Davis* (Cambridge, MA: Harvard University Press, 1960), 290. Although the biographer asserts that Davis "believed that, under the Constitution, Hayes was entitled to the office on the face of the state returns" (thereby suggesting that Davis would have ruled the same way as Bradley eventually did), ibid., that assertion is not the same as demonstrating what Davis would have done if in fact he had been a member of the commission. For one thing, a belief expressed outside the context of the commission's actual deliberations is not the same thing as a judgment formed after presentation of legal argumentation and evidence. For another, determination of the "face of the state returns" would have required consideration of complicated questions arising from the competing returns from the Southern states and Oregon. Thus, the best historical judgment one can reach is that how Davis would have performed had he been the commission's tiebreaker is inherently unknowable with any degree of certainty.
45. Because Bradley played the decisive role, his reasoning shall be the focus of analysis.
46. *Proceedings of the Electoral Commission*, 1021.
47. Ibid., 1020, 1025; U.S. Const., art. II, § 1.
48. Ibid., 1025. The same conclusion applied to any judicial pronouncement after December 6: "Rendered after the [electors'] votes were given, it cannot have the operation to change or affect the vote." "No tampering with the result can be admitted after the day fixed by Congress for casting the electoral votes." Ibid., 1024.
49. Ibid., 1023 (Bradley's emphasis).
50. Ibid., 1025.
51. Ibid., 1023.
52. Ibid., 1024. If Justice Bradley's analysis can be faulted, it is how he ascertained that the canvassing board spoke for the state on December 6. To be sure, as he observed, Florida's statutes explicitly gave the canvassing board the authority it exercised. But the Florida

Supreme Court subsequently said that the canvassing board egregiously abused and exceeded its authority under the statute and that, therefore, its decision should not be taken as the authoritative pronouncement of the state's position on the appointment of presidential electors as of December 6. Even if Bradley was correct that this subsequent judicial decision could not have the legal effect of retroactively reversing the canvassing board's ruling, could (and should) it nonetheless have been taken as the best evidence of what Florida statutory law called for as of that constitutionally determinative date? In other words, as Bradley himself described the issue that he needed to decide, he was obligated to figure out what best represented the will of the Florida legislature on December 6. He could try to make that determination entirely on his own, given the statutes in effect at the time, and the conduct of the state's institutions pursuant to that statute. His own determination, of course, necessarily would be an after-the-fact one, coming on February 7, long after December 6. Therefore, in making that determination, he could have relied on the assistance of the Florida Supreme Court, as a source of special wisdom on the content of Florida law. Even though the Florida Supreme Court's views of Florida law were announced after December 6, they could provide an understanding of what Florida law was on December 6—and perhaps a better understanding than Justice Bradley could determine solely on his own. (Justice Stephen Field, as the leading dissenter on the commission, made an argument along these lines. Ibid., 975.)

Insofar as Justice Bradley did not consider this alternative way of relying on the Florida Supreme Court's decision (not as operationally overturning the canvassing board but as evidence of what was authoritative at the time on December 6), the probable reason is that Bradley did not consider the Florida Supreme Court's analysis of the relevant Florida law persuasive at all. On the contrary, to Bradley's eyes, the Florida Supreme Court's opinion seemed a manipulative distortion of the relevant statutory language that existed on December 6, and not a faithful interpretation of Florida law. In this respect, Bradley's opinion anticipated the same disposition toward the Florida Supreme Court reflected in *Bush v. Gore*. (See Chapter 11.) Whether or not Bradley should have given more credence to the view of Florida law expressed by the Florida Supreme Court, his refusal to do so cannot be taken as evidence of dishonesty or partisanship on his part. Right or wrong, and whatever his previous reputation, Bradley's opinion is consistent with the efforts of a jurist striving to decide a difficult and monumental case, under extreme time pressure, as honestly and impartially as possible. For a further defense of Bradley, see Charles Fairman, *The Five Justices and the Electoral Commission: Supplement to Volume VII, History of the Supreme Court of the United States* (The Oliver Wendell Holmes Devise) (New York: Macmillan, 1988).

53. *Proceedings of the Electoral Commission*, 1023.
54. Ibid., 1036, 1037.
55. Ibid., 1038.
56. Ibid., 1035 (typographical error corrected). Bradley explicitly acknowledged that the public, at least initially, might unhappily perceive his distinction between the Florida and Oregon cases to be "technical." But he trusted that "when the public come to understand (as they will do in time) that the decision come to is founded on the Constitution and the laws, they will be better satisfied than if we should attempt to follow the clamor of the hour." Ibid., 1038–39. Bradley thought it "impossible" to decide the Florida and Oregon cases correctly (and thus fairly) without "deciding the case on technicalities" for the relevant laws required "a close and searching scrutiny" to determine "the true boundary-line between conflicting jurisdictions." Ibid., 1039.
57. Ibid., 1029.
58. Ibid., 1039.
59. Ibid., 1040.
60. Ibid.
61. Ibid., 1041.
62. One particular fact about the South Carolina election seems susceptible to judicial notice: "The number of votes recorded in South Carolina exceeded that state's entire adult male population—a clear indicator of fraud." Holt, *By One Vote*, 167. Insofar as the

conditions in South Carolina were anarchic on Election Day in 1876, the disorder was largely caused by terrorism perpetrated by rifle clubs and Klan-like activity in support of the Democrats, and thus as a matter of equity the Democrats should not have been permitted to profit by their side's own wrongdoing.

63. One objective piece of evidence supporting Bradley's own self-professed claim of integrity was a vote he took on a tangential aspect of the Florida dispute that turned out to be inconsequential. In addition to the main contentions concerning the propriety of the canvassing board's pronouncement in favor of the Hayes electors (and the status of the belated judicial and legislative efforts to undo it), there was a claim that one of the Hayes electors was ineligible to serve as an elector because allegedly he had held a federal office on November 7. (This tangential Florida issue, in other words, bore some similarity to the Oregon dispute.) The Electoral Commission needed to decide how it would handle this issue, and on February 7—the same day as Bradley issued his fateful opinion upholding the claim of the Hayes electors on the main point—Bradley broke with his seven Republican colleagues on the commission and ruled with the seven Democrats that the commission would entertain evidence that this one Hayes elector was ineligible to serve. See Haworth, *Hayes-Tilden*, 234–35.

    Bradley's breach of party unity had the potential to be significant. After all, if even just one electoral vote in favor of Hayes was declared null and void, the most that Hayes could do would be to tie Tilden, sending the election to the House, which was assured to pick Tilden. Had Tilden supporters been able to prove that this one elector had been ineligible on December 6, it might have been momentous. But on February 8, the evidence showed that in fact the elector had resigned his federal office by October 2, and thus factually there was no basis to the allegation of ineligibility. After that digression was resolved, Justice Bradley never parted company with his fellow Republicans on the commission.

64. Haworth, *Hayes-Tilden*, 257–58, 274; see also Frank B. Evans, *Pennsylvania Politics, 1872–1877: A Study in Political Leadership* (Harrisburg: The Pennsylvania Historical and Museum Commission, 1966), 301–03; Michael Les Benedict, "Southern Democrats in the Crisis of 1876–77: A Reconsideration of *Reunion and Reaction*," in *Preserving the Constitution: Essays on Politics and the Constitution in the Reconstruction Era* (New York: Fordham University Press, 2006), 186.

65. Haworth, *Hayes-Tilden*, 274. I have written previously on this Vermont development and Samuel Randall's heroic role in how he handled it. Edward B. Foley, "Virtue over Party: Samuel Randall's Electoral Heroism and Its Continuing Importance," *UC Irvine Law Review* 3 (2013): 475.

66. *Proceedings of the Electoral Commission*, 712.

67. Ibid.

68. Ibid.

69. Haworth, *Hayes-Tilden*, 275.

70. *Proceedings of the Electoral Commission*, 713.

71. Ibid.

72. Ibid., 717.

73. Haworth, *Hayes-Tilden*, 276. See also Frank B. Evans, *Pennsylvania Politics*, 304 (quoting Hubert Bruce Fuller, *The Speakers of the House* (Boston: Little Brown, 1909), 199): "The House session of March 1, 1877, was 'probably the wildest that ever occurred in any American legislative body.'"

74. "Latest Intelligence: the Presidential Election," *The Times (London)*, March 2, 1877, 5; "The Last State Counted," *New York Times*, March 2, 1877, 1.

75. 5 Cong. Rec. 2031 (March 1, 1877) (Hooker of Mississippi).

76. Ibid., 2033 (Tucker of Virginia). A third obstructionist echoed the point: "the preliminary question" of the second certificate "must be determined before we enter upon the two hours' debate on the objections" to the single certificate for this reason: if Vermont properly must go to the commission, then "the two hours' debate upon the objections cannot of course begin." Ibid. (O'Brien of Maryland).

77. 5 Cong. Rec. 2033 (March 1, 1877).

78. Ibid.

79. Haworth, *Hayes-Tilden*, 268–69. On the Wormley Conference and various views of the bargain struck there and its significance, see Holt, *By One Vote*, 240–41; Foner, *Reconstruction*, 580–81; Benedict, "Southern Democrats in the Crisis of 1876–77," 206; Polakoff, *Politics of Inertia*, 310–11; C. Vann Woodward, *Reunion and Reaction: The Compromise of 1877 and the End of Reconstruction* (New York: Doubleday Anchor, 1966), 212–14, 221–25.
80. 5 Cong. Rec. 2047 (1877).
81. 5 Cong. Rec. 2048–49 (1877).
82. Here is a breakdown of the vote on the hardliner resolution:

	Republicans	Northern Democrats	Southern Democrats	Independents	Total
Yea	0	82	34	0	116
Nay	101	31	13	3	148
Abstain	5	10	10	1	26
Total	106	123	57	4	290

Southern Democrats are those from the eleven former Confederate states; Northern Democrats include those from Kentucky and Missouri. The roll is taken from 5 Cong. Rec. 2048–49 (March 1, 1877). For purposes of this chart, Republicans include three members—Simeon Chittenden (NY), Dudley C. Denison (VT), and G. Wiley Wells (MS)—identified as "Independent Republicans," and one Democrat—William H. Felton (GA)—identified as an "Independent Democrat." See Kenneth C. Martis, et al., *The Historical Atlas of Political Parties in the United States Congress, 1789–1989* (New York: Macmillan, 1989), 128. Their classification in this chart is consistent with their congressional careers, both that year and overall. See ibid., 437 (Felton's voting record as a Southern Democrat).
83. The number 139 is the sum of the 116 who actually voted for the resolution plus the 23 additional Southerners who hypothetically might have but for Levy's speech. Conversely, 135 is the result of subtracting the 13 of these Southerners who voted against the resolution from the total of 148 voting nay.
84. Fuller, *Speakers of the House*, 202.
85. Harry Barnard, *Rutherford B. Hayes and His America* (Indianapolis: Bobbs-Merrill, 1954), 394.
86. Woodward, *Reunion and Reaction*, 217–18.
87. On this view, enough Southerners were exhausted with civil war and wanted no part in potentially instigating a second one. Likewise, there were not enough Northern Democrats ultimately willing to risk a second civil war just to install Tilden as president. Even Tilden himself proved unwilling to risk military confrontation over his claim to the White House, although he vacillated until the end. For an analysis of the Southern and Northern Democrats in Congress as they contemplated resistance to completion of the count, see Benedict, "Southern Democrats in the Crisis of 1876–77," 186.
88. "Pandemonium" is how one Randall biographer described the House on March 1. Sidney I. Pomerantz, "Samuel Jackson Randall: Protectionist-Democrat, 1863–1890" (unpublished master's thesis, Columbia University, 1932).
89. In refusing to permit a vote on the hardliner proposal, moreover, it appears that Randall was acting contrary to the wishes, at that particular moment, of the majority of his own Republican caucus in the House. (In this respect, he violated what later would be known as the "Hastert rule," after another Speaker. See Marjorie R. Hershey, *Guide to U.S. Political Parties* (Washington, DC: CQ Press, 2014), 327–28). An overwhelming majority of his caucus supported the hardliner proposal at the end of the two-hour debate: 116 for, 44 against, and 20 abstentions. Although the division within the Democratic caucus might have been closer had a vote on the resolution occurred before the two-hour debate

(because the same resolution would have been much more significantly obstructionist at this point), it is difficult to presume that at least 27 of the eventual yea votes would have been against it at this earlier point. Moreover, if Randall really thought the majority of his Democrats were against the obstructionist maneuver before starting the two-hour clock, it would have been easy for him to permit a quick vote on the hardliner proposal since he knew all the Republicans would be against it and it would have been defeated by a wide margin. Thus, the fact that Randall did not let the House vote on the proposal at that time suggests that he believed it had a chance of passing the whole House precisely because it has strong support within his own caucus at that moment. For the ebbs and flows of the strength of the filibustering group within the Democrats during February of 1877, see Benedict, "Southern Democrats in the Crisis of 1876–77," 199–206.

90. Foner, *Reconstruction*, 581.
91. Roy Morris's one-sided 2003 book, *Fraud of the Century*, briefly describes the events of March 1 (at 235–37), but offers no assessment of Randall's conduct.
92. James Ford Rhodes, *History of the United States: From the Compromise of 1850 to the Final Restoration of Home Rule at the South in 1877*, vol. 7 (New York: Macmillan, 1909), 278, 285.
93. James Monroe, "The Hayes-Tilden Electoral Commission," *Atlantic Monthly*, Oct. 1893, 532–33.
94. Samuel W. McCall, *The Life of Thomas Brackett Reed* (Boston: Houghton Mifflin, 1914), 119.
95. George Rothwell Brown, *The Leadership of Congress* (Indianapolis: Bobbs-Merrill, 1922), 78–79.
96. Randall Papers, Historical Society of Pennsylvania, Philadelphia. When pledging himself to impartiality Randall evidently was concerned about the tariff policy and economic issues, and not just the resolution of the disputed Hayes-Tilden election. He explicitly mentions "finances" among the "every vexed questions" to which he would "give a true expression of the opinions of all the representatives of the people." Yet it is reasonable also to view Randall as pledging himself to impartiality more broadly, beyond the realm of "finance," to the paramount issue of the day: the determination of the presidency. The pledge appears a general one, applying to "every" difficult question "including"—but not limited to—financial ones. (I am indebted to Les Benedict's assistance in analyzing Randall's handwritten words on this document and in assessing their significance.)
97. McCall, *The Life of Thomas Brackett Reed*, 119.
98. Hamilton James Eckenrode, *Rutherford B. Hayes: Statesman of Union* (New York: Dodd & Mead, 1930), 230; Albert Virgil House Jr., "The Political Career of Samuel Jackson Randall" (PhD diss., University of Wisconsin, 1934): 102; Joseph M. Rogers, "How Hayes Became President," *McClure's Magazine*, May 1904, 87; Haworth, *Hayes-Tilden*, 281; Allan Nevins, *Abram S. Hewitt* (New York: Harper & Brothers, 1935), 385; Flick, *Hayes*, 395.
99. 5 Cong. Rec. 2068 (1877); Haworth, *Hayes-Tilden*, 282–83.
100. 5 Cong. Rec. 1012, 2120, 2039 (1877). One clue to the resolution's inoperability is the form that it took. It was a conventional resolution of the House, with each member having a vote. It was *not* the special procedure pursuant to the Twelfth Amendment, in which each state's delegation in the House has a single vote. That special Twelfth Amendment procedure, when properly invoked after no candidate receives a majority of electoral votes, results in the official election of the president. It was that special Twelfth Amendment procedure that the "irreconcilables" attempted to invoke the previous night before Wisconsin's vote and the final tally had been officially declared in the joint session. Had the House attempted to invoke this special procedure on March 3, there would have been a genuine constitutional crisis, because there would have been two conflicting official declarations of who had been duly elected president. But the resolution was carefully worded so that it did not purport to invoke the special Twelfth Amendment procedure. Indeed, another clue was the content of the resolution itself, with the House declaring that Tilden had won 196 electoral votes, a clear

majority, thereby entirely inconsistent with the House having constitutional authority to declare unilaterally that he was officially elected president.

101. Haworth, *Hayes-Tilden*, 285. As unlikely as it was that Tilden would attempt to set up "a rival capital" in New York, Grant gave "instructions to put New York in a state of siege, in such an event, taking military possession of the narrow peninsula connecting it with the mainland, and, with the aid of the Navy, cutting off its supplies of food and water." William Conant Church, *Ulysses S. Grant and the Period of National Preservation and Reconstruction* (New York: G. P. Putnam's Sons, 1897), 421. Similarly, in order to assure that Hayes would be successfully inaugurated in Washington, Grant ordered troops on alert. See also Brands, *The Man Who Saved the Union*, 576.
102. Barnard, *Hayes and His America*, 401–402; Polakoff, *Politics of Inertia*, 313.

Chapter 6

1. Useful sources on Gilded Age politics include Mark Wahlgren Summers, *Party Games: Getting, Keeping, and Using Power in Gilded Age Politics* (Chapel Hill: University of North Carolina Press, 2004); Morton Keller, *Affairs of State: Public Life in Late Nineteenth Century America* (Cambridge, MA: Belknap Press of Harvard University Press, 1977); H. Wayne Morgan, *From Hayes to McKinley: National Party Politics, 1877–1896* (Syracuse, NY: Syracuse University Press, 1969). For a basic introduction, see Robert W. Cherny, *American Poli tics in the Gilded Age, 1868–1900* (Wheaton, IL: Harlan Davidson, 1997). The social background of the era is well captured in H.W. Brands, *American Colossus: The Triumph of Capitalism, 1865–1900* (New York: Doubleday, 2010). An older but still valuable overview is John A Garraty, *The New Commonwealth, 1877–1890* (New York: Harper & Row 1968). See also Peter H. Argersinger, "New Perspectives on Election Fraud in the Gilded Age" (as well as other chapters) in *Structure, Process, and Party: Essays in American Political History* (Armonk, NY: M. E. Sharpe, 1992). For a fascinating and important study on a different electoral issue during this era—the problem of gerrymandering—see Peter H. Argersinger, *Representation and Inequality in Late Nineteenth-Century America* (New York: Cambridge University Press, 2012). Although encompassing the Progressive Era as well as the Gilded Age, an especially significant analysis of the changing political conditions during this period is Michael E. McGerr, *The Decline of Popular Politics: The American North, 1865–1928* (New York: Oxford University Press, 1986).
2. The history of the decade of reform efforts between the Hayes-Tilden dispute and the passage of the Electoral Count Act of 1887 is set forth in Nathan L. Colvin and Edward B. Foley, "Lost Opportunity: Learning the Wrong Lessons from the Hayes-Tilden Dispute," *Fordham Law Review* 79 (2010): 1043. See also Stephen A. Siegel, "The Conscientious Congressman's Guide to the Electoral Count Act of 1887," *Florida Law Review* 56 (2004): 541; Eric Schickler, Terri Bimes, and Robert W. Mickey, "Safe at Any Speed: Legislative Intent, The Electoral Count Act of 1887, and *Bush v. Gore*," *Journal of Law & Politics* 16 (2000): 717.
3. See the sources cited in the relevant notes for each of these states (listed in chronological order) later in this chapter.
4. George Edmunds, "Presidential Elections," *American Law Review* 12 (1877): 1.
5. 45 Cong. Rec. 51 (December 9, 1878).
6. Ibid., 52. This provision put great power in the hands of a Hewlett-like character who offers a purported second return at the last minute. Under the bill, both houses of Congress would need to reject this trumped-up second return in favor of the first; otherwise, the first would be discarded as well. (Alternatively, if some second returns were so frivolous as not to be entitled to consideration, there would need to be a mechanism to make that determination.)
7. See Herman V. Ames, *Proposed Amendments to the Constitution of the United States During the First Century of its History* (Washington, DC: Government Printing Office, 1897), 119–20 (describing three proposals along this line, one of which was Edmunds's).
8. Edmunds, "Presidential Elections," 20.

9. Ames, *Proposed Amendments*, 121.
10. 8 Cong. Rec. 170. (December 13, 1878).
11. See Colvin and Foley, "Lost Opportunity," 1053–56; Ames, *Proposed Amendments*, 96–98.
12. The final certified margin was 21,033. *Presidential Elections, 1789–2000* (Washington, DC: CQ Press, 2002), 126.
13. Herbert J. Clancy, *The Presidential Election of 1880* (Chicago: Loyola University Press, 1958), 243–44.
14. Morgan, *National Party Politics*, 119. See also Kenneth D. Ackerman, *Dark Horse: The Surprise Election and Political Murder of President James A. Garfield* (New York: Carroll & Graf, 2003).
15. Morgan, *National Party Politics*, 119–20; Clancy, *The Presidential Election of 1880*, 246–47.
16. 11 Cong. Rec. 1387 (February 9, 1881); See also Kenneth C. Martis, et al., *The Historical Atlas of Political Parties in the United States Congress, 1789–1989* (New York: Macmillan, 1989), 133.
17. CQ Press, *Presidential Elections*, 127. The best single source on the 1884 election is Mark Wahlgren Summers, *Rum, Romanism & Rebellion: The Making of a President, 1884* (Chapel Hill: University of North Carolina Press, 2000).
18. Francis Lynde Stetson and William Gorham Rice, *Was New York's Vote Stolen?* (New York: North American Review, 1913), 90–91.
19. "A Rock Amidst the Waves," *New York Tribune*, Nov. 17, 1884, 4.
20. David Saville Murray, *James G. Blaine: A Political Idol of Other Days* (New York: Dodd Mead, 1934), 324.
21. Stetson and Rice, *Was New York's Vote Stolen?*, 88; See also Summers, *Rum, Romanism & Rebellion*, 294.
22. Colvin and Foley, "Lost Opportunity," 1076n211.
23. S. 9, 49th Cong. (1886).
24. On Sherman, see Winfield S. Kerr, *John Sherman: His Life and Public Services*, vol. 2 (Boston: Sherman, French, 1908); Theodore E. Burton, *John Sherman* (Boston: Houghton Mifflin, 1908).
25. 17 Cong. Rec. 1021 (1886).
26. Ibid., 1023.
27. Ibid., 1021.
28. Ibid., 1020.
29. Paul Leland Haworth, *The Hayes-Tilden Disputed Presidential Election of 1876* (New York: Russell & Russell, 1906), 197.
30. 17 Cong. Rec. 1022 (1886).
31. Ibid., 1026.
32. Ibid.
33. Ibid., 1025.
34. Ibid., 1022.
35. Hoar made clear that he saw the function of resolving a dispute over a state's submission of electoral votes to be adjudicatory, not legislative or policymaking, in nature: "You are to have a tribunal which is to determine the existing fact and the existing law, in contradistinction from determining the law or creating the fact according to his own desire." He added for emphasis: "This function is to determine the existing fact and apply it to the previously declared and ascertained law. It is a function into which the wish or desire of the person exercising it cannot properly enter." Ibid., 1020.
36. 18 Cong. Rec. 74–77 (1886); ibid., 668 (1887).
37. Report of the Conferees, and Statement of the Conferees, 18 Cong. Rec. 668 (January 14, 1887).
38. John W. Burgess, "The Law of the Electoral Count," *Political Science Quarterly* 3, no. 4 (1888): 643.
39. L. Kinvin Wroth, "Election Contests and the Electoral Vote," *Dickinson Law Review* 65 (1961): 321, 343; See also Jack Maskell, et al., "Counting Electoral Votes in Congress: Multiple Lists of Electors from One State," Congressional Research Service Memorandum (January 2, 2001): 8–9.

40. Maskell approvingly quotes Wroth on this point.
41. Siegel, "Conscientious Congressman's Guide," 663–69.
42. For further discussion of these and related difficulties, see Nathan L. Colvin and Edward B. Foley, "The Twelfth Amendment: A Constitutional Ticking Time Bomb," *University of Miami Law Review* 64 (2010): 475.
43. Burgess, "Law of the Electoral Count," 651.
44. 17 Cong. Rec. 1019–20.
45. John C. Fortier, "The 2000 Election," in *After the People Vote: A Guide to the Electoral College*, ed. John C. Fortier (Washington, DC: AEI Press 2004), 45–46.
46. 17 Cong. Rec. 820, 1057, 1061. Evarts was Hoar's cousin and also had been Hayes's lead counsel before the Electoral Commission. The best biography of Evarts is Chester L. Barrows, *William M. Evarts: Lawyer, Diplomat, Statesman* (Chapel Hill: University of North Carolina Press, 1941); see also Brainerd Dyer, *The Public Career of William M. Evarts* (Berkeley: University of California Press, 1933). An excellent biography of Hoar is Richard E. Welch Jr., *George Frisbie Hoar and the Half-Breed Republicans* (Cambridge, MA: Harvard University Press, 1971). Hoar also wrote interesting and illuminating memoirs. George Frisbie Hoar, *Autobiography of Seventy Years* (Worcester, MA: Scribner's, 1903) (two volumes).
47. Burgess, "Law of the Electoral Count," 651. Judge Richard Posner has expressed the view that "requir[ing] an absolute majority of electoral votes seems to me preferable, for imagine a disaster that prevented all but 10 of the electors from casting their votes on [the constitutionally required date]: could 6 of the 10 elect the President?" Richard A. Posner, *Breaking the Deadlock: The 2000 Election, the Constitution, and the Courts* (Princeton, NJ: Princeton University Press, 2001), 134–35.
48. CQ Press, *Presidential Elections*, 128.
49. The book on this election is Charles W. Calhoun, *Minority Victory: Gilded Age Politics and the Front Porch Campaign of 1888* (Lawrence: University Press of Kansas, 2008).
50. Ibid., 175.
51. Ibid., 174–77.
52. Richard Hofstadter, *The American Political Tradition and the Men Who Made It* (New York: Vintage reprint, 1989), 223.
53. James L. Baumgardner, "The 1888 Presidential Election: How Corrupt?," *Presidential Studies Quarterly* 14, no. 3 (1984): 416–27.
54. 17 Cong. Rec. 1019–20.
55. Edmunds, "Presidential Elections," 20.
56. Keller, *Affairs of* State, 567. Keller calls his chapter "The Crisis of the Nineties."
57. The years in parentheses refer to the date of the election, not the date on which the dispute was resolved. For details, see appendix.
58. For further information on the West Virginia dispute, see James Henry Jacobs, "The West Virginia Gubernatorial Election Contest, 1888–1890," *West Virginia History* 7 (1946): 263; see also John Alexander Williams, *West Virginia: A Bicentennial History* (New York: Norton, 1976), 116; Charles Henry Ambler, *West Virginia: The Mountain State* (New York: Prentice Hall, 1940), 461–62; Richard Ellsworth Fast and Hu Maxwell, *The History and Government of West Virginia* (Morgantown: Acme Publishing, 1901), 201–202.
59. William Alexander MacCorkle, *The Recollections of Fifty Years of West Virginia* (New York: G. P. Putnam's Sons, 1928), 431–44.
60. See Stanley J. Folmsbee, Robert E. Corlew and Enoch L. Mitchell, *Tennessee: A Short History* (Knoxville: University of Tennessee Press, 1969): 403–404; J. Eugene Lewis, "The Tennessee Gubernatorial Campaign and Election of 1894," *Tennessee Historical Quarterly* 13, no. 2 (1954): 99.
61. On this Connecticut dispute, see Albert E. Van Dusen, *Connecticut* (New York: Random House, 1961), 256–58; J. Birney Tuttle, *The Period of Peaceful Anarchy: When Connecticut was Ruled by a Crowbar Governor* (Hartford, CT: New Haven County Bar Association, 1933); Norris G. Osborn, "Political Progress," in *History of Connecticut*, vol. 2 (New York: The States History Company, 1925); Lynde Harrison "The Election

Controversy in Connecticut," *New Englander & Yale Review* 54, no. 4 (1891): 354–78 (series of articles on both sides of issue); see also Kevin Murphy, *Crowbar Governor: The Life and Times of Morgan Gardner Bulkeley* (Middletown, CT: Wesleyan University Press, 2010); Wesley W. Horton and Jeffrey J. White, "The Baldwin-Hamersley Court," *Connecticut Bar Journal* 77 (2003): 245–47.

62. Charles Carroll, *Rhode Island: Three Centuries of Democracy*, vol. 2 (New York: Lewis Historical Publishing, 1932), 660–61; see also Patrick T. Conley and Robert G. Flanders Jr., *The Rhode Island State Constitution: A Reference Guide* (Westport, CT: Praeger, 2007), 144 (discussing the "election fiasco").
63. See James McClellan Hamilton, *History of Montana: From Wilderness to Statehood* (Portland, OR: Binford & Mort, 1970), 561–77; Michael P. Malone, *The Battle for Butte* (Seattle: University of Washington Press, 1981), 91; Michael Malone, Richard B. Roeder and William L. Lang, *Montana: A History of Two Centuries* (Seattle: University of Washington Press, 1991), 198–99; see also John Morrison and Catherine Wright Morrison, *Mavericks: The Lives and Battles of Montana's Political Legends* (Helena: Montana Historical Society Press, 2003), 28–29.
64. Wilbur Fiske Stone, *History of Colorado*, vol. I (Chicago: S. J. Clarke, 1918), 435. See also Frank Hall, *History of the State of Colorado*, vol. 4 (Chicago: Blakely, 1895), 17.
65. William E. Parrish, "The Great Kansas Legislative Imbroglio of 1893," *Journal of the West* 7, no. 4 (1968): 472; William E. Connelley, *Standard History of Kansas and Kansas* (Chicago: Lewis, 1918), 1154–88; see also John D. Bright, *Kansas: The First Century* (New York: Lewis Historical Publishing, 1956), 490.

    On the New Jersey episode of 1894, see *New York Times* coverage, especially: "New Jersey's Two Senates," Jan. 10, 1894, 1; "The Jersey Senate Power," Mar. 10, 1894, 2. See also Richard A. Hogarty, "Leon Abbett's New Jersey: The Emergence of a Modern Governor," in *Memoirs of the American Philosophical Society* (Philadelphia: American Philosophical Society, 2001).
66. Fleming v. Commissioners, 31 W. Va. 608 (1888); Goff v. Wilson, 32 W. Va. 393 (1889); Carr v. Wilson, 32 W.Va. 419 (1889); Morris v. Bulkeley, 61 Conn. 287 (1892); In re Legislative Adjournment, 18 R.I. 824 (1893); see also Horton and White, *Baldwin-Hamersley Court*, 246–47 ("*Morris v. Bulkeley* has to be one of the lowest points in the history of the Connecticut Supreme Court.").
67. State v. Kenney, 9 Mont. 223 (1890).
68. In re Speakership of the House of Representatives, 15 Colo. 520 (1891); In re Gunn, 50 Kan. 155 (1893); Werts v. Rogers, 28 A. 726 (S. Ct. of NJ, 1894).
69. Louis Clinton Hatch, *Maine: A History* (New York: The American Historical Society, 1919; reprinted 1974), 227–29; John Edwards Godfrey, *Memoir of Hon. Edward Kent* (1879), 456, available in *Annals of American Law* (Farmington Hills, MI: Gale, 2015).
70. See appendix.
71. Phyllis Austin, "Curtis Apparently Wins, Erwin Asks Recount," *Bangor Daily News*, Nov. 5, 1970, 1 (the secretary of state "ordered strict security measures to protect the ballots from possible tampering."); Ken Ward, "Senate Presidency Suddenly Crucial," *Bangor Daily News*, Nov. 6, 1970, 1.
72. On the crisis and Chamberlain's role in resolving it, see Louis Clinton Hatch, *Maine: A History*, vol. 2 (New York: American Historical Society, 1919), 553–62; John S. C. Abbott, *The History of Maine* (Augusta, ME: E. E. Knowles, 1892), 562–66; John J. Pullen, *Joshua Chamberlain: A Hero's Life and Legacy*, (Mechanicsburg, PA: Stackpole Books, 1999) (in particular chaps. 8–9); Edward G. Longacre, *Joshua Chamberlain: The Soldier and the Man* (Conshohocken, PA: Combined Publishing, 1999), 279–82; Willard M. Wallace, *Soul of the Lion: A Biography of General Joshua L. Chamberlain* (Gettysburg, PA: Stan Clark Military Books, 1995), 254–68; Jeremiah E. Goulka, ed., *The Grand Old Man of Maine: Selected Letters of Joshua Lawrence Chamberlain, 1865–1914* (Chapel Hill: University of North Carolina Press, 2004), 91–100; Eugene A. Mawhinney, "Joshua Chamberlain and the Twelve Days Which Shook Maine, January 6–17" (unpublished manuscript, University of Maine, 1880); see also Joshua Lawrence Chamberlain[?], *The Twelve*

Days at Augusta (Portland, ME: Smith & Sale, 1906). (Pullen believes Chamberlain wrote this account.)

73. Hatch, *Maine: A History*, vol. 2, 599.
74. Pullen (at 80) suggests that Garcelon left the details of the returns to the council, but other accounts place Garcelon at the center of the council's conduct in the manipulation of the returns. See also Hatch, *Maine: A History*, vol. 2, 602: "Garcelon said he was prouder in his action in the count than anything [else] he ever did in life."
75. Wallace, *Soul of the Lion*, 254–55.
76. Hatch, *Maine: A History*, vol. 2, 599.
77. Ibid., 602.
78. Pullen, *A Hero's Life*, 82. Likewise, votes for "John T. Wallace Jr." were not credited to the same candidate as votes for "John T. Wallace." Ibid. See also Opinions of Justices, 70 Me. 570, 576 (1880) (hereafter *Opinions II*).
79. Pullen, *A Hero's Life*, 83.
80. In re Opinions of the Justices, 70 Me. 560 (1879) (hereinafter *Opinions I*). The case technically arrived at the court upon questions submitted by the governor, but he submitted his questions only in an effort to put the case in a more favorable posture than if it were considered on the Republicans' petition. See Hatch, *Maine: A History*, vol. 2, 608. The gambit failed as the court resoundingly rejected the governor's position. In upholding "the ballot" as "the truest indication of the popular will," the court proclaimed: "The official returns . . . are not required to be written with the scrupulous nicety of a writing master, or with the technical accuracy of a plea in abatement. . . . It is enough if the returns can be understood, and if understood, full effect should be given to their natural and obvious meaning." *Opinions I*, 569.
81. Abbott, *The History of Maine*, 563.
82. Ibid. See also Pullen, *A Hero's Life*, 87–88; *Opinions II*, 578 (the court asserting that the governor "refused" to obey its previous order).
83. Quoted in Pullen, *A Hero's Life*, 84.
84. Hatch, *Maine: A History*, vol. 2, 604.
85. Quoted in Pullen, *A Hero's Life*, 84.
86. On the mob being pro-Fusionist, see Edward Nelson Dingley, *The Life and Times of Nelson Dingley, Jr.* (Kalamazoo, MI: Ihling Brothers & Everard, 1902), 171. Pullen credits Dingley's account as "reliable" despite its Republican "shadings." Pullen, *A Hero's Life*, 92.
87. Longacre, *Chamberlain*, 281; Pullen, *A Hero's Life*, 96.
88. Longacre, *Chamberlain*, 279–82; Pullen, *A Hero's Life*, 93–96.
89. *Opinions II*.
90. Ibid., 586. The court continued in the same vein:

> The doctrine of that act [undertaken by the governor and council] gives to the executive department the power to rob the people of the legislature they have chosen, and force upon them one to serve its own purposes.
>
> It poisons the very fountain of legislation, and tends to corrupt the legislative department of the government. It strikes a death blow at the heart of popular government and renders its foundations and great bulwarks—the will of the people, as expressed by the ballot—a farce.

Ibid., 586–87.

91. Ibid., 583 (court's opinion issued on Jan. 16); see also Hatch, *Maine: A History*, 612; Pullen, *A Hero's Life*, 99 (Jan. 28, the date the Fusionists backed down).
92. See Abbott, *The History of Maine*, 566; Hatch, *Maine: A History*, vol. 2, 626.
93. Pullen, *A Hero's Life*, 81.
94. Ibid., 85.
95. Tracy Campbell, *Deliver the Vote: A History of Election Fraud, an American Political Tradition—1742–2004* (New York: Carroll & Graf, 2005), 108.
96. Hambleton Tapp and James C. Klotter, *Kentucky: Decades of Discord, 1865–1900* (Lexington: University Press of Kentucky, 1977), 453; Campbell, *Deliver the Vote*, 110.

97. 178 U.S. 548 (1900).
98. On John Marshall Harlan's life and legacy, see Linda Przybyszewski, *The Republic According to John Marshall Harlan* (Chapel Hill: University of North Carolina Press, 1999); see also Loren P. Beth, *John Marshall Harlan: The Last Whig Justice* (Lexington: University Press of Kentucky, 1992).
99. This relationship between *Taylor v. Beckham* and *Bush v. Gore* will become clearer after consideration of the "Ballot Box 13" episode of 1948 (in Chapter 8) as well as *Bush v. Gore* itself (in Chapter 11).
100. Lowell Hayes Harrison and James C. Klotter, *A New History of Kentucky* (Lexington: University Press of Kentucky, 1997), 269.
101. See R. E. Hughes, F. W. Schaefer and E. L. Williams, *That Kentucky Campaign; or the Law, the Ballot and the People in the Goebel-Taylor Contest* (Cincinnati: Robert Clarke, 1900), 289–94.
102. Tapp and Klotter, *Decades of Discord*, 410.
103. Campbell, *Deliver the Vote*, 107.
104. Tapp and Klotter, *Decades of Discord*, 441.
105. Ibid.
106. Campbell, *Deliver the Vote*, 107.
107. Tapp and Klotter, *Decades of Discord*, 442–43. Harrison and Klotter, *New Kentucky History*, 271.
108. Campbell, *Deliver the Vote*, 108; Harrison and Klotter, *New Kentucky History*, 272.
109. Campbell, *Deliver the Vote*, 109.
110. Taylor v. Beckham, 56 S.W. 177 (1900). Tapp and Klotter, *Decades of Discord*, 453.
111. *Taylor*, 182.
112. Ibid., 183.
113. Ibid.
114. The one dissenting judge on the Kentucky court thought that the legislature lacked authority to award the election to Goebel if the alleged factual predicate for doing so was that the voters of Louisville had been intimidated at the polls by the invocation of the militia on Election Day. On this factual predicate, the judge argued, the only option was to void the election and declare the office vacant, rather than declaring Goebel the winner. The dissenting judge further asserted that the judiciary had the authority to order this vacancy without violating the constitutional separation of powers. Ibid., 166–68.
115. Taylor v. Beckham, 178 U.S. 548 (1900).
116. Ibid., 580. *Luther v. Borden* is discussed in Chapter 3.
117. Ibid., (emphasis added).
118. Ibid., 578.
119. Ibid., 579–80.
120. 178 U.S. 548, 606 (1900) (emphasis added).
121. Ibid., 606–07.
122. Ibid., 605, 608.
123. 321 U.S. 1, 7 (1944). *Snowden* concerned the exclusion of a candidate from the ballot for a primary election to a state legislative seat, and it reaffirmed the proposition established in *Taylor* that the Fourteenth Amendment could not be invoked by a candidate for public office just because a state's election officials flagrantly deviated from the state's own electoral rules.
124. The otherwise fine biographies of Harlan published in recent decades do not discuss *Taylor*. See Przybyszewski and Beth cited in note 98.
125. *Taylor v. Beckham* shows that Harlan was a progenitor of both parts of the famous philosophy of the Court's role in American society articulated in *U.S. v. Carolene Products Co.*, 304 U.S. 144, 152n4 (1938). This philosophy, reflecting the essence of New Deal jurisprudence, held that although the federal judiciary should generally defer to a legislature's policy choices, such deference was unwarranted when the legislature *either* discriminated against a minority group *or* restricted the equal opportunity of adult citizens

to participate in the election of the legislature. See John Hart Ely, *Democracy and Distrust* (Cambridge, MA: Harvard University Press, 1980).

126. Campbell, *Deliver the Vote*, 131.

Chapter 7

1. For background on the Progressive Era, see Michael McGerr, *A Fierce Discontent: The Rise and Fall of the Progressive Movement in America, 1870–1920* (Oxford: Oxford University Press, 2003). See also Lewis Gould, *America in the Progressive Era, 1890–1914* (New York: Routledge, 2013); Nell Irvin Painter, *Standing at Armageddon: The United States, 1877–1919* (New York: Norton, 1987); Robert H. Wiebe, *The Search for the New Order* (New York: Hill and Wang, 1967). Several valuable essays on Progressive Era politics are in Part Three of Richard L. McCormick, *The Party Period and Public Policy: American Politics from the Age of Jackson to the Progressive Era* (New York: Oxford University Press, 1986).
2. See Eleanor Flexner, *A Century of Struggle: The Woman's Rights Movement in the United States* (Cambridge, MA: Belknap Press of Harvard University Press, 1975). See also Robert Cooney, "Taking a New Look-The Enduring Significance of the American Suffrage Movement," Women's National History Project, accessed March 30, 2015, http://mith.umd.edu/WomensStudies/ReadingRoom/History/Vote/enduring-significance.html.
3. The single best account of the Stolen Senate episode is to be found in Herbert J. Bass, *"I Am a Democrat": The Political Career of David Bennett Hill* (Syracuse, NY: Syracuse University Press, 1961), 191–200. See also De Alva Stanwood Alexander, *The Political History of the State of New York*, vol. 4 (New York: Henry Holt, 1923), 158–64; Roscoe C.E. Brown and Ray Burdick Smith, *Political and Governmental History of the State of New York*, vol. 3 (Syracuse, NY: Syracuse University Press, 1922), chap. 30.
4. These numbers are based on calculations taken from official documents and multiple newspaper reports. There is some confusion about these numbers among the various secondary sources, primarily because some treat the independent candidate as a Republican and others treat him as a Democrat. In truth, neither party could rely upon his support. De Alva Alexander states the numbers correctly, as does Bass. Alexander, *Political History of New York*, 158; Bass, *I Am a Democrat*, 191.
5. People ex rel. Sherwood v. Board of State Canvassers, 129 N.Y. 360, 374 (1891): "We agree that the board of state canvassers act ministerially, and that they have no power or jurisdiction to go outside of the returns of the county canvassers, or to institute an inquiry as to the eligibility of the candidates who were voted for by the electors."
6. Ibid., 370. The court added that although "the state canvassers were bound to canvas the returns from the twenty-seventh senatorial district, and to declare the result in compliance with the law, yet, for reasons we have given, the court will not aid the [Republican candidate]." Ibid., 375.
7. Ibid., 379:

   > The relief he does ask is that the votes for senator cast in his district shall be counted, and the result properly certified. He shows a clear legal right to that relief, for the law awards it, and, as we have held this day, it is immaterial to that relief at the hands of the canvassers whether he is eligible or not.

8. In 1891, New York used an early form of the "Australian" ballot in which the government printed separate tickets, or "strips," for Republican and Democratic candidates, rather than print the names of all candidates from all parties on a single ballot, as has become conventional practice. Still, what distinguished the new regime from what had occurred previously was that the government had assumed responsibility for printing all the ballots, rather than letting the parties prepare their own tickets themselves (a practice that had led to mischief by the parties employing distinctive colors and other features to destroy the secrecy of the ballot). See People ex rel. Nichols v. Board of Canvassers of Onondaga County, 129 N.Y. 395, 402–03, (1891); Bass, *I Am a Democrat*, 151–53 (using the term "strips"), has a description of this hybrid form of ballot, a product of legislative compromise. For the history of New York's adoption of the Australian

ballot in the context of other electoral reforms, see Ronald Hayduk, *Gatekeepers to the Franchise: Shaping Election Administration in New York* (DeKalb: Northern Illinois University Press, 2005), 45; see also Roy G. Saltman, *The History and Politics of Voting Technology: In Quest of Integrity and Public Confidence* (New York: Palgrave MacMillan, 2006), 94, 96–102.

9. There was no proof that the misdistribution of ballots was intentional, although some Democrats speculated that local Republicans might have done this as a way of rewarding loyal voters. By the time the issue was litigated in the state's highest court, the Democrats had expressly waived any claim of intentional wrongdoing. *Nichols*, 129 N.Y., 434–35 (1891). The chief judge nonetheless raised the point in a concurring opinion. Ibid., 416–17.
10. "The result of the decision *Nichols v. Onondaga Board of Canvassers* (129 N.Y. 395) was to convert a majority of 328 in favor of Peck, the Republican in the 25th Senate District, to a majority of 870 for Nichols, the Democrat. This was accomplished by invalidating 1,252 votes cast for Peck." Francis Bergan, *The History of the New York Court of Appeals, 1847–1932* (New York: Columbia University Press, 1985), 177.
11. Ibid., 176: "The votes in the court followed the political background of the judges, five Democrats and two republicans, with a significant exception where the vote was four to three with a vigorous dissent by Judge Peckham, a Democrat, in *Nichols v. Onondaga Board of Canvassers*."
12. *Nichols*, 129 N.Y., 431.
13. Ibid., 408.
14. Ibid.
15. Ibid., 409. Judge O'Brien waffled in a way that makes his opinion in tension with itself. He acknowledged: "It may be freely admitted that no statute regulating the conduct of elections should be so construed as to place arbitrary or unreasonable obstructions in the way of the citizen in the exercise of his right to vote, and, further, that any law fairly open to such an objection would be in conflict with the constitution." Ibid. But he seemed to think that this particular law, as he construed it, did not violate this constitutional standard. Why not? From the face of the concurring opinion it is hard to tell, except that the opinion repeated that "the statute under consideration was intended to prevent corruption." Ibid.
16. See Lochner v. New York, 198 U.S. 45 (1905). On *Lochner* and the era for which it is named, see Owen Fiss, *Troubled Beginnings of the Modern State, 1888–1910*, vol. 8 of *History of the Supreme Court of the United States* (New York: Macmillan, 1993).
17. *Nichols*, 129 N.Y., 445.
18. Ibid., 444.
19. Ibid., 447. Judge Finch joined Judge Peckham's dissent. Ibid., 445, 448–49.
20. Ibid., 443.
21. Ibid., 442.
22. Ibid., 439. Judge Andrews also pointed out that it made no sense to treat the misdirected ballots as marked since as printed they were proper unmarked ballots, they never were perceived at the polls as marked ballots, and the remedy for a marked ballot is to invalidate it only if it was intended to be recognized as marked, which was not the case here. Ibid., 442.
23. Ibid., 443.
24. Richard Hasen, "The Democracy Canon," *Stanford Law Review* 62 (2009): 69.
25. *Nichols*, 129 N.Y., 440.
26. Bergan, *New York Court of Appeals*, 176, 181.
27. The Republican candidate died during the ballot-counting dispute, leaving a vacancy that Hill could have filled at a time of his own choosing. Moreover, the new lieutenant governor was also a Democrat and could break any ties that might have been caused by the one Independent voting with Republicans. See Bass, *I Am a Democrat*, 197–99.
28. Hill's conduct in this respect is additional support for Alberto Simpser's thesis that the goal of manipulating electoral results is often a flexing of political muscle, beyond just winning the election, to intimidate potential opponents. See Alberto Simpser, *Why Governments and Parties Manipulate Elections* (New York: Cambridge University Press, 2013).

29. Here's one account:

> Gilbert A. Dean, candidate of the Republicans in the Dutchess-Columbia district, was clearly favored on the face of the returns, but the Democratic canvassers discovered that some of the ballots cast in the town of Red Hook contained black ink marks made by the pulling up of printers' quads or spaces in the printing. This was reported to James W. Hinkley, then the Democratic leader in Dutchess, who consulted his lawyers and reported it to Governor David B. Hill. The result is that these ballots were thrown out as marked for identification. *Of course, it was impossible that they could have been marked for such purpose for the marking was clearly done in the printing, the result, perhaps of carelessness, but something which happens in every printing office every day.*

Charles E. Fitch, ed., *Official New York: From Cleveland to Hughes*, vol. 3 (New York: Hurd, 1911), 174–75 (emphasis added). This account goes on to say that the lower court judge who issued the writ of mandamus was a "strong Democrat." Ibid.

30. People ex rel. Daley v. Board of State Canvassers, 129 N.Y. 449, 29 N.E. 355 (1891). Technically, the Court of Appeals order is an affirmance of the lower court ruling that the State Canvassing Board refrain from certifying a return that excluded the disputed ballots:

> Upon these facts, standing uncontradicted, we think the court below, in its proper branch, would have the power to command the state canvassers to canvass without regard to such a return. As it contained the result of an illegal and erroneous canvass by the board of county canvassers in excess of its jurisdiction, and which thereby would alter the result of an election, the court should not permit it to be canvassed.

Ibid., 460. This key passage is toward the end of the opinion's lengthy last paragraph. The rest is just procedural technicalities.

31. According to an early historical account, two of the three board members—the secretary of state and the comptroller—were aware of, and approved, the purloining of the corrected return. Brown and Smith, *Political and Governmental History of New York*, 371. The attorney general professed ignorance, but it seems highly unlikely that he would not know when his deputy, Maynard, was at the center of the plot. There was circumstantial evidence that Governor Hill also knew exactly what Maynard was doing as part of his overall plot. See, e.g., Richard L. McCormick, *From Realignment to Reform: Political Change in New York State, 1893–1910* (Ithaca, NY: Cornell University Press, 1981), 42: "Late in 1891, Governor-boss David B. Hill . . . engineered what came to be called the 'steal of the senate.'. . . Hill devised and carried out a plan involving contested returns and court challenges that eventually gave the Democrats the three seats that they needed."
32. People ex rel. Platt v. Rice, 144 N.Y. 249, 259 (1894).
33. Ibid., 260.
34. Brown and Smith, *Political and Governmental History of New York*, 365.
35. Alexander, *The Political History of the State of New York*, 161.
36. *Journal of the Assembly of the State of New York*, vol. 1 (Albany, NY: James B. Lyon, State Printer, 1892) 1274, 1276–77. The report was reprinted in the *New York Daily Tribune*, Oct. 7, 1893.
37. Bergan, *New York Court of Appeals*, 142. See also George Martin, *Causes and Conflicts: The Centennial History of the Association of the Bar of the City of New York, 1870–1970* (Boston: Houghton Mifflin, 1970), 158–59.
38. Peter J. Galie, *Ordered Liberty: A Constitutional History of New York* (New York: Fordham University Press, 1996), 159.
39. Ibid., 159–63; see also Alexander Flick, ed., *History of the State of New York*, vol. 7 (New York: Columbia University Press, 1935), 215–23.
40. McCormick, *From Realignment to Reform*, 53–54; Galie, *Ordered Liberty*, 164–65.

41. Galie, *Ordered Liberty*, 164 (quoting records of convention). The printed version of the records reads "absolute partiality" instead of "absolute impartiality," but the context of the quotation indicates that Galie is correct as to what the sponsor undoubtedly said.
42. Charles Z. Lincoln, *The Constitutional History of New York*, vol. 3 (Rochester: E. R. Andrews, 1906), 127.
43. William H. Steele and Charles E. Fitch, eds., *Revised Record of the Constitutional Convention of the State of New York (May 8, 1894 to September 29, 1894)*, vol. 3 (Albany, NY: Argus, 1900), 259.
44. Ibid.
45. Ibid., 260.
46. Charles Fitch, ed., *Official New York from Cleveland to Hughes*, vol. 2 (New York: Hurd, 1911), 283.
47. William H. Steele and Charles E. Fitch, eds. *Revised Record of the Constitutional Convention of the State of New York (May 8, 1894 to September 29, 1894)*, vol. 2 (Albany, NY: Argus, 1900), 990 (during a discussion of the apportionment issue); see also ibid., vol. 4, 27.
48. See Richard McCormick, *From Realignment to Reform*, 43–48; Galie, *Ordered Liberty*, 164–66.
49. Steele and Fitch, *Revised Record*, vol. III, 254.
50. Ibid.
51. On Roosevelt's role in the Progressive Era, see Doris Kearns Goodwin, *The Bully Pulpit: Theodore Roosevelt, William Howard Taft, and the Golden Age of Journalism* (New York: Simon & Schuster, 2013).
52. McCormick, *From Realignment to Reform*, 196–202.
53. For my understanding and analysis of the 1905 New York City mayoral election and its significance, I am deeply indebted to the work and insights of my student and research assistant Owen Wolfe and especially his manuscript, "'Honest Elections and a Fair Count': Election Reform in New York in the Progressive Era," (unpublished manuscript, Feb. 8, 2012) (on file with author).
54. Robert F. Wesser, *Charles Evans Hughes: Politics and Reform in New York, 1905–1910* (Ithaca, NY: Cornell University Press, 1967), 74–75.
55. See David Nasaw, *The Chief: The Life of William Randolph Hearst* (Boston: Houghton Mifflin, 2000), 200; Kenneth Finegold, *Experts and Politicians: Reform Challenges to Machine Politics in New York, Cleveland and Chicago* (Princeton, NJ: Princeton University Press, 1995).
56. Tracy Campbell, *Deliver the Vote: A History of Election Fraud, an American Tradition, 1742–2004* (New York: Carroll & Graf, 2005), 140; Finegold, *Experts and Politicians*, 46; Ben Procter, *William Randolph Hearst: The Early Years, 1863–1910* (New York: Oxford University Press, 1998), 210.
57. Campbell, *Deliver the Vote*, 140; Nasaw, *The Chief*, 199; Procter, *The Early Years*, 210.
58. Campbell, *Deliver the Vote*, 140–41; Nasaw, *The Chief*, 199; Procter, *The Early Years*, 210.
59. Clarence F. Birdseye, ed., *The Revised Statutes, Codes and General Laws of the State of New York*, vol. 1 (New York: L. K. Strouse, 1901), 1142.
60. In re Hearst, 183 N.Y. 274, 76 N.E. 28 (1905).
61. Ibid.
62. Ibid., 284.
63. Ibid., 291.
64. Henry Beerits, who was employed by Hughes to organize his papers, noted that Hughes accepted the Republican nomination for governor in 1906 precisely because Hearst had appeared robbed in the 1905 mayoral election and, as a sympathetic gubernatorial candidate, needed a formidable opponent. David J. Danelski and Joseph S. Tulchin, eds., *The Autobiographical Notes of Charles Evans Hughes* (Cambridge, MA: Harvard University Press, 1973), 133. If political calculations motivated Hughes's entry into the gubernatorial race, they also may have motivated (at least in part) his support of Hearst's quest for justice in the mayoral race.

65. Charles Evans Hughes, *The Public Papers of Charles E. Hughes*, vol. 1 (Albany: J. B. Lyon, 1907), 24–25.
66. Metz v. Maddox, 189 N.Y. 460, 466 (1907).
67. Ibid., 472–73. Toward the end of its opinion, the court offered an additional reason for finding the statute unconstitutional. Because the new legislation applied retroactively to an election already conducted, it was an attempt of the legislature to undo the electoral process after the fact. This kind of retroactive adjustment of electoral outcomes by the legislature was constitutionally intolerable: "A canvass having been concluded under the statutory provisions for its conduct existing at the time, the Legislature has no power to create a new tribunal with power to recanvass the election and to award possession of the office to another claimant." Ibid., 473. Otherwise, "the legislature might . . . conduct the recanvass and make the determination itself." Ibid. This additional argument was much more cogent than the first two, at least in principle. Retroactive changes in the rules for counting ballots after they have been cast are highly problematic, as courts have recognized both before and since. But in this case, Hughes was not attempting to manipulate the count, only to provide a forum where a fair count could occur. In any event, this point was not the main one on which the Court of Appeals relied.
68. Ibid., 474.
69. "*John Clinton Gray, Ex-Judge, Dies at 71*," *New York Times*, June 29, 1915; "Career of Albert Haight," *New York Times*, Sept. 19, 1894; "Democratic Convention to Nominate Senator," *New York Times*, Sept. 6, 1903; "Candidates of the Parties, Men Who Have Been Nominated on the State Tickets," *New York Times*, Nov. 5, 1893; "Willard Bartlett, Jurist, Dies at 78," *New York Times*, Jan. 18, 1925. See also Bergan, *New York Court of Appeals*, 229; John. R. Russell, "The William E. Werner Collection," University of Rochester, accessed March 30, 2015, www.lib.rochester.edu/index.cfm?PAGE=3423.
70. People v. McClellan, 191 N.Y. 341, 348 (1908).
71. Ibid., 352.
72. Ibid., 355.
73. Ibid.
74. Ibid.
75. This issue would prove crucial in Illinois's disputed gubernatorial election of 1982, over which the Illinois Supreme Court split 4–3 in requiring a candidate to have evidence of improprieties, and not merely allegations, in order to survive a motion to dismiss a judicial contest of the election. In re Contest of the Election for Governor, 93 Ill.2d 463 (1983). More recently, in 2007, the New Jersey Supreme Court also split 4–3 over the same basic issue of how specific the factual basis for challenging an election must be when the challenge is first filed, in order to permit the court's consideration of it. The New Jersey case concerned a mayoral election in a midsize town. In re Contest of November 8, 2005 General Election for the Office of Mayor of the Township of Parsippany-Troy Hills, 192 N.J. 546 (2007).
76. "The Boxes Stuffed, New Hearst Charge," *New York Times*, June 26, 1908.
77. "The delegates at the 1915 convention can fairly claim the distinction of being the most qualified and experienced group of delegates to sit in any constitutional convention held in New York." Peter J. Galie, *Ordered Liberty: A Constitutional History of New York*, (New York: Fordham University Press, 1996), 191. For example, Elihu Root a former US senator, secretary of state, and secretary of war, served again, as he had in 1894.
78. Thomas Schick, *The New York State Constitutional Convention of 1915 and the Modern State Governor* (New York: National Municipal League, 1978), 119.
79. John A Dix, *The Public Papers of John A. Dix, Governor 1911* (Albany, NY: J. B. Lyon, Printers, 1912), 33–34.
80. John G. Saxe, *A Treatise on the New York Laws Relating to Elections* (Albany, NY: J. B. Lyon, 1913), 96.
81. "Smith and Walker Win; Republicans Get Other Places," *New York Times*, Nov. 7, 1918.
82. In re Whitman, 225 N.Y. 21 (1918).
83. In re Whitman, 225 N.Y. 1 (1918).

84. See S. D. Lovell, *The Presidential Election of 1916* (Carbondale: Southern Illinois University Press, 1980). For biographies of Wilson, see John Milton Cooper, *Woodrow Wilson: A Biography* (New York: Knopf, 2009), and Scott Berg, *Wilson* (New York: G. P. Putnam's Sons, 2013). The standard biography of Hughes, in two volumes, is Merlo Pusey, *Charles Evans Hughes* (New York: Macmillan, 1951).
85. Cooper, *Woodrow Wilson*, 338.
86. As a professor, Wilson had written on the Hayes-Tilden election, expressing displeasure that, although the goal had been that the "puzzling and intricate questions involved might be decided with judicial impartiality," the result had been "unhappily" that "every vote of the [Electoral] Commission was a vote upon partisan lines." Because "even members of the Supreme Court had voted as partisans," Wilson's conclusion was that "the whole affair threw profound discredit upon those concerned." Woodrow Wilson, *Division and Reunion, 1829–1889* (New York: Longmans, Green, 1898), 285–86. I have discovered no writings by Hughes on the Hayes-Tilden dispute.
87. *Presidential Elections, 1789–2000* (Washington, DC: CQ Press, 2002), 135. "Charles Evans Hughes did not concede by telegram until November 22, 1916, claiming he had waited for the official count in California to end." Berg, *Wilson*, 417.
88. The election was dramatically close in other states as well. Each candidate took a state with a final margin of under 2,000 votes: Delaware for Hughes (1,258), and North Dakota for Wilson (1,735). Each also took another state with a final margin under 3,000: New Mexico went for Wilson (2,596), and West Virginia for Hughes (2,721). In New Hampshire, where the lead changed hands during the canvassing of returns, Wilson ended up winning by a mere 56 votes. *Presidential Elections*, 135.
89. If California's governor had been called upon to serve as a tiebreaker, as one scenario under the Electoral Count Act contemplates, there was the potential for additional uncertainty. Even though California's governor at the time was a Progressive with roots in the Republican Party, Hiram Johnson, he had become estranged from Hughes during the campaign and thus conceivably might have acted in a way to break a congressional deadlock in favor of Wilson. See Pusey, *Charles Evans Hughes*, 362–63; S. D. Lovell, *The Presidential Election of 1916* (Carbondale: Southern Illinois University Press, 1980), 144–45.
90. See, e.g., Pusey, *Charles Evans Hughes*, 363–66; W. Glen Pierson, "The Role of Federalism in the Disputed Selection of Presidential Electors: 1916 & 2000," *Quinnipiac Law Review* 22 (2003): 295.
91. "Waiting on California, Mr. Hughes Withholds Concession to Wilson," *Washington Post*, Nov. 12, 1916.
92. "G.O.P. Will Contest Election; Wickersham is Collecting Evidence," *Washington Post*, Nov. 10, 1916.
93. "Hughes Silences Hasty Fraud Cry," *New York Times*, Nov. 11, 1916.
94. Ibid.
95. Woodrow Wilson, *Division and Reunion* (New York: Longmans, Green, 1893), 285–86.
96. Cooper, *Wilson*, 356.
97. The failure of the Progressive Era to reform the procedures for resolving a disputed presidential election was underscored two decades later when George Norris's proposed Electoral College amendment was defeated in the Senate by a single vote. Norris, another Progressive Era titan, had been endeavoring to amend the Electoral College since 1916. See Richard W. Lowitt, *George W. Norris: The Persistence of a Progressive, 1913–1933* (Urbana: University of Illinois Press, 1971), 154. His 1933 proposal included this clause: "Congress may by law provide what procedure shall be followed and the method of obtaining a decision in case there shall be more than one certificate of Presidential votes from any State or in case of any other dispute or controversy that may arise in the counting and canvassing of the Presidential votes by [a] joint session of the Senate and House of Representatives." S.J. Res. 29, 71st Cong. (1933). Although this provision did not specify the institution and the method for resolving these disputes, at least it would have given Congress unambiguous authority to enact new procedures, thereby dispelling

all the uncertainties associated with the Twelfth Amendment. But the provision was part of a broader reform of the Electoral College, and although Norris almost garnered the two-thirds necessary for this broader reform to clear the Senate, in the end he came just short. Norris never attempted to adopt just the disputed election provision as a stand-alone measure even though it was lauded as a reform that would "make it impossible for the Nation ever again to be confronted with such a serious crisis as was occasioned in 1876." 73 Cong. Rec. 8946 (1934) (statement of Sen. Fess). A detailed examination of Norris's proposal and its fate can be found in Caitlyn Nestleroth, "Senator George W. Norris's 1934 Constitutional Amendment Relating to Disputed Presidential Elections" (unpublished manuscript on file with author).

Chapter 8

1. The unseated winner was William Vare, a notorious Republican boss of Philadelphia's machine-style politics. See Anne M. Butler and Wendy Wolff, *United States Senate: Election, Expulsion and Censure Cases, 1793–1990* (Washington, DC: GPO, 1995), 323; Samuel J. Astorino, "The Contested Senate Election of William Scott Vare," *Pennsylvania History* 28 (April 1961): 187; J. T. Salter, "The End of Vare," *Political Science Quarterly* 50, no. 2 (1935): 214. See also John Salter, *The People's Choice: Philadelphia's William S. Vare* (New York: Exposition Press, 1971).
2. According to the state's certified result, Vare received 822,187 votes and Wilson 648,680, for a difference of 173,507. "Vare Silent, but Manager Says Inquiry is Welcome," *Washington Post*, Jan. 12, 1927, at 2.
3. Senator George Norris, the progressive from Nebraska, made it his personal mission to keep Vare from being seated. Yet, as the leading biography of Norris acknowledges, Norris could not establish "as fact" that "if the illegal votes could be discounted, the result would show the election of [Vare's opponent]." Richard Lowitt, *George E. Norris: The Persistence of a Progressive, 1913–1933* (Urbana: University of Illinois Press, 1971), 391.
4. The Vare dispute raised novel issues concerning the Senate's authority, pursuant to the new Seventeenth Amendment, to judge the election of its members. These issues required two rulings from the US Supreme Court: *Barry ex rel. Cunningham*, 279 U.S. 597 (1929); *Reed v. County Commissioners of Delaware County*, 277 U.S. 376 (1928). Both decisions, however, addressed relatively narrow questions involving the Senate's power to collect evidence as part of its efforts to decide whether to seat Vare. Both were unanimous in upholding the Senate's investigatory powers. The Court's opinion in *Barry*, by Justice Sutherland, contains the lengthier discussion and broad language about the Senate's prerogatives under the Constitution. For example, *Barry* states unequivocally that the Senate's decision not to seat a member "is beyond the authority of any other tribunal to review." But that phrase was unnecessary to the particular decision in the case and has been cast into doubt by subsequent decisions such as *Powell v. McCormick*, 395 U.S. 486 (1969), which held that the US House of Representatives was without power to exclude an indisputably elected candidate on grounds of collateral improprieties.
5. The closest call came from Minnesota, where the margin of victory for the Republican candidate in the state's 1930 election was little more than 10,000 votes. Butler and Wolff, *Election, Expulsion and Censure Cases, 1793–1990*, 349. But the Democrat did not file a formal contest in the Senate until long after the Republican had been seated, and the Senate needed only a voice vote to reject the contest after its Election Committee unanimously recommended its dismissal. Ibid., 350; see also "Hoidale Loses Election Fight Against Schall," *Washington Post*, Feb. 8, 1933, p.1.
6. See Dayton David McKean, *The Boss: The Hague Machine in Action* (New York: Russel & Russel, 1967), 63; "Hague Policeman Bar Legislators in Quest of Hudson Vote Records," *New York Times*, Jan. 30, 1938; see also McRell v. Kelly, 1 A.2d 926 (N.J. 1938) (blocking legislative investigation of alleged electoral improprieties). As the *Yale Law Journal* observed shortly thereafter, "the disputed New Jersey gubernatorial [election] once again indicates the inadequacy of present governmental machinery and correction of election fraud." "Correction of Election Frauds" (Note), *Yale Law Journal* 48 (1939): 1434, 1434–35.

Wilson's role in the adoption of the Geran Act, New Jersey's major piece of Progressive Era election reform, is chronicled in John Milton Cooper, *Woodrow Wilson: A Biography* (New York: Knopf, 2009); see also Richard P. McCormick, *The History of Voting in New Jersey: A Study in the Development of Electoral Machinery 1644–1911* (New Brunswick, NJ: Rutgers University Press, 1953), 208–13.

7. For a superb and still-valuable study of America's electoral system prior to World War II, see Joseph P. Harris, *Election Administration in the United States* (Washington, DC: Brookings, 1934).
8. For an overview of this era, see James T. Patterson, *Grand Expectations: The United States, 1945–1974* (New York: Oxford University Press, 1996); see also David Halberstam, *The Fifties* (New York: Random House, 1993). On the cultural significance of *Bye Bye Birdie* and *Grease*, as well as similar films portraying the era, see Michael Dunne, *American Musical Films Themes and Forms* (Jefferson, NC: McFarland, 2004).
9. See Tom Brokaw, *The Greatest Generation* (New York: Random House, 1998).
10. See Arthur Herman, *Freedom's Forge: How American Business Produced Victory in World War II* (New York: Random House, 2012).
11. *Public Papers of the Presidents of the United States: John F. Kennedy, January 20 to December 31, 1961*, 3 vols. (Washington, DC: Government Printing Office, 1962), 1–3.
12. See Robert A. Caro, *Means of Ascent: The Years of Lyndon Johnson* (New York: Knopf, 1990). My account of Ballot Box 13 draws primarily from Caro, as well as Robert Dallek, *Lone Star Rising: Lyndon Johnson and His Times, 1908–1960* (New York: Oxford University Press, 1991), and especially Josiah M. Daniel III, "LBJ v. Coke Stevenson: Lawyering for Control of the Disputed Texas Democratic Party Senatorial Primary Election of 1948," *Review of Litigation* 31 (2012): 1–70. Daniel's article is an invaluable resource in understanding this most notorious of disputed elections from a legal perspective. In addition to benefiting directly from the article itself, I've benefited immensely from conversations with Daniel. See also Mary Kahl, *Ballot Box 13: How Lyndon Johnson Won His 1948 Senate Race by 87 Contested Votes* (Jefferson, NC: McFarland, 1983); Ronnie Dugger, *The Politician: The Life and Times of Lyndon Johnson—The Drive for Power, from the Frontier to Master of the Senate* (New York: Norton, 1982).
13. Texas was home to the series of infamous "White Primary Cases" in the US Supreme Court. See Darlene Clark Hine, Steven F. Lawson, and Merline Petre, *Black Victory: The Rise and Fall of the White Primary in Texas*, 2nd ed. (Columbia: University of Missouri Press, 2003); see also Samuel Issacharoff, Pamela Karlan, and Richard Pildes, *The Law of Democracy: Legal Structure of the Political Process*, 4th ed. (Westbury, NY: Foundation Press, 2012), 220–38. For the abject condition of Texas politics in general during this period, see George Norris Green, *The Establishment in Texas Politics: The Primitive Years, 1938–1957* (Westport, CT: Greenwood Press, 1979).
14. Daniel, "Lawyering for Control," 12–13, explains the problem of this deadline.
15. Accounts differ on whether "200" or "202" extra votes were fraudulently added to Johnson's total for Ballot Box 13. Caro generally uses the "200" figure, while Dallek says "202"—although Caro occasionally quotes key participants in the drama (including Luis Salas) saying "202" extra votes were fabricated for Johnson. See Caro, *Means of Ascent*, 344, 346, 394 (Salas), 397 (special master in the federal lawsuit); but see ibid., 324–25 at note* (perplexingly purporting to clarify why "the number of additional votes for Johnson is sometimes given as 200 and sometimes *201*"—emphasis added—not 202).

    The discrepancy appears to stem from some confusion over whether the amended number of votes for Johnson in Precinct 13 of Jim Wells County, as reported on September 3, was 965 or 967. Accounts agree that the initially reported numbers from Precinct 13, on Election Night, had 765 votes for Johnson.

    Although available information does not leave this numerical detail entirely free from doubt, I credit 967 as the more reliable figure for two main reasons. First, Coke Stevenson's own complaint filed in his federal court lawsuit asserts: "Primary election officials of Jim Wells County, Texas, fraudulently changed the vote between Coke R. Stevenson and Lyndon B. Johnson to show that Lyndon B. Johnson had received 967 votes and Coke R. Stevenson had received 61 votes in said election precinct 13." Complaint at 3, Stevenson

v. Johnson, (N.D. Tex. 1948) (No. 1640). Second, Caro's own notes quotes Luis Salas, the perpetrator of the fraud, as telling Caro in an interview: "Later on our party changed the amounts to reach 967, enough for Johnson to defeat Stevenson." Caro, *Means of Ascent*, 495. Other sources also use the 967 figure. See Ronnie Dugger, *The Politician: The Life and Times of Lyndon Johnson—The Drive for Power, from the Frontier to Master of the Senate* (New York: Norton, 1982), 329; see also Mary Kahl, *Ballot Box 13: How Lyndon Johnson Won His 1948 Senate Race by 87 Contested Votes* (Jefferson, NC: McFarland, 1983), 106 (although, unlike other sources, Kahl confusingly has "767" as Johnson's initial total in Precinct 13).

The strongest evidence to support "965" as the amended total for Johnson in Precinct 13 is the testimony of witnesses at the federal court hearing before Judge Davidson on September 21. See Transcript of Hearing on Motion for Temporary Injunction at 17, 42, 44, Stevenson v. Tyson (N.D. Tex. Sept. 21 & 22, 1948) (No. 1640). But that testimony was based on memory of the tally sheets that they had seen several weeks earlier, and their testimony was focused on the fact that the "7" in the initially reported total for Johnson of "765" had been changed into a "9." For example, one witness testified: "The figure 765, on the first figure 7, the 7 had been worked over in pen and ink from a 7 around to a 9." Ibid., 43. Thus, when the same witness said that the new number was "965" (ibid., 42), the witness may have been remembering only the alteration of the "7" to the "9" and overlooking a similar change in the last digit of the original number (from 5 to 7).

Based on this analysis, I have determined that the better course is to follow Dallek, as well as the special master in the federal case, in using "202" as the number of votes falsely added to Johnson's total for Ballot Box 13. See also George Norris Green, *The Establishment in Texas Politics: The Primitive Years, 1938–1957* (Westport, CT: Greenwood Press, 1979), 114: "The amended return from Jim Wells County was even more breathtaking. Box 13 turned up 203 votes that had not been previously counted: 202 were for Johnson, 1 for Stevenson."

16. Caro, *Means of Ascent*, 388–89.
17. Dallek, *Lone Star Rising*, 332; Caro, *Means of Ascent*, 328.
18. Caro, *Means of Ascent*, 391–94. From what Salas has said, relayed by Caro, it does not appear that anyone actually bothered to fill out fake ballots to add to Box 13. Instead, the perpetrators of the fraud thought it sufficed simply to pad the reported vote totals for the precinct and then fictitiously add extra names to the list of individuals who had voted that day (in order to avoid a large gap between the number of votes and the number of voters recorded for the precinct). Salas describes how, having received the instructions to add two hundred extra votes for Johnson, one of his associates—"a jolly man full of jokes"—"added two votes making a total of 202," ibid., 394 (a detail that factors in the reasons for using "202" rather than "200" as the figure for number of fraudulent votes added for Johnson; see note 15, above).
19. Dallek, *Lone Star Rising*, 328.
20. Ibid., 347.
21. Daniel, "Lawyering for Control," 11.
22. Dallek, *Lone Star Rising*, 347.
23. A quantitative analysis of returns in the 1948 runoff between Johnson and Stevenson, compared to a baseline of previous elections in the same precincts, produced results consistent with a hypothesis that "Stevenson's partisans dishonestly added in ballots for their candidate or counted out votes from LBJ's column." Dale Baum and James L. Hailey, "Lyndon Johnson's Victory in the 1948 Texas Senate Race: A Reappraisal," *Political Science Quarterly* 109, no. 4 (1994): 595, 610. But the authors of that study are careful not to claim that their quantitative analysis provides direct evidence of electoral fraud on the part of Stevenson's supporters. In a judicial trial seeking to determine which candidate actually won more valid votes, that kind of statistical evidence would not have provided a sufficient basis for deducting votes counted for Stevenson. (To do so would be a bit like attempting to impeach actual returns in an election based on exit polls—interesting, but not judicially cognizable.) By contrast, Stevenson's direct evidence of 202 fraudulent votes added

to Ballot Box 13 would have been ample proof for a court to deduct those votes from the officially certified count.

The authors of the quantitative study also observe that the net effect of all statewide changes in vote totals during the canvass, from initial returns to final certification, benefited Stevenson by some 400 votes; had none of those changes occurred, "LBJ would have defeated Stevenson by 506 votes." Ibid., 610. But again the authors are quick to acknowledge that these changes "can not automatically be assured to be the result of vote fraud." Ibid. A major purpose of the canvassing of returns is to check and, where necessary, rectify initial Election Night tallies. Anyone experienced with routine error-correction that occurs during this canvassing cannot assume, without additional evidence, that there was anything nefarious about the error-correction that benefited Stevenson.

Thus it is inappropriate to cite this single quantitative study, as one book does, for the proposition that "from the evidence, it appears that if all fraudulent ballots and counts had been thrown out, Johnson would have beaten Stevenson by 506 votes." Randall Bennett Woods, *LBJ: Architect of American Ambition* (New York: Free Press, 2006), 217, 901n95. That assertion is a misreading of the study upon which it relies, ignoring the careful qualifications explicitly made in the study itself. In any event, whatever one concludes from a statistical analysis of precinct returns—or any other information never introduced into evidence in a court in 1948—none of it undercuts the key point: there should have been a straightforward and orderly judicial procedure available to both Stevenson and Johnson to adjudicate their competing claims of electoral fraud.

24. "I firmly believe and have for years that the election was stolen in Precinct 13. I'm now convinced that [the votes] were added, 202 of them, after the polls closed. " Caro, *Means of Ascent*, 397 (quoting oral history; brackets in Caro).
25. Caro, *Means of Ascent*, 317.
26. Dallek, *Lone Star Rising*, 329; Complaint at 3, Stevenson v. Johnson, (N.D. Tex. 1948) (No. 1640) (appears in Complaint as *Stevenson v. Kennedy and Johnson*, and later labeled *Stevenson v. Tyson*, but renamed here *Stevenson v. Johnson* to reflect the real parties in interest).
27. Daniels, "Lawyering for Control," 14.
28. Caro, *Means of Ascent*, 327.
29. Ibid., 328; Dallek, *Lone Star Rising*, 333.
30. Transcript of Hearing on Motion for Temporary Injunction at 44, Stevenson v. Tyson (N.D. Tex. Sept. 21 & 22, 1948) (No. 1640).
31. Caro, *Means of Ascent*, 329.
32. Ibid., 334.
33. In 1932, there had been a dispute over the ballots in the runoff for the Democratic gubernatorial primary, a closely comparable situation to the 1948 runoff for the US Senate primary. One candidate in that dispute had filed an original mandamus petition in the Texas Supreme Court, seeking an order requiring the secretary of state to place that candidate's name on the general election ballot. The court had granted that petition, issuing the writ of mandamus, relying in large part on how little time there was between the date of the runoff and the date that the ballot for the general election needed to be ready. Sterling v. Ferguson, 53 S.W.2d. 753 (Tex. S.Ct. 1932). Based on this precedent, Stevenson could have sought his own original writ of mandamus in the Texas Supreme Court, seeking an order either to examine the election records for Precinct 13 (if they were still withheld from him) or seeking an amended return for Precinct 13 (based on the best available evidence that the extra two hundred votes were fraudulent) or both. If Stevenson had moved fast, he might have been able to get his case before the Texas Supreme Court by Friday, September 10.
34. Dallek, *Lone Star Rising*, 335; Caro, *Means of Ascent*, 348.
35. Under the Texas Constitution, the Texas Supreme Court had the authority to issue writs of certiorari to protect its jurisdiction, and the US Supreme Court occasionally has granted "certiorari before judgment" when time is of the essence. Stevenson could have tried something similar if he thought that preferable to proceeding in front of any trial-level

state judge. (I am indebted to Josiah Daniel for this point, as with so much else regarding my analysis of this disputed election. Any errors are, of course, my own.)

36. Snowden v. Hughes, 321 U.S. 1, 7 (1944).
37. Ibid., 8.
38. "We do not discuss the application of [the statute] to deprivations of the right to equal protection of the laws guaranteed by the Fourteenth Amendment." *United States v. Classic*, 313 U.S. 299, 328 (1941).
39. Caro, *Means of Ascent*, 353; Dallek, *Lone Star Rising*, 336.
40. Johnson v. Brown, 213 S.W.2d 529 (1948); see also Daniel, "Lawyering for Control," 43–44.
41. Daniel, "Lawyering for Control," 46 (quoting the Transcript of Hearing on Motion for Temporary Injunction).
42. T. Whitfield Davidson, *The Memoirs of T. Whitfield Davidson* (Waco, TX: Library Binding, 1972), 103; see Daniel, "Lawyering for Control," 40; Caro, *Means of Ascent*, 363.
43. Daniel, "Lawyering for Control," 47; Caro, *Means of Ascent*, 360.
44. Daniel, "Lawyering for Control," 47–49.
45. Dallek, *Lone Star Rising*, 347; James W. Mangan, "'48 Senate election 'was stolen' for LBJ, ex-vote judge claims," *Houston Post*, July 31, 1977.
46. Caro, *Means of Ascent*, 378.
47. Ibid., 383.
48. Daniel, "Lawyering for Control," 57–59.
49. Dallek, *Lone Star Rising*, 337–39; Caro, *Means of Ascent*, 372.
50. Motion for Stay, *Johnson v. Stevenson*, United States Supreme Court (filed Sept. 27, 1948), in National Archives. See also Daniel, "Lawyering for Control," 55.
51. Roger K. Newman, *Hugo Black: A Biography* (New York: Pantheon Books, 1994), 376.
52. See ibid., 375.
53. Some have suggested that Stevenson went to federal, rather than state, court in order to avoid the possibility that a state court would insist on examining precincts where fraud may have been committed on Stevenson's behalf. See Dallek, *Lone Star Rising*, 336; Green, *Establishment in Texas Politics*, 115. The suggestion rests on the premise that the federal court, if it had been able to consider the case at all, would have confined its inquiry solely to the allegations of fraud perpetrated on Johnson's behalf. But there is no reason to think that the federal court, any more than a state court, would have refused to consider any evidence of pro-Stevenson fraud that Johnson might have tendered to counteract Stevenson's case. On the contrary, Judge Davidson explicitly told Johnson's attorneys that he would "be glad to appoint Masters to investigate any counties" that they would identify for consideration. Caro, *Means of Ascent*, 364.

    The argument is also made that state courts would not have had enough time to consider all the allegations of fraudulent votes that both sides might have presented in this statewide election. See Green, *The Establishment in Texas Politics*, 115. If true, that flaw was not Stevenson's doing, but instead a defect inherent in the state's electoral system. It would mean that Texas, indeed, was incapable of providing a fair procedure to remedy a credible claim that a major statewide election had been stolen.
54. Caro, *Means of Ascent* portrays the culture within the fiefdom of George Parr, Duke of Duval, that would permit such brazen behavior.
55. Caro, *Means of Ascent*, 384. See also Dallek, *Lone Star Rising*, 343 (Johnson was permitted to "shape" the Senate's report on the election).
56. For more on the Kentucky gubernatorial crisis of 1899, see Chapter 6.
57. For a discussion of the impact of *Baker v. Carr*, see Chapter 9.
58. Insofar as *Baker v. Carr* vindicates Justice Harlan's dissent in *Taylor v. Beckham*, it is ironic that Harlan's grandson, who also served on the Supreme Court, dissented in *Baker v. Carr*. Indeed, Harlan the grandson joined Justice Frankfurter's dissent in *Baker*, which in passing cited *Taylor v. Beckham* as one of the many cases that supported the traditional formulation of the "political question doctrine" (now uprooted by *Baker*). There is no indication, however, that Harlan the grandson took notice of the fact that his grandfather had dissented passionately and vigorously in *Taylor*, and thus no indication that Harlan the grandson was intending to rebuke his grandfather's position in that earlier case.

59. Richard M. Nixon, *Six Crises* (Garden City, NY: Doubleday, 1962), 397–98. On Eisenhower's desire for an "investigation" of suspected "Democratic vote fraud," see Edmund F. Kallina Jr., *Kennedy v. Nixon: The Presidential Election of 1960* (Gainesville: University Press of Florida, 2010), 183, 186. See also Gary A. Donaldson, *The First Modern Campaign: Kennedy, Nixon, and the Election of 1960* (New York: Rowman & Littlefield, 2007), 151: "Even Eisenhower wanted him to contest the election."
60. "Texas law made no provision for challenging a presidential election." W.J. Rorabaugh, *The Real Making of the President: Kennedy, Nixon, and the 1960 Election* (Lawrence: University Press of Kansas, 2009), 187. Caro echoes the point: "Texas law gave the [Canvassing] Board no authority to investigate the returns." Robert A. Caro, *The Passage of Power: The Years of Lyndon Johnson* (New York: Knopf, 2012), 154.
61. Richard L. Hasen, "Beyond The Margin of Litigation, Reforming U.S. Election Administration to Avoid Electoral Meltdowns," *Washington & Lee Law Review* 62 (2005): 937.
62. 1844 qualifies as a fourth such case if, as some suggest, the Whigs abandoned thoughts of challenging the result that year because New York provided no mechanism to adjudicate their claim that widespread fraud cost them their victory there and, with it, an overall Electoral College majority. See Chapter 3, note 4.
63. Nixon, *Six Crises*, 382; see also Edward B. Foley, "A Big Blue Shift: Measuring an Asymmetrically Increasing Margin of Litigation," *Journal of Law & Politics* 28 (Summer 2013): 531, 544 at Appendix E.
64. *Presidential Elections, 1789–2000* (Washington, DC: CQ Press, 2002), 146.
65. Rorabaugh, *The Real Making of the President*, 187.
66. Ibid., 187–88.
67. Ibid., 188.
68. Caro, *The Passage of Power*, 152–53.
69. Without Illinois or Texas, Nixon had 219 electoral votes. Adding 27 more from Illinois and 24 more from Texas would have given Nixon an Electoral College majority of 270—and correspondingly would have lowered Kennedy's Electoral College total from 303 to 252. *Presidential Elections, 1789–2000* (Washington, DC: CQ Press), 217.
70. Ibid., 146.
71. Edmund F. Kallina Jr., *Courthouse over White House: Chicago and the Presidential Election of 1960* (Orlando: University of Central Florida Press, 1988), 152.
72. Ibid., 127, 162.
73. "The conclusion that the BEC intentionally misrepresented Adamowski's gains in the discovery recount is inescapable." Ibid., 162.
74. Ibid.
75. See ibid., 170; see also George Tagge, "Top Citizens Lend Support to Check Ballots in Illinois: Kennedy's Lead 9,902 as Voting Recount Opens," *Chicago Tribune*, Nov. 18, 1960.
76. Edmund F. Kallina Jr., *Kennedy v. Nixon: The Presidential Election of 1960* (Gainesville: University Press of Florida, 2010), 258n13.
77. Kallina, *Courthouse*, 167–88. Rorabaugh, on the other hand, seems to credit the early allegations. Rorabaugh, *The Real Making*, 189.
78. Kallina, *Kennedy v. Nixon*, 209.
79. Kallina, *Courthouse*, 185. That amount was not enough to rob Adamowski of the election, since he was certified as being 26,069 votes behind his opponent. Ibid., 152, 235 at Appendix 3.
80. See Roger Biles, *Richard J. Daley: Politics, Race, and the Governing of Chicago* (DeKalb: Northern Illinois University Press, 1995), 71–72. See also Kallina, *Courthouse*, 69.
81. Kallina, *Courthouse*, 110; see also "Paper Ballot is Exception to 'Machine' Rule Tuesday," *Chicago Tribune*, November 6, 1960.
82. See Kallina, *Courthouse*, 177–88; see generally *Report to the Honorable Richard B. Austin, Chief Justice of the Criminal Court of Cook County* (Report of Morris J. Wexler, Special State's Attorney, to investigate and prosecute irregularities arising out of the November 8, 1960 election), accessed July 13, 2015, https://archive.org/details/reporttohonorabl00wexl.

83. The *Chicago Tribune* reported that voters within Chicago proper and other Cook County areas were able to vote straight party tickets on the lever voting machines. "Paper Ballot Is Exception to 'Machine' Rule Tuesday," *Chicago Daily Tribune*, Nov. 6, 1960.
84. Benjamin C. Bradlee, *Conversations with Kennedy* (New York: Norton, 1975), 33.
85. See Kallina, *Nixon v. Kennedy*, 207–12.
86. Ibid., 207.
87. Ibid., 257n13.
88. Kallina, *Courthouse*, 166.
89. Kallina, *Nixon v. Kennedy*, 179.
90. Nixon, *Six Crises*, 385, 398.
91. Ibid., 386, 389.
92. Ibid., 398. Kennedy felt that because of the closeness of the race he could not declare victory until he received Nixon's formal concession. Ibid., 395; Kallina, *Kennedy v. Nixon*, 180.
93. Nixon, *Six Crises*, 412.
94. See note 57, above.
95. Kallina, *Kennedy v. Nixon*, 200.
96. Richard M. Nixon, *RN: The Memoirs of Richard Nixon* (New York: Grosset & Dunlap, 1978), 224.
97. Nixon, *Six Crises*, 413.
98. Ibid.
99. Ibid.
100. Ibid.
101. For more on the 1940 Missouri Gubernatorial Election, see Thomas F. Soaps "The Governorship 'Steal' and the Republican Revival," *Missouri Historical Society Bulletin* 32, no. 3 (April 1976): 158–72; Gerald T. Dunne, *The Missouri Supreme Court: From Dred Scott to Nancy Cruzan* (Columbia: University of Missouri, 1993), 141–49. See also David D. March, *The History of Missouri* (New York: Lewis Historical Publishing, 1967), vol. 2, 1412–19. The Missouri Supreme Court's democracy-vindicating opinion is *State ex rel. Donnell v. Osburn*, 147 S.W.2d 1065 (1941).
102. See Butler and Wolff, *Election, Expulsion and Censure Cases*, 399–403.
103. Senate Report No. 1081, 83d Congress, 2d Session, 3 (1954).
104. See Frederick C. Irion, "The 1958 Election in New Mexico," *Western Political Quarterly* 12, no. 1 (1959). For the 1960 election, see "Republicans Claim Mechem-Bolack Win," *Santa Fe New Mexican*, Nov. 11, 1960; "Official Check Shows Mecham Vote Same, Burroughs Loses," *Las Cruces Sun News*, Nov. 13, 1960; "Bigbee Reiterates Claim of Victory," *Santa Fe New Mexican*, Nov. 23, 1960.
105. See Butler and Wolff, *Election, Expulsion and Censure Cases*, 386–87.
106. Senate Report No. 81-801, 81st Congress, 1st Session, 7–8 (1949).
107. Michigan rebounded in its gubernatorial elections of 1950 and 1952, both of which involved successful recounts. See Samuel J. Eldersveld and Albert A. Applegate, *Michigan's Recounts for Governor, 1950 and 1952: A Systematic Analysis of Election Error* (Ann Arbor: University of Michigan Press, 1954); see also Thomas J. Noer, "A New Deal for Michigan," chap. 3, and "The 'Conscience of the Democratic Party,'" chap. 4, in *Soapy: A Biography of G. Mennen Williams* (Ann Arbor: University of Michigan Press, 2005); Helen W. Berthelot, *Win Some, Lose Some: G. Mennen Williams and the New Democrats* (Detroit: Wayne State University Press, 1995).
108. Senate Report No. 81-802, 8 (1949). See also Butler and Wolff, *Election, Expulsion and Censure Cases*, 383–85.
109. See Tracy Campbell, *Short of the Glory: The Fall and Redemption of Edward F. Prichard, Jr.* (Lexington: University of Kentucky Press, 1998), 137–52.
110. Patrick T. Conley and Robert G. Flanders, *The Rhode Island State Constitution* (New York: Oxford, 2011), 137. See also Elmer E. Cornwell Jr. and Jay S. Goodman, *The Politics of the Rhode Island Constitutional Convention* (New York: National Municipal League, 1968), 4–7.
111. Roberts v. Board of Elections, 129 A.2d 330, 332 (Rhode Island Sup. Ct. 1957).

112. Ibid., 334–35.
113. See Conley and Flanders, *The Rhode Island State Constitution*, 136–37.
114. Ibid., 136.

Chapter 9

1. See Alexander Keyssar, *The Right to Vote: The Contested History of Democracy in the United States*, rev. ed. (New York: Basic Books, 2009), 212. See also Gary May, *Bending Towards Justice: The Voting Rights Act and the Transformation of American Democracy* (New York: Basic Books, 2013).
2. Giles v. Harris, 189 U.S. 475 (1903). See Richard H. Pildes, "Democracy, Anti-Democracy, and the Canon," *Constitutional Commentary* 17 (2000): 295.
3. The Dorr War, which led to the US Supreme Court's articulation of the political question doctrine in *Luther v. Borden*, is discussed in Chapter 3; *Taylor v. Beckham*, in Chapter 5.
4. For discussions of *Baker v. Carr*, see Hasen, *The Supreme Court and Election Law: Judging Equality from* Baker v. Carr *to* Bush v. Gore (New York: New York University Press, 2003); James M. Snyder Jr. and Stephen Ansolabehere, *The End of Inequality: One Person, One Vote and the Reshaping of American Politics* (New York: Norton, 2008). See also Daniel Tokaji and Owen Wolfe, "*Baker, Bush,* and Ballot Boards: The Federalization of Election Administration," *Case Western Law Review* 62 (2012): 969; Guy-Uriel Charles, "Constitutional Pluralism and Democratic Politics: Reflections on the Interpretive Approach in *Baker v. Carr*," *North Carolina Law Review* 80 (2002): 1103.
5. G. Edward White, *Earl Warren: A Public Life* (New York: Oxford University Press, 1987), 337. Warren himself expressed the point this way: "If everyone in this country has an opportunity to participate in government on equal terms with everyone else, and can share in electing representatives who will be truly representative of the entire community and not some special interest, then most of the problems that we are confronted with would be solved through the political process rather than through the courts." Alden Whitman, "Earl Warren, 83, Who Led High Court in Time of Vast Social Change, Is Dead," *New York Times*, July 10, 1974. On *Reynolds v. Sims* generally, see Hasen, *The Supreme Court and Election Law*, 23, 53–54; see also J. Douglas Smith, *On Democracy's Doorstep: The Inside Story of How the Supreme Court Brought "One Person One Vote" to the United States* (New York: Hill and Wang, 2014).
6. Harper v. Virginia Board of Elections, 383 U.S. 663 (1966).
7. Kramer v. Union Free School District No. 15, 395 U.S. 621 (1969). These canonical one-person-one-vote precedents from the Warren Court are included in any Election Law casebook, including Edward B. Foley, Michael J. Pitts, and Joshua A. Douglas, *Election Law and Litigation: The Judicial Regulation of Politics* (New York: Aspen Casebook Series, 2014).
8. "Given that the Supreme Court had previously wiped out malapportioned districting arrangements in a string of decisions following *Baker v. Carr*, it is inconsistent in principle to permit widespread unequal procedures in the voting process." Bruce E. Cain, *Democracy More or Less: America's Political Reform Quandary* (New York: Cambridge University Press, 2015), 199.
9. On the relationship between *Bush v. Gore* and the one-person-one-vote jurisprudence that emerged from *Baker v. Carr* and *Reynolds v. Sims*, see Tokaji, "*Baker, Bush,* and Ballot Boards," 981–86. See also Jack Balkin, *Living Originalism* (Cambridge, MA: Belknap Press of Harvard University Press, 2011), 244: "Vote-counting claims also make sense as equal protection claims: when executive officials use arbitrary methods to count or discard votes, they deny equal protection of the laws."
10. Fortson v. Morris, 385 U.S. 231, 234 (1967).
11. Ibid., 243.
12. See Griffin v. Burns, 570 F.2d 1056 (1st Cir. 1978).
13. Ibid., 1076.
14. See appendix, which includes a table of gubernatorial elections since 1876 that remained unresolved after Election Day, including those in which recounts occurred.

15. The intense scrutiny of absentee ballots in Rhode Island was technically part of the canvass, rather than a separate recount, but it functioned much the same. "Little Rhody's Squeaker," *Boston Globe*, Dec. 1, p. 6 ("show[s] the importance of every vote"). "Chafee Victor in Rhode Island; His Final Margin Is 398 Votes," *New York Times*, Dec. 1, 1962, p.38 (state BOE Chairman criticizing absentee voting laws, which "open[ed] the door to all sorts of legal and political maneuvers which, at times, practically paralyzed the function and efficiency of the board."); see also "Rhode Island Recount Gives Governor Hope," *Los Angeles Times*, Nov. 20, 1962, p. 24.
16. See "Volpe's Suit on Recount to Be Heard Tomorrow," *Boston Globe*, Dec. 11, 1962, p. 32; "Volpe About Ready to Toss in the Towel," *Boston Globe*, Dec. 19, 1962, p. 5; "Volpe's Suit on Recount to Be Heard Tomorrow," *Boston Globe*, Dec. 11, 1962, p. 32; "Bellotti on Defeat: Beginning, Not End," *Boston Globe*, Nov. 10, 1964.
17. My account of Minnesota in 1962 is drawn primarily from Ronald F. Stinnett and Charles H. Backstrom, *Recount* (Washington, DC: Document Publishers, 1964), an invaluable resource on this particularly important episode.
18. Stinnett, *Recount*, 1–3.
19. Ibid.
20. The Kansas percentage is based on the total of Democrat and Republican votes. *Guide to U.S. Elections*, vol. II, 6th ed. (Washington, DC: CQ Press, 2010), 1615. If just Democrat and Republican votes are used to calculate the Minnesota percentage, the 91-vote margin is still 0.0073%.
21. The 2008 US Senate election in Minnesota is discussed in Chapter 12.
22. Rhodes Cook, "The Midterm Election of '62: A Real 'October Surprise,'" *Sabato's Crystal Ball* (blog), *University of Virginia Center for Politics*, accessed July 13, 2015, www.centerforpolitics.org/crystalball/articles/frc2010093001/.
23. Stinnett, *Recount*, 36.
24. Ibid., 63–65.
25. Ibid., 66–68, 76.
26. Stinnett, *Recount*, 76; see also Application of Andersen, 264 Minn. 257, 258–59 (1962).
27. Stinnett, *Recount*, 77–78.
28. Application of Andersen, 264 Minn. 257 (1962).
29. Ibid., 267.
30. Ibid., 269. The majority thus took the opposite position from the Kansas Supreme Court in 1912. Capper v. Stotler, 88 Kan. 387 (1912) (5–2). The Kansas case, involving that state's 1912 gubernatorial election, ended up with local election officials having disqualified—in an admittedly mistaken application of state law—over 100 ballots cast for the Republican candidate, Arthur Capper. These wrongly disqualified ballots were far more than enough to overcome his opponent's 29-vote advantage based on the reported results from the canvassing of the returns. Yet the Kansas Supreme Court, by a 5–2 vote, refused to order the local canvassing boards to correct the error, because their proceedings were already complete, and the error could be corrected in a subsequent *quo warranto* proceeding or formal contest of the election, which would have occurred in the legislature. Ibid., 206. The majority acknowledged that its decision, "certainly rigid and inelastic," appeared "harsh and ill suited to the practical attainment of just results." Ibid., 205. The majority offered a policy justification for its position, on the ground that to reopen the canvass to correct this error would permit reopening the canvass to search for other possible errors, and in a close statewide election that error-correcting power could be subject to partisan temptation and abuse. Once it was known that "the change of a few votes one way or the other might affect the general result, an inflamed partisanship might so warp the judgment of officers as to induce unjustifiable rulings on the new count." Ibid., 206. Better, in the majority's view, to conduct the error-correction systematically in a single proceeding designed to consider all the ballots in the statewide race, rather than attempting to go back to particular local canvassing boards to adjust the canvas there. Ibid., 206–07. After losing in the Kansas Supreme Court, however, Capper declined to pursue any further remedy. Instead, in a move that Alexander Hamilton would have approved, he simply ran again in the next election and won decisively, by more than 45,000 votes. See Homer E. Socolofsky,

Arthur Capper: Publisher, Politician, and Philanthropist (Lawrence: University of Kansas Press, 1962).

31. Application of Andersen, 264 Minn. 257, 277 (1962).
32. Ibid., 278.
33. Ibid., 277.
34. Stinnett, *Recount*, 94.
35. Ibid., 95.
36. Ibid., 95–97.
37. Minnesota Constitution Article V, § 2; Stinnett, *Recount*, 1.
38. Stinnett, *Recount*, 89.
39. Ibid., 99–103.
40. With respect to one precinct Rolvaag alleged that there had been an opportunity to manipulate the count in Anderson's favor, but he disclaimed any evidence that such manipulation actually had occurred. Rolvaag's lawyer explicitly stated that "there is no proof of such fraud but the opportunity existed." Stinnett, *Recount*, 136.
41. Ibid., 119, 126–27, 142, 159.
42. Ibid., 156–57, 170–71; see Fitzgerald v. Morlock, 264 Minn. 417 (1963).
43. Stinnett, *Recount*, 178–82.
44. Stinnett, *Recount*, 138.
45. Ibid., 139.
46. Ibid., 203.
47. Ibid., 97.
48. Ibid., 207.
49. Ibid., 192–93.
50. "Minnesota's Close Election," *Washington Post*, Mar. 26, 1963.
51. Ibid.
52. Ibid.
53. Stinnett, *Recount*, 97.
54. Phyllis Austin, "Curtis Apparently Wins, Erwin Asks Recount," *Bangor Daily News*, Nov. 5, 1970, p. 1.
55. Ken Ward, "Senate Presidency Suddenly Crucial," *Bangor Daily News*, Nov. 6, 1970, p. 1.
56. "Governor Curtis is Reelected in Maine as Recount Gives Him a 500-Vote Margin," *New York Times*, Dec. 16, 1970. If the inauguration had been delayed, the Republican president of the state senate would have served as acting governor for as long as there was a vacancy. Because the Democrat was ahead in the governor's race heading into the recount, the Republicans had an incentive for delay, and there was talk that they would file a lawsuit for this purpose. For reasons explained in the text, this idea evaporated.
57. "287 Votes Unseat Alaska's Governor," *New York Times*, Nov. 29, 1974; "G.O.P. Runoff Bid Gains in New Hampshire Court: Ohio Governor Halts Recount, G.O.P. Victor in North Dakota," *New York Times*, Dec. 14, 1974, p. 27. See also Diane Henry, "Egan and Young Leading in Alaska and in Dakota," *New York Times*, Nov. 8, 1974, p. 18. Election Night in Ohio that year foreshadowed the 2000 presidential election: the television networks called the race incorrectly, causing a candidate to concede prematurely and subsequently retract the concession. Two years later, Ohio almost had a recount in a presidential election: President Ford considered one, but he would have had to overturn Jimmy Carter's victory in Wisconsin as well as in Ohio. Ford's advisers determined that Wisconsin was out of reach, and thus he called off the automatic recount available in Ohio. See James A. Baker III, *"Work Hard, Study . . . and Keep Out of Politics!: Adventures and Lessons from an Unexpected Public Life"* (New York: G.P. Putnam's Sons, 2006), 71.
58. For New Jersey's experience in 1981, see Alvin S Felzenberg, *Governor Tom Kean: From the New Jersey Statehouse to the 9-11 Commission* (New Brunswick, NJ: Rutgers University Press, 2006), 182–84; "Democrats Will Sue G.O.P. Over Voting Patrol in Jersey," *New York Times*, Dec. 14, 1981, p. B1; Robert Hanley, "Panel of Judges Orders Recount of Jersey Vote," *New York Times*, Nov. 14, 1981, p. 26; Joseph F. Sullivan, "Election Law's Weak Spots in Spotlight," *New York Times*, Nov. 15, 1981, p. NJ1.
59. *Gubernatorial Elections, 1787–1997* (Washington, DC: CQ Press, 1998), 50.

60. Senate Hearing 98-672: Hearing Before Subcommittee on the Constitution of S. Judiciary Comm. on the Need for Further Federal Action in the Area of Criminal Vote Fraud, at 6 (Chicago, Sept. 19, 1983), 98th Cong. (Serial No. J-98-68).
61. In re Contest of Election for Offices of Governor and Lieutenant Governor Held at General Election on November 2, 93 Ill.2d 463, 507 (1983).
62. A similar issue arose in the recount of New York City's 1905 mayoral election, but there New York's highest court (by a divided 4–3 vote) permitted the recount to go forward without the kind of particularized showing of errors that the majority of the Illinois Supreme Court required for that state's 1982 gubernatorial election. See Chapter 7.
63. *In re Contest*, at 507.
64. "Virginia: On the Inaugural," *Washington Post*, Dec. 24, 1989, p. C6.
65. Roudebush v. Hartke, 405 U.S. 15 (1972).
66. See Chapter 8, note 1 and sources cited therein.
67. Senate Report 83-1081, at 3, 81, 95 (1952).
68. Ibid., 5.
69. William Moore, "Senate Beats Move to Oust Chavez, 53–36," *Chicago Tribune*, March 24, 1954. See also 100 Cong. Rec. at 3732.
70. In North Dakota, the final margin was only 186, and a faulty ballot design may have cost the Democrat the election (just as the "butterfly ballot" in 2000 was instrumental in Al Gore's defeat). But there was no way to remedy the bad ballot design in the state's recount, and thus the Democrat chose not to press the point in the US Senate. Had he done so, that race also would dragged on for many more months, and might well have ended in a vacant seat, as indicated by how the Senate handled the Oklahoma and New Hampshire elections from the same year. See "N.D. District Judges Still Have Details to Work Out on Conduct of Recount," *The Forum*, Nov. 26, 1974.

    The losing Democrat in the Nevada election that year was Harry Reid, who would go on to win in 1986, eventually becoming majority leader. Reid himself would prevail in a recount in his 1998 reelection bid. These two are part of a trilogy of successful recounts, the first one occurring in 1964. Paul Laxalt, who lost that one, was the winner in 1974. See "Recount Confirms Laxalt as Nevada's Senate Victor," *New York Times*, Dec. 8, 1974.

    Both Laxalt and Reid exemplify the Hamiltonian strategy of staging a successful comeback (as did John Ensign, who lost the 1998 recount but won his own separate seat in 2000). One can wonder, moreover, whether Nevada's gaming culture contributed to its successful recount trilogy: "win some, lose some" is an appropriate motto in politics as well as poker. Perhaps such pragmatism prevented these three recounts from descending into protracted partisan warfare in the Senate.
71. Anne M. Butler and Wendy Wolff, *United States Senate Election, Expulsion and Censure Cases, 1793–1990* (Washington, DC: Government Printing Office, 1995), 421–25, 426–28.
72. For my understanding of this New Hampshire dispute, I have relied primarily on Donn Tibbetts, *The Closest U.S. Senate Race in History:* Durkin v. Wyman (Manchester, NH: Lew A. Cummings, 1976), as well as official documents from the Senate proceedings.
73. Ibid., 14–19, 21–33.
74. Ibid., 29, 32, 38.
75. Ibid., 29, 37–40. Durkin had gone to federal court to try to get the case taken away from the BLC on the ground that, notwithstanding the precedent of *Roudebush v. Hartke*, only the US Senate could review the secretary of state's initial recount. But the federal court rejected that claim, following the Supreme Court's precedent, saying that adding the extra layer of BLC review to the state's proceedings did not diminish the US Senate's ultimate authority. The federal court also observed that the BLC's proceedings comported with due process, thus indicating that the court would be attentive to any claim that the state's procedures violated the Fourteenth Amendment. Durkin, however, had not made any such claim. Meanwhile, Wyman had gone to state court as part of his effort to overturn the result of the initial recount. But the state supreme court also ruled that under state law the case should be left to the BLC, to be followed by the US Senate. Tibbetts, *Closest U.S. Senate Race*, 34–37, 260.

76. Ibid., 58; see also David Rosenbaum, "Senate Refuses Seat for Wyman," *New York Times*, Jan. 29, 1974 (describing "party line vote").
77. Tibbetts, *Closest U.S. Senate Race*, 58.
78. Cannon chaired the Senate's Committee on Rules and Administration, which had jurisdiction over contested elections in the chamber.
79. Ibid., 115.
80. Richard L. Maden, "Senate Refuses to End Debate over New Hampshire Election," *New York Times*, June 24, 1975.
81. "A Squabble in the Senate," *Washington Post*, June 29, 1975.
82. "Resolving the New Hampshire Case," *Washington Post*, July 8, 1975.
83. "The New Hampshire Election Mess," *Washington Post*, July 14, 1975.
84. Ibid.
85. "The Empty Senate Seat," *Washington Post*, July 28, 1975.
86. Ibid.
87. Tibbetts, *Closest U.S. Senate Race*, 191.
88. "Back to New Hampshire," *Washington Post*, Aug. 1, 1975.
89. "U.S. Senate Winners," *Chicago Tribune*, Nov. 7, 1974.
90. Butler and Wolff, *Election, Expulsion and Censure Cases*, 426–27.
91. Senate Report No. 94-597, at 35 (1976) (minority views).
92. Edmondson v. State ex rel. Phelps, 533 P.2d 604, 616 (1974).
93. Ibid. The court's opinion in this sentence contains a common grammatical error (a misplaced modifier), but it is evident that the court meant: "No competent evidence establishes why *not* all the voters *voted* in all the races." (Some voters obviously voted in all the races, just not all voters.) In other words, only some voters engaged in undervoting.
94. After Durkin won the revote in New Hampshire, a sixth Democrat was added to the committee. Senator Allen abstained, thus making the committee's vote on the Oklahoma case five Democrats to three Republicans. See Senate Report No. 94-597, at 6 (majority views); see also "Senate Panel Weighing Disputed '74 Bellmon-Edmondson Election in Oklahoma," *New York Times*, Nov. 25, 1975, p.23.
95. Senate Minority Report, No. 94-597, 27–28.
96. Butler and Wolff, *Election, Expulsion and Censure Cases*, 428.
97. Senate Report No. 94-597, at 51 (Supplemental Views of Mr. Pell).

Chapter 10

1. James T. Patterson, *Restless Giant: The United States from Watergate to Bush v. Gore* (New York: Oxford University Press, 2005), 373. Patterson's *Restless Giant* is a superb overview of this recent period of US history.
2. From 1933 (the first year of FDR's presidency and thus the beginning of the New Deal) until 1981 (the first year of Reagan's presidency), the Democrats controlled both houses of Congress every year except 1947–1949 and 1953–1955. It was a remarkable half-century of one-party dominance. Since 1981, however, when Republicans gained control of both the Senate and the presidency, no party has controlled both houses of Congress for more than eight years in a row (the Democrats from 1987 to 1995, but at a time when the Republicans held the White House except for the last two years). Thus 1981 truly marks the end of New Deal and Great Society epoch, as reflected in the Democratic hegemony in Congress during that time. See History, Art & Archives, US House of Representatives, "Party Divisions of the House of Representatives," accessed March 27, 2015, http://history.house.gov/Institution/Party-Divisions/Party-Divisions/ (House party affiliations); See also United States Senate, "Party Division in the Senate, 1789–Present," accessed March 27, 2015, www.senate.gov/pagelayout/history/one_item_and_teasers/partydiv.htm/ (Senate party affiliations); Lyn Ragsdale, *Vital Statistics on the Presidency: George Washington to Barack Obama*, 4th ed. (Los Angeles: SAGE/CQ Press, 2014), 18–20.
3. Patterson identifies the "heating up of the partisan warfare"—intensified "to unprecedented levels"—as one of the two principal "developments highlighting the last years of

the twentieth century." Patterson, *Restless Giant*, 346. It is clear that Patterson views this development as pernicious, contributing to (among other serious consequences) the failure of the federal government to focus on the growing threat of terrorism. Ibid., 386. Still, one glowing review of the book wished that Patterson had stressed the perniciousness of this trend even more:

> Patterson's tendency to see the glass as half full colors his treatment of the increase in partisanship. When he says there are enough "moderates, independents and centrists" to make the system work, he is not describing today's Washington. He is right to say the people are not as partisan as the politicians, but it is the politicians who make the laws and who determine what government does or doesn't do.

Charles Peters, "'*Restless Giant*': The Rich and the Rest," *New York Times*, Nov. 6, 2005.

4. *Gubernatorial Elections, 1787–1997* (Washington, DC: CQ Press), 11–35.
5. The strength of the Boll Weevils, also sometimes known as "Reagan Democrats," was signified by the passage of Reagan's tax reform bill with the support of 48 House Democrats. Patterson, *Restless Giant*, 156–57. David Stockman's memoir also describes the Reagan administration's use of Boll Weevil Democrats to support Reagan's economic program. See David Stockman, *The Triumph of Politics* (New York: Harper & Row, 1986), 179–84.
6. Tom Mann and Norm Ornstein have drawn the connection between Reagan's courtship of the Boll Weevils and the tenacity with which the Democratic leadership in the House fought to prevail in the fight for the Bloody Eighth:

> Among other attempts to exploit the House rules to their full advantage, the Democrats moved to exaggerate their number on key committees like Ways and Means and Budget, in order to give themselves a working majority and offset any defections by "boll weevil" Democrats. In the process, they did the Republicans out of coveted seats, and provoked immediate and long-lasting outrage.

In this context, what the Democrats did to win Indiana's eighth district was "the last straw" to the Republicans in the House, "a party wandering in the desert of the minority for thirty years with no oasis in sight." Thomas E. Mann and Norman J. Ornstein, *The Broken Branch: How Congress is Failing America and How to Get It Back on Track* (New York: Oxford University Press, 2006), 68–69 (quoting at length an earlier *Atlantic Monthly* piece by Ornstein covering the topic).

7. The absentee ballot fraud in Miami's 1997 mayoral election is detailed in Tracy Campbell, *Deliver the Vote: A History of Election Fraud, An American Political Tradition—1742–2004* (New York: Carroll & Graf, 2005), 286–91. The court's decision is *In re Miami Mayoral Election of 1997*, 707 So.2d 1170 (Fla. Ct. App. 1998).
8. My knowledge of the Bloody Eighth episode has been greatly enhanced by an excellent student seminar paper. See Jared Klaus, "The Bloody Eighth: A Forgotten Stop on the Road to *Bush v. Gore*" (unpublished, on file with author). I have benefitted immensely as well from follow-up research by Jimmy Hafner and Jim Saywell.
9. Tom Keating, "Up, Down, Ahead, Behind in the 8th," *Indianapolis Star*, Dec. 12, 1984 (reporting McIntyre's morning-after-election lead as 190 votes); see also "Declaration Delayed for 8th District Race," *Indianapolis Star*, Dec. 5, 1984 (reporting a then-current McCloskey lead of 72 votes).
10. Patrick J. Traub, "McCloskey Takes New, Slim, Lead," *Indianapolis Star*, Dec.12, 1984.
11. Patrick J. Traub, "McCloskey Files Suit to be Declared Winner in 8th," *Indianapolis Star*, Nov. 28, 1984; see also "McCloskey Loses Two Key Skirmishes as Battle Continues for 8th District," *Indianapolis Star*, Dec. 8, 1984.
12. Margaret Shapiro and Dan Balz, "Partisanship Seen in 99th Congress," *Washington Post*, Jan. 4, 1985.
13. "Republican Called Winner of Indiana Seat in Recount," *Los Angeles Times*, Feb. 6, 1985.
14. Panetta represented Carmel Valley along the coast, while Thomas was from inland Bakersfield. Zach Nauth, "Panetta, Thomas Gain Leadership Points in Bitter House Fight," *Los Angeles Times*, May 5, 1985.

15. Leon Panetta, *Worthy Fights: A Memoir of Leadership in War and Peace* (New York: Penguin Press, 2014), 34. Even before serving in Nixon's Department of Health, Education, and Welfare, Panetta was a legislative aide to Thomas Kuchel, a Republican senator from California. Ibid., 24.
16. Investigation of the Question of the Right of Frank McCloskey or Richard McIntyre, from the Eighth Congressional District of Indiana, to a Seat in the Ninety-Ninth Congress Pursuant to H. Res. 1, 99th Cong. 81–82 (1985) (hereafter Task Force Hearings).
17. Task Force Hearings, 445.
18. Ibid., 440.
19. Patrick J. Traub, "House Panel Meets Today on Disputed Ballots," *Indianapolis Star*, Apr. 18, 1985.
20. "5,000 Indiana Voters Were Disenfranchised," *New York Times*, Mar. 21, 1985.
21. Task Force Hearings, 442.
22. Ibid., 445.
23. Ibid., 440, 444 (inconsequential typo in transcript corrected).
24. Ibid., 441.
25. Ibid., 446–47.
26. Ibid., 447.
27. Ibid.
28. Patrick J. Traub, "McIntyre Already Preparing for 1986," *Indianapolis Star*, Apr. 20, 1985. See *Guide to U.S. Elections* 6th ed., vol. II (Washington, DC: CQ Press, 2010), 928.
29. Task Force Hearings, 473.
30. Ibid., 476.
31. "Indiana Seat Hinged on Uncounted Ballots," *Washington Post*, May 7, 1985.
32. Task Force Hearings, 474. The transcript misspells "hypocrisy" as "hypocracy," but I have corrected it here.
33. Ibid.
34. Ibid., 475.
35. Ibid., 476.
36. Ibid., 477.
37. Ibid., 494.
38. Robert Elder, *States News Service*, Apr. 19, 1985; see also Zack Nauth, "Panetta, Thomas Gain Leadership Points in Bitter House Fight," *Los Angeles Times*, May 5, 1985 ("Talk to a rape victim . . . ask them after it's over if they can just forget about it. I feel personally violated.").
39. H.R. Rep. No 99-58, at 55 (1985).
40. Ibid., 58.
41. Mark Starr and Gloria Borger, "Congress: A House Divided," *Newsweek*, Apr. 22, 1985.
42. Hedrick Smith, "Bitterness on Capitol Hill," *New York Times*, Apr. 24, 1985.
43. Steven V. Roberts, "House Refuses to Order Special Indiana Election," *New York Times*, May 1, 1985. Nineteen Democrats, mostly Boll Weevils, "joined a united Republican bloc in favoring a new election." Ibid. The motion failed 229 to 200.
44. Mann and Ornstein, *Broken Branch*, 67.
45. Morgan v. United States, 801 F.2d 445, 447 (D.C. Cir. Sept. 9, 1986). McIntyre had filed his own separate federal court suit, seeking an injunction to require the House to seat him (at least temporarily), but that too was rejected for the same reason. McIntyre v. O'Neill, 603 F.Supp. 1053 (D.D.C. Mar. 1, 1985), *vacated as moot*, 766 F.2d 535 (D.C. Cir. May 7, 1985). Even earlier, McCloskey had tried to go to federal court in Indiana as part of his effort to prevail in the ballot-counting fight, but he also was rebuffed on *Roudebush v. Hartke* grounds. By the time that case was on appeal, McCloskey had prevailed in the House, and so it too was moot; but Judge Frank Easterbrook wrote to emphasize that the federal judiciary had no role to play given the exclusive authority of the House to judge its own elections. McIntyre v. Fallahay, 766 F.2d 1078 (7th Cir. July 2, 1985). All this litigation, even if unsuccessful, demonstrates the increased desire to litigate election-related issues, especially in federal court, in the aftermath of *Reynolds v. Sims*.

46. "Indiana Seat Hinged on Uncounted Ballots," *Washington Post,* May 7, 1985.
47. Panetta, *Worthy Fights,* 99.
48. Kirk Johnson, "Munster Withdraws Challenge to Gejdenson's Win in 2d District," *New York Times,* Apr. 29, 1995.
49. "Doctors Back Hooper; Hornsby Gets More Money from Lawyers," *Huntsville Times,* Nov. 5, 1994.
50. Winthrop E. Johnson, *Courting Votes in Alabama: When Lawyers Take Over a State's Politics* (Lafayette, LA: Prescott Press, 1999), 75. This book, while containing the details of the dispute, is unabashedly one-sided.
51. Stan Bailey, "Elections Tangled in 4-Court Thicket," *Birmingham News,* Nov. 18, 1994.
52. Ibid.
53. Williams v. Lide, 628 So. 2d 531 (Ala. 1993); Wells v. Ellis, 551 So.2d 382 (Ala. 1989).
54. Stephen Merelman and Michael Har, "Judge Orders Disputed Ballots Opened," *Mobile Register,* Nov. 18, 1984.
55. Two decades after this election, Alabama's obligation under the Voting Rights Act to obtain prior federal approval for any change in its election laws was rendered inoperative by the US Supreme Court in *Shelby County v. Holder,* 133 S. Ct. 2612 (2013).
56. Peggy Sanford, "U.S. Letting Controversial Absentee Votes be Counted," *Birmingham News,* Nov. 23, 1994.
57. Stan Bailey, "GOP Expands Absentee Vote Fight—Asks Federal Judge To Void Ballots Lacking Signatures," *Birmingham News,* Nov. 29, 1994 (quoting the Republicans' complaint).
58. Stan Bailey, "Judge Throws Out Absentee Ballots—Federal Appeals Court Gets Its Turn in Vote Case," *Birmingham News,* Dec. 6, 1994 (quoting judge's oral ruling from the bench).
59. Roe v. Alabama, 43 F.3d 574, 580–81 (11th Cir. 1995).
60. Stan Bailey, "Sessions Wants Bipartisan Court Appointed for Absentee-Ballot Case," *Birmingham News,* Mar. 1, 1995.
61. Phillips Rawls, "Advisory Opinion Questions State High Court's Propriety," *Huntsville Times,* Mar. 18, 1995.
62. Roe v. Mobile Cnty. Appointment Bd., 676 So.2d 1206, 1220 (Ala. 1995).
63. Hornsby and one other formally recused themselves; two others silently chose not to sign either the majority or the dissent.
64. Roe v. Mobile Cnty., 676 So.2d at 1260 (Justice Maddox's March 22 dissent).
65. Roe v. Alabama, 52 F.3d 300, 302–03 (11th Cir. 1995).
66. Stan Bailey, "Hooper Wins in Tally Minus Disputed Ballots," *Birmingham News,* May 15, 1995.
67. Stan Bailey, "Siegelman Testifies for Absentee Voters," *Birmingham News,* Sept. 21, 1995.
68. Ibid.
69. Roe v. Alabama, 43 F.3d 574, 577n2 (11th Cir. 1995).
70. Bailey, "Siegelman Testifies," (internal quotations from Siegelman).
71. Roe v. Mobile Cnty. Appointing Bd., 904 F.Supp. 1315, 1331 (S.D. Ala. 1995) (emphasis added).
72. Ibid., 1330–31.
73. Ibid., 1333 (boldface in original).
74. Ibid., 1330–31, 1336, 1336n10.
75. Ibid., 1336.
76. Roe v. Alabama, 68 F.3d 404, 407 (11th Cir. 1995).
77. Ibid., 406–08.
78. Hellums v. Alabama, No. A-340 (Kennedy, J., in chambers) (order granting stay). See also Stan Bailey, "High Court Grants Stay in Election Certifying," *Birmingham News,* Oct. 15, 1995.
79. Hellums v. Alabama, 516 U.S. 938 (1995); see also Stan Bailey, "State Certifies Perry Hooper as the Winner," *Birmingham News,* Oct. 20, 1995.
80. Some of Chief Justice Rehnquist's papers have been made public, but not those covering any year in which a justice then serving remains alive.

81. Bailey, "State Certifies Perry Hooper."
82. Wells v. Ellis, 551 So.2d 382 (Ala. 1989).
83. Williams v. Lide, 628 So. 2d 531 (Ala. 1993).
84. Ibid., 537.
85. Kenneth Starr, "Federal Judicial Invalidation as a Remedy for Irregularities in State Elections," *New York University Law Review* 49 (1974): 1092.

Chapter 11

1. The literature on *Bush v. Gore* and the dispute over the votes in Florida is vast. Jeffrey Toobin, *Too Close to Call: The Thirty-Six Day Battle to Decide the 2000 Election* (New York: Random House, 2002), is highly readable. More scholarly is Charles L. Zelden, *Bush v. Gore: Exposing the Hidden Crisis in American Democracy* (Lawrence: University Press of Kansas, 2008). Both, however, lean somewhat toward the Gore side of the story in their sympathies. For an account that openly leans the other way, see Robert Zelnick, *Winning Florida: How the Bush Team Fought the Battle* (Stanford, CA: Hoover Institution Press, 2001). The *New York Times* compiled its coverage of the dispute in *Thirty-Six Days: The Complete Chronicle of the 2000 Election Crisis* (New York: Times Books, 2001). The *Washington Post* produced its own summary, *Deadlock: The Inside Story of America's Closest Election* (New York: Public Affairs, 2001), as did the *Miami Herald*, in Martin Merzer, ed., *Democracy Held Hostage* (New York: St. Martin's, 2001).

   Chief Justice Charley Wells of the Florida Supreme Court has written his own memoir about the case: *Inside Bush v. Gore* (Gainesville: University Press of Florida, 2013). Judge Richard Posner, the indefatigable scholar-jurist, wrote a book-length defense of the US Supreme Court's ruling on "pragmatic" grounds: *Breaking the Deadlock: The 2000 Election, the Constitution, and the Courts* (Princeton, NJ: Princeton University Press, 2001). Abner Greene authored a highly useful primer on the legal issues involved: *Understanding the 2000 Election: A Guide to the Legal Battles That Decided the Presidency* (New York: New York University Press, 2001). Richard Hasen helpfully surveyed the field of early works on the topic: "A Critical Guide to *Bush v. Gore* Scholarship," *Annual Review of Political Science* 7 (2004): 297.

   HBO dramatized the dispute in its film *Recount* (2010). The film cannot be taken as literal truth in all its depictions, and it also clearly favors the Gore side of the story (and is particularly vicious in its portrayal of Florida Secretary of State Katherine Harris). Even so, it has a superb cast—including Tom Wilkinson as James Baker, who led Bush's team during the fight—and the film's value is more than just entertainment insofar as it inspires viewers to reflect on what happened, why, and what can be done to prevent a similar debacle from occurring again.
2. The infirmities of the 1887 Act are discussed in Chapter 6.
3. There is a divergence of usage on whether the plural form of the noun "chad" is "chads" or just "chad" (like the plural of "sheep" is "sheep"). One of the most memorable scenes in the HBO movie *Recount* is when Michael Whouley teaches Ron Klain that the "plural of 'chad' is 'chad'"—only later to use the form "chads" and in turn be corrected by Klain on this same point. Whether or not those lines were ever spoken in reality, they are dramatically effective. In any event, the US Supreme Court used the form "chads" in its *Bush v. Gore* opinion, and this book will follow that usage. See also Bryan Garner, *Garner's Modern American Usage* (New York: Oxford University Press, 2003), 139 (endorsing "chads" as the appropriate plural form after the 2000 election).
4. One scholarly analysis, focusing especially on the overvotes, concluded that faulty vote-tabulation systems deprived Gore of 35,000 votes that the voters who cast those ballots intended for him to receive and that, accordingly, that the 2000 presidential election in Florida was not a "statistical tie"—but, instead, "administrative problems turned a clear Gore victory into a narrow loss." Walter R. Mebane Jr., "The Wrong Man is President! Overvotes in the 2000 Presidential Election in Florida," *Perspectives on Politics* 2, no. 3 (2004): 531.

5. The official result is contained on the National Archives and Records Administration (NARA) website, "2000 Presidential Election: Popular Vote Totals," NARA US Electoral College, last modified December 27, 2000, accessed March 17, 2015, www.archives.gov/federal-register/electoral-college/2000/popular_vote.html.
6. Toobin and Greene report the exact vote count in Palm Beach County as 3,407, see Toobin, *Too Close to Call*, 81; Greene, *Understanding the 2000 Election*, 139. Currently available information on the Florida secretary of state's website has the figure of 3,411. See "November 7, 2000 General Election: Available Elections Results Database," Florida Department of State, accessed March 17, 2015, http://doe.dos.state.fl.us/elections/resultsarchive/downloadresults.asp?ElectionDate=11/7/2000&DATAMODE=.
7. Jonathan N. Wand et al., "The Butterfly Did It: The Aberrant Vote for Buchanan in Palm Beach County, Florida," *American Political Science Review* 95 (December 2001); Greene, *Understanding the 2000 Election*, 139.
8. Laura Byrne, "Pat Buchanan: Romney Will Win Florida," *The Daily Caller*, October 16, 2012, http://dailycaller.com/2012/10/16/pat-buchanan-romney-will-win-florida/.
9. Fladell v. Palm Beach County Canvassing Board, 772 So.2d 1240, 1242–43 (Fl. S. Ct. 2000).
10. See, e.g., Bauer v. Souto, 277 Conn. 829, 841–43 (Conn. S. Ct. 2006) (where a faulty voting machine lost votes that might have made a difference in a citywide election, the new election to remedy the problem must also be citywide, not just in the precinct where the faulty voting machine was located in the original election). If one contemplates the idea of holding a "do-over" statewide election in Florida before Monday, December 18—the date that the Constitution required the presidential electors to meet—one quickly sees that it would have been a daunting prospect, if not downright infeasible. Assume the Florida Supreme Court acted within just one week of the original Election Day (November 7) in ordering a new election to be held. That still would have left only five weeks for completing all the steps necessary for conducting the second election, including printing of the ballots and making them available to overseas and military voters. If that second election also had been close and depended upon completion of a recount or counting-related procedures—including the requirement of waiting ten days after the second Election Day for the arrival of absentee ballots from overseas and military voters—it seems that Florida would have run out of time before completion of all the necessary proceedings.

    One author has contended that Florida could have limited a revote to just Palm Beach County, and even further dispensed with absentee voting for the revote. See Steven J. Mulroy, "Right without a Remedy? The 'Butterfly Ballot' Case and Court-Ordered Federal Election 'Revotes'," *George Mason Law Review* 10 (2001): 241–48; see also Steven J. Mulroy, "Substantial Compliance and Reasonable Doubt: How the Florida Courts Got It Wrong in the Butterfly Ballot Case," *Stanford Law & Policy Review* 14 (2003): 203. But this contention seems unsound on the merits, especially with respect to the elimination of absentee voting for the revote. Although it is true that the butterfly ballot did not affect absentee voters (as the author contends), there is the possibility that voters affected by the butterfly ballot will need an absentee ballot for the revote (because they are now out of town on business, for example).
11. For a general discussion on when, if ever, statistical adjustments are appropriate in the context of remedying a problem that occurred in the casting or counting of ballots, see Steven F. Huefner, "Remedying Election Wrongs," *Harvard Journal on Legislation* 44 (2007): 279–83.
12. Fladell v. Palm Beach, at 1242 (internal quotation omitted).
13. The 2000 election in Florida had other serious problems that a fair recount could not have corrected. Perhaps the most egregious of these, at least in terms of moral turpitude, was the effort to purge voter registration rolls even knowing that eligible voters would wrongly be removed from the rolls and thereby unable to cast a ballot when they showed up at the polls. Florida's secretary of state had hired a private company to look for ineligible names, including felons not entitled to vote, among the state's registered voters. The list of felons that the company developed was riddled with errors, in part because it mistakenly classified misdemeanors with felonies (although a misdemeanor was no barrier to

voter eligibility). Yet even after the company reported the problem, the secretary of state's office continued to encourage local election officials to use the company's list as a basis for removing names from the voter registration rolls. It is hard to determine how much of an effect this purge list actually had in the 2000 presidential election, since many localities refused to use it once they became aware of its defects. See Toobin, *Too Close to Call*, 169.

Whatever the magnitude of its effect, any voter wrongly removed from the rolls and denied a ballot as a result was the victim of outright disenfranchisement. Unlike the butterfly ballot, an erroneous purge was not a problem that the voter had the power to prevent through extra vigilance at the polls on Election Day. Thus, the wrong done to this voter, particularly when based on a purge list known to be faulty, is an especially heinous contravention of equal voting rights. Even so, there is no way to remedy this wrongful disenfranchisement in the context of a recount. For this reason, one of the most important features of the Help America Vote Act of 2002, adopted by Congress to redress the wrongs that occurred in the 2000 election, is the requirement that all persons who go to the polls believing themselves to be eligible to cast a ballot must receive at least a provisional ballot, even if the poll workers at that moment are unable to verify the voter's eligibility. See Edward B. Foley, "The Promise and Problems of Provisional Voting," *George Washington Law Review* 73 (2005): 1193.

14. James A. Baker, III, *"Work Hard, Study . . . and Keep Out of Politics!": Adventures and Lessons from an Unexpected Public Life* (New York: G. P. Putnam's Sons, 2006).
15. Ford Fessenden and John M. Broder, "Examining the Vote: The Overview; Study of Disputed Florida Ballots Finds Justices Did Not Cast the Deciding Vote," *New York Times*, November 12, 2001, A1; see also Ford Fessenden, "Examining the Vote: The Method; How the Consortium of News Organizations Conducted the Ballot Review," *New York Times*, November 12, 2001, A17.
16. See Einer Elhauge, "The Lessons of Florida 2000," *Policy Review* 110 (December 2001–January 2002): 18, 22; Einer Elhauge, "Florida 2000: Bush Wins Again!," *Weekly Standard*, November 26, 2001 (op-ed).
17. Fessenden and Broder, "Study of Disputed Ballots."
18. Elhauge, "The Lessons of Florida 2000," 18.
19. Many sources say NBC led the pack at 7:48. Toobin, *Too Close to Call*, 18, has it at 7:49:40 with CBS saying "thirty-one seconds" and ABC at 7:52.
20. Karl Rove, *Courage and Consequence: My Life as a Conservative in the Fight* (New York: Simon & Schuster, 2010), 195.
21. Kathleen Hall Jamieson and Paul Valdman, *The Press Effect: Politicians, Journalists, and the Stories that Shape the Political World* (New York: Oxford University Press, 2004), 78. Dan Rather is also quoted in George W. Bush, *Decision Points* (New York: Crown, 2010), 77.
22. Instead, the networks should have been careful to explain to the public that their projections were unofficial estimates only and that the official ballot-counting process would require weeks to complete, including waiting for overseas absentee ballots to arrive. 1960 was not so long ago in terms of quadrennial presidential elections (there had only been eight between then and 2000) that the networks should have been prepared for the possibility that it might take at least several days before the outcome of the Bush-Gore race could be known with any confidence. The lead might change during the canvassing process in several states, as it did in California in 1960, and if it happened in Florida between Bush and Gore, that back-and-forth might put the entire election on hold until the state settled down. If the networks had taken that kind of responsible posture to their role on Election Night, the public might have been better educated—and prepared—for the days and weeks ahead.
23. Toobin, *Too Close to Call*, 20.
24. Bush, *Decision Points*, 78.
25. Bush v. Gore, 531 U.S. 98, 101 (2000).
26. Toobin, *Too Close to Call*, 36, 124.

27. Contest of Election, Fla. Stat. § 102.168 (West 2000) (hereafter "Contest Statute"); Protest of Election Returns, Procedure, Fla. Stat. § 102.166 (West 2000) (hereafter "Protest Statute").
28. See Protest Statute, §102.166.
29. See Daniel P. Tokaji, "The Paperless Chase: Electronic Voting and Democratic Values," *Fordham Law Review* 73 (March 2005): 1711, 1724–29 (discussing the state of Florida's voting technology in 2000 as well as post 2000 voting technology problems). See also Stephen Ansolabehere and Charles Stewart, III, "Residual Votes Attributable to Technology," *Journal of Politics* 67 (May 2005): 365–89; "Voting: What Is, What Could Be," *Caltech MIT Voting Technology Project* (July 2001): 6–10.
30. Toobin, *Too Close to Call*, 61–62, 69–71.
31. Ibid., 70–76.
32. Elections Canvassing Commission, Fla. Stat. § 102.111(1) (West 2000). In the other statute the exact language was "by 5 p.m. on the 7th day following the . . . general election." Deadline for Submission of County Returns to the Department of State, Penalties, Fla. Stat. § 102.112(1) (West 2000). Both sections are quoted in *Palm Beach County Canvassing Bd. v. Harris*, 772 So.2d, at 1233.
33. Fla. Stat. §102.111(1).
34. Fla. Stat. §102.112(1).
35. At the very least, Gore would have been better off accepting the statutory deadline of November 14 for the completion of the canvass in each county, including any protest, whether or not a manual search for undervotes was finished (or even undertaken at all) as part of a protest in that county.
36. Ron Klain, the leader of Gore's legal team, defends the choice to pursue the recount in the protest rather than moving straight to the contest. His argument is that Gore did gain ground during the protest-based recount, reducing Bush's lead to 537 from the roughly 1,300 that it otherwise would have been. He says this difference was worth the extra days lost. Ronald A. Klain and Jeremy B. Bash, "The Labor of Sisyphus: The Gore Recount Perspective," chap. 7 in *Overtime! The Election 2000 Thriller*, ed. Larry Sabato (New York: Longman, 2002), 171. My judgment is that this is a miscalculation. From all available evidence, the Florida Supreme Court most likely would have insisted upon the same statewide recount if the margin had been 1,300 instead of 537, and Gore needed extra time more than anything else.
37. Toobin, *Too Close to Call*, 38–39, 71–72.
38. David Boies, the celebrated superlawyer who had just flown to Florida to join the Gore team, questioned the wisdom of trying to delay certification to wait for manual recounts that the three counties, exercising their discretion under the protest statute, ultimately might decide not conduct. Gore's other lawyers overruled the newcomer, pointing to a front-page column by the *New York Times* veteran R. W. Apple entitled "The Limits of Patience." Published on Sunday, November 12, 2000 (in the most prominent spot each week of the nation's leading newspaper), Apple's analysis began with this stark warning: "Another week and no more." Apple then continued with a sentence that the Gore team had highlighted with red ink in a copy tacked to a wall of their Florida office: "By next weekend, a group of scholars and senior politicians interviewed this weekend agreed, the presidential race of 2000 must be resolved, without recourse to the courts." It was a spectacularly fallacious prognostication; the nation would soon prove that had much more patience for resolving the Florida vote-counting dispute fairly and accurately, even by using the judiciary as necessary, than Apple and his interviewees were willing to give it credit for. Yet Apple's mistakenly pessimistic perception of the American public carried the day with Gore and his advisers. Consequently, they adopted the short-term tactic of seeking to extend the deadline for a protest-phase administrative recount rather than taking the long-term approach of saving enough time for a contest-phase judicial recount. In his memoirs, David Boies wished he could redo this pivotal decision: "I would second-guess . . . my accepting the critical importance of Secretary Harris's certification, and therefore devoting the time we did to the protest phase." David Boies, *Courting Justice: From the*

NY Yankees v. Major League Baseball to Bush v. Gore, *1997–2000* (New York: Hyperion, 2004), 367.

39. Zelden, *Bush v. Gore*, 91–96.
40. Palm Beach County Canvassing Bd. v. Harris, 772 So.2d, at 1240.
41. "Safe Harbor Provision," Determination of Controversy as to Appointment of Electors, 3 U.S.C. § 5 (2014). (This statute was codified at the same place in 2000.)
42. Toobin, *Too Close to Call*, 156. The protesters saw a Democratic Party official leave the nineteenth floor with a sample ballot, which they mistakenly believed was an actual ballot. Their protests escalated—"Shut it down!" shouted a Congressman participating in the protest—and the three-member county canvassing board complied. Ibid.

    Democrats, in turn, complained that Miami-Dade was caving under the pressure of mob rule. But the Republican protests had been essentially peaceful, well within the American tradition of public assembly to express political grievances. In comparison to the expressions of outrage that occurred over New York's canvassing board in 1792, when John Jay's Federalist supporters took to the streets threatening revolutionary violence, the "Brooks Brothers riot" of 2000 was mild indeed. And of course, it was nothing like the taking up of arms that had occurred in many nineteenth-century electoral disputes. The fundamental point, apparently lost on the Miami-Dade canvassing board as well as on Democrats at the time, was the imperative of conducting a high-stakes recount in a publicly transparent way. The Miami-Dade board never should have attempted to hold the recount on the nineteenth floor in the way that it did—limiting observation to just two individuals from each campaign—with no ability of the press, much less members of the public at large, to watch what was happening. The Republican crowd was entirely justified to holler loudly about what was going on with handling of these all-important ballots in the presidential election.
43. If those eight days had been available after the US Supreme Court's decision in *Bush v. Gore*—in other words, if that decision had occurred on December 4 rather than December 12—the Supreme Court undoubtedly would have given the Florida Supreme Court a second chance to conduct a recount consistently with Equal Protection. (There still would have been eight days left before the safe harbor deadline.) If Gore had been able to prevail in that second-chance recount, the entire course of the dispute would have unfolded differently (perhaps with Congress needing to evaluate two conflicting certificates of electoral votes from Florida, one showing Gore winning the state based on the second-chance recount, while the other asserted that Bush received the state's electoral votes as a result of the Florida legislature's intervention on his behalf). But whatever would have been the ultimate result if those extra eight days had been available after the Court's decision in *Bush v. Gore*, Gore's gamble to seek an extension of the protest-phase deadline deprived him of the opportunity to travel down that potentially more promising road.

    Ron Klain questions whether all of those extra days really would have been available if the contest had begun on November 18. Instead, he thinks they would have been frittered away because in mid-November there was not the same sense of urgency as in early December. But he also thinks that "three or four days" of sustained recounting "could have gotten the job done." Klain and Bash, "The Labor of Sisyphus," 171. Thus, even if frittering had cut the eight days in half, a US Supreme Court ruling on December 8 would have provided enough time for a recount on remand.
44. Palm Beach County Canvassing Bd. v. Harris, 772 So.2d, at 1227.
45. In his memoirs, Baker explains why he thought he had no alternative but to get his case in front of the US Supreme Court: "The only way to deal with the Florida Supreme Court, I believed, was to go over its head." Baker, *Keep Out of Politics*, 379–85. Baker's strategy and the debate within his team on the point are discussed in Zelden, *Bush v. Gore*, 33–34; Zelnick, *Winning Florida*, 82–84. The oral argument at the US Supreme Court in *Bush v. Gore* would begin with Justice Kennedy asking Bush's counsel "where is the federal question here?" Transcript at 4, Bush v. Gore, 531 U.S. 1046 (2000) (No. 00-949).
46. Bush v. Palm Beach County Canvassing Board, 531 U.S. 70, 78 (2000). Alternatively, the state supreme court's decision might have so deviated from the statutory scheme set forth

by the legislature as to deprive Florida of any chance to take advantage of the congressionally provided safe harbor deadline. Ibid., 77. (A precondition of safe harbor status was to resolve ballot-counting disputes in accordance with statutory rules promulgated before Election Day, not new rules concocted after the ballots already had been cast.)

47. Contest Statute, § 102.168 (2000). The critical interpretative issues underlying this reading of the statute were: (1) whether undervotes qualified as "legal votes"; and (2) whether the failure of a properly working machine to record these undervotes qualified as a "rejection" of them. On these two points, there were legal materials favorable to a construction of the statute that would permit manual recounts in a contest.

   First, another provision of Florida's election statutes, section 101.5614(5), suggested that undervotes were a type of "legal votes" even though they could not be detected by machines functioning as designed. This other provision concerned the feeding of paper ballots through voting machines on Election Night after the polls close. Section 101.5614(5) stated that if the paper ballot was "damaged or defective" so that it could not be counted by the voting machine, a duplicate could be made for the machine to read. This provision at least meant that a ballot did not need to be machine-readable, even by a machine functioning as designed, in order to contain a valid vote entitled to be counted. See Canvass of Returns, Fla. Stat. §101.5614(5) (West 2000).

   Second, in 1998 the Florida Supreme Court had rendered an opinion, *Beckstrom v. Volusia County Canvassing Board*, 707 So.2d 720 (1998), which supported the counting of undervotes that were undetectable by a machine functioning as designed. Indeed, *Beckstrom* interpreted section 101.5614(5) so that "defective" ballots, entitled to be remade to become machine-readable, encompassed undervotes detectable by humans even though undetectable by the machines: "We construe 'defective ballot' to include a ballot which is marked in a manner such that it cannot be read by a scanner." *Beckstrom*, 723n4. Although *Beckstrom* did not directly address whether a contest must include a manual recount of undervotes—the question in *Beckstrom* was whether election officials had mishandled undervotes on optical scan ballots, violating the procedures specified in section 101.5614(5), by darkening the ovals on the voted ballots rather than making separate "duplicate" ballots—the opinion indicated that it was appropriate to search for undervotes and to count them when humans were capable of detecting them by a manual examination of the ballots. Ibid., 722–23.

   Thus there was a sound basis in Florida law to interpret the contest statute as requiring a court-ordered manual recount of undervotes.

48. A 50–50 split in the undervotes would follow from the existence of the essentially 50–50 split in all the counted votes in this extraordinarily close election—assuming that undervotes occur randomly and are evenly distributed among all voters. In an election where the two candidates split 60–40 in counted votes, then an evenly random distribution of undervotes would cause them also to split in the same 60–40 ratio.

49. Toobin, *Too Close to Call*, 236. The actual number of undervotes reviewed in the media consortium's analysis turned out to be just shy of 45,000. See Fessenden and Broder, "Study of Disputed Ballots."

50. See note 38, above, for additional details on this point.

51. He also claimed that another county (Nassau) improperly failed to include the results of its mandatory machine recount, relying instead on its Election Night machine tallies. See Toobin, *Too Close to Call*, 196.

52. Judge Sauls, despite his reputation for delay, expedited the case far faster than what the state's statute required. In his memoirs, David Boies credits Judge Sauls with moving the case quickly enough so that the clock did not run out before Gore had a chance to get back to the Florida Supreme Court, where he could again expect a favorable audience. In particular, "Bush's time to answer was reduced from ten to three days." Boies, *Courting Justice*, 415–16, 423. See also, Toobin, *Too Close to Call*, 203–05.

53. Boies, *Courting Justice*, 421. Neither side's witnesses gave stellar performances; rather, their credibility was significantly undermined by cross-examination from opposing counsel. Afterward, Boies "joked" with Bush's attorneys "each of us had done better with the others' witnesses than with our own." Ibid.

54. Gore v. Harris, No. 00-2808, Transcript of Oral Order, December 3, 2000, 9. Gore's failure was twofold: first, he had not shown even the likelihood that he would net enough undervotes in Miami and Palm Beach to overcome Bush's certified victory; but second, and more important, because it was a statewide election, Gore was obligated to show that an examination of undervotes statewide would likely change the outcome, and this showing Gore had not even attempted to make. Judge Sauls emphasized this latter point: "To contest a statewide federal election, the Plaintiff would necessarily have to place at issue and seek as a remedy with the attendant burden of proof, a review and recount on all ballots, and all of the counties in this state with respect to the particular alleged irregularities or inaccuracies in the balloting or counting processes alleged to have occurred." Ibid., 12–13. Elsewhere in his oral opinion, Judge Sauls repeated the same point: "These balloting and counting problems cannot support or effect any recounting necessity with respect to Dade County, absent the establishment of a reasonable probability that the statewide election result would be different, which has not been established in this case." Ibid., 10.
55. See Gore v. Harris, 772 So.2d 1243 (Fl. S. Ct. 2000).
56. Ibid., 1256 (emphasis added) (footnote omitted).
57. Imagine how upset Democrats would have been if *their* certified victory had been open to challenge on such slender evidence. Indeed, in the next chapter, we will consider Democrats in Washington State and Minnesota opposing judicial contests of their certified victories in circumstances where the contests were premised on significantly stronger evidence than what Gore provided in 2000.
58. Gore v. Harris, 772 So.2d, at 1254–66, 1259–60. The majority also rejected Gore's claim regarding Nassau County's failure to include the result of its machine recount. Ibid., 1260.
59. Ibid., 1272 (Harding, J., dissenting). He elaborated: "Appellants failed, however, to provide any meaningful statistical evidence that the outcome of the Florida election would be different if the 'no-vote' in other counties had been counted; their proof that the outcome of the vote in two counties would likely change the results of the election was insufficient." Ibid. Justice Harding continued:

    > It would be improper to permit appellants to carry their burden in a statewide election by merely demonstrating that there were a sufficient number of no-votes that could have changed the returns in isolated counties. Recounting a subset of counties selected by the appellants does not answer the ultimate question of whether a sufficient number of uncounted legal votes could be recovered from the statewide "no-votes" to change the result of the statewide election. At most, such a procedure only demonstrates that the losing candidate would have had greater success in the subset of counties most favorable to that candidate.

    Ibid.
60. Here is the key passage from Chief Justice Wells's opinion:

    > The underlying premise of the majority's rationale is that in such a close race a manual review of ballots rejected by the machines is necessary to ensure that all legal votes cast are counted. The majority, however, ignores the over-votes. Could it be said, without reviewing the over-votes, that the machine did not err in not counting them? It seems patently erroneous to me to assume that the vote-counting machines can err when reading under-votes but not err when reading over-votes. Can the majority say, without having the over-votes looked at, that there are no legal votes among the over-votes?

    Ibid., 1264n26 (Wells, C. J., dissenting).
61. Toobin, 240–43; see also Zelden, 71–72.
62. Toobin, 240–43.
63. Zelden, *Bush v. Gore*, 136. Alan Sipress and Ellen Nakasima, "A Scramble, Interrupted; Order to Stop Stuns Fla. Officials Rushing to Recount," *Washington Post*, December 10. 2000, A1. See also Toobin, 248–51 (placing the time of release of the court order at 2:45 p.m.).

64. The stay order and accompanying concurring and dissenting opinions can be found at *Bush v. Gore*, 531 U.S. 1046 (2000).
65. In this respect, the purpose of a stay, as a form of interim equitable relief, is essentially the same as the purpose of a preliminary injunction. See Charles Alan Wright et al., "Purpose and Scope of Preliminary Injunctions," § 2947 in *Federal Practice & Procedure: Federal Rules of Civil Procedure*, 3rd ed. (updated 2014). "The purpose of an injunction pendente lite is not to determine any controverted right, but to prevent a threatened wrong or any further perpetration of injury, or the doing of any act pending the final determination of the action whereby rights may be threatened or endangered, and to maintain things in the condition in which they are in at the time . . . until the issues can be determined after a full hearing." Ibid. (quoting federal appellate decision).
66. Bush v. Gore, 531 U.S. 1046, 1048 (2000) (internal quotation omitted).
67. Ibid., 1047.
68. Bush's lawyer (and future solicitor general) Ted Olson had led with the argument that the Florida Supreme Court had violated the Florida legislature's authority to establish the method for appointing the state's presidential electors. Justices Kennedy and O'Connor, however, made clear their skepticism of this argument. When Olson acknowledged that this line of attack "may not be the most powerful argument we bring to this Court," Justice Kennedy advised, "I think that's right." Justice O'Connor added, "I have the same problem that Justice Kennedy does." Oral Argument at 6–7, Bush v. Gore, 531 U.S. 1046 (2000) (No. 00-949).
69. Ibid., 53:7–8.
70. Bush v. Gore, 531 U.S. 98, 105–06 (2000).
71. See, e.g., Bruce A. Ackerman, *Bush v. Gore: The Question of Legitimacy* (New Haven, CT: Yale University Press, 2002) (several essays of which, including Post's and Radin's, take the view that the *Bush v. Gore* was unprincipled and illegitimate); Ronald Dworkin, "Introduction," in *A Badly Flawed Election*, Ronald Dworkin, ed. (New York: The New Press, 2002), 1–55; Alan M. Dershowitz, *Supreme Injustice: How the High Court Hijacked Election 2000* (Oxford: Oxford University Press, 2001). See generally Clarke Rountree, *Judging the Supreme Court: Constructions of Motives in* Bush v. Gore (East Lansing: Michigan State University Press, 2007). Bruce Ackerman went so far as to call *Bush v. Gore* a "constitutional coup." Bruce Ackerman, "Anatomy of a Constitutional Coup," chap. 10 in *The Longest Night: Polemics and Perspectives on Election 2000*, Arthur J. Jacobsen and Michael Rosenfeld, eds. (Berkeley: University of California Press, 2002). See also David Strauss, "*Bush v. Gore*: What Where They Thinking?," chap. 9 in *The Vote: Bush, Gore, and the Supreme Court* (Chicago: University of Chicago Press, 2001). According to Strauss, "the best that can be said is that the Court trumped the supposed lawlessness of the Florida Supreme Court with lawlessness of its own." Ibid., 204.

    Further, a full page advertisement ran in the *New York Times* on January 13, 2001, over the names of 554 law professors, proclaiming that the US Supreme Court had acted as political partisans. See Mark S. Brodin, "*Bush v. Gore*: The Worst (or at Least Second-to-the-Worst) Supreme Court Decision Ever," *Nevada Law Journal* 12 (Summer 2012): 568.
72. Bush v. Gore, 531 U.S. 98, 109 (2000).
73. Justice Potter Stewart delivered his famous "I know it when I see it" line in *Jacobellis v. Ohio*, 378 U.S. 184, 197 (1964). In *Riley v. California*, 134 S. Ct. 2473 (2014), the Court confirmed that "search and seizure" law under the Fourth Amendment often turns on "fact-specific" judgments, particularly when applying the "exigent circumstances" exception to the warrant requirement. See also Maryland v. King, 133 S. Ct. 1958, 1978 (2013) ("what is reasonable depends on the context within which a search takes place" [quoting previous precedents]).

    Establishment Clause jurisprudence provides an especially apt comparison. In 1989, in a 5–4 ruling, the Court had invalidated a particular nativity scene as an unconstitutional "endorsement" of Christianity, even though five years earlier the Court had upheld a different nativity scene. County of Allegheny v. ACLU, 492 U.S. 573 (1989); compare with Lynch v. Donnelly, 465 U.S. 668 (1984). Justice Kennedy, dissenting in the 1989 case, accused the majority's "endorsement" test of amounting to a "jurisprudence of minutiae."

Ibid., 674. The majority defended its endorsement test by observing that Justice Kennedy's preferred approach, which would invalidate the government's use of religious imagery only when it amounted to "proselytization," inevitably would also require fine distinctions resting on highly contextual, fact-dependent judgments. Ibid., 606–07. In their back-and-forth exchange, Justice Kennedy acknowledged that the majority indeed had a valid point in this respect: "It is true that the [proselytization] test may involve courts in difficult line drawing in the unusual case where a municipality insists on such extreme use of religious speech that an establishment of religion is threatened." Ibid., 675n11.

This truth was confirmed in 2005, when the Court split 5–4 over two different cases involving governmental displays of the Ten Commandments. With Justice Breyer serving as the crucial swing vote in these two cases, the Court invalidated the courthouse display of the Ten Commandments in Kentucky, while upholding their display in a monument on the statehouse grounds in Texas. Compare McCreary County v. ACLU, 545 U.S. 844 (2005), with Van Orden v. Perry, 545 U.S. 677 (2005). Recognizing "one will inevitably find difficult borderline cases," Justice Breyer explained what he saw as the key distinction in making this "fact-intensive" judgment: "The short (and stormy) history of the courthouse Commandments' displays demonstrates the substantially religious objectives of those who mounted them," whereas the Texas statehouse display "conveys a predominantly secular message." Van Orden v. Perry, at 700–03.

Then, in 2014, the Court again divided 5–4 in upholding the particular practice of prayers before town meetings held in a suburb of Rochester, New York. Town of Greece v. Galloway, 134 S.Ct. 1811 (2014). As Justice Breyer's dissent in that "fact-sensitive" case observed, all nine Justices acknowledged the need to make fine factual distinctions, because if the town's prayers were to "over time denigrate, proselytize or betray an impermissible government purpose," then even the Court's majority (which included Justice Kennedy this time) would have ruled them unconstitutional. Ibid., 1825, 1838.

When the Court in *Bush v. Gore* said that its "consideration is limited to the present circumstances, for the problem of equal protection in election processes generally presents many complexities," the Court was doing no more than it did in saying each governmental invocation of religious imagery must be evaluated on its own specific facts—because one particular nativity scene, or one particular Ten Commandments display, will be invalid whereas another one will not.

74. While *Bush v. Gore* was pending in the US Supreme Court, the Florida Supreme Court released an opinion declaring (among other things) that Florida law, properly construed, indicated a desire on the part of the state to take full advantage of the safe harbor that Congress had provided in 3 U.S.C. § 5—and thus Florida law should be construed to enable the state to comply with the safe harbor deadline. See Palm Beach County Canvassing Board v. Harris, 772 So.2d 1273, 1289–90 (2000). The majority of the US Supreme Court took that assertion from the Florida Supreme Court as justification for declaring that there was to be no further recounting: "Because it is evident that any recount seeking to meet the December 12 date will be unconstitutional for the reasons we have discussed, we reverse the judgment of the Supreme Court of Florida ordering a recount to proceed." Bush v. Gore, 531 U.S. 98, 110.
75. Bush v. Gore, 531 U.S. 98, 146 (Breyer, J., dissenting).
76. Ibid., 111 (majority opinion).
77. Jan Crawford Greenburg, *Supreme Conflict: The Inside Story of the Struggle for Control of the Unites States Supreme Court* (New York: Penguin Press, 2007), 176. See also Toobin, *Too Close to Call*, 264 (on effort to persuade Kennedy); David Margolick, "The Path to Florida," *Vanity Fair*, October 2004 (describing behind-the-scenes drama at the Court during deliberations on the case).
78. Some of Gore's advisers urged him to fight on, and even drafted another brief to file in the Florida Supreme Court, but after "sleeping on it," Gore declined to make that move. See Toobin, *Too Close to Call*, 268.
79. The *New York Times* published a transcript of Gore's speech: "In His Remarks, Gore Says He Will Help Bush 'Bring American[s] Together,'" *New York Times*, December 14, 2000,

A26. (The headline mistakenly omitted the "s" in "Americans.") In this kind of hortatory address, it was appropriate for Gore to invoke the historical examples that did end "peacefully and in a spirit of reconciliation," like Jay's concession of 1792, leaving unmentioned the counterexamples that did not, like the assassination of a gubernatorial candidate during the dispute over the counting of votes in Kentucky's 1899 election.

80. Gore was required to gavel down members of the Congressional Black Caucus who attempted to disrupt the ceremony. Alison Mitchell, "Over Some Objections, Congress Certifies Electoral Vote," *New York Times*, January 7, 2001, 1.
81. See Diane H. Mazur, "The Bullying of America: A Cautionary Tale about Military Voting and Civilian-Military Relations," *Election Law Journal* 4 (2005): 105; Steve Bickerstaff, "Post-Election Legal Strategy in Florida: The Anatomy of Defeat and Victory," *Loyola U. (Chicago) Law Journal* 34 (2002): 149.
82. Zelden, *Bush v. Gore*, 58.
83. David Barstow and Dan Van Natta Jr., "How Bush Took Florida: Mining the Overseas Absentee Vote," *New York Times*, July 15, 2001, § 1, at 1. See also Josh Barbanel, "How the Ballots Were Examined," *New York Times*, July 15, 2001, 16.
84. Boardman v. Esteva, 323 So.2d 259 (1975).
85. Even the political scientists employed by the *New York Times* concluded that "our results suggest that it is unlikely that illegal overseas absentee ballots alone changed the election outcome" (although they did contend "that Bush's margin of victory would likely have been much narrower if those flawed ballots had not been counted"). Kosuke Imai and Gary King, "Did Illegal Overseas Absentee Ballots Decide the 2000 U.S. Presidential Election?," *Perspectives on Politics* 2, no. 3 (2004): 537.
86. Jacobs v. Seminole County Canvassing Board, 773 So.2d 519 (2000); Taylor v. Martin County Canvassing Board, 773 So.2d 517 (2000).
87. Boies, *Courting Justice*, 407–10.
88. Cass Sunstein doubts that "the four dissenters would have been willing to press a constitutional objection on Gore's behalf," but as Jack Balkin observes, this contention is belied by the fact that Souter and Breyer embraced the Equal Protection claim when *Bush* raised it, and it is conceivable to think that Justice Stevens and Ginsburg would have also if Gore, instead of Bush, had been the claimant. Compare Sunstein, "Lawless Order and Hot Cases," in *A Badly Flawed Election* at 87, with Jack Balkin, "*Bush v. Gore* and the Boundary between Law and Politics," *Yale Law Journal* 110 (2001): 1435n92. Indeed, "it is entirely plausible that all nine Justices would have reversed the positions they actually took in a reverse *Gore v. Bush*, had Vice President Gore been attempting to halt a recount ordered by an apparently partisan Michigan Supreme Court." Mark Tushnet, "Renormalizing *Bush v. Gore*: An Anticipatory Intellectual History," *Georgetown Law Journal* 90 (2001): 113, 117n36. See also Laurence Tribe, "Freeing eroG v. hsuB from its Hall of Mirrors," in *A Badly Flawed Election*.
89. I have written previously about the potential of *Bush v. Gore* to produce a principled Equal Protection jurisprudence that guarantees the equal treatment of voters and their ballots in the counting processes that election officials employ. See Edward B. Foley, "The Future of *Bush v. Gore*?," *Ohio State Law Journal* 68 (2007): 925, and Edward B. Foley, "Refining the *Bush v. Gore* Taxonomy," *Ohio State Law Journal* 68 (2007): 1035. See also Edward B. Foley, "Voting Rules and Constitutional Law," *George Washington Law Review* 81 (2013): 1836.

Chapter 12

1. For the events of the decade since 2000, see Richard L. Hasen, *The Voting Wars: From Florida 2000 to the Next Great Meltdown* (New Haven, CT: Yale University Press, 2012); Martha Kropf and David Kimball, *Helping America Vote: The Limits of Election Reform* (New York: Routledge, 2011); Charles Stewart, "What Hath HAVA Wrought?," chap. 4 in *Election Administration in the United States: The State of Reform after Bush v. Gore*, eds. Michael Alvarez and Bernard M. Grofman (New York: Cambridge University Press, 2014), 79–101; Daniel P. Tokaji, "HAVA in Court: A Summary and Analysis of Litigation," *Election Law Journal* 12 (2013): 203.

I have written previously about the new rules of provisional voting. See Edward B. Foley, "Uncertain Insurance: The Ambiguities and Complexities of Provisional Voting," in *Voting in America: American Voting Systems in Flux—Debacles, Dangers and Brave New Designs*, ed. Morgan Felchner (Westport, CT: Praeger, 2008); Edward B. Foley, "The Promise and Problems of Provisional Voting," *George Washington Law Review* 73 (2005): 1193.

2. The National Commission on Federal Election Reform, *Final Report*, 62–63 (2001), accessed July 13, 2015, http://web1.millercenter.org/ commissions/comm_2001.pdf.
3. Ibid., 60.
4. Ibid.
5. "Provisional Ballots: November 2, 2004," The Ohio Secretary of State's Office, accessed February 15, 2015, www.sos.state.oh.us/sos/elections/Research/electResultsMain/2004ElectionsResults/04-1102ProvisionalBallots.aspx.
6. Edward B. Foley, "A Big Blue Shift: Measuring an Asymmetrically Increasing Margin of Litigation," *Journal of Law and Politics* 28 (2013): 501, accessed July 14, 2015, http://files.www.lawandpolitics.org/content/vol-xxviii-no-4/Foley_Color_1110.pdf.
7. Richard L. Hasen, "Beyond the Margin of Litigation: Reforming U.S. Election Administration to Avoid Electoral Meltdown," *Washington & Lee Law Review* 62 (2005): 937.
8. Jodi Wilogren, "At Finish Line, a Bit Late, Kerry Bows to Cold Numbers," *New York Times*, Nov. 4, 2004.
9. In this respect the 2004 presidential election was similar to the US Senate's situation in 1931, as discussed in Chapter 8.
10. *Presidential Elections, 1789–2000* (Washington, DC: CQ Press, 2002) 143, 150.
11. The election was Ohio's 15th Congressional District, and the Democratic challenger, Mary Jo Kilroy, eventually beat the Republican incumbent Steve Stivers by 2,312 votes. "Representative to Congress: November 4, 2008," Ohio Secretary of State, accessed February 14, 2015, www.sos.state.oh.us/sos/elections/Research/electResultsMain/2008ElectionResults/congress110408.aspx.

    The election was litigated in both federal and state courts. See Ohio ex rel. Skaggs v. Brunner, 588 F. Supp. 2d 828 (S.D. Ohio 2008); Ohio ex rel. Skaggs v. Brunner, 120 Ohio St. 3d 506, 900 N.E.2d 982 (2008).
12. Election Day was November 2, 2010. The appeal in the lawsuit over this local judicial election was dismissed on July 12, 2012 (after a trial and an earlier visit to the appeals court). The court documents are available on the *Election Law @ Moritz* website: accessed July 14, 2015, http://moritzlaw.osu.edu/electionlaw/litigation/Hunter.php.
13. Hunter v. Hamilton County Board of Elections, 635 F.3d 219 (6th Cir. 2011). The two judges in the majority were appointed by President Clinton; the judge dissenting on the *Bush v. Gore* issue was appointed by President George W. Bush. The *Hunter* precedent is discussed extensively in Daniel Tokaji and Owen Wolfe, "*Baker, Bush,* and Ballot Boards: The Federalization of Election Administration," *Case Western Law Review* 62 (2012): 969.
14. The trial court found that several poll workers were confused by the fact that odd-numbered houses were on the opposite side of the street from even-numbered houses and in one extreme instance the poll worker apparently did not understand the distinction between odd and even numbers. When asked whether the house number 798 was even or odd, the poll worker responded: "A. Odd. Q. . . . Why do you think her address is an odd address? A. Because it begins with an odd number." Hunter v. Hamilton County Board of Elections, 850 F.Supp.2d 795, 820 (S.D. Ohio 2012).
15. James v. Bartlett, 607 S.E.2d 638 (2005); Jack Betts, "N.C. Voters Now Punished For Others' Errors," *Charlotte Observer*, Feb. 13, 2005; Sharif Durham and Mark Johnson, "N.C. Election Bills Advance-Legislature Aims To Assure Itself Final Say On Disputed Ballots," *Charlotte Observer*, Mar. 1, 2005; N.C.S.L. 2005-2 (S.B. 133).
16. Roe v. Alabama, 68 F.3d 404 (11th Cir. 1995). See Chapter 10.
17. For more on this point, see Edward B. Foley, "How Fair Can Be Faster: The Lessons of *Coleman v. Franken*," *Election Law Journal* 10 (2011): 187.
18. "The maxim that justice must not only be done, but be seen to be done, holds good not only in law but in free public reason." John Rawls, "The Idea of an Overlapping Consensus," *Oxford Journal of Legal Studies* 7, no. 1 (Spring 1987): 21. Not surprisingly, the US Supreme

Court has echoed the same point: "The Court must, of course, speak in terms of the perception of fairness rather than its reality." Powers v. Ohio, 499 U.S. 400, 426 (1991).

19. Jim Brunner, "Hutchison elected to lead 'ragtag army' of state GOP," *Seattle Times*, Aug. 25, 2013.
20. A book on Washington's 2004 gubernatorial election has been written by the person who served as the secretary of state's communications director at the time; aimed for a general audience, this book provides an overview of the basic facts. Trova Heffernan, *An Election for the Ages, Ross vs. Gregoire, 2004* (Pullman: Washington State University Press, 2010). See also Joaquin Avila, "The Washington 2004 Gubernatorial Election Crisis: The Necessity of Restoring Public Confidence in the Electoral Process," *Seattle University Law Review* 29 (2005): 313.
21. Washington Secretary of State, *Washington State's Vote-by-Mail Experience* (2007), 2–4.
22. Susan Gilmore, Andrew Garber, and Ralph Thomas, "Rossi Leading; Gregoire Allies Win in Court," *Seattle Times*, Nov. 13, 2004.
23. 52 U.S.C. § 21082(a) (formerly cited as 42 U.S.C. § 15482(a)).
24. Cook, "Rossi Back in the Lead, Barely," *Seattle Times*, Nov. 17, 2004.
25. Washington State Republic[an] Party v. Washington State Democratic Committee, Washington Superior Court (King County), No. 04-2-36048-0 SEA (Wash. Sup. Ct., Nov. 16, 2004), 2, accessed July 14, 2015, http://moritzlaw.osu.edu/electionlaw/docs/WSDCC/WSDCCorder2.pdf.
26. Gilmore et al., "Rossi Leading." See also Angela Galloway and Mike Lewis, "Democrats Win In Court Over Ballots but Rossi Still Leads For Governor," *Seattle Post-Intelligencer*, Nov. 13, 2004.
27. Angela Galloway, "Governor Race Slips Closer To A Recount. As Of Last Night, Gregoire Held 158-Vote Lead Over Rossi," *Seattle Post-Intelligencer*, Nov. 15, 2004; Ralph Thomas and Keith Ervin, "More Ballots Found in King County Gregoire Back in Lead," *Seattle Times*, Nov. 16, 2004.
28. Keith Ervin, "'Sudden' County Ballots Were There All Along," *Seattle Times*, Nov. 17, 2004.
29. Rebecca Cook, "Rossi Apparent Winner in Governor's Race; Recount Next," *Seattle Times*, November 17, 2004.
30. Washington State Republican Party v. Sam Reed, No. 2: 2004-CV-02350 (W.D. Wash. Nov. 20, 2004). Unlike in Minnesota four years later, the recount was not supervised by a single statewide authority; instead, more like Florida in 2000, each county was responsible for conducting its own recount.
31. Washington State Republican Party v. Sam Reed, No. 2: 2004-CV-02350 (W.D. Wash. Nov. 20, 2004).
32. Heffernan, *An Election for the Ages*, 44, 55.
33. Washington State Republican Party v. King County Division of Records, 103 P.3d 725 (Wash. S. Ct. 2004).
34. Ibid.; Wash. Rev. Code Ann. § 29A.60.210.
35. David Postman, "Error Discovery Could Give Gregoire Election," *Seattle Times*, Dec. 14, 2004.
36. Heffernan, *An Election for the Ages*, 69, 72; Rebecca Cook, "King County Board Votes to Move Forward with 573 Ballots," *Seattle Times*, December 15, 2004.
37. Editorial, "Right Court Move; Recount Goes On," *Seattle Times*, December 15, 2004.
38. Washington State Republican Party v. Kings County Division of Records No. 04-2-14599-1 (Wash. Sup. Ct. Dec. 17, 2004).
39. Susan Gilmore and Ralph Thomas, "Judge Blocks Count of Disputed Ballots," *Seattle Times*, December 18, 2004.
40. Washington State Republican Party v. King County, 153 Wash. 2d 220, 103 P.3d 725 (Wash. S. Ct. 2004).
41. Rebecca Cook, "King County Reports Recount Results, Gregoire By 10," *Seattle Times*, Dec. 22, 2004; Rebecca Cook, "Final Washington State Recount Results: Gregoire by 130," *Seattle Times*, Dec. 23, 2004.

42. The margin at the end of the hand recount on November 24 was thought to be 130, but it was subsequently reduced to 129 upon disqualification by the secretary of state of one ballot outside King County. See Heffernan, *An Election for the Ages*, 79.
43. The *Seattle Times* reported that the Republicans identified these extra ballots in batches, 91 in a first batch and an unspecified number later. David Postman, Ralph Thomas and Keith Ervin, "It's Gregoire by 130," *Seattle Times*, Dec. 24, 2004.
44. David Ammos, "Gregoire Sworn in as Washington governor," *Seattle Times*, Jan. 12, 2005.
45. Oral Decision of Judge John E. Bridges, Borders v. King County et al., No.05-2-00027-3 (Wash. Super. Ct. Feb. 4, 2005).
46. The trial judge announced his decision from the bench. See Oral Decision of Judge John E. Bridges, Borders v. King County, No.05-2-00027-3 (Wash. Super. Ct. June 6, 2005), available on the *Election Law @ Moritz* website: accessed July 14, 2015, http://moritzlaw.osu.edu/electionlaw/litigation/documents/oraldecision.pdf.
47. The trial judge further divided these 252 ballots into three subcategories: 96, 77, and 76, and spoke somewhat inconsistently about a couple of these subcategories at different points in his oral opinion delivered from the bench. The best understanding is that the three subcategories corresponded to different localities within the state and different particular reasons why the provisional voters could not be verified. For example, the subcategory of 96 was provisional ballots in King County that had been improperly fed through vote-counting machines before the eligibility of the provisional voters had been checked.
48. Wash. Rev. Code Ann. § 29A.68.110:

    > No election may be set aside on account of illegal votes, unless it appears that an amount of illegal votes has been given to the person whose right is being contested, that, if taken from that person, would reduce the number of the person's legal votes below the number of votes given to some other person for the same office, after deducting therefrom the illegal votes that may be shown to have been given to the other person.

49. This example appears in Heffernan, *An Election for the Ages*, 129.
50. *Borders*, 17 (June 6th oral decision).
51. Ibid., 21.
52. Heffernan, *An Election for the Ages*, 147.
53. I have written extensively on the 2008 Minnesota election. I detailed the events in Edward B. Foley, "The Lake Wobegon Recount: Minnesota's Disputed 2008 U.S. Senate Election," *Election Law Journal* 10 (2011): 129, and the account here is a substantially condensed and revised version of that narrative. I analyzed the election's implications in Edward B. Foley, "How Fair Can Be Faster: The Lessons of *Coleman v. Franken*," *Election Law Journal* 10 (2011): 187. I have also benefited immensely from Jay Weiner's reporting, both as the dispute was unfolding and in his subsequent book. See Jay Weiner, *This is Not Florida: How Al Franken Won the Minnesota Senate Recount* (Minneapolis: University of Minnesota Press, 2010). For my review essay on the book, see Edward B. Foley, "A Tale of Two Teams," *Election Law Journal* 10 (2011): 475.
54. Editorial, "A Gracious Finish to an Epic Drama," *Star Tribune*, July 1, 2009; Editorial, "A Senator at Long Last," *Pioneer Press*, June 30, 2009.
55. Jim Ragsdale, "Overtime: Chapter 4: In Minnesota's Coleman vs. Franken U.S. Senate Race, the System Worked. But Here's How to Make it Better," *Pioneer Press*, September 24, 2009.
56. Weiner describes the process by which the members of the Minnesota Supreme Court conferred on the selection of the three-judge panel, quoting one of them as publicly acknowledging that they deliberated for "about two weeks" in order to successfully yield an evenly balanced and highly qualified trio. Weiner, *This is Not Florida*, 143–44.
57. Coleman v. Richie, 758 N.W.2d 306 (Minn. S. Ct. 2008). Weiner said that the Minnesota Supreme Court "had embarrassed itself" with this 3–2 ruling. Weiner, *This is Not Florida*, 125.
58. For details, see Foley, "Lake Wobegon Recount," 133.

59. Minn. Stat. Ann. § 204C.31; "2008 Minnesota Recount Guide," Office of the Minnesota Secretary of State, accessed February 14, 2015, www.leg.state.mn.us/docs/2009/other/090983.pdf.
60. "It was Magnuson who set the tone early on the first day of evaluating challenges" to specific ballots in the recount. Weiner, *This is Not Florida*, 112.
61. Foley, "Lake Wobegon Recount," 140.
62. *Coleman*, 758 N.W.2d, 308–09.
63. Foley, "Lake Wobegon Recount," 135, 145.
64. Ibid., 131, 145–46.
65. For the Bloody Eighth episode and the 1994 Alabama chief justice election, see Chapter 10.
66. Franken v. Pawlenty, 762 N.W.2d 558 (Minn. S. Ct. 2009). On the political effect of not seating Franken provisionally during the pendency of the contest, see Gregory Koger, *Filibustering: A Political History of Obstruction in the House and Senate* (Chicago: University of Chicago Press, 2010), 4.
67. Weiner, *This Is Not Florida*, 143, 225.
68. Ibid., 209 (quoting Denise Reilly).
69. Contestants' Memorandum of Law in Support of Motion for Summary Judgment, Coleman v. Franken, 62-CV-09-56, 42, 49 (Minn. Dist. Ct. Jan. 21, 2009), accessed July 14, 2015, http://moritzlaw.osu.edu/electionlaw/litigation/ColemanvFranken-Contest.php.
70. Foley, "Lake Wobegon Recount," 153 (emphasis added).
71. See George McCrary, *A Treatise on the American Law of Elections*, 4th ed. (Chicago: E. B. Myers, 1897), 522–23.
72. See Foley, "How Fair Can Be Faster," 217. The US Court of Appeals for the Sixth Circuit, in an important 2012 case concerning provisional ballots in Ohio, relied heavily on this distinction between official error and voter error, ruling that the US Constitution at least in some contexts protects voters from disenfranchisement caused by voter error, but not from self-induced disenfranchisement caused by the voter's own mistake. Northeast Ohio Coalition for the Homeless v. Husted, 696 F.3d 580 (6th Cir. 2012).
73. Coleman v. Franken, 62-CV-09-56, 25 (Minn. Dist. Ct. Apr. 7, 2009).
74. Foley, "Lake Wobegon Recount," 152, 155; Bell v. Gannaway, 227 N.W.2d 797 (Minn. S. Ct. 1975).
75. Foley, "Lake Wobegon Recount," 154.
76. Coleman v. Franken, 767 N.W.2d 453, 462 (Minn. S. Ct. 2009) (internal quotation omitted).
77. Ibid., 466.
78. Ibid., 468, n19.
79. Ibid., 458–62.
80. Eric Black, "What Coleman said," *MinnPost*, June 30, 2009, accessed July 14, 2015, www.minnpost.com/eric-black-ink/2009/06/what-coleman-said.
81. Editorial, "A Gracious Finish to an Epic Drama; Unanimous Supreme Court Decision Legitimizes Franken Win," *Star Tribune*, July 1, 2009; Editorial, "A Senator at Long Last," *Pioneer Press*, June 30, 2009.
82. I analyze this point in Edward B. Foley, "The Future of *Bush v. Gore*?," *Ohio State Law Journal* 68 (2007): 925; see also Edward B. Foley, "Voting Rules and Constitutional Law," *George Washington Law Review* 81 (2013): 1836.
83. See notes 11 and 12 and accompanying text. See also Richard Hasen, "The 2012 Voting Wars, Judicial Backstops, and the Resurrection of *Bush v. Gore*," George *Washington Law Review* 81 (2013): 1865.
84. Katie Zezima, "Vermont: Recount Changes Auditor's Race," *New York Times*, Dec. 22, 2006. See also Bob Audette, "Victory Goes to Salmon," *Brattleboro Reformer*, Dec. 22, 2006.
85. Laura Vozzella and Ben Pershing, "Obenshain Concedes Virginia Attorney General's Race to Herring," *Washington Post*, Dec. 19, 2013; "Recount Confirms McDonnell as Winner; The Attorney General Election is Decided by 360-Vote Margin," *Richmond Times-Dispatch*, Dec. 22, 2005.

86. Ben Pershing, "Virginia Attorney General Race Becomes Even Closer," *Washington Post*, Nov. 10, 2013. See also Abby D. Phillip, "How Twitter Helped Make the Va. Attorney General Race's One of the Closest in History," *ABC News*, Nov. 11, 2013.
87. Laura Vozzella, "Democrat Wins Virginia Senate Recount, Giving Gov. Terry McAuliffe's Agenda a Crucial Boost," *Washington Post*, Jan. 27, 2014. The Democrat was Lynwood Lewis; the Republican, Ralph Northam.

Conclusion

1. Charles Evans Hughes, *The Public Papers of Charles E. Hughes*, vol. 1 (Albany, NY: J. B. Lyon, 1907), 24–25.
2. 3 Annals of Cong. 476–77 (March 20, 1792).
3. Paul Revere Frothingham, *Edward Everett: Orator and Statesman* (Boston: Houghton Mifflin, 1925), 153.
4. George W. McCrary, *A Treatise on the American Law of Elections* (Keokuk, IA: R. B. Ogden, 1875), 283–84.
5. Paul Leland Haworth, *The Hayes-Tilden Disputed Presidential Election of 1876* (New York: Russell & Russell, 1906), 331. Whether or not Grant himself would later adhere faithfully to that principle as the dispute over the election unfolded, Barlow considered it his "duty" to abide by it.
6. Robert A. Caro, *Means of Ascent: The Years of Lyndon Johnson* (New York: Knopf, 1990), 355, 362–63 (quoting the court proceeding).
7. Roe v. Mobile Cnty. Appointing Bd., 904 F.Supp. 1315, 1335 (S.D. Alabama 1995).
8. Howard Gillman, *The Votes That Counted: How the Court Decided the 2000 Presidential Election* (Chicago: University of Chicago Press, 2001), 126 (quoting David Boies). In his memoirs, James Baker emphasizes his belief that his side had "the moral high ground" because it was arguing for counting the votes according to "the rules as they existed *before* the game was played." James A. Baker, III, *"Work Hard, Study . . . and Keep Out of Politics!" Adventures and Lessons from an Unexpected Public Life* (New York: G. P. Putnam's Sons, 2006), 375.
9. See Tracy Campbell, *Short of the Glory: The Fall and Redemption of Edward F. Prichard, Jr.* (Lexington: University of Kentucky Press, 1998), 137–52.
10. George W. McCrary, *A Treatise on the American Law of Elections* (Keokuk, IA: R. B. Ogden, 1875), 322–23.
11. See also Steven F. Huefner, "Remedying Election Wrongs," *Harvard Journal on Legislation* 44 (2007): 302.
12. Caro, *Means of Ascent*, 193.
13. McCrary, *American Law of Elections*, 252.
14. Alexander Keyssar, *The Right to Vote: The Contested History of Democracy in the United States*, rev. ed. (New York: Basic Books, 2009), 301.
15. Mary Fulbrook, *Historical Theory* (New York: Routledge, 2002), 122.
16. Steven Pinker, *The Better Angels of Our Nature* (New York: Viking, 2001).
17. See also Keyssar, *The Right to Vote*, xxii:

> By the middle of the twentieth century, [the] sense of conflict and contingency [over the right to vote] had receded; perhaps because women finally had gained the franchise and because cold war liberalism provided a congenial ideological climate, the idea of an inexorable march toward universal suffrage became preeminent.

18. The Alabama case is thus especially strong evidence for the proposition advanced by my colleague Dan Tokaji that the federal judiciary is the best existing institution for the protection of equal voting rights and the integrity of the electoral process. See Daniel Tokaji and Owen Wolfe, "*Baker, Bush*, and Ballot Boards: The Federalization of Election Administration," *Case Western Reserve Law Review* 62 (2012): 969.
19. For a more pessimistic assessment of the role that Twitter might play in vote-counting disputes (an assessment made before Virginia's highly successful experience with Twitter

in 2013), see Richard Hasen, "Tweeting the Next Meltdown," in *The Voting Wars* (New Haven, CT: Yale University Press, 2012), 182–201.

20. I discuss this potential innovation in Edward B. Foley, "The Speaking Ballot," *New York University Law Review Online* 89 (2014): 52. It is also addressed in Presidential Commission on Election Administration, *The American Voting Experience: Report and Recommendations of the Presidential Commission on Election Administration* (January 2014), 65.
21. Requiring ballots cast at home to be scanned at a polling location on or before Election Day would also curtail a phenomenon that has grown considerably since 2000, with the increased use of both absentee and provisional ballots. Prior to 2000, most ballots in an election were counted on Election Night. Since 2000, however, a growing number of ballots are *not* part of the initial Election Night count, but instead counted for the first time during the canvassing period after Election Night. These initially uncounted ballots tend to be one of two types: mailed-in absentee ballots that, as long as they are postmarked by Election Day, are permitted to arrive afterward; and provisional ballots needing verification of their eligibility before being counted. If the Election Night count produces a tight margin, this pile of uncounted ballots becomes an obvious and immediate target of disputation, with the trailing candidate wanting to count more of these ballots and the leading candidate wanting to disqualify more of them. See Edward Foley, "A Big Blue Shift: Measuring an Asymmetrically Increasing Margin of Litigation," *Journal of Law and Politics* 28 (2013): 501.
22. Frederick C. Brightly, *A Collection of Leading Cases on the Law of Elections in the United States* (Philadelphia: Kay & Bro., 1871), 448–49, 501; McCrary, *American Law of Elections*, 301.
23. Richard Hasen, "Democracy Canon," *Stanford Law Review* 62 (2009): 69; Justin Levitt, "Resolving Election Error: The Dynamic Assessment of Materiality," *William & Mary Law Review* 54 (2012): 83.
24. Brightly saw elected judges as especially inconsistent with respect to the doctrine that "mere irregularities," if committed by "the election officers," "would not be sufficient cause for setting aside the election." Brightly, *Leading Cases*, 320. Because "it would require more than human virtue and independence," Brightly explained, "to hold the scales of justice with an even hand, in cases appealing so strongly to the political prejudices of themselves," this doctrine had "been departed from in practice." Ibid., 333–34. For emphasis, he added: "This departure from the ancient landmarks is but another proof of the vicious policy of vesting discretionary powers, in political cases, in an elective judiciary." Such cases over time—where "the fear of offending the body of their partisans" causes judicial rulings based on "political prejudice"—"combine to destroy the independence of the courts." Ibid., 359.
25. See Edward B. Foley, "The Future of *Bush v. Gore*?," *Ohio State Law Journal* 68 (2007): 925.
26. See Edward B. Foley, "Voting Rules and Constitutional Law," *George Washington Law Review* 81 (2013): 1836.
27. A major aim of the American Law Institute's Election Law Project, of which I am very fortunate (and honored) to play a part, is to provide guidance to states on how they might provide greater clarity and consistency in their election codes. See Steven F. Huefner and Edward B. Foley, "The Judicialization of Politics," *Brooklyn Law Review* 79 (2014): 551.
28. The Texas gubernatorial election of 2014 was essentially a 60–40 landslide in favor of Greg Abbott, the incumbent. See Office of the Secretary of State, "Race Summary Report: 2014 General Election," accessed March 28, 2015, http://elections.sos.state.tx.us/elchist175_state.htm. Even if Texas will not be purple as quickly as some may think, however, "there will be a date when the state will be competitive." Aaron Blake, "A Purple Texas. Not So Fast," *Washington Post*, Feb. 7, 2014.
29. Steve Bickerstaff, *Lines in the Sand: Congressional Redistricting in Texas and the Downfall of Tom DeLay* (Austin: University of Texas Press, 2007), 112.
30. "Texas Appeals Court Upholds Reversal of Tom DeLay's Money Laundering Convictions," *Dallas Morning News*, Oct. 1, 2014; see also Edward B. Foley, "The Federalism Defect in the Prosecution of Tom DeLay," *Roll Call*, Nov. 28, 2005; "Rick Perry Charges Clarified by

Prosecutor," *Statesman*, Feb. 13, 2015; see also Eugene Volokh, "Amicus Brief Supporting Dismissal of Rick Perry Prosecution in Texas," *Washington Post*, Nov. 10, 2014.

31. Texas law provides: "The senate and the house of representatives, in joint session, have exclusive jurisdiction of a contest of a general election for governor." Tex. Elec. Code Ann. § 221.002(b). The only thing worse would be if this provision failed to specify that the legislature acts in joint session, as otherwise a stalemate between the two chambers could result. See generally Joshua A. Douglas, "Procedural Fairness in Election Contests," *Indiana Law Journal* 88 (2013): 1.
32. In this respect, a future disputed gubernatorial election in Texas might look more like the three that occurred in the Border States during the Gilded Age, as the Democratic Party became newly ascendant. None of those three were handled fairly, and all three of them involve serious threats of civil disorder. Texas presumably would not wish to emulate those experiences.
33. See "*Hurley v. Chavez*," in Anne M. Butler and Wendy Wolff, *United States Senate Election, Expulsion and Censure Cases, 1793–1990* (Washington, DC: Government Printing Office, 1995), 399.
34. On the exercise of the so-called nuclear option, see Jeremy Peters, "In Landmark Vote, Senate Limits the Use of the Filibuster," *New York Times*, Nov. 21, 2013; Paul Kane, "Reid, Democrats Trigger 'Nuclear' Option; Eliminate Most Filibusters on Nominees," *Washington Post*, Nov. 21, 2013.

    The Constitution requires a majority of Senators for a quorum. If the Senate were split 50–49 with one seat disputed (and if the vice president of the United States belonged to the same party as the 49), the party of 49 might try to defeat a quorum so as to prevent the other party from awarding itself the disputed seat and thereby taking control of the body. If the Senate were unable to break the impasse, it might face a circumstance comparable to the Broad Seal War that afflicted the House of Representatives in 1838. Would the vice president, as the body's presiding officer, be entitled to make unilateral rulings, even if of dubious legality, in an effort to get the Senate up and running, in a way roughly analogous to what John Quincy Adams did in that early episode? Would the vice president even be able to prevail if the opposing party, in turn, attempted to defeat a quorum?
35. S. Rep., No. 94-597, 51. In 1890, Speaker Thomas Reed recommended that federal courts act as a tribunal to make *prima facie* determinations of disputed elections in the House of Representatives. Thomas B. Reed, "Contested Elections," *North American Review* 151, no. 404 (1890): 112. That idea, however, was subsequently defeated in the 53rd and 54th Congresses. C. H. Rammelkamp, "Contested Congressional Elections," *Political Science Quarterly* 20, no. 3 (1905): 439–40.
36. Even worse that a stalemate in the Senate over another situation like the 1952 New Mexico election would be that situation combined with a disputed presidential election. The nation does not remember how close it came to that "double whammy" in 2000. Not only was the presidential election in doubt that year, but for several weeks so too was the US Senate election in Oregon, and with it the determination of which party would control the Senate on January 6, 2001, the date for Congress to officially count the Electoral College votes from the states. Had the Senate been unable to function that date because of a deadlock over the Oregon seat, and if Gore had not conceded after the Supreme Court's decision in *Bush v. Gore*, the constitutional crisis that the nation would have faced would have been unparalleled. Not even in the Hayes-Tilden dispute was the Senate (or the House) incapable of convening, deliberating, and acting on the issues needing resolution. Avoiding even the remote possibility that this kind of double whammy might actually materialize in the future is reason enough for the Senate (and the House) to develop adequate contingency plans that avert the inability of the chamber to organize itself at the beginning of the new Congress because of one or more disputed seats in the chamber.
37. Cf. "chaos" in Nate Silver, "Democrats Need Chaos," *FiveThirtyEight*, November 3, 2014, accessed July 15, 2015, http://fivethirtyeight.com/datalab/democrats-need-chaos/.
38. For further details, see Edward B. Foley, "How Fair Can Be Faster: The Lessons of *Coleman v. Franken*," *Election Law Journal* 10 (2011): 187.

39. Steven Thomma, "Bush, Gore Are Quietly Planning Transitions," *Philadelphia Inquirer*, Nov. 19, 2000; "Gore Has Decided to Start Engines of His Transition," *New York Times*, November 23, 2000.
40. Congress, at the same time, could consider the creation of a special three-judge court to adjudicate any claims arising under federal law relating to a state's counting of presidential ballots. This special three-judge federal court, in other words, would exercise the jurisdiction of the federal judiciary over any equal protection or due process claims based on the precedents of *Bush v. Gore* and *Roe v. Alabama*. As valuable as that special three-judge court might be, however, its creation is not as pressing as an impartial tribunal capable of assisting Congress in its constitutional function under the Twelfth Amendment.

    The jurisdiction of the federal judiciary already exists to hear equal protection and due process claims based on the precedents of *Bush v. Gore* and *Roe v. Alabama*, with the availability of review in the Supreme Court. Congress could make the Supreme Court's appellate review of these cases mandatory, to remove any uncertainty about whether or not the Court will become involved in this type of ballot-counting dispute. But fine-tuning the existing jurisdiction of the federal judiciary in this way is no substitute for fixing the fundamental flaws that lie in procedures if and when a disputed presidential election reaches Congress under the Twelfth Amendment. At that point the federal judiciary no longer has a role, and Congress is susceptible to a stalemate between its two houses and controversy over how the unintelligible Electoral Count Act of 1887 is to apply in particular circumstances. It is to eliminate this set of potential problems that the creation of an impartial Electoral Count Tribunal, as an auxiliary to Congress's own authority under the Twelfth Amendment, is a necessity.
41. Although representative of the two parties, the two panelists on the tribunal who are not the neutral tiebreaker should still "take an oath to decide the case on the law and facts, not their loyalties to the candidate." Douglas, "Procedural Fairness in Election Contests," 53. The goal is for candidates and their partisan supporters to see themselves visibly represented on the adjudicatory tribunal in the person of one of the judges. That individual will look out for partisan interests of one side to the extent of objecting if the other panelists appear to deviate from a fair-minded adjudication. But a judge can play that kind of monitoring role while at the same time honor a commitment that the judge's own decisions will be as impartial as humanly possible.
42. Douglas, "Procedural Fairness in Election Contests," 51.
43. The unanimity of all nine Supreme Court justices in the selection of the neutral member of tribunal would assure that the individual selected was genuinely impartial toward both sides. The Supreme Court currently, and historically, has members appointed by presidents of opposing political parties. Currently, John Roberts and Elena Kagan would need to concur on the selection of the impartial individual, as would Samuel Alito and Sonia Sotomayor. It is difficult to envision the circumstance in which all nine justices come from the same political party, and if that circumstance ever were to occur the statutory mechanism for the appointment of the Electoral Count Tribunal could be revisited. (As for the objection that all nine justices could not be expected to agree upon the choice of a neutral arbiter, we must have confidence that the justices—despite their differences—have sufficient good will and public spiritedness to undertake the collective effort to identify a mutually acceptable individual, especially when statutorily required to do so.)
44. For further details on this experiment, see Edward B. Foley, "The *McCain v. Obama* Simulation: A Fair Tribunal for Disputed Presidential Elections," *New York University Journal of Legislation and Public Policy* 13 (2010): 471–509.
45. The members of the tribunal, at the time of their appointment, could be instructed that they are expected to refrain from voting in the upcoming presidential election. I am inclined to think that such a measure would be largely symbolic: an individual could be psychologically biased toward one candidate in the election even if the individual refrained from voting; conversely, a rigorously self-disciplined individual could set aside preferences expressed in casting a ballot for one of the candidates when called upon to impartially adjudicate the dispute between the two candidates. Nonetheless, symbolism

matters, and although obviously it is a sacrifice to self-disenfranchise by serving on this tribunal, it is a sacrifice that just a few individuals would make for the sake of the country.

This extra degree of impartiality (or at least increased appearance of impartiality) could not occur if the members of tribunal were appointed after Election Day, once a dispute had arisen. By that point, anyone chosen to serve likely would have voted for one of the candidates. The argument can be made that the crucible of the dispute will prompt the identification of the most impartial individual possible for the occasion, whereas appointment before Election Day might be more cavalier given the unlikelihood of a ballot-counting dispute arising in any particular presidential election. But the counterargument also can be made that there is a much greater risk of deadlock if membership on the tribunal is not determined until after the dispute has arisen. On balance, it seems more prudent to opt for the preappointed panel.

46. If Congress refuses to adopt this institutional reform, as seems likely given the incapacity of Congress to overcome partisan gridlock on a wide variety of fronts, it is possible that the Supreme Court might be able to adopt a version of this reform on its own initiative. The Supreme Court has the power to appoint Special Masters to assist in the adjudication of cases within its jurisdiction. The Court thus unanimously could create a three-member Special Master Panel to adjudicate any case within its jurisdiction concerning the counting of ballots in a presidential election. Although the Court's use of Special Masters traditionally has been confined to cases within its original jurisdiction, meaning that the Court acts as a trial rather than appellate court in the case, there is no reason in principle why the Court could not appoint a Special Master Panel to assist in the exercise of its appellate jurisdiction. After all, Special Masters are entirely advisory. They are a bit like law clerks hired for just one case. There is no reason why the Court should not be entitled to employ such a Special Master Panel if the Court believed it could be helpful. The argument would be that a specially designed three-member panel, with a neutral tiebreaker, would help the Court itself avoid an ugly partisan split in a case involving counting presidential ballots.

The Court, moreover, could induce lower courts to employ the same Special Master Panel at an earlier stage of any litigation that might occur over presidential ballots. The Court could announce in advance that it will use the designated Special Master Panel for any presidential ballot case that might come its way if *but only if* the same designated Special Master Panel has not already been employed by a lower court in the same case. This announcement would incentivize the lower courts to employ the designated Special Master Panel because, if they do, they get to review its determination in the case, rather than the other way around. (The Special Master Panel would be the last step in the process before the US Supreme Court's review of the case unless the Special Master Panel was employed by a lower court; if not, then the Special Master Panel would be reviewing all the lower court determinations in the case.) Most courts would rather have the opportunity to review the decision of another tribunal than have their own decisions reviewed by that tribunal. Thus the lower courts could be enticed into using the Special Master Panel, so that they could avoid being reviewed by it.

As valuable as the Court's announcement of this Special Master Panel policy would be, it would not directly apply to proceedings in Congress under the Twelfth Amendment. For that, a congressional statute, to amend the Electoral Count Act of 1887, would be necessary. But even without such a statute, the Supreme Court's promulgation of a Special Master Panel for litigation over presidential ballots might have a salutary effect in any proceedings arising in Congress over a disputed presidential election. If the Special Master Panel performs its function of demonstrating how the dispute can be resolved impartially, Congress might be shamed into setting aside any temptation to overrule the impartial decision based on rank partisanship. Congress might just look too corrupt if it were to attempt to override a fair decision from the impartial tribunal.

Of course, to adopt this kind of Special Master Panel the Supreme Court would need to be convinced that employing a specially designed advisory tribunal would be preferable to relying on its own capacity for impartial adjudication. But perhaps the Court's experience with *Bush v. Gore* has imparted the lesson that the Court could benefit from some nonpartisan assistance for this kind of uniquely high-stakes political case. The Court would not be divesting itself of any jurisdiction, just obtaining the assistance of three individuals most trustworthy for the adjudication of this kind of case. One would hope that the nine Justices could see the wisdom, or at least prudence, of seeking such assistance.

47. A copy of their unanimous opinion is appended to Foley, "*McCain v. Obama* Simulation," 497.
48. Rick Pildes has put the point this way: "The constitutional obligation is to design recount processes, and perhaps voting or democratic processes more generally, that sufficiently cabin the risk of partisan, self-interested manipulation." Rick Pildes, "The Constitutionalization of Democratic Politics," *Harvard Law Review* 118 (2004): 49.

INDEX

Note: Page numbers in *italics* indicate figures and tables.